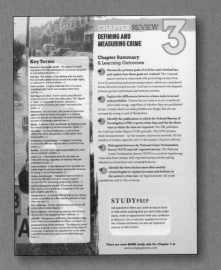

Chapter-in-Review Cards at the back of the Student Edition provide a portable study tool containing concepts for review and a list of landmark cases. Additional cards show a flow chart of the CJ system, and offer career information.

THE
SOLUTION

CJ Are you in?

ONLINE RESOURCES INCLUDED!

CourseMate   Engaging. Trackable. Affordable.

CourseMate brings course concepts to life with interactive learning, study, and exam preparation tools that support CJ2.

FOR INSTRUCTORS:
- Everything available to students
- Engagement Tracker

CJ2 resources also include Custom Options through the 4LTR+ Program, and an Instructor Web site with:
- First Day of Class Instructions
- Lecture Booster
- Instructor's Manual
- Test Bank
- PowerPoint® Slides
- Instructor Prep Cards

FOR STUDENTS:
- Interactive eBook
- Auto-Graded Quizzes
- Flashcards
- Beat the Clock
- PowerPoint® Slides
- Animations, Videos, Simulations
- Web Links

WADSWORTH
CENGAGE Learning™

CJ 2
Larry K. Gaines and **Roger LeRoy Miller**

Editor-in-Chief: Michelle Julet

Senior Publisher: Linda Schreiber Ganster

Senior Acquisitions Editor:
Carolyn Henderson Meier

Assistant Editor: Erin Abney

Editorial Assistant: Virginette Acacio

Product Development Manager,
4LTR Press: Steven E. Joos

Executive Brand Marketing Manager,
4LTR Press: Robin Lucas

Senior Marketing Manager:
Michelle Williams

Marketing Coordinator: Jack Ward

Marketing Communications Manager:
Heather Baxley

Senior Content Project Manager:
Ann Borman

Photo Researcher: Anne Sheroff,

Copyeditor: Mary Berry

Indexer: Terry Casey

Media Editor: Andy Yap

Manufacturing Coordinator: Judy Inouye

Art Director: Maria Epes

Interior Designer: RHDG

Cover Design Credit: Riezebos Holzbaur/
Brieanna Hattey

Cover images: Highway patrol:
jacomstephens/iStockphoto;
female officer: iofoto/Shutterstock.
com; female scientist: Leah-Anne
Thompson /Shutterstock.com;
CSI investigator: Luis Louro/
Shutterstock.com; man in suit:
prism68/Shutterstock.com; Judge:
Ross Anania/Digital Vision; Columns:
Corbis/Photolibrary.com

For product information and technology assistance, contact us at
Cengage Learning Customer & Sales Support 1-800-423-0563

For permission to use material from this text or product,
submit all requests online at **www.cengage.com/permissions**
Further permissions questions can be emailed to
permissionrequest@cengage.com

Library of Congress Control Number: 2011937666

SE ISBN-13: 978-1-111-84087-7

Wadsworth Cengage Learning
20 Davis Drive
Belmont, CA 94002-3098
USA

Cengage Learning products are represented in Canada by Nelson Education, Ltd.

For your course and learning solutions, visit **academic.cengage.com**
Purchase any of our products at your local college store or at our preferred online store **www.cengagebrain.com**

Printed in the United States of America
2 3 4 5 6 7 14 13 12

BRIEFCONTENTS

CONTENTS

mipan/iStockphoto

Katrina Brown/iStockphoto

Contents   **v**

spxChrome/iStockphoto

James Steidl/iStockphoto

Nikolay Mamluke/iStockphoto

PART FOUR
CORRECTIONS

CHAPTER 12
PROBATION AND COMMUNITY CORRECTIONS 218

Light Rap for Lil Wayne? 219

CHAPTER 13
PRISONS AND JAILS 236

Incarceration Nation 237

CHAPTER 14
BEHIND BARS: THE LIFE OF AN INMATE 256

Threepeat 257

Susan Farley/New York Times/Redux

PART FIVE
SPECIAL ISSUES

CHAPTER 15
THE JUVENILE JUSTICE SYSTEM 276

Forever Young 277

CHAPTER 16
HOMELAND SECURITY 296

Wrong Number 297

Mario Aguilar/iStockphoto.com

CHAPTER 17
CYBER CRIME AND THE FUTURE OF CRIMINAL JUSTICE 318

René Mansi/iStockphoto

SKILL PREP
A STUDY SKILLS MODULE

WHAT'S INSIDE

After reading through and practicing the material in this study skills module, you will be better prepared to . . .

Welcome!

With this course and this textbook, you've begun what we hope will be a fun, stimulating, and thought-provoking journey into the world of criminal justice. In this course, you will learn all the basics about crime, like law enforcement, the court system, corrections, and other special issues like justice for juveniles, homeland security, and cyber crime. Knowledge of these basics will get you well on your way to a great future in criminal justice.

To help you get the most out of this course, and this textbook, we have developed this study skills module. You may be a recent high school graduate, or a working professional continuing your education, or an adult making your way back to the classroom after a few years. Whatever type of student you are, you want RESULTS when you study. You want to be able to understand the issues and ideas presented in the textbook, to be able to talk about them intelligently during class discussions, and to be able to remember them as you prepare for exams and papers.

This kind of knowledge doesn't just come from natural talent. Instead, it comes from the use of good study skills. This module is designed to help you develop the skills and habits you'll need to get the results that you want from this course. With tips on lifestyle decisions, how to manage your time more effectively, how to be more engaged when you study, how to get the most out of your textbook, how to prepare for quizzes and exams, how to write papers, and how to prepare and deliver a speech, this guide will help you become the best learner you can be!

LIFEprep

It takes several things to succeed in a class—hard work, concentration, and commitment to your studies. In order to work hard, concentrate, and demonstrate commitment, you need energy. When you are full of energy, time seems to pass quickly, and it is easier to get things done. When you don't have energy, time feels as if it is standing still, and even your favorite activities can feel like a burden. To have the energy you need to be a great learner, it is important to make good lifestyle choices. You need to get enough sleep, eat well, take care of yourself, and maintain good relationships. An important part of being a successful student is to pay attention to what goes on in your life so that you have all the ingredients you need to maintain your focus and energy.

Here are some suggestions that you can use to keep up your energy so that you can succeed in everything you do.

- Too often, we become so busy with other aspects of our lives that we neglect our health. It is crucial that you eat a balanced diet, exercise regularly, and get enough sleep. If you don't take care of your physical well-being, other areas of your life will inevitably suffer.

- Hearing is not the same thing as listening. Many people are not good listeners. We often hear what we want to hear as we filter information through our own experiences and interests. When talking with friends, instructors, or family members, focus carefully on what they say—it may reveal something unexpected.

Most people who succeed have a plan.

- Be very careful about what you post on the Internet. A good rule of thumb is "Don't post anything that you wouldn't want the world to know." Many employers search the Internet for information concerning potential employees, and one embarrassing photo or tweet can have long-term damaging consequences.

- Most people who succeed have a plan—what they want to accomplish and when. Do you have a life plan? If not, you can start by making a list of your lifetime goals, even though they may change later on. You can also create a career plan that includes a list of skills you will need to succeed. Then, choose classes and extracurricular activities that will help you develop these skills.

- When we start doing something new, whether in school or in other areas of life, we usually aren't very good at it. We need feedback from those who are good in that area—such as instructors—to improve and succeed. Therefore, you should welcome feedback, and if it isn't given, you should ask for it.

- Exercise not only benefits the body, but the mind as well. A study at Naperville Central High School, in Naperville, Illinois, showed that students who participated in a morning gym class performed significantly better on math and reading standardized tests than those who did not. So take a little time to exercise each day—it'll help you feel great and it'll make you a better learner. (Vanessa Richardson, "A Fit Body Means a Fit Mind," Edutopia, May 27, 2009, www.edutopia.org/exercise-fitness-brain-benefits-learning).

- Do you want to become a better writer? Your college or university probably has a writing center with resources to help you with your writing assignments. If not, you should be able to find a tutor who will help you figure out what you are trying to communicate and how to put it effectively on paper.

- Filing systems are an easy way to keep track of your money. First, label file folders for different categories of income, such as paycheck stubs, bank statements, and miscellaneous. Then, do the same for expenses, such as clothes, food, and entertainment. If you find you need another category, just set up a new folder.

- Do you want to become a better public speaker? Consider using your campus's audiovisual resources to develop this difficult but rewarding skill. Record yourself speaking and then critique your performance. Join a school organization such as a debate or drama club to gain confidence in front of a live audience.

- If you feel that you are overly dependent on family or friends, nurture skills that lead to independence. For example, learn how to cook for yourself. Get a job that does not interfere (too much) with your schoolwork. Save money and pay your own bills. Rent your own living space. Most important, have confidence in yourself.

- More often than not, in school and life, things do not go as planned. When this happens, you need to be flexible. Do not focus on your disappointment. Instead, try to accept the situation as it is, and deal with it by looking at the future rather than dwelling on the past.

- Be thankful for the people who care about you. Your family and good friends are a precious resource. When you have problems, don't try to solve them by yourself. Talk to the people in your life who want you to succeed and be happy, and listen to their advice.

- Critical thinking is a crucial skill, and, as with any other skill, one gets better at it with practice. So, don't jump to conclusions. Whether you are considering a friend's argument, a test question, a major purchase, or a personal problem, carefully weigh the evidence, balance strengths and weaknesses, and make a reasoned decision.

- Rather than constantly seeking approval from others, try to seek approval from the person who matters the most—yourself. If you have good values, then your conscience will tell you when you are doing the right thing. Don't let worries about what others think run, or ruin, your life.

> If you don't take care of your **physical well-being**, other areas of your life will inevitably suffer.

> *"Twenty years from now you will be more disappointed by the things that you didn't do than by the ones you did. So throw off the bowlines. Sail away from the safe harbor. Catch the trade winds in your sails. Explore. Dream. Discover."*

Mark Twain
(American author, 1835–1910)

TIME PREP

Taking a college-level course involves a lot of work. You have to go to class, read the textbook, pay attention to lectures, take notes, complete homework assignments, write papers, and take exams. On top of that, there are other things in the other areas of your life that call for your time and attention. You have to take care of where you live, run daily errands, take care of family, spend time with friends, work a full- or part-time job, and find time to unwind. With all that you're involved in, knowing how to manage your time is critical if you want to succeed as a learner.

Skip Odonnell/iStockphoto.com

The key to managing your time is to know how much time you have and to use it well. At the beginning of every term, you should evaluate how you use your time. How much time is spent working? How much caring for your home and family? On entertainment? How much time do you spend studying? Keep a record of what you do hour by hour for a full week. Once you see where all your time goes, you can decide which activities you might modify in order to have "more" time.

To manage your time well, you need to know where it is going.

Here are some other helpful tips on how to make the most of your time.

- Plan your study schedule in advance. At the beginning of each week, allocate time for each subject that you need to study. If it helps, put your schedule down on paper or use one of the many "calendar" computer programs for efficient daily planning.
- Don't be late for classes, meetings with professors, and other appointments. If you find that you have trouble being on time, adjust your planning to arrive fifteen minutes early to all engagements. That way, even if you are "late," in most cases you will still be on time.
- To reduce the time spent looking for information on the Internet, start with a clear idea of your

Paul Ijsendoorn/iStockphoto.com

research task. Use a trusted search engine and focus only on that subject. Do not allow yourself to be sidetracked by other activities such as checking e-mail or social networking.

- Set aside a little time each day to assess whether you are going to meet the deadlines for all of your classes—quizzes, papers, and exams. It is critical to ensure that deadlines don't "sneak up" on you. A great way to do this is to use a calendar program or app, which can help you keep track of target dates and even give you friendly reminders.
- Nothing wastes more time—or is more aggravating—than having to redo schoolwork that was somehow lost on your computer. Back up all of your important files periodically. You can copy them onto an external hard drive, a DVD, or a USB flash drive.

Concentrate on doing one thing at a time.

- Concentrate on doing one thing at a time. Multitasking is often a trap that leads you to do several things quickly but poorly. When you are studying, don't carry on a text conversation with a friend or have one eye on the Internet at the same time.
- Set deadlines for yourself, not only with schoolwork but also with responsibilities in other areas of your life. If you tell yourself, "I will have this task done by Monday at noon and that other task finished before dinner on Wednesday," you will find it much easier to balance the many demands on your time.
- Regularly checking e-mail and text messages not only interrupts the task at hand, but also is an easy excuse for procrastination. Set aside specific times of the day to check and answer e-mail, and, when necessary, make sure that your cell phone is off or out of reach.
- Sometimes, a task is so large that it seems impossible, making it more tempting to put off. When given a large assignment, break it into a

series of small assignments. Then, make a list of the assignments, and as you finish each one, give yourself the satisfaction of crossing it off.

- Many of us have a particular time of day when we are most alert—early morning, afternoon, or night. Plan to do schoolwork during that time, when you will be most efficient, and set aside other times of the day for activities that do not require such serious concentration.

- Because we like to be helpful, we may have a hard time saying "no" when others ask for favors that take up our time. Sometimes, though, unless the person is experiencing a real emergency, you have to put your schoolwork or job first. If you are worried that the person will be offended, explain why and trust that they will understand how important your schoolwork or job is.

- Slow down. You may think that you are getting more work done by rushing, but haste inevitably leads to poor decisions, mistakes, and errors of judgment, all of which waste time. Work well, not quickly, and you will wind up saving time.

- If you can, outsource! Give someone else some of your responsibilities. If you can afford to, hire someone to clean your house. Send your dirty clothes to a laundry. If money is tight, split chores with friends or housemates so that you can

better manage your work-life responsibilities.

- In marketing, *to bundle* means to combine several products in one. In time management, it means combining two activities to free up some time. For example, if you need to exercise and want to socialize, bundle the two activities by going on a jog with your friends. Take along some schoolwork when you head to the laundromat—you can get a lot done while you're waiting for the spin cycle. Or, you can record class lectures (ask the professor for permission) so that you can review class material while you're out running errands.

- Develop a habit of setting time limits for tasks, both in and out of school. You will find that with a time limit in mind, you will waste less time and work more efficiently.

- Even the best time management and organization can be waylaid by forgetfulness. Most e-mail systems have free calendar features that allow you to send e-mail reminders to yourself concerning assignments, tests, and other important dates.

- A Chinese adage goes, "The longest journey starts with a single step." If you are having trouble getting started on a project or assignment, identify the first task that needs to be done. Then do it! This helps avoid time-wasting procrastination.

Paul Ijsendoorn/iStockphoto.com

Bundling, or combining two activities, will help you save time.

Rubberball/iStockphoto.com

STUDY PREP

What does it take to be a successful student? Like many people, you may think that success depends on how naturally smart you are, that some people are just better at school than others. But in reality, successful students aren't born, they're made. What this means is that even if you don't consider yourself naturally "book smart," you can do well in this course by developing study skills that will help you understand, remember, and apply key concepts.

There are five things you can do to develop good study habits:

be engaged
ask questions
take notes
make an outline
mark your text

BE ENGAGED

If you've ever heard elevator music, you know what easy listening is like—it stays in the background. You know it's there, but you're not really paying attention to it, and you probably won't remember it after a few minutes. That is *not* what you should be doing in class. You have to be engaged. Being *engaged* means listening to discover (and remember) something. In other words, listening is more than just hearing. Not only do you have to hear what the professor is saying in class, you have to pay attention to it. And as you listen with attention, you will hear what your instructor believes is important. One way to make sure that you are listening attentively is to take notes. Doing so will help you focus on the professor's words and will help you identify the most important parts of the lecture.

ASK QUESTIONS

If you are really engaged in your criminal justice course, you will ask a question or two whenever you do not understand something. You can also ask a question to get your instructor to share her or his opinion on a subject. However you do it, true engagement requires you to be a participant in your class. The more you participate, the more you will learn (and the more your instructor will know who you are!).

TAKE NOTES

Note-taking has a value in and of itself, just as outlining does. The physical act of writing makes you a more efficient learner. In addition, your notes provide a guide to what your instructor thinks is important. That means you will have a better idea of what to study before the next exam if you have a set of notes that you took during class.

MAKE AN OUTLINE

As you read through each chapter of your textbook, you might want to make an outline—a simple method for organizing information. You can create an outline as part of your reading or at the end of your reading. Or you can make an outline when you reread a section before moving on to the next. The act of physically writing an outline for a chapter will help you retain the material in this text and master it, thereby obtaining a higher grade in class. Even if you make an outline that is no more than the headings in this text, you will be studying more efficiently than you would be otherwise.

To make an effective outline, you have to be selective. Outlines that contain all the information in the text are not very useful. Your objectives in outlining are, first, to identify the main concepts and, then, to add the details that support those main concepts.

Your outline should consist of several levels written in a standard format. The most important concepts are assigned Roman

iStockphoto.com

numerals; the second most important, capital letters; the third most important, numbers; and the fourth most important, lowercase letters. Here is a quick example:

I. What Is The Criminal Justice System?
  A. The Purpose of the Criminal Justice System
    1. Controlling and Preventing Crime
    2. Maintaining Justice
  B. The Structure of the Criminal Justice System
    1. Law Enforcement
      a. Local and County Law Enforcement
      b. State Law Enforcement
      c. Federal Law Enforcement
    2. The Courts
    3. Corrections
  C. The Criminal Justice Process
    1. The Assembly Line
    2. The Formal Criminal Justice Process
    3. The Informal Criminal Justice Process
      a. Discretionary Basics
      b. Discretionary Values
      c. The "Wedding Cake" Model of Criminal Justice

MARK YOUR TEXT

Now that you own your own textbook for this course, you can greatly improve your learning by (marking) your text. By doing so, you will identify the most important concepts of each chapter, and at the same time, you'll be making a handy study guide for reviewing material at a later time.

DIFFERENT WAYS OF MARKING The most commonly used form of marking is to underline impor-

tant points. The second most commonly used method is to use a felt-tipped highlighter, or marker, in yellow or some other transparent color. Marking also includes circling, numbering, using arrows, jotting brief notes, or any other method that allows you to remember things when you go back to skim the pages in your textbook prior to an exam.

IMPORTANT

WHY MARKING IS IMPORTANT Marking is impor-
tant for the same reason that outlining is—it helps you to organize the information in the text. It allows you to become an active participant in the mastery of the material. Researchers have shown that the physical act of marking, just like the physical acts of note-taking during class and outlining, helps you better retain the material. The better the material is organized in your mind, the more you'll remember. There are two types of readers—passive and active. The active reader outlines or marks. Active readers typically do better on exams. Perhaps one of the reasons that active readers retain more than passive readers is because the physical act of outlining and/or marking requires greater concentration. It is through greater concentration that more is remembered.

TWO POINTS TO REMEMBER WHEN MARKING

 Read one section at a time before you do any extensive marking. You can't mark a section until you know what is important, and you can't know what is important until you read the whole section.

Don't over mark. Just as an outline cannot contain everything that is in a text (or, with respect to note-taking, in a lecture), marking can't be of the whole book. Don't fool yourself into thinking that you have done a good job just because each page is filled up with arrows, asterisks, circles, and underlines. If you do mark the whole book, when you go back to review the material, your markings will not help you remember what was important.

Take a look at the two paragraphs below:

Parole, a conditional release, is the most common form of prison release. About two-thirds of all inmates who leave incarceration do so under the supervision of a parole officer. The remaining one third are subject to various other release mechanisms. Prisoners receive an unconditional release when they have completed the terms of their sentence and no longer require incarceration or supervision. One form of unconditional release is mandatory release (also known as "maxing out"), which occurs when an inmate has served the maximum amount of time on the initial sentence, minus reductions for good-time credits.

Parole, a conditional release, is the most common form of prison release. About two-thirds of all inmates who leave incarceration do so under the supervision of a parole officer. The remaining one third are subject to various other release mechanisms. Prisoners receive an unconditional release when they have completed the terms of their sentence and no longer require incarceration or supervision. One form of unconditional release is mandatory release (also known as "maxing out"), which occurs when an inmate has served the maximum amount of time on the initial sentence, minus reductions for good-time credits.

The second paragraph, with all of the different markings, is hard to read and understand because there is so much going on. There are arrows and underlines and highlights all over the place, and it is difficult to identify the most important parts of the paragraph. The first paragraph, by contrast, has highlights only on a few important words, making it much easier to identify quickly the important elements of the paragraph. The key to marking is *selective* activity. Mark each page in a way that allows you to see the most important points at a glance. You can follow up your marking by writing out more in your subject outline.

With these skills in hand, you will be well on your way to becoming a great student. Here are a few more hints that will help you develop effective study skills.

We study **best** when we are **free from distractions**.

- Read textbook chapters actively! Underline the most important topics. Put a check mark next to material that you do not understand. After you have completed the entire chapter, take a break. Then, work on better comprehension of the check-marked material.

- As a rule, do school work as soon as possible when you get home after class. The longer you wait, the more likely you will be distracted by television, video games, phone calls from friends, or social networking.

- Many students are tempted to take class notes on a laptop computer. This is a bad idea for two reasons. First, it is hard to copy diagrams or take other "artistic" notes on a computer. Second, it is easy to get distracted by checking e-mail or surfing the Web.

- We study best when we are free from distractions such as the Internet, cell phones, and our friends. That's why your school library is often the best place to work. Set aside several hours a week of "library time" to study in peace and quiet.

- Reward yourself for studying! From time to time, allow yourself a short break for surfing the Internet, going for a jog, taking a nap, or doing something else that you enjoy. These interludes will refresh your mind and enable you to study longer and more efficiently.

- When you are given a writing assignment, make sure you allow yourself enough time to revise and polish your final draft. Good writing takes time—you may need to revise a paper several times before it's ready to be handed in.

- A neat study space is important. Staying neat forces you to stay organized. When your desk is covered with piles of papers, notes, and textbooks, things are being lost even though you may not realize it. The only work items that should be on your desk are those that you are working on that day.

- Often, studying involves pure memorization. To help with this task, create flash (or note) cards. On one side of the card, write the question or term. On the other side, write the answer or definition. Then, use the cards to test yourself on the material.

- Mnemonic (ne-mon-ik) devices are tricks that increase our ability to memorize. A well-known mnemonic device is the phrase ROY G BIV, which helps people remember the colors of the rainbow— Red, Orange, Yellow, Green, Blue, Indigo, Violet. Of course, you don't have to use mnemonics that other people made. You can create your own for whatever you need to memorize. The more fun you have coming up with mnemonics for yourself, the more useful they will be.

- Take notes twice. First, take notes in class. Then, when you get back home, rewrite your notes. The rewrite will act as a study session by forcing you to think about the material. It will also, invariably, lead to questions that are crucial to the study process.

- Notice that each major section heading in this textbook has been written in the form of a question. By turning headings or subheadings in all of your textbooks into questions—and then answering them—you will increase your understanding of the material.

- Multitasking while studying is generally a bad idea. You may think that you can review your notes and watch television at the same time, but your ability to study will almost certainly suffer. It's OK to give yourself TV breaks from schoolwork, but avoid combining the two.

= BAD IDEA!

TEST PREP

You have worked hard throughout the term, reading the book, paying close attention in class, and taking good notes. Now it's test time, when all that hard work pays off. To do well on an exam, of course, it is important that you learn the concepts in each chapter as thoroughly as possible; however, there are additional strategies for taking exams. You should know which reading materials and lectures will be covered. You should also know in advance what type of exam you are going to take—essay or objective or both. (Objective exams usually include true/false, fill-in-the-blank, matching, and multiple-choice questions.) Finally, you should know how much time will be allowed for the exam. By taking these steps, you will reduce any anxiety you feel as you begin the exam, and you'll be better prepared to work through the entire exam.

Petek ARICI/iStockphoto.com

FOLLOW DIRECTIONS

Students are often in a hurry to start an exam, so they take little time to read the instructions. The instructions can be critical, however. In a multiple-choice exam, for example, if there is no indication that there is a penalty for guessing, then you should never leave a question unanswered. Even if only a few minutes are left at the end of an exam, you should guess on the questions that you remain uncertain about.

Additionally, you need to know the weight given to each section of an exam. In a typical multiple-choice exam, all questions have equal weight. In other types of exams, particularly those with essay questions, different parts of the exam carry different weights. You should use these weights to apportion your time accordingly. If the essay portion of an exam accounts for 20 percent of the total points on the exam, you should not spend 60 percent of your time on the essay.

Finally, you need to make sure you are marking the answers correctly. Some exams require a No. 2 pencil to fill in the dots on a machine-graded answer sheet. Other exams require underlining or circling. In short, you have to read and follow the instructions carefully.

Jesus Jauregui/iStockphoto.com

OBJECTIVE EXAMS

An objective exam consists of multiple-choice, true/false, fill-in-the-blank, or matching questions that have only one correct answer. Students usually commit one of two errors when they read objective-exam questions: (1) they read things into the questions that do not exist, or (2) they skip over words or phrases. Most test questions include key words such as:

- all
- never
- always
- only

If you miss any of these key words, you may answer the question wrong even if you know the information. Consider the following example:

> True or False?
> All cases in which one person kills another person are considered murder.

In this instance, you may be tempted to answer "True," but the correct answer is "False," because the charge of murder is only brought in cases in which one person *intentionally* killed another. In cases in which a person unintentionally killed another, the charge is manslaughter.

Whenever the answer to an objective question is not obvious, start with the process of elimination. Throw out the answers that are clearly incorrect. Typically, the easiest way to eliminate incorrect answers is to look for those that are meaningless, illogical, or inconsistent. Often test authors put in choices that make perfect sense and are indeed true, but they are not the answer to the question under study.

If you follow the above tips, you will be well on your way to becoming an efficient, results-oriented student. Here are a few more that will help you get there.

- Instructors usually lecture on subjects they think are important, so those same subjects are also likely to be on the exam. Therefore, be sure to take extensive notes in class. Then, review your notes thoroughly as part of your exam preparation.

- At times, you will find yourself studying for several exams at once. When this happens, make a list of each study topic and the amount of time needed to prepare for that topic. Then, create a study schedule to reduce stress and give yourself the best chance for success.

- When preparing for an exam, you might want to get together a small group (two or three other students) for a study session. Discussing a topic out loud can improve your understanding of that topic and will help you remember the key points that often come up on exams.

- If the test requires you to read a passage and then answer questions about that passage, read the questions first. This way, you will know what to look for as you read.

- When you first receive your exam, look it over quickly to make sure that you have all the pages. If you are uncertain, ask your professor or exam proctor. This initial scan may uncover other problems as well, such as illegible print or unclear instructions.

- Grades aren't a matter of life and death, and worrying too much about a single exam can have a negative effect on your performance. Keep exams in perspective. If you do poorly on one test, it's not the end of the world. Rather, it should motivate you to do better on the next one.

- Review your lecture notes immediately after each class, when the material is still fresh in your mind. Then, review each subject once a week, giving yourself an hour to go back over what you have learned. Reviews make tests easier because you will feel comfortable with the material.

- Some professors make old exams available, either by posting them online or putting them on file in the library. Old tests can give you an idea of the kinds of questions the professor likes to ask. You can also use them to take practice exams.

- With essay questions, look for key words such as "compare," "contrast," and "explain." These will guide your answer. If you have time, make a quick outline. Most important, get to the point without wasting your time (or your professor's) with statements such as "There are many possible reasons for . . ."

- Cramming just before the exam is a dangerous proposition. Cramming tires the brain unnecessarily and adds to stress, which can severely hamper your testing performance. If you've studied wisely, have confidence that the information will be available to you when you need it.

- When you finish a test early, your first instinct may be to hand it in and get out of the classroom as quickly as possible. It is always a good idea, however, to review your answers. You may find a mistake or an area where some extra writing will improve your grade.

- Be prepared. Make a list of everything you will need for the exam, such as a pen or pencil, watch, and calculator. Arrive at the exam early to avoid having to rush, which will only add to your stress. Good preparation helps you focus on the task at hand.

- Be sure to eat before taking a test. Having food in your stomach will give you the energy you need to concentrate. Don't go overboard, however. Too much food or heavy foods will make you sleepy during the exam.

Grades aren't a matter of life and death, and worrying about them can have a negative effect on your performance.

Cramming
just before the exam is a **dangerous** *proposition.*

READPREP

This textbook is the foundation for your introduction to criminal justice. It contains key concepts and terms that are important to your understanding of what criminal justice is all about. This knowledge will be important not only for you to succeed in this course, but for your future as you pursue a career in criminal justice. For this reason, it is essential that you develop good reading skills so that you can make the most out of this textbook.

Of course, all students know how to read, but reading for a college-level course goes beyond being able to recognize words on a page. As a student, you must read to learn. You have to be able to read a chapter with the goal of understanding its key points and how it relates to other chapters. In other words, you have to be able to read your textbook and be able to explain what it is all about. To do this, you need to develop good reading habits and reading skills.

READING FOR LEARNING REQUIRES FOCUS

Reading (and learning from) a textbook is not like reading a newspaper or a magazine or even a novel. The point of reading for learning isn't to get through the material as fast as you can or to skip parts to get to the stuff you're interested in. A textbook is a source of information about a subject, and the goal of reading a textbook is to learn as much of that information as you can. This kind of reading requires attention. When you read to learn, you have to make an effort to focus on the book and tune out other distractions so that you can understand and remember the information it presents.

READING FOR LEARNING TAKES TIME

When reading your textbook, you need to go slow. The most important part of reading for learning is not how many pages you get through or how fast you get through them. Instead, the goal is to learn the key concepts of criminal justice that are presented in each chapter. To do that, you need to read slowly, carefully, and with great attention.

Andrzej Tokarski/iStockphoto.com

READING FOR LEARNING TAKES REPETITION

Even the most well-read scholar will tell you that it's difficult to learn from a textbook just by reading through it once. To read for learning, you have to read your textbook a number of times. This doesn't mean, though, that you just sit and read the same section three or four times. Instead, you should follow a preview-read-review process. Here's a good guide to follow:

THE FIRST TIME The first time you read a section of the book, you should preview it. During the preview, pay attention to how the chapter is formatted. Look over the title of the chapter, the section headings, and high-lighted or bolded words. This will give you a good preview of the important ideas in the chapter. You should also pay close attention to any graphs, pictures, illustrations, or figures that are used in the chapter, since these provide a visual illustration of important concepts. You should also pay special attention to the first and last sentence of each paragraph. First sentences usually introduce the main point of the paragraph, while last sentences usually sum up what was presented in each paragraph.

The goal of previewing the section is to answer the question "What is the main idea?" Of course, you may not be able to come up with a detailed answer yet, but that's not the point of previewing. Instead, the point is to develop some general ideas about what the section is about so that when you do read it in full, you can have a guide for what to look for.

THE SECOND TIME After the preview, you'll want to read through the passage in detail. During this phase, it is important to read with a few of questions in mind: What is the main point of this paragraph? What does the author want me to learn from this? How does this relate to what I read before? Keeping these questions in mind will help you to be an attentive reader who is actively focusing on the main ideas of the passage.

It is helpful to take notes while reading in detail. There are several different methods of doing this—you can write notes in the margin, highlight important words and phrases, or write an outline. Whatever method you prefer, taking notes will help you read actively, identify important concepts, and remember them. Then when it comes time to review for the exam, the notes you've made will make your studying more efficient. Instead of reading through the entire chapter again, you can focus your studying energy on the areas that you've identified as most important.

After you have completed a detailed read of the chapter, take a break so that you can rest your mind (and your eyes). Then you should write up a summary or paraphrase of what you just read. You don't need to produce a detailed, lengthy summary of the whole chapter. Instead, try to produce a brief paraphrase that covers the most important ideas of the chapter. This paraphrase will help you remember the main points of the chapter, check the accuracy of your reading, and provide a good guide for later review.

THE THIRD TIME (AND BEYOND) After you've finished a detailed reading of the chapter, you should take the time to review the chapter (at least once, but maybe even two, three, or more times). During this step, you should review each paragraph and the notes you made, asking this question: "What was this paragraph about?" At this point, you'll want to answer the question in some detail; that is, you should develop a fairly good idea of the important points of what you read before.

A reading group is a great way to review the chapter. After completing the reading individually, group members should meet and take turns sharing

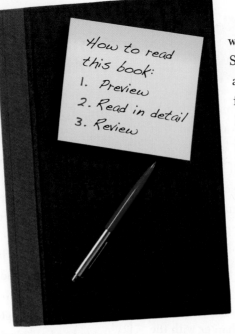

clu/iStockphoto.com

what they learned from their reading. Sharing what you learned from reading and explaining it to others will reinforce and clarify what you already know. It also provides an opportunity to learn from others. Getting a different perspective on a passage will increase your knowledge, since different people will find different things important during a reading.

Whether you're reading your textbook for the first time or reviewing it for the final exam, here are a couple of tips that will help you be an attentive and attuned reader.

Set aside time and space.

To read effectively, you need to be focused and attentive, and that won't happen if your phone is ringing every two minutes, if the TV is on in the background, if you're updating Twitter, or if you're surrounded by friends or family. Similarly, you won't be able to focus on your book if you're trying to read in a room that is too hot or too cold, or sitting in an uncomfortable chair. So when you read, find a quiet, comfortable place that is free from distractions where you can focus on one thing—learning from the book.

Take frequent breaks.

Reading your textbook shouldn't be a test of endurance. Rest your eyes and your mind by taking a short break every twenty to thirty minutes. The concentration you need to read attentively requires lots of energy, and you won't have enough energy if you don't take frequent breaks.

brave-carp/iStockphoto.com

Keep reading.

Effective reading is like playing sports or a musical instrument—practice makes perfect. The more time that you spend reading, the better you will be at learning from your textbook. Your vocabulary will grow, and you'll have an easier time learning and remembering information you find in textbooks.

WRITE PREP

A key part of succeeding as a student is learning how to write well. Whether writing papers, presentations, essays, or even e-mails to your instructor, you have to be able to put your thoughts into words and do so with force, clarity, and precision. In this section, we outline a three-phase process that you can use to write virtually anything.

1. Getting ready to write
2. Writing a first draft
3. Revising your draft

PHASE 1: GETTING READY TO WRITE

First, make a list. Divide the ultimate goal—a finished paper—into smaller steps that you can tackle right away. Estimate how long it will take to complete each step. Start with the date your paper is due and work backwards to the present: For example, if the due date is December 1, and you have about three months to write the paper, give yourself a cushion and schedule November 20 as your targeted completion date. Plan what you want to get done by November 1, and then list what you want to get done by October 1.

PICK a TOPIC To generate ideas for a topic, any of the following approaches work well:

- **Brainstorm with a group.** There is no need to create in isolation. You can harness the energy and the natural creative power of a group to assist you.
- **Speak it.** To get ideas flowing, start talking. Admit your confusion or lack of clear ideas. Then just speak. By putting your thoughts into words, you'll start thinking more clearly.
- **Use free writing.** Free writing, a technique championed by writing teacher Peter Elbow, is also very effective when trying to come up with a topic. There's only one rule in free writing: Write without stopping. Set a time limit—say, ten minutes—and keep your fingers dancing across the keyboard the whole time. Ignore the urge to stop and rewrite. There is no need to worry about spelling, punctuation, or grammar during this process.

REfine your idea After you've come up with some initial ideas, it's time to refine them:

- **Select a topic and working title.** Using your instructor's guidelines for the paper or speech, write down a list of topics that interest you. Write down all of the ideas you think of in two minutes. Then choose one topic. The most common pitfall is selecting a topic that is too broad. "Terrorism" is probably not a useful topic for your paper. Instead, consider "The Financing of Terrorist Activities."
- **Write a thesis statement.** Clarify what you want to say by summarizing it in one concise sentence. This sentence, called a *thesis statement*, refines your working title. A thesis is the main point of the paper; it is a declaration of some sort. You might write a thesis statement such as "Drug trafficking and other criminal activities are often used to finance terrorism."

SET GOALS Effective writing flows from a purpose. Think about how you'd like your reader or listener to respond after considering your ideas.

- If you want someone to think differently, make your writing clear and logical. Support your assertions with evidence.
- If your purpose is to move the reader into action, explain exactly what steps to take and offer solid benefits for doing so.

To clarify your purpose, state it in one sentence—for example, "The purpose of this paper is to discuss and analyze the various explanations for the nation's decreasing crime rate."

BEGIN RESEARCH At the initial stage, the objective of your research is not to uncover specific facts about your topic. That comes later. First, you want to gain an overview of the subject. Say that you want to persuade the reader to vote against the death penalty in your state. You must first learn enough about the death penalty to summarize for your reader its history, application, effectiveness as a deterrent, and so on.

MAKE AN OUTLINE An outline is a kind of map. When you follow a map, you avoid getting lost. Likewise, an outline keeps you from wandering off topic. To create your outline, follow these steps:

1. Review your thesis statement and identify the three to five main points you need to address in your paper to support or prove your thesis.

2. Next, look closely at those three to five major points or categories and think about what minor points or subcategories you want to cover in your paper. Your major points are your big ideas; your minor points are the details you need to fill in under each of those ideas.

3. Ask for feedback. Have your instructor or a classmate review your outline and offer suggestions for improvement. Did you choose the right categories and subcategories? Do you need more detail anywhere? Does the flow from idea to idea make sense?

DO IN-DEPTH RESEARCH Three-by-five-inch index cards are an old-fashioned but invaluable tool for in-depth research. Simply write down one idea or piece of information per card. This makes it easy to organize—and reorganize—your ideas and information. Organizing research cards as you create them saves time. Use rubber bands to keep *source cards* (cards that include the bibliographical information for a source) separate from *information cards* (cards that include nuggets of information from a source) and to maintain general categories.

When creating your cards, be sure to:

- Copy all of the information correctly.
- Always include the source and page number on information cards.
- Be neat and organized. Write legibly, using the same format for all of your cards.

In addition to source cards and information cards, generate *idea cards*. If you have a thought while you are researching, write it down on a card. Label these cards clearly as containing your own ideas.

PHASE 2: WRITING A FIRST DRAFT

To create your draft, gather your index cards and confirm that they are arranged to follow your outline. Then write about the ideas in your notes. It's that simple. Look at your cards and start writing. Write in paragraphs, with one idea per paragraph. As you complete this task, keep the following suggestions in mind:

- **Remember that the first draft is not for keeps.** You can worry about quality later; your goal at this point is simply to generate lots of words and lots of ideas.

- **Write freely.** Many writers prefer to get their first draft down quickly and would advise you to keep writing, much as in free writing. Of course, you may pause to glance at your cards and outline. The idea is to avoid stopping to edit your work.

- **Be yourself.** Let go of the urge to sound "official" or "scholarly" and avoid using unnecessarily big words or phrases. Instead, write in a natural voice.

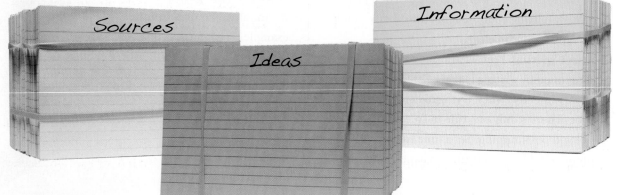

Address your thoughts not to the teacher but to an intelligent student or someone you care about. Visualize this person, and choose the three or four most important things you'd say to her about the topic.

- **Make writing a habit.** Don't wait for inspiration to strike. Make a habit of writing at a certain time each day.

- **Get physical.** While working on the first draft, take breaks. Go for a walk. Speak or sing your ideas out loud. From time to time, practice relaxation techniques and breathe deeply.

- **Hide it in your drawer for a while.** Schedule time for rewrites before you begin, and schedule at least one day between revisions so that you can let the material sit. The brain needs that much time to disengage itself from the project.

PHASE 3: REVISING YOUR DRAFT

During this phase, keep in mind the saying "Write in haste; revise at leisure." When you are working on your first draft, the goal is to produce ideas and write them down. During the revision phase, however, you need to slow down and take a close look at your work. One guideline is to allow 50 percent of writing time for planning, researching, and writing the first draft. Then use the remaining 50 percent for revising.

There are a number of especially good ways to revise your paper:

1. Read it out loud.

The combination of voice and ears forces us to pay attention to the details. Is the thesis statement clear and supported by enough evidence? Does the introduction tell your reader what's coming? Do you end with a strong conclusion that expands on what's in your introduction rather than just restating it?

2. Have a friend look over your paper.

This is never a substitute for your own review, but a friend can often see mistakes you miss. Remember, when other people criticize or review your work, they are not attacking you. They're just commenting on your paper. With a little

practice, you will learn to welcome feedback because it is one of the fastest ways to approach the revision process.

3. Cut.

Look for excess baggage. Avoid at all costs and at all times the really, really terrible mistake of using way too many unnecessary words, a mistake that some student writers often make when they sit down to write papers for the various courses in which they participate at the fine institutions of higher learning that they are fortunate enough to attend. (Example: The previous sentence could be edited to "Avoid unnecessary words.") Also, look for places where two (or more) sentences could be rewritten as one. Resist the temptation to think that by cutting text you are losing something. You are actually gaining—a clearer, more polished product. For maximum efficiency, make the larger cuts first—sections, chapters, pages. Then go for the smaller cuts—paragraphs, sentences, phrases, words.

4. Paste.

In deleting both larger and smaller passages in your first draft, you've probably removed some of the original transitions and connecting ideas. The next task is to rearrange what's left of your paper or speech so that it flows logically. Look for consistency within paragraphs and for transitions from paragraph to paragraph and section to section.

5. **Fix.**

Now it's time to look at individual words and phrases. Define any terms that the reader might not know, putting them in plain English whenever you can. In general, focus on nouns and verbs. Using too many adjectives and adverbs weakens your message and adds unnecessary bulk to your writing. Write about the details, and be specific. Also, check your writing to ensure that you are:

- Using the active voice. Write *"The research team began the project"* rather than (passively) *"A project was initiated."*

- Writing concisely. Instead of *"After making a timely arrival and perspicaciously observing the unfolding events, I emerged totally and gloriously victorious,"* be concise with *"I came, I saw, I conquered."*

- Communicating clearly. Instead of *"The speaker made effective use of the television medium, asking in no uncertain terms that we change our belief systems,"* you can write specifically, *"The reformed criminal stared straight into the television camera and shouted, 'Take a good look at what you're doing! Will it get you what you really want?'"*

6. **Prepare.**

In a sense, any paper is a sales effort. If you hand in a paper that is wearing wrinkled jeans, its hair tangled and unwashed and its shoes untied, your instructor is less likely to buy it. To avoid this situation, format your paper following accepted standards for margin widths, endnotes, title pages, and other details. Ask your instructor for specific instructions on how to cite the sources used in writing your paper. You can find useful guidelines in the *MLA Handbook for Writers of Research Papers*, a book from the Modern Language Association. If you cut and paste material from a Web page directly into your paper, be sure to place that material in quotation marks and cite the source. Before referencing an e-mail message, verify the sender's identity. Remember that anyone sending e-mail can pretend to be someone else. Use quality paper for the final version of your paper. For an even more professional appearance, bind your paper with a plastic or paper cover.

7. **Proof.**

As you ease down the home stretch, read your revised paper one more time. This time, go for the big picture and look for the following:

Feng Yu/iStockphoto.com

Proofreading checklist

☐ A clear thesis statement.

☐ Sentences that introduce your topic, guide the reader through the major sections of your paper, and summarize your conclusions.

☐ Details—such as quotations, examples, and statistics—that support your conclusions.

☐ Lean sentences that have been purged of needless words.

☐ Plenty of action verbs and concrete, specific nouns.

☐ Finally, look over your paper with an eye for spelling and grammar mistakes. Use contractions sparingly if at all. Use your word processor's spell-check by all means, but do not rely on it completely as it will not catch everything.

When you are through proofreading, take a minute to savor the result. You've just witnessed something of a miracle—the mind attaining clarity and resolution. That's the *aha!* in writing.

ACADEMIC INTEGRITY: AVOIDING PLAGIARISM

Joanne Harris and Daniel Bubnich/iStockphoto.com

Using another person's words, images, or other original creations without giving proper credit is called *plagiarism*. Plagiarism amounts to taking someone else's work and presenting it as your own—the equivalent of cheating on a test. The consequences of plagiarism can range from a failing grade to expulsion from school. Plagiarism can be unintentional. Some students don't understand the research process. Sometimes they leave writing until the last minute and don't take the time to organize their sources of information. Also, some people are raised in cultures where identity is based on group membership rather than individual achievement. These students may find it hard to understand how creative work can be owned by an individual.

To avoid plagiarism, ask an instructor where you can find your school's written policy on this issue. Don't assume that you can resubmit a paper you wrote for another class for a current class; many schools will regard this as plagiarism even though you wrote the paper. The basic guidelines for preventing plagiarism are to cite a source for each phrase, sequence of ideas, or visual image created by another person. While ideas cannot be copyrighted, the specific way that an idea is *expressed* can be. You also need to list a source for any idea that is closely identified with a particular person. The goal is to clearly distinguish your own work from the work of others. There are several ways to ensure that you do this consistently:

- **Identify direct quotes.** If you use a direct quote from another writer or speaker, put that person's words in quotation marks. If you do research online, you might find yourself copying sentences or paragraphs from a Web page and pasting them directly into your notes. This is the same as taking direct quotes from your source. To avoid plagiarism, identify such passages in an obvious way.

- **Paraphrase carefully.** Paraphrasing means restating the original passage in your own words, usually making it shorter and simpler. Students who copy a passage word for word and then just rearrange or delete a few phrases are running a serious risk of plagiarism. Remember to cite a source for paraphrases, just as you do for direct quotes. When you use the same sequence of ideas as one of your sources—even if you have not paraphrased or directly quoted—cite that source.

- **Note details about each source**. For books, details about each source include the author, title, publisher, publication date, location of publisher, and page number. For articles from serial print sources, record the article title and the name of the magazine or journal as well. If you found the article in an academic or technical journal, also record the volume and issue number of the publication. A librarian can help identify these details. If your source is a Web page, record as many identifying details as you can find—author, title, sponsoring organization, URL, publication date, and revision date. In addition, list the date that you accessed the page. Be careful when using Web resources, as not all Web sites are considered legitimate sources. Wikipedia, for instance, is not regarded as a legitimate source; the National Institute of Justice's Web site, however, is.

- **Cite your sources as endnotes or footnotes to your paper.** Ask your instructor for examples of the format to use. You do not need to credit wording that is wholly your own. Nor do you need to credit general ideas, such as the suggestion that people use a to-do list to plan their time. When you use your own words to describe such an idea, there's no need to credit a source. But if you borrow someone else's words or images to explain the idea, do give credit.

SPEECH PREP

In addition to reading and writing, your success as a student will depend on how well you can communicate what you have learned. Most often, you'll do so in the form of speeches. Many people are intimidated by the idea of public speaking, but it really is just like any other skill—the more often you do it, the more you practice, the better you will get. Developing a speech is similar to writing a paper. Begin by writing out your topic, purpose, and thesis statement. Then carefully analyze your audience by using the strategies listed below.

If your topic is new to listeners . . .

- Explain why your topic matters to them.
- Relate the topic to something that they already know and care about.
- Define any terms that they might not know.

If listeners already know about your topic . . .

- Acknowledge this fact at the beginning of your speech.
- Find a narrow aspect of the topic that may be new to listeners.

- Offer a new perspective on the topic, or connect it to an unfamiliar topic.

If listeners disagree with your thesis . . .

- Tactfully admit your differences of opinion.
- Reinforce points on which you and your audience agree.
- Build credibility by explaining your qualifications to speak on your topic.
- Quote experts who agree with your thesis—people whom your audience is likely to admire.
- Explain to your audience that their current viewpoint has costs for them and that a slight adjustment in their thinking will bring significant benefits.

If listeners might be uninterested in your topic . . .

- Explain how listening to your speech can help them gain something that matters deeply to them.
- Explain ways to apply your ideas in daily life.

Remember that audiences generally have one question in mind: *So what?* They want to know how your presentation relates to their needs and desires. To convince people that you have something worthwhile to say, think of your main topic or point. Then see if you can complete this sentence: I'm telling you this because . . .

Jacob Wackerhausen/IStockphoto.com / JazzIRT/iStockphoto.com

ORGANIZE YOUR PRESENTATIONS

Consider the length of your presentation. Plan on delivering about one hundred words per minute. Aim for a lean presentation—enough words to make your point but not so many as to make your audience restless. Leave your listeners wanting more. When you speak, be brief and then be seated. Speeches are usually organized in three main parts: the introduction, the main body, and the conclusion.

1. The introduction.

Rambling speeches with no clear point or organization put audiences to sleep. Solve this problem by making sure your introduction conveys the point of your presentation. The following introduction, for example, reveals the thesis and exactly what's coming. It reveals that the speech will have three distinct parts, each in logical order:

Prison overcrowding is a serious problem in many states. I intend to describe prison conditions around the country, the challenges these conditions create, and how various states are addressing the issue.

Some members of an audience will begin to drift during any speech, but most people pay attention for at least the first few seconds.

Highlight your main points in the beginning sentences of your speech. People might tell you to open your introduction with a joke, but humor is tricky. You run the risk of falling flat or offending somebody. Save jokes until you have plenty of experience with public speaking and know your audiences well. Also avoid long, flowery introductions in which you tell people how much you like them and how thrilled you are to address them. If you lay it on too thick,

your audience won't believe you. Draft your introduction, and then come back to it after you have written the rest of your speech. In the process of creating the main body and conclusion, your thoughts about the purpose and main points of your speech might change.

2. The main body.

The main body of your speech accounts for 70 to 90 percent of your speech. In the main body, you develop your ideas in much the same way that you develop a written paper. Transitions are especially important in speeches. Give your audience a signal when you change points. Do so by using meaningful pauses, verbal emphasis, and transitional phrases: "On the other hand, until the public realizes what is happening to children in these countries . . ." or "The second reason police officers use *Miranda* cards is . . ." In long speeches, recap from time to time. Also preview what's to come. Hold your audience's attention by using facts, descriptions, expert opinions, and statistics.

3. The conclusion.

At the end of the speech, summarize your points and draw your conclusion. You started with a bang; now finish with drama. The first and last parts of a speech are the most important. Make it clear to your audience when you have reached the end. Avoid endings such as "This is the end of my speech." A simple standby is "So, in conclusion, I want to reiterate three points: First . . ." When you are finished, stop speaking. Although this sounds quite obvious, a good speech is often ruined by a speaker who doesn't know when, or how, to wrap things up.

Speeches are usually organized in three main parts: the **introduction**, the **main body**, and the **conclusion**.

SUPPORT YOUR SPEECH WITH NOTES AND VISUALS

To create speaking notes, you can type out your speech in full and transfer key words or main points on a few three-by-five-inch index cards. Number the cards so that if you drop them, you can quickly put them in order again. As you finish the information on each card, move it to the back of the pile. Write information clearly and in letters large enough to be seen from a distance. The disadvantage of the index card system is that it involves card shuffling—so some speakers prefer to use standard outlined notes.

You can also create supporting visuals. Presentations often include visuals such as PowerPoint slides or hand-written flip charts. These visuals can reinforce your main points and help your audience understand how your presentation is organized. Use visuals to *complement* rather than *replace* speech. If you use too many visuals or visuals that are too complex, your audience might focus on them and forget about you. To avoid this fate:

OVERCOME FEAR OF PUBLIC SPEAKING

You may not be able to eliminate fear of public speaking entirely, but you can take steps to reduce and manage it.

PREPARE THOROUGHLY Research your topic thoroughly. Knowing your topic inside and out can create a baseline of confidence. To make a strong start, memorize the first four sentences that you plan to deliver, and practice them many times. Delivering them flawlessly when you're in front of an audience can build your confidence for the rest of your speech.

ACCEPT YOUR PHYSICAL SENSATIONS You have probably experienced the physical sensations that are commonly associated with stage fright: dry mouth, a pounding heart, sweaty hands, muscle jitters, shortness of breath, and a shaky voice. One immediate way to deal with such sensations is to simply notice them. Tell yourself, "Yes, my hands are clammy. Yes, my stomach is upset. Also, my face feels numb." Trying to deny or

- *Use fewer visuals rather than more. For a fifteen-minute presentation, a total of five to ten slides is usually enough.*

- *Limit the amount of text on each visual. Stick to key words presented in short sentences or phrases and in bulleted or numbered lists.*

- *Use a consistent set of plain fonts. Make them large enough for all audience members to see.*

- *Stick with a simple, coherent color scheme. Use light-colored text on a dark background or dark text on a light background.*

gehringj/iStockphoto.com

ignore such facts can increase your fear. In contrast, when you fully accept sensations, they start to lose power.

Focus on content, not delivery

If you view public speaking simply as an extension of an one-to-one conversation, the goal is not to perform but to communicate your ideas to an audience in the same ways that you would explain them to a friend. This can reduce your fear of public speaking. Instead of thinking about yourself, focus on your message. Your audience is more interested in what you have to say than in how you say it. Forget about giving a "speech." Just give people valuable ideas and information that they can use.

PRACTICE YOUR PRESENTATION

The key to successful public speaking is practice.

- [ ] **Use your "speaker's voice."** When you practice, do so in a loud voice. Your voice sounds different when you talk loudly, and this fact can be unnerving. Get used to it early on.
- [ ] **Practice in the room in which you will deliver your speech.**
- [ ] **Get familiar with the setting.** If you can't practice your speech in the actual room in which it will be given, at least visit the site ahead of time. Also make sure that the materials you will need for your speech, including any audiovisual equipment, will be available when you want them.
- [ ] **Make a recording.** Many schools have video recording equipment available for student use. Use it while you practice. Then view the finished recording to evaluate your presentation. Pay special attention to your body language—how you stand, your eye contact, how you use your hands.
- [ ] **Listen for repeated words and phrases.** Examples include *you know, kind of,* and *really,* plus any instances of *uh, umm,* and *ah.* To get rid of them, tell yourself that you intend to notice every time they pop up in your daily speech.
- [ ] **Keep practicing.** Avoid speaking word for word, as if you were reading a script. When you know your material well, you can deliver

it in a natural way. Practice your presentation until you could deliver it in your sleep. Then run through it a few more times.

DELIVER YOUR PRESENTATION

Before you begin, get the audience's attention. If people are still filing into the room or adjusting their seats, they're not ready to listen. Wait for the audience to settle into their seats before you begin.

For a great speech, keep these tips in mind:

Dress for the occasion

The clothing you choose to wear on the day of your speech delivers a message that's as loud as your words. Consider how your audience will be dressed, and then choose a wardrobe based on the impression you want to make.

Project your voice

When you speak, talk loudly enough to be heard. Avoid leaning over your notes or the podium.

Maintain eye contact

When you look at people, they become less frightening. Remember, too, that it is easier for the audience to listen to someone when that person is looking at them. Find a few friendly faces around the room, and imagine that you are talking to each of these people individually.

NOTICE YOUR NONVERBAL COMMUNICATION, YOUR BODY LANGUAGE Be aware of what your body is telling your audience. Contrived or staged gestures will look dishonest. Hands in pockets, twisting your hair, chewing gum, or leaning against a wall will all make you appear less polished than you want to.

WATCH THE TIME You can increase the impact of your words by keeping track of the time during your speech. It's better to end early than to run late.

PAUSE WHEN APPROPRIATE Beginners sometimes feel that they have to fill every moment with the sound of their voice. Release that expectation. Give your listeners a chance to make notes and absorb what you say.

HAVE FUN Chances are that if you lighten up and enjoy your presentation, so will your listeners.

REFLECT ON YOUR PRESENTATION

Review and reflect on your performance. Did you finish on time? Did you cover all of the points you intended to cover? Was the audience attentive? Did you handle any nervousness effectively? Welcome evaluation from others. Most of us find it difficult to hear criticism about our speaking. Be aware of resisting such criticism, and then let go of your resistance. Listening to feedback will increase your skill.

TALKING ABOUT PRACTICE

When practicing your speech, you'll need to do more than just read through it silently. While it's good to use practice sessions to memorize the contents of your speech, they are also important times to work on how you use your voice and body as you speak. To make your practice time efficient and beneficial, follow the two-step process shown below and repeat it two or three (or more times) until you're ready to deliver a masterful speech.

1. Practice

- If possible, practice your speech in the location where you will be actually giving it. If this is not possible, make your practice setting as similar to the actual setting as possible.
- Record your practice so that you can analyze it later.
- Working from your outline or notes, go through the entire speech without stopping. If you make mistakes, try to fix them as you go along.

2. Review

Watch the recording of your first practice and ask yourself:

- Did I leave out important ideas?
- Did I focus too much on one point and not enough on others?
- Did I talk too fast or too slow?
- Did I speak clearly?
- Was my body language distracting or helpful?
- Did I maintain good eye contact?

After watching the recording, write down three or four specific changes that you will make to improve your speech.

1 CRIMINAL JUSTICE TODAY

Learning Outcomes

After studying this chapter, you will be able to . . .

 LO 1 Define crime and identify the different types of crime.

 LO 2 Outline the three levels of law enforcement.

 LO 3 List the essential elements of the corrections system.

LO 4 Explain the difference between the formal and informal criminal justice processes.

LO 5 Contrast the crime control and due process models.

Warning Signs

During his time at Pima Community College in Tucson, Arizona, Jared Loughner was hardly a model student. Over a seven-month stretch in 2010, Loughner had no fewer than seven contacts with campus police. In one classroom incident, which led an officer to suggest that school administrators "keep an eye" on Loughner, he blurted out that dynamite ought to be strapped to baby suicide bombers. In another, Loughner confronted a teacher for giving him a B in her Pilates course. Following a bizarre argument over the meaning of the "number 6," math instructor Ben McGahee began watching Loughner out of the corner of his eye. "I was afraid he was going to pull out a weapon," said McGahee.

College officials finally suspended Loughner in late September after he made a YouTube video describing Pima as "my genocide school" and calling it "one of the biggest scams in America." The suspension did little to curtail Loughner's pattern of disturbing behavior. He had a 9-millimeter bullet tattooed on his right shoulder blade. He posted incomprehensible tutorials concerning U.S. currency on the Internet. He purchased a Glock 19 semiautomatic pistol and took pictures of himself posing with the gun while wearing nothing but a bright red G-string.

Then, at 5 a.m. on the morning of January 8, 2011, Loughner posted a chilling message on his Myspace page: "Goodbye. Dear friends . . . please don't be mad at me." Several hours later, he opened fire with his Glock 19 into a crowd that had gathered outside a supermarket to "meet-and-greet" Arizona congresswoman Gabrielle Giffords. Before being wrestled to the ground, Loughner killed six of the attendees and wounded thirteen, including Giffords, who was shot in the head. "It wasn't a case of 'Gee, no one saw this coming,'" said Randy Borum, a violent crime expert at the University of South Florida, referring to Loughner's behavior leading up to the tragedy. "People saw it. But the question then was, what do you do about it? Who do you call?"

ARCHIE CARPENTER/UPI /Landov

In what ways were the violent actions of Jared Loughner, who killed nine-year-old Christina Green (memorialized here) and five others, foreseeable? In what ways were Loughner's crimes unpredictable? (Photo by John Moore/Getty Images)

Crime An act that violates criminal law and is punishable by criminal sanctions.

By all accounts, Pima Community College officials had taken the threat posed by Jared Loughner seriously. The school's Behavior Assessment Committee had identified him as a "person of concern," which led to his eventual suspension. Just a week before Loughner's shooting rampage, college police commander Manny Amado announced plans to circulate the twenty-two-year-old's photo to staff members as a precautionary measure.[1] The problem, perhaps, was that Pima officials had failed to warn local law enforcement about Loughner's behavior. Even if they had issued a warning, it seems unlikely that it would have been heeded. "Students get kicked out of school for a multitude of reasons," says security expert Dan Borelli. "That doesn't necessarily mean that they're going to go kill somebody."[2]

The Loughner case raises several other interesting issues. First, a number of observers believe that his odd behavior in the months leading up to the massacre can be attributed to a form of delusional thinking known as schizophrenia. In Chapter 2, we will address the question of whether mental illness causes criminal behavior. Second, if Loughner is mentally ill, how should he be punished for his actions? In Chapter 4, you will learn about the insanity defense and its place in American criminal courts. Finally, if ultimately found guilty on several charges of murder and attempted murder, should Loughner be put to death? As we shall see in Chapter 11, capital punishment is one of the more hotly debated topics in criminal justice.

As you proceed through this textbook, you will see that few aspects of crime and justice are ever simple, even though you may have clear opinions about them. In this first chapter, we will introduce you to the criminal justice system by discussing its structure, the values that it is designed to promote, and the most challenging issues it faces today.

¿WHAT IS CRIME?

Three years before he opened fire on Gabrielle Giffords and his other victims, Jared Loughner was arrested on a minor drug charge related to marijuana use. For all his "creepy," "very hostile," and "suspicious" behavior, this was the only *criminal* wrongdoing in Loughner's past. Throughout this textbook, the word *crime* will only be used to describe a certain category of behavior that goes beyond making inappropriate comments in a classroom or on the Internet. In general, a **crime** can be defined as a wrong against society proclaimed by law and, if committed under certain circumstances, punishable by society. One problem with this definition, however, is that it obscures the complex nature of societies. A society is not static—it evolves and changes, and its concept of criminality evolves and changes as well. Different societies can have vastly different ideas of what constitutes a crime. In 2010, for example, Thai police arrested Thanthawut Thaweevarodomkul for operating a Web

Thirty states have laws banning texting while driving, with penalties ranging from fines to jail sentences. What are the arguments for and against making the sort of behavior shown in this photo a crime and punishing it with criminal sanctions?

(AP Photo/Elaine Thompson)

site that allegedly disparaged King Bhumibol Adulyadej. Thailand's criminal code prohibits anyone from "defaming" or "insulting" a member of the country's royal family. Such legislation protecting public figures from criticism would not be allowed in the United States because of our country's long tradition of free speech.

To more fully understand the concept of crime, it will help to examine the two most common models of how society "decides" which acts are criminal: the consensus model and the conflict model.

THE CONSENSUS MODEL

The term *consensus* refers to general agreement among the majority of any particular group. Thus, the **consensus model** rests on the assumption that as people gather together to form a society, its members will naturally come to a basic agreement with regard to shared norms (standards of behavior) and values. Those individuals whose actions are *deviant* (do not conform to the established norms and values) are considered to pose a threat to the well-being of society as a whole and must be sanctioned (punished). The society passes laws to control and prevent deviant behavior, thereby setting the boundaries for acceptable behavior within the group.[3]

Public Morality The consensus model, to a certain extent, assumes that a diverse group of people can have similar **morals**. That is, they share an ideal of what is "right" and "wrong." Consequently, as public attitudes toward morality change, so do laws. In colonial times, those found guilty of adultery were subjected to corporal punishment. A century ago, one could walk into a pharmacy and purchase heroin. Today, social attitudes have shifted to consider adultery a personal issue, beyond the authority of the state, and to consider the sale of heroin a criminal act.

Public Pressure Sometimes, a consensus forces the government to move more quickly. In the autumn of 2010, national media outlets began to focus on the negative effects of Four Loko, a 23.5-ounce canned beverage that combined the alcohol content of nearly six servings of beer and a strong dose of caffeine. Popular on college campuses, this "blackout in a can" was blamed for the hospitalization of nearly two dozen students with alcohol poisoning. By the end of the year, bowing to public pressure, the federal government and several state governments had banned the sale of Four Loko and other similar drinks. (CAREER TIP: The federal government employs law enforcement agents called *consumer safety officers* to investigate reports of injury, illness, or death caused by certain consumer products.)

Source: www.fda.com

Consensus Model A criminal justice model in which the majority of citizens in a society share the same values and beliefs.

Morals Principles of right and wrong behavior, as practiced by individuals or by society.

Conflict Model A criminal justice model in which the content of criminal law is determined by the groups that hold economic, political, and social power in a community.

THE CONFLICT MODEL

Some people reject the consensus model on the ground that moral attitudes are not constant or even consistent. In large, democratic societies such as the United States, different groups of citizens have widely varying opinions on controversial issues of morality and criminality, including abortion, the war on drugs, immigration, and assisted suicide. These groups and their elected representatives are constantly coming into conflict with one another. According to the **conflict model**, then, the most politically powerful segments of society—based on class, income, age, and race—have the most influence on criminal laws and are therefore able to impose their values on the rest of the community.

Consequently, what activity is deemed criminal is determined by whichever group happens to be holding power at any given time. Because certain groups do not have access to political power, their interests are not served by the criminal justice system. To give one example, with the exception of Oregon and Washington

Deviance Behavior that is considered to go against the norms established by society.

State, physician-assisted suicide is illegal in the United States. Although opinion polls show that the general public is evenly divided on the issue,[4] several highly motivated interest groups have been able to convince lawmakers that the practice goes against America's shared moral and religious values.

AN INTEGRATED DEFINITION OF CRIME

LO| Considering both the consensus and conflict models, we can construct a definition of crime that will be useful throughout this textbook. For our purposes, crime is an action or activity that is

1. Punishable under criminal law, as determined by the majority or, in some cases, by a powerful minority.

2. Considered an *offense against society as a whole* and prosecuted by public officials, not by victims and their relatives or friends.

3. Punishable by sanctions based on law that bring about the loss of personal freedom or life.

At this point, it is important to understand the difference between crime and **deviance**, or behavior that does not conform to the norms of a given community or society. Deviance is a subjective concept, in that some segments of society may think that smoking marijuana or killing animals for clothing and food is deviant behavior. Deviant acts become crimes only when society as a whole, through its legislatures, determines that those acts should be punished—as is the situation today in the United States with using illegal drugs but not with eating meat. Furthermore, not all crimes are considered particularly deviant. For example, little social disapproval is attached to those who fail to follow the letter of parking laws. In essence, criminal law reflects those

CAREERPREP

CRIME SCENE PHOTOGRAPHER

JOB DESCRIPTION:

- Photograph physical evidence and crime scenes related to criminal investigations.
- Be able to compose reports, testify in court, and operate digital and fluorescent camera equipment.

WHAT KIND OF TRAINING IS REQUIRED?

- One year in law enforcement or commercial photography OR a degree or certificate in photography OR some combination of the above training or experience totaling one year.
- Must be willing to work irregular hours, weekends, holidays, and evenings.

ANNUAL SALARY RANGE?

- $45,780–$53,290

For additional information, visit:
www.crime-scene-investigator.net/csi-photo.html

Korhan Hasim Isik/iStockphoto.com/
Rich H. Legg/iStockphoto

CRIME SCENE DO NOT CROSS

> **"There is no such crime as a crime of thought; there are only crimes of action."**
>
> CLARENCE DARROW,
> American Attorney (1857 – 1938)

As you will see in Chapter 4, these violent crimes are further classified by *degree*, depending on the circumstances surrounding the criminal act. These circumstances include the intent of the person committing the crime, whether a weapon was used, and (in cases other than murder) the level of pain and suffering experienced by the victim.

Murder The unlawful killing of one human being by another.

Sexual Assault Forced or coerced sexual intercourse (or other sexual acts).

Assault A threat or an attempt to do violence to another person that causes that person to fear immediate physical harm.

Battery The act of physically contacting another person with the intent to do harm, even if the resulting injury is minor.

Robbery The act of taking property from another person through force, threat of force, or intimidation.

acts that we, as a society, agree are so unacceptable that steps must be taken to prevent them from occurring.

TYPES OF CRIME

The manner in which crimes are classified depends on their seriousness. Federal, state, and local legislation has provided for the classification and punishment of hundreds of thousands of different criminal acts, ranging from jaywalking to first degree murder. For general purposes, we can group criminal behavior into six categories: violent crime, property crime, public order crime, white-collar crime, organized crime, and high-tech crime.

Violent Crime Crimes against persons, or *violent crimes*, have come to dominate our perspectives on crime. There are four major categories of violent crime:

- **Murder,** or the unlawful killing of a human being.
- **Sexual assault,** or *rape*, which refers to forced actions of a sexual nature against an unwilling participant.
- **Assault** and **battery,** two separate acts that cover situations in which one person physically attacks another (battery) or, through threats, intentionally leads another to believe that he or she will be physically harmed (assault).
- **Robbery,** or the taking of funds, personal property, or any other article of value from a person by means of force or fear.

Property Crime The most common form of criminal activity is *property crime*, or those crimes in which the goal of the offender is some form of economic

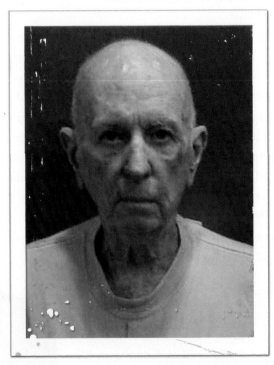

In 2010, eighty-eight-year-old Roy Charles Laird performed what a family member described as a "mercy killing" by fatally shooting his ill, long-suffering, eighty-six-year old wife, Clara, at her nursing home in Seal Beach, California. Why is it important that Laird be charged with the crime of murder, whatever his motives? (AP Photo/Orange County Sheriff's Department)

Larceny The act of taking property from another person without the use of force with the intent of keeping that property.

Burglary The act of breaking into or entering a structure (such as a home or office) without permission for the purpose of committing a crime.

Public Order Crime Behavior that has been labeled criminal because it is contrary to shared social values, customs, and norms.

White-Collar Crime Nonviolent crimes committed by business entities or individuals to gain a personal or business advantage.

gain or the damaging of property. Pocket picking, shoplifting, and the stealing of any property that is not accomplished by force are covered by laws against **larceny**, also known as *theft*. **Burglary** refers to the unlawful entry of a structure with the intention of committing a serious crime such as theft. *Motor vehicle theft* describes the theft or attempted theft of a motor vehicle, including all cases in which automobiles are taken by persons not having lawful access to them.

Arson, also a property crime, involves the willful and malicious burning of a home, automobile, commercial building, or any other construction.

Public Order Crime The concept of **public order crimes** is linked to the consensus model discussed earlier. Historically, societies have always outlawed activities that are considered contrary to public values and morals. Today, the most common public order crimes include public drunkenness, prostitution, gambling, and illicit drug use. These crimes are sometimes referred to as *victimless crimes* because they often harm only the offender. As you will see throughout this textbook, however, that term is rather misleading. Public order crimes may create an environment that gives rise to property and violent crimes.

White-Collar Crime Business-related crimes are popularly referred to as **white-collar crimes**. The term *white-collar crime* is broadly used to describe an illegal act or series of acts committed by an

Jesus Jauregui/iStockphoto

individual or business entity using some nonviolent means to obtain a personal or business advantage. Examples include various types of fraud and embezzlement, in which an individual uses her or his position within an organization to steal the employer's funds or other property. Although the extent of white-collar crime is difficult to determine with any certainty, the Association of Certified Fraud Examiners estimates that this criminal activity costs businesses as much as $3 trillion a year worldwide.[5] The issue of white-collar crime was thrust into the spotlight several years ago when Bernard L. Madoff (see photo below) was sentenced to 150 years behind bars for defrauding investors of $65 billion.

What are some of the justifications for punishing white-collar criminals such as Bernard L. Madoff, right, with lengthy prison sentences? (Timothy A. Clary/AFP/Getty Images)

Organized Crime White-collar crime involves the use of legal business facilities and employees to commit illegal acts. For example, a bank teller can't embezzle unless he or she is first hired as a legal employee of the bank. In contrast, **organized crime** describes illegal acts by illegal organizations, usually geared toward satisfying the public's demand for unlawful goods and services. Organized crime broadly implies a conspiratorial and illegal relationship among any number of persons engaged in unlawful acts. More specifically, groups engaged in organized crime employ criminal tactics such as violence, corruption, and intimidation for economic gain. The hierarchical structure of organized crime operations often mirrors that of legitimate businesses, and, like any corporation, these groups attempt to capture a sufficient percentage of any given market to make a profit. For organized crime, the traditional preferred markets are gambling, prostitution, illegal narcotics, and loan sharking (lending funds at higher-than-legal interest rates), along with more recent ventures into counterfeiting and credit-card scams.

High-Tech Crime The newest variation on crime is directly related to the increased presence of computers in everyday life. The Internet, with approximately 2 billion users worldwide, is the site of numerous *cyber crimes*, such as selling pornographic materials, soliciting minors, and defrauding consumers through bogus financial investments. The dependence of businesses on computer operations has left corporations vulnerable to sabotage, fraud, embezzlement, and theft of proprietary data. We will address cyber crime in much greater detail in Chapter 17.

¿WHAT IS THE CRIMINAL JUSTICE SYSTEM?

Defining which actions are to be labeled "crimes" is only the first step in safeguarding society from criminal behavior. Institutions must be created to apprehend alleged wrongdoers, to determine whether these persons have indeed committed crimes, and to punish

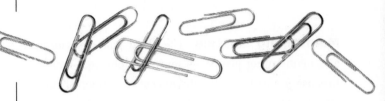

"Organized crime *takes in over forty billion dollars a year. This is quite a profitable sum, especially when one considers that the Mafia spends very little for office supplies."*

—WOODY ALLEN, AMERICAN HUMORIST

those who are found guilty according to society's wishes. These institutions combine to form the **criminal justice system**. As we begin our examination of the American criminal justice system in this introductory chapter, it is important to have an idea of its purpose.

THE PURPOSE OF THE CRIMINAL JUSTICE SYSTEM

In 1967, the President's Commission on Law Enforcement and Administration of Justice stated that the criminal justice system is obliged to enforce accepted standards of conduct so as to "protect individuals and the community."[6] Given this general mandate, we can further separate the purpose of the modern criminal justice system into three general goals:

1. To control crime.
2. To prevent crime.
3. To provide and maintain justice.

Controlling and Preventing Crime Although many observers differ on the precise methods of reaching them, the first two goals are fairly straightforward. By arresting, prosecuting, and punishing wrongdoers, the criminal justice system attempts to *control* crime. In the

Organized Crime Illegal acts carried out by illegal organizations engaged in the market for illegal goods or services.

Criminal Justice System The interlocking network of law enforcement agencies, courts, and corrections institutions designed to enforce criminal laws.

Justice The quality of fairness that must exist in the processes designed to determine whether citizens are guilty of criminal wrongdoing.

Federalism A form of government in which a written constitution provides for a division of powers between a central government and several regional governments.

process, the system also hopes to *prevent* new crimes from taking place. The prevention goal is often used to justify harsh punishments for wrongdoers, which some see as deterring others from committing similar criminal acts.

Maintaining Justice The third goal—providing and maintaining justice—is more complicated, largely because *justice* is a difficult concept to define. Broadly stated, **justice** means that all citizens are equal before the law and that they are free from arbitrary arrest or seizure as defined by the law. In other words, the idea of justice is linked with the idea of fairness. Above all, we want our laws and the means by which they are carried out to be fair.

Justice and fairness are subjective terms. Different people may have different concepts of what is just and fair. If a woman who has been beaten by her husband retaliates by killing him, what is her just punishment? Reasonable persons could disagree, with some thinking that the homicide was justified and that the woman should be treated leniently. Others might insist that she should not have taken the law into her own hands. Police officers, judges, prosecutors, prison administrators, and other employees of the criminal justice system must decide what is "fair." Sometimes, their course of action is obvious. Often as we shall see, it is not.

Society places the burden of controlling crime, preventing crime, and determining fairness on those citizens who work in the three main institutions of the criminal justice system: law enforcement, courts, and corrections. In the next section, we take an introductory look at these institutions and their roles in the criminal justice system as a whole.

THE STRUCTURE OF THE CRIMINAL JUSTICE SYSTEM

To understand the structure of the criminal justice system, you must understand the concept of **federalism,** which means that government powers are shared by the national (federal) government and the states. The framers of the U.S. Constitution, fearful of tyranny and a too-powerful central government, chose the system of federalism as a compromise. The appeal of federalism was that it established a strong national government capable of handling large-scale problems while allowing for state powers and local traditions. For example, earlier in the chapter we noted that physician-assisted suicide, banned in most of the country, is legal in Oregon and Washington State. Several years ago, the federal government challenged the decision made by voters in those two states to allow the practice. The United States Supreme Court sided with the states, ruling that the principle of federalism supported their freedom to differ from the majority viewpoint in this instance.[7]

The Constitution gave the national government certain express powers, such as the power to coin money, raise an army, and regulate interstate commerce. All other powers were left to the states, including police power, which allows the states to enact whatever laws are necessary to protect the health, morals, safety, and welfare of their citizens. As the American criminal justice system has evolved, the ideals of federalism have ebbed somewhat. In particular, the powers of the national government have expanded significantly. Crime is still primarily a local concern, however, and the majority of all employees in the criminal justice system work for local government (see **Figure 1.1** on the facing page).

Law Enforcement The ideals of federalism can be clearly seen in the local, state, and federal levels of law enforcement. Although agencies from the different levels cooperate if the need arises, they have their own organizational structures and tend to operate independently of one another. We briefly introduce each level of law enforcement here and cover the levels in more detail in Chapters 5, 6, and 7.

LO2

Local and County Law Enforcement On the local level, the duties of law enforcement agencies are split between counties and municipalities. The chief law enforcement officer of most counties is the county sheriff. The sheriff is usually an elected post, with a two- or four-year term. In some areas, where city and county governments have merged, there is a county police force, headed by a chief of police. The bulk of

Figure 1.1   Local, State, and Federal Employees in Our Criminal Justice System

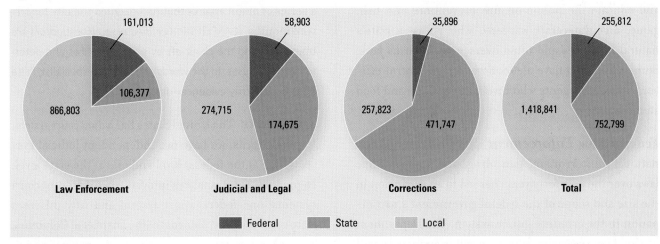

| | Federal | State | Local |

Law Enforcement: 161,013 · 106,377 · 866,803

Judicial and Legal: 58,903 · 174,675 · 274,715

Corrections: 35,896 · 471,747 · 257,823

Total: 255,812 · 752,799 · 1,418,841

Source: Bureau of Justice Statistics, *Justice Expenditure and Employment in the United States, 2006* (Washington, D.C.: U.S. Department of Justice, December 2008), Table 2.

all police officers in the United States are employed by municipalities. The majority of these forces consist of fewer than ten officers, though a large city such as New York may have a police force of about 38,000.

Local police are responsible for the nuts and bolts of law enforcement work. They investigate most crimes and attempt to deter criminal activity through patrol activities. They apprehend criminals and participate in trial proceedings, if necessary. Local police are also charged with keeping the peace, a broad set of duties that includes crowd and traffic control and the resolution of minor conflicts between citizens. In many areas, local police have the added obligation of providing social services such as dealing with domestic violence and child abuse.

State Law Enforcement Hawaii is the only state that does not have a state law enforcement agency. Generally, there are two types of state law enforcement agencies: those designated simply as *state police* and those designated as *highway patrols.* State highway patrols concern themselves mainly with infractions on public highways and freeways. Other state law enforcers

CAREER PREP   LOCAL POLICE OFFICER

JOB DESCRIPTION:

- Protect the lives and property of citizens in the community.

- Maintain order, catch those who break the law, and strive to prevent crimes.

- Testify at trials and hearings.

WHAT KIND OF TRAINING IS REQUIRED?

- Almost every police department requires that applicants be high school graduates, and an increasing number of departments expect a college degree.

- Minimum height, weight, eyesight, and hearing requirements, as well as the passage of physical examinations and background checks.

- Graduation from a police academy.

ANNUAL SALARY RANGE?

- $30,000–$80,000

For additional information, visit:
www.bls.gov/oco/ocos160.htm.

include fire marshals, who investigate suspicious fires and educate the public on fire prevention; and fish, game, and watercraft wardens, who police a state's natural resources and often oversee its firearms laws. Some states also have alcoholic beverage control officers, as well as agents who investigate welfare and food stamp fraud.

Federal Law Enforcement

The enactment of new national antiterrorism, gun, drug, and violent crime laws over the past forty years has led to an expansion in the size and scope of the federal government's participation in the criminal justice system. The Department of Homeland Security, which we will examine in detail in Chapters 5 and 16, combines the police powers of twenty-four federal agencies to protect the United States from terrorist attacks. Other federal agencies with police powers include the Federal Bureau of Investigation (FBI), the Drug Enforcement Administration, the U.S. Secret Service, and the Bureau of Alcohol, Tobacco, Firearms and Explosives (ATF).

In fact, almost every federal agency, including the postal and forest services, has some kind of police power. Unlike their local and state counterparts, federal law enforcement agencies operate throughout the United States. In November 2010, for example, the FBI conducted a nationwide sweep to remove children from the illegal sex trade, rescuing sixty-nine teenage prostitutes and arresting more than 880 suspects in cities from Miami to Detroit to Seattle. Federal agencies are also available to provide support for overworked local police departments, as was necessary several years ago when agents from the ATF joined forces with the

Coatesville (Pennsylvania) Police Department to combat a series of arson attacks that had plagued the city for fifteen months. (CAREER TIP: *Certified arson investigators* are trained to read the clues left by suspicious fires and determine their causes. In the words of one arson specialist, "Fire does not destroy evidence—it creates it.")

The Courts

The United States has a *dual court system*. In other words, we have two independent judicial systems, one at the federal level and one at the state level. In practice, this translates into fifty-two different court systems: one federal court system and fifty different state court systems, plus that of the District of Columbia. The federal system consists of district courts, circuit courts of appeals, and the United States Supreme Court. The state systems include trial courts, intermediate courts of appeals, and state supreme courts.

The *criminal court* and its work group—the judge, prosecutors, and defense attorneys—are charged with the weighty responsibility of determining the innocence or guilt of criminal suspects. We will cover these important participants, their roles in the criminal trial, and the court system as a whole in Chapters 8, 9, 10, and 11.

A sheriff's deputy, left, and a local police officer open fire on a trailer in Enon Beach, Ohio, on January 1, 2011. What is the main difference between local and federal law enforcement agents? How does this difference reflect the concept of federalism? (AP Photo/Springfield News-Sun, Marshall Gorby)

> "It is the **spirit** and not the form of the law that keeps justice alive."
>
> EARL WARREN,
> American jurist
> 1891–1974

(Paul Kooi/iStockphoto)

U.S. Army Photo by Jeffrey Castro

Corrections Once the court system convicts and sentences an offender, she or he is delegated to the corrections system. Depending on the seriousness of the crime and their individual needs, offenders are placed on probation, incarcerated, or transferred to community-based corrections facilities.

LO 3

- *Probation*, the most common correctional treatment, allows the offender to return to the community and remain under the supervision of an agent of the court known as a probation officer. While on probation, the offender must follow certain rules of conduct. When probationers fail to follow these rules, they may be incarcerated.

- If the offender's sentence includes a period of *incarceration*, he or she will be remanded (ordered to go) to a correctional facility for a certain amount of time. *Jails* hold those convicted of minor crimes with relatively short sentences, as well as those awaiting trial or involved in certain court proceedings. *Prisons* house those convicted of more serious crimes serving longer sentences. Generally speaking, counties and municipalities administer jails, while prisons are the domain of federal and state governments.

- *Community-based corrections* have increased in popularity as jails and prisons have been plagued with problems of funding and overcrowding. Community-based correctional facilities include halfway houses, residential centers, and work-release centers; they operate on the assumption that all convicts do not need, and are not benefited by, incarceration in jail or prison.

The majority of those inmates released from incarceration are not finished with the correctional system. The most frequent type of release from a jail or prison is *parole*, in which an inmate, after serving part of his or her sentence in a correctional facility, is allowed to serve the rest of the term in the community. Like someone on probation, a parolee must conform to certain conditions of freedom, with the same consequences if these conditions are not followed. Issues of probation, incarceration, community-based corrections, and parole will be covered in Chapters 12, 13, and 14.

THE CRIMINAL JUSTICE PROCESS

In its 1967 report, the President's Commission on Law Enforcement and Administration of Justice asserted that the criminal justice system

> is not a hodgepodge of random actions. It is rather a continuum—an orderly progression of events—some of which, like arrest and trial, are highly visible and some of which, though of great importance, occur out of public view.[8]

The commission's assertion that the criminal justice system is a "continuum" is one that many observers would challenge.[9] Some liken the criminal justice system to a sports team, which is the sum of

CAREER TIP: For those interested in both a military and a law enforcement career, the U.S. Army's *Criminal Investigation Command* is responsible for investigating crimes involving military personnel.

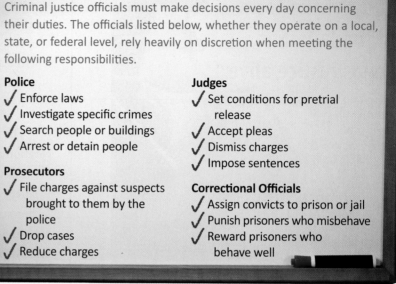

Figure 1.2 Discretion in the Criminal Justice System

Criminal justice officials must make decisions every day concerning their duties. The officials listed below, whether they operate on a local, state, or federal level, rely heavily on discretion when meeting the following responsibilities.

Police
✓ Enforce laws
✓ Investigate specific crimes
✓ Search people or buildings
✓ Arrest or detain people

Prosecutors
✓ File charges against suspects brought to them by the police
✓ Drop cases
✓ Reduce charges

Judges
✓ Set conditions for pretrial release
✓ Accept pleas
✓ Dismiss charges
✓ Impose sentences

Correctional Officials
✓ Assign convicts to prison or jail
✓ Punish prisoners who misbehave
✓ Reward prisoners who behave well

Mark Stahl/iStockphoto.com

an indeterminable number of decisions, relationships, conflicts, and adjustments.[10] Such a volatile mix is not what we generally associate with a "system." For most, the word **system** indicates a certain degree of order and discipline. That we refer to our law enforcement agencies, courts, and correctional facilities as part of a system may reflect our hopes rather than reality.

The Assembly Line Just as there is an idealized image of the criminal justice system as a smooth continuum, there also exists an idealized version of the *criminal justice process*, or the procedures through which the criminal justice system meets the expectations of society. Professor Herbert Packer, for example, compared the idealized criminal justice process to an assembly line,

> down which moves an endless stream of cases, never stopping, carrying the cases to workers who stand at fixed stations and who perform on each case as it comes by the same small but essential operation that brings it one stop closer to being a finished product, or, to exchange the metaphor for the reality, a closed file.[11]

As Packer himself was wont to point out, the daily operations of criminal justice are not nearly so perfect. In this textbook, the criminal justice process will be examined as the end product of thousands of decisions made by police officers, courtroom workers, and correctional administrators. It should become clear that, in fact, the criminal justice process functions as a continuous balancing act between its formal and informal nature.

The Formal Criminal Justice Process In Packer's image of assembly-line justice, each step of the

LO4 formal process "involves a series of routinized operations whose success is gauged primarily by their tendency to pass the case along to a successful conclusion."[12]

The Informal Criminal Justice Process Each step in the process is the result of a series of decisions that must be made by those who work in the criminal justice system. This **discretion**—which can be defined as the authority to choose between and among alternative courses of action—leads to the development of the informal criminal justice process, discussed below.

Discretionary Basics One New York City public defender called his job "a pressure cooker." That description could apply to the entire spectrum of the criminal justice process. Law enforcement agencies do not have the staff or funds to investigate *every* crime; they must decide where to direct their restricted resources. Increasing caseloads and a limited amount of time in which to dispose of them constrict many of our nation's courts. Overcrowding in prisons and jails affects both law enforcement agencies and the courts—there is simply not enough room for all convicts.

The criminal justice system uses discretion to alleviate these pressures. Police decide whether to arrest a suspect; prosecutors decide whether to prosecute; magistrates decide whether there is sufficient probable cause for a case to go to a jury; and judges decide on sentencing, to mention only some of the occasions when discretion is used. (See **Figure 1.2** on the facing page for a description of some of the more important discretionary decisions.) Collectively, these decisions are said to produce an *informal criminal justice system* because discretion is informally exercised by the individual and is not enclosed within the rigid confines of the law.

Even if prosecutors believe that a suspect is guilty, they may decide not to prosecute if the case is weak or if they know that the police erred in the investigative process. In most instances, prosecutors will not squander the scarce resource of court time on a case they might not win. Some argue that the informal process has made our criminal justice system more just. Given the immense pressure of limited resources, the argument goes, only rarely will an innocent person end up before a judge and jury.[13]

Discretionary Values Of course, not all discretionary decisions are dictated by the scarcity of resources. Sometimes, discretion is based on policy considerations. For example, many participants in Hempfest, an annual festival in Seattle, Washington, smoke marijuana in public without fear of arrest because that city's police department de-emphasizes arrests for minor drug possession.[14] Furthermore, employees of the criminal justice system may make decisions based on their personal values, which, depending on what those values are, may make the system less just in the eyes of some observers. For that reason, discretion is closely connected to questions of *ethics* in criminal justice and will be discussed in that context throughout this textbook.

The "Wedding Cake" Model of Criminal Justice Some believe that the prevailing informal approach to criminal justice creates a situation in which all cases are not treated equally. As anecdotal evidence, they point to a cultural landmark in the American criminal justice system—the highly publicized O. J. Simpson trial of 1995, during which the wealthy, famous defendant had an experience far different from that of most double-murder suspects. To describe this effect, criminal justice researchers Lawrence M. Friedman and Robert V. Percival came up with a **"wedding cake" model** of criminal justice.[15] This model posits that

discretion comes to bear depending on the relative importance of a particular case to the decision makers. Like any wedding cake, Friedman and Percival's model has the smallest layer at the top and the largest at the bottom (see **Figure 1.3** below).

> **"Wedding Cake" Model** A wedding cake–shaped model that explains how different cases receive different treatment in the criminal justice system.

1. The "top" layer consists of a handful of "celebrated" cases that attract the most attention and publicity. Recent examples of top-level cases include the trials of Brian David Mitchell, convicted of kidnapping fourteen-year-old Elizabeth Smart in Salt Lake City, Utah; of Rachel Wade of Pinellas Park, Florida, who was sentenced to twenty-seven years in prison for murdering a romantic rival (see photo on the next page); and of Casey Anthony, found not guilty by a Clearwater, Florida, jury of suffocationg her two-year-old daughter and dumping the girl's body in the woods. (CAREER TIP: If you are more interested in writing or talking about crimes than solving them, you could report on these types of stories for the media as an *investigative crime journalist.*)

2. The second layer consists of "high-profile" felonies. A *felony* is a serious crime such as murder,

Figure 1.3 The Wedding Cake Model

1. The "celebrated" cases

2. Serious or "high-profile" felonies

3. Less serious or "ordinary" felonies

4. Misdemeanors

Steven Miric/iStockphoto.com

rape, or burglary. This layer includes crimes committed by persons with criminal records, crimes in which the victim was seriously injured, and crimes in which a weapon was used, as well as crimes in which the offender and victim were strangers. These types of felonies are considered high profile because they usually draw a certain amount of public attention, which puts pressure on the prosecutors to bring such a case to trial instead of accepting a guilty plea for a lesser sentence.

3. The third layer consists of "ordinary" felonies, which include less violent crimes such as burglaries and thefts or even robberies in which no weapon was used. Because of the low profile of the accused—usually a first-time offender who has had a prior relationship with his or her victim—these "ordinary" felonies often do not receive the full formal process of a trial.

Why do high-profile trials, such as the one involving Rachel Wade, below, give the public an unrealistic view of the average criminal trial? (s70/ZUMA Press/ Newscom)

4. Finally, the fourth layer consists of *misdemeanors*, or crimes less serious than felonies. Misdemeanors include petty offenses such as shoplifting, disturbing the peace, and violations of local ordinances. More than three-quarters of all arrests made by police are for misdemeanors.

The irony of the wedding cake model is that the cases on the top level come closest to meeting our standards of ideal criminal justice. In these celebrated trials, we get to see committed (and expensive) attorneys argue minute technicalities of the law, sometimes for days on end. The further one moves down the layers of the cake, the more informal the process becomes. Though many of the cases in the second layer are brought to trial, only rarely does this occur for the less serious felonies in the third level of the wedding cake. By the fourth level, cases are dealt with almost completely informally, and the end goal appears to be speed rather than what can be called "justice."

Public fascination with celebrated cases obscures a truth of the informal criminal justice process: trial by jury is relatively rare (only about 5 percent of those arrested for felonies go to trial). Indeed, most cases are disposed of with an eye more toward convenience than ideals of justice or fairness. Consequently, the summary of the criminal justice system provided by the wedding cake model is much more realistic than the impression many Americans have obtained from the media.

¿WHICH IS MORE IMPORTANT— PUNISHMENT OR RIGHTS?

If the general conclusion of the wedding cake model—that some defendants are treated differently from others—bothers you, then you probably question the values of the system. Just as individuals have values—a belief structure governing individual conduct—our criminal justice system can be said to have values, too. These values form the foundation for Herbert Packer's two models of the criminal justice system, which we discuss next.

CRIME CONTROL AND DUE PROCESS: TO PUNISH OR PROTECT?

In his landmark book *The Limits of the Criminal Sanction*, Herbert Packer introduced two models for the American criminal justice system: the crime control model and the due process model.[16] The underlying value of the crime control model is that the most important function of the criminal justice process is to punish and repress criminal conduct. Though not in direct conflict with crime control, the underlying values of the due process model focus more on protecting the **civil rights** of the accused through legal restraints on the police, courts, and corrections. Civil rights are those rights guaranteed to all Americans in the U.S. Constitution.

LO5

The Crime Control Model Under the **crime control model**, law enforcement must be counted on to control criminal activity. Doing so is at best difficult, and probably impossible. For the crime control model to operate successfully, Packer writes, it

> must produce a high rate of apprehension and conviction, and must do so in a context where the magnitudes being dealt with are very large and the resources for dealing with them are very limited.[17]

In other words, the system must be quick and efficient. In the ideal crime control model, any suspect who most likely did not commit a crime is quickly jettisoned from the system, while those who are transferred to the trial process are convicted as quickly as possible. It was in this context that Packer referred to the criminal justice process as an assembly line.

The crime control model also assumes that the police are in a better position than the courts to determine the guilt of arrested suspects. Therefore, judges should operate on a "presumption of guilt" (that is, any suspect brought before the court is more likely guilty than not). Furthermore, as few restrictions as possible should be placed on police investigative and fact-gathering activities. The crime control model relies on the informality in the criminal justice system, as discussed earlier.

The Due Process Model Packer likened the **due process model** to an obstacle course instead of an assembly line. Rather than expediting cases through the system, as is preferable in the crime control model, the due process model strives to make it more difficult to prove guilt. It rests on the belief that it is more desirable for society that ninety-nine guilty suspects go free than that a single innocent person be condemned.[18]

The due process model is based on the assumption that the absolute efficiency that is the goal of the crime control model can be realized only if the power of the state is absolute. Because fairness, and not efficiency, is the ultimate goal of the due process model, it rejects the idea of a criminal justice system with unlimited powers. As a practical matter, the model also argues that human error in any process is inevitable. As a result, the criminal justice system should recognize its own capability of making mistakes and take all measures necessary to ensure that this fallibility does not impinge on the rights of citizens.

Finally, whereas the crime control model relies heavily on the police, the due process model relies just

Civil Rights The personal rights and protections guaranteed by the Constitution, particularly the Bill of Rights.

Crime Control Model A criminal justice model that places primary emphasis on the right of society to be protected from crime and violent criminals.

Due Process Model A criminal justice model that places primacy on the right of the individual to be protected from the power of the government.

STUDYPREP

Read textbook chapters actively! Underline the most important topics. Put a check mark next to material that you do not understand. After you have completed the entire chapter, take a break. Then, work on better comprehension of the check-marked material.

iStockphoto

CJ and Technology

BIOMETRICS

The science of biometrics involves identifying a person through her or his unique physical characteristics. In the criminal justice context, the term *biometrics* refers to the various technological devices that read these characteristics and report the identity of the subject to the authorities. Today, there are four leading biometric technologies:

1. *Fingerprint readers* take photographic images of fingerprints to determine patterns based on the points where the ridges of the fingertips begin, terminate, or split. These patterns are then mathematically encoded and the information stored.
2. *Iris recognition systems* capture about 240 minute details of the eye in a similar manner.
3. *Face recognition systems* use a camera to record from thirty to eighty "markers" on a subject's face, such as cheekbone formations, the width of the nose bridge, and the space between the eyes.
4. *Hand geometry scanners* take and store as many as ninety different measurements, such as vein patterns, distance between knuckles, and the length and width of fingers.

The use of biometrics is becoming more common in law enforcement. More than 2,100 sheriff's departments in twenty-seven states are using iris recognition technology. Most take digital pictures of the eyes of people with Alzheimer's disease and of children to help identify the subjects should they be abducted or become lost. Law enforcement officials in New Mexico scan the irises of convicted sex offenders to keep them from avoiding detection under false names. Experts predict that face recognition systems will eventually allow hidden cameras to check the identities of thousands of people shopping in a mall or taking a stroll in a city park. Furthermore, someday police officers will be able to take a photo of a suspect and instantaneously check the biometric markers against a database of millions for an identifying match.

THINKING ABOUT BIOMETRICS

What would be the benefits and drawbacks of a database that contained biometric information on every person in the United States? Why would the creation of such a database by the government signify adherence to the crime control model rather than the due process model?

as heavily on the courts and their role in upholding the legal procedures of establishing guilt. The due process model is willing to accept that a person who is factually guilty will go free if the criminal justice system does not follow legally prescribed procedures in proving her or his guilt.[19] Therefore, the due process model relies on formality in the criminal justice system.

WHICH MODEL PREVAILS TODAY?

Although both the crime control and the due process models have always been present to a certain degree, during different periods one has taken precedence over the other. The 1950s and 1960s, for instance, experienced a "due process revolution." During those decades, the United States Supreme Court placed severe limits on the ability of the police to gather evidence[20] (discussed in Chapter 7) and provided those suspected of criminal behavior with unprecedented rights[21] (discussed in Chapter 9). Rising crime rates in the late 1970s and early 1980s led to increased pressure on politicians and judges to "get tough on crime," which slowed down the due process revolution considerably. The result was an explosion in the number of criminal suspects arrested, convicted, and incarcerated, a trend that we will reference often in this textbook. (Look at **Figure 1.4** below to see how the number of prison and jail inmates in the United States has increased since the mid-1980s.)

The events of September 11, 2001, when terrorists hijacked four commercial airliners and used the planes to kill more than 3,000 people in New York City, northern Virginia, and rural Pennsylvania, further cemented the crime control principles of the U.S. criminal justice system. In the wake of the attacks, new laws designed to protect America against further acts of **terrorism** gave law enforcement agents greater powers to investigate and incarcerate suspects. As we will discuss in Chapter 16, the **homeland security** movement has, in many ways, transformed our criminal justice system. Due process ideals did finally resurface near the end of the past decade, in large part due to the recent financial crisis. As we will see later in this textbook, because of the high costs of incarceration, state officials are finding ways to keep offenders—especially nonviolent ones—out of prison.

> **Terrorism** The use or threat of violence to achieve political objectives.
>
> **Homeland Security** A concerted national effort to prevent terrorist attacks within the United States and reduce the country's vulnerability to terrorism.

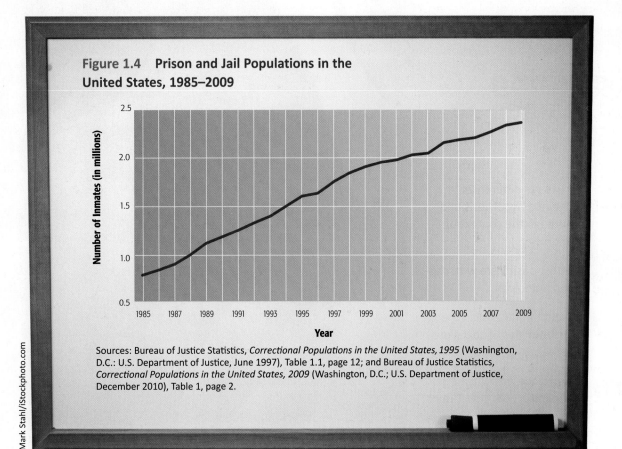

Figure 1.4   **Prison and Jail Populations in the United States, 1985–2009**

Sources: Bureau of Justice Statistics, *Correctional Populations in the United States, 1995* (Washington, D.C.: U.S. Department of Justice, June 1997), Table 1.1, page 12; and Bureau of Justice Statistics, *Correctional Populations in the United States, 2009* (Washington, D.C.; U.S. Department of Justice, December 2010), Table 1, page 2.

Mark Stahl/iStockphoto.com

2 CAUSES OF CRIME

Learning Outcomes

After studying this chapter, you will be able to . . .

 LO 1 Discuss the difference between a hypothesis and a theory in the context of criminology.

 LO 2 Contrast positivism with classical criminology.

 LO 3 List and briefly explain the three branches of social process theory.

 LO 4 Contrast the medical model of addiction with the criminal model of addiction.

LO 5 Explain the theory of the chronic offender and its importance for the criminal justice system.

Ronaldo Schemidt/AFP/Getty Images

No Fun and Games

There was little mystery as to *who* killed Kimmie Daily. Tyler Savage admitted to law enforcement officers that on August 17, 2010, he convinced the sixteen-year-old girl to follow him to a vacant lot in Puyallup, Washington, where he attacked and murdered her. The mystery was *why* he did it. Savage, eighteen years old, had a clean record and could provide no motive for investigators. "His criminal history went from 0 to 100 miles an hour with one crime," said Pierce County prosecutor Mark Lindquist.

The only clue to Savage's behavior came from his confession that after killing Daily, he returned home to play the online fantasy video game *Dungeons and Dragons*. "The defendant admitted some kind of connection between the murder and the video game," Lindquist said. "I'm not clear at this point what exactly that connection is." Savage is not the only young man to attribute his violent behavior to video games. In recent years, both Daniel Petric of Wellington, Ohio (a seventeen-year-old who shot his parents, killing his mother), and Patrick Morris of Klamath Falls, Oregon (a twenty-year-old who murdered Diego Aguilar with a shotgun), raised an addiction to violent video games as an explanation for their crimes in court.

Many observers fear that by desensitizing users to acts of killing, dismembering, maiming, and sexual assault, video games such as *Postal 2* and *Grand Theft Auto IV* can lead to violent conduct by frequent players. Lorain County common pleas judge James Burge, who presided over the trial of Daniel Petric mentioned in the previous paragraph, blamed *Halo 3* for warping the teenager's sense of reality. In this particular video game, the judge noted, the player "can shoot these aliens, and they're there again the next day." Consequently, Burge concluded that Petric "had no idea, at the time he hatched this plot, that if he killed his parents, they would be dead forever."

What explanation did Tyler Savage, shown here being led into a Pierce County (Washington) criminal court, give for murdering Kimmie Daily?
(AP Photo/The News Tribune, Drew Perine)

Criminology The scientific study of crime and the causes of criminal behavior.

Criminologist A specialist in the field of crime and the causes of criminal behavior.

Correlation The relationship between two measurements or behaviors that tend to move in the same direction.

If violent video games are so dangerous, why isn't their sale banned, or at least restricted? In fact, a number of states have tried to do so. The latest, California, passed a law several years ago that prohibited businesses from selling or renting "violent" video games to minors. The statute defined a "violent" video game, in part, as one that allows the player to inflict serious injury "in an especially heinous, cruel or depraved manner that involves torture or serious physical abuse to the victim."[1] In passing this law, California lawmakers relied heavily on research done by experts showing the negative psychological effects on minors of repeated exposure to video game violence. In certain circumstances, these experts contended, such exposure greatly increases the risk of antisocial, aggressive, and even criminal behavior.[2]

The study of crime, or **criminology**, is rich with different theories as to why people commit crimes. In this chapter, we will discuss the most influential of these theories, some of which complement each other and some of which do not. We will also look at the various factors most commonly, if not always correctly, associated with criminal behavior. Finally, this chapter will address the question of relevance: What effect do theories of why wrongdoing occurs have on efforts to control and prevent crime?

¿WHAT IS A THEORY?

Criminologists, or researchers who study the causes of crime, warn against using models to predict violent behavior. After all, not every male teenager who spends an inordinate amount of time playing violent video games is a likely criminal, and it would be wrong to treat him as such. In the example given at the beginning of this chapter, there may have been a **correlation**

CAREER PREP

CRIMINOLOGIST

JOB DESCRIPTION:
- Analyze criminal and delinquent behavior and provide theoretical explanations for such behavior.
- Work with and for law enforcement agencies to prevent crime by offering profiles of criminal behavior and scrutinizing crime statistics.

WHAT KIND OF TRAINING IS REQUIRED?
- Research skills, computer proficiency, and expertise in statistics.
- An undergraduate degree in a field relating to criminal justice with, preferably, a minor in psychology or sociology. A postgraduate degree is necessary for an academic career in criminology.

ANNUAL SALARY RANGE?
- $32,000–$76,000

For additional information, visit: www.princetonreview.com/Careers.aspx?cid=47.

zhang bo/iStockphoto

between Tyler Savage's obsession with *Dungeons and Dragons* and his murder of Kimmie Daily, but very few criminologists would go so far as to say that this obsession **caused** him to murder her.

CORRELATION AND CAUSATION

Correlation between two variables means that they tend to vary together. Causation, in contrast, means that one variable is responsible for the change in the other. Research conducted by Dan Immergluck and Geoff Smith, for example, shows that when levels of single-family mortgage foreclosures rise in a neighborhood, so do levels of violent crime. The researchers are careful, however, not to imply that the increased foreclosure rates cause the boost in violent crime rates. Rather, they focus on the overall negative impact on neighborhoods when families lose their homes.[3]

The difference between correlation and causation is the main reason why the nation's courts, up to this point, have rejected all state laws restricting the sale of violent video games. Experts can argue that there is a correlation between violent behavior and certain characteristics of the lives of excessive gamers. But it is very difficult to determine what actually caused Tyler Savage, Daniel Petric, and Patrick Morris to commit their crimes without knowing much more about their backgrounds and environments, and possibly not even then. In addition, the vast majority of minors who play these games do not become violent criminals. Therefore, courts are unwilling to limit the freedom of consumers to purchase these products unless, as one federal judge put it, criminologists are able to "establish a *solid causal link* between video game exposure and aggressive thinking and behavior. [emphasis added]"[4]

THE ROLE OF THEORY

As the violent video game controversy shows, criminologists find themselves in a quandary. The question that is the underpinning of criminology—What causes crime?—may be impossible to answer definitively. Criminologists have, however, uncovered a wealth of information concerning a different, and more practically applicable, inquiry: Given a certain set of circumstances, why do individuals commit criminal acts? This information has allowed criminologists to develop a number of *theories* concerning the causes of crime. Most of us tend to think of a *theory* as some sort of guess or a statement that is lacking in credibility. In the academic world, and therefore for our purposes, a **theory** is an explanation of a happening or circumstance that is based on observation, experimentation, and reasoning. Scientific and academic researchers observe events and their consequences to develop *hypotheses* about what will occur when a similar fact pattern is present in the future. A **hypothesis** is a proposition that can be tested by researchers or observers to determine if it is valid. If enough authorities do find the hypothesis valid, it will be accepted as a theory. See **Figure 2.1** on the next page for an example of this process, known as the *scientific method*, in action.

Cause The relationship in which a change in one measurement or behavior creates a recognizable change in another measurement or behavior.

Theory An explanation of a happening or circumstance that is based on observation, experimentation, and reasoning.

Hypothesis A possible explanation for an observed occurrence that can be tested by further investigation.

¿WHICH THEORIES OF CRIME ARE MOST WIDELY ACCEPTED?

As you read this chapter, keep in mind that theories are not the same as facts, and most, if not all, of the criminological theories described in these pages have their detractors. Over the past century, however, a number of theories of crime have gained wide, if not total, acceptance and are deserving of our attention. These include choice theories, trait theories, sociological theories, social process theories, and social conflict theories.

CRIME AND FREE WILL: CHOICE THEORIES OF CRIME

For the purposes of the American criminal justice system, the answer to why a person commits a crime is rather straightforward: because that person chooses

Choice Theory A school of criminology that holds that wrongdoers act as if they weigh the possible benefits of criminal or delinquent activity against the expected costs of being apprehended.

Classical Criminology A school of criminology based on the belief that individuals have free will to engage in any behavior, including criminal behavior.

Utilitarianism An approach to ethical reasoning in which the "correct" decision is the one that results in the greatest amount of good for the greatest number of people affected by that decision.

to do so. This application of **choice theory** to criminal law is not absolute. If a defendant can prove that she or he lacked the ability to make a rational choice, in certain circumstances the defendant will not be punished as harshly for a crime as would normally be the case. But such allowances are relatively recent. From the early days of this country, the general presumption in criminal law has been that behavior is a consequence of free will.

Figure 2.1 The Scientific Method

The scientific method is a process through which researchers test the accuracy of a hypothesis. This simple example should provide an idea of how the scientific method works.

Observation: I left my home at 7:00 this morning, and I was on time for class.

Hypothesis: If I leave home at 7:00 every morning, then I will never be late for class. (Hypotheses are often presented in this "If . . . , then . . ." format.)

Test: For three straight weeks, I left home at 7:00 every morning. Not one time was I late for class.

Verification: Four of my neighbors have the same morning class. They agree that they are never late if they leave by 7:00 A.M.

Theory: As long as I leave home at 7:00 A.M., I don't have to worry about being late for class.

Prediction: Tomorrow morning I'll leave at 7:00, and I will be on time for my class.

Note that even a sound theory supported by the scientific method such as this one does not *prove* that the prediction will be correct. Other factors not accounted for in the test and verification stages, such as an unexpected traffic jam, may disprove the theory. Predictions based on complex theories such as the criminological ones we will be discussing in this chapter are often challenged in such a manner.

Theories of Classical Criminology An emphasis on free will and human rationality in the realm of criminal behavior has its roots in **classical criminology**. Classical theorists believed that crime was an expression of a person's rational decision-making process: before committing a crime, a person would weigh the benefits of the crime against the costs of being apprehended. Therefore, if punishments were stringent enough to outweigh the benefits of crime, they would dissuade people from committing the crime in the first place.

The earliest popular expression of classical theory came in 1764, when the Italian Cesare Beccaria (1738–1794) published his *Essays on Crime and Punishments*. Beccaria criticized existing systems of criminal law as irrational and argued that criminal procedures should be more consistent with human behavior. He believed that, to be just, criminal law should reflect three truths:

1. All decisions, including the decision to commit a crime, are the result of rational choice.
2. Fear of punishment can have a deterrent (discouraging) effect on the choice to commit crime.
3. The more swift and certain punishment is, the more effective it will be in controlling crime.[5]

Beccaria believed that any punishment that purported to do anything other than deter crime was cruel and arbitrary. This view was shared by his contemporary, Britain's Jeremy Bentham (1748–1832). In 1789, Bentham pronounced that "nature has placed man under the governance of two sovereign masters, *pain* and *pleasure*." Bentham applied his theory of **utilitarianism** to the law by contending that punishment should use the threat of pain against criminal individuals to ensure the pleasure of society as a whole. As a result, Bentham felt that punishment should have four goals:

1. To prevent all crime.
2. When it cannot prevent crime, to ensure that a criminal will commit a lesser crime to avoid a harsher punishment.
3. To give the criminal an incentive not to harm others in the pursuit of crime.
4. To prevent crime at the least possible cost to society.[6]

(To get a better idea of how a convicted criminal's ability to choose might affect his or her punishment, see the feature *You Be the Judge—The Tumor Made Me Do It* below.)

Positivism and Modern Rational Choice Theory

By the end of the nineteenth century, the positivist school of criminologists had superseded classical criminology. According to **positivism**, criminal behavior is determined by biological, psychological, and social forces and is beyond the control of the individual. The

 Italian physician Cesare Lombroso (1835–1909), an early adherent of positivism who is known as the "Father of Criminology," believed that criminals were throwbacks to the savagery of early humankind and could therefore be identified by certain physical characteristics such as sharp teeth and large jaws. He also theorized that criminality was similar to mental illness and could be genetically passed down from generation to generation in families that had cases of insanity, syphilis, epilepsy, and even deafness. Such individuals, according to Lombroso and his followers, had no free choice when it came to wrongdoing—their criminality had been predetermined at birth.

Positivist theory lost credibility as crime rates began to climb in the 1970s. If crime was caused by social factors, critics asked, why had the proactive social programs of the 1960s not brought about a decrease in criminal activity? An updated version of classical criminology, known as *rational choice theory*, found renewed acceptance. James Q. Wilson, one of the more prominent critics of the positivist school, sums up rational choice theory as follows:

> At any given moment, a person can choose between committing a crime and not committing it. The consequences of committing a crime consist of rewards (what psychologists call "reinforcers") and punishments; the consequences of not committing the crime also entail gains and losses. The larger the ratio of the net rewards of crime to the net rewards of [not committing a crime], the greater the tendency to commit a crime.[7]

Positivism A school of the social sciences that sees criminal and delinquent behavior as the result of biological, psychological, and social forces. Because wrongdoers are driven to deviancy by external factors, they should not be punished but treated to lessen the influence of those factors.

YOU BE THE JUDGE
The Tumor Made Me Do It

THE FACTS Philip, a forty-year-old schoolteacher with no history of deviant behavior, suddenly became obsessed with sex. He began collecting child pornography, soliciting prostitutes, and making sexual advances to young girls, including his stepdaughter. Eventually, Philip's wife reported his behavior, and he was tried and found guilty of child molestation. The judge ruled that Philip must complete a rehabilitation program or face jail time. When Philip was expelled from the program for lewdly propositioning the nurses, the judge had no choice but to order him to jail. The evening before his sentence was to begin, Philip checked himself into a hospital, complaining of headaches and an urge to rape his landlady. Doctors removed an egg-sized tumor from Philip's brain, and the overpowering sexual urges disappeared.

THE LAW The ability to choose is an important element in determining punishment under American law. If a person has no control over his or her actions, then no "choice" to commit a crime has been made, and a court will often hand down a lesser punishment or no punishment if the defendant agrees to seek medical treatment.

YOUR DECISION There is no doubt that Philip committed the crimes of which he was convicted. The presence of the tumor, however, suggests that he failed to choose to be a sexual deviant, and therefore he might reasonably escape blame for his actions. In light of his dramatic personality change following removal of the tumor, should Philip be required to serve his jail term? How does the basic premise of rational choice theory influence your decision?

[To see how a Virginia judge ruled in a case with similar facts, go to Example 2.1 on page 350.]

Gina Sanders/Shutterstock

According to rational choice theory, we can hypothesize that many criminal actions, including acts of violence and even murder, are committed *as if* individuals had this ratio in mind. For example, when Vernon Hills (Illinois) police began investigating Daniel Baker for killing Marina Aksman with an aluminum baseball bat in April 2010 (see photo below), they started with the assumption that Baker chose to commit the crime, even though a strong possibility existed that he would be punished for his actions. An early theory to explain the murder was that Baker was angry with Aksman for her efforts to break up the relationship between him and Aksman's daughter, Kristina.

"BORN CRIMINAL": BIOLOGICAL AND PSYCHOLOGICAL THEORIES OF CRIME

As we have seen, Cesare Lombroso believed in the "criminal born" man and woman and was confident that he could distinguish criminals by their apelike physical features. Such far-fetched notions have long been relegated to scientific oblivion. Nevertheless, many criminologists do believe that *trait theories* have validity. These theories suggest that certain *biological* or *psychological* traits in individuals could incline them toward criminal behavior given a certain set of circumstances. **Biology** is a very broad term that refers to the scientific study of living organisms, while **psychology** pertains more specifically to the study of the mind and its processes. "All behavior is biological," pointed out psychologist David C. Rowe. "All behavior is represented in the brain, in its biochemistry, electrical activity, structure, and growth and decline."[8]

Genetics and Crime Criminologists who study biological theories of crime often focus on the effect that *genes* have on human behavior. Genes are coded sequences of DNA that control every aspect of our biology, from the color of our eyes and hair to the type of emotions we have. Every person's genetic makeup is determined by genes inherited from his or her parents. Consequently, when scientists study ancestral or evolutionary developments, they are engaging in **genetics,** a branch of biology that deals with traits that are passed from one generation to another through genes. (CAREER TIP: A scientist who studies genes and counsels patients with genetic disorders is known as a *geneticist.*)

Twin Studies Genetics is at the heart of criminology's "nurture versus nature" debate. In other words, are traits such as aggressiveness and antisocial behavior, both of which often lead to criminality, a result of a person's environment (nurture) or her or his genes (nature)? To tip the balance toward "nature," a criminologist must be able to prove that, all other things being equal, the offspring of aggressive or antisocial parents are at risk to exhibit those same traits.

Many criminologists have turned to *twin studies* to determine the relationship between genetics and criminal behavior. If the "nature" argument is correct, then twins should exhibit similar antisocial tendencies. The problem with twin studies is that most twins grow up in the same environ-

How does rational choice theory apply to the action of suspects such as Daniel Baker, shown here on the left, being escorted by a member of the Lake County (Illinois) Major Crimes Task Force? (Chicago Tribune/MCT/ LANDOV)

Cameron Whitman/iStockphoto.com/Andrey Prokhorov/iStockphoto.com

ment, so it is difficult, if not impossible, to determine whether their behavior is influenced by their genes or by their surroundings. To overcome this difficulty, criminologists compare identical twins, known as MZ twins, and fraternal twins of the same sex, known as DZ twins. Because MZ twins are genetically identical while DZ twins share only half of their genes, the latter should be less likely to have similar behavior patterns than the former.

Adoption Studies The results of such twin studies have been decidedly mixed. Some show that MZ pairs are considerably more likely to exhibit similar criminal behavior than DZ pairs,[9] but others discredit this hypothesis.[10] Because of the inconsistencies of twin studies, some criminologists have turned to *adoption studies*, which eliminate the problem of family members sharing the same environment. A number of well-received adoption studies have shown a correlation between rates of criminality among adopted children and antisocial or criminal behavior by their biological parents.[11]

Furthermore, such studies have shown a genetic basis for such traits as attention deficit hyperactivity disorder (ADHD) and aggressiveness, both of which have been linked to antisocial behavior and crime.[12] Keep in mind, however, that no single gene or trait has been proved to lead to criminality. As a result, the best that genetics can

do is raise the possibility for a predisposition (tendency) toward aggression or violence in an individual based on her or his family background.[13]

Hormones and Aggression Chemical messengers known as **hormones** have also been the subject of much criminological study. Criminal activity in males has been linked to elevated levels of hormones—specifically **testosterone,** which controls secondary sex characteristics such as growth of facial and pubic hair and has been associated with traits of aggression. Testing of inmate populations shows that those imprisoned for violent crimes exhibit higher testosterone levels than other prisoners.[14] Elevated testosterone levels have also been used to explain the age-crime relationship, as the average testosterone level of men under the age of twenty-eight is double that of men between thirty-one and sixty-six years old.[15]

A very specific form of female violent behavior is also believed to stem from hormones. In 2010, defense attorneys for Stephanie Rochester of Superior, Colorado, claimed that their client was not responsible for smothering her six-month-old son to death because she was suffering from *postpartum depression* at the time of her actions. This temporary illness, believed to be caused partly by the hormonal changes that women experience after childbirth, triggers abnormal behavior in a small percentage of new mothers.[16] (CAREER TIP: Often, women do not know that they are suffering from postpartum depression. *Public health nurses*—who work in the community, rather than in a hospital or a doctor's office—are frequently in the best position to identify and treat this condition.)

CJ and Technology

MAPPING THE BRAIN

Today, technology has made it relatively easy (if not always inexpensive) for scientists (and defense attorneys) to show brain irregularities such as frontal lobe damage. Computed tomography (CT) scans combine X-ray technology with computer technology to provide an exact three-dimensional image of the brain. Magnetic resonance imaging (MRI) technology uses a very powerful magnet to create a magnetic field, which is then bombarded with radio waves. These waves can provide a very detailed image of brain tissue, allowing doctors to determine whether the tissue is damaged or diseased. Positron emission tomography (PET) permits researchers to study the function of the brain rather than its structure. A small amount of radioactive matter is injected into a PET subject's bloodstream, which is then measured to determine which parts of the brain respond to various activities and functions. Finally, single photon emission computed tomography (SPECT) measures levels of a sugar called glucose in certain areas of the brain. Because glucose gives the brain the energy to function, tracing which areas of the brain "light up" under SPECT gives scientists clues as to the subject's thoughts and emotions.

THINKING ABOUT BRAIN-SCANNING DEVICES

Numerous studies using these techniques have shown that the brains of violent offenders differ in important ways from "normal" brains. Most of the offenders tested, however, were adults and had already committed criminal acts. What would be the benefits of mapping the brains of children or adolescents to determine if any criminal-tendency abnormalities were present? Would there be any drawbacks to this practice, particularly for the test subjects?

Neurotransmitter A chemical that transmits nerve impulses between nerve cells and from nerve cells to the brain.

The Brain and Crime

The study of brain activity, or *neurophysiology*, has also found a place in criminology. Cells in the brain known as *neurons* communicate with each other by releasing chemicals called **neurotransmitters.** Criminologists have isolated three neurotransmitters that seem to be particularly related to aggressive behavior:

1. Serotonin, which regulates moods, appetite, and memory.
2. Norepinephrine, which regulates sleeping cycles and controls how we respond to anxiety, fear, and stress.

3. Dopamine, which regulates perceptions of pleasure and reward.[17]

Researchers have established that under certain circumstances, low levels of serotonin and high levels of norepinephrine are correlated with aggressive behavior.[18]

In addition, research seems to have shown a strong connection between violent behavior and damage to a part of the brain known as the *frontal lobe*.[19] Located in the part of the brain just behind the forehead, the frontal lobe appears to regulate our ability to behave properly in social situations. Thus, people whose frontal lobes do not function properly—due to birth defect or injury—tend to act more impulsively and violently. Experts testifying in court often use frontal lobe trauma to explain the horrific actions of defendants. In 2010, for example, defense attorneys emphasized damage to Kemar Johnston's frontal lobe—caused by a childhood playground accident—when arguing that their client should not be executed for torturing, mutilating, and murdering two teenagers in Cape Coral, Florida.

Psychology and Crime As with biological theories of crime, psychological theories of crime operate under the assumption that individuals have traits that make them more or less predisposed to criminal activity. To a certain extent, however, psychology rests more heavily on abstract ideas than does biology. Even Sigmund Freud (1856–1939), perhaps the most influential of all psychologists, considered the operations of the mind to be, like an iceberg, mostly hidden.

Freud's Psychoanalytic Theory For all his accomplishments, Freud rarely turned his attention directly toward the causes of crime. His **psychoanalytic theory**, however, has provided a useful approach for thinking about criminal behavior. According to Freud, most of our thoughts, wishes, and urges originate in the *unconscious* region of the mind, and we have no control of—or even awareness of—these processes. Freud believed that, on an unconscious level, all humans have criminal tendencies and that each of us is continually struggling against these tendencies.

To explain this struggle, Freud devised three abstract systems that interact in the brain: the *id*, the *ego*, and the *superego*. The id is driven by a constant desire for pleasure and self-gratification through sexual and aggressive urges. The ego, in contrast, stands for reason and common sense, while the superego "learns" the expectations of family and society and acts as the conscience. When the three systems fall into disorder, the id can take control, causing the individual to act on his or her antisocial urges and, possibly, commit crimes.[20]

Social Psychology and "Evil" Behavior Another branch of psychology—**social psychology**—focuses on human behavior in the context of how human beings relate to and influence one another. Social psychology rests on the assumption that the way we view ourselves is shaped to a large degree by how we think others view us. Generally, we act in the same manner as those we like or admire because we want them to like or admire us. Thus, social psychology tries to explain the influence of crowds on individual behavior.

In March 2010, a "flash mob" of thousands of teenagers and young adults, summoned via text-messages, tweets, and e-mails, swarmed the South Street corridor of Philadelphia, threatening onlookers and forcing shops and restaurants to close early. How does social psychology explain the possibility of violent behavior in such situations? (Laurence Kesterson/The Philadephia Inquirer)

About three decades ago, psychologist Philip Zimbardo highlighted the power of group behavior in dramatic fashion. Zimbardo randomly selected some Stanford University undergraduate students to act as "guards" and other students to act as "inmates" in an artificial prison environment. Before long, the students began to act as if these designations were real, with the "guards" physically mistreating the "inmates," who rebelled with equal violence. Within six days, Zimbardo was forced to discontinue the experiment out of fear for its participants' safety.[21] One of the basic assumptions of social psychology is that people are able to justify improper or even criminal behavior by convincing themselves that it is actually acceptable behavior. This delusion, researchers have found, is much easier to accomplish with the support of others behaving in the same manner.[22] (CAREER TIP: *Psychologists* study how a person's mental functions cause him or her to think or act in certain ways. Many psychologists, such as Philip Zimbardo, apply their knowledge to the mysteries of criminal behavior.)

SOCIOLOGICAL THEORIES OF CRIME

The problem with trait theory, many criminologists contend, is that it falters when confronted with certain crime patterns. Why is the crime rate in Detroit, Michigan, twenty-five times that of Sioux Falls, South Dakota? Do high levels of air pollution cause an increase in abnormal brain activity or higher levels of testosterone? As no evidence has been found that would suggest that such biological factors can be so easily influenced, several generations of criminologists have instead focused on social and physical environmental factors in their study of criminal behavior.

The Chicago School The importance of sociology (the study of human social behavior) in the study of criminal behavior was established by a group of scholars who were associated with the Sociology Department at the University of Chicago in the early 1900s. These sociologists, known collectively as the Chicago School, gathered empirical evidence from low-income areas of the city that showed a correlation between conditions of poverty, such as inadequate housing and poor sanitation, and high rates of crime.

Chicago School members Ernest Burgess (1886–1966) and Robert Ezra Park (1864–1944) argued that neighborhood conditions, be they of wealth or poverty, had a much greater determinant effect on criminal behavior than ethnicity, race, or religion.[23] The methods and theories of the Chicago School, which stressed that humans are social creatures whose behavior reflects their environment, have had a profound effect on criminology over the past century. (CAREER TIP: A *sociologist* is someone who studies human social behavior. Because crime is such an important—and interesting—facet of human behavior, sociologists often study criminality.)

The study of crime as correlated to social structure revolves around three specific theories: (1) social disorganization theory, (2) strain theory, and (3) cultural deviance theory.

Social Disorganization Theory Park and Burgess introduced an *ecological* analysis of crime to criminology. Just as ecology studies the relationships between animals and their environments, the two Chicago School members studied the relationship between inner-city residents and their environment. In addition, Clifford Shaw and Henry McKay, contemporaries of the Chicago School and researchers in juvenile crime, popularized the idea of ecology in criminology through **social disorganization theory**. This theory states that crime is largely a product of unfavorable conditions in certain communities.[24]

Disorganized Zones Studying juvenile delinquency in Chicago, Shaw and McKay discovered certain "zones" that exhibited high rates of crime. These zones were characterized by "disorganization," or a breakdown of the traditional institutions of social control such as family, school systems, and local businesses. In contrast, in the city's "organized" communities, residents had developed implicit agreements about fundamental values and norms. Shaw and McKay found that residents in high-crime neighborhoods had to a large degree abandoned these fundamental values and norms. Also, a lack of social controls had led to increased levels of antisocial, or criminal, behavior.[25] According to social disorganization theory, ecological factors that lead to crime in these neighborhoods are perpetuated by continued elevated levels of high school dropouts, unemployment, deteriorating infrastructures, and single-parent families. (See **Figure 2.2** below to better understand social disorganization theory.)

The Value of Role Models In the late 1990s, sociologist Elijah Anderson of the University of Pennsylvania took Shaw and McKay's theories one step further. According to Anderson, residents in high-crime, African American "disorganized" zones separate themselves into two types of families: "street" and "decent." "Street" families are characterized by a lack of consideration for others and poorly disciplined children. In contrast, "decent" families are community minded, instill values of hard work and education in their children, and generally have "hope for the future."[26]

Spending time in these disadvantaged areas, Anderson discovered that most "decent" families included an older man who held a steady job, performed his duties as husband and father, and was interested in the community's well-being. When external factors such as racial discrimination and lack of employment opportunities reduce the presence of these traditional role models, Anderson theorizes, "street" codes fill the void and youth violence escalates.[27] In 2008, criminologists Karen F. Parker and Amy Reckdenwald tested Anderson's theories. They studied data from nearly two hundred urban areas and found that, indeed, areas with fewer older African American male role models had higher levels of black juvenile violence.[28]

Strain Theory Another self-perpetuating aspect of disorganized neighborhoods is that once residents gain the financial means to leave a high-crime community, they usually do so. This desire to escape the inner city is related to the second branch of social structure theory: **strain theory**. Most Americans have similar life goals, which include

Strain Theory
The assumption that crime is the result of frustration felt by individuals who cannot reach their financial and personal goals through legitimate means.

Figure 2.2   The Stages of Social Disorganization Theory

Social disorganization theory holds that crime is related to the environmental pressures that exist in certain communities or neighborhoods. These areas are marked by the desire of many of their inhabitants to "get out" at the first possible opportunity. Consequently, residents tend to ignore the important institutions in the community, such as businesses and education, causing further erosion of social controls and an increase in the conditions that lead to crime.

Source: Adapted from Larry J. Siegel, *Criminology,* 10th ed. (Belmont, CA: Wadsworth/Cengage Learning, 2009), 180.

Anomie A condition in which the individual suffers from the breakdown or absence of social norms.

Cultural Deviance Theory A theory based on the assumption that members of certain subcultures reject the values of the dominant culture through deviant behavior patterns.

Subculture A group exhibiting certain values and behavior patterns that distinguish it from the dominant culture.

Social Process Theories A school of criminology that considers criminal behavior to be the predictable result of a person's interaction with his or her environment.

Learning Theory The hypothesis that delinquents and criminals must be taught both the practical and emotional skills necessary to participate in illegal activity.

gaining a certain measure of wealth and financial freedom. The means of attaining these goals, however, are not universally available. Many citizens do not have access to the education or training necessary for financial success. This often results in frustration and anger, or *strain*.

Strain theory has its roots in the works of French sociologist Emile Durkheim (1858–1917) and his concept of *anomie* (derived from the Greek word for "without norms"). Durkheim believed that *anomie* resulted when social change threw behavioral norms into a flux, leading to a weakening of social controls and an increase in deviant behavior.[29] Another sociologist, American Robert K. Merton, expanded on Durkheim's ideas in his own theory of strain. Merton believed that *anomie* was caused by a social structure in which all citizens have similar goals without equal means to achieve them.[30] One way to alleviate this strain is to gain wealth by the means that are available to the residents of disorganized communities: drug trafficking, burglary, and other criminal activities.

Cultural Deviance Theory Combining certain aspects of social disorganization and strain theories, **cultural deviance theory** asserts that people adapt to the values of the subculture to which they belong. A **subculture** (a subdivision that exists within the dominant culture) has its own standards of behavior, or norms. By definition, a disorganized neighborhood is isolated from society at large, and the strain of this isolation encourages the formation of subcultures within its boundaries. According to cultural deviance theory, members of low-income subcultures are more likely to conform to value systems that celebrate behavior, such as violence, that directly confronts the value system of

society at large and therefore draws criminal sanctions.

FAMILY, FRIENDS, AND THE MEDIA: SOCIAL PROCESSES OF CRIME

Some criminologists find sociological theories of crime overly narrow. Surveys that ask people directly about their criminal behavior have shown that the criminal instinct is pervasive in middle- and upper-class communities, even if it is expressed differently. Anybody, these criminologists argue, has the potential to act out criminal behavior, regardless of class, race, or gender.

Philip Zimbardo conducted a well-known, if rather unscientific, experiment to make this point. Zimbardo placed an abandoned automobile with its hood up on the campus of Stanford University. The car remained in place, untouched, for a week. Then, the psychologist smashed the car's window with a sledgehammer. Within minutes, passersby had joined in the destruction of the automobile, eventually stripping its valuable parts.[31] **Social process theories** function on the same basis as Zimbardo's "interdependence of decisions experiment": the potential for criminal behavior exists in everyone and will be realized depending on an individual's interaction with various institutions and processes of society. Social process theory has three main branches: (1) learning theory, (2) control theory, and (3) labeling theory.

LO 3

Learning Theory Popularized by Edwin Sutherland in the 1940s, **learning theory** contends

to commit crimes if she or he saw an older sibling or a parent doing so. A good deal of data backs these theories. In a recent survey, a high percentage of boys involved in aggressive delinquent behavior reported having friends who sold drugs or carried a knife or gun.[33] Furthermore, according to the U.S. Department of Justice, nearly 50 percent of inmates in state prisons have relatives who have also been incarcerated.[34]

that criminal activity is a learned behavior. In other words, a criminal is taught both the practical methods of crime (such as how to pick a lock) and the psychological aspects of crime (how to deal with the guilt of wrongdoing). Sutherland's *theory of differential association* held that individuals are exposed to the values of family and peers such as school friends or co-workers. If the dominant values a person is exposed to favor criminal behavior, then that person is more likely to mimic such behavior.[32] Sutherland concentrated particularly on familial relations, believing that a child was more likely

As we saw at the beginning of this chapter, learning theory has been expanded to include the growing influence of the media. For instance, psychologists at the University of Michigan's Institute for Social Research released data in 2003 showing that exposure to high levels of televised violence erodes a natural aversion to violence and increases aggressive behavior among young children.[35] Such findings have spurred a number of legislative attempts to curb violence on television.[36]

Control Theory Criminologist Travis Hirschi focuses on the reasons why individuals *do not* engage in

CAREER PREP

SOCIAL WORKER

JOB DESCRIPTION:

- Help people cope with issues in their everyday lives, deal with relationships, and solve personal and family problems. Assist families that have serious domestic conflicts, sometimes involving child or spousal abuse.
- Conduct research on services in a particular area and act as an advocate for improvement of those services.

WHAT KIND OF TRAINING IS REQUIRED?

- A bachelor's degree in social work is the minimum requirement, and a master's degree in social work or a related field has become the standard for many positions.
- Essential qualities include emotional maturity; sensitivity to people and their problems; and the ability to handle responsibility, work independently, and maintain good relationships with clients and co-workers.

ANNUAL SALARY RANGE?

- $32,500–$56,500

For additional information, visit:
www.socialworkers.org.

Control Theory
A series of theories that assume that all individuals have the potential for criminal behavior, but are restrained by the damage that such actions would do to their relationships with family, friends, and members of the community.

Labeling Theory The hypothesis that society creates crime and criminals by labeling certain behavior and certain people as deviant.

Social Conflict Theories A school of criminology that views criminal behavior as the result of class conflict.

criminal acts, rather than why they do. According to Hirschi, social bonds promote conformity to social norms. The stronger these social bonds—which include attachment to, commitment to, involvement with, and belief in societal values—the less likely that any individual will commit a crime.[37] **Control theory** holds that although we all have the potential to commit crimes, most of us are dissuaded from doing so because we care about the opinions of our family and peers. James Q. Wilson and George Kelling describe control theory in terms of the "broken windows" effect. Neighborhoods in poor condition are filled with cues of lack of social control (for example, broken windows) that invite further vandalism and other deviant behavior.[38] If these cues are removed, according to Wilson and Kelling, so is the implied acceptance of crime within a community.

Labeling Theory James Caston was a big fan of the James Gang, a group of outlaws famous for robbing trains, banks, and stagecoaches in southern and midwestern states near the end of the nineteenth century. Consequently, Caston decided to name his first two sons after gang members "Jesse" and "Frank." Today, both brothers are serving life sentences in a Louisiana state prison for murder. "We never had a chance," said Jesse James Caston when asked about the influence of his name.[39]

The Caston brothers serve as a rather literal example of a third social process theory. **Labeling theory** focuses on perceptions of criminal behavior rather than the behavior itself. Labeling theorists study how being labeled a criminal—a "whore," or a "junkie," or a "thief"—affects that person's future behavior. Sociologist Howard Becker contends that deviance is

a consequence of the application by others of rules and sanctions to an offender. The deviant is one to whom that

TEST PREP

At times, you will find yourself studying for several exams at once. When this happens, make a list of each study topic and the amount of time needed to prepare for that topic. Then create a study schedule to reduce stress and give yourself the best chance for success.

label has successfully been applied; deviant behavior is behavior that people so label.[40]

Such labeling, some criminologists believe, becomes a self-fulfilling prophecy. Someone labeled a "junkie" will begin to consider himself or herself a deviant and continue the criminal behavior for which he or she has been labeled. Following this line of reasoning, the criminal justice system is engaged in artificially creating a class of criminals by labeling victimless crimes such as drug use, prostitution, and gambling as "criminal."

SOCIAL CONFLICT THEORIES

A more recent movement in criminology focuses not on psychology, biology, or sociology but on *power*. Those who identify power—seen as the ability of one person or group of persons to control the economic and social positions of other people or groups—as the key component in explaining crime entered the mainstream of American criminology during the 1960s.

These theorists saw social ills such as poverty, racism, sexism, and destruction of the environment as the "true crimes," perpetrated by the powerful, or ruling, classes. Burglary, robbery, and even violent crimes were considered justifiable reactions by the powerless against laws that were meant to repress, not protect, them. Supporters of these ideas aligned themselves with Marxist, radical, conflict, and feminist schools of criminology. Collectively, they have constructed the **social conflict theories** of crime causation.

Marxism versus Capitalism The origin of social conflict theory can be found in the political philosophy of a German named Karl Marx (1818–1883). Marx believed that capitalist economic systems necessarily produce income inequality and lead to the exploitation of the working classes.[41] Consequently, social conflict theory is often associated with a critique of our capitalist economic system. Capitalism is seen as leading to high levels of violence and crime because of the disparity of income that results. The poor commit property crimes for reasons of need and because, as members of a capitalist society, they desire the same financial rewards as everybody else. They commit violent crimes because of the frustration and rage they feel when these rewards seem unattainable.

Laws, instead of reflecting the values of society as a whole, reflect only the values of the segment of society that has achieved power and is willing to use the criminal justice system as a tool to keep that power.[42] Thus, the harsh penalties for "lower-class" crimes such as burglary can be seen as a means of protecting the privileges of the "haves" from the aspirations of the "have-nots."

The Social Reality of Crime It is important to note that according to social conflict theory, power is not synonymous with wealth. Women and members of minority groups can be wealthy and yet still be disassociated from the benefits of power in our society. Richard Quinney, one of the more influential social conflict theorists of the past forty years, encompasses issues of race, gender, power, and crime in a theory known as the **social reality of crime.**[43] For Quinney, along with many of his peers, criminal law does not reflect a universal moral code, but instead is a set of "rules" through which those who hold power can control and subdue those who do not. Any conflict between the haves and the have-nots, therefore, is bound to be decided in favor of the haves, who make the law and control the criminal justice system. Following this reasoning, Quinney sees violations of the law not as inherently criminal acts but rather as political ones—as revolutionary acts against the power of the state.

Angel Herrero de Frutos / iStockphoto.com

"Poverty is the mother of crime."
MARKUS AURELIUS
Roman emperor, 121–180

Issues of Race and Gender Thinking along racial lines, many observers would assert that African Americans as a group have been have-nots since the earliest days of this country. Today, the median income of an African American family is about $22,000 less than that of a non-Hispanic Caucasian family.[44] In 2010, only five of the nation's five hundred most profitable companies had a black chief executive. Similarly, women have run up against what has been called the "glass ceiling" as they attempt to assume positions of power in corporations: only fifteen major U.S. corporations have a female chief executive. Furthermore, those women most likely to be arrested and imprisoned have exactly the characteristics—low income, often raising children without the aid of a partner—that social conflict theorists would predict.

Historical Injustices Those who perceive the criminal justice system as an instrument of social control point to a number of historical studies and statistics to support their argument. In the nineteenth century, nearly three-quarters of female inmates had been incarcerated for sexual misconduct; they were sent to institutions such as New York's Western House of Refuge at Albion to be taught the virtues of "true" womanhood.[45] Today, about 70 percent of the nearly 57,000 Americans arrested for prostitution each year are women.[46] After the Civil War (1861–1865), many African Americans were driven from the South by "Jim Crow laws" designed to keep them from attaining power in the postwar period. Today, the criminal justice system performs a similar function. One out of every eight black men in their twenties is in prison or jail on any given day,[47] and black males are incarcerated at about 6.5 times the rate of white males.[48]

Riot police subdue a protester following the sentencing of Johannes Mehserle for killing Oscar Grant III. If you were a proponent of social conflict theory, how would you interpret Grant's death and Mehserle's punishment? (AP Photo/ Noah Berger)

Apparent injustices past and present only add to the sense of oppression in minority communities. In November 2010, for example, Bay Area Rapid Transit (BART) police officer Johannes Mehserle was sentenced to two years in prison for the death of African American Oscar Grant III. Nearly two years earlier, Mehserle had shot a prone and unresisting Grant in the back during an incident at a BART station. Although Mehserle was able to convince a jury that he had mistakenly pulled his gun, many Oakland, California, residents felt that Grant's race contributed to Mehserle's relatively light punishment (see photo alongside.)

¿WHAT IS THE CONNECTION BETWEEN DRUG USE AND CRIME?

Criminologists have long studied the link between crime and drugs. In general, offenders who use greater amounts of alcohol and illegal drugs have significantly higher crime rates than those who are less involved with these substances. Actually, alcohol falls under the broadest possible definition of a drug, which is any substance that modifies biological, psychological, or social behavior. In popular usage, however, the word **drug** has a more specific connotation. When people speak of the *drug* problem, or the war on *drugs*, or *drug* abuse, they are referring specifically to illegal **psychoactive drugs**, which affect the brain and alter consciousness or perception. Almost all of the drugs that we will be discussing in this textbook, such as

marijuana, cocaine, heroin, and amphetamines, are illegal and psychoactive.

Figure 2.3 on the facing page provides a useful picture of the extent of illegal drug use in the United States. For criminologists, these data raise two questions. First, why do people use drugs? Second, what are the consequences for the criminal justice system?

THE CRIMINOLOGY OF DRUG USE

At first glance, the reason people use drugs, including legal drugs such as alcohol, is obvious: such drugs give the user pleasure and provide a temporary escape for those who may feel tension or anxiety. Ultimately, though, such explanations are unsatisfactory because they fail to explain why some people use drugs while others do not.

Theories of Drug Use Several of the theories we discussed earlier in the chapter have been used by experts to explain drug use. *Social disorganization theory* (page 30) holds that rapid social change can cause people to become disaffiliated from mainstream society, causing them to turn to drugs. *Subculture theory* (page 32), particularly as applied to adolescents, sees drug use as the result of peer pressure. *Control theory* (pages 33–34) suggests that a lack of social control, as provided by entities such as the family or school, can lead to antisocial behavior.

Drugs and the "Learning Process"

Focusing on the question of why first-time drug users become habitual users, sociologist Howard Becker sees three factors in the "learning process." He believes first-time users do the following:

1. Learn the techniques of drug use.
2. Learn to perceive the pleasurable effects of drug use.
3. Learn to enjoy the social experience of drug use.[49]

Figure 2.3   Drug Use in the United States

According to the National Survey on Drug Use and Health, approximately 21.8 million Americans, or almost 9 percent of those over twelve years old, can be considered "illicit drug users." As you can see, most of these people used marijuana exclusively. Furthermore, eighteen- to twenty-five-year-olds were more likely to have used illegal drugs than any other segment of the population.

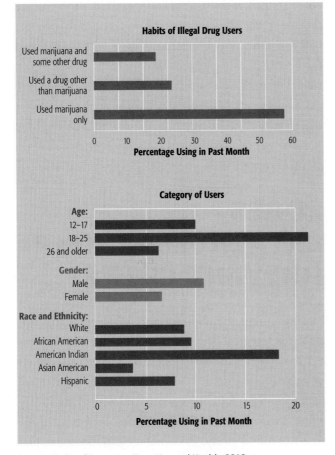

Source: National Survey on Drug Use and Health, 2010.

Becker's assumptions are evident in the widespread belief that positive images of drug use in popular culture "teach" adolescents that such behavior is not only acceptable but desirable. The entertainment industry, in particular, has been criticized for glamorizing various forms of drug use. (CAREER TIP: Teen drug abuse is a significant problem in the United States, and you can work toward alleviating it by becoming a *substance abuse counselor.*)

> **Drug Abuse** The use of drugs that results in physical or psychological problems for the user or third parties.

Drug Use and Drug Abuse

Another theory rests on the assumption that some people possess overly sensitive drug receptors in their brains and are therefore biologically disposed toward drug use.[50] Though there is little conclusive evidence that biological factors can explain initial drug experimentation, scientific research has provided a great deal of insight into patterns of long-term drug use.

In particular, science has aided in understanding the difference between drug *use* and drug *abuse*. **Drug abuse** can be defined as the use of any drug—licit or illicit—that causes either psychological or bodily harm to the abuser or to third parties. Just as most people who drink beer or wine avoid abusing alcohol, most users of illegal substances are not abusers. For most drugs, only between 7 and 20 percent of all users suffer from compulsive abuse.[51]

Despite their relatively small numbers, drug abusers have a disparate impact on the drug market. The 20 percent of Americans, for example, who drink the most consume more than 80 percent of all alcoholic beverages sold in the United States. The data are similar for illicit substance abusers, leading to the conclusion that to a large extent, abusers and addicts sustain the market for illegal drugs.

THE DRUG-CRIME RELATIONSHIP

Of course, because many drugs are illegal, anybody who sells, uses, or in any way promotes the use of these drugs is, under most circumstances, breaking the law. The drug-crime relationship is much more complex than the language of criminal drug statutes, however.

Around two-thirds of jail inmates are dependent on or abuse alcohol or drugs.[52] According to one recent study, more than two-thirds of all arrestees in ten major American cities tested positive for illicit drugs at the time of their arrest.[53] As we will see throughout this textbook, the prosecution of illegal drug users and suppliers has been one of the primary factors in the enormous growth of the American correctional industry.

Models of Explanation Epidemiologist Paul Goldstein has devised three models to explain the relationship between drugs and crime:

- The *psychopharmacological model* holds that individuals act violently or criminally as a direct result of the drugs they have ingested.

Do you feel that the behavior of celebrities such as socialite Paris Hilton, who was arrested for cocaine possession in Las Vegas on August 27, 2010, "teaches" adolescents that such behavior is acceptable or even desirable? Explain your answer. (AP Photo/Mark Damon)

- The *economically impulsive model* holds that drug abusers commit crimes to obtain the funds to purchase drugs.
- The *systemic model* suggests that violence is a by-product of the interpersonal relationships within the drug-using community, such as when a dealer is assaulted by a buyer for selling "bad" drugs.[54]

The strength of the drug-crime relationship has provided justification for increased law enforcement efforts to criminalize drug use by harshly punishing offenders of controlled substance laws.

Models of Addiction Is criminal conviction and incarceration the best way for society to deal with addicts? Those who follow the **medical model of addiction** believe that addicts are not criminals, but mentally or physically ill individuals who are forced into acts of petty crime to "feed their habit." Those who believe in the *enslavement theory of addiction* advocate treating addiction as a disease. They also hold that society should not punish addicts but rather attempt to rehabilitate them, as would be done for any other unhealthy person.[55] Although a number of organizations, including the American Medical Association, recognize alcoholism and other forms of drug dependence as diseases, the criminal justice system tends to favor the **criminal model of addiction** over the medical model. The criminal model holds that drug abusers and addicts endanger society with their behavior and should be punished the same as any other persons who commit crimes that are not drug related.[56]

¿DOES CRIMINOLOGY HELP PREVENT CRIME?

You have almost completed the only chapter in this textbook that deals primarily with theory. What follows will concentrate on the more practical and legal aspects of the criminal justice system: how law enforcement agencies fight crime, how our court systems determine guilt or innocence, and how we punish those who are found guilty. Criminology can, however, play a crucial role in the criminal justice system. "A lot of

the problem. Legislators have also reacted to this research: habitual offender laws that provide harsher sentences for repeat offenders have become quite popular. We will discuss these statutes, including the controversial "three-strikes-and-you're-out" laws, in Chapter 11.

Can criminologists help law enforcement agents such as this Boston police officer prevent crime? If so, how? (Rick Friedman/Boston/Corbis/iStockphoto.com)

my colleagues just want to write scholarly articles for scholarly journals," notes Professor James Alan Fox of Northeastern University in Boston. "But I think if you're in a field with specialized knowledge that can be useful to the community, you should engage the public and policymakers."[57]

CRIMINOLOGY AND THE CHRONIC OFFENDER

Perhaps the most useful criminological contribution to crime fighting in the past half century was *Delinquency in a Birth Cohort*, published by the pioneering trio of Marvin Wolfgang, Robert Figlio, and Thorsten Sellin in 1972. This research established the idea of the **chronic offender**, or career criminal, by showing that a small group of juvenile offenders—6 percent—was responsible for a disproportionate amount of the violent crime attributed to a group of nearly 10,000 young males: 71 percent of the murders, 82 percent of the robberies, 69 percent of the aggravated assaults, and 73 percent of the rapes.[58]

Further research has supported the idea of a "chronic 6 percent,"[59] and law enforcement agencies and district attorneys' offices have devised specific strategies to apprehend and prosecute repeat offenders, with dozens of local police agencies forming career criminal units to deal with

CRIMINOLOGY AND THE CRIMINAL JUSTICE SYSTEM

There is a sense, however, that criminology has not done enough to make our country a safer place. Eminent criminologist James Q. Wilson, for one, has criticized his peers for trying to understand crime rather than to reduce it.[60] Many law enforcement officials also argue that too much of the research done by criminologists is inaccessible to them. As Sarah J. Hart, director of the National Institute of Justice, has noted, an overwhelmed police chief simply does not have the time or patience to wade through the many scientific journals in which crime research appears.[61]

These criticisms notwithstanding, John H. Laub of the American Society of Criminology defends modern criminology's practical benefits.[62] He points out that the work of Clifford Shaw and Henry McKay (page 30) focused law enforcement efforts on the community, while Travis Hirschi's research in the 1960s on the root causes of delinquency has had a wide impact on the juvenile justice system. As we will discuss further in Chapter 6, Wilson himself (in collaboration with George Kelling) developed the "broken windows" theory, which reshaped police strategy in the 1990s and the first decade of the twenty-first century. Following the premises of the medical model of addiction (page 38), state and federal governments spend $15 billion on substance abuse services each year, in part to keep abusers from becoming or staying involved in crime.[63] Indeed, in the opinion of many observers, researchers know more today about "what works" in criminology than at any other time in our nation's history.[64]

LO 5

3 DEFINING AND MEASURING CRIME

Learning Outcomes

After studying this chapter, you will be able to . . .

LO 1 Discuss the primary goals of civil law and criminal law, and explain how these goals are realized.

LO 2 Explain the differences between crimes *mala in se* and *mala prohibita*.

LO 3 Identify the publication in which the Federal Bureau of Investigation (FBI) reports crime data and list the three ways in which the data are reported.

LO 4 Distinguish between the National Crime Victimization Survey (NCVS) and self-reported surveys.

LO 5 Identify the three factors most often used by criminologists to explain increases and declines in the nation's crime rate.

AP Photo/Joseph Kaczmarek

Highways to Hell

Patty Peterson was last seen alive more than five years ago at a truck stop in Tulsa, Oklahoma. Then in 2009, a hiker stumbled across Peterson's skeleton near a rest stop in Lupton, Arizona, just across the state border from New Mexico. She had been beaten to death, her skull crushed on the right side and her nose broken. When Peterson's remains were finally identified in September 2010, her name was added to a growing—and disturbing—list of crime victims. According to data compiled by the Federal Bureau of Investigation (FBI), over the past four decades at least 450 people have died at the hands of serial killers who operate along the nation's highways.

Many of these victims share a common profile. Like Peterson, they are women involved in high-risk activities such as substance abuse and prostitution who spend time at truck stops or gas stations. They are picked up and then sexually assaulted, murdered, and discarded along interstates and highways. The prime suspects in these crimes, as identified by the FBI, are long-haul truck drivers, who have the ability to abduct the women in one state, dispose of their bodies in another, return to the highway, and disappear. Given the mobile nature of these suspects and the long distances involved, it has proved very difficult for local and state law enforcement agencies to track them down and link them to any criminal activity.

Why do law enforcement officials suspect long-haul truckers in the abductions and murders of hundreds of women from roadside locations such as the truck stop shown here? (Thinkstock Images/Comstock Images/Getty Images/Selahattin Bayram/iStockphotos)

For these reasons, several years ago the FBI started the Highway Serial Killings Initiative. As part of this program, local police departments send information about unsolved murders that fit the "roadside serial killer" profile to the FBI. Analysts at the agency then process the data and send out e-mail alerts when evidence matches a known suspect with a known victim. "It's a great resource for us," says George Cronin of the Pennsylvania State Police. "For a long time, police departments were operating in a bubble [and did not know] what was going on in neighboring jurisdictions."

Civil Law The branch of law dealing with the definition and enforcement of all private or public rights, as opposed to criminal matters.

Plaintiff The person or institution that initiates a lawsuit in civil court proceedings by filing a complaint.

Defendant In a civil court, the person or institution against whom an action is brought. In a criminal court, the person or entity who has been formally accused of violating a criminal law.

Crunching numbers is rarely considered exciting police work. As the Highway Serial Killings Initiative shows, however, it can be a crucial aspect of law enforcement. Using a definition of serial killing that identifies offenders as those who "murder two or more victims . . . in separate events,"[1] FBI analysts have gathered information on two hundred potential suspects. The movement of each suspect is tracked via technology such as the GPS system in his truck and credit-card retrieval records, allowing the experts to create time lines of the suspect's movements. To date, the program has helped solve more than two dozen murders, including that of Monica Massaro, killed while sleeping in her bedroom by a trucker named Adam Lane. (Massaro's home was located near a truck stop off Interstate 78 in Hunterdon County, New Jersey.)

As we will see in this chapter, definitions and measurements of crime are tools that both the police and other criminal justice professionals can use to help fight crime. We will start our examination of these subjects with an overview of how crimes are classified, move on to the various methods of measuring crime, and end with a discussion of some statistical trends that give us a good idea of the "state of crime" in the United States today.

¿WHAT ARE THE DIFFERENT CATEGORIES OF CRIME??

The huge body of the law can be broken down according to various classifications. Three of the most important distinctions are those between (1) civil law and criminal law, (2) felonies and misdemeanors, and (3) crimes *mala in se* and *mala prohibita*.

CIVIL LAW AND CRIMINAL LAW

All law can be divided into two categories: civil law and criminal law. As U.S. criminal law has evolved, it has diverged from U.S. civil law. The two categories of law are distinguished by their primary goals. The criminal justice system is concerned with protecting society from harm by preventing and prosecuting crimes. A crime is an act so reprehensible that it is considered a wrong against society as a whole, as well as against the individual victim. Therefore, the state prosecutes a person who commits a criminal act. If the state is able to prove that a person is guilty of a crime, the government will punish her or him with imprisonment or fines, or both.

Civil law, which includes all types of law other than criminal law, is concerned with disputes between private individuals and between entities. Proceedings in civil lawsuits are normally initiated by an individual or a corporation (in contrast to criminal proceedings, which are initiated by public prosecutors). Such disputes may involve, for example, the terms of a contract, the ownership of property, or an automobile accident. Under civil law, the government provides a forum for the resolution of *torts*—or private wrongs—in which the injured party, called the **plaintiff,** tries to prove that a wrong has been committed by the accused party, or the **defendant.** (Note that the accused party in both criminal and civil cases is known as the *defendant*.)

Guilt and Responsibility A criminal court is convened to determine whether the defendant is *guilty*—that is, whether the defendant has, in fact, committed the offense charged. In contrast, civil law is concerned with *responsibility*, a much more flexible concept. For example, after William Hensley died of an allergic reaction to bee stings, a civil court partially blamed emergency room physician Allen Retirado for his death. Retirado had mistakenly attributed Hensley's unconsciousness on arrival at St. Clare's Hospital in Sussex Borough, New Jersey, to heat stroke. Even though Retirado was never charged with any crime, the civil court decided that he was **liable**, or legally responsible, for Hensley's death because of his improper diagnosis.

Most civil cases involve a request for monetary damages to compensate for the wrong that has been committed. Thus, in 2010, the civil court ordered Allen Retirado to pay nearly $1 million to William Hensley's family as compensation for the financial and emotional consequences of his death. (See **Figure 3.1** below for a comparison of civil and criminal law.)

The Burden of Proof Although criminal law proceedings are completely separate from civil law proceedings in the modern legal system, the two systems do have some similarities. Both attempt to control behavior by imposing sanctions on those who violate society's definition of acceptable behavior. Furthermore, criminal and civil law often supplement each other. In certain instances, a victim may file a civil suit against an individual who is also the target of a criminal prosecution by the government.

Because the burden of proof is much greater in criminal trials than civil ones, it is almost always easier to win monetary damages than a criminal conviction. In 2008, for example, truck driver George Albright was found not guilty of any criminal wrongdoing in connection with a traffic accident near Columbia, Missouri, that left four women dead. In 2010, however, a civil court decided that Albright was responsible for the death of Anita Gibbs, one of the four crash victims, and ordered a $32.25 million payment to Gibbs's family. In the earlier trial, the criminal court did not find enough evidence to prove **beyond a reasonable doubt** (the burden of proof in criminal cases) that Albright was guilty of any crime. Nevertheless, the civil trial established by a **preponderance of the evidence** (the burden of proof in civil cases) that Albright was responsible for Gibbs's death. (CAREER TIP: When attorneys are gathering evidence to use in civil trials, they will often engage a *private investigator* [PI] to find important evidence that the police might have missed. In this case, a private investigation determined that Albright falsified his trucking logs to indicate that he had gotten sufficient rest before the accident.)

Liability In a civil court, legal responsibility for one's own or another's actions.

Beyond a Reasonable Doubt The degree of proof required to find the defendant in a criminal trial guilty of committing the crime.

Preponderance of the Evidence The degree of proof required to decide in favor of one side or the other in a civil case. In general, this requirement is met when a plaintiff proves that a fact is more likely than not true.

Figure 3.1   Civil Law versus Criminal Law

Area of Concern	CIVIL LAW Rights and duties between individuals	CRIMINAL LAW Offenses against society as a whole
Wrongful Act	Harm to a person or business entity	Violation of a criminal statute
Party who brings suit	Person who suffered harm (plaintiff)	The state (prosecutor)
Party who responds	Person who supposedly caused harm (defendant)	Person who allegedly committed a crime (defendant)
Standard of proof	Preponderance of the evidence	Beyond a reasonable doubt
Remedy	Damages to compensate for the harm	Punishment (fine or incarceration)

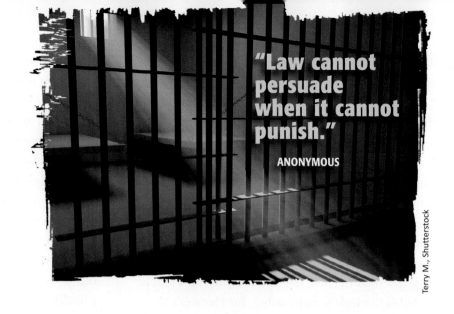

Felony A serious crime, punishable by imprisonment for a year or longer or, on rare occasions, death.

Malice Aforethought A depraved state of mind in which the offender's behavior shows a lack of concern for the well-being of his or her victims.

"Law cannot persuade when it cannot punish."

ANONYMOUS

FELONIES AND MISDEMEANORS

Depending on their degree of seriousness, crimes are classified as *felonies* or *misdemeanors*. **Felonies** are serious crimes punishable by death or, more commonly, by imprisonment in a federal or state penitentiary for one year or longer (though some states, such as North Carolina, consider felonies to be punishable by at least two years' incarceration). The Model Penal Code, a general guide for criminal law, provides for four degrees of felony:

1. Capital offenses, for which the maximum penalty is death.
2. First degree felonies, punishable by a maximum penalty of life imprisonment.
3. Second degree felonies, punishable by a maximum of ten years' imprisonment.
4. Third degree felonies, punishable by a maximum of five years' imprisonment.[2]

Degrees of Crime Although specifics vary from state to state, some general rules apply when grading crimes. For example, most criminal codes punish a burglary that involves a nighttime forced entry into a home more seriously than one that takes place during the day and involves a nonresidential building. Furthermore, the seriousness of any crime is usually determined by the mental state of the offender. That is, the law punishes those who plan and intend to do harm more harshly than it does those who act wrongfully because of strong emotions or other extreme circumstances. We will address the importance of mental state in crime more extensively in the next chapter, but here we can see how it affects the degrees of murder.

Murder in the first degree occurs under two circumstances:

1. When the crime is *premeditated*, or considered (contemplated) beforehand by the offender, instead of being a spontaneous act of violence.
2. When the crime is *deliberate*, meaning that it was planned and decided on after a process of decision making. Deliberation does not require a lengthy planning process. A person can be found guilty of first degree murder even if she or he made the decision to murder only seconds before committing the crime.

Second degree murder, generally punishable by fifteen years to life in prison, occurs when no premeditation or deliberation was present, but the offender did have **malice aforethought** toward the victim. In other words, the offender acted with wanton disregard of the consequences of his or her actions. The difference between first and second degree murder is clearly illustrated in a case involving a California man who beat a neighbor to death with a partially full brandy bottle. The crime took place after Ricky McDonald, the victim, complained to Kazi Cooksey, the offender, about the noise coming from a late-night barbecue Cooksey and his friends were holding. The jury could not find sufficient evidence that Cooksey's actions were premeditated, but he certainly acted with wanton disregard of his victim's safety. Therefore, the jury convicted Cooksey of second degree murder rather than first degree murder.

Types of Manslaughter A homicide committed without malice toward the victim is known as

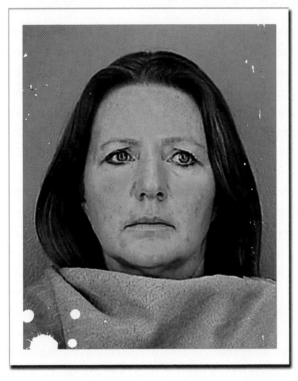

Why was former day-care center operator Jeanette Lawrence, pictured here, convicted of involuntary manslaughter rather than murder or voluntary manslaughter for her role in the death of eighteen-month-old Ava Patrick? (Johnson County Sheriff's Office)

manslaughter and is usually punishable by up to fifteen years in prison. **Voluntary manslaughter** occurs when the intent to kill may be present, but malice, as described in the previous section, was lacking. Voluntary manslaughter covers crimes of passion, such as when the emotion of an argument between two friends may lead to a homicide. Voluntary manslaughter can also occur when the victim provoked the offender to act violently.

Involuntary manslaughter covers incidents in which the offender's acts may have been careless, but she or he had no intent to kill. In 2010, for example, Jeanette Lawrence was convicted of involuntary manslaughter for her role in the death of eighteen-month-old Ava Patrick. A year earlier, Lawrence lost track of Ava at the day-care center she operated in Olathe, Missouri. Unattended, the child suffocated when her neck got caught in the slats of a wooden fence. Although Lawrence certainly did not intend for Ava to die,

she was held criminally responsible and sentenced to forty-one months in prison (see the photo alongside).

Degrees of Misdemeanor Under federal law and in most states, any crime that is not a felony is considered a **misdemeanor**. Misdemeanors are crimes punishable by a fine or by confinement for up to a year. If imprisoned, the guilty party usually goes to a local jail instead of a prison. Disorderly conduct and trespassing are common misdemeanors. Like felonies, misdemeanors are graded by level of seriousness. In Illinois, for example, misdemeanors are either Class A (confinement for up to a year), Class B (not more than six months), or Class C (not more than thirty days).

Most states similarly distinguish between *gross misdemeanors*, which are offenses punishable by thirty days to a year in jail, and *petty misdemeanors*, or offenses punishable by fewer than thirty days in jail. Whether a crime is a felony or a misdemeanor can also determine whether the case is tried in a magistrate's court (for example, by a justice of the peace) or in a general trial court (for example, a superior court).

Infractions The least serious form of wrongdoing is often called an **infraction** and is punishable only by a small fine. Even though infractions such as parking tickets or traffic violations technically represent illegal activity, they generally are not considered "crimes." Therefore, infractions rarely lead to jury trials and are deemed to be so minor that they do not appear on the offender's criminal record. In some jurisdictions, the terms *infraction* and *petty offense* are interchangeable. In

> **Voluntary Manslaughter** A homicide in which the intent to kill was present in the mind of the offender, but malice was lacking.
>
> **Involuntary Manslaughter** A negligent homicide in which the offender had no intent to kill his or her victim.
>
> **Misdemeanor** A criminal offense that is not a felony; usually punishable by a fine and/or a jail term of less than one year.
>
> **Infraction** In most jurisdictions, a noncriminal offense for which the penalty is a fine rather than incarceration.

others, however, they are different. Under federal guidelines, for example, an infraction can be punished by up to five days of prison time, while a petty offender is only liable for a fine.[3] Finally, those who string together a series of infractions (or fail to pay the fines that come with such offenses) are in danger of being criminally charged. In Illinois, having three or more speeding violations in one year is considered criminal behavior.[4]

MALA IN SE AND *MALA PROHIBITA*

Criminologists often express the social function of criminal law in terms of *mala in se* or *mala prohibita* crimes. A criminal act is referred to as **mala in se** if it would be considered wrong even if there were no law prohibiting it. *Mala in se* crimes are said to go against "natural laws"—that is, against the "natural, moral, and public" principles of a society. Murder, rape, and theft are examples of *mala in se* crimes. These crimes are generally the same from country to country or culture to culture. In contrast, the term **mala prohibita** refers to acts that are considered crimes only because they have been codified as such through statute—"human-made" laws. A *mala prohibita* crime is considered wrong only because it has been prohibited. The act is not inherently a wrong, though it may reflect the moral standards of a society at a given time. Thus, the definition of a *mala prohibita* crime can vary from country to country and even from state to state. Bigamy, or having two spouses at the same time, could be considered a *mala prohibita* crime.

Some observers question the distinction between *mala in se* and *mala prohibita*. In many instances, it is difficult to define a "pure" *mala in se* crime. That is, it is difficult to separate a crime from the culture that has deemed it a crime.[5] Even murder, under certain cultural circumstances, is not considered a criminal act. In a number of poor, traditional areas of the Middle East and Asia, the law excuses "honor killings" in which men kill female family members suspected of sexual indiscretion. Our own legal system excuses homicide in extreme situations, such as self-defense or when a law enforcement agent kills in the

CAREER PREP   PARALEGAL/LEGAL ASSISTANT

JOB DESCRIPTION:

- Assist lawyers in many aspects of legal work, including preparing for trial, researching legal documents, drafting contracts, and investigating cases.

- In addition to criminal law, work includes civil law, corporate law, intellectual property, bankruptcy, immigration, family law, and real estate.

WHAT KIND OF TRAINING IS REQUIRED?

- A community college–level paralegal program that leads to an associate degree.

- For those who already have a college degree, a certificate in paralegal studies.

ANNUAL SALARY RANGE?

- $30,000–$75,000

For additional information, visit:
www.nala.org/AboutParalegals.aspx.

©Andresr/iStockphoto

Uniform Crime Report (UCR) An annual report compiled by the FBI to give an indication of criminal activity in the United States.

Part I Offenses Crimes reported annually by the FBI in its Uniform Crime Report.

course of upholding the law. Therefore, "natural" laws can be seen as culturally specific. Similar difficulties occur in trying to define a "pure" *mala prohibita* crime.

¿HOW DOES THE GOVERNMENT MEASURE CRIME?

Suppose that a firefighter dies while fighting a fire at an office building. Later, police discover that the building manager intentionally set the fire. All of the elements of the crime of arson have certainly been met, but can the manager be charged with murder? In some jurisdictions, the act might be considered a form of manslaughter. According to the U.S. Department of Justice, however, arson-related deaths and injuries of police officers and firefighters due to the "hazardous natures of their professions" are not murders.[6]

The distinction is important because the Department of Justice provides the most far-reaching and oft-cited set of national crime statistics. Each year, the department releases the **Uniform Crime Report (UCR)**. Since its inception in 1930, the UCR has attempted to measure the overall rate of crime in the United States by organizing "offenses known to the police."[7] To produce the UCR, the FBI relies on the voluntary participation of local law enforcement agencies. These agencies—approximately 17,500 in total, covering 95 percent of the population—base their information on three measurements:

LO 3

1. The number of persons arrested.
2. The number of crimes reported by victims, witnesses, or the police themselves.
3. The number of officers and support law enforcement specialists.[8]

Once this information has been sent to the FBI, the agency presents the crime data in two important ways:

1. As a *rate* per 100,000 people. In 2009, for example, the crime rate was 3,465. In other words, for every 100,000 inhabitants of the United States, 3,465 *Part I offenses* (explained below) were reported to the FBI. This statistic is known as the *crime rate* and is often cited by media sources when discussing the level of crime in the United States.

2. As a *percentage* change from the previous year or other time periods. From 2008 to 2009, there was a 6.1 percent decrease in the violent crime rate and a 5.5 percent decrease in the property crime rate.[9]

The Department of Justice publishes these data annually in *Crime in the United States.* Along with the basic statistics, this publication offers an exhaustive array of crime information, including breakdowns of crimes committed by city, county, and other geographic designations and by the demographics (gender, race, age) of the individuals who have been arrested for crimes. (CAREER TIP: With their expert knowledge of statistics and their ability to organize numerical data, *statisticians* are crucial employees for the FBI and other federal and state law enforcement agencies that regularly publish crime reports.)

PART I OFFENSES

The UCR divides the criminal offenses it measures into two major categories: Part I and Part II offenses. **Part I offenses** are those crimes that, due to their seriousness and frequency, are recorded by the FBI to give a general

Part II Offenses
All crimes recorded by the FBI that do not fall into the category of Part I offenses.

idea of the "crime picture" in the United States in any given year. For a description of the eight crimes that can be considered Part I offenses, see **Figure 3.2** below.

Part I offenses are those most likely to be covered by the media and, consequently, inspire the most fear of crime in the population. These crimes have come to dominate crime coverage to such an extent that, for most Americans, the first image that comes to mind at the mention of crime is one person physically attacking another person or a robbery taking place with the use or threat of force.[10] Furthermore, in the stereotypical crime, the offender and the victim usually do not know each other.

Given the trauma of violent crimes, this perception is understandable. It is not, however, accurate. According to UCR statistics, a relative or other acquaintance of the victim commits at least 56 percent of the homicides in the United States.[11] Furthermore, as is evident from **Figure 3.3** on the facing page, the majority of Part I offenses committed are property crimes. Notice that almost 60 percent of all reported Part I offenses are larceny/thefts, and about another 20 percent are burglaries.[12]

PART II OFFENSES

Not only do violent crimes represent the minority of Part I offenses, but Part I offenses are far outweighed by **Part II offenses**, which include all crimes recorded by the FBI that do not fall into the category of Part I offenses. The most common Part II offenses include drug abuse violations, driving under the influence, assaults that do not result in injury, disorderly conduct, and drunkenness. While information gathered on Part I offenses reflects those offenses "known," or reported to the FBI by local agencies, Part II offenses are measured only by arrest data. In 2009, the FBI recorded about 2.3 million arrests for Part I offenses in the United States. That same year, more than 11.3 million arrests for Part II offenses took place.[13] In other words, a Part II offense was about five times more common than a Part I offense. Such statistics have prompted Marcus Felson, a professor at Rutgers University School of Criminal Justice, to comment that "most crime is very ordinary."[14]

Figure 3.2 Part I Offenses

Every month, local law enforcement agencies voluntarily provide information on serious offenses in their jurisdiction to the FBI. These serious offenses, known as Part I offenses, are defined here. The FBI collects data on Part I offenses to present an accurate picture of criminal activity in the United States. Arson is not included in national crime rate figures, but it is sometimes considered a Part I offense nonetheless, so it is included here.

Criminal homicide.
   a. **Murder and nonnegligent manslaughter:** The willful (non-negligent) killing of one human being by another.
   b. **Manslaughter by negligence:** The killing of another person through gross negligence.

Forcible rape. The carnal knowledge of a female forcibly and against her will. Included are rapes by force and attempted rapes or assaults as part of a rape.

Robbery. The taking or attempting to take anything of value from the care, custody, or control of a person or persons by force or threat of force or violence and/or by putting the victim in fear.

Aggravated assault. An unlawful attack by one person on another for the purpose of inflicting severe, or aggravated, bodily injury.

Burglary—breaking or entering. The unlawful entry of a structure to commit a felony or a theft. Attempted forcible entry is included.

Larceny/theft (except motor vehicle theft). The unlawful taking, carrying, leading, or riding away of property from the possession of another.

Motor vehicle theft. The theft or attempted theft of a motor vehicle.

Arson. Any willful or malicious burning or attempt to burn, with or without intent to defraud, a dwelling house, public building, motor vehicle or aircraft, personal property of another, and the like.

Source: Federal Bureau of Investigation, *Crime in the United States, 2009* (Washington, D.C.: U.S. Department of Justice, 2010), at **www2.fbi.gov/ucr/cius2009/about/offense_definitions.html.**

Figure 3.3 Composition of Part I Offenses

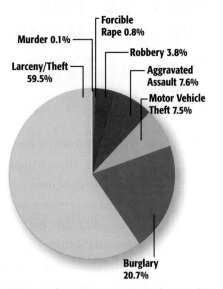

- Murder 0.1%
- Forcible Rape 0.8%
- Robbery 3.8%
- Larceny/Theft 59.5%
- Aggravated Assault 7.6%
- Motor Vehicle Theft 7.5%
- Burglary 20.7%

Source: Federal Bureau of Investigation, *Crime in the United States,* 2009 (Washington, D.C.: U.S. Department of Justice, 2010), at **www2.fbi.gov/ucr/cius2009/data/table_01.html.**

¿IN WHAT OTHER WAYS CAN CRIME BE MEASURED?

The UCR is generally considered the "official" record of crime in the United States, but it is only one of many sources of crime data in this country. Law enforcement professionals and academics also rely on victim surveys and self-reported surveys to collect such data, and we discuss these two popular crime measurement methods in this section.

VICTIM SURVEYS

One alternative source of data collecting attempts to avoid the distorting influence of the "intermediary," or the local police agencies. In **victim surveys**, criminologists or other researchers ask the victims of crime directly about their experiences, using techniques such as interviews or e-mail and phone surveys. The first large-scale victim survey took place in 1966, when members of 10,000 households answered questionnaires as part of the President's Commission on Law Enforcement and the Administration of Justice. The results indicated a much higher victimization rate than had been previously

expected, and researchers felt the process gave them a better understanding of the **dark figure of crime**, or the actual amount of crime that occurs in the country.

Criminologists were so encouraged by the results of the 1966 experiment that the federal government decided to institute an ongoing victim survey. The result was the National Crime Victimization Survey (NCVS), which started in 1972. Conducted by the U.S. Bureau of the Census in cooperation with the Bureau of Justice Statistics of the Justice Department, the NCVS conducts an annual survey of more than 40,000 households with nearly 75,000 occupants over twelve years of age. Participants are interviewed twice a year concerning their experiences with crimes in the prior six months. As you can see in **Figure 3.4** on the next page, the questions try to be as specific as possible.

> **Victim Survey** A method of gathering crime data that directly surveys participants to determine their experiences as victims of crime.
>
> **Dark Figure of Crime** A term used to describe the actual amount of crime that takes place. The "figure" is "dark," or impossible to detect, because a great number of crimes are never reported to the police.
>
> **Self-Reported Survey** A method of gathering crime data that relies on participants to reveal and detail their own criminal or delinquent behavior.

Supporters of the NCVS highlight a number of aspects in which the victim survey is superior to the UCR:

1. It measures both reported and unreported crime.
2. It is unaffected by police bias and distortions in reporting crime to the FBI.
3. It does not rely on victims directly reporting crime to the police.[15]

Most important, some supporters say, is that the NCVS gives victims a voice in the criminal justice process.

SELF-REPORTED SURVEYS

Based on many of the same principles as victim surveys, but focusing instead on offenders, **self-reported surveys** are a third source of data for criminologists. In this form of data collection, persons are asked directly—through personal interviews or questionnaires, or over the telephone—about specific criminal activity to which they may have been a party. Self-reported surveys are most useful in situations in

Figure 3.4   Sample Questions from the NCVS (National Crime Victimization Survey)

36a. Was something belonging to YOU stolen, such as:
  a. Things that you carry, like luggage, a wallet, purse, briefcase, book.
  b. Clothing, jewelry, or cell phone.
  c. Bicycle or sports equipment.
  d. Things in your home, like a TV, stereo, or tools.
  e. Things from outside your home, such as a garden hose or lawn furniture.
  f. Things belonging to children in the household.
  g. Things from a vehicle, such as a package, groceries, camera, or CDs.
  h. Did anyone ATTEMPT to steal anything belonging to you?

41a. Has anyone attacked or threatened you in any of these ways:
  a. With any weapon, for instance, a gun or knife.
  b. With anything like a baseball bat, frying pan, scissors, or stick.
  c. By something thrown, such as a rock or bottle.
  d. Include any grabbing, punching, or choking.
  e. Any rape, attempted rape, or other type of sexual attack.
  f. Any face-to-face threats—OR
  g. Any attack or threat or use of force by anyone at all? Please mention it even if you are not certain it was a crime.

Source: U.S. Department of Justice, *National Crime Victimization Survey 2006* (Washington, D.C.: Bureau of Justice Statistics, 2008).

which the group to be studied is already gathered in an institutional setting, such as a juvenile facility or a prison. One of the more widespread self-reported surveys in the United States, the Drug Use Forecasting Program, collects information on narcotics use from arrestees who have been brought into booking facilities.

Because there is no penalty for admitting to criminal activity in a self-reported survey, subjects tend to be more forthcoming in discussing their behavior. Researchers interviewing a group of male students at a state university, for example, found that a significant number of the students admitted to committing minor crimes for which they had never been arrested. This fact points to the most striking finding of self-reported surveys: the *dark figure of crime*, a term that refers to the *actual* amount of crime that takes place, appears to be much larger than the UCR or NCVS would suggest.

¿WHAT IS THE STATE OF CRIME IN THE UNITED STATES?

The UCR, NCVS, and other statistical measures we have discussed so far in this chapter, though important, represent only the tip of the iceberg of crime data. Thanks to the efforts of government law enforcement agencies, educational institutions, and private individuals, more information on crime is available today than at any time in the nation's history. Pure statistics, however, do not always tell the whole story, and crime rates often fail to behave in the ways criminologists predict. In this section, we will look at how crime patterns in the United States have shifted over the past five decades and how trends from the immediate past may or may not help us understand what to expect in the immediate future.

ON THE RISE: CRIME IN THE 1960s AND 1970s

Since the early 1960s, the United States has suffered two large-scale crime increases. The first, long term and relatively gradual, lasted through the 1970s. The second, shorter and more dramatic, peaked in 1991. In attempting to explain the first increase, experts relied principally on what Franklin Zimring calls the three "usual suspects" of crime fluctuation:

1. *Imprisonment*, based on the principle that (a) an offender in prison or jail is unable to commit a crime on the street, and (b) a potential offender on the street will not commit a crime because he or she does not want to wind up behind bars.
2. *Youth populations*, because offenders commit fewer crimes as they grow older.
3. The *economy*, because when legitimate opportunities to earn income become scarce, some people will turn to illegitimate methods such as crime.[16]

To a certain extent, evidence from the 1960s and 1970s, when the first crime increase occurred, sup-

CJ and Technology

TRANSDERMAL ALCOHOL TESTING

Sweat, it seems, is one source of self-reported data that never lies, at least when it comes to alcohol consumption. That's the logic behind the Secure Continuous Remote Alcohol Monitor, otherwise known as the SCRAM bracelet or the "bling with a ping." This eight-ounce bracelet, usually worn around the subject's ankle, relies on a process called *transdermal alcohol testing* to measure the levels of alcohol vapor that show up in perspiration when alcohol has been consumed. The measurements are then transmitted and posted on a Web site via wireless modem, allowing the subject to prove—or disprove—that he or she remains sober. The SCRAM bracelet gained notoriety several years ago when actress and socialite Lindsay Lohan voluntarily donned one to show her commitment to sobriety. Most wearers, however, are not celebrities but rather offenders who are required by a court to undergo the testing after an arrest for drunken driving, domestic violence, or some other alcohol-related wrongdoing.

THINKING ABOUT TRANSDERMAL ALCOHOL TESTING

Coming soon: passive transdermal detectors in steering wheels. These devices will measure the sweat on the driver's hands to determine whether she or he has been ingesting drugs or alcohol. How could this technology be used to keep someone from driving under the influence?

ports the influence of each of these usual suspects. For example, levels of imprisonment in the United States were relatively low during the 1960s. By the early 1970s, the public outcry at violent crime rates that had doubled in the previous decade started a "get tough on crime" political movement that resulted in harsher sentences for a wider range of offenders.[17] In fact, 1972 would mark the last time that the number of Americans behind bars dropped for the next thirty years, leading many to believe that the massive expansion of the corrections industry has played a crucial role in subsequent reductions in crime.

Age and Crime: The Peak Years Writing in 1974, criminologist James Q. Wilson pointed out a trend that seemed to have an obvious connection to the crime increases of the era. Between 1960 and 1973, the num-

ber of Americans between the ages of eighteen and twenty-four increased by 13 million, bringing the total to more than 40 million.[18] Wilson found these data highly relevant because the strongest statistical determinant of criminal behavior appears to be age. Numerous studies show that criminal behavior peaks in the teenage years. Indeed, juvenile arrest rates did increase in the 1960s and early 1970s before leveling off for the remainder of the decade.[19] As **Figure 3.5** on the next page shows, the eighteen- to twenty-four-year-old group targeted by Wilson remains responsible for a greater percentage of total arrests than any other age group.

Why is the crime rate dramatically higher for young people? There is no single, simple answer. As noted in Chapter 2, biological theories of crime point to high testosterone levels in young males, which increase rates of aggression and violence (see page 27). Adolescents are

Crack Cocaine A highly addictive form of cocaine, crystallized into "rock" and smoked rather than snorted.

also more susceptible to peer pressure, and studies show that juvenile delinquents tend to socialize with other juvenile delinquents.[20] In Chapter 15, we will take a much closer look at the many *risk factors* that are associated with youthful offending.

Crime and the Economy

The 1970s were also a difficult period for the American economy, and criminologists have pointed to high unemployment rates and falling wages as contributing to the crime increases of that decade.[21] While few observers would question the existence of some correlation between crime and the economy, the overall equation is not quite so simple. The 1960s, for example, were a time of concurrent general economic prosperity and increasing crime rates.[22] Indeed, none of the usual suspects—imprisonment, demographics, and the economy—has consistently mirrored crime trends. In Chapter 13, we will look at the often contradictory relationship between incarceration and crime. Furthermore, later in this section we will see that predictions based on youth populations have often been wrong—sometimes spectacularly so.

DRUG WARS: CRIME IN THE 1980s

Another reason often cited for the crime increases of the 1970s was rising heroin use, particularly in inner cities of the United States. The drug-crime relationship, which we first examined in Chapter 2 (see pages 37–38), also appeared to be a leading factor in the crime spike of the late 1980s and early 1990s. Those years saw the

Figure 3.5   Percentage of Arrests by Age

As this graph shows, the majority of persons arrested for property crimes in the United States are under twenty-five years old, and more violent crimes are committed by eighteen- to twenty-four-year-olds than by any other age group.

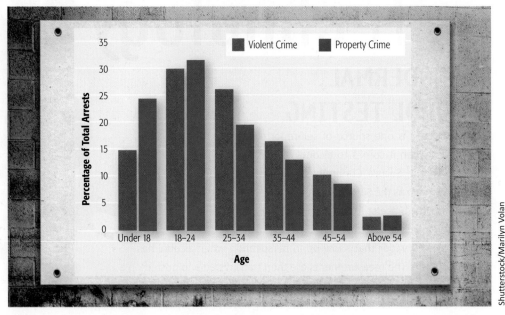

Source: Federal Bureau of Investigation, *Crime in the United States, 2009* (Washington, D.C.: U.S. Department of Justice, 2010), at **www2.fbi.gov/ucr/cius2009/data/table_38.html.**

introduction of **crack cocaine**, which is more powerful than the powdered form of the drug and quickly became a staple of the illegal drug market.

The Impact of Crack According to Professor Alfred Blumstein of Pittsburgh's Carnegie Mellon University, the introduction of crack cocaine set off a series of events with disastrous consequences for young, low-income males. First, drug kingpins hired them to sell the drug on the street. Because firearms were necessary to protect a dealer's territory, the crack trade led to a flood of handguns in poorer neighborhoods of the United States. These handguns then began to spread to the rest of the youth population and were used to commit crimes

is relatively easy to make in home laboratories using the ingredients of common cold medicines and farm chemicals. Consequently, the drug provides a "cheap high" for the consumer and has become the scourge of many of the nation's poor rural areas.

Several years ago, 98 percent of Washington State law enforcement agencies reported a significant meth presence in their jurisdictions. The vast majority of these agencies also reported that crimes such as robbery/burglary, identity theft, domestic violence, and assault increased as a direct result of the meth trade.[25] In addition, the spread of the drug has had significant secondary effects. Children who have been taken away from parents caught using or making the substance, known as "meth orphans," are overwhelming foster homes and social services in Washington and several other states. (CAREER TIP: Many law enforcement agencies require *emergency medical technicians* to provide on-the-spot health services such as assessing the condition of a child who has been removed from a meth lab site.)

LOOKING GOOD: CRIME IN THE 1990s AND 2000s

In 1995, James Q. Wilson, noting that the number of young males was set to increase dramatically over the next decade, predicted that "30,000 more young muggers, killers, and thieves" would be on the streets by 2000. "Get ready," he warned.[26] Other criminologists offered their own dire projections. John DiIulio foresaw a swarm of "juvenile super-predators" on the streets,[27] and James A. Fox prophesied a "blood bath" by 2005.[28] Given previous data, these experts could be fairly confident in their predictions. Fortunately for the country, they were wrong. As is evident from **Figure 3.6** on the following page, starting in 1994 the United States experienced a steep crime decline that we are still enjoying, though to a somewhat lesser degree, today.

The Great Crime Decline The crime statistics of the 1990s are startling. Even with the upswing at the beginning of the decade, from 1990 to 2000 the homicide rate dropped 39 percent, the robbery rate

Drug Enforcement Administration agents collect evidence at a meth lab in Liverpool, Ohio. Why has this particular drug flourished in poor, rural areas? (AP Photo/Wayne Maris/*East Liverpool Review*/Korhan Karacan/iStockphoto.com)

such as homicide and robbery.[23] Further research by Blumstein showed that the homicide rates by young offenders in large cities began to increase in 1985 and began to fall in 1993, a trend that reflected the ebb and flow of crime rates in general at that time.[24]

The Methamphetamine Scourge Although nothing as dramatic and far reaching as the crack cocaine epidemic has occurred in the first decades of the twenty-first century, the drug-crime relationship can still be seen in concentrated geographic areas. Many of these crime pockets have formed as a result of the manufacture and sale of **methamphetamine (meth)**, a highly addictive stimulant to the central nervous system. Meth

Figure 3.6 Violent Crime in the United States

According to statistics gathered each year by the FBI, American violent crime rates have varied over time. As you can see, the numbers ebb and flow, with increases in the early 1990s and decreases in the mid to late 1990s. The first decade of the 2000s was, in the words of one expert, "impressively flat."

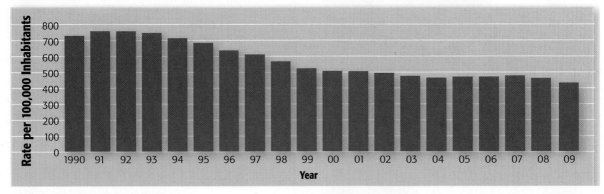

Source: Federal Bureau of Investigation.

44 percent, the burglary rate 41 percent, and the auto theft rate 37 percent. By most measures, this decline was the longest and deepest of the twentieth century.[29] In retrospect, the 1990s seem to have encompassed a "golden era" for the leading indicators of low crime rates. The economy was robust. The incarceration rate was skyrocketing. Plus, despite the misgivings of James Q. Wilson and many of his colleagues, the percentage of the population in the high-risk age bracket in 1995 was actually lower than it had been in 1980.[30]

Several other factors also seemed to favor lower crime rates. Police tactics, many of which we will discuss in Chapter 6, became more efficient—thanks in no small part to "zero-tolerance" policies inspired by Wilson's writings. Furthermore, many of those most heavily involved in the crack cocaine boom of the late 1980s had been killed or imprisoned, or were no longer offending. Without their criminal activity, the United States became a much safer place.[31]

A "Welcome Puzzle" In the early years of the 2000s, the nation's crime rate flattened for a time before resuming its downward slope. In 2009, property crime rates dropped for the seventh straight year, and violent crime rates shrank to their lowest levels since the early 1970s. Given that, in recent years, the economy has been mired in a recession, unemployment has been unusually high, and many local police departments have been reducing their budgets, the decreasing crime rates have come as something of a surprise.

Richard Rosenfeld, president of the American Society of Criminology, calls the trend "one of those welcome puzzles" and suggests that his colleagues reconsider "under what conditions economic activity influences crime."[32]

CRIME, RACE, AND POVERTY

One group has noticeably failed to benefit from the improved crime trends of the past fifteen years: young African American males. According to data compiled by criminologists James A. Fox and Marc L. Swatt of Northeastern University in Boston, from 2002 to 2007 the number of murders committed by black males under the age of eighteen rose 43 percent. Over the same time period, the number of young black males who were victims of murder also increased significantly, by 31 percent. In both categories, levels for young white males remained the same or declined.[33]

Race and Crime Youth homicide rates are not the only area in which there is a "worrisome divergence"[34]—to use Professor Fox's term—in crime trends between the races. Official crime data seem to indicate a strong correlation between minority status and crime: African Americans—who make up 13 percent of the population—constitute 39 percent of those arrested for violent crimes and 30 percent of those arrested for property crimes.[35] A black man is almost twelve times more likely than a white man to be sent to prison for a drug-related conviction, while black women are about five times more likely than white women to be incarcerated for a drug offense.[36] An African American male born in 2001 in the United States has a one in three chance of going to prison at some point in his life. The national average for American men of all races is one in fifteen. Furthermore, although less than half of those arrested for violent crimes are African American, blacks account for just over half of all convictions and approximately 60 percent of prison admissions.[37] (CAREER TIP: If you are interested in remedying unequal treatment of minorities in the criminal justice system, you should consider becoming a *civil rights lawyer*.)

The racial differences in the crime rate are one of the more controversial areas of the criminal justice system. At first glance, crime statistics seem to support the idea that the subculture of African Americans in the United States is disposed toward criminal behavior. Not all of the data, however, support that assertion. A recent research project led by sociologist Robert J. Sampson of Harvard University collected extensive data on more than 11,000 residents living in 180 Chicago neighborhoods. Sampson and his colleagues found that 60 percent of the "gap" in levels of violence between whites and African Americans could be attributed to neighborhood and family conditions. In other words, regardless of race, a person would have a much higher risk of violent behavior if he or she lived in a poverty-stricken, disorganized neighborhood or in a household run

Mourning friends carry a portrait of Bobby Tillman, who was beaten to death in a random attack outside a Douglasville, Georgia, house party on November 7, 2010. How have young black males failed to benefit from the positive crime trends that currently exist in the United States? (AP Photo/Atlanta Journal & Constitution, Brant Sanderlin)

by a single parent.[38] (CAREER TIP: Under certain circumstances, when home life becomes unhealthful for a child, the state can decide to place him or her in a foster home. The professionals who oversee this process and look out for the best interests of the children, and their families, are called *foster care case workers*.)

Class and Crime Indeed, a wealth of information suggests that income level is more important than skin color when it comes to crime trends. A 2002 study of nearly 900 African American children (400 boys and 467 girls) from neighborhoods with varying income levels showed that family earning power had the only significant correlation with violent

"**41%** of all inmates in state and federal prisons **do not have a high school diploma,** compared with 18% of the general population."

behavior.[39] More recent research conducted by William A. Pridemore of Indiana University found a "positive and significant association" between poverty and homicide.[40] Lack of education, another handicap most often faced by low-income citizens, also seems to correlate with criminal behavior. Forty-one percent of all inmates in state and federal prisons failed to obtain a high school education, compared with 18 percent of the population at large.[41]

It might seem logical that those without the financial means to acquire the consumer goods and services that dominate our society would turn to illegal methods to "steal" purchasing power. But, logic aside, many criminologists are skeptical of such an obvious class-

crime relationship. After all, poverty does not *cause* crime. The majority of residents in low-income neighborhoods are law-abiding. Furthermore, self-reported surveys indicate that high-income citizens are involved in all sorts of criminal activities[42] and are far more likely to commit white-collar crimes, which are not included in national crime statistics. These facts tend to support the theory that high crime rates in low-income communities are at least partly the result of a greater willingness of police to arrest poor citizens and of the court system to convict them.

Ethnicity and Crime Another point to remember when reviewing statistical studies of minority offenders and victims is that these studies tend to focus on *race*, which distinguishes groups based on physical characteristics such as skin color, rather than *ethnicity*, which denotes national or cultural background. Thus, the bulk of criminological research in this area has focused on the differences between European Americans and African Americans, both because the latter have been the largest minority group in the United States for most of its history and because the racial differences between the two groups are easily identifiable. Americans of Hispanic descent have either been excluded from many crime studies or

CAREER PREP   GANG INVESTIGATOR

JOB DESCRIPTION:

- Conduct assessments and refer at-risk youth to appropriate activities, programs, or agencies as an alternative to their becoming involved in criminal activity. Also, counsel troubled youths and their families.
- Serve as a liaison between the police department and schools and community organizations regarding gangs and other youth-related matters.

WHAT KIND OF TRAINING IS REQUIRED?

- At a minimum, a high school diploma and any combination of training, education, and experience equivalent to three to five years' social service employment involving youth. A law enforcement background is also very helpful.

- Preferred candidates will have a bachelor's degree in counseling, criminal justice, or another social science field. Bilingual (English/Spanish) skills are desired.

ANNUAL SALARY RANGE?

- $40,000–$49,000

For additional information, visit: www.nagia.org.

been linked with whites or blacks based on racial characteristics. Other minority groups, such as Asian Americans, Native Americans, and immigrants from the South Pacific or Eastern Europe, have been similarly underreported in crime studies.

This state of affairs will more than likely change in the near future. Latinos are the fastest-growing minority group in the U.S. prison population, and because of immigration offenses, they now account for 40 percent of those convicted of federal crimes.[43] In fact, criminologists have already begun to focus on issues of Hispanic criminality. For example, Robert Sampson's research project, mentioned earlier on page 55, found lower rates of violence among Mexican Americans than among either whites or blacks living in Chicago. The authors theorize that strong social ties in immigrant populations create an environment that is antithetical to crime.[44]

James McQuillan/iStockphoto.com

WOMEN AND CRIME

To put it bluntly, crime is an overwhelmingly male activity. More than 65 percent of all murders involve a male victim and a male perpetrator. In only 2.4 percent of homicides are both the offender

"You can't get **involved** *in a bar fight if you're* **not allowed** *in the bar."*

and the victim female.[45] A mere 12 percent of the national jail population and 7 percent of the national prison population are female, and in 2009 only 24 percent of all arrests involved women.[46] These statistics, however, fail to convey the startling rate at which the female presence in the criminal justice system has been increasing. In 1970, there were about 6,000 women in federal and state prisons; today, there are more than 113,000.[47]

There are two possible explanations for these increases. Either (1) the life circumstances and behavior of women have changed dramatically in the past forty years, or (2) the criminal justice system's attitude toward women has changed over that time period.[48] In the 1970s, when female crime rates started surging upward, many observers accepted the former explanation. "You can't get involved in a bar fight if you're not allowed in the bar," said feminist theorist Freda Adler in 1975.[49] It has become clear, however, that a significant percentage of women arrested are involved in a narrow band of wrongdoing, mostly drug- and alcohol-related offenses or property crimes.[50] Research shows that as recently as the 1980s, many of the women now in prison would not have been arrested or would have received lighter sentences for committing the same crimes.[51] Consequently, more scholars are convinced that rising female criminality is the result of a criminal justice system that is "more willing to incarcerate women."[52]

Brandon Laufenberg/iStockphoto

TEST PREP

When preparing for an exam, you might want to get together a small group (two or three other students) for a study session. Discussing a topic out loud can improve your understanding of that topic and will help you remember the key points that often come up on exams.

4 INSIDE CRIMINAL LAW

Deadly Heat

As a nationally known self-help guru, financial wizard, and motivational speaker, James Arthur Ray prides himself on being right. Ray was tragically wrong, however, on an autumn day in 2009 when he told more than fifty participants in a sweat lodge ceremony he was leading, "You are not going to die. You might think you are, but you're not going to die." About halfway through the two-hour-long ceremony, the end piece of Ray's five-day "Spiritual Warrior" retreat near Sedona, Arizona, people began to vomit and pass out in the extreme heat. When it was over, despite Ray's words of assurance, Kirby Brown, James Shore, and Liz Neuman never regained consciousness and died in a local hospital. Twenty other participants required medical treatment, suffering from burns, dehydration, kidney failure, and respiratory arrest.

"I did everything I could to help," Ray told an interviewer following the incident. "I held people's hands, I stroked their hair, I talked to them, I held the IV for paramedics." According to some witnesses, Ray was not quite so helpful during the ceremony. Beverly Bunn, who was inside the sweat lodge, said that people were gasping for air, collapsing, and crying out for water while Ray, positioned near the entrance, "did nothing. He just stood there." Megan Frederickson, an employee at the Angel Valley Retreat (the site of the sweat lodge), admitted that before the ceremony, Ray told her not to worry if participants vomited or fainted, because such responses were to be expected.

After a four-month investigation, law enforcement officials decided that the sweat lodge was, in fact, a crime scene. On February 3, 2010, Yavapai County sheriff's deputies arrested Ray and charged him with three counts of manslaughter for the deaths of Brown, Shore, and Neuman. Sixteen months later, a Campe Verde jury found Ray guilty of three counts of negligent homicide, and he faced a maximum penalty of twelve years behind bars. (CAREER TIP: The *paramedics* who arrived at the scene of the sweat lodge are certified health-care providers trained to treat victims of emergencies.)

REUTERS/Jessica Rinaldi

What risks did James Arthur Ray—shown here in a Camp Verde, Arizona, courtroom—overlook during a sweat lodge ceremony in which three participants died? (AP Photo/Ross D. Franklin, Pool)

Was James Arthur Ray treated fairly? Nobody involved with the situation believes that he wanted any of the Spiritual Warriors to die. The sweat lodge, built in 2008, had been used numerous times without incident. "This was a terrible accident," said Luis Ri, Ray's attorney, "but it was an accident, not a criminal act."[1] In this chapter, we will learn that a defendant usually must have a guilty state of mind, or *mens rea*, to have committed a crime. Ray may have acted irresponsibly, but he certainly had no intent to injure or kill.

At the same time, society needs to protect its citizens from harm, even if that harm was not intentionally inflicted. According to the criminal code of Arizona, a person is guilty of manslaughter if he or she "recklessly" causes the death of another person.[2] Later in the chapter, we define *recklessness* as ignoring an obvious risk. Given the circumstances of the sweat lodge ceremony, Arizona officials felt that Ray *should have known* that he was placing others in grave danger, and therefore he had committed a criminal act. As this example suggests, criminal law must be flexible enough to encompass behavior that is not marked by criminal intent yet still poses a threat to society and therefore, in the eyes of some, merits punishment. In this chapter, we will examine how these "threats to society" are identified and focus on the guidelines that determine how the criminal justice system resolves and punishes criminal guilt.

Jurisdiction is the authority of a court to hear and decide cases within an area of the law or a geographic territory.

¿WHAT ARE THE WRITTEN SOURCES OF AMERICAN CRIMINAL LAW?

LO 1

Originally, American criminal law was *uncodified*. In other words, it relied primarily on judges following precedents, and the body of the law was not written down in any single place. Uncodified law, however, presents a number of drawbacks. For one, if the law is not recorded in a manner or a place in which the citizenry has access to it, then it is difficult, if not impossible, for people to know exactly which acts are legal and which acts are illegal. Furthermore, citizens have no way of determining or understanding the procedures that must be followed to establish innocence or guilt. Consequently, U.S. history has seen the development of several written sources of American criminal law, also known as "substantive" criminal law. These sources include

1. The U.S. Constitution and the constitutions of the various states.
2. Statutes, or laws, passed by Congress and by state legislatures, plus local ordinances.
3. Regulations created by regulatory agencies, such as the federal Food and Drug Administration.
4. Case law (court decisions).

We describe each of these important written sources of law in the following pages.

CONSTITUTIONAL LAW

The federal government and the states have separate written constitutions that set forth the general organization and powers of, and the limits on, their respective governments. **Constitutional law** is the law as expressed in these constitutions.

The U.S. Constitution is the supreme law of the land. As such, it is the basis of all law in the United States. Any law that violates the Constitution, as ultimately determined by the United States Supreme Court, will be declared unconstitutional and will not be enforced. The Tenth Amendment, which defines the powers and limitations of the federal government, reserves to the states all powers not granted to the federal government. Under our system of federalism (see Chapter 1), each state also has its own constitution. Unless they conflict with the U.S. Constitution or a federal law, state constitutions are supreme within their respective borders. (You will learn more about how constitutional law applies to our criminal justice system in later chapters.)

Edward Grajeda/iStockphoto.com

STATUTORY LAW

Statutes enacted by legislative bodies at any level of government make up another source of law, which is generally referred to as **statutory law.** *Federal statutes* are laws that are enacted by the U.S. Congress. *State statutes* are laws enacted by state legislatures, and statutory law also includes the ordinances passed by cities and counties. A federal statute, of course, applies to all states. A state statute, in contrast, applies only within that state's borders. City or county ordinances (statutes) apply only to those jurisdictions where they are enacted. As mentioned, statutory law found by the Supreme Court to violate the U.S. Constitution will be overturned. In the late 1980s, for example, the Court ruled that any state laws banning the burning of the American flag were unconstitutional because they impinged on the individual's right to freedom of expression.[3]

On a state and local level, voters can write or rewrite criminal statutes through a form of direct democracy known as the **ballot initiative.** In this process, a group of citizens draft a proposed law and then gather a certain number of signatures to get the proposal on that year's ballot. If a majority of the voters approve the measure, it is enacted into law. Currently, twenty-four states and the District of Columbia accept ballot initiatives, and these special elections have played a crucial role in shaping criminal law in those jurisdictions. In the mid-1990s, for example, California voters approved a "three-strikes" measure (discussed in Chapter 11) that increased penalties for third-time felons, transforming the state's criminal justice system in the process. In 2008, Massachusetts voters decided that possession of small amounts of marijuana would no longer be a crime within state limits. Two years later, a ballot initiative required Arizona to join thirteen other states and Washington, D.C., in allowing the use of marijuana for medicinal purposes.[4]

ADMINISTRATIVE LAW

A third source of American criminal law consists of **administrative law**—the rules, orders, and decisions of *regulatory agencies*. A regulatory agency is a federal, state, or local government agency established to perform a specific function. The Occupational Safety and Health Administration (OSHA), for example, oversees the safety and health of American workers; the Environmental Protection Agency (EPA) is concerned with protecting the natural environment; and the Food and Drug Administration (FDA) regulates food and drugs produced in the United States.

Disregarding certain laws created by regulatory agencies can be a criminal violation. Federal statutes, such as the Clean Water Act, designate authority to a specific regulatory agency, such as the EPA,

Statutory Law The body of law enacted by legislative bodies.

Ballot Initiative A procedure in which the citizens of a state, if they collect enough signatures, can force a public vote on a proposed change to state law.

Administrative Law The body of law created by administrative agencies (in the form of rules, regulations, orders, and decisions) in order to carry out their duties and responsibilities.

George Washington, standing at right, presided over the constitutional convention of 1787, which resulted in the U.S. Constitution. Why is this document considered the supreme law of the United States?

(The Granger Collection/Rich Koele/iStockphoto.com)

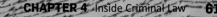

Case Law The rules of law announced in court decisions.

Precedent A court decision that is used as a guideline for deciding a subsequent case with similar facts.

to enforce regulations to which criminal sanctions are attached.[5] So, after the April 20, 2010, explosion on the Deepwater Horizon drilling rig, which led to a spill that dumped 205 million gallons of crude oil into the Gulf of Mexico, the EPA opened an investigation to determine if any criminal activity had contributed to the environmental disaster. (CAREER TIP: A number of local police departments, particularly those serving large metropolitan areas, employ *environmental police officers,* whose sole duty is to enforce local environmental laws. These laws cover issues such as automobile pollution and recycling requirements.)

CASE LAW

Another basic source of American law consists of the rules of law announced in court decisions, or *precedents*. These rules of law include interpretations of constitutional provisions, of statutes enacted by legislatures, and of regulations created by administrative agencies. Today, this body of law is referred to variously as the common law, judge-made law, or **case law.**

Case law relies to a certain extent on how courts interpret a particular statute. If you wanted to learn about the coverage and applicability of a particular statute, for example, you would need to locate the statute and study it. You would also need to see how the courts in your jurisdiction have interpreted the statute—in other words, what *precedents* have been established in regard to that statute. A **precedent** is a judge-made decision that furnishes an example or authority for deciding subsequent cases involving similar legal principles or facts. The use of precedent means that case law varies from jurisdiction to jurisdiction. (For a summary of the four different sources of American law, see **Figure 4.1** below.)

¿WHY DO SOCIETIES NEED LAWS?

Many criminologists believe that criminal law has two basic functions: one relates to the legal requirements of a society, and the other pertains to its need to maintain and promote social values.

PROTECT AND PUNISH: THE LEGAL FUNCTION OF THE LAW

LO2 The primary legal function of the law is to maintain social order by protecting citizens from *criminal harm*. This term refers to a variety of harms that can be generalized to fit into two categories:

1. Harms to individual citizens' physical safety and property, such as the harm caused by murder, theft, or arson.
2. Harms to society's interests collectively, such as the harm caused by unsafe foods and consumer products, a polluted environment, or poorly constructed buildings.[6]

The first category is self-evident, although even murder has different degrees, or grades, of offense to which different punishments are assigned. The second category, however, has proved more problematic, for it is difficult to measure society's "collective" interests. Often, laws passed to reduce such harms seem overly intrusive and marginally necessary. An extreme example would seem to be the Flammable

Figure 4.1 **Sources of American Law**

1 **Constitutional law** The law as expressed in the U.S. Constitution and the various state constitutions.

2 **Statutory law** Laws or ordinances created by federal, state, and local legislatures and governing bodies.

3 **Administrative law** The rules, orders, and decisions of federal or state government administrative agencies.

4 **Case law** Judge-made law, including interpretations of constitutional provisions, of statutes enacted by legislatures, and of regulations created by administrative agencies.

Fabrics Act, which makes it a crime for a retailer to willfully remove a precautionary instruction label from a mattress that is protected with a chemical fire retardant.[7]

Yet even in this example, a criminal harm is conceivable. Suppose a retailer removes the tags before selling a large number of mattresses to a hotel chain. Employees of the chain then unknowingly wash the mattresses with an agent that lessens their flame-resistant qualities. After the mattresses have been installed in rooms, a guest falls asleep while smoking a cigarette, starting a fire that burns down the entire hotel and causes several deaths.

MAINTAIN AND TEACH: THE SOCIAL FUNCTION OF THE LAW

If criminal laws against acts that cause harm or injury to others are almost universally accepted, the same cannot be said for laws that criminalize "morally" wrongful activities that may do no obvious, physical harm outside the families of those involved. Why criminalize gambling or prostitution, for example, if the participants are consenting?

Expressing Public Morality The answer lies in the social function of criminal law. Many observers believe that the main purpose of criminal law is to reflect the values and norms of society, or at least of those segments of society that hold power. Legal scholar Henry Hart has stated that the only justification for criminal law and punishment is "the judgment of community condemnation."[8]

Take, for example, the misdemeanor of bigamy, which occurs when someone knowingly marries a second person without terminating her or his marriage to an original husband or wife. Apart from moral considerations, there would appear to be no victims in a bigamous relationship, and indeed many societies have

How do criminal prohibitions against practices such as cockfighting, which may be favored by a minority, reflect the social function of criminal law? (Al Bello/Getty Images)

allowed and continue to allow bigamy to exist. In the American social tradition, however, as John L. Diamond of the University of California's Hastings College of the Law points out:

> Marriage is an institution encouraged and supported by society. The structural importance of the integrity of the family and a monogamous marriage requires unflinching enforcement of the criminal laws against bigamy. The immorality is not in choosing to do wrong, but in transgressing, even innocently, a fundamental social boundary that lies at the core of social order.[9]

When discussing the social function of criminal law, it is important to remember that a society's views

STUDY PREP

Many students are tempted to take class notes on a laptop computer. This is a bad idea for two reasons. First, it is hard to copy diagrams or take other "artistic" notes on a computer. Second, it is easy to get distracted by checking e-mail or surfing the Web.

Corpus Delicti The body of circumstances that must exist for a criminal act to have occurred.

Actus Reus (pronounced *ak-*tus *ray-*uhs). A guilty (prohibited) act.

of morality change over time. Seventeenth-century Puritan New England society not only had strict laws against adultery, but also considered lying and idleness to be criminal acts.[10] Today, such acts may carry social stigmas, but only in certain extreme circumstances do they elicit legal sanctions.

Teaching Societal Boundaries Some scholars believe that criminal laws not only express the expectations of society, but "teach" them as well. Professor Lawrence M. Friedman of Stanford University thinks that just as parents teach children behavioral norms through punishment, criminal justice "'teaches a lesson' to the people it punishes, and to society at large." Making burglary a crime, arresting burglars, putting them in jail—each step in the criminal justice process reinforces the idea that burglary is unacceptable and is deserving of punishment.[11]

This teaching function can also be seen in traffic laws. There is nothing "natural" about most traffic laws. Americans drive on the right side of the street and the British on the left side, with no obvious difference in the results.

These laws, such as stopping at intersections, using headlights at night, and following speed limits, do lead to a more orderly flow of traffic and fewer accidents— certainly socially desirable goals. The laws can also be updated when needed. Over the past few years, several states have banned the use of handheld cell phones while driving because of the safety hazards associated with them. Various forms of punishment for breaking traffic laws teach drivers the social order of the road. (CAREER TIP: Often, those who violate the rules of the road are required to attend mandatory traffic classes. Consequently, state and local governments need *traffic school instructors* to lead these classes.)

SCHOOL SPEED LIMIT 25 WHEN FLASHING

¿WHAT ARE THE ELEMENTS OF A CRIME?

In fictional accounts of police work, the admission of guilt is often portrayed as *the* crucial element of a criminal investigation. Although an admission is certainly useful to police and prosecutors, it alone cannot establish the innocence or guilt of a suspect. Criminal law normally requires that the **corpus delicti**, a Latin phrase for "the body of the crime," be proved before a person can be convicted of wrongdoing.[12] *Corpus delicti* can be defined as "proof that a specific crime has actually been committed by someone."[13] It consists of the basic elements of any crime, which include (1) *actus reus*, or a guilty act; (2) *mens rea*, or a guilty intent; (3) concurrence, or the coming together of the criminal act and the guilty mind; (4) a link between the act and the legal definition of the crime (causation); (5) any attendant circumstances; and (6) the harm done, or the result of the criminal act.

CRIMINAL ACT: *ACTUS REUS*

Suppose Mr. Smith walks into a police department and announces that he just killed his wife. In and of itself the confession is insufficient for conviction unless the police find Mrs. Smith's corpse with, for example, a bullet in her brain and establish through evidence that Mr. Smith fired the gun. (This does not mean that an actual dead body has to be found in every homicide case. Rather, it is the fact of the death that must be established in such cases.)

Most crimes require an act of *commission*. That is, a person must *do* something in order to be accused of a crime. The prohibited act is referred to as the **actus reus**, or guilty act. Furthermore, the act of commission must be voluntary. For example, if Mr. Smith had an epileptic seizure while holding a hunting rifle and accidentally shot his wife, he normally would not be held criminally liable

Rob Byron/Shutterstock

CJ and Technology

Two men set a couch on fire in downtown Indiana, Pennsylvania, as part of a Super Bowl celebration. A scorned twenty-one-year-old woman vandalizes her ex-boyfriend's apartment. A student in Baltimore assaults a teacher. These offenders, and many others, might have escaped detection except for one very silly move: they posted photos or videos of their wrongdoing on social networks such as MySpace and Facebook. Numerous criminals and victims—particularly young ones—often leave clues of criminal behavior on the Internet. As a result, surfing the Web has become an important part of law enforcement efforts to enforce real-world criminal laws. Police officers have also begun placing fake profiles on social-networking Web sites, posing as young children or gang members in order to make contact with wrongdoers. "We get a lot of information in terms of what's going on this weekend because kids think they are talking to another buddy or friend," says Detective Sergeant Victor Flaherty of the West Bridgewater (Connecticut) Police Department. "[The Internet] is like any community," adds Indiana state trooper Charles Cohen. "There are going to be criminals in it."

THINKING ABOUT SOCIAL NETWORK INVESTIGATIONS

Can you think of any problems that might arise from police officers using this particular "undercover" strategy on the Internet? For a police officer, what is the difference between the *actus reus* of a crime that he or she has witnessed in person and a crime that has been posted on the Internet?

---

for her death. If, however, Mr. Smith knew that he was prone to such attacks, the outcome might be different. In one case, a Buffalo, New York, man suffered an epileptic seizure while driving and struck a group of six schoolgirls, killing four. Because he had a history of epileptic blackouts, he was charged with homicide. Thus, the *actus reus* in this crime was not the defendant's driving into the girls, but his reckless decision to get behind the wheel in the first place.

A Legal Duty In some cases, an **act of omission** can be a crime, but only when a person has a legal duty to perform the omitted act. One such legal duty is assumed to exist based on a "special relationship" between two parties, such as a parent and child, adult children and

their aged parents, and spouses.[14] Those persons involved in contractual relationships with others, such as physicians and lifeguards, must also perform legal duties to avoid criminal penalty. Rhode Island, Vermont, and Wisconsin have even passed "duty to aid" statutes requiring their citizens to report criminal conduct and help victims of such conduct if possible.[15] Another example of a criminal act of omission is failure to file a federal income tax return when required by law to do so.

> **Act of Omission** The act of neglecting or forgetting to do something that is required by law.

A Plan or Attempt The guilty act requirement is based on one of the premises of criminal law—that a

Attempt The act of taking substantial steps toward committing a crime while having the ability and the intent to commit the crime, even if the crime never takes place.

Mens Rea (pronounced *mehns ray*-uh). Mental state, or intent.

Negligence A failure to exercise the standard of care that a reasonable person would exercise in similar circumstances.

person is punished for harm done to society. Planning to kill someone or to steal a car may be wrong, but the thoughts do no harm and are therefore not criminal until they are translated into action. Of course, a person can be punished for *attempting* murder or robbery, but normally only if he or she took substantial steps toward the criminal objective and the prosecution can prove that the desire to commit the crime was present. Furthermore, the punishment for an **attempt** normally is less severe than if the act had succeeded.

MENTAL STATE: *MENS REA*

A wrongful mental state—*mens rea*—is usually as necessary as a wrongful act in establishing guilt. The mental state, or requisite *intent*, required to establish guilt of a crime is indicated in the applicable statute or law. For theft, the wrongful act is the taking of another person's property, and the required mental state involves both the awareness that the property belongs to another and the desire to deprive the owner of it.

The Categories of *Mens Rea* A guilty mental state includes elements of purpose, knowledge, negligence, and recklessness.[16] A defendant is said to have *purposefully* committed a criminal act when he or she desires to engage in certain criminal conduct or to cause a certain criminal result. For a defendant to have *knowingly* committed an illegal act, he or she must be aware of the illegality, must believe that the illegality exists, or must correctly suspect that the illegality exists but fail to do anything to dispel (or confirm) his or her belief. Criminal **negligence** involves the mental state in which the defendant grossly deviates from the standard of care that a reasonable person would use under the same circumstances. The defendant is accused of taking an unjustified, substantial, and foreseeable risk that resulted in harm. In Texas, for example, a parent commits a felony if she or he fails to lock up a loaded

CAREERPREP   ANIMAL CONTROL OFFICER

JOB DESCRIPTION:

- Work to protect stray, injured, abused, and unwanted animals. This includes rescuing the animals, aiding in the prosecution of individuals who abused them, and providing impounded animals with humane care.

- Educate the public about animal overpopulation and responsible pet ownership.

WHAT KIND OF TRAINING IS REQUIRED?

- On-the-job training is a common condition for entry-level positions in this field.

- Desirable backgrounds include an associate's degree or study in law enforcement, criminology, animal behavior, and/or veterinary technology.

ANNUAL SALARY RANGE?

- $23,236–$44,149

For additional information, visit:
www.nacanet.org.

firearm or otherwise leaves it in such a manner that it could easily be accessed by a child.[17]

A defendant who commits an act *recklessly* is more blameworthy than one who is criminally negligent. The Model Penal Code, a general guide for criminal law, defines criminal **recklessness** as "consciously disregard[ing] a substantial and unjustifiable risk."[18] Some courts, particularly those adhering to the Model Penal Code, will not find criminal recklessness on the part of a defendant who was subjectively unaware of the risk when she or he acted. Sometimes, however, awareness can tip the balance against a defendant. For instance, Marjorie Knoller owned two aggressive dogs that continually terrorized her neighbors. Finally, one day the dogs attacked Diane Whipple (see the photo below) in the hallway of Knoller's San Francisco apartment building, killing the young woman. A judge determined that Knoller's level of *mens rea* was recklessness because, even though she did not intend for Whipple to die, she was conscious of the risk posed by her vicious pets and refused to take any steps to lessen that risk. Knoller was found guilty of second degree murder and sentenced to fifteen years to life in prison. (CAREER TIP: The responsibility for dealing with dangerous dogs often falls to local *animal control officers*, who also protect pets from abuse and educate citizens about animal rights.)

Criminal Liability Intent plays an important part in allowing the law to differentiate among varying degrees of criminal liability for similar, though not identical, guilty acts. The role of intent is clearly seen in the different classifications of homicide, defined generally as the willful killing of one human being by another. It is important to emphasize the word *willful*, as it precludes (rules out) deaths caused by accident or negligence and those deemed justifiable. A death that results from negligence or accident generally is considered a private wrong and a matter for civil law. Nevertheless, some statutes allow for culpable negligence, which permits certain negligent homicides to be criminalized. As we saw in Chapter 3, when the act of killing is willful, deliberate, and premeditated (planned beforehand), it is considered first degree murder. When premeditation does not exist but intent does, the act is considered second degree murder.

Different degrees of criminal liability for various categories of homicide lead to different punishments. The distinction between murder and manslaughter is often evident in **domestic violence** cases, which involve physical abuse at the hands of a spouse, partner, or other close relation. Because of the highly complex and emotional circumstances that surround

> **Recklessness** The state of being aware that a risk does or will exist and nevertheless acting in a way that consciously disregards this risk.
>
> **Domestic violence** The act of willful neglect or physical violence that occurs within a familial or other intimate relationship.

Why did a judge determine that Marjorie Knoller's level of *mens rea* was recklessness following an incident in which Knoller's dogs attacked and killed lacrosse coach Diane Whipple, pictured here? (Courtesy of Saint Mary's College of California/ Jessica Dold/Mark Strozier/ iStockphoto.com)

Strict Liability Crimes Certain crimes, such as traffic violations, in which the defendant is guilty regardless of her or his state of mind at the time of the act.

Statutory Rape A strict liability crime in which an adult engages in a sexual act with a minor.

"It is easier to **COMMIT MURDER** than to justify it."

—PAPINIAN (142-212)
A CELEBRATED ROMAN JURIST

these cases, judges and juries can be reluctant to find the willfulness or intent required for a murder conviction. In 2010, for example, sixty-five-year-old Verna Sewell of Dorchester, Massachusetts, was convicted of involuntary manslaughter and sentenced to two years in prison for the killing of her partner, seventy-four-year-old Julius Scott. Prosecutors had charged Sewell with second degree murder, which can carry a life prison term. The jury, however, believed Sewell's claim that she *unintentionally* stabbed Scott in the chest after he attacked her with the knife in a drunken rage, and they opted for the lesser charge. (CAREER TIP: Many cities have shelters that provide therapeutic and practical services for both victims and perpetrators of domestic violence. These organizations rely on *domestic violence counselors* to provide such services.)

Strict Liability For certain crimes, criminal law holds the defendant to be guilty even if intent to commit the offense is lacking. These acts are known as **strict liability crimes** and generally involve endangering the public welfare in some way.[19] Drug-control statutes, health and safety regulations, and traffic laws are all strict liability laws.

Protecting the Public To a certain extent, the concept of strict liability is inconsistent with the traditional principles of criminal law, which hold that *mens rea* is required for an act to be criminal. The goal of strict liability laws is to protect the public by eliminating the possibility that wrongdoers could claim ignorance or mistake to absolve themselves of criminal responsibility.[20] Thus, a person caught dumping waste in a protected pond or driving 70 miles per hour in a

55-miles-per-hour zone cannot plead a lack of intent in his or her defense.

The principle is often applied in more serious situations as well. Several years ago twenty-year-old Kieran Hunt of Piscataway, New Jersey, was charged with a first degree felony after he accidentally injected his friend, eighteen-year-old Justin Warfield, with a fatal dose of heroin. Because Hunt had no intention of killing Warfield, in many jurisdictions he would have been charged with involuntary manslaughter. Under New Jersey law, however, strict liability is imposed on anybody who helps another person obtain drugs that lead to a fatal overdose. As a result, Hunt's *mens rea* concerning Warfield's death was irrelevant.[21]

Protecting Minors One of the more controversial strict liability crimes is **statutory rape**, which occurs when an adult has a sexual encounter with a minor. In most states, even if the minor consents to the sexual act, the crime still exists because, being underage, he or she is considered incapable of making a rational decision on the matter.[22] Therefore, statutory rape has been committed even if the adult was unaware of the minor's age or was misled to believe that the minor was older.

Accomplice Liability Under certain circumstances, a person can be charged with and convicted of a crime that he or she did not actually commit. This occurs when the suspect acted as an *accomplice* to a crime. In other words, he or she helped another person commit the crime. Generally, to be found guilty as an accomplice, a person must have the "dual intent" (1) to aid the person who committed the crime and (2) that such aid would lead to the commission of the crime.[23] As for the *actus reus*, the accomplice must have helped the primary actor

stocksnap/Shutterstock

in either a physical sense (for example, by providing the getaway car) or a psychological sense (for example, by encouraging her or him to commit the crime).[24]

Felony-Murder In some states, a person can be convicted as an accomplice even without intent if the crime was a "natural and probable consequence" of his or her actions.[25] This principle has led to a proliferation of **felony-murder** legislation. Felony-murder is a form of first degree murder that applies when a person participates in any of a list of serious felonies that results in the unlawful killing of a human being. Under felony-murder law, a person can be convicted as an accomplice to an intentional killing even when there is no intent. So, for example, if a person intentionally burns down a building, unintentionally killing an inhabitant, he or she will be charged with first degree murder because, in most jurisdictions, arson is a felony.

The felony-murder rule can have odd consequences. Several years ago, for example, Devon Gallagher and his older brother attempted to rob a discount grocery store in Fort Myers, Florida, using a handgun. The shop manager fired at them and killed the older boy. Because Gallagher was involved in a felony (armed robbery) that resulted in a death, he was convicted of first degree murder, even though the victim was his accomplice. These kinds of laws have come under criticism because they punish individuals for acts committed by others. Regardless, the criminal codes of more than thirty states include some form of the felony-murder rule.[26]

CONCURRENCE

According to criminal law, there must be *concurrence* between the guilty act and the guilty intent. In other words, the guilty act and the guilty intent must occur together.[27] Suppose, for example, that a woman intends to murder her husband with poison in order to collect his life insurance. Every evening, this woman drives her husband home from work. On the night she plans to poison him, however, she swerves to avoid a cat crossing the road and runs into a tree. She survives the accident, but her husband is killed. Even though her intent was realized, the incident would be considered an accidental death because she had not planned to kill him by driving the car into a tree.

CAUSATION

Criminal law also requires that the criminal act cause the harm suffered. In 1989, for example, nineteen-year-old Mike Wells shook his two-year-old daughter, Christina, so violently that she suffered brain damage. Soon after, Wells served prison time for aggravated child abuse. Then, in 2006, seventeen years later, Christina died. When a coroner ruled that the cause of death was the earlier brain injury, Pasco County (Florida) authorities decided that despite the passage of time, Wells had killed his daughter. In 2010, Wells, then forty-two-years old, pleaded guilty to second degree murder and received a fifteen-year prison sentence. (CAREER TIP: In court proceedings, children such as Christina who are harmed by their parents are often represented by trained community volunteers called *child advocates*.)

ATTENDANT CIRCUMSTANCES

In certain crimes, **attendant circumstances**—also known as accompanying circumstances—are relevant to the *corpus delicti*. Most states, for example, differentiate between simple assault and the more serious offense of aggravated assault depending on whether the defendant used a weapon such as a gun or a knife while committing the

Felony-Murder An unlawful homicide that occurs during the commission of a felony.

Attendant Circumstances The facts surrounding a criminal event.

Frances Twitty/iStockphoto

Figure 4.2 Offenses Motivated by Bias

In 2009, the Federal Bureau of Investigation reported almost 7,800 bias-motivated offenses. This chart shows the percentage distribution of the motivating factors.

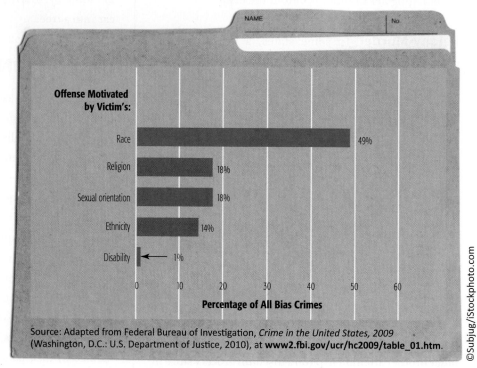

Source: Adapted from Federal Bureau of Investigation, *Crime in the United States, 2009* (Washington, D.C.: U.S. Department of Justice, 2010), at **www2.fbi.gov/ucr/hc2009/table_01.htm**.

crime. Criminal law also classifies degrees of property crimes based on the amount stolen. According to federal statutes, the theft of less than $1,000 from a bank is a misdemeanor, while the theft of any amount over $1,000 is a felony.[28]

HATE CRIME LAWS

In most cases, a person's motive for committing a crime is irrelevant—a court will not try to read the accused's mind. Over the past few decades, however, nearly every state and the federal government have passed *hate crime laws* that make the suspect's motive an important attendant circumstance to his or her criminal act. In general, **hate crime laws** provide for greater sanctions against those who commit crimes motivated by bias against a person or a group based on race, ethnicity, religion, sexual orientation, or disability (see **Figure 4.2** above).

In 2010, for example, nineteen-year-old Jeffrey Conroy became the first person charged with homicide under New York's hate crime statute. Two years earlier, Conroy and several of his friends who shared the same white-supremacist outlook ended a night of "Mexican hunting" by attacking Ecuadorean immigrant Marcelo Lucero. During the fight, Conroy stabbed Lucero with a knife, killing him. Conroy was found guilty of first degree manslaughter as a hate crime, and a judge sentenced him with the maximum possible penalty: twenty-five years in prison.[29]

HARM

For most crimes to occur, some harm must have been done to a person or to property. A certain number of crimes are actually categorized depending on the harm done to the victim, regardless of the intent behind the criminal act. Take two offenses, both of which involve one person hitting another in the back of the head with a tire iron. In the first instance, the victim dies, and the offender is charged with murder. In the second, the victim is only knocked unconscious, and the offender is charged with battery. Because the harm in the second instance was less severe, so was the crime with which the offender was charged, even though the act was exactly the same. Furthermore, most states have different degrees of battery depending on the extent of the injuries suffered by the victim.

Many acts are deemed criminal if they could do harm that the laws try to prevent. Such acts are called **inchoate offenses.** They exist when only an attempt at a criminal act was made. If Jenkins solicits Peterson to murder Jenkins's business partner, this is an inchoate offense on the part of Jenkins, even though Peterson fails to carry out the act. Conspiracies also fall into the category of inchoate offenses. In 2003, the United States

Supreme Court ruled that a person could be convicted of criminal conspiracy even though police intervention made the completion of the illegal plan impossible.[30]

¿WHICH DEFENSES ARE AVAILABLE UNDER CRIMINAL LAW?

When Tammy Gibson of Tacoma, Washington, saw a convicted sex offender named William A. Baldwin talking to her ten-year-old daughter, she leaped into action. Grabbing a baseball bat, she went after Baldwin, striking him repeatedly in the arm. At her trial, a local judge rejected Gibson's excuse that her victim "got what was coming to him" and sentenced the overly protective mother to three months behind bars for committing assault. A number of other defenses for wrongdoing, however, can be raised in the course of a criminal trial. These defenses generally rely on one of two arguments: (1) the defendant is not responsible for the crime, or (2) the defendant was justified in committing the crime.

CRIMINAL RESPONSIBILITY AND THE LAW

The idea of responsibility plays a significant role in criminal law. In certain circumstances, the law recognizes that even though an act is inherently criminal, society will not punish the actor because he or she does not have the requisite (suitable) mental condition. In other words, the law "excuses" the person for his or her behavior. Insanity, intoxication, and mistake are the most important excuse defenses today, but we start our discussion of the subject with one of the first such defenses recognized by American law: infancy.

Infancy Under the earliest state criminal codes of the United States, children younger than seven years of age could never be held legally responsible for crimes. Those between seven and fourteen years old were presumed to lack the capacity for criminal behavior, while anyone over the age of fourteen was tried as an adult. Thus, early American criminal law recognized **infancy** as a defense in which the accused's wrongdoing is excused because he or she is too young to fully understand the consequences of his or her actions.

With the creation of the juvenile justice system in the early 1900s, the infancy defense became redundant, as youthful delinquents were automatically treated differently from adult offenders. Today, most states either designate an age (seventeen or eighteen) under which wrongdoers are sent to juvenile court or allow prosecutors to decide whether a minor will be charged as an adult on a case-by-case basis. We will explore the concept of infancy as it applies to the modern American juvenile justice system in much greater detail in Chapter 15.

Insanity After Ashley Von Hadnagy fatally stabbed Riga Quaglino, her eighty-five-year-old grandmother, she told investigators that the voice of Cuban revolutionary leader Fidel Castro had ordered her to kill Quaglino. In 2010, a St. Tammany Parish (Louisiana) judge found that Von Hadnagy's severe mental problems kept her from knowing that her actions were wrong. As a result, Von Hadnagy was sent to a psychiatric hospital rather than prison. Thus, **insanity** may be a defense to a criminal charge when the defendant's state of mind is

Infancy A condition that, under early American law, excused young wrongdoers of criminal behavior because presumably they could not understand the consequences of their actions.

Insanity A defense for criminal liability that asserts a lack of criminal responsibility.

TEST PREP

Make sure you are answering exam questions correctly! Some exams require a No. 2 lead pencil to fill in the dots. Other exams ask you to underline, circle, or fill in the blanks. In short, the first thing you should do is read the instructions. Then read them again to be sure you understand them.

M'Naghten Rule A common law test of criminal responsibility that relies on the defendant's inability to distinguish right from wrong.

Substantial-Capacity Test (ALI/MPC Test) A test that states that a person is not responsible for criminal behavior if he or she had no awareness of wrongdoing or was unable to control his or her actions.

Irresistible-Impulse Test A test for the insanity defense under which a defendant who knew his or her action was wrong must establish that he or she was unable to resist the urge to commit the crime.

such that she or he cannot claim legal responsibility for her or his actions.

Measuring Sanity The general principle of the insanity defense is that a person is excused for his or her criminal wrongdoing if, as a result of a mental disease or defect, he or she

- Does not perceive the physical nature or consequences of his or her conduct;
- Does not know that his or her conduct is wrong or criminal; or

After eighty-two-year-old ex-wrestler Verne Gagne body-slammed and killed a fellow patient in a Minnesota nursing home, authorities determined that he was suffering from mental illness and declined to charge him with a crime. Why is someone like Gagne "not responsible" for behavior that would, under normal circumstances, be considered criminal?

(*Star Tribune*/MCT/Landov)

- Is not sufficiently able to control his or her conduct so as to be held accountable for it.[31]

Although criminal law has traditionally accepted the idea that an insane person cannot be held responsible for criminal acts, society has long debated what standards should be used to measure sanity for the purposes of a criminal trial. This lack of consensus (agreement) is reflected in the diverse tests employed by different American jurisdictions to determine insanity. The tests include the following:

1. *The* M'Naghten *rule.* Derived from an 1843 British murder case, the ***M'Naghten* rule** states that a person is legally insane and therefore not criminally responsible if, at the time of the offense, he or she was not able to distinguish between right and wrong. As **Figure 4.3** on the facing page shows, half of the states still use a version of the *M'Naghten* rule.[32]

2. *The ALI/MPC test.* In the early 1960s, the American Law Institute (ALI) included an insanity standard in its Model Penal Code (MPC). Also known as the **substantial-capacity test**, the **ALI/MPC test** requires that the defendant lack "substantial capacity" to either "appreciate the wrongfulness" of his or her conduct or to conform that conduct "to the requirements of the law."[33]

3. *The irresistible-impulse test.* Under the **irresistible-impulse test**, a person may be found insane even if he or she was aware that a criminal act was "wrong," provided that some "irresistible impulse" resulting from a mental deficiency drove him or her to commit the crime.[34]

The ALI/MPC test is considered the easiest standard of the three for a defendant to meet because the defendant needs only to show a lack of "substantial capacity" to be released from criminal responsibility. Defense attorneys generally consider it more difficult to prove that the defendant could not distinguish right from wrong or that he or she was driven by an irresistible impulse.

Competency for Trial The insanity defense is raised in only 1 percent of

Figure 4.3 Insanity Defenses

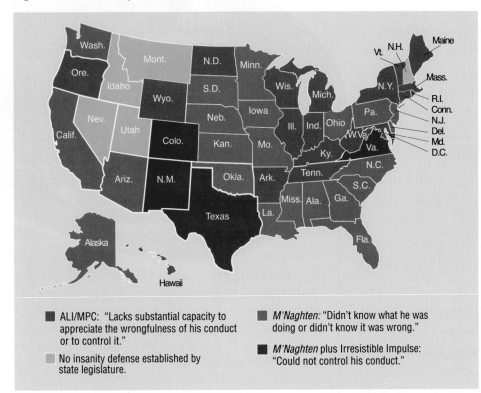

- **ALI/MPC:** "Lacks substantial capacity to appreciate the wrongfulness of his conduct or to control it."
- No insanity defense established by state legislature.
- **M'Naghten:** "Didn't know what he was doing or didn't know it was wrong."
- **M'Naghten plus Irresistible Impulse:** "Could not control his conduct."

Source: "State Insanity Defense Laws," *Frontline,* at **www.pbs.org/wgbh/pages/frontline/shows/crime/trial/ states.html**.

felony trials. Even then, it is successful only one out of every four times it is raised. More often, a defendant is found not *mentally competent* to stand trial. That is, the defendant is not sane enough to understand the case against him or her. When this occurs, the defendant is usually returned to a mental health facility for further treatment. If, after a certain amount of time, the defendant's mental health improves to the point where competency is restored, the criminal trial resumes. Under certain circumstances, however, a judge may decide that the defendant will never be mentally competent enough to stand tried. In these cases, the judge must dismiss the charges against the defendant, who will then be released. At that point, local authorities can petition to have the defendant committed to a mental institution.[35]

Intoxication The law recognizes two types of **intoxication**, whether from drugs or from alcohol: *voluntary* and *involuntary*. Involuntary intoxication occurs when a person is physically forced to ingest or is injected with an intoxicating substance, or is unaware that a substance contains drugs or alcohol. Involuntary intoxication is a viable defense to a crime if the substance leaves the person unable to form the mental state necessary to understand that the act committed while under the influence was wrong.[36] In Colorado, for example, the murder conviction of a man who shot a neighbor was overturned on the basis that the jury in the initial trial was not informed of the possibility of involuntary intoxication. At the time of the crime, the man had been taking a prescription decongestant that contained phenylpropanolamine, which has been known to cause psychotic episodes.

Mistake Everyone has heard the saying, "Ignorance of the law is no excuse." Ordinarily, ignorance of the law or a *mistaken idea* about what the law requires is not a valid defense.[37] For example, Gilbert A. Robinson appealed a conviction for possession of sexually explicit photographs of teenage boys by claiming that he did not know that such an act had become illegal. Chief Judge Juan R. Torruella del Valle of the Fifth Circuit Court of Appeals upheld Robinson's

> **"***You know how it is, Dr. Ellsworth. You go to a party, have a few drinks,* **somebody gets killed."**
>
> —LETTER FROM A DEATH ROW INMATE TO PROFESSOR PHOEBE ELLSWORTH, UNIVERSITY OF MICHIGAN

Gorgev/Shutterstock.com

Duress Unlawful pressure brought to bear on a person, causing the person to perform an act that he or she would not otherwise perform.

conviction, stating that child pornography is "inherently deleterious" and that the "probability of regulation is so great that anyone who is aware that he is in possession of [it] . . . must be presumed to be aware of the regulation."[38]

Mistake of Law In some states, however, the mistake rule has been modified to allow for a mistake-of-law defense. People who claim that they honestly did not know that they were breaking a law may have a valid defense if (1) the law was not published or reasonably known to the public or (2) the person relied on an official statement of the law that was erroneous.[39]

Mistake of Fact A *mistake of fact*, as opposed to a *mistake of law*, operates as a defense if it negates the mental state necessary to commit a crime. If, for example, Oliver mistakenly walks off with Julie's briefcase because he thinks it is his, there is no theft. Theft requires knowledge that the property belongs to another. The mistake-of-fact defense has proved very controversial in rape and sexual assault cases, in which the accused claims that the sex was consensual while the alleged victim claims it was coerced.

JUSTIFICATION CRIMINAL DEFENSES AND THE LAW

In certain instances, a defendant will accept responsibility for committing an illegal act, but contend that—given the circumstances—the act was justified.

 In other words, even though the guilty act and the guilty intent are present, the particulars of the case relieve the defendant of criminal liability. In 2009, for example, there were 667 "justified" killings of those who were in the process of committing a felony: 406 were killed by law enforcement officers and 261 by private citizens.[40] The four most important justification defenses are duress, self-defense, necessity, and entrapment.

Duress **Duress** exists when the *wrongful* threat of one person induces another person to perform an act that she or he would otherwise not perform. In such a situ-

Before it detonated and killed him, Brian Douglas Wells claimed that the bomb attached to his neck was placed there by men who forced him to rob a bank in Summit Township, Pennsylvania. If this is true and he had survived, why would Wells have been able to claim duress as a defense? (AP Photo/Janet B. Campbell/ *Erie Times-News*/iStockphoto.com)

ation, duress is said to negate the *mens rea* necessary to commit a crime. For duress to qualify as a defense, the following requirements must be met:

1. The threat must be of serious bodily harm or death.
2. The harm threatened must be greater than the harm caused by the crime.
3. The threat must be immediate and inescapable.
4. The defendant must have become involved in the situation through no fault of his or her own.[41]

When ruling on the duress defense, courts often examine whether the defendant had the opportunity to avoid the threat in question. In one case, the defendant claimed that an associate threatened to kill him and his wife unless he participated in a marijuana deal. Although this contention was proved true during the course of the trial, the court rejected the duress defense because the defendant made no apparent effort to escape, nor did he report his dilemma to the police. In sum, the drug deal was avoidable—the defendant could have made an effort to extricate (remove) himself, but he did not, thereby giving up the protection of the duress defense.[42]

Justifiable Use of Force—Self-Defense A person who believes he or she is in danger of being harmed by another is justified in defending himself or herself with the use of force, and any criminal act committed in such circumstances can be justified as **self-defense.** Other situations that also justify the use of force include the defense of one's dwelling, the defense of other property, and the prevention of a crime. In all these situations, it is important to distinguish between deadly and nondeadly force. Deadly force is likely to result in death or serious bodily harm.

Generally speaking, people can use the amount of nondeadly force that seems necessary to protect themselves, their dwellings, or other property or to prevent the commission of a crime. Deadly force can be used in self-defense if there is a *reasonable belief* that imminent death or bodily harm will otherwise result, if the attacker is using unlawful force (an example of lawful force is that exerted by a police officer), if the defender has not initiated or provoked the attack, and if there is no other possible response or alternative way out of the life-threatening situation.[43] Deadly force normally can be used to defend a dwelling only if the unlawful entry is violent and the person believes deadly force is necessary to prevent imminent death or great bodily harm or—in some jurisdictions—if the person believes deadly force is necessary to prevent the commission of a felony (such as arson) in the dwelling.

When a person is outside the home or in a public space, the rules for self-defense change somewhat. In almost thirty states, someone who is attacked under these circumstances has a duty to "retreat to the wall" before fighting back. In other words, under this **duty to retreat,** one who is being assaulted may not resort to deadly force if she or he has a reasonable opportunity to "run away" and thus avoid the conflict. Once this person has run into a "wall," literally or otherwise, then deadly force may be used in self-defense.

Self-Defense The legally recognized privilege to protect one's self or property from injury by another.

Duty to Retreat The requirement that a person claiming self-defense prove that she or he first took reasonable steps to avoid the conflict that resulted in the use of deadly force.

Necessity A defense against criminal liability in which the defendant asserts that circumstances required her or him to commit an illegal act.

Necessity In 2009, Jennifer Greenwood of North Pole, Alaska, was charged with felony driving while intoxicated. In her defense, she claimed that on the night in question, she had no choice but to drive drunk because she needed to warn her boyfriend's parents that he planned to burn down their house. A local judge, noting Greenwood's two earlier DUI convictions, sentenced her to forty-eight months in prison and suspended her driver's license for life.[44]

Under different circumstances, however, the **necessity** defense can be used to justify otherwise illegal behavior. In most jurisdictions, the necessity defense is viable if "the harm or evil sought to be

---

CAREER**PREP**

CRIMINAL COURT JUDGE

PhotoDisc

JOB DESCRIPTION:

- Preside over trials and hearings in federal, state, and local courts. Ensure that all proceedings are fair and protect the legal rights of everyone involved.
- Rule on admissibility of evidence, monitor the testimony of witnesses, and settle disputes between prosecutors and defense attorneys.

WHAT KIND OF TRAINING IS REQUIRED?

- A law degree and several years of legal experience.
- Depending on the jurisdiction, judges are either appointed or elected.

ANNUAL SALARY RANGE?

- $93,000–$162,000

For additional information, visit:
education-portal.com/become_a_judge.html.

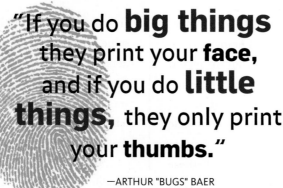

> "If you do **big things** they print your **face,** and if you do **little things,** they only print your **thumbs.**"
>
> —ARTHUR "BUGS" BAER
> AMERICAN JOURNALIST

Entrapment A defense in which the defendant claims that he or she was induced by a public official—usually an undercover agent or police officer—to commit a crime that he or she would otherwise not have committed.

Substantive Criminal Law Law that defines the rights and duties of individuals with respect to one another.

Procedural Criminal Law Rules that define the manner in which the rights and duties of individuals may be enforced.

avoided by such conduct is greater than that sought to be prevented by the law defining the offense charged." In another driving case from 2009, for example, Jason Blair of Brooksville, Florida, successfully used the necessity defense to justify leaving the scene of a car accident involving a death. After accidentally hitting a pedestrian who later died from injuries suffered in the collision, Blair claimed that he heard someone yell, "I'm going to kill you." Fearing for his life, Blair fled the scene. A jury agreed that a "greater evil" existed—a threat to his own life—and acquitted Blair of a crime that carries a maximum of thirty years in state prison.[45]

The one crime for which the necessity defense is not acceptable under any circumstances is murder.[46]

Entrapment Entrapment is a justification defense that criminal law allows when a police officer or government agent deceives a defendant into wrongdoing. Although law enforcement agents can legitimately use various forms of deception—such as informants or undercover agents—to gain information or apprehend a suspect in a criminal act, the law places limits on these strategies. Police cannot persuade an innocent person to commit a crime, nor can they coerce a suspect into doing so, even if they are certain she or he is a criminal.

According to the United States Supreme Court, entrapment occurs if a defendant who is not predisposed to commit a crime is enticed to do so by an agent of the government. In a 1992 case, for example, over a two-year period agents from the U.S. Postal Investigation Service sent the defendant seven letters inquiring about his sexual preference, two sex catalogues, and two sexual-attitude surveys, all from fictitious organizations. (CAREER TIP: The *U.S. Postal Investigation Service,* made up of about 650 uniformed agents, is the law enforcement arm of the U.S. Postal Service.) Eventually, the defendant ordered a publication called *Boys Who Love Boys* and was arrested and convicted for breaking child pornography laws.[47] The Supreme Court overturned the conviction, ruling that entrapment had taken place because the defendant had showed no predisposition to order the illicit publication in the absence of the government's efforts. (For more examples involving justification and excuse defenses, see **Figure 4.4** on the facing page.)

¿HOW DO CRIMINAL PROCEDURES PROTECT OUR CONSTITUTIONAL RIGHTS?

To this point, we have focused on **substantive criminal law,** which defines the acts that the government will punish. We will now turn our attention to **procedural criminal law.** (The section that follows will provide only a short overview of criminal procedure. In later chapters, many other constitutional issues will be examined in more detail.) Criminal law brings the force of the state, with all its resources, to bear against the individual. Criminal procedures, drawn from the ideals stated in the Bill of Rights, are designed to protect the constitutional rights of individuals and to prevent the arbitrary use of power by the government.

THE BILL OF RIGHTS

For various reasons, proposals related to the rights of individuals were rejected during the framing of the U.S. Constitution in 1787. In fact, the original constitution

Dmitry Terentjev/Shutterstock.com

76 **PART 1** The Criminal Justice System

Figure 4.4 Justification and Excuse Defenses

EXCUSE DEFENSES: *Based on a defendant admitting that she or he committed the criminal act but asserting that she or he cannot be held criminally responsible for the act due to lack of criminal intent.*

	Example
INFANCY (see page 71)	A thirteen-year-old takes a handgun from his backpack at school and begins shooting at fellow students, killing three. (In such cases, the offender is often processed by the juvenile justice system rather than the criminal justice system.)
INSANITY (see page 71)	A man with a history of mental illness pushes a woman in front of an oncoming subway train, which kills her instantly.
INTOXICATION (see page 73)	A woman who had been drinking malt liquor and vodka stabs her boyfriend to death after a domestic argument. She claims to have been so drunk as to not remember the incident.
MISTAKE (see page 73)	A woman, thinking that her divorce in another state has been finalized when it has not, marries for a second time, thereby committing bigamy.

JUSTIFICATION DEFENSES: *Based on a defendant admitting that he or she committed the particular criminal act but asserting that under the circumstances, the criminal act was justified.*

	Example
DURESS (see page 74)	A mother assists her boyfriend in committing a burglary after he threatens to kill her children if she refuses to do so.
SELF-DEFENSE (see page 75)	A husband awakes to find his wife standing over him, pointing a shotgun at his chest. In the ensuing struggle, the firearm goes off, killing the wife.
NECESSITY (see page 75)	Four people physically remove a friend from her residence on the property of a religious cult, arguing that the crime of kidnapping was justified in order to remove the victim from the damaging influence of cult leaders.
ENTRAPMENT (see page 76)	The owner of a boat marina agrees to allow three federal drug enforcement agents, posing as drug dealers, to use his dock to unload shipments of marijuana from Colombia.

contained only three provisions that referred to criminal procedure. Article I, Section 9, Clause 2, states that the "privilege of the Writ of Habeas Corpus shall not be suspended." As will be discussed in Chapter 10, a writ of *habeas corpus* is an order that requires jailers to bring a person before a court or judge and explain why the person is being held in prison. Article I, Section 9, Clause 3, holds that no "Bill of Attainder or ex post facto Law shall be passed." A bill of attainder is a legislative act that targets a particular person or group for punishment without a trial, while an ***ex post facto* law** operates retroactively, making an event or action illegal even though it took place before the law was passed. Finally, Article III, Section 2, Clause 3, maintains that the "Trial of all Crimes" will be by jury and that "such Trial shall be held in the State where the said Crimes shall have been committed."

Amending the Constitution The need for a written declaration of rights of individuals eventually caused the first Congress to draft twelve amendments to the Constitution and submit them for approval by the states. Ten of these amendments, commonly known as the **Bill of Rights**, were adopted in 1791. Since then, seventeen more amendments have been added.

The Bill of Rights, as interpreted by the United States Supreme Court, has served as the basis for procedural safeguards of the accused in this country. These safeguards include the following:

1. The Fourth Amendment protection from unreasonable searches and seizures.
2. The Fourth Amendment requirement that no warrants for a search or an arrest can be issued without good reason.
3. The Fifth Amendment requirement that no one can be deprived of life, liberty, or property without "due process" of law.

> **Ex Post Facto Law**
> Latin for "after the fact," it refers to a law making a certain act illegal after that act was committed. That is, when the act took place, it was still legal.
>
> **Bill of Rights** The first ten amendments to the U.S. Constitution.

4. The Fifth Amendment prohibition against *double jeopardy* (trying someone twice for the same criminal offense).

5. The Fifth Amendment guarantee that no person can be required to be a witness against (incriminate) himself or herself.

6. The Sixth Amendment guarantees of a speedy trial, a trial by jury, a public trial, the right to confront witnesses, and the right to a lawyer at various stages of criminal proceedings.

7. The Eighth Amendment prohibitions against excessive bails and fines and cruel and unusual punishments. (Each of these amendments will be referenced numerous times over the course of this textbook.)

Expanding the Constitution The Bill of Rights initially offered citizens protection only against the federal government. Shortly after the end of the Civil War, in 1868, three-fourths of the states ratified the Fourteenth Amendment to expand the protections of the Bill of Rights. For our purposes, the most important part of the amendment reads:

> No State shall make or enforce any law which shall abridge the privileges or immunities of citizens of the United States; nor shall any State deprive any person of life, liberty, or property, without due process of law; nor deny to any person within its jurisdiction the equal protection of the laws.

The United States Supreme Court did not immediately interpret the Fourteenth Amendment as extending the procedural protections of the Bill of Rights to people who had been charged with breaking state criminal law. Indeed, it would be nearly a hundred years before those accused of crimes on the state level would enjoy all the same protections as those accused of breaking federal laws.[48] As these protections are crucial to criminal justice procedures in the United States, they will be afforded much more attention in Chapter 6, with regard to police action, and in Chapter 10, with regard to the criminal trial.

DUE PROCESS

Both the Fifth and Fourteenth Amendments provide that no person should be deprived of "life, liberty, or property without due process of law." This **due process clause** basically requires that the government not act unfairly or arbitrarily. In other words, the govern-

Why do most citizens accept certain steps taken by the government—such as limiting the amount of liquids and gels passengers can carry on airplanes to protect against terrorist attacks—that restrict our individual freedoms?

(AP Photo/Gene Blyth)

ment cannot rely on individual judgment and impulse when making decisions, but must stay within the boundaries of reason and the law. Of course, disagreements as to the meaning of these provisions have plagued courts, politicians, and citizens since this nation was founded and will undoubtedly continue to do so.

To understand due process, it is important to consider its two types: procedural due process and substantive due process.

Procedural Due Process According to **procedural due process**, the law must be carried out by a *method* that is fair and orderly. Procedural due process requires that certain procedures be followed in administering and executing a law so that an individual's basic freedoms are never violated.

For example, Hank Skinner, currently residing on Texas's death row for committing a triple murder in 1993, believes new DNA testing of evidence from the crime scene will prove his innocence (see the photo alongside). Texas officials, however, had refused to allow the DNA tests, saying that Skinner's defense attorneys did not file a proper and timely request. Skinner then sued the state, claiming that it is only fair that he be given every chance to prove his innocence. In 2011, the United States Supreme Court gave Skinner a partial victory on procedural due process grounds. The Court ruled that Skinner and other inmates did have the right to bring—though not necessarily win—lawsuits demanding DNA testing of evidence relevant to their cases.[49]

Substantive Due Process Fair procedures would obviously be of little use if they were used to administer unfair laws. For example, suppose a law requires everyone to wear a red shirt on Mondays. You wear a blue shirt on Monday, and you are arrested, convicted, and sentenced to one year in prison. The fact that all proper procedures were followed and your rights were given their proper protections would mean very little because the law that you broke was unfair and arbitrary.

Thus, **substantive due process** requires that the laws themselves be reasonable. The idea is that if a law is unfair or arbitrary, even if properly passed by a legislature, it must be declared unconstitutional. In the 1930s,

for example, Oklahoma instituted the Habitual Criminal Sterilization Act. Under this statute, a person who had been convicted of three felonies could be "rendered sexually sterile" by the state (that is, the person would no longer be able to produce children). The United States Supreme Court held that the law was unconstitutional, as there are "limits to the extent which a legislatively represented majority may conduct biological experiments at the expense of the dignity and personality and natural powers of a minority."[50]

Procedural Due Process A provision in the Constitution that states that the law must be carried out in a fair and orderly manner.

Substantive Due Process The constitutional requirement that laws used in accusing and convicting persons of crimes must be fair.

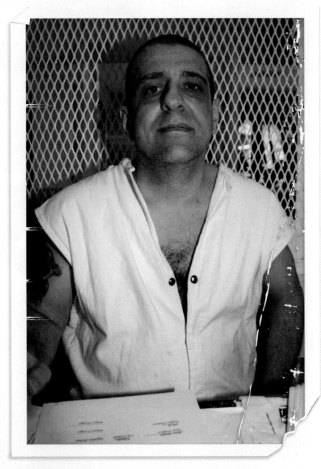

Why did Hank Skinner, shown here in a West Livingston prison, believe that his procedural due process rights were being violated by the state of Texas? (AP Photo/Michael Graczyk)

5 LAW ENFORCEMENT TODAY

Learning
Outcomes

After studying this chapter,
you will be able to . . .

LO 1   List the four basic responsibilities of the police.

LO 2   List five main types of law enforcement agencies.

LO 3   Indicate some of the most important law enforcement agencies under the control of the Department of Homeland Security.

LO 4   Analyze the importance of private security today.

LO 5   Indicate why patrol officers are allowed discretionary powers.

John Moore/Getty Images

"Primed, Prepared, and Precise"

Over the course of twenty years in law enforcement, Feris Jones had not once fired her gun in the line of duty. Then, on the evening of October 23, 2010, Winston Cox burst into Sabine's Hallway Beauty Salon, where the fifty-year-old New York police officer was getting her hair done. Brandishing a .44-caliber revolver, Cox herded the four women present—including Jones—into a back bathroom. "This ain't no joke!" Cox shouted as he collected the women's valuables in a black bag. "This is a robbery! I will kill you!"

When Cox returned to the main room of the Brooklyn salon, Jones decided to take action. She pulled out her Smith & Wesson five-shot pistol, told the other women to get down, and identified herself as a police officer. Cox responded by opening fire, which Jones returned in kind. At a distance of about twelve feet, all four of Cox's shots missed. Jones, thanks to hundreds of hours of training, had better results. Of her five rounds, two bullets struck Cox—one fracturing his right middle finger and another grazing his left hand—and a third shattered the salon doorknob, blocking a potential avenue of escape. The would-be robber finally did get free by kicking out a window, but police were easily able to track him down, partially due to the trail of blood he left behind.

Until the incident at the beauty salon, Jones had spent most of her time at the New York Police Department behind a desk. Following this display of bravery and marksmanship, however, she was promoted to the rank of detective. "Her quick thinking and sharp aim stopped an armed robbery, or worse," said New York mayor Michael Bloomberg at Jones's promotion ceremony. "She was primed, prepared, and precise." Afterward, a reporter asked Jones if it was common practice for her to take a weapon to a beauty salon. "I'm always armed," the newly minted detective said with a smile.

Why was New York police officer Feris Jones, shown here leaving a press conference, promoted to the rank of detective? (AP Photo/Frank Franklin II)

Law enforcement holds endless surprises. Officer Feris Jones certainly did not expect to find herself in a firefight in the middle of a routine Saturday night haircut. She probably did not expect to become the focus of so much media attention, either. Her promotion ceremony was broadcast live in New York City, and the story of the "Salon Hero's Brave Stand" was an Internet sensation. (CAREER TIP: Many law enforcement agencies—even small local police departments—employ *public relations specialists* to develop goodwill in the community and provide information to the media.)

In many ways, though, the public's response to Detective Jones was no surprise at all. Police officers are the most visible representatives of our criminal justice system. Indeed, they symbolize the system for many Americans who may never see the inside of a courtroom or a prison cell. The police are entrusted with immense power to serve and protect the public good: the power to use weapons and the power to arrest. But that same power alarms many citizens, who fear that it may be turned arbitrarily against them. The role of the police is constantly debated as well. Is their primary mission to fight crime, or should they also be concerned with the social conditions that presumably lead to crime?

This chapter will lay the foundation for our study of law enforcement agents and the work that they do. We will start by looking at the various responsibilities of police officers, followed by an examination of the many different agencies that make up the American law enforcement system. We will also discuss the expanding presence of private policing and the crucial role of discretion in law enforcement.

¿WHAT DO THE POLICE DO?

For the most part, the incidents that make up a police officer's daily routine would not make it onto television dramas such as *Law & Order.* Besides catching criminals, police spend a great deal of time on such mundane tasks as responding to noise complaints, confiscating firecrackers, and poring over paperwork. Sociologist Egon Bittner warned against the tendency to see the police primarily as agents of law enforcement and crime control. A more inclusive accounting of "what the police do," Bittner believed, would recognize that they provide "situationally justified force in society."[1] In other words, the function of the police is to solve any problem that may *possibly*, though not *necessarily*, require the use of force.

Within Bittner's rather broad definition of "what the police do," we can pinpoint four basic responsibilities of the police:

1. To enforce laws.
2. To provide services.
3. To prevent crime.
4. To preserve the peace.

As will become evident over the next two chapters, there is a great deal of debate among legal and other scholars and law enforcement officers over which responsibilities deserve the most police attention and what methods should be employed by the police in meeting those responsibilities.

ENFORCE LAWS

In the public mind, the primary role of the police is to enforce society's laws—hence, the term *law enforcement officer.* In their role as "crime fighters," police officers have a clear mandate to seek out and apprehend those who have violated the law. The crime-fighting responsibility

Naomi Bassitt/iStockphoto

This police officer was called to help capture two of nine American bison that escaped from a farm in Stevenson, Maryland. What are some other responsibilities of the police that have little to do with preventing crime? (AP Photo/Steve Ruark/ iStockphoto.com)

is so dominant that all police activity—from the purchase of new automobiles to a plan to hire more minority officers—must often be justified in terms of its law enforcement value.[2]

Police officers also primarily see themselves as crime fighters, or "crook catchers," a perception that often leads people into what they believe will be an exciting career in law enforcement. Although the job certainly offers challenges unlike any other, police officers normally do not spend the majority of their time in law enforcement duties. After surveying a year's worth of dispatch data from the Wilmington (Delaware) Police Department, researchers Jack Greene and Carl Klockars found that officers spent only about half of their time enforcing the law or dealing with crimes. The rest of their time was taken up with order maintenance, providing services, traffic patrol, and medical assistance.[3] Furthermore, information provided by the Uniform Crime Report shows that most arrests are made for "crimes of disorder" or public annoyances rather than violent or property crimes.[4]

In 2009, for example, police made 11 million arrests for drunkenness, liquor law violations, disorderly conduct, homelessness, loitering, and other minor offenses but only about 580,000 arrests for violent crimes.[5]

PROVIDE SERVICES

The popular emphasis on crime fighting and law enforcement tends to overshadow the fact that a great deal of a police officer's time is spent providing services for the community. The motto "To Serve and Protect" has been adopted by thousands of local police departments, and the *Law Enforcement Code of Ethics* recognizes the duty "to serve the community" in its first sentence.[6] The services that police provide are numerous—a partial list would include directing traffic, performing emergency medical procedures, counseling those involved in domestic disputes, providing directions to tourists, and finding lost children. Along with firefighters, police officers are among the first public servants to arrive at disaster scenes to conduct search and rescue operations. This particular duty adds considerably to the dangers faced by law enforcement agents (discussed in more detail in Chapter 6).

In addition, a number of police departments have adopted the strategy of community policing (also discussed in the next chapter). As a consequence, many officers find themselves providing assistance in areas that have not until recently been their domain.[7] Along these lines, police are expected to deal with the problems of the homeless and the mentally ill to a greater extent than in past decades.

PREVENT CRIME

Perhaps the most controversial responsibility of the police is to *prevent* crime, a difficult task under the best of circumstances. According to Jerome Skolnick, co-director of the Center for Research in Crime and Justice at the New York University School of Law, there are two predictable public responses when crime rates begin to rise in a community. The first is to punish convicted criminals with stricter laws and more severe penalties. The second is to demand that the police "do something" to prevent crimes from occurring in the first place. Is it, in fact, possible for the police to prevent crimes? The strongest response that Professor Skolnick is willing to give to this question is "maybe."[8]

> "That's the only thing that made me feel safe last night when I came home from work."
>
> —PENNY BAILY, RESIDENT OF INDIANAPOLIS, COMMENTING ON THE POLICE CAR PATROLLING HER NEIGHBORHOOD

Maciej Korzekwa/iStockphoto.com

On a limited basis, police can certainly prevent some crimes. If a rapist is dissuaded from attacking a solitary woman because a patrol car is cruising the area, then the police officer behind the wheel has prevented a crime. Furthermore, exemplary police work can have an effect. The nation's two largest cities—New York and Los Angeles—have both experienced sharp declines in crime in recent years, a trend many attribute in large part to aggressive and innovative law enforcement.[9]

In general, however, the deterrent effects of police presence are unclear. Carl Klockars has written that the "war on crime" is a war that the police cannot win because they cannot control the factors—such as unemployment, poverty, immorality, inequality, political change, and lack of educational opportunities—that lead to criminal behavior in the first place.[10] As we shall see in the next chapter, police authorities are engaged in a number of different strategies in an attempt to better prevent crime.

PRESERVE THE PEACE

To a certain extent, the fourth responsibility of the police, that of preserving the peace, is related to preventing crime. Police have the legal authority to use the power of arrest, or even force, in situations in which no crime has yet occurred but might occur in the immediate future.

In the words of James Q. Wilson, the police's peacekeeping role (which Wilson believes is the most important role of law enforcement officers) often takes on a pattern of simply "handling the situation."[11] For example, when police officers arrive on the scene of a loud late-night house party, they may feel the need to disperse the party and even arrest some of the party-goers for disorderly conduct. By their actions, the officers have lessened the chances of serious and violent crimes taking place later in the evening. The same principle is often used when dealing with domestic disputes, which, if escalated, can lead to homicide. Such situations are in need of, to use Wilson's terminology again, "fixing up," and police can use the power of arrest, or threat, or coercion, or sympathy, to do just that.

¿WHAT ARE THE DIFFERENT KINDS OF LAW ENFORCEMENT AGENCIES?

At times, police officers encounter a task that requires the "multilayering" of law enforcement. For example, a wide network of local, state, and federal law enforcement agencies was involved in the extensive search for eight members of the Vagos motorcycle gang responsible for setting off a brutal brawl in Bullhead City, Arizona. Taking part in "Operation Sand Castle"—which ended successfully with eight arrests on December 8, 2010—were law enforcement agents from local police and sheriffs' departments in Bullhead City, Kingman, Lake Havasu, and Mohave County; tribal police from Fort Mohave; the Arizona Department of Public Safety; and U.S. Immigration and Customs Enforcement (ICE).

The manhunt illustrates how many agencies can become involved in a single incident. There are more than 15,000 law enforcement agencies in the United States, employing nearly 1 million people.[12] These various agencies include the following:

- Local police departments.
- Sheriffs' departments.
- Special police agencies, limited to policing parks, schools, airports, and other areas.
- State police departments.
- Federal law enforcement agencies.

Each level has its own set of responsibilities, which we shall discuss starting with local police departments.

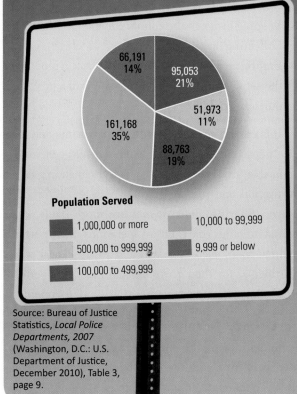

Figure 5.1 Full-Time Police Personnel, by Size of Population Served

66,191
14%

95,053
21%

51,973
11%

161,168
35%

88,763
19%

Population Served

- 1,000,000 or more
- 500,000 to 999,999
- 100,000 to 499,999
- 10,000 to 99,999
- 9,999 or below

Source: Bureau of Justice Statistics, *Local Police Departments, 2007* (Washington, D.C.: U.S. Department of Justice, December 2010), Table 3, page 9.

Stan Rohrer/iStockphoto.com

MUNICIPAL LAW ENFORCEMENT AGENCIES

According to the FBI, there are 2.3 state and local police officers for every 1,000 citizens in the United States.[13] This average somewhat masks the discrepancies between the police forces in urban and rural America. As noted in Chapter 1, the vast majority of all police officers work in small and medium-sized police departments (see **Figure 5.1** above). While the New York City Police Department employs about 38,000 police officers, 50 percent of all local police departments have ten or fewer law enforcement officers.[14]

Of the three levels of law enforcement, municipal agencies have the broadest authority to apprehend criminal suspects, maintain order, and provide services to the community. Whether the local officer is part of a large force or the only law enforcement officer in the community, he or she is usually responsible for a wide spectrum of duties, from responding to noise complaints to investigating homicides. Much of the criticism of local police departments is based on the belief that local police are too underpaid or poorly trained to handle these various responsibilities. Reformers have suggested that residents of smaller American towns would benefit from greater statewide coordination of local police departments.[15]

Sheriff The primary law enforcement officer in a county, usually elected to the post by a popular vote.

SHERIFFS AND COUNTY LAW ENFORCEMENT

The **sheriff** is still an important figure in American law enforcement. Almost every one of the more than three thousand counties in the United States (except those in Alaska) has a sheriff. In every state except Rhode Island and Hawaii, sheriffs are elected by members of the community for two- or four-year terms and are paid a salary set by the state legislature or county board. As elected officials who do not necessarily need a background in law enforcement, sheriffs must also be politicians. When a new sheriff is elected, she or he will sometimes repay political debts by appointing new deputies or promoting those who have given her or him support. This high degree of instability and personnel turnover in many states is seen as one of the weaknesses of county law enforcement.[16]

Size and Responsibility of Sheriffs' Departments
Like municipal police forces, sheriffs' departments

STUDY PREP

We study best when we are free from distractions such as the Internet, cell phones, and our friends. That's why your school library is often the best place to work. Set aside several hours a week of "library time" to study in peace and quiet. Remember to turn off your cell phone and other Web devices.

Coroner The medical examiner of a county, usually elected by popular vote.

vary in size. The largest is the Los Angeles County Sheriff's Department, with more than 8,400 deputies. Of the approximately 3,000 sheriffs' departments in the country, 13 employ more than 1,000 officers, while 19 have only 1.[17]

The image of the sheriff as a powerful figure patrolling vast expanses is not entirely misleading. Most sheriffs' departments are assigned their duties by state law. About 80 percent of all sheriffs' departments have the primary responsibility for investigating violent crimes in their jurisdictions. Other common responsibilities of a sheriff's department include:

☑ Investigating drug crimes.
☑ Maintaining the county jail.

A local police officer operates a roadblock as part of the search for Jason Lee Wheeler, who killed one Lake County (Florida) sheriff's deputy and wounded two others. Why would local law enforcement agencies seek the aid of federal law enforcement agencies in a situation such as this one? (AP Photo/Phil Sandlin)

☑ Carrying out civil and criminal processes within county lines, such as serving eviction notices and court summonses.
☑ Keeping order in the county courthouse.
☑ Collecting taxes.
☑ Enforcing orders of the court, such as overseeing the sequestration (forced seclusion) of a jury during a trial.[18]

It is easy to confuse sheriffs' departments and local police departments. Both law enforcement agencies are responsible for many of the same tasks, including crime investigation and routine patrol. There are differences, however. Sheriffs' departments are more likely to be involved in county court and jail operations and to perform certain services such as search and rescue. Local police departments, for their part, are more likely to perform traffic-related functions than are sheriffs' departments.[19]

The County Coroner Another elected official on the county level is the **coroner**, or medical examiner. Duties vary from county to county, but the coroner has a general mandate to investigate "all sudden, unexplained, unnatural, or suspicious deaths" reported to the office. The coroner is ultimately responsible for determining the cause of death in these cases. Coroners also perform autopsies and assist other law enforcement agencies in homicide investigations.[20] In certain rare circumstances, such as when the sheriff is arrested or otherwise forced to leave his or her post, the coroner becomes the leading law enforcement officer of the county. (CAREER TIP: Some counties or districts employ *medical examiners* instead of coroners. Although they perform many of the same duties, medical examiners are licensed physicians, unlike coroners, and are usually appointed rather than elected.)

STATE POLICE AND HIGHWAY PATROLS

The most visible state law enforcement agency is the state police or highway patrol agency. Historically, state police agencies were created for four reasons:

1. To assist local police agencies, which often did not have adequate resources or training to handle some of their law enforcement tasks.

CJ and Technology

HIGH-TECH COP CARS

The capabilities of the patrol car, perhaps the most important piece of policing technology of the past half-century, continue to expand. Project 54, a voice-recognition system developed at the University of New Hampshire, allows police officers to multitask without having to divert their attention from the road or take a hand off the wheel. The officer simply presses a button, and all the technological equipment in the car becomes voice activated. Four Andrea digital array microphones positioned in the cab of the automobile cancel all noise except the sound of the officer's voice. So, for example, if the officer witnesses a hit-and-run accident, he or she simply says the word "pursuit" to activate the automobile's siren and flashing lights. Then the officer can call for an ambulance and run a check on the suspect's license plate—all by voice command. Other recent innovations include Automatic License Plate Recognition, a three-camera computer-operated system that performs a "20-millisecond" background check on every license plate it sees, and the StarChase launcher, a small, laser-guided cannon that shoots a small, sticky radio transmitter at a fleeing vehicle. Once the offending car has been tagged with this device, police can track the fugitive at a safe distance without the need for a dangerous, high-speed pursuit.

Project 54: Dura Tech, USA, Inc./Octavian Florentin Babusi/iStockphoto.com

THINKING ABOUT POLICE AUTOMOBILE TECHNOLOGY

American automobile manufacturers do not produce ready-made police cars. Law enforcement agencies must add technologies such as the ones discussed here after the car has been purchased. What might be some of the benefits of large-scale production of a car that would be sold only for law enforcement purposes?

2. To investigate criminal activities that crossed jurisdictional boundaries (such as when bank robbers committed a crime in one county and then fled to another part of the state).

3. To provide law enforcement in rural and other areas that did not have local or county police agencies.

4. To break strikes and control labor movements.

Today, there are twenty-three state police agencies and twenty-six highway patrols in the United States. State police agencies have statewide jurisdiction and

A Connecticut State Police officer provides advice for a motorist stuck in a snowstorm on Interstate 84 in East Hartford. In what ways do state law enforcement officers supplement the efforts of local police officers? (AP Photo/Jessica Hill)

are authorized to perform a wide variety of law enforcement tasks. Thus, they provide the same services as city or county police departments and are limited only by the boundaries of the state. In general, state police are complementary (supplemental) to local law enforcement agencies. They maintain crime labs to assist in local investigations and also keep statewide intelligence files.

State officers in some instances also provide training to local police and will assist local forces when needed.[21] In contrast, highway patrols have limited authority. They are limited either by their jurisdiction or by the specific types of offenses they have the authority to control. As their name suggests, most highway patrols concentrate primarily on regulating traffic. Specifically, they enforce traffic laws and investigate traffic accidents. Furthermore, highway patrols usually limit their activity to patrolling state and federal highways.

FEDERAL LAW ENFORCEMENT AGENCIES

Statistically, employees of federal agencies do not make up a large part of the nation's law enforcement force. In fact, the New York City Police Department has about one-third as many employees as all of the federal law enforcement agencies combined.[22] Nevertheless, the influence of these federal agencies is substantial. Unlike local police departments, which must deal with all forms of crime, federal agencies have been authorized, usually by Congress, to enforce specific laws or attend to specific situations. The U.S. Coast Guard, for example, patrols the nation's waterways, while U.S. Postal Inspectors investigate and prosecute crimes perpetrated through the use of the U.S. mail.

As mentioned in Chapter 1, the most far-reaching reorganization of the federal government since World War II took place in the early 2000s. These changes, particularly the formation of the Department of Homeland Security, have had a significant effect on federal law enforcement. (See **Figure 5.2** below for the current federal law enforcement "lineup.") In Chapter 16, we will take a close look at just how profound this effect has been. Here, you will learn the basic elements of the most important federal law enforcement agencies, which are grouped according to the federal department or bureau to which they report.

The Department of Homeland Security On November 25, 2002, President George W. Bush signed the Homeland Security Act.[23] This legislation created the Department of Homeland Security (DHS), a new cabinet-level department designed to coordinate federal efforts to protect the United States against international and domestic terrorism. The new department has no new agencies. Rather, twenty-two existing agencies were shifted under the control of the secretary of homeland security, a post now held

Figure 5.2 Federal Law Enforcement Agencies

A number of federal agencies employ law enforcement officers who are authorized to carry firearms and make arrests. The most prominent ones are under the control of the U.S. Department of Homeland Security, the U.S. Department of Justice, or the U.S. Department of the Treasury.

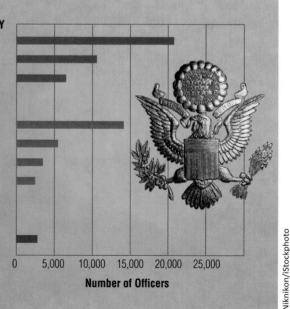

Sources: U.S. Department of Homeland Security, U.S. Department of Justice, and U.S. Department of the Treasury.

Border Patrol agents make their rounds of the United States' shared boundary with Mexico on all-terrain vehicles (ATVs). What are the primary duties of U.S. Customs and Border Protection, which oversees the Border Patrol? (James Tourtellotte/CBP.gov/ Laura Young/iStockphoto. com/Blent Gültek/ iStockphoto.com)

U.S. Customs and Border Protection (CBP) The federal agency responsible for protecting U.S. borders and facilitating legal trade and travel across those borders.

U.S. Border Patrol The mobile law enforcement branch of U.S. Customs and Border Protection, responsible for protecting this country's borders with Mexico and Canada.

U.S. Immigration and Customs Enforcement (ICE) The federal agency that enforces the nation's immigration and customs laws.

by Janet Napolitano. For example, the Transportation Security Administration, which was formed in 2001 to revive the Federal Air Marshals program placing undercover federal agents on commercial flights, was moved from the Department of Transportation to the DHS. U.S. Customs and Border Protection, U.S. Immigration and Customs Enforcement, and the U.S. Secret Service are the three most visible agencies under the direction of the DHS.

U.S. Customs and Border Protection (CBP)

One of the most important effects of the Homeland Security Act was the termination of the Immigration and Naturalization Service (INS), which had monitored and policed the flow of immigrants into the United States since 1933. Many of the INS's duties have been transferred to **U.S. Customs and Border Protection (CBP)**, which polices the flow of goods and people across U.S. international borders. In general terms, this means that the agency has two primary goals: (1) to keep illegal immigrants (including potential terrorists), drugs, and

drug traffickers from crossing our borders, and (2) to facilitate the smooth flow of legal trade and travel. Consequently, CBP officers are stationed at every port of entry and exit to the United States. The officers have widespread authority to investigate and search all international passengers, whether they arrive on airplanes, ships, or other forms of transportation.

The **U.S. Border Patrol**, a branch of the CBP, has the burden of policing both the Mexican and Canadian borders between official ports of entry. In 2009, Border Patrol agents caught nearly 560,000 people entering the country illegally and confiscated more than 4.75 million pounds of narcotics.[24] Today, about 21,000 Border Patrol agents guard 19,000 miles of land and sea borders, about double the number on duty ten years earlier.

U.S. Immigration and Customs Enforcement (ICE)

The CBP shares responsibility for locating and apprehending those persons in the United States illegally with special agents from **U.S. Immigration and Customs Enforcement (ICE)**. While the CBP focuses almost exclusively on the nation's borders, ICE has a broader mandate to investigate and to enforce our country's immigration and customs laws. Simply stated, the CBP covers the borders, and ICE covers everything else. The latter agency's duties include detaining illegal immigrants and deporting (removing) them from the United States, ensuring that those without permission do not work or gain other benefits in this country, and disrupting human trafficking operations. Recently, ICE has become more aggressive in its efforts to apprehend and remove illegal immigrants with criminal records. In 2009, ICE officers blanketed California searching for these individuals and arrested nearly three hundred of them over the course of three days. That year, in total, ICE removed about 300,000 illegal immigrants from this country.[25] As we shall see in Chapter 16, both the CBP and ICE are crucial elements of the nation's antiterrorism strategy.

The U.S. Secret Service When it was created in 1865, the U.S. Secret Service was primarily responsible for combating currency counterfeiters. In 1901, the agency was given the added responsibility of protecting the president of the United States, the president's family, the vice president, the president-elect, and former presidents. These duties have remained the cornerstone of the agency, with several expansions. After a number of threats against presidential candidates in the 1960s and early 1970s, including the shootings of Senator Robert Kennedy of New York and Governor George Wallace of Alabama, in 1976 Secret Service agents became responsible for protecting those political figures as well.

In addition to its special plainclothes agents, the agency also directs two uniformed groups of law enforcement officers. The Secret Service Uniformed Division protects the grounds of the White House and its inhabitants, and the Treasury Police Force secures the Treasury Building in Washington, D.C. This responsibility includes investigating threats against presidents and those running for presidential office.

The Department of Justice The U.S. Department of Justice, created in 1870, is still the primary federal law enforcement agency in the country. With the responsibility of enforcing criminal law and supervising the federal prisons, the Justice Department plays a leading role in the American criminal justice system. To carry out its responsibilities to prevent and control crime, the department has a number of law enforcement agencies, including the Federal Bureau of Investigation, the federal Drug Enforcement Administration, the Bureau of Alcohol, Tobacco, Firearms and Explosives, and the U.S. Marshals Service.

CAREERPREP — FEDERAL BUREAU OF INVESTIGATION (FBI) AGENT

JOB DESCRIPTION:

- Primary role is to oversee intelligence and investigate federal crimes. Agents might track the movement of stolen goods across state lines, examine accounting and business records, listen to legal wiretaps, and conduct undercover investigations.
- Special agent careers are divided into five paths: intelligence, counterintelligence, counterterrorism, criminal, and cyber crime.

WHAT KIND OF TRAINING IS REQUIRED?

- A bachelor's and/or master's degree, plus three years of work experience, along with a written and oral examination, medical and physical examinations, a psychological assessment, and an exhaustive background investigation.

- Critical skills required in one or more of the following areas: accounting, finance, computer science/information technology, engineering, foreign language(s), law, law enforcement, intelligence, military, and/or physical sciences.

ANNUAL SALARY RANGE?

- $61,100–$69,900

For additional information, visit:
www.fbijobs.gov.

Courtesy Federal Bureau of Investigation/Department of Justice

The Federal Bureau of Investigation (FBI)

Initially created in 1908 as the Bureau of Investigation, this agency was renamed the **Federal Bureau of Investigation (FBI)** in 1935. One of the primary investigative agencies of the federal government, the FBI has jurisdiction over nearly two hundred federal crimes, including a number of white-collar crimes, espionage (spying), kidnapping, extortion, interstate transportation of stolen property, bank robbery, interstate gambling, and civil rights violations. With its network of agents across the country and the globe, the FBI is also uniquely positioned to combat worldwide criminal activity such as terrorism and drug trafficking.

The agency also provides valuable support to local and state law enforcement agencies. The FBI's Identification Division maintains a large database of fingerprint information and offers assistance in finding missing persons and identifying the victims of fires, airplane crashes, and other disfiguring disasters. The services of the FBI Laboratory, the largest crime laboratory in the world, are available at no charge to other agencies. Finally, the FBI's National Crime Information Center (NCIC) provides lists of stolen vehicles and firearms, missing license plates, vehicles used to commit crimes, and other information to local and state law enforcement officers who may access the NCIC database. The FBI employs about 34,000 people and has an annual budget of approximately $8 billion.

The Drug Enforcement Administration (DEA)

With a $2.6 billion annual budget and about 5,200 special agents, the **Drug Enforcement Administration (DEA)** is one of the more important law enforcement agencies in the country. The mission of the DEA is to enforce domestic drug laws and regulations and to assist other federal and foreign agencies in combating illegal drug manufacture and trade on an international level. The agency also enforces the provisions of the Controlled Substances Act, which governs the manufacture, distribution, and dispensing of legal drugs, such as prescription drugs.

DEA agents often work in conjunction with local and state authorities to prevent illicit drugs from reaching communities. The agency also conducts extensive operations with law enforcement entities in other drug-producing countries. Recently, for example, the DEA joined forces with the Mexican military to target that country's various and powerful drug cartels. In November 2010, acting on information from

the U.S. agency, Mexican authorities sent 660 Marines to Matamoros—just across the U.S. border from Brownsville, Texas—to apprehend drug boss Antonio Ezequiel Cardenas Guillen, also known as Tony Tormenta, or Tony the Storm.[26] (Guillen was killed in the ensuing firefight.)

Like the FBI, the DEA also operates a network of six regional laboratories used to test and categorize seized drugs. Local law enforcement agencies have access to the DEA labs and often use them to ensure that information about particular drugs that will be presented in court is accurate and up to date. (CAREER TIP: Illegal drug manufacturers often try to outwit the DEA by creating new psychoactive substances that are not yet illegal under federal law. Consequently, the agency employs *forensic chemists* to identify these new illegal drugs and support their investigation by DEA special agents.)

> **Federal Bureau of Investigation (FBI)** The branch of the Department of Justice responsible for investigating violations of federal law.
>
> **Drug Enforcement Administration (DEA)** The federal agency responsible for enforcing the nation's laws and regulations regarding narcotics and other controlled substances.

A suspected Colombian drug dealer is escorted by a U.S. Marshal and a U.S. DEA agent on his arrival in Florida to face U.S. drug trafficking and money laundering charges in federal court. How do the duties of DEA and FBI agents differ? How are they similar? (AP Photo/Alan Diaz)

The Bureau of Alcohol, Tobacco, Firearms and Explosives (ATF) As its name suggests, the **Bureau of Alcohol, Tobacco, Firearms and Explosives (ATF)** is primarily concerned with the illegal sale, possession, and use of firearms and the control of untaxed tobacco and liquor products. The Firearms Division of the agency has the responsibility of enforcing the Gun Control Act of 1968, which sets the circumstances under which firearms may be sold and used in this country. The bureau also regulates all gun trade between the United States and foreign nations and collects taxes on all firearm importers, manufacturers, and dealers. In keeping with these duties, the ATF additionally is responsible for policing the illegal use and possession of explosives. Furthermore, the ATF is charged with enforcing federal gambling laws.

Because it has jurisdiction over such a wide variety of crimes, especially those involving firearms and explosives, the ATF is a constant presence in federal criminal investigations. So, in January 2011, following the shooting rampage in Tucson, Arizona, that left six people dead and U.S. representative Gabrielle Giffords critically injured, the ATF investigated the handgun used by the suspect, Jared Loughner. Furthermore, the ATF is engaged in an ongoing and crucial operation to keep American firearms out of the hands of Mexican drug cartels. The ATF has also formed multijurisdictional antigang task forces with other federal and local law enforcement agencies to investigate gang-related crimes involving firearms.

The U.S. Marshals Service The oldest federal law enforcement agency is the **U.S. Marshals Service**. In 1789, President George Washington assigned thirteen U.S. Marshals to protect his attorney general. That same year, Congress created the office of the U.S. Marshals and Deputy Marshals. Originally, the U.S. Marshals acted as the main law enforcement officers in the western territories. Following the Civil War (1861–1865), when most of these territories had become states, these agents were assigned to work for the U.S. district courts, where federal crimes are tried. The relationship between the U.S. Marshals Service and the federal courts continues today and forms the basis for the officers' main duties, which are listed in the CAREERprep feature below.

The Department of the Treasury The Department of the Treasury, formed in 1789, is mainly

CAREERPREP — U.S. MARSHAL

JOB DESCRIPTION:

- Provide security at federal courts, control property that has been ordered seized by federal courts, and protect government witnesses who put themselves in danger by testifying against the targets of federal criminal investigations.

- Transport federal prisoners to detention institutions and hunt and capture fugitives from federal law.

WHAT KIND OF TRAINING IS REQUIRED?

- A bachelor's degree or three years of qualifying experience, which includes work in law enforcement, correctional supervision, and volunteer teaching or counseling.

- A rigorous seventeen-and-a-half-week basic training program at the U.S Marshals Service Training Academy in Glynco, Georgia.

ANNUAL SALARY RANGE?

- $37,000–$47,000

For additional information, visit:
www.usmarshals.gov/careers/index.html.

Stephen Mulcahey/iStockphoto.com

responsible for all financial matters of the federal government. It pays all the federal government's bills, borrows funds, collects taxes, mints coins, and prints paper currency.

The largest bureau of the Treasury Department, the Internal Revenue Service (IRS), is concerned with violations of tax laws and regulations. The bureau has three divisions, only one of which is involved in criminal investigations. The examination branch of the IRS audits the tax returns of corporations and individuals. The collection division attempts to collect taxes from corporations or citizens who have failed to pay the taxes they owe. The criminal investigation division investigates cases of tax evasion and tax fraud. Criminal investigation agents can make arrests. The IRS has long played a role in policing criminal activities such as gambling and selling drugs for one simple reason: those who engage in such activities almost never report any illegally gained income on their tax returns. Therefore, the IRS is able to apprehend them for tax evasion. The most famous instance of this took place in the early 1930s, when the IRS finally arrested famed crime boss Al Capone—responsible for numerous violent crimes—for not paying his taxes.

¿WHY IS THERE A DEMAND FOR PRIVATE SECURITY?

LO 4

Even with increasing numbers of local, state, and federal law enforcement officers, the police do not have the ability to prevent every crime. Recognizing this, many businesses and citizens have decided to hire private guards for their properties and homes. In fact, according to the Freedonia Group, an industry-research firm, demand for **private security** in 2010 created revenues of $48 billion.[27] More than 10,000 firms employing around

Christopher Steer/iStockphoto

1.1 million people provide private security services in this country, compared with about 700,000 public law enforcement agents.

> **Private Security** The practice of private corporations or individuals offering services traditionally performed by police officers.

PRIVATIZING LAW ENFORCEMENT

In the eyes of the law, a private security guard is the same as any other private person when it comes to police powers such as being able to arrest or interrogate a person suspected of committing a crime. Ideally, a security guard—lacking the training of a law enforcement agent—should only observe and report criminal activity unless use of force is needed to prevent a felony.[28]

Citizens' Arrests Any private citizen (including private security guards) may perform a "citizen's arrest" under certain circumstances. The California Penal Code, for example, allows a private person to arrest another

- For a public offense committed in his or her presence.
- When the person arrested has committed a felony, even if it was not in the arrester's presence, if the arrester has reasonable cause to believe that the person committed the felony.[29]

Obviously, these are not very exacting standards, and in reality, private security guards have many, if not most, of the same powers to prevent crime that a police officer does.

The Deterrence Factor

As a rule, however, private security is not designed to replace law enforcement. It is intended to deter crime rather than stop it.[30] A uniformed security guard patrolling a shopping mall parking lot or a bank lobby has one primary function—to convince a potential criminal to search out a shopping mall or bank that does not have private security. For the same reason, many citizens hire security personnel to drive marked cars through their neighborhoods, making them less attractive targets for burglaries, robberies, vandalism, and other crimes.

PRIVATE SECURITY TRENDS

Despite the increased use of private security, many questions remain about this largely unregulated industry. Several years ago, Jessie Walker, a sixty-four-year-old security guard for Markman's Diamonds & Fine Jewelry in West Knoxville, Tennessee, was charged with aggravated assault for shooting Kevin Bowman and Elizabeth Day. Walker had intervened when he heard the couple having a loud argument in the store's parking lot. When the fighting continued, Walker eventually drew his handgun and shot Bowman and Day, neither of whom was armed, sending them to the hospital in critical condition. The only requirement for becoming a weapons-licensed security guard in Tennessee is eight hours of training.[31]

Lack of Standards As there are no federal regulations regarding private security, each state has its own rules for employment as a security guard. In several states, including California and Florida, prospective guards must have at least forty hours of training. Twenty-nine states, however, have no specific training requirements, and ten states do not regulate the private security industry at all. By comparison, Spain mandates 160 hours of theoretical training, 20 hours of practical training, and 20 hours of annual continuing education for anybody hoping to find employment as a security guard.[32]

The quality of employees is also a problem for the U.S. private security industry. Given the low pay (see **Figure 5.3** below) and lack of benefits such as health insurance, paid vacation time, and sick days, the industry does not always attract highly qualified and motivated recruits.[33] "At those wages," notes one industry specialist, "you're competing with McDonald's."[34] To make matters worse, fewer than half of the states require a fingerprint check for applicants,

Figure 5.3   Average Salaries in Law Enforcement

In New York City, servers in restaurants, landscapers, hotel desk clerks, and domestic workers all earn more than private security guards. Nationwide, as this figure shows, security guards are the lowest paid of the "protective service occupations."

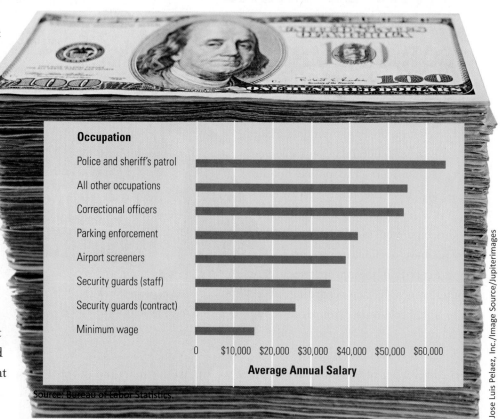

Source: Bureau of Labor Statistics.

Jose Luis Pelaez, Inc./Image Source/Jupiterimages

making it relatively easy for a person with a criminal record in one state to obtain a security guard position in another state (or even the home state in some cases).[35]

The security industry is finding it much easier to uncover past convictions of employees and job applicants thanks to the Private Security Officer Employment Authorization Act of 2004.[36] The legislation, which authorizes the FBI to provide background checks for security firms, was spurred by congressional concern over possible terrorist attacks on shipping ports, water treatment facilities, telecommunications facilities, power plants, and other strategic targets that are often secured by private guards. In the first year of this program, the FBI found that 990,000 of the estimated 9 million applicants for private security positions (about 11 percent) had criminal records.[37]

Continued Growth in the Industry Issues surrounding private security promise to gain even greater prominence in the criminal justice system, as indicators point to higher rates of growth for the industry. The Hallcrest Report II, a far-reaching overview of private security trends funded by the National Institute of Justice, identifies four factors driving this growth:

1. An increase in fear on the part of the public triggered by media coverage of crime.

2. The problem of crime in the workplace. According to the University of Florida's National Retail Security Survey, American retailers lose about $34 billion a year because of shoplifting and employee theft.[38] (CAREER TIP: *Loss prevention* is a catchall phrase used by retail companies to describe their efforts to reduce shoplifting and cash theft in their stores. Retailers need *loss prevention security officers* to keep an eye on suspicious shoppers and *loss prevention detectives* to investigate shoplifting and employee theft.)

3. Budget cuts in states and municipalities that have forced reductions in the number of public police, thereby raising the demand for private ones.

4. A rising awareness of private security products (such as home burglar alarms) and services as cost-effective protective measures.[39]

Another reason for the industry's continued profitability is terrorism. Private security is responsible for pro-

tecting more than three-fourths of the nation's likely terrorist targets such as power plants, financial centers, dams, malls, oil refineries, and transportation hubs. When several dozen private security guards were caught sleeping on the job at the John F. Kennedy International Airport in Queens, New York, in December 2010, the incident was greeted not with chuckles but with alarm. Nine of the employees, who are responsible for guarding the tarmac, inspecting vehicles, and providing other security services at the airport, lost their jobs.

To avoid this kind of negative publicity, private security companies are becoming more professional, with better screened and trained employees. "The importance of [the industry] has resulted in a crackdown on those who think they can sit around and do nothing," says Gregory A. Thomas, a senior manager at Columbia University's National Center for Disaster Preparedness.[40]

¿HOW DO LAW ENFORCEMENT AGENTS USE DISCRETION?

Leading up to World Naked Bike Ride Day on June 19, 2010, in Madison, Wisconsin, one particular question was on the minds of participants: What would the police do? In Madison, as in most of the United States, public nudity is against the law. Local officials would only warn that nude bikers ran the risk of being ticketed or arrested, depending on decisions made by individual police officers. As it turned out, Madison law enforcement, using megaphones, ordered participants to "cover their genitalia" and handed out $429 disorderly conduct citations to a number of riders who failed to do so.

As noted in Chapter 1, when law enforcement officers use their judgment in deciding which offenses to punish and which to ignore, they are said to be using *discretion*. Whether this discretion applies to controlling public nudity or other, more serious areas of the law, it is a crucial aspect of policing.

JUSTIFICATION FOR POLICE DISCRETION

One of the ironies of law enforcement is that patrol officers—who are often the lowest-paid members of an agency and have the least amount of authority—have the greatest amount of discretionary power. Part of the explanation for this is practical. Patrol officers spend most of the day on the streets, beyond the control of their supervisors. Usually, only two people are present when a patrol officer must make a decision: the officer and the possible wrongdoer. In most cases, the law enforcement officer has a great deal of freedom to take the action that he or she feels best corresponds to the situation.[41]

This is not to say that police discretion is misplaced. In general, courts have recognized that a patrol officer is in a unique position to be allowed discretionary powers, as explained in the following list:

- Police officers are considered trustworthy and are therefore assumed to make honest decisions, regardless of contradictory testimony by a suspect.
- Experience and training give officers the ability to determine whether a certain activity poses a threat to society, and to take any reasonable action necessary to investigate or prevent such activity.
- Due to the nature of their jobs, police officers are extremely knowledgeable in human, and by extension criminal, behavior.
- Police officers may find themselves in danger of personal, physical harm and

must be allowed to take reasonable and necessary steps to protect themselves.[42]

Anthony J. Pinizzotto, a psychologist with the FBI, and Charles E. Miller, an instructor in the bureau's Criminal Justice Information Services Division, take the justification for discretion one step further, arguing that many police officers have a "sixth sense," or intuition, that helps them handle on-the-job challenges. Pinizzotto and Miller believe that although "intuitive policing" is often difficult to explain to those outside law enforcement, it is a crucial part of policing and should not be discouraged by civilian administrators.[43]

MAKING THE DECISION

There is no doubt that subjective factors influence police discretion. The officer's beliefs, values, personality, and background all enter into his or her decisions. To a large extent, however, a law enforcement agent's actions are determined by the rules of policing set down in the U.S. Constitution and enforced by the courts. These rules are of paramount importance and will be discussed in great detail in Chapter 7.

Three Factors of Police Discretion Assuming that most police officers stay on the right side of the Constitution in most instances, three other factors generally enter the discretion equation in any particular situation. First, obviously and importantly, is the nature of the criminal act. The less serious a crime, the more likely a police officer is to ignore it. A person driving 60 miles per hour in a 55-miles-per-hour zone, for example, is much less likely to be ticketed than someone doing 80 miles per hour. A second element often considered is the attitude of the wrongdoer toward the officer. A motorist who is belligerent toward a highway patrol officer is much more likely to be ticketed than one who is remorseful and apologetic. Third, departmental policy can place limits on discretion. For example, many police departments have **mandatory arrest policies** under which officers *must* arrest a person who has been

Katrina Brown/iStockphoto

involved in a particular activity, such as abusing a spouse or domestic partner. No discretion is involved. (To learn more about what "mandatory" actually means, see the feature *You Be the Judge—Duty Bound?* below.)

Discretion and High-Speed Pursuits

Departmental policy has played a large role in shaping the discretionary behavior during incidents such as when, on March 24, 2010, Henrico County (Virginia) police ordered Darryl Harris to stop at a traffic checkpoint. Harris refused and led officers on a high-speed chase. Although such drastic action is often necessary, the results can be tragic. This particular chase ended when Harris ran a stop sign and crashed his car into a van driven by Apostle Anthony Taylor, a local pastor. Taylor was killed on impact. In fact, police chases cause about 360 fatalities each year, and one-third of the victims are drivers of other cars or pedestrians who were present merely as innocent bystanders.[44]

In response to these deaths, 94 percent of the nation's local police departments have implemented police pursuit policies, with 61 percent restricting the discretion of officers to engage in a high-speed chase.[45] The success of such policies can be seen in the results from Los Angeles, which features more high-speed chases than any other city in the country by a wide margin. In 2003, Los Angeles police officers were ordered to conduct dangerous pursuits only if the fleeing driver was suspected of a serious crime. Within a year, the number of high-speed pursuits decreased by 62 percent, and injuries to third parties dropped by 58 percent.[46]

While police departments are trying to limit the use of high-speed chases, the United States Supreme Court has shown that it will support a police officer's discretionary use of the tactic. In 1998, the Court held that an officer can be sued in civil court for damages caused by a high-speed pursuit only if her or his conduct was so outrageous that it "shocks the conscience."[47] Then, in 2007, the Court ruled in favor of a Georgia police officer who intentionally caused a crash involving the plaintiff, a nineteen-year-old who was trying to avoid arrest by driving 90 miles per hour on a two-lane road. Even though the plaintiff was paralyzed in the accident, the Court held that the officer was justified in his drastic effort to protect other drivers.[48] (CAREER TIP: Many police departments use helicopters to give officers on the ground an eye in the sky during high-speed chases. If you are interested in aviation, a career as a *police helicopter pilot* is always a possibility.)

YOU BE THE JUDGE
Duty Bound?

THE FACTS Simon was under court order to stay one hundred yards away from the house of his estranged ex-wife, Jessica. One summer evening, Jessica called the Castle Rock (Colorado) Police Department and reported that Simon had entered her home and abducted their three daughters, ages seven, nine, and ten. A few hours later, Jessica called the police department again with new information: Simon was with the children at a local park. The police failed to take action on either call, and Simon killed the three girls.

THE LAW The preprinted text on the back of Simon's restraining order included the following: "A KNOWING VIOLATION OF A RESTRAINING ORDER IS A CRIME" and "YOU MAY BE ARRESTED WITHOUT NOTICE IF A LAW ENFORCEMENT OFFICER HAS PROBABLE CAUSE TO BELIEVE THAT YOU HAVE KNOWINGLY VIOLATED THIS ORDER."

YOUR DECISION Jessica wants to sue the Castle Rock Police Department in civil court. She claims the language of the restraining order and the circumstances of her case created a situation in which Simon's arrest was mandatory. If you allow her lawsuit to go forward, you are essentially saying that citizens have a right to win monetary awards when police officers fail to use their discretion properly. What is your decision?

[To see how the United States Supreme Court ruled in this case, go to Example 5.1 on page 350.]

6 CHALLENGES TO EFFECTIVE POLICING

Learning Outcomes

After studying this chapter, you will be able to . . .

LO1 Identify the differences between the police academy and field training as learning tools for recruits.

LO2 List the three primary purposes of police patrol.

LO3 Describe how forensic experts use DNA fingerprinting to solve crimes.

LO4 Determine when police officers are justified in using deadly force.

LO5 Explain what an ethical dilemma is and name four categories of ethical dilemmas typically facing a police officer.

Open Wounds

According to Seattle police officer Ian Birk, while patrolling on the night of August 30, 2010, he "clearly saw" John T. Williams carrying a knife with a three-inch blade "in the open position." In response, Birk got out of his car, drew his handgun, and repeatedly and loudly ordered Williams to put the knife down. When Williams failed to do so, Birk shot the man four times from a distance of about nine feet, killing him. Video recordings from Birk's car measured an interval of approximately four seconds between the first command to drop the knife and the first gunshot. Later, Birk explained that although four seconds may seem like a short time to most people, he had been trained to recognize that it was long enough for Williams to attack him with the knife. "I was not left with any reasonable alternative but to fire at Mr. Williams," Birk said.

As is customary with such shootings, the Seattle Police Department launched an investigation into the incident. Its findings did not support Birk's version of the events. First, witnesses said that Williams, a street alcoholic and woodcarver well known in downtown Seattle, made no threatening movement toward the police officer or anyone else. Second, an autopsy showed that Williams was shot in the side, indicating that he had not been facing Birk at that point in the confrontation. Third, and most damning, when police recovered Williams's knife, they found it in a closed position. The department's Firearms Review Board eventually ruled that the shooting was unjustified and relieved Birk of his badge and gun pending further review.

For the local Native American community, this action did not go far enough. They noted that Williams, a member of the Canadian Ditidaht tribe, was partially deaf and may not have heard Birk's instructions. Furthermore, even if Birk had felt threatened, why hadn't he called for backup or used his patrol car as cover? "It's not just about John Williams," said Jack Thompson, chief of the Ditidaht tribe. "It's about the way people are treated on the street. I'm sure this could have been avoided."

© The Star-Ledger / Sarah Rice / The Image Works

Why did the fatal shooting of John T. Williams by a Seattle police officer set off demonstrations by outraged citizens such as the one shown here? (AP Photo/Ted S. Warren)

Following John T. Williams's death, Seattle police chief John Diaz said of encounters between police and civilians, "We can't get them right 99 percent of the time. We have to get them right 100 percent of the time."[1] For many observers, Diaz's police force had been operating at well below this lofty goal. In April 2010, a gang detective was caught on video kicking a Latino man while saying, "I'm going to beat the . . . Mexican piss out of you, Homey."[2] That June, another video showed an officer punching a teenage African American girl in the face following a jaywalking dispute. Finally, the Williams shooting was just one of five involving Seattle police officers in 2010, and one of three that proved fatal for the citizen involved.

Ideally, police would like to be seen as an integral part of the community, with the same goals of crime prevention and public safety as everybody else. When the relationship between police officers and those they serve—such as many minorities in Seattle—is marked by ill will and mistrust, these goals become more difficult to reach.

Most Americans cannot imagine the on-the-job situations that the average law enforcement officer faces. As one-time police officer and later professor James Fyfe explained, by telling police officers that we expect them to eradicate crime, we are putting them in a "no win war." Like some soldiers in such combat, Fyfe adds, "they commit atrocities."[3] In this chapter, we will examine some of these "atrocities," such as police brutality and corruption. We will also consider the possible causes of police misconduct and review the steps that are being taken to limit these problems. Our discussion begins with a look at how a person becomes a police officer—a process that can have a significant impact on the quality of law enforcement in cities such as Seattle and in the United States as a whole.

¿HOW DOES SOMEONE BECOME A POLICE OFFICER?

In 1961, police expert James H. Chenoweth commented that the methods used to hire police officers had changed little since 1829, when the first modern police force, the Metropolitan Police of London, was created.[4] The past half-century, however, has seen a number of improvements in the way that police administrators handle the task of **recruitment**, or the development of a pool of qualified applicants from which to select new officers. Efforts have been made to diversify police rolls, and recruits in most police departments undergo a substantial array of screening tests—discussed below—to determine their aptitude. Furthermore, annual starting salaries that exceed $50,000, along with the opportunities offered by an interesting profession in the public service field, have attracted a wide variety of applicants to police work.

BASIC REQUIREMENTS

The selection process involves a number of steps, and each police department has a different method of choosing candidates. Most agencies, however, require at a minimum that a police officer

☑ Be a U.S. citizen.

☑ Not have been convicted of a felony.

☑ Have or be eligible to have a driver's license in the state where the department is located.

☑ Be at least twenty-one years of age.

☑ Meet weight and eyesight requirements.

Beyond these minimum requirements, police departments usually conduct (1) extensive background checks, including drug tests; (2) a review of the applicant's educational, military, and driving records; (3) credit checks; (4) interviews with spouses, acquaintances, and previous employers; and (5) a background search to determine whether the applicant has been convicted of any criminal acts.[5] Police agencies generally require certain physical attributes in applicants. Normally, they must be able to pass a physical agility or fitness test. (For an example of one such test, see **Figure 6.1** on the facing page.)

Age is also a factor, as few departments will accept candidates younger than twenty-one years of age or older than forty-five. In some departments, the applicant must take a polygraph (lie-detector) exam in conjunction with the background check. The results of the polygraph exam are often compared with the informa-

Figure 6.1

Physical Agility Exam for the Henrico County (Virginia) Division of Police

Those applying for the position of police officer must finish this physical agility exam within 3 minutes, 30 seconds. During the test, applicants are required to wear the equipment (with a total weight of between 9 and 13 pounds) worn by patrol officers, which includes the police uniform, leather gun belt, firearm, baton, portable radio, and ballistics vest.

1. Applicant begins test seated in a police vehicle, door closed, seat belt fastened.
2. Applicant must exit vehicle and jump or climb a six-foot barrier.
3. Applicant then completes a one-quarter-mile run or walk, making various turns along the way, to simulate a pursuit run.
4. Applicant must jump a simulated five-foot culvert/ditch.
5. Applicant must drag a "human simulator" (dummy) weighing 155 pounds a distance of 30 feet (to simulate a situation in which an officer is required to pull or carry an injured person to safety).
6. Applicant must draw his or her weapon and fire five rounds with the strong hand and five rounds with the weak hand.

> **Probationary Period** A period of time at the beginning of a police officer's career during which she or he may be fired without cause.

tion from the background check to ensure that the applicant has not been deceptive.

Educational Requirements One of the more dramatic differences between today's police recruits and those of several generations ago is their level of education. In the 1920s, when reformers first began promoting the need for higher education in police officers, few had attended college. Today, 82 percent of all local police departments require at least a high school diploma, and 9 percent require a degree from a two-year college.[6] Recruits with college or university experience are generally thought to have an advantage in hiring and promotion.

Not all police observers believe that education is a necessity for police officers, however. In the words of one police officer, "effective street cops learn their skills on the job, not in a classroom."[7] By emphasizing a college degree, say some, police departments discourage those who would make solid officers but lack the education necessary to apply for positions in law enforcement.

Probationary Period If an applicant successfully navigates the application process, he or she will be hired on a *probationary* basis. During this **probationary period**, which can last from six to eighteen months depending on the department, the recruit is in jeopardy of being dismissed without cause if he or she proves inadequate to the challenges of police work.

THE TRAINING PERIOD

Almost every state requires that police recruits pass through a training period while on probation. During this time, they are taught the basics of police work and are under constant supervision by superiors. The training period usually has two components: the police academy and field training. On average, local police departments require 922 hours of training—613 hours in the classroom and 309 hours in the field.[8]

Academy Training The *police academy*, run by either the state or a police agency, provides recruits with a controlled, militarized environment in which they receive their introduction to the world of the police officer. They are taught the essentials of police work, such as the laws of search, seizure, arrest, and interrogation. Cadets also learn how to secure a crime scene and interview witnesses, along with the basics of first aid and self-defense. Nine in ten police academies also provide terrorism-related training to teach recruits how to respond to terrorist incidents, including those involving weapons of mass destruction.[9] Academy instructors evaluate the recruits' performance and send intermittent progress reports to police administrators. (CAREER TIP: *Police academy instructors are often experienced in a wide variety of law* enforcement areas, from sex crimes to crowd control to traffic investigation. Many continue to work in policing in addition to their instructor duties.)

In the Field Field training takes place outside the confines of the police academy. A recruit is paired with an experienced police officer known as a field training officer (FTO). The goal of field training is to help rookies apply the concepts they have learned in the academy to the streets, with the FTO playing a supervisory role to make sure that nothing goes awry. According to many, the academy introduces recruits to the formal rules of police work, but field training gives the rookies their first taste of the informal rules. In fact, the initial advice to recruits from some FTOs is often along the lines of "O.K., kid. Forget everything you learned in the classroom. You're in the real world now." Nonetheless, the academy is a critical component in the learning process, as it provides rookies with a road map to the job.

¿HOW DO POLICE OFFICERS FIGHT CRIME?

After finishing their training, most new police officers start their careers in a *field service*. Also known as "operations" or "line services," field services include patrol activities, investigations, and special operations. According to Henry M. Wrobleski and Karen M. Hess, most police departments are "generalists." That is, police officers are assigned to general areas and perform all field service functions within the boundaries of their beats. Larger departments may be more specialized, with personnel assigned to specific types of crime, such as illegal drugs or white-collar crime, rather than geographic locations. Smaller departments, which make up the bulk of local law enforcement agencies, rely almost exclusively on general patrol.[10]

POLICE ON PATROL:
THE BACKBONE OF THE DEPARTMENT

One of the great ironies of the police organization is that the people lowest on the hierarchical "stepladder"—the patrol officers—are considered the most valuable members of the force. (Many patrol officers, considering their pay and work hours, would call the situation unjust, not ironic.) Nearly two-thirds of the **sworn officers**—those officers authorized to make arrests and use force—in some large police departments are patrol officers, and every department has a patrol unit.

"Life on the street" is not easy. Patrol officers must be able to handle any number of difficult situations, and experience is often the best and, despite training programs, the only teacher. As one patrol officer commented:

> You never stop learning. You never get your street degree. The person who says . . . they've learned it all is the person that's going to wind up dead or in a very compromising position. They've closed their minds.[11]

It may take a patrol officer years to learn when a gang is "false flagging" (trying to trick rival gang members into the open) or what to look for in a suspect's eyes to sense if he or she is concealing a weapon. This learning process is the backdrop to a number of different general functions that a patrol officer must perform on a daily basis.

A recruit performs pushups under duress at the Cleveland Police Academy. Why are police academies an important part of the learning process for a potential police officer? (MARVIN FONG/The Plain Dealer/Landov)

The Purpose of Patrol In general, patrol officers do not spend most of their shifts chasing, catching, and handcuffing suspected criminals. The vast majority of patrol shifts are completed without a single arrest.[12] Officers spend a great deal of time meeting with other officers, completing paperwork, and patrolling with the goal of preventing crime in general rather than focusing on any specific crime or criminal activity.

 As Samuel Walker has noted, the basic purposes of the police patrol have changed very little since 1829, when the first modern police department was established. These purposes include:

1. The deterrence of crime by maintaining a visible police presence.
2. The maintenance of public order and a sense of security in the community.
3. The twenty-four-hour provision of services that are not crime related.[13]

The first two goals—deterring crime and keeping order—are generally accepted as legitimate police functions. The third, however, has been more controversial.

Community Concerns The extent to which non-crime incidents dominate patrol officers' time is evident in the Police Services Study, a survey of 26,000 calls to police in sixty different neighborhoods. The study found that only one out of every five calls involved the report of criminal activity.[14] There is some debate over whether community services should be allowed to dominate patrol officers' duties. The question, however,

remains: If the police do not handle these problems, who will? Few cities have the financial resources to hire public servants to deal specifically with, for example, finding shelter for homeless persons. Furthermore, the police are the only public servants on call twenty-four hours a day, seven days a week, making them uniquely accessible to citizen needs.

Patrol Activities To recap, the purposes of police patrols are to prevent and deter crime and also to provide social services. How can the police best accomplish these goals? Of course, each department has its own methods and strategies, but William Gay, Theodore Schell, and Stephen Schack are able to divide routine patrol activity into four general categories:

1. *Preventive patrol.* By maintaining a presence in a community, either in a car or on foot, patrol officers attempt to prevent crime from occurring. This strategy, which O. W. Wilson called "omnipresence," was a cornerstone of early policing philosophy and still takes up roughly 40 percent of patrol time.
2. *Calls for service.* Patrol officers spend nearly a quarter of their time responding to 911 calls for emergency service or other citizen problems and complaints.
3. *Administrative duties.* Paperwork takes up nearly 20 percent of patrol time.
4. *Officer-initiated activities.* Incidents in which the patrol officer initiates contact with citizens, such as stopping motorists and pedestrians and questioning them, account for 15 percent of patrol time.[15]

The category estimates made by Gay, Schell, and Schack are not universally accepted. Professor of law enforcement Gary W. Cordner argues that administrative duties account for the largest percentage of patrol officers' time and that when these officers are not consumed with paperwork and meetings, they are either

Why are police officers on patrol so often required to provide services that have little or nothing to do with preventing and fighting crime? (David Turnley/Corbis)

Detective The primary police investigator of crimes.

answering calls for service (which takes up 67 percent of the officers' time on the street) or initiating activities themselves (the remaining 33 percent).[16]

"Noise, Booze, and Violence" Indeed, there are dozens of academic studies that purport to answer the question of how patrol officers spend their days and nights. Perhaps it is only fair, then, to give a police officer the chance to describe the duties patrol officers perform. In the words of Anthony Bouza, a former police chief:

> [Patrol officers] hurry from call to call, bound to their crackling radios, which offer no relief—especially on summer weekend nights. . . . The cops jump from crisis to crisis, rarely having time to do more than tamp one down sufficiently and leave for the next. Gaps of boredom and inactivity fill the interims, although there aren't many of these in the hot months. Periods of boredom get increasingly longer as the nights wear on and the weather gets colder.[17]

Bouza paints a picture of a routine beat as filled with "noise, booze, violence, drugs, illness, blaring TVs, and human misery." This may describe the situation in high-crime neighborhoods, but it certainly does not represent the reality for the majority of patrol officers in the United States. Duties that all patrol officers have in common, whether they work in Bouza's rather nightmarish city streets or in the quieter environment of

"One night . . . it was so slow that **three patrol cars showed up** *for a dispute between two crackheads over a shopping cart."*

—MARCUS LAFFEY, NEW YORK POLICE OFFICER

Yegor Tsyba/iStockphoto.com

rural America, include controlling traffic, conducting preliminary investigations, making arrests, and patrolling public events.

POLICE INVESTIGATIONS

Investigation is the second main function of police, along with patrol. Whereas patrol is primarily preventive, investigation is reactive. After a crime has been committed and the patrol officer has gathered the preliminary information from the crime scene, the responsibility of finding "who dunnit" is delegated to the investigator, generally known as the **detective.**

The most common way for someone to become a detective is to be promoted from patrol officer. Detectives have not been the focus of nearly as much reform attention as their patrol counterparts, mainly because the scope of the detective's job is limited to law enforcement, with less emphasis given to social services or order maintenance.

Detectives in Action The detective's job is not quite as glamorous as it is sometimes portrayed by the media. Detectives spend much of their time investigating common crimes such as burglaries and are more likely to be tracking down stolen property than a murderer. They must also prepare cases for trial, which involves a great deal of time-consuming paperwork. Furthermore, a landmark RAND Corporation study estimated that more than 97 percent of cases that are solved can be attributed to a patrol officer making an arrest at the scene, witnesses or victims identifying the perpetrator, or detectives undertaking routine investigative procedures that could easily be performed by clerical personnel.[18] For example, it was not detective work but an informant's tip that led to the arrest several years ago of two men responsible for twenty-four random attacks—seven of which resulted in death—over a period of nearly fifteen months in the Phoenix, Arizona, area. "There is no Sherlock Holmes," said one investigator. "The good detective on the street is the one who knows all the weasels and one of the weasels will tell him who did it."[19]

Aggressive Investigation Strategies Detective bureaus also have the option of implementing more aggressive strategies. For example, if detectives suspect that a person was involved in the robbery of a Mercedes-Benz parts warehouse, one of them might pose as a "fence"—or purchaser of stolen goods. In what is known as a sting operation, the suspect is deceived into thinking that the detective (fence) wants to buy stolen car parts. Then, after the transaction takes place, the suspect can be arrested.

Perhaps the most dangerous and controversial operation a law enforcement agent can undertake is to go *undercover*, or to assume a false identity in order to obtain information concerning illegal activities. Although each department has its own guidelines on when undercover operations are necessary, all that is generally required is the suspicion that illegal activity is taking place. Today, undercover officers are used to infiltrate large-scale narcotics enterprises or those run by organized crime.

Although dangerous, undercover operations can yield impressive results. In March 2010, "Operation: Safe Campus," which involved undercover Memphis, Tennessee, police officers, led to the arrest of more than three hundred suspects as part of an ongoing effort to cut down on gun crime near city high schools. In some cases, a detective bureau may not want to take the risk of exposing an officer to undercover work or may believe that an outsider cannot infiltrate an organized crime network. When the police need access and information, they have the option of turning to a **confidential informant (CI)**. A CI is a person who is involved in criminal activity and gives information about that activity and those who engage in it to the police.

CLEARANCE RATES AND COLD CASES

The ultimate goal of all law enforcement activity is to *clear* a crime, or secure the arrest and prosecution of the offender. Even a quick glance at **clearance rates,** which show the percentage of reported crimes that have been cleared, reveals that investigations succeed only part of the time. In 2009, just 67 percent of homicides and 42 percent of total violent crimes were solved, while police cleared only 19 percent of property crimes.[20] To a large extent, the different clearance rates for different crimes reflect the resources that a law enforcement agency expends on each type of crime. The police generally investigate a murder or a rape more vigorously than the theft of an automobile or a computer.

Despite the best efforts of detectives and other police officers, the clearance rate for violent crimes has been dropping for decades. In the early 1960s, the clearance rate for homicides was as high as 91 percent.[21]

By posing as a "Muggable Mary," this undercover New York detective is using herself as bait to lure would-be muggers. Why are undercover operations such as this one considered particularly dangerous for the law enforcement agents involved? (Corbis/Bettmann)

Cold Case A criminal investigation that has not been solved after a certain amount of time.

Forensics The application of science to establish facts and evidence during the investigation of crimes.

Trace Evidence Evidence such as a fingerprint, blood, or hair found in small amounts at a crime scene.

According to law enforcement officials, the main reason for this decline is a change in the demographics of murder. Forty years ago, the majority of killers and victims knew each other, and investigations focused on finding clues to this relationship. Today, police are dealing with a large number of impersonal and anonymous drug- and gang-related slayings, and the clues no longer exist. "With the gangs and the drugs," said one expert, "we don't have that ability to establish motive, opportunity, and means."[22]

As a result of low clearance rates, police departments are saddled with an increasing number of **cold cases,** or criminal investigations that are not cleared after a certain amount of time. (The length of time before a case becomes cold varies from department to department. In general, a cold case must be "somewhat old" but not "so old that there can be no hope of ever solving" it.)[23] More than 80 percent of large-city police departments have cold case squads dedicated to unsolved crimes.[24]

FORENSIC INVESTIGATIONS AND DNA

Although the crime scene typically offers a wealth of evidence, some of it is incomprehensible to a patrol officer or detective without assistance. For that aid, law enforcement officers rely on experts in **forensics,** or the practice of using science and technology to investigate crimes. Forensic experts apply their knowledge to items found at the crime scene to determine crucial facts such as:

- The cause of death or injury.
- The time of death or injury.
- The type of weapon or weapons used.
- The identity of the crime victim, if that information is unavailable.
- The identity of the offender (in the best-case scenario).[25]

To assist forensic experts, many police departments operate or are affiliated with crime laboratories. As we noted in the previous chapter, the FBI also offers the services of its crime lab, the largest in the world, to agencies with limited resources.

Crime Scene Forensics The first law enforcement agent to reach a crime scene has the important task of protecting any **trace evidence** from contamination. Trace evidence is generally very small—often invisible to the naked human eye—and thus requires technological aid for detection. Hairs, fibers, blood, fingerprints, broken glass, and footprints are all examples of trace evidence. (CAREER TIP: A *bloodstain pattern analyst* can learn a great deal about a violent

CAREER PREP

FORENSIC SCIENTIST

JOB DESCRIPTION:

- Examine, test, and analyze tissue samples, chemical substances, physical materials, and ballistics evidence collected at a crime scene.
- Testify as an expert witness on evidence or laboratory techniques in criminal trials.

WHAT KIND OF TRAINING IS REQUIRED?

- A bachelor's degree in science, particularly chemistry, biology, biochemistry, or physics.
- Certification programs (usually two years' additional study) can help prospective applicants specialize as forensic consultants, fingerprint technicians, forensic investigators, and laboratory technicians.

ANNUAL SALARY RANGE?

$25,100–$65,000

For additional information, visit: **www.aafs.org.**

Nancy Catherine Walker/iStockphoto.com

CJ and Technology

THE FUTURE OF FINGERPRINTING

Lifting fingerprints can be a tedious process, involving painstaking work with fine powder and small brushes at the crime scene and then further drudgery in the crime lab. Now, however, researchers at Purdue University in Indiana have developed a new technique that may make the process less laborious and more reliable. First, the fingerprint is sprayed with an electrically charged mixture of water and alcohol. Then, the mixture is heated until it evaporates, which transfers the electrical charge to the fingerprint molecules. A device called a mass spectrometer reads the charge and, in seconds, produces a two-dimensional image of the fingerprint. Because the mass spectrometer picks up chemical rather than visual information, it can also discover what the person touched before leaving the print. In tests, researchers have identified traces of marijuana, cocaine, and explosives within the swirls of fingerprints.

THINKING ABOUT THE MASS SPECTROMETER

This technology is too expensive to be of practical use today, but smaller, portable versions of the mass spectrometer fingerprint analyzer will probably be available in several years. What are some other areas, besides testing fingerprints, in which it could be used? For example, how could the device be used for drug testing without a suspect's knowledge?

Ed Vigil/Los Alamos National Laboratory

---

crime by examining where blood landed at the scene, the size and consistency of the drops, and the pattern of the blood spatter.)

Police will also search a crime scene for bullets and spent cartridge casings. These items can provide clues as to how far the shooter was from the target. They can also be compared with information stored in national firearms databases to determine, under some circumstances, the gun used and its most recent owner. The study of firearms and its application to solving crimes goes under the general term **ballistics**.

For more than a century, the most important piece of trace evidence has been the human fingerprint. Because no two fingerprints are alike, they are considered reliable sources of identification. Forensic scientists compare a fingerprint lifted from a crime scene with that of a suspect and declare a match if there are between eight and sixteen "points of similarity." This method of identification is not infallible, however. It is often difficult to lift a suitable print from a crime scene.

Researchers have uncovered numerous cases in which innocent persons were convicted based on evidence obtained through faulty fingerprinting procedures.[26]

The DNA Revolution The technique of **DNA fingerprinting**, or using a suspect's DNA to match the suspect to a crime, emerged in the mid-1990s and has now all but replaced fingerprint evidence in many types of criminal investigations. The shift has been a boon to crime fighters: one law enforcement agent likened DNA fingerprinting to "the finger of God pointing down" at a guilty suspect.[27]

DNA, which is the same in each cell of a person's body, provides a "genetic blueprint" or "code" for every living organism. DNA fingerprinting is useful in criminal investigations because no two people, save for identical

Ballistics The study of firearms, including the firing of the weapon and the flight of the bullet.

DNA Fingerprinting The identification of a person based on a sample of her or his DNA, the genetic material found in the cells of all living things.

twins, have the same genetic code. Therefore, lab technicians can compare the DNA sample of a suspect to the evidence found at the crime scene. If the match is negative, it is certain that the two samples did not come from the same source. If the match is positive, the lab will determine the odds that the DNA sample could have come from someone other than the suspect. Those odds are so high—sometimes reaching 30 billion to one—that a match is practically conclusive.[28]

LO3

The initial use of DNA to establish criminal guilt took place in Britain in 1986. The FBI used it for the first time in the United States two years later. The process begins when forensic technicians gather blood, semen, skin, saliva, or hair from the scene of a crime. Blood cells and sperm are rich in DNA, making them particularly useful in murder and rape cases, but DNA has also been extracted from sweat on dirty laundry, skin cells on eyeglasses, and saliva on used envelope seals. Once a suspect is identified, her or his DNA can determine whether she or he can be placed at the crime scene.

DNA in Action The ability to "dust" for genetic information on such a wide variety of evidence, as well as that evidence's longevity and accuracy, greatly increases the chances that a crime will be solved. Indeed, police no longer need a witness or even a suspect in custody to solve crimes. What they do need is a piece of evidence and a database.

In 2010, for example, Samuel Roshard Cole was convicted of abducting and raping a woman in Petersburg, Virginia, eight years earlier. During most of that time, law enforcement had been unable to identify a suspect in the case. When Cole was arrested for an unrelated charge in 2008, however, he was required to provide authorities with a sample of his DNA. Technicians entered the sample into the state's database, where it matched DNA evidence taken from the earlier rape victim's T-shirt.

The identification of Samuel Cole is an example of what police call a **cold hit**, which occurs when law enforcement finds a suspect "out of nowhere" by comparing DNA evidence from a crime scene against the contents of a database. The largest and most important database is the National Combined DNA Index System (CODIS). Operated by the FBI since 1998, CODIS gives local and state law enforcement agencies access to the DNA profiles of those who have been convicted of various crimes. CODIS contains DNA records of more than 9.6 million people, and as of April 2011, the database had produced almost 143,000 cold hits nationwide.[29]

A technician processes blood from a DNA collection kit at a laboratory in Richmond, California. How does DNA evidence help police solve cold cases in which witnesses are no longer available and no suspect has even been identified? (AP Photo/Noah Berger/Andrey Prokhorov/iStockphoto.com)

¿HOW DO POLICE PREVENT CRIME?

No matter how miraculous DNA fingerprinting may appear, the technology does have its limitations. Forensic evidence, including DNA fingerprinting, is the primary factor in only about 30 percent of solved cold cases.[30] Furthermore, any evidence, forensic or otherwise, can only help police solve a crime that has already taken place. It does little to prevent crime that has yet to occur.

PATROL STRATEGIES

Even though law enforcement officers do not like to think of themselves as being at the beck and call of citizens, that is the operational basis of much police work. All police departments practice **incident-driven policing**, in which calls for service are the primary instigators of action. Between 40 and 60 percent of police activity is the result of 911 calls or other citizen requests, which means that police officers in the field initiate only about half of such activity.[31] (CAREER TIP: Although they are responsible for a crucial aspect of policing, *911 dispatchers* generally are not sworn police officers and do not need any law enforcement experience. Rather, they receive special training in dealing with emergency calls.)

General and Directed Patrol Of course, officers do not sit at the station waiting for incident calls. Earlier in this chapter, we noted that the majority of police officers are assigned to patrol duties. Most of these officers work **general patrol,** making the rounds of a specific area with the purpose of carrying out the various patrol functions. Every police department in the United States patrols its jurisdiction using automobiles. In addition, 55 percent utilize foot patrols, 32 percent bicycle patrols, 16 percent motorcycle patrols, 4 percent boat patrols, and 1 percent horse patrols.[32] (CAREER TIP:

TESTPREP

When you first receive an exam, look it over quickly to make sure that you have all the pages. If you are uncertain, ask your professor or the exam proctor. This initial scan may uncover other problems as well, such as illegible print or unclear instructions.

Mounted police officers are often considered to have the most enjoyable patrol assignments, as they work on horseback. In most mounted divisions, however, officers must complete a grueling training regimen and care for their animals in addition to performing their regular police duties.)

General patrols are *random* because the officers spend a substantial amount of their shifts hoping to notice any crimes that may be occurring. In contrast, **directed patrols** are specifically designed to deal with crimes that commonly occur in certain locations and under circumstances that provide police with opportunity for preparation.

The Pittsburgh (Pennsylvania) Police Department's recent decision to set up weekend traffic checkpoints and send undercover detectives into "nuisance" bars in some of the city's high-violence neighborhoods is a good example of a directed patrol. Like this one, most directed patrols are limited in time and scope because of the strain they place on departmental resources.

"Hot Spots" and Crime Mapping Lawrence W. Sherman, director of the Jerry Lee Center of Criminology at the University of Pennsylvania, believes that evidence of the effectiveness of directed patrol is quite strong.[33] The target areas of directed patrols are often labeled **hot spots** because these areas contain a greater number of criminals and have higher-than-average levels of victimization. Needless to say, police administrators are no longer sticking pins in maps to determine where hot spots exist. Rather, police departments now use geographical information system (GIS) **crime mapping** technology to locate and identify hot spots and "cool" them down.

Incident-Driven Policing A reactive approach to policing that emphasizes a speedy response to calls for service.

General Patrol
A patrol strategy that relies on police officers monitoring a certain area with the goal of detecting crimes in progress or preventing crime due to their presence; also known as *random* or *preventive patrol*.

Directed Patrol
A patrol strategy that is designed to focus on a specific type of criminal activity at a specific time.

Hot Spot
A concentrated area of high criminal activity that draws a directed police response.

Crime Mapping
Technology that allows crime analysts to identify trends and patterns of criminal behavior within any given area.

Computerized crime mapping was popularized when the New York Police Department first launched CompStat in the mid-1990s. Still in use, CompStat starts with police officers reporting the exact location of crime and other crime-related information to department officials. These reports are then fed into a computer, which prepares grids of a particular city or neighborhood and highlights areas with a high incidence of serious offenses. (See **Figure 6.2** below for an example of a GIS crime map.) In New York and many other cities, the police department holds "Crime Control Strategy Meetings" during which precinct commanders are held accountable for CompStat's data-based reports in their districts. In theory, this system provides the police with accurate information about patterns of crime and gives them the ability to "flood" hot spots with officers at short notice. About two-thirds of large departments now employ some form of computerized crime mapping.[34] Wesley Skogan, a criminologist at Northwestern University, believes that CompStat and similar technologies are the most likely cause of recent declines in big-city crime.[35]

ARREST STRATEGIES

Like patrol strategies, arrest strategies can be broken into two categories that reflect the intent of police administrators. **Reactive arrests** are those arrests made by police officers, usually on general patrol, who observe a criminal act or respond to a call for service. **Proactive arrests** occur when the police take the initiative to target a particular type of criminal or behavior. Proactive arrests are

often associated with directed patrols of hot spots, and thus are believed by many experts to have a greater influence on an area's crime rates.[36]

To a certain extent, the popularity of proactive strategies was solidified by a magazine article that James Q. Wilson and George L. Kelling wrote in 1982.[37] In this article, entitled "Broken Windows," Wilson and Kelling argued that policing strategies at the time focused on violent crime to the detriment of the vital police role of promoting the quality of life in neighborhoods. As a result, many communities, particularly in large cities, had fallen into a state of disorder and disrepute, with two very important consequences. First, these neighborhoods—with their broken windows, dilapidated buildings, and lawless behavior by residents—send out signals that criminal activity is tolerated. Second, this disorder spreads fear among law-abiding citizens, discouraging them from leaving their homes or attempting to improve their surroundings.

"Why aren't we thinking more about 'wheredunit' rather than 'whodunit'?"
—LAWRENCE SHERMAN, AMERICAN CRIMINOLOGIST

Figure 6.2   A GIS Crime Map for a Neighborhood in Chicago
This crime map shows the incidence of various crimes during a two-week period in the Hyde Park neighborhood of Chicago.

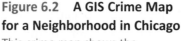

Clear Map.com/Korhan Karacan/iStockphoto.com/iStockphoto.com

Thus, the **broken windows theory** is based on "order maintenance" of neighborhoods by cracking down on "quality-of-life" crimes such as panhandling (begging on the streets), public drinking and urinating, loitering, and graffiti painting. Only by encouraging directed arrest strategies with regard to these quality-of-life crimes, the two professors argued, could American cities be rescued from rising crime rates.

COMMUNITY POLICING

In "Broken Windows," Wilson and Kelling insisted that to reduce fear and crime in high-risk neighborhoods, police had to rely on the cooperation of citizens. Today, a majority of American police departments rely on a broad strategy known as **community policing** to improve relations with citizens and fight crime at the same time. Community policing can be defined as an approach that promotes community-police partnerships, proactive problem solving, and community engagement to address issues such as fear of crime and the causes of such fear in a particular area.[38] Under community policing, patrol officers have much more freedom to improvise. They are expected to develop personal relationships with residents and to encourage those residents to become involved in making the community a safer place.

For example, the Columbia (South Carolina) Police Department has adopted the Japanese *koban* system. A *koban* is a mini-police station where police officers live as well as work. Officers stay rent-free in the upper floor of the building, while the lower floor is a police station/community center. Residents are encouraged to report crimes at the *koban*, which also serves as a work station for social and educational services.

Community policing has been criticized—not least by police officials—as having more to do with public relations than with actual crime fighting. Having law enforcement establish a cooperative presence in the community, however, is a crucial part of a different strategy that does focus on long-term crime prevention.

SOLVING PROBLEMS

Introduced by Herman Goldstein of the Police Executive Research Forum in the 1970s, **problem-oriented policing** is based on the premise that police departments devote too many of their resources to reacting to calls for service and too few to "acting on their own initiative to prevent or reduce community problems."[39] To rectify this situation, problem-oriented policing moves beyond simply responding to incidents and attempts instead to control or even solve the root causes of criminal behavior.

Goldstein's theory encourages police officers to stop looking at their work as a day-to-day proposition. Rather, they should try to shift the patterns of criminal behavior in a positive direction. For example, instead of responding to a 911 call concerning illegal drug use by simply arresting the offender—a short-term response—the patrol officers should also look at the long-term implications of the situation. They should analyze the pattern of similar arrests in the area

A Drug Enforcement Administration special agent adjusts a fifth-grader's helmet at an elementary school in Tucson, Arizona. How can establishing friendly relations with citizens help law enforcement agencies reduce crime?

(James Wood/*Arizona Daily Star*)

and interview the arrestee to determine the reasons, if any, that the site was selected for drug activity.[40] Then additional police action should be taken to prevent further drug sales at the identified location.

¿WHAT ARE THE CHALLENGES OF BEING A POLICE OFFICER?

Each year, the Guardian Civil League, a group of experienced Philadelphia police officers, presents a program to Philadelphia Police Academy cadets entitled "Steer Straight." The purpose of the course is to warn the cadets about the various self-imposed hazards of policing, including domestic violence, improper use of force, alcohol abuse, corruption, and racial insensitivity. In other words, all the things that could get them fired. "It takes one slip to lose everything you've worked so hard for," cautions Inspector Cynthia Dorsey, a veteran officer with the department's internal affairs division.[41]

Philadelphia's Steer Straight program covers many of the on-the-job issues that make law enforcement such a challenging and often difficult career. When faced with

"We have a hard enough time dealing with real crime, let alone somebody's fantasy of it."

—LOS ANGELES PATROL OFFICER, COMPLAINING ABOUT THE DIFFICULTY IN IMPLEMENTING COMMUNITY POLICING PROGRAMS

these issues, sometimes police officers make the right decisions, and sometimes they make the wrong ones. Indeed, it may often be difficult to tell the two apart.

POLICE SUBCULTURE

During a recent Steer Straight presentation, Philadelphia cadets were shown a video, taken by a local news station, showing about a dozen of the city's police officers kicking and punching three suspects at a traffic stop. Eventually, four of the officers were fired and several others demoted. "Don't even think about privacy," a Philadelphia official warned the cadets. "You are going to have to remember that everybody is watching you."[42]

Mistrust of the media and of civilians is one of the hallmarks of **police subculture**, a broad term used to describe the basic assumptions and values that run deep in law enforcement agencies and are taught to new members of a law enforcement agency as the proper way to think, perceive, and act. Every organization has a subculture, with values shaped by the particular aspects and pressures of that organization. In the police subculture, those values are formed in an environment characterized by danger, stress, boredom, and violence.

From the first day on the job, rookies begin the process of **socialization**, in which they are taught the values and rules of police work. This process is aided by a number of rituals that are common to the law enforcement experience. Police theorist Harry J. Mullins believes that the following rituals are critical to the police officer's acceptance, and even embrace, of police subculture:

- Attending a police academy.
- Working with a senior officer, who passes on the "lessons" of police work and life to the younger officer.
- Making the initial felony arrest.
- Using force to make an arrest for the first time.
- Using or witnessing deadly force for the first time.
- Witnessing major traumatic incidents for the first time.[43]

Each of these rituals makes it clear to the police officer that this is not a "normal" job. The only other people who can understand the stresses of police work are fellow officers, and consequently law enforcement officers tend to isolate themselves from civilians. Eventually, this insulation

A fellow officer pays his respects during the 2010 funeral of Chattahoochee Hills, Georgia, police officer Mike Vogt, who was shot and killed while on patrol. Besides physical violence, what are some of the other occupational threats that police officers face on a daily basis? (AP Photo/Brant Sanderlin)

breeds mistrust, and the police officer develops an "us versus them" outlook toward those outside the force. In turn, this outlook creates what sociologist William Westly called the **blue curtain**, also known as the "blue wall of silence" or simply "the code."[44] This curtain separates the police from the civilians they are meant to protect.

THE PHYSICAL AND MENTAL DANGERS OF POLICE WORK

Police officers learn early in their careers that nothing about their job is "routine"—they face the threat of physical harm every day. According to the U.S. Bureau of Labor Statistics, police have one of the ten most dangerous jobs in the United States.[45] In 2010, 162 police officers were killed in the line of duty, and nearly 10,000 were assaulted while working.[46] Surprisingly, the number of officers killed in vehicle crashes has increased by 30 percent over the past three decades, while death by firearms has decreased by 54 percent.[47] Today, almost half of all law enforcement deaths are caused by accidents.[48]

In addition to physical dangers, police work entails considerable mental pressure and stress. Any number of factors can contribute to chronic stress for a police officer, including the rigors of the job, constant fear for personal safety, depressing on-the-job conditions, and inconsistent sleep patterns.[49] Stress, in turn, leads to other problems. After a decade of studying police officer health, researchers at the University of Buffalo have found that the pressures of law enforcement lead to high blood pressure, heart problems, posttraumatic stress disorder (PTSD), and even suicide.[50]

"No one takes into consideration the human being behind the cop."

—COLLEAGUE OF NEW YORK POLICE OFFICER MICHAEL W. PIGOTT, WHO COMMITTED SUICIDE IN 2008 AFTER HAVING ORDERED THE FATAL TASERING OF AN EMOTIONALLY DISTURBED SUSPECT

Thomas Vogel/iStockphoto

AUTHORITY AND THE USE OF FORCE

If the police subculture is shaped by the dangers of the job, it often finds expression through **authority**. The various symbols of authority that decorate a police officer—including the uniform, badge, nightstick, and firearm—establish the power she or he holds over civilians. For better or for worse, both police officers and civilians tend to equate terms such as *authority* and *respect* with the ability to use force.

In general, the use of physical force by law enforcement personnel is very rare, occurring in only about 1.6 percent of some 43.5 million police–public encounters. Still, the Department of Justice estimates that law enforcement officers threaten to use force or use force in encounters with 700,000 Americans a year, and 14.8 percent of those incidents result in an injury.[51] Federal authorities also report that about 650 deaths occur in the process of an arrest on an annual basis.[52]

Without doubt, police officers are often justified in using force to protect themselves and other citizens. As we noted in the previous section, they are the targets of nearly 10,000 assaults each year. At the same time, few observers would be naïve enough to believe that the police are *always* justified in the use of force. A 2009 survey of emergency room physicians found that 98 percent believed that they had treated patients who were victims of excessive police force.[53] How, then, is "misuse" of force to be defined? One attempt to define excessive force that has been lauded by legal scholars, if not necessarily by police officers, was offered by the

Christopher Commission. Established in Los Angeles in 1991 after the beating of African American motorist Rodney King, the commission advised that "an officer may resort to force only where he or she faces a credible threat, and then may only use the minimum amount necessary to control the subject."[54]

The Phoenix Study Terms such as *credible* and *necessary* are quite subjective, of course, rendering the previous definitions of excessive force too vague to be practical. To better understand the subject, the Phoenix (Arizona) Police Department, in partnership with Rutgers University and Arizona State University, conducted a study to measure how often police officers used force. The results showed that police used some form of "physical force"—defined as any "weaponless tactic" (such as kicking or shoving) or the threatened or actual use of any weapon—in 22 percent of the surveyed arrests.[55] The study also examined the predictors of force—that is, the factors that were present in the situations in which force was used. As one might expect, the study found that the best predictor of police use of force was the civilian's use of force.[56] To provide guidance for officers in this tricky area, nearly every law enforcement agency designs a *use of force matrix*. As the example in **Figure 6.3** on the facing page shows, such a model presents officers with the proper force options depending on the escalating nature of contact with a civilian.

Types of Force To comply with the various, and not always consistent, laws concerning the use of force, a police officer must understand that there are two kinds of force: *nondeadly force* and *deadly force*. Most force used by law enforcement is **nondeadly force**. In most states, the use of nondeadly force is regulated by the concept of **reasonable force**, which allows the use of nondeadly force when a reasonable person would assume that such force was necessary. In contrast, **deadly force** is force that an objective police officer realizes will place the subject in direct threat of serious injury or death.

> "The police subculture permits and sometimes demands deception of courts, prosecutors, defense attorneys, and defendants."
>
> —JEROME SKOLNICK, CRIMINOLOGIST

iStockphoto.com

Figure 6.3 The San Diego Police Department's Use-of-Force Matrix

The San Diego Police Department has a mission to "train its officers in the use of the safest, most humane restraint procedures and force options currently known." As part of this mission, the department provides its officers with this use-of-force matrix, which details the appropriate response to various forms of suspect behavior.

RUNG 5

Suspect's Behavior: **Life Threatening**

Officer's Response: Firearms and hard impact with weapons.

RUNG 4

Suspect's Behavior: **Assaultive**

Officer's Response: Hard impact with weapons such as nightsticks and flashlights and personal body weapons such as head, hands, elbows, knees, and feet.

RUNG 3

Suspect's Behavior: **Active Resistance**

Officer's Response: Tasers, neck restraints, takedown techniques, chemical agents such as pepper spray, and K-9.

RUNG 2

Suspect's Behavior: **Passive Resistance**

Officer's Response: Light pushes or jabs with impact weapons such as nightsticks and flashlights, control holds with or without light impact weapons, and body strength.

RUNG 1

Suspect's Behavior: **Compliant**

Officer's Response: Touch and verbal control such as orders, explanations, and requests.

Spectral-Design, 2009. Used under license from Shutterstock.com

Source: San Diego Police Department.

The United States Supreme Court and Use of Force

 The United States Supreme Court set the limits for the use of deadly force by law enforcement officers in *Tennessee v. Garner* (1985).[57] The case involved an incident in which Memphis police officer Elton Hymon shot and killed a suspect who was trying to climb over a fence after stealing ten dollars from a residence. Hymon testified that he had been trained to shoot to keep a suspect from escaping, and indeed Tennessee law at the time allowed police officers to apprehend fleeing suspects in this manner.

In reviewing the case, the Court focused not on Hymon's action but on the Tennessee statute itself, ultimately finding it unconstitutional:

When the suspect poses no immediate threat to the officer and no threat to others, the use of deadly force is unjustified. . . . It is not better that all felony suspects die than that they escape.[58]

The Court's ruling forced twenty-three states to change their fleeing felon rules. It did not, however, completely eliminate police discretion in such situations. Police officers may use deadly force if they have probable cause to believe that the fleeing suspect poses a threat of serious injury or death to the officers or others. (We will discuss the concept of probable cause in the next chapter.) In essence, the Court recognized that police officers must be able to make split-second decisions without worrying about the legal ramifications.

Four years after the *Garner* case, the Court tried to clarify this concept in *Graham v. Connor* (1989), stating that the use of any force should be judged by the "reasonableness of the moment."[59] In 2004, the Court modified this rule by suggesting that an officer's use of force could be "reasonable" even if, by objective measures, the force was not needed to protect the officer or others in the area.[60]

¿HOW IMPORTANT IS ETHICS IN POLICING?

If excessive force is a "strong" misuse of authority by law enforcement, then "soft" misuse of this authority manifests itself in *police corruption*. For general purposes,

Police Corruption The abuse of authority by a law enforcement officer for personal gain.

Ethics The rules or standards of behavior governing a profession; aimed at ensuring the fairness and rightness of actions.

police corruption is the misuse of authority by a law enforcement officer "in a manner designed to produce personal gain." An obvious form of police corruption is *bribery*, in which the police officer accepts money or other forms of payment in exchange for "favors." These services may include allowing a certain criminal activity to continue or misplacing a key piece of evidence before trial. Related to bribery are *payoffs*, in which an officer demands payment from an individual in return for certain services.

More serious corruption occurs when police engage directly in criminal activity, such as narcotics trafficking. This often leads to further misuse of authority, as the offending officers may resort to brutality and lying in court to protect their illicit activities. Sometimes, police corruption occurs to cover up other misconduct. In December 2010, for example, a federal jury found former New Orleans police officer David Warren guilty of fatally shooting a civilian in the aftermath of Hurricane Katrina five years earlier. Two other New Orleans police officers (see photo alongside) were also convicted for helping Warren try to cover up his crime, first by burning a car with the victim's body in it and then by falsifying paperwork relating to the homicide. (CAREER TIP: Within police departments, *internal affairs officers* are charged with investigating corruption, ethics violations, and other misconduct on the force.)

ETHICAL DILEMMAS

Police corruption is intricately connected with the ethics of law enforcement officers. **Ethics** has to do with fundamental questions of the fairness, justice, rightness, or wrongness of any action. Some police actions are obviously unethical, such as the behavior of a Pennsylvania officer who paid a woman he was dating $500 to pretend to be an eyewitness in a murder trial. The majority of ethical dilemmas that a police officer will face are not so clear-cut. Criminologists Joycelyn M. Pollock

and Ronald F. Becker define an ethical dilemma as a situation in which law enforcement officers:

- Do not know the right course of action;
- Have difficulty doing what they consider to be right; and/or
- Find the wrong choice very tempting.[61]

These ethical dilemmas can occur often in police work, and it is how an officer deals with them that determines to what extent he or she is behaving ethically.

ELEMENTS OF ETHICS

Pollock and Becker, both of whom have extensive experience as ethics instructors for police departments, further identify four categories of ethical dilemmas, involving discretion, duty, honesty, and loyalty:[62]

- *Discretion.* The law provides rigid guidelines for how police officers must act and how they cannot act, but it does not offer guidelines for how officers *should* act in many circumstances. As mentioned in Chapter 5, police officers often use discretion to determine how they should act, and ethics plays an important role in guiding discretionary actions.

How do the ethical breaches committed by New Orleans police officers Travis McCabe, left, and Gregory McCrae, undermine public confidence in law enforcement? (AP Photo/ Cheryl Gerber, File) left (AP Photo/Cheryl Gerber, File) right

- *Duty.* The concept of discretion is linked with **duty**, or the obligation to act in a certain manner. Society, by passing laws, can make a police officer's duty clearer and, in the process, help eliminate discretion from the decision-making process. But an officer's duty will not always be obvious, and ethical considerations can often supplement "the rules" of being a law enforcement agent.

- *Honesty.* Of course, honesty is a critical trait for an ethical police officer. A law enforcement agent must make hundreds of decisions in a day, and most of them require him or her to be honest in order to properly do the job.

- *Loyalty.* What should a police officer do if he or she witnesses a partner using excessive force on a suspect? The choice often sets loyalty against ethics, especially if the officer does not approve of the violence.

Although there is no easy "formula" to guide police officers through ethical challenges, experts Linda S. Miller and Karen M. Hess have come up with several questions that can act as personal "checks" for police officers. Miller and Hess suggest that officers, when considering a particular action, ask themselves:

Duty The moral sense of a police officer that she or he should apply authority in a certain manner.

1. Is it legal?
2. Is it fair?
3. How would my family and friends feel about my decision?
4. How does it make me feel about myself?[63]

CAREER PREP

FISH AND WILDLIFE SERVICE OFFICER

JOB DESCRIPTION:

- Protect the integrity of America's natural habitat by policing the millions of acres of public land in this country, including wildlife refuges, fish hatcheries, waterfowl management areas, and wetland districts.

- Investigate wildlife crimes, particularly the illegal hunting, poaching, and sale of federally protected resources such as endangered species, migratory birds, marine mammals, and species of international concern.

WHAT KIND OF TRAINING IS REQUIRED?

- Completion of an eighteen-week basic Land Management Police Training Academy course, a two-week Refuge Officer Basic School course, and a ten-week Field Training and Evaluation Program.

- The U.S. Fish and Wildlife Service offers students summer jobs that provide the experience necessary for a career in this field, with either a federal or a state agency.

ANNUAL SALARY RANGE?

- $27,000–$53,200

For additional information, visit: www.fws.gov/jobs/wwd_law.html.

John and Karen Hollingsworth/US Fish and Wildlife Service

7 POLICE AND THE CONSTITUTION: THE RULES OF LAW ENFORCEMENT

Learning Outcomes

After studying this chapter, you will be able to . . .

 LO1 Outline the four major sources that may provide probable cause.

LO2 Distinguish between a stop and a frisk, and indicate the importance of the case *Terry v. Ohio.*

 LO3 List the four elements that must be present for an arrest to take place.

 LO4 Explain when searches can be made without a warrant.

LO5 Indicate situations in which a *Miranda* warning is unnecessary.

House Call

Jeremy Fisher obviously did not want the police, or anybody else, to bother him. Not only had he locked the back door to his Brownstown, Michigan, home, but he had also shoved a couch up against the front door to block access. Still, Officer Christopher Goolsby and his partner felt a need to look inside. They had just received a call that someone was "going crazy" at Fisher's residence, and when they arrived at the home they found "considerable chaos." The wreckage included a smashed pickup truck in the driveway, a damaged fence post on the side lawn, three broken house windows, and blood on the hood of a pickup truck and on one of the doors of the house.

The officers knocked on the front door, but Fisher refused to answer. They could hear him screaming, however, and they caught sight of him bleeding from a cut on his hand. Goolsby yelled to Fisher, asking if he needed medical attention. The wounded man responded with a profanity. The officer then pushed the front door partway open and entered the home. The first thing he saw was Fisher pointing a rifle at him. Goolsby quickly retreated and called for backup. Fisher was eventually arrested and charged under Michigan law with assault with a dangerous weapon and possession of a firearm during the commission of a felony.

During his trial, Fisher argued that Goolsby had had no right to enter his house, and therefore any evidence gathered during this entry could not be used against him. Several years ago, the case reached the United States Supreme Court, which rejected Fisher's claims and sided with Goolsby. According to the Supreme Court, requiring police officers to "walk away" from a situation such as the one they encountered at Fisher's house would not "meet the needs of law enforcement or the demands of public safety."

Why does the United States Supreme Court sometimes allow law enforcement officers to enter a private home without the consent of the person living there? (Michael Matthews—Police Images/Alamy)

AP Photo/David Kohl

Searches and Seizures The legal term that generally refers to the searching for and the confiscating (taking) of evidence by law enforcement agents.

Probable Cause Reasonable grounds to believe the existence of facts warranting certain actions, such as the search or arrest of a person.

Reasonable In the context of criminal law, an action by a law enforcement agent that is appropriate under the circumstances.

Jeremy Fisher's argument that the police officers overstepped the boundaries of their authority was not a fanciful one. The "right of a man to retreat to his own home" is one the cornerstones of the U.S. Constitution.[1] In most cases, law enforcement agents cannot enter any sort of dwelling without written permission from a judge called a *warrant*, which you will learn about later in the chapter. There are several exceptions to this warrant requirement, however, including "the need to assist persons who are seriously injured or threatened with such injury."[2] Given the circumstances in *Michigan v. Fisher*, the Supreme Court found that the police officers were reasonable in their belief that Fisher could have posed a threat to himself or someone else in the house.[3]

In Chapter 5, we discussed the importance of discretion in the criminal justice system. Certainly, as in this case, police officers have a great deal of discretion to make the decisions they feel are necessary to protect themselves and the public. This discretion is not absolute, however. For the most part, a law enforcement agent's actions are determined by the rules for policing set down in the U.S. Constitution and enforced by the courts. In this chapter we will examine the extent to which police behavior is controlled by the law, starting with a discussion of the constitutional principles on which such control is grounded.

¿HOW DOES THE CONSTITUTION LIMIT POLICE BEHAVIOR?

In *Michigan v. Fisher*, the Supreme Court did not address whether Jeremy Fisher was guilty or innocent of the weapons charges against him. That was for a trial court to decide. Rather, the Court ruled that Officer Christopher Goolsby had not overstepped the boundaries of his authority in entering and "searching" Fisher's house. To understand these boundaries, law enforcement officers must understand the Fourth Amendment, which reads as follows:

> The right of the people to be secure in their persons, houses, papers, and effects, against unreasonable searches and seizures, shall not be violated, and no Warrants shall issue, but upon probable cause, supported by Oath or affirmation, and particularly describing the place to be searched, and the persons or things to be seized.

This amendment contains two critical legal concepts: a prohibition against *unreasonable* **searches and seizures** and the requirement of **probable cause** to issue a warrant (see **Figure 7.1** on the facing page).

REASONABLENESS

Law enforcement personnel use searches and seizures to look for and collect the evidence needed to convict individuals suspected of crimes. As you have just read, when police are conducting a search or seizure, they must be *reasonable*. Though courts have spent innumerable hours scrutinizing the word, no specific meaning for **reasonable** exists. A thesaurus can provide useful synonyms—*logical, practical, sensible, intelligent, plausible*—but because each case is different, those terms are relative.

In the *Fisher* case, the Supreme Court rejected the argument that the search had been so unreasonable as to violate the Fourth Amendment's prohibition against unreasonable searches and seizures. That does not mean that the police officers' actions would have been reasonable under any circumstances. What if there had been no evidence of carnage at Jeremy Fisher's home and he had, in fact, been quietly watching television when the police officers arrived? In this situation, Officer Goolsby's conduct would almost certainly have been considered unreasonable, as American courts go to great lengths to protect against overzealous searches of homes. The Supreme Court has even ruled that homicide detectives cannot enter a house without a warrant when it contains a dead body, if no emergency requires them to do so.[4]

PROBABLE CAUSE

The concept of reasonableness is linked to probable cause. The Supreme Court has ruled, for example, that any arrest or seizure is unreasonable unless it is supported by probable cause.[5] The burden of probable cause requires more than mere suspicion on a police officer's part. That officer must know of facts and circumstances that would reasonably lead to "the belief that an offense has been or is being committed."[6]

Sources of Probable Cause If no probable cause existed when a police officer took a certain action, that justification cannot be retroactively applied. If, for example, a police officer stops a person for jaywalking and then (without the help of a drug-sniffing dog) finds several ounces of marijuana in that person's pocket, the arrest for marijuana possession would probably be disallowed. Remember, suspicion does not equal probable cause. If, however, an informant had tipped the officer off that the person was a drug dealer, probable cause might exist and the arrest could be valid. Informants are one of several sources that may provide probable cause. Others include:

1. *Personal observation.* Police officers may use their personal training, experience, and expertise to infer probable cause from situations that may not be obviously criminal. If, for example, a police officer observes several people in a car slowly circling a certain building in a high-crime area, that officer may infer that the people are "casing" the building in preparation for a burglary. Probable cause could be established for detaining the suspects.

2. *Information.* Law enforcement officers receive information from victims, eyewitnesses, informants, and official sources such as police bulletins or broadcasts. Such information, as long as it is believed to be reliable, is a basis for probable cause.

3. *Evidence.* In certain circumstances, which will be examined later in this chapter, police have probable cause for a search or seizure based on evidence—such as a shotgun—in plain view.

4. *Association.* In some circumstances, if the police see a person with a known criminal background in a place where criminal activity is openly taking place, they have probable cause to stop that person. Generally, however, association is not adequate to establish probable cause.[7]

Figure 7.1 The Meaning of Reasonable Searches and Seizures and Probable Cause

AP Photo/Noah Berger

For a law enforcement officer to **reasonably** search a suspect or his or her premises (including an automobile) and **seize** any evidence found during that search, the law enforcement officer must first

- **Establish that probable cause exists that the suspect committed a crime, and**
- **Produce a document called a warrant from a judge stating that such probable cause exists.**

Probable cause exists if there is a **substantial likelihood** that

- **A crime was committed** and
- **The suspect committed that crime.**

Note that

- **Probable cause involves a likelihood—not just a probability—that the suspect committed the crime, and**
- **Law enforcement officers can conduct searches and seizures without a warrant from a judge under certain circumstances,** described later in the chapter.

The Probable Cause Framework

In a sense, the concept of probable cause allows police officers to do their job effectively. Most arrests are made without a warrant, because most arrests are the result of quick police reaction to the commission of a crime. Indeed, it would not be practical to expect a police officer to obtain a warrant before making an arrest on the street. Thus, probable cause provides a framework that limits the situations in which police officers can make arrests, but it also gives officers the freedom to act within that framework. In 2003, the Supreme Court reaffirmed this freedom by ruling that Baltimore (Maryland) police officers acted properly when they arrested all three passengers of a car in which cocaine had been hidden in the back seat. "A reasonable officer," wrote Chief Justice William H. Rehnquist, "could conclude that there was probable cause to believe" that the defendant, who had been sitting in the front seat, was in "possession" of the illicit drug despite his protests to the contrary.[8]

Once an arrest is made, the arresting officer must prove to a judge that probable cause existed. In *County of Riverside v. McLaughlin* (1991),[9] the Supreme Court ruled that this judicial determination of probable cause must be made within forty-eight hours after the arrest, even if this two-day period includes a weekend or holiday. (CAREER TIP: Once a suspect is arrested, he or she is subject to standard booking procedure, which includes providing personal information, being photographed, and being fingerprinted. This process is overseen by a *booking technician*, who may or may not be a sworn officer.)

THE EXCLUSIONARY RULE

Historically, the courts have looked to the Fourth Amendment for guidance in regulating the activity

How does the concept of probable cause limit a police officer's ability to make an arrest? How does it allow the same police officer to do his or her job effectively? (Kim Kulish/Corbis/iStockphoto.com)

of law enforcement officers, as the language of the Constitution does not expressly do so. The courts' most potent legal tool in this endeavor is the **exclusionary rule,** which prohibits the use of illegally seized evidence. According to this rule, any evidence obtained by an unreasonable search or seizure is inadmissible (may not be used) against a defendant in a criminal trial.[10] Even highly incriminating evidence, such as a knife stained with the victim's blood, usually cannot be introduced at a trial if illegally obtained. Furthermore, any physical or verbal evidence that police are able to acquire by using illegally obtained evidence is known as the **fruit of the poisoned tree** and is also inadmissible. For example, if the police use the existence of the bloodstained knife to get a confession out of a suspect, that confession will be excluded as well.

One of the hoped-for consequences of the exclusionary rule is that it forces police to gather evidence properly. If they follow appropriate procedures, they

Theo Hawkins/iStockphoto.com

are more likely to be rewarded with a conviction. If they are careless or abuse the rights of the suspect, they are unlikely to get a conviction. Critics of the exclusionary rule, however, argue that its strict application may permit guilty people to go free because of police carelessness or innocent errors.

¿WHEN CAN POLICE STOP AND FRISK CITIZENS?

On April 23, 2010, Arizona governor Jan Brewer signed one of the nation's toughest immigration laws. Known as S.B. 1070, the new law requires a state law enforcement officer to check the immigration status of any person detained if the officer has "reasonable suspicion" to believe that person is in the country illegally.[11] Controversy surrounding the law has focused on exactly what factors would trigger a police officer's reasonable suspicion of a person's illegal immigration status. Latino groups and lawmakers, in particular, worry that police will target Arizona residents who look Hispanic or have Hispanic surnames. This tactic is called **racial profiling** because the police action is based on the race, nationality, or national origin of the suspect rather than on evidence or information that the suspect has broken the law.

Supporters of S.B. 1070 point out that the statute specifically forbids racial profiling and only applies after police have legally stopped a suspect for a different reason. Regardless, Georgetown University law professor David Cole believes that such profiling is "inevitable" under the new Arizona law. "People don't wear signs saying that they are illegal immigrants," Cole points out. "So police officers will not stop white people, and [they] will stop Latinos, especially poor Latinos."[12]

No fewer than seven lawsuits have been filed challenging S.B. 1070, and the law's fate may rest on the courts' view of its reasonable suspicion provision. When such reasonable suspicion does exist, police officers are well within their rights to *stop and frisk* a suspect. In a stop and frisk, law enforcement officers (1) briefly detain a person they reasonably believe to be suspicious and (2) if they believe the person to be armed, proceed to pat down, or "frisk," that person's outer clothing.[13]

Racial Profiling The practice of targeting people for police action based solely on their race, ethnicity, or national origin.

THE ELUSIVE DEFINITION OF REASONABLE SUSPICION

Like so many elements of police work, the decision of whether to stop a suspect is based on the balancing of conflicting priorities. On the one hand, a police officer feels a sense of urgency to act when he or she believes that criminal activity is occurring or is about to occur. On the other hand, law enforcement agents do not want to harass innocent individuals, especially if doing so runs afoul of the U.S. Constitution. In stop-and-frisk law, this balancing act rests on the focal point of reasonable suspicion.

Terry v. Ohio The precedent for the ever-elusive definition of a "reasonable" suspicion in stop-and-frisk situations was established by the Supreme Court in *Terry v. Ohio* (1968).[14] In that case, a detective named McFadden observed two men (one of whom was Terry) acting strangely in downtown Cleveland. The men would walk past a certain store, peer into the window, and then stop at a street corner and confer. While they were talking, another man joined the conversation and then left quickly. Several minutes later the three men met again at another corner a few blocks away. Detective McFadden believed the trio was planning to break into the store. He approached them, told them who he was, and asked for identification. After receiving a mumbled response, the detective frisked the three men and found handguns on two of them, who were tried and convicted of carrying concealed weapons.

The Supreme Court upheld the conviction, ruling that Detective McFadden had reasonable cause to believe that the men were armed and dangerous and that swift action was necessary to protect himself and other citizens in the area.[15] The Court accepted McFadden's interpretation of the unfolding scene as based on objective facts and practical conclusions. It therefore concluded that his suspicion was reasonable. In contrast, critics of Arizona's S.B. 1070, described earlier, believe that the law requires state police officers to stop citizens for reasons—their skin color or

Stop A brief detention of a person by law enforcement agents for questioning.

general appearance—that are not reasonable.

The "Totality of the Circumstances"

Test For the most part, the judicial system has refrained from placing restrictions on police officers' ability to make stops. In the *Terry* case mentioned earlier, the Supreme Court did say that an officer must have "specific and articulable [able to be stated] facts" to support the decision to make a stop, but added that the facts may be "taken together with rational inferences."[16] The Court has consistently ruled that because of their practical experience, law enforcement agents are in a unique position to make such inferences and should be given a good deal of freedom in doing so.

In the years since the *Terry* case was decided, the Court has settled on a "totality of the circumstances"

test to determine whether a stop is based on reasonable suspicion.[17] In 2002, for example, the Court ruled that a U.S. Border Patrol agent's stop of a minivan in Arizona was reasonable.[18] On being approached by the Border Patrol car, the driver had stiffened, slowed down his van, and avoided making eye contact with the agent. Furthermore, the children in the van waved at the officer in a mechanical manner, as if ordered to do so. The agent pulled over the van and found 128 pounds of marijuana. In his opinion, Chief Justice William Rehnquist pointed out that such conduct might have been unremarkable on a busy city highway, but on an unpaved road thirty miles from the Mexican border it was enough to reasonably arouse the agent's suspicion.[19] The justices also made clear that the need to prevent terrorist attacks is part of the "totality of the circumstances" and, therefore, law enforcement agents will have more leeway to make stops near U.S. borders.

A STOP

The terms *stop* and *frisk* are often used in concert, but they describe two separate acts. A **stop** takes place when a law enforcement officer has reasonable suspicion that a criminal activity is about to take place. Because an investigatory stop is not an arrest, there are limits to the extent police can detain someone who has been stopped. For example, in one situation an airline traveler and his luggage were detained for ninety minutes while the police waited for a drug-sniffing dog to arrive. The Supreme Court ruled that the initial stop of the passenger was constitutional, but that the ninety-minute wait was excessive.[20]

In 2004, the Court held that police officers could require suspects to identify themselves during a stop that is otherwise valid under the *Terry* ruling.[21] The case involved a Nevada rancher who was fined $250 for refusing to give his name to a police officer investigating a possible assault. The defendant argued that such requests force citizens to incriminate themselves against their will, which is prohibited by the Fifth Amendment, as we shall see later in the chapter. Justice Anthony Kennedy wrote, however, that "asking questions is an essential part of police investigations" that would be made much more difficult if officers could not determine the identity of a suspect.[22] The ruling

Frisk A pat-down or minimal search by police to discover weapons.

Arrest The taking into custody of a person suspected of criminal activity.

validated "stop-and-identify" laws in twenty states and numerous cities and towns.

A FRISK

The Supreme Court has stated that a **frisk** (a pat-down or other minimal search) should be a protective measure. Police officers cannot conduct a frisk as a "fishing expedition" simply to try to find items besides weapons, such as illegal narcotics, on a suspect.[23] A frisk does not necessarily follow a stop. In fact, it may occur only when the officer is justified in thinking that the safety of police officers or other citizens may be endangered.

Again, the question of reasonable suspicion is at the heart of determining the legality of frisks. In the *Terry* case (on page 123), the Court accepted that Detective McFadden reasonably believed that the three suspects posed a threat. The suspects' refusal to answer McFadden's questions, though within their rights because they had not been arrested, provided him with sufficient motive for the frisk. In 2009, the Court extended the "stop and frisk" authority by ruling that a police officer could order a passenger in a car that had been pulled over for a traffic violation to submit to a pat-down.[24] To do so, the officer must have a reasonable suspicion that the suspect may be armed and dangerous.

¿WHAT IS REQUIRED TO MAKE AN ARREST?

As in the *Terry* case, a stop and frisk may lead to an **arrest**. An arrest is the taking into custody of a citizen for the purpose of detaining him or her on a criminal charge. It is important to understand the difference between a stop and an arrest. In the eyes of the law, a stop is a relatively brief intrusion on a citizen's rights, whereas an arrest—which involves a deprivation of liberty—is deserving of a full range of constitutional protections, which we shall discuss throughout the chapter. (See **Figure 7.2** on the next page for a more detailed description of the differences between stops and arrests.) Consequently, while a stop can be made based on reasonable suspicion, a law enforcement officer needs probable cause, as defined earlier, to make an arrest.[25]

ELEMENTS OF AN ARREST

When is somebody under arrest? The easy—and incorrect—answer would be whenever the police officer says so. In fact, the state of being under arrest is dependent not only on the actions of the law enforcement officers but also on the perception of the suspect. Suppose Mr. Jones is stopped by plainclothes detectives, driven to the police station, and detained for three hours for questioning. During this time, the police never tell Mr. Jones he is under arrest, and in fact, he is free to leave at any time. But if Mr. Jones or any other reasonable person *believes* he is not free to leave, then, according to the Supreme Court, that person is in fact under arrest and should receive the necessary constitutional protections.[26]

Criminal justice professor Rolando V. del Carmen of Sam Houston State University has identified four elements that must be present for an arrest to take place:

Figure 7.2   The Differences between a Stop and an Arrest

Both stops and arrests are considered seizures because both police actions involve the restriction of an individual's freedom to "walk away." Both must be justified by a showing of reasonableness as well. You should be aware, however, of the differences between a stop and an arrest.

During a stop, police can interrogate the person and make a limited search of his or her outer clothing. If anything occurs during the stop, such as the discovery of an illegal weapon, then officers may arrest the person. **If an arrest is made,** the suspect is now in police custody and is protected by the U.S. Constitution in a number of ways that will be discussed later in the chapter.

	STOP	ARREST
Justification	Reasonable suspicion only	Probable cause
Warrant	None	Required in some, but not all, situations
Intent of Officer	To investigate suspicious activity	To make a formal charge against the suspect
Search	May frisk or "pat down" for weapons	May conduct a full search for weapons or evidence
Scope of Search	Outer clothing only	Area within the suspect's immediate control or "reach"

1. The *intent* to arrest. In a stop, though it may entail slight inconvenience and a short detention period, there is no intent on the part of the law enforcement officer to take the person into custody. Therefore, there is no arrest. As *intent* is a subjective term, it is sometimes difficult to determine whether the police officer intended to arrest. In situations when the intent is unclear, courts often rely—as in our hypothetical case of Mr. Jones—on the perception of the person arrested.[27]

2. The *authority* to arrest. State laws give police officers the authority to place citizens under custodial arrest, or take them into custody. Like other state laws, the authorization to arrest varies among the fifty states. Some states, for example, allow off-duty police officers to make arrests, while others do not.

3. *Seizure or detention.* A necessary part of an arrest is the detention of the subject. Detention is considered to have occurred as soon as the arrested individual submits to the control of the officer, whether peacefully or under the threat or use of force.

4. The *understanding* of the person that she or he has been arrested. Through either words—such as "you are now under arrest"—or actions, the person taken into custody must understand that an arrest has taken place. If a subject has been forcibly subdued by the police, handcuffed, and placed in a patrol car, that subject is believed to understand that an arrest has been made. This understanding may be lacking if the person is intoxicated, insane, or unconscious.[28]

ARRESTS WITH A WARRANT

When law enforcement officers have established probable cause to arrest an individual who is not in police custody, they obtain an **arrest warrant** for that person. An arrest warrant contains information such as the name of the person suspected and any crimes he or she is suspected of having committed. Judges or magistrates issue arrest warrants after first determining that the law enforcement officers have indeed established probable cause.

Entering a Dwelling There is a perception that an arrest warrant gives law enforcement officers the authority to enter a dwelling without first announcing themselves. This is not accurate. In *Wilson v. Arkansas* (1995),[29] the Supreme Court restated the requirement that police officers must knock and announce their identity and purpose before entering a dwelling. Under certain conditions, known as **exigent circumstances,**

law enforcement officers need not announce themselves. These circumstances include situations in which the officers have a reasonable belief of any of the following:

- The suspect is armed and poses a strong threat of violence to the officers or others inside the dwelling.
- Persons inside the dwelling are in the process of destroying evidence or escaping because of the presence of the police.
- A felony is being committed at the time the officers enter.[30]

The Waiting Period The Supreme Court severely weakened the practical impact of the "knock and announce" rule with its decision in *Hudson v. Michigan* (2006).[31] In that case, Detroit police did not knock before entering the defendant's home with a warrant. Instead, they announced themselves and then waited only three to five seconds before making their entrance, not the fifteen to twenty seconds suggested by a prior Court ruling.[32] Hudson argued that the drugs found during the subsequent search were inadmissible because the law enforcement agents did not follow proper procedure. By a 5–4 margin, the Court disagreed. In his majority opinion, Justice Antonin Scalia stated that an improper "knock and announce" is not unreasonable enough to provide defendants with a "get-out-of-jail-free card" by disqualifying evidence uncovered on the basis of a valid search warrant.[33] Thus, the exclusionary rule, discussed earlier in this chapter, would no longer apply under such circumstances. Legal experts still advise, however, that police observe a reasonable waiting period after knocking and announcing to be certain that any evidence found during the subsequent search will be admitted during trial.[34]

ARRESTS WITHOUT A WARRANT

Arrest warrants are not always required, and in fact, most arrests are made on the scene without a warrant.[35] A law enforcement officer may make a **warrantless arrest** if:

1. The offense is committed in the presence of the officer, or

Warrantless Arrest An arrest made without first seeking a warrant for the action.

2. The officer has knowledge that a crime has been committed and probable cause to believe the crime was committed by a particular suspect.[36]

The type of crime also comes to bear in questions of arrests without a warrant. As a general rule, officers can make a warrantless arrest for a crime they did not see if they have probable cause to believe that a felony has been committed. For misdemeanors, the crime must have been committed in the presence of the officer for a warrantless arrest to be valid. In 2001, the Supreme Court examined a case involving a Texas mother who was handcuffed, taken away from her two young children, and placed in jail for failing to wear her seat belt. The Court ruled that even an arrest for a misdemeanor that involves "gratuitous humiliations" imposed by a police officer "exercising extremely poor judgment" is valid as long as the officer can satisfy probable cause requirements.[37]

¿WHAT ARE THE RULES FOR SEARCHES AND SEIZURES?

How far can law enforcement agents go in searching and seizing private property? Consider the steps taken by Jenny Stracner, an investigator with the Laguna Beach (California) Police Department. After receiving information that a suspect, Greenwood, was engaged in drug trafficking, Stracner enlisted the aid of the local trash collector in procuring evidence. Instead of taking Greenwood's trash bags to be incinerated, the collector agreed to give them to Stracner. The officer found enough drug paraphernalia in the garbage to obtain a warrant to search Greenwood's home. Subsequently, he was arrested and convicted on narcotics charges.[38]

Remember, the Fourth Amendment is quite specific in forbidding unreasonable searches and seizures. Were Stracner's search of Greenwood's garbage and her seizure of its contents "reasonable"? The U.S. Supreme Court thought so, holding that Greenwood's garbage was not protected by the Fourth Amendment.[39]

THE ROLE OF PRIVACY IN SEARCHES

A crucial concept in understanding search and seizure law is *privacy*. By definition, a **search** is a governmental intrusion on a citizen's reasonable expectation of privacy. The recognized standard for a "reasonable expectation of privacy" was established in *Katz v. United States* (1967).[40] The case dealt with the question of whether the defendant was justified in his expectation of privacy in the calls he made from a public phone booth. The Supreme Court held that "the Fourth Amendment protects people, not places," and Katz prevailed.

STUDY PREP

When you are given a writing assignment, make sure you allow yourself enough time to revise and polish your final draft. Good writing takes time—you may need to revise a paper several times before you are satisfied with its quality.

In his concurring opinion, Justice John Harlan, Jr., set a two-pronged test for a person's expectation of privacy:

1. The individual must prove that she or he expected privacy, and
2. Society must recognize that expectation as reasonable.[41]

Accordingly, the Court agreed with Katz's claim that he had a reasonable right to privacy in a public phone booth. (Remember, however, that the *Terry* case allows for conditions under which a person's privacy rights are superseded by a reasonable suspicion on the part of a law enforcement officer that a threat to public safety is present.)

In contrast, in *California v. Greenwood* (1988),[42] described earlier, the Court did not believe that the suspect had a reasonable expectation of privacy when it came to his garbage bags. The Court noted that when we place our trash on a curb, we expose it to any number of intrusions by "animals, children, scavengers, snoops, and other members of the public."[43] In other words, if Greenwood had truly intended for the contents of his garbage bags to remain private, he would not have left them on the side of the road. To give another example, the Court also upheld the search in a case in which a drug-sniffing dog was used to detect marijuana in the trunk of a car after the driver was stopped for speeding. The Court ruled that no one has a legitimate privacy interest in possessing illegal drugs or other contraband such as explosives in the trunk of his or her car.[44]

SEARCH AND SEIZURE WARRANTS

To protect against charges that they have unreasonably infringed on privacy rights during a search, law enforcement officers can obtain a **search warrant**. (See **Figure 7.3** on the facing page for an example of a search warrant.) Similar to an arrest warrant, a search warrant is a court order that authorizes police to search a certain area. Before a judge or magistrate will issue a search warrant, law enforcement officers must provide the following:

- Information showing probable cause that a crime has been or will be committed.
- Specific information on the premises to be searched, the suspects to be found and the illegal

Figure 7.3 Example of a Search Warrant

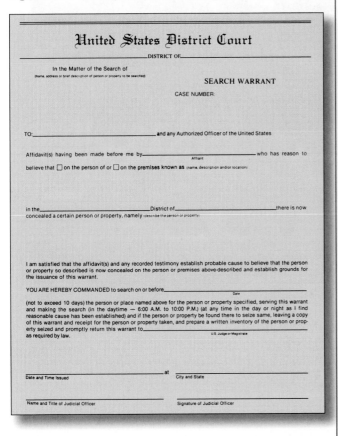

United States District Court

DISTRICT OF

In the Matter of the Search of
(Name, address or brief description of person or property to be searched)

SEARCH WARRANT

CASE NUMBER:

TO:_____ and any Authorized Officer of the United States

Affidavit(s) having been made before me by_____ who has reason to
                                                      Affiant
believe that ☐ on the person of or ☐ on the premises known as (name, description and/or location)

in the_____District of_____there is now
concealed a certain person or property, namely (describe the person or property)

I am satisfied that the affidavit(s) and any recorded testimony establish probable cause to believe that the person
or property so described is now concealed on the person or premises above-described and establish grounds for
the issuance of this warrant.

YOU ARE HEREBY COMMANDED to search on or before_____
                                                                       Date
(not to exceed 10 days) the person or place named above for the person or property specified, serving this warrant
and making the search (in the daytime — 6:00 A.M. to 10:00 P.M.) (at any time in the day or night as I find
reasonable cause has been established) and if the person or property be found there to seize same, leaving a copy
of this warrant and receipt for the person or property taken, and prepare a written inventory of the person or property seized and promptly return this warrant to_____
                                                                   U.S. Judge or Magistrate
as required by law.

Date and Time Issued   at   City and State

Name and Title of Judicial Officer   Signature of Judicial Officer

activities taking place at those premises, and the items to be seized.

The purpose of a search warrant is to establish, before the search takes place, that a *probable cause to search* justifies infringing on the suspect's reasonable expectation of privacy.

Particularity of Search Warrants

The members of the First Congress specifically did not want law enforcement officers to have the freedom to make "general, exploratory" searches through a person's belongings.[45] Consequently, the Fourth Amendment requires that a warrant describe with "particularity" the place to be searched and the things—either people or objects—to be seized.

This particularity requirement places a heavy burden on law enforcement officers. Before going to a judge to ask for a search warrant, they must prepare an **affidavit** in which they provide specific, written information on the property that they wish to search and seize. They must know the specific address of any place they wish to search; general addresses of apartment buildings or office complexes are not sufficient. Furthermore, courts generally frown on vague descriptions of goods to be seized.

"Stolen goods" would most likely be considered unacceptably imprecise; "one MacBook Pro laptop computer" would be preferred.

A **seizure** is the act of taking possession of a person or property by the government because of a (suspected) violation of the law. In general, four categories of items can be seized by use of a search warrant:

1. Items resulting from the crime, such as stolen goods.
2. Items that are inherently illegal for anybody to possess (with certain exceptions), such as narcotics and counterfeit currency.
3. Items that can be called "evidence" of the crime, such as a bloodstained sneaker or a ski mask.
4. Items used in committing the crime, such as an ice pick or a printing press used to make counterfeit bills.[46]

Affidavit A written statement of facts, confirmed by the oath or affirmation of the party making it.

Seizure The forcible taking of a person or property in response to a violation of the law.

Reasonableness during a Search and Seizure

No matter how particular a warrant is, it cannot provide

CAREER TIP: Law enforcement dogs provide invaluable services—detecting bombs, mines, illegal narcotics, and even cell phones in jails and prisons. These animals are prepared for their law enforcement duties by *K-9 (canine) trainers*.

Jan Tyler/iStockphoto.com

Search Incidental to an Arrest Searches for weapons and evidence of persons who have just been arrested.

Michigan state and federal law enforcement officers take part in a predawn raid of a Detroit residence. Why is a search warrant generally required before such a drastic action can be taken? (AP Photo/Charles V. Tines/*Detroit News*/iStockphoto.com)

for all the conditions that are bound to come up during its service. Consequently, the law gives law enforcement officers the ability to act "reasonably" during a search and seizure in the event of unforeseeable circumstances. For example, if a police officer is searching an apartment for a stolen MacBook Pro laptop computer and notices a vial of crack cocaine sitting on the suspect's bed, that contraband is considered to be in "plain view" and can be seized. (See *You Be the Judge—A Valid Search?* on the facing page.)

Note that if law enforcement officers have a search warrant that authorizes them to search for a stolen laptop computer, they would *not* be justified in opening small drawers. Because a computer could not fit in a small drawer, an officer would not have a basis for reasonably searching one. Hence, officers are restricted in terms of where they can look by the items for which they are searching.

SEARCHES AND SEIZURES WITHOUT A WARRANT

Although the Supreme Court has established the principle that searches conducted without warrants are *per se* (by definition) unreasonable, it has set "specifically established" exceptions to the rule.[47] In fact, most searches, like most arrests, take place in the absence of a judicial order. Warrantless searches and seizures can be lawful when police are in "hot pursuit" of a subject or when they search bags of trash left at the curb for regular collection. Because of the magnitude of smuggling activities in border areas such as airports, seaports, and international boundaries, a warrant normally is not needed to search property in those places.

Furthermore, in 2006 the Court held unanimously **LO 4** that police officers do not need a warrant to enter a private home in an emergency, such as when they reasonably fear for the safety of the inhabitants.[48] The two most important circumstances in which a warrant is not needed, though, are (1) searches incidental to an arrest and (2) consent searches.

Searches Incidental to an Arrest The most frequent exception to the warrant requirement involves **searches incidental to arrests**, so called because nearly every time police officers make an arrest, they also search the suspect. As long as the original arrest was based on probable cause, these searches are valid for two reasons, established by the Supreme Court in *United States v. Robinson* (1973):

1. The need for a police officer to find and confiscate any weapons a suspect may be carrying.
2. The need to protect any evidence on the suspect's person from being destroyed.[49]

Law enforcement officers, however, are limited in the searches they may make during an arrest. These limits were established by the Supreme Court in *Chimel v. California* (1969).[50] In that case, police arrived at Chimel's home with an arrest warrant but not a search warrant. Even though Chimel refused their request to "look around," the officers searched the entire three-bedroom house for nearly an hour, finding stolen coins in the process. Chimel was convicted of burglary and appealed, arguing that the evidence of the coins should have been suppressed. (CAREER TIP: Law enforcement agents who concentrate on recovering stolen fine art and other collectibles such as rare coins are known as *art intelligence officers*.)

The Supreme Court held that the search was unreasonable. In doing so, the Court established guidelines as to the acceptable extent of searches incidental to an arrest. Primarily, the Court ruled that police may search any area within the suspect's "immediate control" to confiscate any weapons or evidence that the suspect could destroy. The Court found, however, that there was no justification

> for routinely searching rooms other than that in which the arrest occurs—or, for that matter, for searching through all desk drawers or other closed or concealed areas in that room itself. Such searches, in the absence of well-recognized exceptions, may be made only under the authority of a search warrant.[51]

The exact interpretation of the "area within immediate control" has been left to individual courts, but in general it has been taken to mean the area within the reach of the arrested person. Thus, the Court is said to have established the "arm's reach doctrine" in its *Chimel* decision.

Searches with Consent Consent searches, the second most common type of warrantless searches, take place when individuals voluntarily give law enforcement officers permission to search their persons, homes, or belongings. The most relevant factors in determining whether consent is voluntary follow:

1. The age, intelligence, and physical condition of the consenting suspect.
2. Any coercive behavior by the police, such as the language used to request consent.
3. The length of the questioning and its location.[52]

If a court finds that a person has been physically threatened or otherwise coerced (forced) into giving consent, the search is invalid.[53] Furthermore, the search consented to must be reasonable. Several years ago, the North Carolina Supreme Court invalidated a consent search that turned up a packet of cocaine because the police pulled down the suspect's underwear and shined a flashlight on his groin. The court ruled that a reasonable person in the defendant's position would not consent to such an intrusive examination.[54]

Consent Search
A police search that is made after the subject of the search has agreed to the action.

YOU BE THE JUDGE
A Valid Search?

THE FACTS Baltimore police officers obtained a valid warrant to search Larry's apartment for marijuana. Larry's address, as described on the warrant, was "the premises known as 2036 Park Avenue third floor apartment." When the officers conducted the search, they reasonably believed that there was only one apartment on the third floor of the building. In fact, the third floor was divided into two apartments, the second one rented by Harold. Before the officers became aware that they were actually searching Harold's apartment, for which they had no warrant, they discovered illegal drugs there. Harold was eventually charged with possession of heroin with intent to distribute.

THE LAW To prevent general searches, the Fourth Amendment requires warrants to describe with particularity "the place to be searched." Police officers are required to make a "reasonable effort" to make sure that the place they are searching is the place specified in the warrant.

YOUR DECISION Harold claims that the evidence against him is invalid, because "the officers, not having a warrant for [his] apartment, had no right to go into that apartment." Do you agree?

[To see how the United States Supreme Court ruled in this case, go to Example 7.1 on page 350.]

SEARCHES OF AUTOMOBILES

In *Carroll v. United States* (1925),[55] the Supreme Court ruled that the law would distinguish among automobiles, homes, and persons in questions involving police searches. In the years since its *Carroll* decision, the Court has established that the Fourth Amendment does not require police to obtain a warrant to search an automobile or other movable vehicle when they have probable cause to believe that the vehicle contains contraband or evidence of criminal activity.[56]

The reasoning behind such leniency is straightforward: requiring a warrant to search an automobile places too heavy a burden on police officers. By the time the officers could communicate with a judge and obtain the warrant, the suspects could have driven away and destroyed any evidence. Consequently, the Court has consistently held that someone in a vehicle does not have the same reasonable expectation of privacy as someone at home or even in a phone booth.

Warrantless Searches of Automobiles

For nearly three decades, police officers believed that when they made a lawful arrest of a person driving a car, they could legally make a warrantless search of the car's entire front and back compartments. This understanding was based on the Supreme Court's ruling in *New York v. Benton* (1981),[57] which seemed to allow this expansive interpretation of the "area within immediate control" with regard to automobiles. In *Arizona v. Gant* (2009), however, the Court announced that its *Benton* decision had been misinterpreted. Such warrantless searches are allowed only if (1) the person being arrested is close enough to the car to grab or destroy evidence or a weapon inside the car or (2) the arresting officer reasonably believes that the car contains evidence pertinent to the same crime for which the arrest took place.[58]

So, for example, police will no longer be able to search an automobile for contraband if the driver has been arrested for failing to pay previous speeding tickets—unless the officer reasonably believes the suspect has the ability to destroy any such contraband within his or her reach. As you can imagine, the law enforcement community reacted negatively to this new, more demanding set of rules.[59] Police officers, however, still have the ability to conduct a warrantless search of an automobile based on circumstances other than the search-incidental-to-an-arrest doctrine. These circumstances include probable cause of criminal activity, consent of the driver, and "protective searches" to search for weapons if police officers have a reasonable suspicion that such weapons exist.[60]

Pretextual Stops

Despite the Supreme Court's ruling in the *Gant* case, police officers still have a great deal of leeway in situations involving automobile searches. In *Whren v. United States* (1996),[61] the Supreme Court ruled that the "true" motivation of police officers in making traffic stops was irrelevant as long as they had probable cause to believe that a traffic law had been broken. In other words, police may stop a driver they believe to be drunk in order to issue a speeding citation. The fact that the officers are using the speeding ticket as a pretext to conduct a drunk driving investigation (and would not have stopped the driver otherwise) does not matter, as long as the driver actually was speeding. (CAREER TIP: In many jurisdictions, only a licensed *phlebotomist*—not a police officer—is authorized to draw blood from a person suspected of driving under the influence.)

One year after the *Whren* case, in *Maryland v. Wilson* (1997),[62] the Court further expanded police power by ruling that an officer may order passengers as well as the driver out of a car during a traffic stop. The Court reasoned that the danger to an officer is increased when there is a passenger in the automobile.

TEST PREP

Read each question on the exam carefully. "Speed" reading can cause you to skip over key words or phrases. Many test questions include words such as *all*, *always, never,* and *only.* If you miss these words, you are missing the "trick" part of the question.

THE PLAIN VIEW DOCTRINE

The Constitution, as interpreted by our courts, provides very little protection to contraband *in plain view.* For example, suppose a traffic officer pulls over a person for speeding, looks in the driver's side window, and clearly sees what appears to be a bag of heroin resting on the passenger seat. In this instance, under the **plain view doctrine,** the officer would be justified in seizing the drugs without a warrant.

The plain view doctrine was first enunciated by the Supreme Court in *Coolidge v. New Hampshire* (1971).[63] The Court ruled that law enforcement officers may make a warrantless seizure of an item if four criteria are met:

1. The item is positioned so as to be detected easily by an officer's sight or some other sense.
2. The officer is legally in a position to notice the item in question.
3. The discovery of the item is inadvertent. That is, the officer had not intended to find the item.
4. The officer immediately recognizes the illegal nature of the item. No interrogation or further investigation is allowed under the plain view doctrine.

ELECTRONIC SURVEILLANCE

During the course of a criminal investigation, law enforcement officers may decide to use **electronic surveillance,** or electronic devices such as wiretaps or hidden microphones ("bugs"), to monitor and record conversations, observe movements, and trace or record telephone calls.

Basic Rules: Consent and Probable Cause

Given the invasiveness of electronic surveillance, the Supreme Court has generally held that the practice is prohibited by the Fourth Amendment. In *Burger v. New York* (1967),[64] however, the Court ruled that it was permissible under certain circumstances. That same year, *Katz v. United States* (mentioned on page 128 in our discussion of the role of privacy in searches) established that recorded conversations are inadmissible as evidence unless certain procedures are followed.

In general, law enforcement officers can use electronic surveillance only if:

1. Consent is given by one of the parties to be monitored, or
2. There is a warrant authorizing the use of the devices.[65]

Note that the consent of only one of the parties being monitored is needed to waive the reasonable expectation of privacy. The Court has ruled that people whose conversations have been recorded by supposed friends who turn out to be police informers have not been subjected to an unreasonable search.[66] Therefore, at least theoretically, a person always assumes the risk that whatever he or she says to someone else may be monitored by the police. A number of states, however, have

> **Plain View Doctrine** The legal principle that objects in plain view of a law enforcement agent who has the right to be in a position to have that view may be seized without a warrant.
>
> **Electronic Surveillance** The use of electronic equipment to record or observe conduct that is meant to be private.

Early on the morning of September 21, 2010, New York police officers pulled over professional football player Braylon Edwards for having excessive tinting on his car windows. The officers then arrested him for driving while intoxicated. Why might this be considered a "pretextual stop"? What is your opinion of such tactics by police? (AP Photo/Louis Lanzano)

CJ and Technology

THE DRAGANFLY

It looks like a toy, but the Draganfly X6 is expected to do serious work for the Saskatoon (Canada) police. A small remote-controlled helicopter, the Draganfly X6 has a built-in camera that is designed to take aerial photographs of crime scenes and collision sites. The unmanned aerial vehicle (UAV) is remote controlled by an operator who wears video goggles that allow him or her to see through the machine's camera. Although the U.S. Customs and Border Protection agency has used UAVs to patrol the U.S. border with Mexico for years, the Draganfly X6 will be the first such device in North America designed to aid crime investigations in a city. Although the surveillance possibilities for police-operated UAVs seem endless, the federal government has not approved them for widespread use in the United States. The problem, according to the Federal Aviation Administration, is that these devices are not yet reliably able to sense and avoid obstacles in their path. "You don't want one of these coming down on grandma's windshield when she's on her way to the grocery store," said one official. Consequently, cities such as Miami and North Little Rock, Arkansas, have had to test surveillance UAVs over less populated areas, including abandoned buildings and national parks.

THINKING ABOUT SURVEILLANCE UAVS

Researchers at Harvard University are working on a tiny robot that weighs 0.002 ounces, has a wingspan of 1.2 inches, and flies by flapping its wings like a real insect. How would this "flybot" resolve some of the problems caused by larger UAVs operating in cities? What new problems would such a small and agile surveillance device introduce?

---

statutes that forbid private citizens from electronically recording another person's conversation without her or his knowledge. In Maryland, for example, such an act is a felony.

If consent exists, then law enforcement officers are not required to obtain a warrant before engaging in electronic surveillance. In most other instances, however, a warrant is required. For the warrant to be valid, it must:

1. Detail with "particularity" the conversations that are to be overheard.
2. Name the suspects and the places that will be under surveillance.
3. Show with probable cause that a specific crime has been or will be committed.[67]

Once the specific information has been gathered, the law enforcement officers must end the electronic surveillance immediately.[68] In any case, the surveillance cannot last more than thirty days without a judicial extension. (CAREER TIP: *Electronic surveillance officers carry out court-approved intercepts by hooking up the necessary equipment and listening in on the wiretap. These experts then pass on all pertinent information to the investigating officers.*)

Video and Digital Surveillance Many Americans would be surprised to learn how often they are under the watchful eye of law enforcement via another form of electronic surveillance: closed-circuit television (CCTV) cameras. CCTV surveillance relies on strategically placed video cameras to record and transmit all activity in a targeted area. The images are monitored in real time so that law enforcement personnel can investigate any suspicious or criminal behavior captured by the cameras. Private businesses such as office buildings, banks, and casinos have long used CCTV to observe their customers, but CCTV for crime-fighting purposes has only become common in the past decade. Because of terrorism concerns, authorities are installing three thousand cameras in lower Manhattan, and hundreds of cameras also operate in large cities such as Baltimore, Boston, and Chicago.[69]

Critics of the rapid spread of CCTV systems contend that they are easily abused to infringe on individual privacy, allowing law enforcement to create "digital dossiers" on people without probable cause.[70] American courts, however, have consistently held that there is no right to privacy in public. Indeed, so long as a suspect does not take steps to conceal information, a court will generally refuse to find a legitimate privacy interest. In one case, a police officer used binoculars to read the license plate of a stolen car parked in an open garage. A Michigan court approved of this "search," holding that the defendants "could not reasonably expect that passers-by would shut their eyes to what was clearly visible from the sidewalk or from across the street."[71]

¿WHAT ARE THE MIRANDA RIGHTS?

After the Pledge of Allegiance, there is perhaps no recitation that comes more readily to the American mind than the *Miranda* warning:

> You have the right to remain silent. If you give up that right, anything you say can and will be used against you in a court of law. You have the right to speak with an attorney and to have the attorney present during questioning. If you so desire and cannot afford one, an attorney will be appointed for you without charge before questioning.

The *Miranda* warning is not a mere prop. It strongly affects one of the more important aspects of any criminal investigation—the **interrogation**, or questioning of a suspect from whom the police want to

get information concerning a crime and perhaps a confession.

THE LEGAL BASIS FOR *MIRANDA*

The Fifth Amendment guarantees protection against self-incrimination. In other words, as we shall see again in Chapter 10, a defendant cannot be required to provide information about his or her own criminal activity. A defendant's choice *not* to incriminate himself or herself cannot be interpreted as a sign of guilt by a jury in a criminal trial. A confession, or admission of guilt, is by definition a statement of self-incrimination. How, then, to reconcile the Fifth Amendment with the critical need of law enforcement officers to gain confessions? The answer lies in the concept of **coercion**. When torture or brutality is involved, it is relatively easy to determine that a confession was improperly coerced and is therefore invalid.

The *Miranda* Case The Supreme Court first asserted that a confession could not be physically coerced in a 1936 case concerning a defendant who was beaten and whipped until he confessed to a murder.[72] It was not until 1966, however, that the Court handed down its landmark decision in *Miranda v. Arizona*.[73] The case involved Ernesto Miranda, a produce worker, who had been arrested three years earlier in Phoenix and charged with kidnapping and rape. Detectives questioned Miranda for two hours before gaining a confession of guilt. At no time was Miranda informed that he had a right to have a lawyer present. The Court overturned Miranda's conviction, stating that police interrogations are, by their very nature, coercive and therefore deny suspects their constitutional right against self-incrimination by "forcing" them to confess.

Miranda Rights The concept of *Miranda* **rights**, established in this case, is based on what University of Columbia law professor H. Richard Uviller called

Interrogation
The direct questioning of a suspect to gather evidence of criminal activity and to try to gain a confession.

Coercion The use of physical force or mental intimidation to compel a person to do something—such as confess to committing a crime—against her or his will.

Miranda **Rights** The constitutional rights of accused persons taken into custody by law enforcement officials.

Custody The forceful detention of a person, or the perception that a person is not free to leave the immediate vicinity.

Custodial Interrogation The questioning of a suspect after that person has been taken into custody.

inherent coercion. This term refers to the assumption that even if a police officer does not lay a hand on a suspect, the general atmosphere of an interrogation is in and of itself coercive.[74] Although the *Miranda* case is best remembered for the procedural requirement it spurred, at the time the Supreme Court was more concerned about the treatment of suspects during interrogation.

The Court found that routine police interrogation strategies, such as leaving suspects alone in a room for several hours before questioning them, were inherently coercive. Therefore, the Court reasoned, every suspect—not just those who had been physically abused—needed protection from coercion. The *Miranda* warning is a result of this need. In theory, if the warning is not given to a suspect before an interrogation, the fruits of that interrogation, including a confession, are invalid.

WHEN A *MIRANDA* WARNING IS REQUIRED

As we shall see, a *Miranda* warning is not necessary under several conditions, such as when no questions are asked of the suspect. Generally, *Miranda* requirements apply only when a suspect is in *custody.* In a series of rulings since *Miranda,* the Supreme Court has defined **custody** as an arrest or a situation in which a reasonable person would not feel free to leave.[75] For example, if four police officers enter a suspect's bedroom at 4:00 A.M., wake him, and form a circle around him during questioning, then they must first read him a *Miranda* warning. Even though the suspect has not been arrested, he will "not feel free to go where he pleased."[76] Consequently, a **custodial interrogation** occurs when a suspect is under arrest or is deprived of her or his freedom in a significant manner.

What aspects of the situation shown here indicate that the Aspen (Colorado) police officer is required to "Mirandize" the suspect before asking him any questions, even if he never formally places the suspect under arrest? (Photo by Chris Hondros/Getty Images)

Remember, a *Miranda* warning is required only before a custodial interrogation takes place.

WHEN A *MIRANDA* WARNING IS NOT REQUIRED

A *Miranda* warning is not necessary in a number of situations:

1. When the police do not ask the suspect any questions that are *testimonial* in nature. Such questions are designed to elicit information that may be used against the suspect in court. Note that "routine booking questions," such as the suspect's name, address, height, and eye color, do not require a *Miranda* warning. Even though answering these questions may provide incriminating evidence (especially if the person answering is a prime suspect), the Supreme Court has held that they are absolutely necessary if the police are to do their jobs.[77] (Imagine the officer not being able to ask a suspect her or his name.)

2. When the police have not focused on a suspect and are questioning witnesses at the scene of a crime.

3. When a person volunteers information before the police have asked a question.

4. When the suspect has given a private statement to a friend or some other acquaintance.

Miranda does not apply to these statements so long as the government did not orchestrate the situation.

5. During a stop and frisk, when no arrest has been made.
6. During a traffic stop.[78]

Furthermore, suspects can *waive* their Fifth Amendment rights and speak to a police officer, but only if the *Miranda* waiver is made voluntarily. Silence on the part of a suspect does not mean that his or her *Miranda* protections have been taken away. To waive their rights, suspects must state—either in writing or orally—that they understand those rights and that they will voluntarily answer questions without the presence of counsel.

Clear Waiver To ensure that the suspect's rights are upheld, prosecutors are required to prove that the suspect "knowing and intelligently" waived his or her *Miranda* rights.[79] To make the waiver perfectly clear, police will ask suspects two questions in addition to giving the *Miranda* warning:

1. Do you understand your rights as I have read them to you?
2. Knowing your rights, are you willing to talk to another law enforcement officer or me?

Clear Intent If the suspect indicates that she or he does not want to speak to the officer, thereby invoking her or his right to silence, the officer must *immediately* stop any questioning.[80] Similarly, if the suspect requests a lawyer, the police can ask no further questions until an attorney is present.[81]

The suspect must be clear about this intention, however. In *Davis v. United States* (1994),[82] the Supreme Court upheld the interrogation of a suspect after he said, "Maybe I should talk to a lawyer." The Court found that this statement was too ambiguous, stating that it did not want to force police officers to "read the minds" of suspects who make vague declarations. Along these same lines, in *Berghuis v. Thompkins* (2010),[83] the Court upheld the conviction of a suspect who implicated himself in a murder after remaining mostly silent during nearly three hours of police questioning. The defendant claimed that he had invoked his *Miranda* rights by being uncommunicative with the interrogating officers. The Court disagreed, saying that silence is not enough—a suspect must actually state that he or she wishes to cut off questioning for the *Miranda* protections to apply.

> **Miranda Waiver**
> A decision by a suspect to voluntarily give up his or her right to remain silent, with the understanding that his or her answers may be used as evidence in criminal court.

CAREERPREP DETECTIVE

JOB DESCRIPTION:
- Collect evidence and obtain facts pertaining to criminal cases.
- Conduct interviews, observe suspects, examine records, and help with raids and busts. Some detectives are assigned to multiagency task forces that deal with specific types of crime, like drug trafficking or gang activity.

WHAT KIND OF TRAINING IS REQUIRED?
- Two to five years of experience as a police officer are required before taking the test to become a detective.

- Larger departments require sixty units of college credit or an associate's degree.

ANNUAL SALARY RANGE?
- $43,920–$76,350

For additional information, visit:
www.bls.gov/oco/ocos160.htm.

Karen Mower/iStockphoto.com

8 COURTS AND THE QUEST FOR JUSTICE

Learning Outcomes

After studying this chapter, you will be able to . . .

LO1 Define and contrast the four functions of the courts.

LO2 Define *jurisdiction* and contrast geographic and subject-matter jurisdiction.

LO3 Explain the difference between trial and appellate courts.

LO4 Explain briefly how a case is brought to the U.S. Supreme Court.

LO5 List and describe the members of the courtroom work group.

Innocent Abroad?

Shortly after police discovered the knifed, lifeless body of twenty-one-year-old British student Meredith Kercher in her apartment in Perugia, Italy, local prosecutors focused on Amanda Knox, Kercher's twenty-year-old American roommate, as the primary suspect. They believed that Knox, Knox's Italian boyfriend Raffaele Sollecito, and an African immigrant named Rudy Guede had engaged in a "drug fueled" orgy in the apartment. Then, after the trio forced Kercher to have sex with them, Sollecito and Guede held her down "while the American slit her throat."

Knox, then a junior at the University of Washington, maintained that she had spent the night in question at Sollecito's apartment, where the two had smoked hashish and watched a movie. Initially, this report meshed with Guede's admission that he and Kercher had been alone that evening, and that a stranger who snuck into the apartment while Guede was using the bathroom had killed the British woman. Then, after unsuccessfully trying to avoid arrest by fleeing to Germany, Guede changed his story to implicate Knox and Sollecito. The main piece of concrete evidence against Knox was a knife found in Sollecito's kitchen. Authorities claimed that this murder weapon had traces of DNA belonging to both Knox—not surprisingly, given how much time she spent with her boyfriend—and, more damningly, the murder victim.

During Knox's trial, her attorneys argued that the trace amounts of "mystery" DNA on the knife were so small that it was impossible to determine their origin. Furthermore, the lawyers pointed out, the shape of the blade did not match a knife-shaped bloodstain on Kercher's bed. Nonetheless, on December 4, 2009, more than two years after Kercher's death, an Italian jury found Knox guilty of murder and sentenced her to twenty-six years in prison. The verdict caused an outcry among Knox's supporters, including many in the American media. One CBS News commentator called the trial "the railroad job from hell."

(AP Photo/Michael P. King, Pool)

Why do some observers believe that Amanda Knox, shown here in an Italian courtroom, was unfairly convicted of murdering Meredith Kercher, her roommate? (Photo by Giuseppe Bellini/Getty Images)

Critics of Amanda Knox's guilty verdict were not shy about damning Italy's criminal justice system.[1] First, they pointed out, Italian police questioned Knox for more than fifty-three hours without providing her access to an attorney—a situation that, as we will learn in the next chapter, would not be allowed in the United States. Then, Knox was held in an Italian jail for more than a year before being charged with a crime.

The jury in her trial gathered for only two days a week, which, in addition to a long summer break, added to the overall length of the proceedings. More important, the jury was not *sequestered*, or shielded from the influence of a local media that reveled in lurid and possibly untrue tales of Knox's unseemly behavior as a foreign student caught in a whirlpool of drugs, booze, and sex.

"I am innocent. Raffaele [Sollecito] is innocent," Knox told an Italian judge on December 11, 2010, during an appeal in which her lawyers argued for retesting several key pieces of evidence. "It doesn't do justice to Meredith [Kercher] and her loved ones to take our lives from us."[2] Do the circumstances listed in the previous paragraphs mean that the Italian court system denied Knox, Sollecito, and Kercher justice? Would the American courts have done better?

Famed jurist Roscoe Pound characterized "justice" as society's demand "that serious offenders be convicted and punished," while at the same time "the innocent and unfortunate are not oppressed."[3] We can expand on this noble, if idealistic, definition. Citizens expect their courts to discipline the guilty, discourage illegal activities, protect civil liberties, and rehabilitate criminals—all simultaneously. Over the course of the next four chapters, we shall examine these lofty goals and the extent to which they can be reached. We start with a discussion of how courts in the United States work.

¿WHAT ROLES DO COURTS PLAY IN SOCIETY?

Simply stated, a court is a place where arguments are settled. The argument may be between the federal government and a corporation accused of violating environmental regulations, between business partners, between a criminal and the state, or between any number of other parties. The court provides an environment in which the basis of the argument can be decided through the application of the law.

Courts have extensive powers in our criminal justice system: they can bring the authority of the state to seize property and to restrict individual liberty. Given that the rights to own property and to enjoy personal freedom are

A prosecutor (standing, right) speaks to the jury in a Cape May, New Jersey, court room. In simple terms, what happens during a trial in a courtroom? What expectations does society have of court proceedings? (AP Photo/Dale Gerhard/The Press of Atlantic City)

enshrined in the U.S. Constitution, a court's *legitimacy* in taking such measures must be unquestioned by society. This legitimacy is based on two factors: impartiality and independence.[4] In theory, each party involved in a courtroom dispute must have an equal chance to present its case and must be secure in the belief that no outside factors are going to influence the decision rendered by the court. In reality, as we shall see over the next four chapters, it does not always work that way.

DUE PROCESS AND CRIME CONTROL IN THE COURTS

As mentioned in Chapter 1, the criminal justice system has two sets of underlying values: due process and crime control. Due process values focus on protecting the rights of the individual, while crime control values stress the punishment and repression of criminal conduct.[5] The competing nature of these two value systems is often evident in the nation's courts.

The Due Process Function The primary concern of early American courts was to protect the rights of the individual against the power of the state. Memories of injustices suffered at the hands of the British monarchy were still strong, and most of the procedural rules that we have discussed in this textbook were created with the express purpose of giving the individual a fair chance against the government in any courtroom

proceedings. Therefore, the due process function of the courts is to protect individuals from the unfair advantages that the government—with its immense resources—automatically enjoys in legal battles. Seen in this light, constitutional guarantees such as the right to counsel, the right to a jury trial, and protection from self-incrimination are equalizers in the "contest" between the state and the individual. The idea that the two sides in a courtroom dispute are adversaries (rivals) is, as we shall discuss in the next chapter, fundamental in American courts.

The Crime Control Function Advocates of crime control distinguish between the court's obligation to be fair to the accused and its obligation to be fair to society.[6] The crime control function of the courts emphasizes punishment and retribution—criminals must suffer for the harm done to society, and it is the courts' responsibility to see that they do so.

Given these responsibilities to protect the public, discourage criminal behavior, and "get criminals off the streets," the courts should not be concerned solely with giving the accused a fair chance. Rather than using due process rules as "equalizers," the courts should use them as protection against blatantly unconstitutional acts. For example, a detective who beats a suspect with a tire iron to get a confession has obviously infringed on the suspect's constitutional rights. If, however, the detective uses trickery to gain a confession, the court should allow the confession to stand because it is not in society's interest that law enforcement agents be deterred from outwitting criminals.

THE REHABILITATION FUNCTION

A third view of the court's responsibility is based on the "medical model" of the criminal justice system. In this model, criminals are comparable to patients, and the courts perform the role of physicians who dispense "treatment."[7] The criminal is seen as sick, not evil, and therefore treatment is morally justified. Of course, treatment varies from case to case, and some criminals require harsh penalties such as incarceration. In other cases, however, it may not be in society's best interest for the criminal to be punished according to the formal rules of the justice system. Perhaps the criminal

> **Jurisdiction** The authority of a court to hear and decide cases within an area of the law or a geographic territory.

can be rehabilitated to become a productive member of society and thus save taxpayers the costs of incarceration or other punishment.

THE BUREAUCRATIC FUNCTION

To a certain extent, the crime control, due process, and rehabilitation functions of a court are secondary to its bureaucratic function. In general, a court may have the goal of protecting society or protecting the rights of the individual, but on a day-to-day basis that court has the more pressing task of dealing with the cases brought before it. Like any bureaucracy, a court is concerned with speed and efficiency, and loftier concepts such as justice can be secondary to a judge's need to wrap up a particular case before six o'clock so that administrative deadlines can be met. Indeed, many observers feel that the primary adversarial relationship in the courts is not between the two parties involved but between the ideal of justice and the reality of bureaucratic limitations.[8]

¿HOW DO AMERICAN COURTS OPERATE?

One of the more often cited limitations of the American judicial system is its complex nature. In truth, the United States does not have a single judicial system, but fifty-two different systems—one for each state, for the District of Columbia, and for the federal government. Each state has its own unique judiciary with its own set of rules, some of which may be in conflict with the federal judiciary. Thus, it may be helpful at this point to discuss some basics—jurisdiction, trial and appellate courts, and the dual court system.

> " *The punishment of criminals should be of use;* **when a man is hanged, he is good for nothing.** "
>
> —VOLTAIRE
> (FRENCH PHILOSOPHER AND WRITER, 1694–1778)

JURISDICTION

In Latin, *juris* means "law," and *diction* means "to speak." Thus, **jurisdiction** literally refers to the power "to speak the law." Before any court can hear a case, it must have jurisdiction over the persons involved in the case or its subject matter. The jurisdiction of every court, even the United States Supreme Court, is limited in some way.

Geographic Jurisdiction One limitation is geographic. Generally, a court can exercise its authority over residents of a certain area. A state trial court, for example, normally has jurisdictional authority over crimes committed in a particular area of the state, such as a county or a district. A state's highest court (often called the state supreme court) has jurisdictional authority over the entire state, and the United States Supreme Court has jurisdiction over the entire country.

For the most part, criminal jurisdiction is determined by legislation. The U.S. Congress or a state legislature can determine what acts are illegal within the geographic boundaries it controls, thus giving federal or state courts jurisdiction over those crimes. What happens, however, when more than one court system has jurisdiction over the same criminal act?

LO2

Federal versus State Jurisdiction Under the principles of federalism (see page 10), crime is considered a state and local issue. Nonetheless, because of laws passed by the U.S. Congress, federal courts have jurisdiction over about 4,400 crimes, including drug trafficking, kidnapping, bank robbery, and illegal gambling.[9] Many acts that are illegal under federal law are also illegal under state law. As a general rule, when Congress "criminalizes" behavior that is already prohibited under a state criminal code, the federal and state courts both have jurisdiction over that crime unless Congress states otherwise in the initial legislation. Thus, **concurrent jurisdiction**, which occurs when two different court systems have simultaneous jurisdiction over the same case, is quite common.

Less common is a situation in which federal law and state law contradict each other. Today, fifteen states allow the use of marijuana for medicinal purposes (see photo below), even though federal law considers the possession, sale, or distribution of marijuana a crime.[10] This contradiction can place citizens of those states in a difficult position. For example, at an airport in Montana—which allows medical marijuana—state employees at an airport might ignore possession of marijuana while baggage screeners, who work for the federal government, would be required to notify law enforcement when finding marijuana used for medical purposes.

State versus State Jurisdiction Multiple states can also claim jurisdiction over the same defendant or criminal act, depending on state legislation and the circumstances of the crime. For example, if Billy is standing in State A and shoots Frances, who is standing in State B, the two states could have concurrent jurisdiction to try Billy for murder. Similarly, if a property theft takes place in State A but police recover the stolen goods in State B, concurrent jurisdiction could exist. Some states have even passed laws stating that they have jurisdiction over their own citizens who commit crimes in other states, even if there is no other connection between the home state and the criminal act.[11]

Accordingly, rules of jurisdiction can give a state court power over an individual who has had only minor contact with that state. Consider the case of Phillip R. Greaves II, of Pueblo, Colorado. In 2010, Greaves touched off national outrage by publishing a book about pedophilia (sexual desire felt by adults for children). Although his jurisdiction was far from Colorado, a law enforcement agent in Polk County, Florida, ordered a copy of *The Pedophile's Guide to Love and Pleasure: A Child-Lover's Code of Conduct* over the Internet.

As soon as the book arrived, Polk County officials claimed jurisdiction over Greaves and issued a warrant for his arrest on charges of distributing obscene material in Florida. Cooperating, Colorado law enforcement agents *extradited* Greaves to Florida, where he was found guilty in state court and sentenced to two months' probation. **Extradition** is the formal process by which one legal authority, such as a state or a nation, transfers a fugitive to another legal authority that has a valid claim on the suspect. (CAREER TIP: To become a *U.S. Extradition Service agent*, a federal law enforcement officer must complete 120 hours of training in areas such as prisoner transportation, contraband control, and defensive driving.)

Concurrent Jurisdiction The situation that occurs when two or more courts have the authority to preside over the same criminal case.

Extradition The process by which one jurisdiction surrenders a person accused or convicted of violating another jurisdiction's criminal law to the second jurisdiction.

At the Dr. Reefer dispensary in Boulder, Colorado, a saleswoman packages medical marijuana for a customer. How does medical marijuana represent a situation in which federal and state law is contradictory? (Photo by Chris Hondros/Getty Images)

Multiple Trials When different courts share jurisdiction over the same defendant, multiple trials can result. In late 2007, for example, professional football player Michael Vick was convicted in federal court for operating a dogfighting ring and was sentenced to twenty-three months in federal prison. Nearly a year into his sentence, Vick traveled to Surry County, Virginia—where his crimes had taken place—and pleaded guilty to similar charges, receiving as punishment a suspended sentence (discussed in Chapter 12).

Similarly, from 2007 to 2010, religious sect leader Warren Jeffs appeared in the courts of three different states—Arizona, Texas, and Utah—to face charges related to sex with underage girls. Because officials in each state had probable cause that he had committed crimes within state limits, each state had jurisdiction over him and the right to conduct a criminal trial. Although some believe that these multiple trials are a waste of taxpayer money, state and county prosecutors often argue that local victims of crimes deserve the "sense of closure" that comes with criminal proceedings.[12]

In addition, as we will see in Chapter 10, guilty verdicts can be appealed and reversed, and extra convictions serve as "insurance" against that possibility. In most situations, however, convictions in one jurisdiction end the prosecution of the same case in another jurisdiction.

Subject-Matter Jurisdiction Jurisdiction over subject matter also acts as a limitation on the types of cases a court can hear. State court systems include courts of *general* (unlimited) *jurisdiction* and courts of *limited jurisdiction*. Courts of general jurisdiction have no restrictions on the subject matter they may address, and therefore deal with the most serious felonies and civil cases. Courts of limited jurisdiction, also known as lower courts, handle misdemeanors and civil matters under a certain amount, usually $1,000. To lighten caseload pressures in lower courts, many states have created special subject-matter courts that only dispose of cases involving a specific crime. For example, a number of jurisdictions have established drug courts to handle an overload of illicit narcotics arrests, and several years ago California created the first court specifically designed for crimes involving U.S. military veterans.

TRIAL AND APPELLATE COURTS

Another distinction is between courts of original jurisdiction and courts of appellate, or review, jurisdiction. Courts having *original jurisdiction* are courts of the first instance, or **trial courts**. Almost every case begins in

Why are some defendants, such as professional football player Michael Vick, shown here while awaiting trial in Richmond, Virginia, tried twice for the same crime? (Doug Mills/*The New York Times*/Redux/James Pauls/iStockphoto)

a trial court. It is in this court that a trial (or a guilty plea) takes place, and the judge imposes a sentence if the defendant is found guilty. Trial courts are primarily concerned with

 questions of fact. That is, they are designed to determine exactly what events occurred that are relevant to questions of the defendant's guilt or innocence.

Courts having *appellate jurisdiction* act as reviewing courts, or **appellate courts.** In general, cases can be brought before appellate courts only on appeal by one of the parties in the trial court. (Note that because of constitutional protections against being tried twice for the same crime, prosecutors who lose in *criminal* trial court *cannot* appeal the verdict.) An appellate court does not use juries or witnesses to reach its decision. Instead, its judges make a decision on whether the case should be *reversed* and *remanded*, or sent back to the court of original jurisdiction for a new trial. Appellate judges present written explanations for their decisions, and these **opinions** of the court are the basis for a great deal of the precedent in the criminal justice system.

It is important to understand that appellate courts do not determine the defendant's guilt or innocence—they only make judgments on questions of procedure. In other words, they are concerned with *questions of law* and normally accept the facts as established by the trial court. Only rarely will an appeals court question a jury's decision. Instead, the appellate judges will review the manner in which the facts and evidence were provided to the jury and rule on whether errors were made in the process.

THE DUAL COURT SYSTEM

Like many other aspects of American government, the structure of the judicial system was the result of a compromise. During the framing of the U.S. Constitution, two camps emerged with different views on the courts. The Anti-Federalists, interested in limiting the power of the federal government, wanted the Supreme Court to be the only *national* court, with the states handling the majority of judicial work. The Federalists, dedicated

> ## "Justice is open to everyone
> *. . . in the same way as the Ritz Hotel*"
>
> —JUDGE STURGESS
> (BRITISH, 1920)

to ensuring that the states did not have too much power, wanted all cases to be heard in federal courts. Both sides eventually made concessions, and the outcome is reflected in the **dual court system** that we have today (see **Figure 8.1** on the following page).[13]

Federal and state courts both have limited jurisdiction. Generally, federal courts preside over cases involving violations of federal law, and state courts preside over cases involving violations of state law. The distinction is not always clear, however. A number of crimes—such as kidnapping and transportation of narcotics—are deemed illegal by both federal and state statutes, and persons accused of such crimes can be tried in either court system. In these instances, federal and state prosecutors must decide among themselves who will handle the case—a decision based on a number of factors, including publicity surrounding the crime and the relative caseloads of the respective court systems. Prosecutors will often steer a suspect toward the harsher penalty. Thus, if the punishment for a particular crime is more severe under federal law than state law, then law enforcement officials may decide to try the defendant in federal court (and vice versa).

¿HOW DO STATES ORGANIZE THEIR COURTS?

Typically, a state court system includes several levels, or tiers, of courts. State courts may include (1) lower courts, or courts of limited jurisdiction; (2) trial courts of general jurisdiction; (3) appellate courts; and (4) the

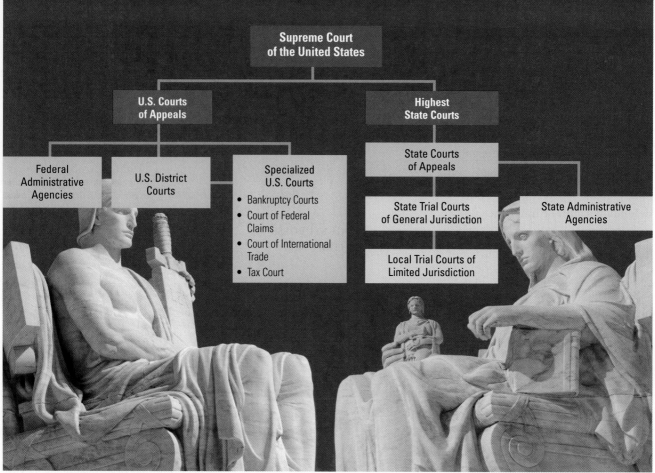

Figure 8.1   The Dual Court System

The chart shows:

Supreme Court of the United States

Branching to:
- **U.S. Courts of Appeals**
  - Federal Administrative Agencies
  - U.S. District Courts
  - Specialized U.S. Courts
    - Bankruptcy Courts
    - Court of Federal Claims
    - Court of International Trade
    - Tax Court
- **Highest State Courts**
  - State Courts of Appeals
    - State Trial Courts of General Jurisdiction
    - Local Trial Courts of Limited Jurisdiction
    - State Administrative Agencies

Gary Blakeley/iStockphoto.com

Specialty Court
A lower court that has jurisdiction over one specific area of criminal activity, such as illegal drugs or domestic violence.

state's highest court. As previously mentioned, each state has a different judicial structure, in which different courts have different jurisdictions, but there are enough similarities to allow for a general discussion. **Figure 8.2** on the facing page shows a typical state court system.

COURTS OF LIMITED JURISDICTION

Most states have local trial courts that are limited to trying cases involving minor criminal matters, such as traffic violations, prostitution, and drunk and disorderly conduct. Although these minor courts usually keep no written record of the trial proceedings and cases are decided by a judge rather than a jury, defendants have the same rights as those in other trial courts.

The majority of all minor criminal cases are decided in these lower courts. Courts of limited jurisdiction can also be responsible for the preliminary stages of felony cases. Arraignments, bail hearings, and preliminary hearings often take place in these lower courts. (CAREER TIP: Some jurisdictions, notably in Texas, continue to use justice courts to settle minor disputes between private individuals and crimes punishable by small fines or jail terms. These courts of limited jurisdiction are presided over by a judge called a *justice of the peace* [mostly in rural areas] or a *magistrate* [mostly in cities].)

Many states have also created **specialty courts** that have jurisdiction over very narrowly defined areas of criminal justice. Not only do these courts remove many cases from the existing court systems, but they also allow court personnel to become experts in a particular subject. Specialty courts include the following:

1. Drug courts, which deal only with illegal substance crimes.

2. Gun courts, which have jurisdiction over crimes that involve the illegal use of firearms.

3. Juvenile courts, which specialize in crimes committed by minors. (We will discuss juvenile courts in more detail in Chapter 15.)

4. Domestic courts, which deal with crimes of domestic violence, such as child and spousal abuse.

5. Elder courts, which focus primarily on the special needs of the elderly victims rather than the offenders.

As we will see in Chapter 12, many state and local governments are searching for cheaper alternatives to locking up nonviolent offenders in prison or jail. Because specialty courts offer a range of treatment options for wrongdoers, these courts are becoming increasingly popular in today's more budget-conscious criminal justice system. For example, about two thousand drug courts are now operating in the United States, a number that is expected to increase as the financial benefits of diverting drug law violators from correctional facilities become more evident.

TRIAL COURTS OF GENERAL JURISDICTION

State trial courts that have general jurisdiction may be called county courts, district courts, superior courts, or circuit courts. In Ohio, the name is the court of common pleas and in Massachusetts, the trial court. (The name sometimes does not correspond with the court's functions. For example, in New York the trial court is called the supreme court, whereas in most states the supreme court is the state's highest court.) Courts of general

Figure 8.2 **A Typical State Court System**

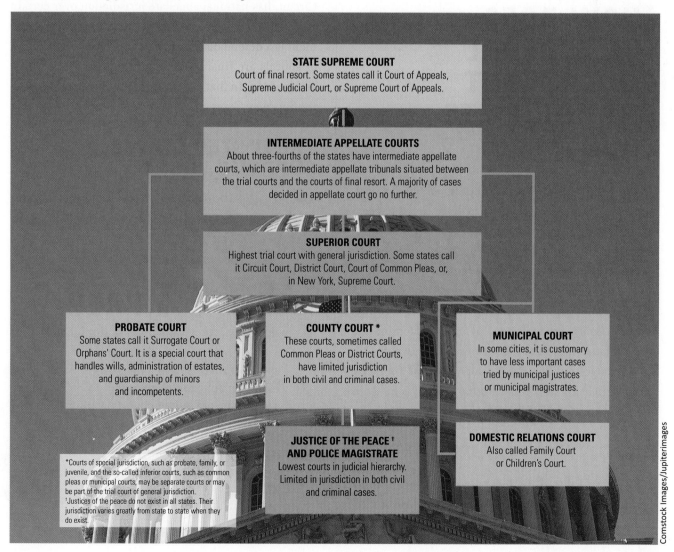

STATE SUPREME COURT
Court of final resort. Some states call it Court of Appeals, Supreme Judicial Court, or Supreme Court of Appeals.

INTERMEDIATE APPELLATE COURTS
About three-fourths of the states have intermediate appellate courts, which are intermediate appellate tribunals situated between the trial courts and the courts of final resort. A majority of cases decided in appellate court go no further.

SUPERIOR COURT
Highest trial court with general jurisdiction. Some states call it Circuit Court, District Court, Court of Common Pleas, or, in New York, Supreme Court.

PROBATE COURT
Some states call it Surrogate Court or Orphans' Court. It is a special court that handles wills, administration of estates, and guardianship of minors and incompetents.

COUNTY COURT *
These courts, sometimes called Common Pleas or District Courts, have limited jurisdiction in both civil and criminal cases.

MUNICIPAL COURT
In some cities, it is customary to have less important cases tried by municipal justices or municipal magistrates.

**JUSTICE OF THE PEACE †
AND POLICE MAGISTRATE**
Lowest courts in judicial hierarchy. Limited in jurisdiction in both civil and criminal cases.

DOMESTIC RELATIONS COURT
Also called Family Court or Children's Court.

*Courts of special jurisdiction, such as probate, family, or juvenile, and the so-called inferior courts, such as common pleas or municipal courts, may be separate courts or may be part of the trial court of general jurisdiction.
†Justices of the peace do not exist in all states. Their jurisdiction varies greatly from state to state when they do exist.

Comstock Images/Jupiterimages

jurisdiction have the authority to hear and decide cases involving many types of subject matter, and they are the setting for criminal trials (discussed in Chapter 10).

STATE COURTS OF APPEALS

Every state has at least one court of appeals (known as an appellate, or reviewing, court), which may be an intermediate appellate court or the state's highest court. About three-fourths have intermediate appellate courts. The highest appellate court in a state is usually called the supreme court, but in both New York and Maryland, the highest state court is called the court of appeals. The decisions of each state's highest court on all questions of state law are final. Only when issues of federal law or constitutional procedure are involved can the United States Supreme Court overrule a decision made by a state's highest court.

¿HOW DOES THE FEDERAL GOVERNMENT ORGANIZE ITS COURTS?

The federal court system is basically a three-tiered model consisting of (1) U.S. district courts (trial courts of general jurisdiction) and various courts of limited jurisdiction, (2) U.S. courts of appeals (intermediate courts of appeals), and (3) the United States Supreme Court.

Unlike state court judges, who are usually elected, federal court judges—including the justices of the Supreme Court—are appointed by the president of the United States, subject to the approval of the Senate. All federal judges receive lifetime appointments (because under Article III of the Constitution they "hold their offices during Good Behavior").

U.S. DISTRICT COURTS

On the lowest tier of the federal court system are the U.S. district courts, or federal trial courts. These are the courts in which cases involving federal laws begin, and a judge or, if it is a jury trial, a jury decides the case. Every state has at least one federal district court, and there is one in the District of Columbia. The number of judicial districts varies over time, primarily owing to population changes and corresponding caseloads. At the present time, there are ninety-four judicial districts. The federal system also includes other trial courts of limited jurisdiction, such as the Tax Court and the Court of International Trade.

U.S. COURTS OF APPEALS

In the federal court system, there are thirteen U.S. courts of appeals—also referred to as U.S. circuit courts of appeals. The federal courts of appeals for twelve of the circuits hear appeals from the district courts located within their respective judicial circuits (see **Figure 8.3** on the facing page). The Court of Appeals for the Thirteenth Circuit, called the Federal Circuit, has national appellate jurisdiction over certain types of cases, such as cases in which the U.S. government is a defendant. The decisions of the circuit courts of appeals are final unless a further appeal is pursued and granted. In that event, the matter is brought before the Supreme Court.

THE UNITED STATES SUPREME COURT

Although the United States Supreme Court reviews a minuscule percentage of the cases decided in the

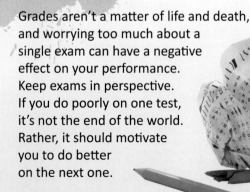

TEST PREP

Grades aren't a matter of life and death, and worrying too much about a single exam can have a negative effect on your performance. Keep exams in perspective. If you do poorly on one test, it's not the end of the world. Rather, it should motivate you to do better on the next one.

United States each year, its decisions profoundly affect our lives. The impact of Court decisions on the criminal justice system is equally far reaching: *Gideon v. Wainwright* (1963)[14] established every American's right to be represented by counsel in a criminal trial; *Miranda v. Arizona* (1966)[15] transformed pretrial interrogations; *Furman v. Georgia* (1972)[16] ruled that the death penalty was unconstitutional (temporarily); and *Gregg v. Georgia* (1976)[17] spelled out the conditions under which the death penalty could be allowed. As you have no doubt noticed from the discussions in this textbook, the Court has addressed nearly every important facet of criminal law.

The Supreme Court in Action The Supreme Court "makes" criminal justice policy in two important ways: through *judicial review* and through its authority to interpret the law. **Judicial review** refers to the power of the Court to determine whether a law or action by the other branches of the government is constitutional. For example, in the late 1990s Congress passed a law restricting Internet sales of "crush" videos, which showed women crushing small animals to death with their bare feet or high heels.[18] The wording of the statute prohibited the sale of videos showing any form of graphic violence against animals. Several years after the law's passage, Robert Stevens of Pittsville, Virginia, was sentenced to three years in prison for distributing videos that featured pit bull fights. In 2010, the Supreme Court overturned Stevens's conviction and

Judicial Review
The power of a court to review the actions of the executive and legislative branches.

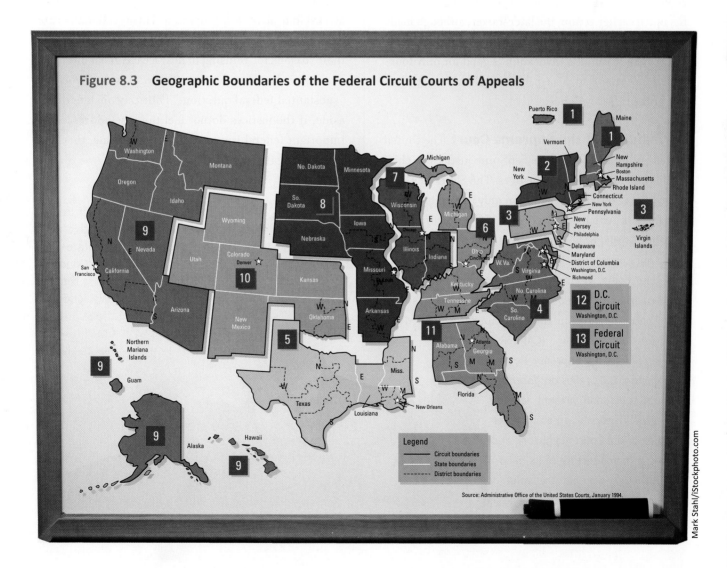

Figure 8.3   **Geographic Boundaries of the Federal Circuit Courts of Appeals**

Legend
— Circuit boundaries
— State boundaries
- - - District boundaries

Source: Administrative Office of the United States Courts, January 1994.

Mark Stahl/iStockphoto.com

invalidated the federal law as unconstitutional on the ground that it violated First Amendment protections of freedom of expression.[19]

As the final interpreter of the Constitution, the Supreme Court must also determine how established law applies to specific situations. In the previous chapter, you learned that a law enforcement officer must immediately stop questioning a suspect who requests her or his *Miranda* rights (see pages 134–135).

In *Maryland v. Shatzer* (2010),[20] the Court considered a situation in which a sexual abuse suspect invoked his *Miranda* rights, spent more than two years in prison (for an unrelated crime), and then waived his *Miranda* rights. The Court rejected the suspect's claim that due to his much earlier action, the later waiver, although made willingly, "did not count." Instead, the Court decided on a new rule: A *Miranda* invocation is good for only fourteen days. After that, a suspect must clearly reestablish her or his right to silence.

Jurisdiction of the Supreme Court The United States Supreme Court consists of nine justices—a chief justice and eight associate justices. The Supreme Court has original, or trial, jurisdiction only in rare instances (set forth in Article III, Section 2, of the Constitution). In other words, only rarely does a case originate at the Supreme Court level. Most of the Court's work is as an appellate court. It has appellate authority over cases decided by the U.S. courts of appeals, as well as over some cases decided in the state courts when federal questions are at issue. (CAREER TIP: The United States Supreme Court in Washington, D.C., relies on *docents* to conduct tours and present lectures that give visitors a greater understanding of the Court, its history, and the art and architecture of its building. Although docents are volunteers, the position provides public speaking and customer service experience—valuable additions to any résumé.)

Which Cases Reach the Supreme Court? There is no absolute right to appeal to the United States Supreme Court. Although thousands of cases are filed with the Supreme Court each year, in 2009–2010 the Court heard only eighty. With a **writ of *certiorari*** (pronounced sur-shee-uh-*rah*-ree), the Supreme Court orders a lower court to send it the record of a case for review. A party can petition the Supreme Court to issue a writ of *certiorari*, but whether the Court will do so is entirely within its discretion.

More than 90 percent of the petitions for writs of *certiorari* (or "certs," as they are popularly called) are denied. A denial is not a decision on the merits of a case, nor does it indicate agreement with the lower court's opinion. Therefore, the denial of the writ has no value as a precedent.[21] The Court will not issue a writ unless at least four justices approve of it. This is called the **rule of four.** Although the justices are not required to give their reasons for refusing to hear a case, most often the decision is based on whether the legal issue involves a "substantial federal question." Political considerations aside, if the justices do not feel the case addresses an important federal law or constitutional issue, they will vote to deny the writ of *certiorari*.

John G. Roberts, Jr., pictured here, is the seventeenth chief justice of the United States Supreme Court. What is the jurisdiction of the Supreme Court? (AP Photo/Lawrence Jackson)

Supreme Court Decisions Like all appellate courts, the Supreme Court normally does not hear any evidence. The Court's decision in a particular case is based on the written record of the case and the written arguments (briefs) that the attorneys submit. The attorneys also present **oral arguments**—arguments presented in person rather than on paper—to the Court, after which the justices discuss the case in *conference*. The conference is strictly private—only the justices are allowed in the room.

When the Court has reached a decision, the chief justice, if in the majority, assigns the task of writing the Court's opinion to one of the justices. When the chief justice is not in the majority, the most senior justice voting with the majority assigns the writing of the Court's opinion. The opinion outlines the reasons for the Court's decision, the rules of law that apply, and the decision.

Often, one or more justices who agree with the Court's decision may do so for different reasons than those outlined in the majority opinion. These justices may write **concurring opinions** setting forth their own legal reasoning on the issue. Frequently, one or more justices disagree with the Court's conclusion. These justices may write **dissenting opinions** outlining the reasons why they feel the majority erred. Although a dissenting opinion does not affect the outcome of the case before the Court, it may be important later. In a subsequent case concerning the same issue, a justice or attorney may use the legal reasoning in the dissenting opinion as the basis for an argument to reverse the previous decision and establish a new precedent.

Oral Arguments
The verbal arguments presented in person by attorneys to an appellate court.

Concurring Opinion A separate opinion prepared by a judge who supports the decision of the majority.

Dissenting Opinion A separate opinion in which a judge disagrees with the conclusion reached by the majority of the court.

¿HOW DO JUDGES FUNCTION IN THE CRIMINAL JUSTICE SYSTEM?

Supreme Court justices are the most visible and best-known American jurists, but in many ways they are unrepresentative of the profession as a whole. Few judges enjoy three-room office suites fitted with a fireplace and a private bath, as do the Supreme Court justices. Few judges have four clerks to assist them. Few

CAREER PREP — LAW CLERK

JOB DESCRIPTION:

- Assist judges in courtroom matters such as managing evidence, interacting with court personnel, and communicating with attorneys and the public.

- Analyze complex legal issues regarding information submitted by the two parties before the court, help the judge research and write opinions, prepare reports for the judge on the legal issues of a case, and make recommendations directly to the judge concerning the outcome of the trial or appeal.

WHAT KIND OF TRAINING IS REQUIRED?

- Despite the job title, law "clerks" are almost always recent law school graduates who have either passed or are expected to pass the state bar examination, a prerequisite to becoming a lawyer.

- Law clerks must have superior writing and research skills and a solid knowledge of the law, court procedures, jurisdictional rules, and the court system.

ANNUAL SALARY RANGE?

- $54,000–$105,000

For additional information, visit:
www.judicialclerkships.com.

© Katherine Moffitt/iStockphoto

Docket The list of cases entered on a court's calendar and thus scheduled to be heard by the court.

judges get a yearly vacation that stretches from July through September. Most judges, in fact, work at the lowest level of the system, in criminal trial courts, where they are burdened with overflowing caseloads and must deal daily with the pettiest of criminals.

One attribute a Supreme Court justice and a criminal trial judge in any small American city do have in common is the expectation that they will be just. Of all the participants in the criminal justice system, no single person is held to the same high standards as the judge. From her or his lofty perch in the courtroom, the judge is counted on to be "above the fray" of the bickering defense attorneys and prosecutors. When the other courtroom contestants rise at the entrance of the judge, they are placing the burden of justice squarely on that judge's shoulders.

THE ROLES AND RESPONSIBILITIES OF TRIAL JUDGES

One of the reasons why judicial integrity is considered so important is the amount of discretionary power a judge has over the court proceedings. Nearly every stage of the trial process includes a decision or action to be taken by the presiding judge.

Before the Trial A great deal of the work done by a judge takes place before the trial even starts, free from public scrutiny. These duties, some of which you have seen from a different point of view in the section on law enforcement agents, include determining the following:

- ☑ Whether there is sufficient probable cause to issue a search or arrest warrant.
- ☑ Whether there is sufficient probable cause to authorize electronic surveillance of a suspect.
- ☑ Whether enough evidence exists to justify the temporary incarceration of a suspect.
- ☑ Whether a defendant should be released on bail, and if so, the amount of the bail.
- ☑ Whether to accept pretrial motions by prosecutors and defense attorneys.
- ☑ Whether to accept a plea bargain.

During these pretrial activities, the judge takes on the role of the *negotiator*.[22] As most cases are decided through plea bargains rather than through trial proceedings, the judge often offers his or her services as a negotiator to help the prosecution and the defense "make a deal." The amount at which bail is set is often negotiated as well. Throughout the trial process, the judge usually spends a great deal of time in his or her *chambers*, or office, negotiating with the prosecutors and defense attorneys.

During the Trial When the trial starts, the judge takes on the role of *referee*. In this role, she or he is responsible for seeing that the trial unfolds according to the dictates of the law and that the participants in the trial do not overstep any legal or ethical bounds. In this role, the judge is expected to be neutral, determining the admissibility of testimony and evidence on a completely objective basis. The judge also acts as a *teacher* during the trial, explaining points of law to the jury.

If the trial is not a jury trial, then the judge must also make decisions concerning the guilt or innocence of the defendant. If the defendant is found guilty, the judge must decide on the length of the sentence and the type of sentence. (Different types of sentences, such as incarceration, probation, and other forms of community-based corrections, will be discussed in Chapters 11 and 12.)

The Administrative Role Judges are also *administrators*. That is, they are responsible for the day-to-day functioning of their courts. A primary administrative task of a judge is scheduling. Each courtroom has a **docket**, or calendar of cases, and it is the judge's responsibility to keep the docket current. This entails not only scheduling the trial but also setting pretrial motion dates and deciding whether to grant attorneys' requests for *continuances*, or additional time to prepare for a case.

Judges must also keep track of the immense load of paperwork generated by each case and manage the various employees of the court. In some instances, judges are even responsible for the budgets of their courtrooms.[23] Congress, recognizing the burden of such tasks, created the Administrative Office of the United States Courts in 1939 to provide administrative assistance for federal court judges.[24] Most state court judges, however, do not have the luxury of similar aid, though they are supported by a court staff.

CJ and Technology

"TWEETING" ON TRIAL

For the most part, nothing happens in a criminal courtroom without the judge's approval. As you will see in the next chapter, the judge keeps a particularly close eye on the members of the jury, who are supposed to reach their decision based solely on the evidence presented at trial. In recent years, however, this control is being challenged by technology. Jurors can, and do, use small (and easily hidden) wireless devices to text, tweet, blog, take photos, and conduct Internet research on the case before them. "Dozens of people a day are sending tweets or Facebook updates from courthouses all over America," says one social networking expert. This technology also poses a problem for witnesses, who are supposed to testify in court without knowing anything about what has occurred during the trial. For this reason, many judges have banned journalists from blogging live during a trial. The judges fear that witnesses waiting to testify might follow the proceedings on their cell phones from the courthouse lobby.

THINKING ABOUT WIRELESS DEVICES IN THE COURTROOM

Some judges do allow reporters to use Twitter to provide constant updates of cases. For example, one journalist covering a gang trial in Wichita, Kansas, sent tweets such as "Defendants are chatting and laughing among themselves" to his readers. What are the positive aspects of reporters being able to tweet and blog live during a criminal trial?

SELECTION OF JUDGES

In the federal court system, all judges are appointed by the president and confirmed by the Senate. It is difficult to make a general statement about how judges are selected in state court systems, however, because the procedure varies widely from state to state. In some states, such as New Jersey, all judges are appointed by the governor and confirmed by the upper chamber of the state legislature. In other states, such as Alabama, **partisan elections** are used to choose judges. In these elections, a judicial candidate declares allegiance to a political party, usually the Democrats or the Republicans, before the election. States that conduct **nonpartisan elections** such as Kentucky do not require a candidate to affiliate herself or himself with a political party in this manner.

In 1940, Missouri became the first state to combine appointment and election in a single merit selection. When all jurisdiction levels are counted, twenty-one states and the District of Columbia now utilize the **Missouri Plan**, as merit selection has been labeled. The Missouri Plan consists of three basic steps:

- When a vacancy on the bench arises, candidates are nominated by a nonpartisan committee of citizens.
- The names of the three most qualified candidates are sent to the governor or executive of the state

Partisan Election An election in which candidates are affiliated with and receive support from political parties.

Nonpartisan Election An election in which candidates are presented on the ballot without any party affiliation.

Missouri Plan A method of selecting judges that combines appointment and election.

judicial system, and that person chooses who will be the judge.

- A year after the new judge has been installed, a "retention election" is held so that voters can decide whether the judge deserves to keep the post.[25]

The goal of the Missouri Plan is to eliminate partisan politics from the selection procedure, while at the same time giving the citizens a voice in the process. One noted drawback of the merit system—and indeed of any elective method of selecting judges—is that voters may lack knowledge not only of the issues of a judicial election, but also of the identities of the candidates. A poll in Michigan found that nine out of ten voters could not identify any sitting state supreme court justice, and an equal number did not know how many justices served on the state's highest court or the length of their term in office.[26]

¿WHAT IS THE COURTROOM WORK GROUP?

Television dramas often depict the courtroom as a battle-field, with prosecutors and defense attorneys spitting fire at each other over the loud and insistent protestations of a frustrated judge. Consequently, many people are somewhat disappointed when they witness a real courtroom at work. Rarely does anyone raise his or her voice, and the court-room professionals appear—to a great extent—to be coop-erating with one another. In Chapter 6, we discussed the existence of a police subculture, based on the shared values of law enforcement agents. A courtroom subculture exists as well, centered on the **courtroom work group**. The most important feature of any work group is that it is a *cooperative* unit whose members establish shared values and methods that help the group efficiently reach its goals. Though coop-eration is not a concept usually associated with criminal courts, it is in fact crucial to the adjudication process.[27]

CAREERPREP

BAILIFF

Alina Solovyova-Vincent/iStockphoto.com

JOB DESCRIPTION:

- Maintain order and provide security in the courtroom during trials, and escort and guard jurors and prevent them from having improper contact with the public.
- Open and close court, call cases, call witnesses, and generally "direct the traffic" of the trial.

WHAT KIND OF TRAINING IS REQUIRED?

- At minimum, a high school diploma or GED.
- Supplemental training at a vocational school or a police academy, or a two- or four-year college degree with an emphasis on criminal justice.

ANNUAL SALARY RANGE?

- $30,000–$38,000

For additional information, visit:
www.criminaljusticeusa.com/bailiff.html.

MEMBERS OF THE COURTROOM WORK GROUP

The courtroom work group is made up of those individuals who are involved with the defendant from the time she or he is arrested until sentencing. The most prominent members are the judge, the prosecutor, and the defense attorney (the latter two will be discussed in detail in the next chapter). Three other court participants complete the work group:

1. The **bailiff of the court** is responsible for maintaining security and order in the judge's chambers and the courtroom. Bailiffs lead the defendant in and out of the courtroom and attend to the needs of the jurors during the trial. A bailiff, often a member of the local sheriff's department but sometimes an employee of the court, also delivers summonses in some jurisdictions. (CAREER TIP: In some states, such as New York, the court system hires law enforcement agents known as *court officers* to protect judges, court employees, and the public in courthouses.)

2. The **clerk of the court** has an exhaustive list of responsibilities. Any plea, motion, or other matter to be acted on by the judge must go through the clerk. The large amount of paperwork generated during a trial, including transcripts, photographs, evidence, and any other records, is maintained by the clerk. The clerk also issues subpoenas for jury duty and coordinates the jury selection process. In the federal court system, judges select clerks, while state clerks are either appointed or, in nearly a third of the states, elected.

3. **Court reporters** record every word that is said during the course of the trial. They also record any *depositions,* or pretrial question-and-answer sessions in which a party or a witness answers an attorney's questions under oath.

FORMATION OF THE COURTROOM WORK GROUP

The premise of the work group is based on constant interaction that fosters relationships among the members. As legal scholar David W. Neubauer describes:

Every day, the same group of courthouse regulars assembles in the same courtroom, sits or stands in the same places, and performs the same tasks as the day before. The types of defendants and the nature of the crimes they are accused of committing also remain constant. Only the names of the victim, witnesses, and defendants are different.[28]

Bailiff of the Court A law enforcement officer from the local sheriff's department who maintains courtroom order and oversees the activities of the jurors.

Clerk of the Court A court employee whose main duties include maintaining court records, coordinating jury selection, and managing case flow.

Court Reporter Also known as a stenographer, a court employee who provides a word-for-word written record of all court proceedings.

After a period of time, the members of a courtroom work group learn how the others operate. The work group establishes patterns of behavior and norms, and cooperation allows the adjudication process to function informally and smoothly.[29] In some cases, the members of the work group may even form personal relationships, which only strengthen the courtroom culture.

CAREER TIP: Court reporters are also known as *stenographers* because many of them use a stenotype machine—with a keyboard based on the phonetic sound of words—to take down court proceedings.

What is the role of the court reporter during a criminal trial? Why are court reporters necessary?
(Michael Newman/ PhotoEdit)

One way in which the courtroom work group differs from a traditional work group at a company such as Apple Computer, Inc., is that each member answers to a different sponsoring organization. Although the judge has ultimate authority over a courtroom, he or she is not the "boss" of the attorneys. The prosecutor works for the district attorney's office, while the defense attorney is hired by a private individual or the public defender's office. For her or his part, the judge works for the court system itself. (See **Figure 8.4** below for an overview of the main participants in the courtroom work group.)

THE JUDGE IN THE COURTROOM WORK GROUP

The judge is the dominant figure in the courtroom and therefore exerts the most influence over the values and norms of the work group. A judge who runs a tight ship follows procedure and restricts the freedom of attorneys to deviate from regulations, while a *laissez-faire* judge allows more leeway to members of the work group. A judge's personal philosophy also affects the court proceedings. If a judge has a reputation for being tough on crime, both prosecutors and defense attorneys will alter their strategies accordingly. In fact, a lawyer may be able to manipulate the system to "shop" for a judge whose philosophy best fits the attorney's goals in a particular case.[30] If a lawyer is caught trying to influence the assignment of judges, however, she or he is said to be "corrupting judicial independence" and may face legal proceedings.

Figure 8.4 The Courtroom Work Group
The major figures of the courtroom work group—judges, prosecutors, and defense attorneys—each have very important and very different responsibilities and pressures.

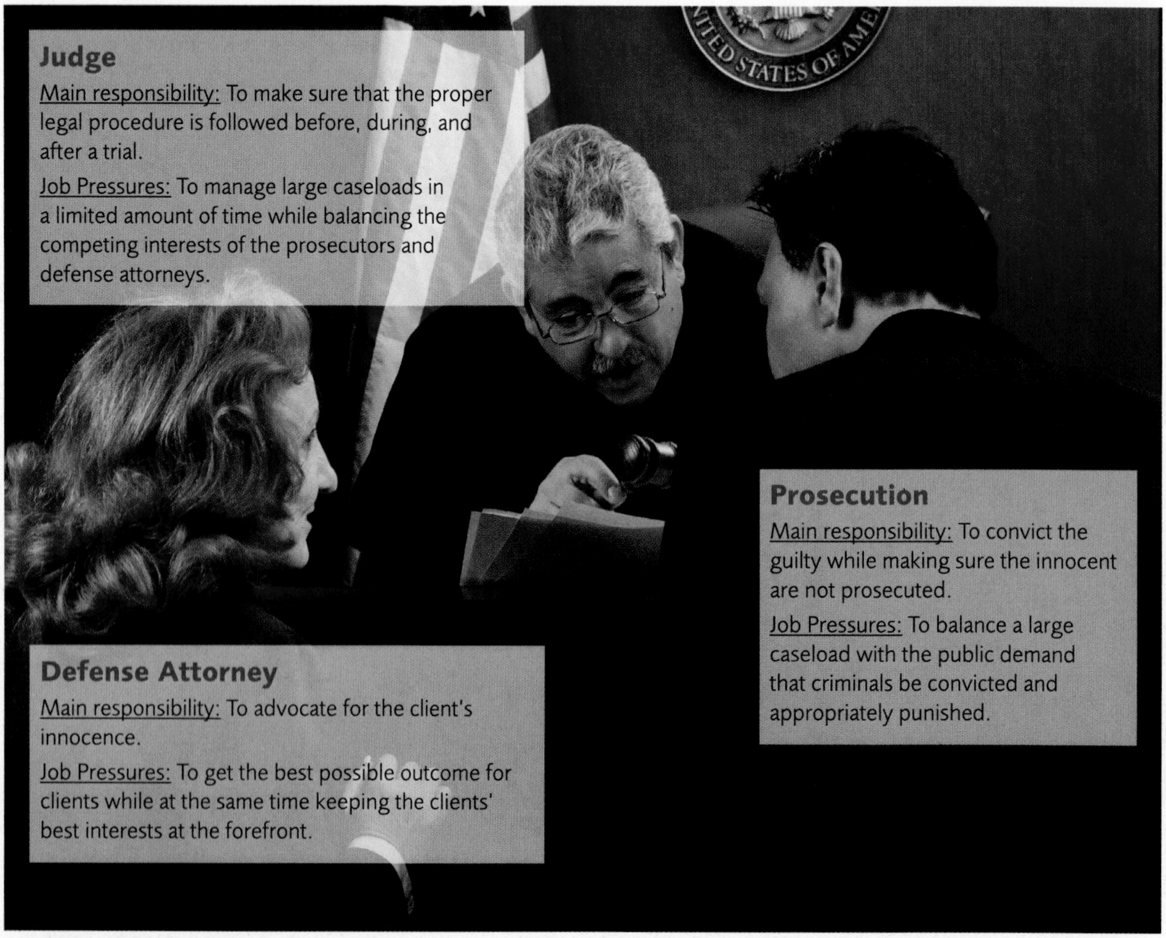

Judge

Main responsibility: To make sure that the proper legal procedure is followed before, during, and after a trial.

Job Pressures: To manage large caseloads in a limited amount of time while balancing the competing interests of the prosecutors and defense attorneys.

Prosecution

Main responsibility: To convict the guilty while making sure the innocent are not prosecuted.

Job Pressures: To balance a large caseload with the public demand that criminals be convicted and appropriately punished.

Defense Attorney

Main responsibility: To advocate for the client's innocence.

Job Pressures: To get the best possible outcome for clients while at the same time keeping the clients' best interests at the forefront.

Deborah L. Cheramie/iStockphoto.com

4LTR Press solutions are designed for today's learners through the continuous feedback of students like you. Tell us what you think about **CJ** and help us improve the learning experience for future students.

YOUR FEEDBACK MATTERS.

Complete the Speak Up survey in CourseMate at www.cengagebrain.com

Follow us at www.facebook.com/4ltrpress

9 PRETRIAL PROCEDURES: THE ADVERSARY SYSTEM IN ACTION

Learning Outcomes

After studying this chapter, you will be able to . . .

 LO 1 List the different names given to public prosecutors and indicate the general powers that they have.

 LO 2 Delineate the responsibilities of defense attorneys.

 LO 3 List the three basic features of an adversary system of justice.

LO 4 Explain how a prosecutor screens potential cases.

LO 5 List and briefly explain the different forms of plea bargaining agreements.

To Sleep No More

Michael Jackson, like many who suffer from insomnia, would ask for some milk when he had trouble sleeping. The famous pop singer was not, however, referring to the nutritious liquid that comes from cows. Rather, he wanted a dose of a white solution called *propofol,* a powerful anesthetic used to render patients unconscious during surgery. For six weeks in the spring and summer of 2009, Dr. Conrad Murray, Jackson's personal physician, administered propofol to the singer daily, despite growing concerns that his patient was addicted to the drug. On the morning of June 25, Murray tried to help Jackson sleep using milder sedatives. When that did not work, Jackson again demanded his "milk," and Murray again provided it. Within twelve minutes, the fifty-year-old singer was dead.

Murray initially informed paramedics that he had given Jackson only one sedative— the antianxiety drug lorazepam—and failed to mention anything about propofol. "That [was] a telling omission," said Dr. Bryan A. Liang, a physician and professor at San Diego's California Western School of Law. "He knows he is not supposed to be fooling around with propofol." Because the drug is so powerful, it is generally used only in a hospital setting, where heart monitors and breathing machines can deal with any unexpected side effects. Furthermore, noted another expert, "The concept of using propofol for insomnia is completely crazy. It's like trying to swat a fly with a bomb."

On February 9, 2010, about five months after the Los Angeles County coroner ruled that Jackson died of "acute propofol intoxication," Murray was arrested and charged with involuntary manslaughter. The exact language of the criminal complaint contended that the physician "did unlawfully, and without malice, kill Michael Joseph Jackson" by acting "without due caution." After watching Murray plead not guilty to the manslaughter charge, Joe Jackson, the singer's father, gave his own verdict on what had happened: "My son was murdered."

Joe Burbank/MCT /Landov

Why was Dr. Conrad Murray, center, charged with manslaughter in the death of pop star Michael Jackson? (Irfan Khan/Reuters /Landov)

Public Prosecutor
A lawyer who initiates and conducts cases in the government's name and on behalf of the people.

The police had done their job. They had investigated the circumstances surrounding Michael Jackson's death, interviewed those involved, and recorded the results. Now, the case was in the hands of the lawyers, who got their first chance to square off at a *preliminary hearing* before Los Angeles County Superior Court judge Michael Pastor in early January 2011. As you will learn later in the chapter, the preliminary hearing is designed so that a judge can decide whether enough evidence exists for a case to go to trial. In general, a preliminary hearing is short. It features few, if any, witnesses, and has almost a routine feel.

There was nothing routine about this particular pretrial hearing, though. Over the course of six days, Deputy District Attorney David Walgren summoned twenty-two witnesses to show that "[b]ecause of Dr. Murray's actions, Michael's children are left without a father."[1] Joseph Low IV, Murray's defense attorney, dismissed the parade of accusers, hinting that Jackson self-medicated to the point of overdose.[2] Eventually, Low asked Pastor to dismiss the charges, arguing that the prosecution had failed to conclusively link Jackson's death to his client's actions. The judge refused, ruling that there was sufficient evidence to try Murray for involuntary manslaughter.

"Dueling lawyers" such as Walgren and Low are the main combatants of the American adversary system. Contrary to public perception, however, these struggles start well before the beginning of the criminal trial. As we saw in Chapter 8, cases rarely make it that far. Indeed, the issue of guilt and innocence is usually settled beforehand through the efforts of the legal representatives of the state and the defendant. Thus, we will start this chapter—which focuses on "negotiated justice"—with a discussion of these key players: the prosecutor and the defense attorney.

> "*We do not prosecute* **morals.** *We prosecute* **crimes.**"
>
> —OCMULGEE CIRCUIT (GEORGIA) DISTRICT ATTORNEY FRED BRIGHT, explaining his decision not to charge professional football player Ben Roethlisberger with sexually assaulting a twenty-year-old college student (2010)

¿WHAT DO PROSECUTORS DO?

Criminal cases are tried by **public prosecutors**, who are employed by the government. The public prosecutor in federal criminal cases is called a *U.S. attorney*. In cases tried in state or local courts, the public prosecutor may be referred to as a *prosecuting attorney*, *state prosecutor*, *district attorney*, *county attorney*, or *city attorney*. Given their great autonomy, prosecutors are generally considered the most dominant figures in the American criminal justice system. In some jurisdictions, the district attorney is the chief law enforcement officer, with broad powers over police operations. Prosecutors have the power to bring the resources of the state against the individual and hold the legal keys to measuring out or withholding punishment.[3] Ideally, this power is balanced by a duty of fairness and a recognition that the prosecutor's ultimate goal is not to win cases but to see that justice is done. In *Berger v. United States* (1935), Justice George Sutherland called the prosecutor

LO

in a peculiar and very definite sense the servant of the law, the twofold aim of which is that guilt shall not escape or innocence suffer. He may prosecute with earnestness and vigor—indeed, he should do so. But, while he may strike hard blows, he is not at liberty to strike foul ones. It is as much his duty to refrain from improper methods calculated to produce a wrongful conviction as it is to use every legitimate means to bring about a just one.[4]

THE OFFICE OF THE PROSECUTOR

When he or she is acting as an *officer of the law* during a criminal trial, there are limits on the prosecutor's conduct, as we shall see in the next chapter. During the pretrial process, however, prosecutors hold a great deal of discretion in deciding the following:

1. Whether an individual who has been arrested by the police will be charged with a crime.
2. The level of the charges to be brought against the suspect.
3. If and when to stop the prosecution.[5]

There are more than eight thousand prosecutor's offices around the country, serving state, county, and municipal jurisdictions. Even though the **attorney general** is the chief law enforcement officer in any state, she or he has limited (and in some states, no) control over prosecutors within the state's boundaries.

Each jurisdiction has a chief prosecutor, who is sometimes appointed but most often elected. As an elected official, he or she typically serves a four-year term, though in some states, such as Alabama, the term is six years. (CAREER TIP: In smaller jurisdictions, the chief prosecutor has several assistants, and they work closely together. In larger ones, the chief prosecutor may have numerous *assistant prosecutors,* many of whom he or she rarely meets. Assistant prosecutors—for the most part young attorneys recently graduated from law school—may be assigned to particular sections of the organization, such as criminal prosecutions in general, or areas of *special prosecution,* such as narcotics or gang crimes.)

Attorney General The chief law officer of a state. Also, the chief law officer of the nation.

THE PROSECUTOR AS ELECTED OFFICIAL

The chief prosecutor's autonomy is not complete: as an elected official, she or he must answer to the voters. (There are exceptions: U.S. attorneys are nominated by the president and approved by the Senate, and chief prosecutors in Alaska, Connecticut, New Jersey, Rhode Island, and the District of Columbia are either appointed or hired as members of the attorney general's office.)

The prosecutor may be part of the political machine. In many jurisdictions the prosecutor must declare a party affiliation and is expected to reward fellow party members with positions in the district attorney's office if elected. The post is often seen as a stepping-stone to higher political office, and many prosecutors have gone on to serve in legislatures or as judges. Arlen Specter, a Democratic senator from Pennsylvania; Ron Castille, who sits on the state's supreme court; and Ed Rendell, a former mayor of Philadelphia and now governor of the state, all served as Philadelphia district attorneys early in their careers. Sonia Sotomayor (see the photo alongside), who in 2009 became the first Hispanic member of the United States Supreme Court, started her career as an assistant district attorney in New York City from 1979 to 1984.

Give several reasons why experience as a prosecutor would make someone such as U.S. Supreme Court justice Sonia Sotomayor a more effective judge. (AP Photo/Pablo Martinez Monsivais)

¿WHAT DO DEFENSE ATTORNEYS DO?

The media provide most people's perception of defense counsel: the idealistic public defender who nobly serves the poor, the "ambulance chaser," or the celebrity

Defense Attorney The lawyer representing the defendant.

Public Defender A court-appointed attorney who is paid by the state to represent defendants who are unable to hire private counsel.

attorney in the $3,000 suit. These stereotypes, though not entirely fictional, tend to obscure the crucial role that the **defense attorney** plays in the criminal justice system. Most persons charged with crimes have little or no knowledge of criminal procedure. Without assistance, they would be helpless in court. By acting as a staunch advocate for her or his client, the defense attorney (ideally) ensures that the government proves every point against that client beyond a reasonable doubt, even for cases that do not go to trial. In sum, the defense attorney provides a counterweight against the state in our adversary system.

THE RESPONSIBILITIES OF THE DEFENSE ATTORNEY

The Sixth Amendment right to counsel is not limited to the actual criminal trial. In a number of instances, the United States Supreme Court has held that defendants are entitled

 LO 2 to representation as soon as their rights may be denied, which includes the custodial interrogation and lineup identification procedures.[6]

Therefore, an important responsibility of the defense attorney is to represent the defendant at the various stages of the custodial process, such as arrest, interrogation, lineup, and arraignment. Other responsibilities include:

- Investigating the incident for which the defendant has been charged.
- Communicating with the prosecutor, which includes negotiating plea bargains.
- Preparing the case for trial.
- Submitting defense motions, including motions to suppress evidence.
- Representing the defendant at trial.
- Negotiating a sentence, if the client has been convicted.
- Determining whether to appeal a guilty verdict.[7]

"Look at the stakes. In civil law, if you screw up, it's just money. Here, it's the client—his life, his time in jail—and you **never know how much time** people have in their life."

—CRIMINAL DEFENSE ATTORNEY STACEY RICHMAN

Comstock Images/Jupiterimages

DEFENDING THE GUILTY

At one time or another in their careers, all defense attorneys will face a difficult question: Must I defend a client whom I know to be guilty? According to the American Bar Association's code of legal ethics, the answer is almost always, "yes."[8] The most important responsibility of the criminal defense attorney is to be an advocate for her or his client. As such, the attorney is obligated to use all ethical and legal means to achieve the client's desired goal, which is usually to avoid or lessen punishment for the charged crime.

As Supreme Court justice Byron White once noted, defense counsel has no "obligation to ascertain or present the truth." Rather, our adversarial system insists that the defense attorney "defend the client whether he is innocent or guilty."[9] Indeed, if defense attorneys refused to represent clients whom they believed to be guilty, the Sixth Amendment guarantee of a criminal trial for all accused persons would be rendered meaningless. (**CAREER TIP:** Attorneys who specialize in representing clients in court are called *trial lawyers*. Note, though, that many lawyers rarely or never do trial work, focusing instead on drafting legal documents and doing legal research.)

THE PUBLIC DEFENDER

Generally speaking, there are two different types of defense attorneys: (1) private attorneys, who are hired by individuals, and (2) **public defenders**, who work for the government. The distinction is not absolute, as many private attorneys accept employment as public defenders, too. The modern role of the public defender was established by the Supreme Court's interpretation of the Sixth Amendment in *Gideon v. Wainwright* (1963).[10] In that case, the Court ruled that no defendant can be "assured a fair trial unless counsel is provided for him," and therefore the state must provide a public defender to those who cannot afford to hire one for themselves.

Subsequently, the Court extended the **Gideon protection** to juveniles in *In re Gault* (1967)[11] and to those faced with imprisonment for committing misdemeanors in *Argersinger v. Hamlin* (1972).[12] The impact of these decisions has been substantial: about 90 percent of all criminal defendants in the United States are represented by public defenders or other appointed counsel.[13]

Effectiveness of Public Defenders Under the U.S. Constitution, a defendant who is paying for her or his defense attorney has a right to choose that attorney without interference from the court.[14] This right of choice does not extend to all defendants. According to the United States Supreme Court, "a defendant may not insist on an attorney he cannot afford."[15] In other words, an indigent defendant (one who cannot afford to pay) must accept the public defender provided by the court system. (Note that, unless the presiding judge rules otherwise, a person can waive her or his Sixth Amendment rights and act as her or his own defense attorney.) This lack of control contributes to the widespread belief that public defenders do not provide an acceptable level of defense to indigents. Statistics show, however, that conviction rates of defendants with private counsel and those represented by publicly funded attorneys are generally the same. The difference comes during sentencing, when a higher percentage of defendants with public defenders are sent to prison.[16]

The *Strickland* Standard In one Louisiana murder trial, not only did the court-appointed defense attorney spend only eleven minutes preparing for trial on a charge that carries a mandatory life sentence, but she also represented the victim's father and had been representing the victim at the time of his death. Not surprisingly, her defendant was found guilty.[17] Such

The *Gideon* Protection The rule, established in the 1963 Supreme Court case *Gideon v. Wainwright*, that the government must provide a public defender for those defendants too poor to hire one for themselves.

CAREERPREP   PUBLIC DEFENDER

Comstock Images/Jupiterimages

JOB DESCRIPTION:
- Interview low-income applicants for legal services and, if they are eligible, engage in negotiation, trial, and /or appeal of legal issues on their behalf.
- Exercise initiative, sound judgment, and creativity in attempting to solve the legal problems of the poor.

WHAT KIND OF TRAINING IS REQUIRED?
- A law degree and membership in the relevant state bar association.
- Commitment and dedication to the needs of low-income and elderly clients.

ANNUAL SALARY RANGE?
- $44,000–$92,000

For additional information, visit:
www.nlada.org/Jobs.

behavior raises a critical question: When a lawyer does such a poor job, has the client essentially been denied his or her Sixth Amendment right to assistance of counsel? In *Strickland v. Washington* (1984),[18] the Supreme Court set up a two-pronged test to determine whether constitutional requirements have been met. To prove that prior counsel was not sufficient, a defendant must show (1) that the attorney's performance was deficient *and* (2) that this deficiency *more likely than not* caused the defendant to lose the case.

In practice, it has been very difficult to prove the second prong of this test. A prosecutor can always argue that the defendant would have lost the case even if his or her lawyer had not been inept.

Several years ago, for example, the U.S. Court of Appeals for the Sixth Circuit declined to overturn the death sentence of Jeffrey Leonard (see the photo alongside) even though his public defender's investigation of the case was so superficial that it did not even uncover Leonard's real name. Despite the court's finding that the public defender's performance was so lax as to violate the Constitution, it held that the evidence against Leonard was strong enough that he would have suffered the same fate even if he had enjoyed the services of a relatively competent defense attorney.[19]

Why did a court of appeals uphold the death sentence of Jeffrey Leonard, shown here, even though his public defender was so incompetent as to be unaware of Leonard's true name?

(AP Photo/Kentucky State Dept. of Corrections/ Korhan Karacan/iStockphoto.com)

ATTORNEY-CLIENT PRIVILEGE

To defend a client effectively, a defense attorney must have access to all the facts concerning the case, even those that may be harmful to the defendant. To promote the unrestrained flow of information between the two parties, legislatures and lawyers themselves have constructed rules of **attorney-client privilege**. These rules require that communications between a client and his or her attorney be kept confidential, unless the client consents to the disclosure.

Privilege and Confessions Attorney-client privilege does not stop short of confessions.[20] Indeed, if, on hearing any statement that points toward guilt, the defense attorney could alert the prosecution or try to resign from the case, attorney-client privilege would be rendered meaningless. Even if the client says, "I have just killed seventeen women. I selected only pregnant women so I could torture them and kill two people at once. I did it. I liked it. I enjoyed it," the defense attorney must continue to do his or her utmost to serve that client.[21]

Without attorney-client privilege, observes legal expert John Kaplan, lawyers would be forced to give their clients the equivalent of *Miranda* warnings before representing them.[22] In other words, lawyers would have to make clear what clients could or could not say in the course of preparing for trial, because any incriminating statement might be used against the client in court. Such a development would have serious ramifications for the criminal justice system.

The Exception to the Privilege

The scope of attorney-client privilege is not all encompassing. In *United States v. Zolin* (1989),[23] the Supreme Court ruled that lawyers may disclose the contents of a conversation with a client if the client has provided information concerning a crime that has yet to be committed. This exception applies only to communications involving a crime that is ongoing or will occur in the future. If the client reveals a past crime, the privilege is still in effect, and the attorney may not reveal any details of that particular criminal act.

CJ and Technology

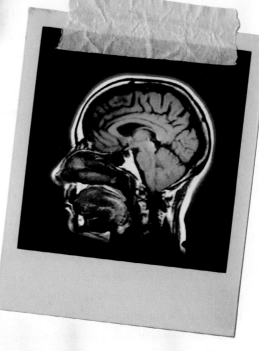

NEUROTECHNOLOGICAL LIE DETECTION

Almost a hundred years ago, the *New York Times* predicted an end to the American adversary system. "There will be no jury, no horde of detectives and witnesses, no charges and countercharges, and no attorney for the defense," the newspaper reported. This prediction was a reaction to the invention of the polygraph, a lie detector that purports to read a subject's stress levels during questioning to ascertain if the answers are truthful. Today, though widely used in criminal investigations, polygraph results are inadmissible in criminal court and therefore have had minimal impact on the criminal justice system. Nevertheless, scientists have not given up the search for a reliable lie detector. The latest research has focused on neurotechnological lie detection (NTLD), particularly functional magnetic resonance imaging (fMRI) and functional near-infrared neuroimaging (fNIR). Both devices measure blood flow in the brain, on the assumption that we access certain parts of our brains when we lie. Although this theory has yet to be proved, many experts believe that NTLD has the potential to transform the American courtroom—eventually.

THINKING ABOUT NEUROTECHNOLOGICAL LIE DETECTION

An fMRI device requires the subject to lie still while being magnetically scanned. Movement by the subject might render the scan unreadable. In contrast, fNIR uses an infrared light scan of the brain to measure blood flow, and its results are unaffected by a subject's movement. Why do these differences make fNIR more practical than fMRI for eventual use in the criminal justice system?

¿WHICH IS MORE IMPORTANT IN COURT—VICTORY OR THE TRUTH?

LO3 In strictly legal terms, three basic features characterize the **adversary system:**

1. A neutral and passive decision maker, either the judge or the jury.
2. The presentation of evidence from both parties.
3. A highly structured set of procedures (in the form of constitutional safeguards) that must be followed in the presentation of that evidence.[24]

Some critics of the American court system believe that it has been tainted by overzealous prosecutors and defense attorneys. Gordon Van Kessel, a professor at Hastings College of Law in California, complains that American lawyers see themselves as "prize fighters, gladiators, or, more accurately, semantic warriors in a verbal battle," and points out the atmosphere of "ritualized aggression" that is commonplace in the courts.[25]

Our discussion of the courtroom work group in the last chapter, however, seems to contradict this image of ritualized aggression. As political scientists Herbert

> **Adversary System** A legal system in which the prosecution and defense are opponents, or adversaries, and present their cases in the light most favorable to themselves. The court arrives at a just solution based on the evidence presented by the contestants and determines who wins and who loses.

Jacob and James Eisenstein have written, "Pervasive conflict is not only unpleasant; it also makes work more difficult."[26] The image of the courtroom work group as negotiators rather than prize fighters seems to be supported by the fact that more than nine out of every ten cases conclude with negotiated "deals" rather than trials.

Jerome Skolnick of the University of California at Berkeley found that work group members grade each other according to "reasonableness"[27]—a concept criminal justice scholar Abraham S. Blumberg embellished by labeling the defense attorney a "double agent." Blumberg believed that a defense attorney is likely to cooperate with the prosecutor in convincing a client to accept a negotiated plea of guilty because the defense attorney's main object is to finish the case quickly so as to collect the fee and move on.[28]

Perhaps the most useful definition of the adversary process softens Professor Van Kessel's criticism with the realities of the courtroom work group. University of California at Berkeley law professor Malcolm Feeley observes:

> In the adversary system the goal of the advocate is not to determine truth but to win, to maximize the interests of his or her side within the confines of the norms governing the proceedings. This is not to imply that the theory of

the adversary process has no concern for the truth. Rather, the underlying assumption of the adversary process is that truth is most likely to emerge as a by-product of vigorous conflict between intensely partisan advocates, each of whose goal is to win.[29]

Blumberg took a more cynical view when he called the court process a "confidence game" in which "victory" is achieved when a defense attorney—with the unspoken aid of the prosecutor and judge—is able to persuade the defendant to plead guilty.[30] As you read the rest of the chapter, which deals with pretrial procedures, keep in mind Feeley's and Blumberg's contentions concerning "truth" and "victory" in the American courts.

¿WHAT HAPPENS AFTER ARREST?

After an arrest has been made, the first step toward determining the suspect's guilt or innocence is the **initial appearance**. During this brief proceeding, a magistrate (see Chapter 8) informs the defendant of the charges that have been brought against him or her and explains his or her constitutional rights—particularly, the right to remain silent (under the Fifth Amendment) and the right to be represented by counsel (under the Sixth Amendment). At this point, if the defendant cannot afford to hire a private attorney, a public defender may be appointed, or private counsel may be hired by the state to represent the defendant.

As the U.S. Constitution does not specify how soon a defendant must be brought before a magistrate after arrest, it has been left to the judicial branch to determine the timing of the initial appearance. The Supreme Court has held that the initial appearance must occur "promptly," which in most cases means within forty-eight hours of booking.[31]

In misdemeanor cases, a defendant may decide to plead guilty and be sentenced during the initial appearance. Otherwise, the magistrate will usually release those charged with misdemeanors on their promise to return at a later date for further proceedings. For felony cases, however, the defendant is not permitted to make a plea at the initial appearance because a magistrate's court does not have jurisdiction to decide felonies. Furthermore, in most cases the defendant will be released only if she or he posts **bail**—an amount paid by the defendant to the court and retained by the court until the defendant returns for further proceedings. Defendants who cannot afford bail are generally kept in a local jail or lockup until the date of their trial, though many jurisdictions are searching for alternatives to this practice because of overcrowded incarceration facilities. Government statisticians estimate that 62 percent of felony defendants are released before their trials.[32]

THE PURPOSE OF BAIL

Bail is provided for under the Eighth Amendment. The amendment does not, however, guarantee the right to bail. Instead, it states that "excessive bail shall not be required." This has come to mean that in all cases except those involving a death-penalty eligible crime (where bail is prohibited), the amount of bail required must be reasonable compared with the seriousness of the wrongdoing. It does *not* mean that the amount of bail must be within the defendant's ability to pay.

The vagueness of the Eighth Amendment has encouraged a second purpose of bail: to protect the community by preventing the defendant from committing another crime before trial. To achieve this purpose, a judge can simply set bail at a level that the suspect cannot possibly afford. As we shall see, several states and the federal government have passed laws that allow judges to detain suspects deemed a threat to the community without going through the motions of setting relatively high bail.

SETTING BAIL

There is no uniform system for pretrial detention. Each jurisdiction has its own *bail tariffs*, or general guidelines concerning the proper amount of bail. For misdemeanors, the police usually follow a preapproved bail schedule created by local judicial authorities. In felony cases, the primary responsibility to set bail lies with the judge. **Figure 9.1** alongside shows typical bail amounts for violent offenses.

The Judge and Bail Setting Bail tariffs can be quite extensive. In Illinois, for example, a judge is required to take thirty-eight different factors into account when setting bail. Fourteen of these factors involve the crime itself, two refer to the evidence gathered, four to the defendant's record, nine to the defendant's flight risk and immigration status, and nine to the defendant's general character.[33] For the most part, however, judges are free to use such tariffs as loose guidelines, and they have a great deal of discretion in setting bail according to the circumstances in each case.

Other Influences on the Bail Decision Extralegal factors may also play a part in bail setting. University of

> **Bail** The amount or conditions set by the court to ensure that an individual accused of a crime will appear for further criminal proceedings.

Figure 9.1 **Average Bail Amounts for Violent Felonies**
These figures represent the mean bail figures for the seventy-five largest counties in the nation.

Comstock Images/Jupiterimages

Source: Adapted from Bureau of Justice Statistics, *Felony Defendants in Large Urban Counties, 2007* (Washington, D.C.: U.S. Department of Justice, May 2010), Table 7, page 7.

New Orleans political scientist David W. Neubauer has identified three contexts that may influence a judge's decision-making process:[34]

1. *Uncertainty.* To a certain extent, predetermined bail tariffs are unrealistic, given that judges are required to set bail within forty-eight hours of arrest. It is often difficult to get information on the defendant in that period of time, and even if a judge can obtain a "rap sheet," or list of prior arrests ("priors"), she or he will probably not have an opportunity to verify its accuracy. Due to this uncertainty, most judges have no choice but to focus primarily on the seriousness of the crime in setting bail.

2. *Risk.* There is no way of knowing for certain whether a defendant released on bail will return for his or her court date, or whether he or she will commit a crime while free. Judges are aware of the criticism they will come under from police groups, prosecutors, the press, and the public if the defendant commits a crime during that time. Consequently, especially if the judge is up for reelection, she or he may prefer to play it safe and set a high bail to detain a suspect or refuse outright to offer bail when legally able to do so.

In general, risk avoidance also dictates why those who are charged with a violent crime such as murder are usually less likely to be released prior to trial than those who are charged with property crimes such as larceny or motor vehicle theft.

3. *Overcrowded jails.* As we will discuss in detail in Chapter 13, many of the nation's jails are overcrowded. This may force a judge to make a difficult distinction between those suspects she or he believes must be detained and those who might need to be detained. To save jail space, a judge might be more lenient in setting bail for members of the latter group.[35]

In the case featured at the beginning of this chapter, Judge Michael Pastor set bail for Conrad Murray at $75,000, which is three times the standard for involuntary manslaughter in Los Angeles County.[36] Most likely, the publicity surrounding this high-profile case had an impact on the judge's decision.

GAINING PRETRIAL RELEASE

Earlier, we mentioned that many jurisdictions are looking for alternatives to the bail system. One of the most popular options is **release on recognizance (ROR)**. This is used when the judge, based on the advice of trained personnel, decides that the defendant is not at risk to "jump" bail and does not pose a threat to the community. The defendant is then released at no cost with the understanding that he or she will return at the time of the trial. The Vera Institute, a nonprofit organization in New York City, introduced the concept of ROR as part of the Manhattan Bail Project in the 1960s, and such programs are now found in nearly every jurisdiction. When properly administered, ROR programs seem to be successful, with less than 5 percent of the participants failing to show for trial.[37]

Posting Bail Those suspected of committing a felony, however, are rarely released on recognizance. These defendants may post, or pay, the full amount of the bail in cash to the court. The money will be returned when the suspect appears for trial. Given the large amount of funds required and the relative lack of wealth of many criminal defendants, a defendant can rarely post bail in cash. One option is to use personal property as collateral. These **property bonds** are also rare, because most courts require property valued at double the bail amount. Thus, if bail is set at $5,000, the defendant (or the defendant's family and friends) will have to produce property valued at $10,000.

Bail Bond Agents If unable to post bail with cash or property, a defendant may arrange for a **bail bond agent** to post a bail bond on the defendant's behalf. The bond agent, in effect, promises the court that he or she will turn over to the court the full amount of bail if the defendant fails to return for further proceedings.

The defendant usually must give the bond agent a certain percentage of the bail (frequently 10 percent) in cash. This amount, which is often not returned to the defendant later, is considered payment for the bond agent's assistance and assumption of risk. Depending on the amount of the bail bond, the defendant may also be required to sign over to the bond agent rights to certain property (such as a car, a valuable watch, or other asset) as security for the bond. (**CAREER TIP:** When a defendant "skips" bail, the bail bond agent has the option

of hiring a *bounty hunter* [see the photo on the next page] to track the fugitive down. Typically, a bounty hunter charges 10 percent of the bail amount for a successful recovery.)

PREVENTIVE DETENTION

Judges who believe that suspects pose a danger to the community or are high flight risks have always had the power to detain them by setting bail at a prohibitively high level. This strategy does involve some risk, however. In 2009, a Washington State judge set bail for Maurice Clemons, arrested on charges of assaulting a police officer and raping a child, at $190,000. To the surprise of Pierce County law enforcement and court personnel, Clemons's family was able to raise the bail amount, and Clemons was set free. Six months later, he killed four police officers at a Seattle-area coffee shop.

In an attempt to prevent such scenarios, more than thirty states have directly authorized judges to act "in

Property Bond The defendant gains pretrial release with property valued at double the bail amount that the defendant provides to the court as assurance that he or she will return for trial.

Bail Bond Agent A businessperson who agrees, for a fee, to pay the bail amount if the accused fails to appear in court as ordered.

CAREERPREP

BAIL BOND AGENT

JOB DESCRIPTION:

- Enter into contractual agreements with defendants who have posted bail. On behalf of the client/ defendant, guarantee that he or she will appear in court whenever required by the judge.
- Ensure that clients do not leave the jurisdiction to avoid court appearances and undertake the sometimes dangerous task of seeking out and capturing fugitive clients.

WHAT KIND OF TRAINING IS REQUIRED?

- Successful completion of educational courses and examinations as required by state regulation to earn the necessary license.
- Given that bail bond agents often find themselves in perilous situations and may have to use force in dealing with clients, self-defense and weapons training are strongly suggested.

ANNUAL SALARY RANGE?

- $24,000–$150,000

For additional information, visit: www.pbus.com.

Oscar Williams/iStockphoto.com

Bounty hunters such as the ones shown here are often paid substantial sums by bail bond agents to capture bond-jumping clients. What services does a bond agent offer a person facing trial?

(Hemis/Alamy)

Preventive Detention The retention of an accused person in custody due to fears that she or he will commit a crime if released before trial.

Preliminary Hearing An initial hearing in which a judge decides if there is probable cause to believe that the defendant committed the crime with which he or she is charged.

the best interests of the community" by passing **preventive detention** legislation. These laws allow judges to deny bail to arrestees with prior records of violence, thus keeping them in custody prior to trial. The federal Bail Reform Act of 1984 similarly states that federal offenders can be held without bail to ensure "the safety of any other person and the community."[38]

Critics of the 1984 act believe that it violates the U.S. Constitution by allowing the freedom of a citizen to be restricted before he or she has been proved guilty in a court of law. For many, the act also brings up the troubling issue of *false positives*—erroneous predictions that defendants, if given pretrial release, would commit a crime, when in fact they would not.

In *United States v. Salerno* (1987),[39] however, the Supreme Court upheld the act's premise. Then chief justice William Rehnquist wrote that preventive detention was not a "punishment for dangerous individuals" but a "potential solution to a pressing social problem." Therefore, "there is no doubt that preventing danger to the community is a legitimate . . . goal." In fact, about 21 percent of released defendants are rearrested before their trials begin, 13 percent for violent felonies.[40]

¿HOW DOES A PROSECUTOR LINK THE DEFENDANT TO THE CRIME?

Once the initial appearance has been completed and bail has been set, the prosecutor must establish *probable cause.* That is, the prosecutor must prove that a crime was committed and link the defendant to that crime. There are two formal procedures for establishing probable cause at this stage of the pretrial process: preliminary hearings and grand juries.

THE PRELIMINARY HEARING

During the **preliminary hearing**, the defendant appears before a judge who decides whether the evidence presented is sufficient for the case to proceed to trial. Normally, every person arrested has a right to this hearing within a reasonable amount of time after his or her initial arrest[41]—usually, no later than ten days if the defendant is in custody or within thirty days if he or she has gained pretrial release.

The Preliminary Hearing Process The preliminary hearing is conducted in the manner of a mini-trial. Typically, a police report of the arrest is presented by a law enforcement officer, supplemented with evidence provided by the prosecutor.

Because the burden of proving probable cause is relatively light (compared with proving guilt beyond a reasonable doubt), prosecutors rarely call witnesses during the preliminary hearing, saving them for the trial. During this hearing, the defendant has a right to be represented by counsel, who may cross-examine witnesses (if there are any) and challenge any evidence offered by the prosecutor. In most states, defense attorneys can take advantage of the preliminary hearing to begin the process of **discovery**, in which they are entitled to have access to any evidence in the possession of the prosecution relating to the case. Discovery is considered a keystone in the adversary process, as it allows the defense to see the evidence against the defendant prior to making a plea.

Waiving the Hearing The preliminary hearing often seems rather routine, although in some jurisdictions it replaces grand jury proceedings. It usually lasts no longer than five minutes, and the judge rarely finds that probable cause does not exist. For this reason, defense attorneys commonly advise their clients to waive their right to a preliminary hearing. Once a judge has ruled affirmatively on probable cause, the defendant is bound over to (passed along to) the *grand jury* in many jurisdictions. If the grand jury believes there are grounds for a trial, it issues an *indictment*. In other jurisdictions, the government prosecutor issues an **information**, which replaces the police complaint as the formal charge against the defendant for the purposes of a trial.

THE GRAND JURY

The federal government and about one-third of the states require a grand jury to make the decision as to whether a case should go to trial. A **grand jury** is a group of citizens called to decide whether probable cause exists. Grand juries are *impaneled*, or created, for a period of time usually not exceeding three months.

During that time, the grand jury sits in closed (secret) session and hears only evidence presented by the prosecutor—the defendant cannot present evidence at this hearing. The prosecutor presents to the grand jury whatever evidence the state has against the defendant, including photographs, documents, tangible objects, the testimony of witnesses, and other items.

If the grand jury finds that probable cause exists, it issues an **indictment** (pronounced in-*dyte*-ment) against the defendant. Like an information in a preliminary hearing, the indictment becomes the formal charge against the defendant. (CAREER TIP: If a grand jury needs more evidence, it can issue a document called a subpoena, ordering a person to appear in court and answer its questions. The task of delivering the subpoena is often left to a *process server*, whose career is based on the challenge of finding people who do not want to be found.)

The "Shield" and the "Sword" The grand jury has a long history in the United States, having been brought over from England by the colonists and codified in the Fifth Amendment to the U.S. Constitution. Historically, it has acted as both a "shield" and a "sword" in the criminal justice process. By giving citizens the chance to review government charges of

Discovery Formal investigation prior to trial.

Information The formal charge against the accused issued by the prosecutor after a preliminary hearing has found probable cause.

Grand Jury The group of citizens called to decide whether probable cause exists.

Indictment A written accusation that probable cause exists to believe that a named person has committed a crime.

Jim Jurca/iStockphoto

Case Attrition The process through which prosecutors effect an overall reduction in the number of persons prosecuted.

Nolle Prosequi (nol-é pro-sekwi) A Latin term describing the prosecutor's decision not to prosecute a defendant based on his or her determination that a conviction is either unlikely or undesirable.

wrongdoing, it "shields" the individual from the power of the state. At the same time, the grand jury offers the government a "sword"—the opportunity to provide evidence against the accused—in its efforts to fight crime and protect society.[42]

A "Rubber Stamp" Today, the protective function of the grand jury is in doubt—critics say that the "sword" aspect works too well and the "shield" aspect not at all. Statistically, the grand jury is even more prosecutor friendly than the preliminary hearing. Defendants are indicted at a rate of more than 99 percent,[43] leading to the common characterization of the grand jury as little more than a "rubber stamp" for the prosecution. Certainly, the procedural rules of the grand jury favor prosecutors. The exclusionary rule (see Chapter 7) does not apply in grand jury investigations, so prosecutors can present evidence that would be disallowed at any subsequent trial. Furthermore, because the grand jury is given only one version of the facts—the prosecution's—it is likely to find probable cause. In the words of one observer, a grand jury would indict a "ham sandwich" if the government asked it to do so.[44] As a result of these concerns, more than half of the jurisdictions have abolished grand juries.

Ken Glaser/Corbis

CASE ATTRITION

Prosecutorial discretion also includes the power *not* to prosecute cases. For example, federal prosecutors decline to bring charges in nearly three out of every four computer fraud cases referred to them by investigators.[45] **Figure 9.2** on the facing page depicts the average outcomes of one hundred felony arrests in the United States. As you can see, of the sixty-five adult arrestees brought before the district attorney, only

thirty-five are prosecuted, and only eighteen of these prosecutions lead to incarceration. Consequently, fewer than one in three adults arrested for a felony see the inside of a prison or jail cell. This phenomenon is known as **case attrition**, and it is explained in part by prosecutorial discretion.

Scarce Resources A large percentage of the adult felony cases brought to prosecutors by police are dismissed through a ***nolle prosequi*** (Latin for "unwilling to pursue"). Why are these cases "nolled," or not prosecuted by the district attorney? In the section on law enforcement, you learned that the police do not have the resources to arrest every lawbreaker in the nation. Similarly, district attorneys do not have the resources to prosecute every arrest. They must choose how to distribute their scarce resources.

Several years ago, for example, Contra Costa County (California) district attorney Robert Kochly announced that, due to budget shortfalls, his office would no longer prosecute anyone caught with less than a gram of methamphetamine or cocaine, less than half a gram of heroin, and fewer than five pills of Ecstasy.[46]

In some cases, the decision is made for prosecutors, such as when police break procedural law and negate important evidence. This happens rarely—less than 1 percent of felony arrests are dropped because of the exclusionary rule, and almost all of these are the result of illegal drug searches.[47]

Screening Factors Most prosecutors have a *screening process* for deciding when to prosecute and when to "noll." This process varies a bit from jurisdiction to jurisdiction, but most prosecutors consider several factors in making the decision:

LO 4

- The most important factor in deciding whether to prosecute is not the prosecutor's belief in the guilt of the suspect, but whether there is *sufficient evidence for conviction*.[48] If prosecutors have strong physical evidence and a number of reliable and

Figure 9.2   Following One Hundred Felony Arrests: The Criminal Justice Funnel

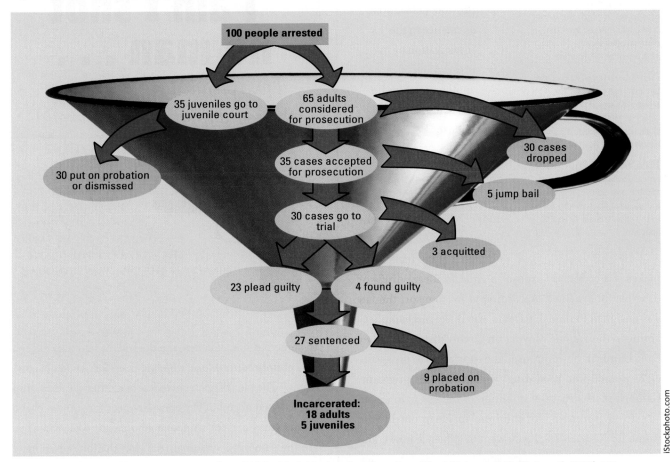

Source: Adapted from Todd R. Clear, George F. Cole, and Michael D. Reisig, *American Corrections,* 9th ed. (Belmont, Calif.: Wadsworth, 2011), 134.

believable witnesses, they are quite likely to prosecute.

- Prosecutors also tend to establish *case priorities.* In other words, everything else being equal, a district attorney will prosecute a rapist instead of a jaywalker because the former presents a greater threat to society than does the latter. A prosecutor will also be more likely to prosecute someone with an extensive record of wrongdoing than a first-time offender. Often, in coordination with the police, a district attorney's office will target a single area of crime, such as illegal drug use or drunk driving.

- Sometimes a case is dropped even when it involves a serious crime and a wealth of evidence exists against the suspect. These situations usually involve **uncooperative victims.** Domestic violence cases are particularly difficult to prosecute because the victims may want to keep the matter private, fear

reprisals, or have a strong desire to protect their abuser.[49] In some jurisdictions, as many as 80 percent of domestic violence victims refuse to cooperate with the prosecution.[50]

- *Unreliability of victims* can also affect a charging decision. If the victim in a rape case is a crack addict and a prostitute, while the defendant is the chief executive officer of a large corporation, prosecutors may be hesitant to have a jury decide which one is more trustworthy.

- A prosecutor may be willing to drop a case or reduce the charges against *a defendant who is willing to testify against other offenders.* Federal law encourages this kind of behavior by offering sentencing reductions

Uncooperative Victim A crime victim who decides, for reasons of her or his own, not to provide information concerning the alleged crime to police or prosecutors, therefore making it difficult or impossible to pursue a conviction.

Arraignment A court proceeding in which the suspect is formally charged with the criminal offense stated in the indictment or information.

Nolo Contendere Latin for "I will not contest it." A criminal defendant's plea, in which he or she chooses not to challenge, or contest, the charges brought by the government.

Plea Bargaining The process by which the accused and the prosecutor work out a mutually satisfactory conclusion to the case, subject to court approval.

to defendants who provide "substantial assistance in the investigation or prosecution of another person who has committed an offense."[51]

A prosecutor also has great discretion to interpret the criminal codes under which he or she operates. In Alabama, for example, state legislation makes it a crime to "expose" a child to illegal drugs or drug paraphernalia.[52] According to its sponsor, the law was designed to punish parents who make methamphetamine in their home. Covington County district attorney Greg Gambril, however, used the legislation to prosecute eight women who used drugs while they were pregnant. Gambril insists that the intention of the law is to create "a safe environment" for children "inside or outside the womb."[53] (CAREER TIP: If you want to influence how criminal law is written in your state, you should consider running for office as a *state legislator* at some point in your career.)

¿WHY DO SO MANY DEFENDANTS PLEAD GUILTY?

Based on the information (delivered during the preliminary hearing) or indictment (handed down by the grand jury), the prosecutor submits a motion to the court to order the defendant to appear before the trial court for an **arraignment**. Due process of law, as guaranteed by the Fifth Amendment, requires that a criminal defendant be informed of the charges brought against her or him and be offered an opportunity to respond to those charges. The arraignment is one of the ways in which due process requirements are satisfied by criminal procedure law.

At the arraignment, the defendant is informed of the charges and must respond by pleading not guilty or guilty.

"I ain't shot no man . . .

I just pleaded guilty because they said if I didn't they would gas me for it, and that is all."

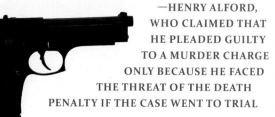

—HENRY ALFORD, WHO CLAIMED THAT HE PLEADED GUILTY TO A MURDER CHARGE ONLY BECAUSE HE FACED THE THREAT OF THE DEATH PENALTY IF THE CASE WENT TO TRIAL

Comstock Images/Jupiterimages

In some but not all states, the defendant may also enter a plea of **nolo contendere**, which is Latin for "I will not contest it." The plea of *nolo contendere* is neither an admission nor a denial of guilt. (The consequences for someone who pleads guilty and for someone who pleads *nolo contendere* are the same in a criminal trial, but the latter plea cannot be used in a subsequent civil trial as an admission of guilt.) Most frequently, the defendant pleads guilty to the initial charge or to a lesser charge that has been agreed on through *plea bargaining* between the prosecutor and the defendant. If the defendant pleads guilty, no trial is necessary, and the defendant is sentenced based on the crime he or she has admitted committing.

PLEA BARGAINING IN THE CRIMINAL JUSTICE SYSTEM

Plea bargaining usually takes place after the arraignment and before the beginning of the trial. In its simplest terms, it is a process by which the accused, represented by the defense counsel, and the prosecutor work out a mutually satisfactory disposition of the case, subject to court approval. Plea bargaining agreements can take several different forms:

- *Charge bargaining.* In charge bargaining, the defendant pleads guilty in exchange for a reduction of the charges. A felony burglary charge, for example, could be reduced to the lesser offense of breaking and entering. The more serious the initial charge, the more an accused has to gain by bargaining: pleading guilty to second degree murder can save the defendant from the risk of being convicted of first degree murder, which carries the death penalty in some states.

- *Sentence bargaining.* In sentence bargaining, the defendant pleads guilty in exchange for a lighter sentence, which may include a shorter prison term or probation. In most jurisdictions, the judge makes the final decision on whether to accept this agreement. The prosecutor can only recommend a lighter sentence. The prosecutor may also suggest that the defendant be placed in a counseling program, such as a drug rehabilitation center, in return for the guilty plea.

- *Count bargaining.* A person can be charged with multiple counts, either for committing multiple crimes or for different aspects of a single incident. A person who goes on a killing spree that results in seven deaths, for example, would be charged with seven counts of first degree murder. A person who breaks into a home, sexually assaults the inhabitants, and then takes their credit cards could be charged with counts of rape, aggravated burglary, misdemeanor theft, felony theft, and criminal use of a credit card. In count bargaining, a defendant pleads guilty in exchange for a reduction in the counts against him or her.

In a sense, count bargaining is a form of sentence bargaining. If a person is convicted of multiple counts, her or his prison time is calculated by combining the attendant sentence of each count (which is why some criminals are sentenced to a seemingly ridiculously long prison term, well past their life expectancies). If a count is dropped, so is the prison time that goes with it.

In *Santobello v. New York* (1971),[54] the Supreme Court held that plea bargaining "is not only an essential part of the process but a highly desirable part for many reasons." Some observers would agree, but with reservations. They understand that plea bargaining offers the practical benefit of saving court resources but question whether it is the best way to achieve justice.[55]

MOTIVATIONS FOR PLEA BARGAINING

Given the high rate of plea bargaining—accounting for 94 percent of criminal convictions in state courts[56]—it follows that the prosecutor, defense attorney, and defendant each have strong reasons to engage in the practice.

Prosecutors and Plea Bargaining In most cases, a prosecutor has a single goal after charging a defendant with a crime: conviction. If a case goes to trial, no matter how certain a prosecutor may be that the defendant is guilty, there is always a chance that a jury or judge will disagree. Plea bargaining removes this risk.

Furthermore, the prosecutorial screening process described earlier in the chapter is not infallible. Sometimes, a prosecutor will find that the evidence against the accused is weaker than first thought or will uncover new information that changes the complexion of the case. In these situations, the prosecutor may decide to drop the charges or, if he or she still feels that the defendant is guilty, turn to plea bargaining to "save" a questionable case.

The prosecutor's role as an administrator also comes into play. She or he may be interested in the quickest, most efficient manner to dispose of caseloads, and plea bargains reduce the time and money spent on each case. Personal philosophy can affect the proceedings as well. A prosecutor who feels that the probable sentence for a particular crime, such as marijuana possession, is too strict may plea bargain to lessen the penalty. Similarly, some prosecutors will consider plea bargaining only in certain instances—for burglary and theft, for example, but not for more serious felonies such as rape and murder.[57]

Defense Attorneys and Plea Bargaining Political scientist Milton Heumann has said that the most important lesson that a defense attorney learns is that "most of his [or her] clients are guilty."[58] Given this stark reality, favorable plea bargains are often the best a defense attorney can do for clients, aside from helping them to gain acquittals. Some have suggested that defense attorneys have other, less savory motives for convincing a client to plead guilty, such as a desire to increase profit margins by quickly disposing of cases[59] or a wish to please the other members of the courtroom work group by showing their "reasonableness."[60]

Why did John Albert Gardner agree to plead guilty to murdering two teenagers? What incentives might the San Diego prosecutors have had for accepting Gardner's guilty plea and declining to seek his execution? (AP Photo/San Diego Union-Tribune, Nelvin C. Cepeda, Pool)

Defendants and Plea Bargaining The plea bargain allows the defendant a measure of control over her or his fate. In 2010, for example, John Albert Gardner was convicted of killing fourteen-year-old Amber Dubois and seventeen-year old Chelsea King (see the photo alongside). Despite the violent nature of the crimes, San Diego County prosecutors agreed not to seek the death penalty if Gardner pleaded guilty to both murders. He did so, and a judge sentenced him to life in prison without parole. As **Figure 9.3** below shows, defendants who plea bargain receive significantly lighter sentences on average than those who are found guilty at trial.

GOING TO TRIAL

The pretrial process does not definitely lead to a guilty plea. Just as prosecutors, defense attorneys, and defendants have reasons to negotiate, they may also be motivated to take a case to trial. If either side is confident in the strength of its arguments and evidence, it will obviously be less likely to accept a plea bargain. Both prosecutors and defense attorneys may favor a trial to gain publicity, and sometimes public pressure after an extremely violent or high-profile crime will force a chief prosecutor (who is, remember, normally an elected official) to take a weak case to trial. Also, some defendants may insist on their right to a trial, regardless of their attorneys' advice. In the next chapter, we will examine what happens to the roughly 5 percent of indictments that do lead to the courtroom.

Figure 9.3 Sentencing Outcomes for Guilty Pleas

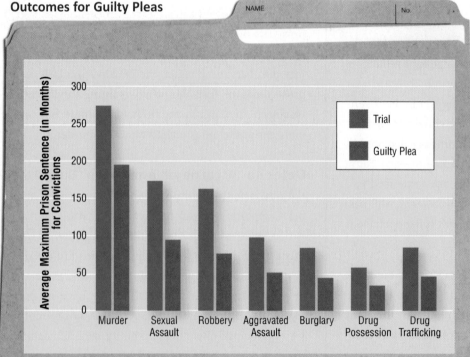

Source: Adapted from Bureau of Justice Statistics, *Felony Sentences in State Courts, 2006—Statistical Tables* (Washington, D.C.: U.S. Department of Justice, December 2009), Table 4.3.

THE IN-CROWD

Share your 4LTR Press story on Facebook at
www.facebook.com/4ltrpress for a chance to win.

To learn more about the
In-Crowd opportunity 'like'
us on Facebook.

© Go Media

10 THE CRIMINAL TRIAL

Learning Outcomes

After studying this chapter, you will be able to . . .

 LO 1 Identify the basic protections enjoyed by criminal defendants in the United States.

LO 2 Explain what "taking the Fifth" really means.

 LO 3 Contrast challenges for cause and peremptory challenges during *voir dire*.

 LO 4 List the standard steps in a criminal jury trial.

LO 5 List the five basic steps of an appeal.

JUDGE BOB R. McGEE

Star Witness

The jury had been sitting in a District of Columbia court for nearly two weeks, watching the trial of Ingmar Guandique for the first degree murder of Chandra Levy. In that time, very little had happened. Of the prosecution's thirty-seven witnesses, most were forensic experts who offered detailed testimony about highly technical subjects such as DNA testing and body decomposition. Plainly put, the jurors were bored. One of them even appeared to be nodding off.

Then, witness number thirty-eight took the stand and woke things up. Handcuffed and wearing an orange jail jumpsuit, Armando Morales testified about a conversation he had had with Guandique four years earlier, when the two shared a prison cell in Kentucky. Guandique had been incarcerated for attacking two female joggers in Rock Creek Park in Washington, D.C., during the spring of 2001—about the same time that Levy, a twenty-four-year-old government intern, had disappeared. Morales recalled Guandique's words about Levy, whose body was found in Rock Creek Park a year after she vanished: "I killed that bitch, but I didn't rape her."

"Mr. Morales is a pretty smart guy," Santha Sonenberg, Guandique's public defender, told the jurors. Sonenberg was trying to convince them that Morales, serving a ten-year prison term for gang-related drug and weapons crimes, had made up his testimony to "get in good" with government corrections officials. This strategy didn't work. On November 22, 2010, the jury found Guandique guilty of killing Levy during an attempted robbery and kidnapping, and he was sentenced to sixty years in prison. After the verdict, Susan Levy, Chandra's mother, hugged lead prosecutor Amanda Haines. "Thank you," Levy said. "That was a miracle."

What evidence most likely convinced a Washington, D.C., jury that Ingmar Guandique, shown here, was guilty of murdering Chandra Levy? (AP Photo/Jacquelyn Martin, File)

Susan Levy certainly had reason to be pleased with Ingmar Guandique's conviction. The mystery of her daughter's death had lasted nearly a decade—mental torture for any parent. To make matters worse, the initial police investigation had focused on married California congressman Gary Condit, with whom Chandra had been having an affair when she disappeared, generating a stressful media circus. But was the verdict really a "miracle?"

In a way, perhaps. No forensic evidence linked Guandique to the crime scene in Rock Creek Park. There was no murder weapon, no eyewitnesses, and no definitive ruling as to how Chandra Levy actually died. The police did find DNA on Chandra's running tights, but it did not belong to Guandique. Indeed, the only link between the victim and the defendant was Armando Morales. For juror Sharae Bacon, that was enough. "There were no holes in [Morales's] testimony," she said.[1]

Throughout the proceedings, Guandique's lawyers complained that their client was being made a scapegoat for the prosecution's earlier failures, particularly the embarrassing investigation of Condit.[2] Whenever a defendant, even one with a criminal past, is convicted without direct evidence, the fairness of a criminal trial's result inevitably comes into question. Fairness, of course, is a crucial component of the criminal trial. Protection against the arbitrary abuse of power is at the heart of the U.S. Constitution, and the right to a criminal trial before a jury is one means of ensuring this protection.

In this chapter, we will examine the fairness of the criminal trial in the context of the current legal environment. Because fairness can only be defined subjectively, we will also make an effort to look into the effect human nature has on the adversary process. Trials may be based on fact finding, but as Judge Jerome Frank once asserted, when it comes to a jury, "facts are guesses."[3] (CAREER TIP: Ingmar Guandique, an

immigrant from El Salvador, spent the trial wearing headphones into which a *court interpreter* translated the proceedings from English to Spanish. These interpreters are often required so that a defendant, witness, or other key participant can understand what is being said at court.

¿WHAT ARE THE SPECIAL FEATURES OF CRIMINAL TRIALS?

Civil trials (see Chapter 4) and criminal trials have many similar features. In both types of trials, attorneys from each side select a jury, make their opening statements to the court, examine and cross-examine witnesses, and summarize their positions in closing arguments. The jury is charged (instructed), and if it reaches a verdict, the trial comes to an end.

The principal difference is that in civil trials, the adversaries are persons (including corporations, which are legal persons, and businesses), one of whom often is seeking a remedy in the form of damages from the other. In a criminal trial, it is the state, not the victim of the crime, that brings the action against an alleged wrongdoer. Criminal trial procedures reflect the need to protect criminal defendants against the power of the state by providing them with a number of rights. Many of the significant rights of the accused are spelled out in the Sixth Amendment, which reads, in part, as follows:

> In all criminal prosecutions, the accused shall enjoy the right to a speedy and public trial, by an impartial jury of the State and the district wherein the crime shall have been committed, . . . and to be informed of the nature and cause of the accusation; to be confronted with

> " *Law is not justice and a trial is not a scientific inquiry into truth.*
> **A trial is the resolution of a dispute."**
>
> —EDISON HAINES

LO

the witnesses against him; to have compulsory process for obtaining witnesses in his favor; and to have the Assistance of Counsel for his defense.

In the last chapter, we discussed the Sixth Amendment's guarantee of the right to counsel. In this section, we will examine the other aspects of the criminal trial that make it unique, beginning with two protections explicitly stated in the Sixth Amendment: the right to a speedy trial by an impartial jury.

A "SPEEDY" TRIAL

As you have just read, the Sixth Amendment requires a speedy trial for those accused of a criminal act. The reason for this requirement is obvious: depending on various factors, the defendant may lose his or her right to move freely and may be incarcerated prior to trial. Also, the accusation that a person has committed a crime jeopardizes that person's reputation in the community. If the defendant is innocent, the sooner the trial is held, the sooner his or her innocence can be established in the eyes of the court and the public.

The Definition of a Speedy Trial The Sixth Amendment does not specify what is meant by the term *speedy*. The United States Supreme Court has refused to quantify "speedy" as well, ruling instead in *Barker v. Wingo* (1972)[4] that only in situations in which the delay is unwarranted and proved to be prejudicial can the accused claim a violation of Sixth Amendment rights.

As a result, all fifty states have their own speedy-trial statutes. For example, the Illinois Speedy Trial Act states that a defendant must be tried within 120 days of arrest unless both the prosecution and the defense agree otherwise.[5] At the national level, the Speedy Trial Act of 1974[6] (amended in 1979) specifies the following time limits for those in the federal court system:

1 No more than thirty days between arrest and indictment.

2 No more than ten days between indictment and arraignment.

3 No more than sixty days between arraignment and trial.

Federal law allows extra time for hearings on pretrial motions, mental competency examinations, and other procedural actions.

Statutes of Limitations Note that the Sixth Amendment's guarantee of a speedy trial does not apply until a person has been accused of a crime. Citizens are protected against unreasonable delays before accusation by **statutes of limitations**, which are legislative time limits that require prosecutors to charge a defendant with a crime within a certain amount of time after the allegedly illegal

Statute of Limitations A law limiting the amount of time prosecutors have to bring criminal charges against a suspect after the crime has occurred.

CAREERPREP

TRIAL COURT ADMINISTRATOR

JOB DESCRIPTION:

- Oversee court operations, budget and accounting, technology, emergency management, and human resources.
- Establish and maintain working relationships with judges, state attorneys, public defenders, clerks, other state and federal courts (including the United States Supreme Court), law enforcement agencies, and the public.

WHAT KIND OF TRAINING IS REQUIRED?

- A bachelor of arts in court administration, management, or a related area, and five years of professional experience in court administration or government administration, plus five years in a supervisory capacity.
- A law degree, master's degree, or certification by the Institute of Court Management may substitute for nonsupervisory experience.

ANNUAL SALARY RANGE?

- $66,000–$116,000

For additional information, visit: www.ncsc.org.

PhotoDisc

Jury Trial A trial before a judge and a jury.

Bench Trial A trial conducted without a jury, in which a judge makes the determination of the defendant's guilt or innocence.

Acquittal A declaration following a trial that the individual accused of the crime is innocent.

Immunity A special status, granted by the prosecutor, protecting a witness from being prosecuted for any acts about which the witness testifies in criminal court.

act took place. If the statute of limitations on a particular crime is ten years, and the police do not identify a suspect until ten years and one day after the criminal act occurred, then that suspect cannot be charged with that particular offense.

In general, prosecutions for murder and other offenses that carry the death penalty do not have a statute of limitations. This exception provides police with the ability to conduct cold case investigations (see page 106) that last for decades. In 2011, for example, Federal Bureau of Investigation agents were still interviewing suspects in the arson-related 1964 murder of Frank Morris. Morris died when his Ferriday, Louisiana, shoe shop was set on fire by members of the local Ku Klux Klan. The main problem with such cases concerns the amount of time that has passed since the criminal act. During the interval, witnesses may have died or forgotten key aspects of the case, and important evidence may also have been lost.

THE ROLE OF THE JURY

The Sixth Amendment also states that anyone accused of a crime shall be judged by "an impartial jury." In *Duncan v. Louisiana* (1968),[7] the Supreme Court solidified this right by ruling that in all felony cases, the defendant is entitled to a **jury trial**. The Court has, however, left it to the individual states to decide whether juries are required for misdemeanor cases.[8] If the defendant waives her or his right to trial by jury, a **bench trial** takes place in which a judge decides questions of legality and fact, and no jury is involved.

The typical American jury consists of twelve persons. In most jurisdictions, a jury verdict in a criminal case must be *unanimous* for **acquittal**—a declaration of innocence—or conviction. In other words, all twelve jurors must agree on the defendant's fate. There are some exceptions, however. About half the states allow fewer than twelve persons on criminal juries, though the United States Supreme

Court has struck down attempts to use juries with fewer than six members. Furthermore, two states—Louisiana and Oregon—permit nonunanimous trial verdicts, though neither allows more than three dissenting votes for convictions by twelve-person juries.

THE PRIVILEGE AGAINST SELF-INCRIMINATION

In addition to the Sixth Amendment, which specifies the protections we have just discussed, the Fifth Amendment to the Constitution also provides important safeguards for the defendant. The Fifth Amendment states that no person "shall be compelled in any criminal case to be a witness against himself." Therefore, a defendant has the right *not* to testify at a trial if to do so would implicate him or her in the crime. Witnesses may also refuse to testify on this ground.

For example, if a witness, while testifying, is asked a question and the answer would reveal her or his own criminal wrongdoing, the witness may "take the Fifth." In other words, she or he can refuse to testify on the ground that such testimony may be self-incriminating. This rarely occurs, however, as witnesses are often granted **immunity** before testifying, meaning that no information they disclose can be used to bring criminal charges against them. Witnesses who have been granted immunity cannot refuse to answer questions on the basis of self-incrimination.

It is important to note that not only does the defendant have the right to take the Fifth, but also that the decision to do so should not prejudice the jury in the prosecution's favor. The Supreme Court came to this controversial decision while reviewing *Adamson v. California* (1947),[9] a case involving the convictions of two defendants who had declined to testify in their own defense against charges of robbery, kidnapping, and murder. The prosecutor in the *Adamson* proceedings frequently and insistently brought this silence to the notice of the jury in his closing argument, implying that if the pair had been innocent, they would not have been afraid to testify. The Court ruled that such tactics effectively invalidated the Fifth Amendment by using the defendants' refusal to testify against them. Now judges are required to inform the jury that an accused's decision to remain silent cannot be held against him or her.

THE PRESUMPTION OF A DEFENDANT'S INNOCENCE

The presumption in criminal law is that a defendant is innocent until proved guilty. The burden of proving guilt falls on the state (the public prosecutor). Even if a defendant did in fact commit the crime, she or he will be innocent in the eyes of the law unless the prosecutor can substantiate the charge with sufficient evidence to convince a jury (or judge, in a bench trial) of the defendant's guilt.[10] Sometimes, especially when a case involves a high-profile violent crime, pretrial publicity may have convinced many members of the community—including potential jurors—that a defendant is guilty. In these instances, a judge has the authority to change the venue (location) of the trial to ensure an unbiased jury. The judge can also import an impartial jury, as was the case for the high-profile trial of Casey Anthony, charged with killing her two-year-old daughter, Caylee. Although the trial took place in Orlando, Florida, the presiding judge, Belvin Perry, Jr., decided to bring in a jury from Clearwater—about 100 miles away. Perry was worried that Orlando residents would have found it difficult, if not impossible, to act impartially toward Anthony (see the photo above). In 2011, the Clearwater jury found Anthony not guilty of first degree murder.

Why did the presiding judge choose to import an impartial jury in the high-profile trial of Casey Anthony? What is your opinion of the judge's decision to do so? (AP Photo/Red Huber, Pool)

A STRICT STANDARD OF PROOF

In a criminal trial, the defendant is not required to prove his or her innocence. As mentioned earlier, the burden of proving the defendant's guilt lies entirely with the state. Furthermore, the state must prove the defendant's guilt *beyond a reasonable doubt*. That is, the prosecution must show that, based on all the evidence, the defen-

dant's guilt is clear and unquestionable. In *In re Winship* (1970),[11] a case involving the due process rights of juveniles, the Supreme Court ruled that the Constitution requires the reasonable doubt standard because it reduces the risk of convicting innocent people and therefore reassures Americans of the law's moral force and legitimacy.

This high standard of proof in criminal cases reflects a fundamental social value—the belief that it is worse to convict an innocent individual than to let a guilty one go free. The consequences to the life, liberty, and reputation of an accused person from an erroneous conviction for a crime are substantial, and these consequences have been factored into the process. Placing a high standard of proof on the prosecutor reduces the margin of error in criminal cases (at least in one direction).

¿HOW IS THE JURY SELECTED?

The initial step in a criminal trial involves choosing the jury. The main goal of jury selection is to produce a cross section of the population in the jurisdiction where the crime was committed. Besides having to live in the jurisdiction where the case is being tried, there are very few restrictions on eligibility to serve on a jury. State legislatures generally set the requirements, and they are similar in most states. For the most part, jurors must be:

Master Jury List The list of citizens in a court's district from which a jury can be selected.

Venire The group of citizens from which the jury is selected.

Voir Dire The process that allows trial attorneys to determine the qualifications and suitability of prospective jurors.

Challenge for Cause A *voir dire* challenge in which an attorney states the reason why a prospective juror should not be included on the jury.

1. Citizens of the United States.
2. Over eighteen years of age.
3. Free of felony convictions.
4. Healthy enough to function in a jury setting.
5. Sufficiently intelligent to understand the issues of a trial.
6. Able to read, write, and comprehend

the English language (with one exception—New Mexico does not allow non-English-speaking citizens to be eliminated from jury lists simply because of their lack of English-language skills).

The **master jury list**, sometimes called the *jury pool*, is made up of all the eligible jurors in a community. This list is usually drawn from voter-registration lists or driver's license rolls, which have the benefit of being easily available and timely.

The next step in gathering a jury is to draw together the *venire* (Latin for "to come"). The *venire* is composed of all those people who are notified by the clerk of the court that they have been selected for jury duty. Those selected to be part of the *venire* are ordered to report to the courthouse on the date specified by the notice.

VOIR DIRE

At the courthouse, prospective jurors are gathered, and the process of selecting those who will actually hear the case begins. This selection process is not haphazard. The court ultimately seeks jurors who are free of any biases that may affect their willingness to listen to the facts of the case impartially. To this end, both the

"A jury consists of twelve persons **chosen to decide** *who has the better lawyer."*

—ROBERT FROST, AMERICAN POET (1874–1963)

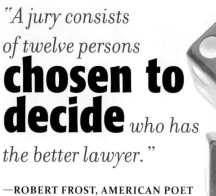

Brent Melton/IStockphoto.com

prosecutor and the defense attorney have some input into the ultimate makeup of the jury. Each attorney questions prospective jurors in a proceeding known as **voir dire** (French for "to speak the truth"). During *voir dire*, jurors are required to provide the court with a significant amount of personal information, including home address, marital status, employment status, arrest record, and life experiences.

Questioning Potential Jurors The *voir dire* process involves both written and oral questioning of potential jurors. Attorneys fashion their inquiries in such a manner as to uncover any biases on the parts of prospective jurors and to find persons who might identify with the plights of their respective sides. As one attorney noted, though a lawyer will have many chances to talk to a jury as a whole, *voir dire* is his or her only chance to talk with the individual jurors. (To better understand the specific kinds of questions asked during this process, see **Figure 10.1** on the facing page.)

Increasingly, attorneys are also conducting virtual *voir dires* on the Internet, using social-networking sites such as MySpace and Facebook to learn valuable information about potential jurors.

Challenging Potential Jurors During *voir dire*, the attorney for each side may exercise a certain number of challenges to prevent particular persons from serving on the jury. Both sides can exercise two types of challenges: challenges "for cause" and peremptory challenges.

LO 3

Challenges for Cause If a defense attorney or prosecutor concludes that a prospective juror is unfit to serve, the attorney may exercise a **challenge for cause** and request that that person not be included on the jury. Attorneys must provide the court with a sound, legally justifiable reason for why potential jurors are "unfit" to serve. For example, jurors can be challenged for cause

Figure 10.1 Sample Juror Questionnaire

In 2010, Brian David Mitchell went on trial in Salt Lake City, Utah, for kidnapping fourteen-year-old Elizabeth Smart and keeping the girl in captivity for "nine months of hell." Mitchell held a number of extreme religious views, including the belief that he was a godlike figure who would play a prominent role in the upcoming "end of the world." As Mitchell's religion would play a significant part in the criminal proceedings, both the prosecution and the defense were interested in any potential juror's own religious beliefs, as this excerpt from the juror questionnaire shows.

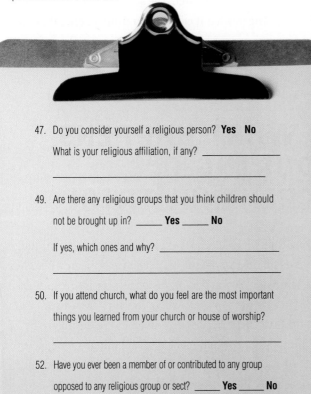

AP Photo/Isaac Brekken, Pool/Image Source

47. Do you consider yourself a religious person? **Yes No**

What is your religious affiliation, if any? _____

_____

49. Are there any religious groups that you think children should not be brought up in? _____ **Yes** _____ **No**

If yes, which ones and why? _____

_____

50. If you attend church, what do you feel are the most important things you learned from your church or house of worship?

_____

52. Have you ever been a member of or contributed to any group opposed to any religious group or sect? _____ **Yes** _____ **No**

If yes, what groups and how long have you participated? _____

_____

if they are mentally incompetent, do not understand English, or are proved to have a prior link—be it personal or financial—with the defendant or victim.

Jurors can also be challenged if they are outwardly biased in some way that would prejudice them for or against the defendant. Jury selection for the trial of José Padilla, charged several years ago with providing material support to al Qaeda, took more than a month because so many potential jurors had to be dismissed for harboring negative feelings against the defendant. "I try to keep an open mind, but it's difficult with so many

Arabs tied to terrorist organizations," wrote one man on his juror questionnaire,[12] even though Padilla is a U.S. citizen of Puerto Rican birth. The Supreme Court has ruled that individuals may also be legally excluded from a jury in a capital case if they would under no circumstances vote for a guilty verdict if it carried the death penalty.[13]

At the same time, potential jurors cannot be challenged for cause if they have "general objections" or have "expressed conscientious or religious scruples" against capital punishment.[14] The final responsibility for deciding whether a potential juror should be excluded rests with the judge, who may choose not to act on an attorney's request.

Peremptory Challenges Each attorney may also exercise a limited number of **peremptory challenges**. These challenges are based solely on an attorney's subjective reasoning. That is, the attorney is usually not required to give any legally justifiable reason for wanting to exclude a particular person from the jury. Because of the rather random nature of peremptory challenges, each state limits the number that an attorney may utilize: between five and ten for felony trials (depending on the state) and between ten and twenty for capital trials (also depending on the state). Once an attorney's peremptory challenges are used up, he or she must accept forthcoming jurors, unless a challenge for cause can be used.

> **Peremptory Challenge** A *voir dire* challenge to exclude potential jurors from serving on the jury without any supporting reason or cause.

RACE AND GENDER ISSUES IN JURY SELECTION

For many years, prosecutors used their peremptory challenges as an instrument of *de facto* segregation in juries. Prosecutors were able to keep African Americans off juries in cases in which an African American was the defendant. The argument that African Americans—or members of any other minority group—would be partial toward one of their own was tacitly supported by the Supreme Court. Despite its own assertion, made in *Swain v. Alabama* (1965),[15] that blacks have the same right to appear on a jury as whites, the Court mirrored the apparent racism of society as a whole by protecting the questionable actions of many prosecutors.

The *Batson* Reversal The Supreme Court reversed this policy in 1986 with *Batson v. Kentucky*.[16] In this case, the Court declared that the equal protection clause prohibits prosecutors from using peremptory challenges to strike possible jurors on the basis of race. Under the rules established in the *Batson* case, the defendant must prove that the prosecution's use of a peremptory challenge was racially motivated to overturn that challenge.

The Court has revisited the issue of race a number of times in the years since its *Batson* decision. In *Powers v. Ohio* (1991),[17] it ruled that a defendant may contest race-based peremptory challenges even if the defendant is not of the same race as the excluded jurors. In *Georgia v. McCollum* (1992),[18] the Court placed defense attorneys under the same restrictions as prosecutors when making race-based peremptory challenges. Finally, in 2008, the Court, reaffirming the *Batson* ruling of twenty-two years earlier, overturned the conviction of an African American death row inmate because a Louisiana prosecutor improperly picked an all-white jury for his murder trial.[19] These rulings do not mean that a black defendant can never be judged by a jury made up entirely of whites. Rather, they indicate that

attorneys cannot use peremptory challenges to reject a prospective juror because of her or his race.

Women on the Jury In *J.E.B. v. Alabama ex rel. T. B.* (1994),[20] the Supreme Court extended the principles of the *Batson* ruling to cover gender bias in jury selection. The case was a civil suit for paternity and child support brought by the state of Alabama. Prosecutors used nine of their ten challenges to remove men from the jury, while the defense made similar efforts to remove women. When confronted, the state defended its actions by referring to what it called the rational belief that men and women might have different views on the issues of paternity and child support. The Court disagreed and held this approach to be unconstitutional.

¿WHAT HAPPENS DURING A CRIMINAL TRIAL?

Once the jury members have been selected, the judge swears them in and the trial itself can begin. A rather pessimistic truism among attorneys is that every case "has been won or lost when the jury is sworn." This reflects the belief that a juror's values are the major, if not dominant, factor in the decision of guilt or innocence.[21]

In actuality, it is difficult to predict how a jury will go about reaching a decision. Despite a number of studies on the question, researchers have not been able to identify any definitive consistent patterns of jury behavior. Sometimes, jurors in a criminal trial will follow instructions to find a defendant guilty unless there is a reasonable doubt, and sometimes they seem to follow instinct or prejudice and apply the law anyway they choose.[22]

LO4

OPENING STATEMENTS

Attorneys may choose to open the trial with a statement to the jury, though they are not required to do so. In these **opening statements,** the attorneys give a brief version of the facts and the supporting evidence that they will present during the trial. Because some trials can drag on for weeks or even months, it is extremely helpful for jurors to

STUDYPREP

An outline should consist of several levels written in a standard format. The most important concepts are assigned Roman numerals; the second most important, capital letters; the third most important, numbers; and the fourth most important, lowercase letters.

hear a summary of what will unfold. In short, the opening statement is a kind of road map that describes the destination that each attorney hopes to reach and outlines how she or he plans to reach it. The danger for attorneys is that they will offer evidence during the trial that might contradict an assertion made during the opening statement. Such inconsistencies may cause jurors to disregard the evidence or shift their own thinking further away from the narrative being offered by the attorney.[23]

THE ROLE OF EVIDENCE

Once the opening statements have been made, the prosecutor begins the trial proceedings by presenting the state's evidence against the defendant. Courts have complex rules about what types of evidence may be presented and how the evidence may be brought out during the trial. **Evidence** is anything that is used to prove the existence or nonexistence of a fact. For the most part, evidence can be broken down into two categories: testimony and real evidence. **Testimony** consists of statements by competent witnesses. **Real evidence,** presented to the court in the form of exhibits, includes any physical items—such as the murder weapon or a bloodstained piece of clothing—that affect the case.

Rules of evidence are designed to ensure that testimony and exhibits presented to the jury are relevant, reliable, and not unfairly prejudicial against the defendant. One of the tasks of the defense attorney is to challenge evidence presented by the prosecution by establishing that the evidence is not reliable. Of course, the prosecutor also tries to demonstrate the irrelevance or unreliability of evidence presented by the defense. The final decision on whether evidence is allowed before the jury rests with the judge, in keeping with his or her role as the "referee" of the adversary system.

Evidence Anything that is used to prove the existence or nonexistence of a fact.

Testimony Verbal evidence given by witnesses under oath.

Real Evidence Evidence that is brought into court and seen by the jury.

Lay Witness A witness who can truthfully and accurately testify on a fact in question without having specialized training or knowledge.

Expert Witness A witness with professional training or substantial experience qualifying her or him to testify on a certain subject.

Testimonial Evidence A person who is called to testify on factual matters that would be understood by the average citizen is referred to as a **lay witness**. If asked about the condition of a victim of an assault, for example, a lay witness could relate certain facts, such as "she was bleeding from her forehead" or "she was unconscious on the ground for several minutes." A lay witness, however, could not give information about the medical extent of the victim's injuries, such as whether she suffered from a fractured skull or internal bleeding. Coming from a lay witness, such testimony would be inadmissible. When the matter in question requires scientific, medical, or technical skill beyond the scope of the average person, prosecutors and defense attorneys may call an **expert witness** to

A Marion County (Oregon) deputy district attorney presents sections of a bomb used by Bruce Turnbridge and his son, Joshua Turnbridge, to kill two law enforcement officers. Why is it important that jurors see physical evidence related to a crime? (AP Photo/Brent Wojahn, Pool)

Direct Evidence
Evidence that establishes the existence of a fact that is in question without relying on inference.

Circumstantial Evidence Indirect evidence that is offered to establish, by inference, the likelihood of a fact that is in question.

Relevant Evidence
Evidence tending to make a fact in question more or less probable than it would be without the evidence.

the stand. The expert witness is an individual who has professional training, advanced knowledge, or substantial experience in a specialized area, such as medicine, computer technology, or ballistics. (CAREER TIP: Digital computer data—such as e-mail exchanges or Internet search records—often play an important role in criminal trials. Consequently, *information technology experts* are now in high demand to act as witnesses and explain such matters to juries.

Direct versus Circumstantial Evidence

Two types of testimonial evidence may be brought into court: direct evidence and circumstantial evidence. **Direct evidence** is evidence that has been witnessed by the person giving testimony. "I saw Bill shoot Chris" is an example of direct evidence. **Circumstantial evidence** is indirect evidence that, even if believed, does not establish the fact in question but only the degree of likelihood of the fact. In other words, circumstantial evidence can create an inference that a fact exists.

Suppose that the defendant owns a gun that shoots bullets of the type found in the victim's body. This circumstantial evidence, by itself, does not establish that the defendant committed the crime. Combined with other circumstantial evidence, however, it may do just that. For instance, if other circumstantial evidence indicates that the defendant had a motive for harming the victim and was at the scene of the crime when the shooting occurred, the jury might conclude that the defendant committed the crime. The prosecutor's successful case against Ingmar Guandique for the murder of Chandra Levy, described in the opening of this chapter, was based entirely on circumstantial evidence.

Relevance

Evidence will not be admitted in court unless it is relevant to the case being considered. **Relevant evidence** is evidence that tends to prove or disprove a fact in question. Forensic proof that the bullets found in a victim's body were fired from a gun discovered in the suspect's pocket at the time of arrest, for example, is certainly relevant. The suspect's prior record showing a conviction for armed robbery ten years earlier is, as we shall soon see, irrelevant to the case at hand and in most instances will be ruled inadmissible by the judge.

Prejudicial Evidence Evidence may be excluded if it would tend to distract the jury from the main issues of the case, mislead the jury, or cause jurors to decide the issue on an emotional basis.

Real Evidence In most cases involving a violent crime, prosecutors try to offer as much physical evidence of the crime as possible. For example, they will show the jury touching photographs of the victim before the crime and graphic photos of the victim after the crime, bloody pieces of clothing, and other items that tend to cause strong emotional reactions. Defense attorneys usually try to exclude these items on the ground that they unfairly prejudice the jury against the defendant.

Judges generally will permit such evidence so long as it is not blatantly prejudicial. In 2010, for example, Edward B. Fleury faced manslaughter charges after an eight-year-old boy named Christopher Bizilj accidentally killed himself at a gun show sponsored by Fleury. During the trial, Judge Peter A. Velis of Hampden Superior Court in Springfield, Massachusetts, allowed jurors to see a video of the incident, in which a bullet from a 9-millimeter Micro UZI pierces Bizilj's head. Velis, however, turned the audio track off so that jurors would not hear the boy's screams. "The greatest risk in this case is invoking any sympathy" for young Christopher, the judge explained.[24] (CAREER TIP: *Evidence technicians* help the police and prosecutors gain convictions by identifying, securing, collecting, cataloguing, and storing evidence found at a crime scene.)

Evil Character Defense attorneys are likely to have some success keeping prosecutors from using prior supposed criminal activities or actual convictions to show that the defendant has criminal tendencies or an "evil character."[25] This concept is codified in the Federal Rules of Evidence, which state that evidence of "other crimes, wrongs, or acts is not admissible to prove the character of a person in order to show action in

CJ and Technology

THE CSI EFFECT

Letalvis Cobbins and Lemaricus Davidson, half brothers, were prime suspects in the brutal kidnapping, torture, rape, and murder of a University of Tennessee student named Channon Christian. As part of its case during Cobbins's trial, the prosecution planned to present a key piece of evidence: a strand of hair found on Christian's body. There was only one problem. Because of the family relationship between Cobbins and Davidson, a DNA fingerprinting expert could not say which brother was the source of the hair. The judge in the case was leaning toward keeping the hair from the jury, so as not to confuse the jurors. Prosecutor Leland Price did not like this idea. "If they hear the victim was in that house for twelve hours and we didn't find a fiber, hair, or something, that's going to weigh against us," he said.

Price was worried about the "CSI effect," a phenomenon that takes its name from the popular television series *CSI: Crime Scene Investigation* and its two spin-offs, *CSI: Miami* and *CSI: NY*. According to many prosecutors, these shows have fostered unrealistic notions among jurors as to what forensic science can accomplish as part of a criminal investigation. In reality, the kind of physical evidence used to solve crimes on *CSI* is often not available to the prosecution, which must rely instead on witnesses and circumstantial evidence. Prosecutors such as Price fear that jurors, expecting the high-tech physical clues they have become accustomed to on television, will wrongfully acquit guilty defendants when this expectation is not met. Indeed, one recent study of jurors in Washtenaw County, Michigan, found that nearly half "expected the prosecutor to present scientific evidence in every criminal case."

THINKING ABOUT THE CSI EFFECT

In general, why are prosecutors taking a risk when they present *only* circumstantial evidence to a jury? How might the CSI effect have a positive impact on criminal trials, from the standpoint of both prosecutor preparation and juror interest?

---

conformity therewith." Such evidence is allowed only when it does not apply to character construction and focuses instead on "motive, opportunity, intent, preparation, plan, knowledge, identity, or absence of mistake or accident."[26] Though this legal concept has come under a great deal of criticism, it is consistent with the presumption-of-innocence standards discussed earlier. Presumably, if a prosecutor is allowed to establish that the defendant has shown antisocial or even violent character traits, this will prejudice the jury against the defendant.

THE PROSECUTION'S CASE

Because the burden of proof is on the state, the prosecution is generally considered to have a more difficult task than the defense. The prosecutor attempts to establish guilt beyond a reasonable doubt by presenting the *corpus delicti* ("body of the offense" in Latin) of the crime to the jury.

The *corpus delicti* is simply a legal term that refers to the substantial facts that show a crime has been committed. By establishing such facts through the presentation of relevant and nonprejudicial evidence, the prosecutor hopes to convince the jury of the defendant's guilt.[27]

Direct Examination of Witnesses Witnesses are crucial to establishing the prosecutor's case against the defendant. The prosecutor will call witnesses to the stand and ask them questions pertaining to the sequence of events that the trial is addressing. This form of questioning is known as **direct examination**. During

> **Direct Examination** The examination of a witness by the attorney who calls the witness to the stand to testify.

Hearsay An oral or written statement made by an out-of-court speaker that is later offered in court by a witness (not the speaker) concerning a matter before the court.

Confrontation Clause The part of the Sixth Amendment that guarantees all defendants the right to confront witnesses testifying against them during the criminal trial.

Cross-Examination The questioning of an opposing witness during trial.

Redirect Examination The questioning of a witness following cross-examination, designed to reestablish the credibility of the witness in the minds of the jurors.

direct examination, the prosecutor will usually not be allowed to ask *leading questions*—questions that might suggest to the witness a particular desired response. A leading question might be something like, "So, Mrs. Williams, you noticed the defendant threatening the victim with a broken beer bottle?" If Mrs. Williams answers "yes" to this question, she has, in effect, been "led" to the conclusion that the defendant was, in fact, threatening with a broken beer bottle. (A properly worded query would be, "Mrs. Williams, please describe the defendant's manner toward the victim during the incident.") The fundamental purpose behind testimony is to establish what actually happened, not what the trial attorneys would like the jury to believe happened.

"This is a court of law, young man, not a court of justice."

—OLIVER WENDELL HOLMES, JR., ASSOCIATE JUSTICE OF THE SUPREME COURT OF THE UNITED STATES, 1902–1932

question the same witnesses. The Sixth Amendment states, "In all criminal prosecutions, the accused shall enjoy the right . . . to be confronted with witnesses against him." This **confrontation clause** gives the accused, through his or her attorneys, the right to cross-examine witnesses. **Cross-examination** refers to the questioning of an opposing witness during trial, and both sides of a case are allowed to do so (see **Figure 10.2** on the facing page). Cross-examination allows the attorneys to test the truthfulness of opposing witnesses and usually entails efforts to create doubt in the jurors' minds that the witness is reliable.

After the defense has cross-examined a prosecution witness, the prosecutor may want to reestablish any reliability that might have been lost. The prosecutor can do so by again questioning the witness, a process known as **redirect examination**. Following the redirect examination, the defense attorney will be given the opportunity to ask further questions of prosecution witnesses, or recross-examination. Thus, each side has two opportunities to question a witness. The attorneys need not do so, but only after each side has been offered the opportunity will the trial move on to the next witness or the next stage.

Hearsay When interviewing a witness, both the prosecutor and the defense attorney will make sure that the witness's statements are based on the witness's own knowledge and not hearsay. **Hearsay** can be defined as any testimony given in court about a statement made by someone else. Literally, it is what someone heard someone else say. For the most part, hearsay is not admissible as evidence. It is excluded because the listener may have misunderstood what the other person said, and without the opportunity of cross-examining the originator of the statement, the misconception cannot be challenged.

CROSS-EXAMINATION

After the prosecutor has directly examined her or his witnesses, the defense attorney is given the chance to

THE DEFENDANT'S CASE

After the prosecutor has finished presenting evidence against the defendant, the defense attorney may offer the defendant's case. Because the burden is on the state to prove the accused's guilt, the defense is not required to offer any case at all. It can simply "rest" without calling any witnesses or producing any real evidence and ask the jury to judge the merits of the case on what it has seen and heard from the prosecution.

Creating a Reasonable Doubt Defense lawyers most commonly defend their clients by attempting to expose weaknesses in the prosecutor's case. Remember that if the defense attorney can create reasonable doubt concerning the client's guilt in the mind of just a single juror, the defendant has a good chance of gain-

Figure 10.2 The Cross-Examination

The following is a transcript of a cross-examination of a government witness during a drug trial. Note that the defense attorney is not trying to establish any facts concerning the alleged crime. Instead, he is trying to create a negative picture of the witness in the minds of the jurors.

Defense: You have thirteen children?

Witness: Unh huh (affirmative).

Defense: Made by thirteen different women?

Witness: Unh huh (affirmative).

Defense: Now, and you are twenty-four years old?

Witness: Yes, sir.

Defense: So, out of the twenty-four years that you have been living, twenty years has [sic] been on the street, and almost four have been in prison?

Witness: Yes, you can say so.

Defense: And out of the [last] two years that you have been on the street you had thirteen children?

Witness: Yes.

Source: **www.thesmokinggun.com/archive/years/2009/0813091alfamega1.html**.

ing an acquittal or at least a *hung jury*, a circumstance explained later in the chapter.

Even if the prosecution can present seemingly strong evidence, a defense attorney may succeed by creating reasonable doubt. In an illustrative case, Jason Korey bragged to his friends that he had shot and killed Joseph Brucker in Pittsburgh, Pennsylvania, and a great deal of circumstantial evidence linked Korey to the killing. The police, however, could find no direct evidence: they could not link Korey to the murder weapon, nor could they match his footprints to those found at the crime scene. Michael Foglia, Korey's defense attorney, explained his client's bragging as an attempt to gain attention, not a true statement. Although this explanation may strike some as unlikely, in the absence of physical evidence it did create doubt in the jurors' minds, and Korey was acquitted. (CAREER TIP: By using various methods such as making plaster casts or measuring impressions in the ground, *forensic footprint experts* can match footprints found at a crime scene with a suspect's bare foot or shoe.)

This strategy is also very effective in cases that essentially rely on the word of the defendant against the word of the victim. In sexual-assault cases, for example, if the defense attorneys can create doubt about the victim's credibility—in other words, raise the possibility that he or she is lying—then they may prevail at trial. According to the Alcohol and Rape Study, carried out by researchers at Rutgers University and the University of New Hampshire, juries acquit about 90 percent of the time when the defendant says the sex was consensual and there is evidence that the alleged victim was drinking alcohol before the incident in question.[28]

Other Defense Strategies The defense can choose among a number of strategies to generate rea-

sonable doubt in the jurors' minds. It can present an *alibi defense*, by submitting evidence that the accused was not at or near the scene of the crime at the time the crime was committed. Another option is to attempt an *affirmative defense*, by presenting additional facts to the ones offered by the prosecution. Possible affirmative defenses, which we discussed in detail in Chapter 4, include the following:

1. Self-defense.
2. Insanity.
3. Duress.
4. Entrapment.

With an affirmative defense strategy, the defense attempts to prove that the defendant should be found not guilty because of extenuating (moderating) circumstances surrounding the crime. An affirmative strategy can be difficult to carry out because it forces the defense to prove the truthfulness of its own evidence, not simply disprove the evidence offered by the prosecution.

The defense is often willing to admit that a certain criminal act took place, especially if the defendant has already confessed. In this case, the primary question of the trial becomes not whether the defendant is guilty, but what the defendant is guilty of. In these situations, the defense strategy focuses on obtaining the lightest possible penalty for the defendant. As we saw in the last chapter, this strategy is responsible for the high percentage of proceedings that end in plea bargains.

REBUTTAL AND SURREBUTTAL

After the defense closes its case, the prosecution is permitted to bring new evidence forward that was not

Rebuttal Evidence given to counteract or disprove evidence presented by the opposing party.

Closing Arguments An argument made by each side's attorney after the cases for the plaintiff and defendant have been presented.

Charge The judge's instructions to the jury following the attorneys' closing arguments.

Sequestration A judge's decision during a high-profile case to isolate the jury so that the jurors' opinions concerning the case will not be swayed by the news media or any other source of information.

used during its initial presentation to the jury. This is called the **rebuttal** stage of the trial. When the rebuttal stage is finished, the defense is given the opportunity to cross-examine the prosecution's new witnesses and introduce new witnesses of its own. This final act is part of the *surrebuttal*. After these stages have been completed, the case is closed, and the opposing sides offer their closing arguments.

CLOSING ARGUMENTS

In their **closing arguments**, the attorneys summarize their presentations and argue one final time for their respective cases. In most states, the defense attorney goes first, and then the prosecutor. (In Colorado, Kentucky, and Missouri, the order is reversed.) An effective closing argument includes all of the major points that support the government's or the defense's case. It also emphasizes the shortcomings of the opposing party's case.

Jurors will view a closing argument with some skepticism if it merely recites the central points of a party's claim or defense without also responding to the unfavorable facts or issues raised by the other side. Of course, neither attorney wants to focus too much on the other side's position, but the elements of the opposing position do need to be acknowledged and their flaws highlighted.

¿WHAT HAPPENS AT THE END OF A CRIMINAL TRIAL?

After closing arguments, the outcome of the trial is in the hands of the jury. Before the jurors begin their deliberations, the judge gives the jury a **charge**, summing up the case and instructing the jurors on the

rules of law that apply to the issues in the case. These charges, also called jury instructions, are usually prepared during a special *charging conference* involving the judge and the trial attorneys. In this conference, the attorneys suggest the instructions they would like to see be sent to the jurors, but the judge makes the final decision as to the charges submitted.[29] If the defense attorney disagrees with the charges sent to the jury, he or she can enter an objection, thereby setting the stage for a possible appeal.

The judge usually begins by explaining basic legal principles, such as the need to find the defendant guilty beyond a reasonable doubt. Then the jury instructions narrow to the specifics of the case at hand, and the judge explains to the jurors what facts the prosecution must have proved to obtain a conviction. If the defense strategy centers on an affirmative defense such as insanity or entrapment, the judge will discuss the relevant legal principles that the defense must have proved to obtain an acquittal. The final segment of the charges discusses possible verdicts. These always include "guilty" and "not guilty," but some cases also allow for the jury to find "guilt by reason of insanity" or "guilty but mentally ill." Juries are often charged with determining the seriousness of the crime as well, such as deciding whether a homicide is murder in the first degree, murder in the second degree, or manslaughter.

JURY DELIBERATION

After receiving the charge, the jury begins its deliberations. Jury deliberation is a somewhat mysterious process, as it takes place in complete seclusion. One of the most important instructions that a judge normally gives the jurors is that they should seek no outside information during deliberation. The idea is that jurors should base their verdict *only* on the evidence that the judge has deemed admissible. In extreme cases, the judge will order that the jury be **sequestered**, or isolated from the public, during the trial and deliberation stages of the proceedings. Sequestration is used when deliberations are expected to be lengthy, or the trial is attracting a high amount of interest and the judge wants to keep the jury from being unduly influenced.

Juries are usually sequestered in hotels and kept under the watch and guard of officers of the court.

The importance of *total* sequestration is reflected in a recent Colorado Supreme Court decision to overturn the death penalty of a man who was sentenced after the jurors consulted a Bible during deliberations. The court held that a Bible constituted an improper outside influence and a reliance on a "higher authority."[30]

THE VERDICT

Once it has reached a decision, the jury issues a **verdict**. The most common verdicts are guilty and not guilty, though, as we have seen, juries may signify different degrees of guilt if instructed to do so. Following the announcement of a guilty or not guilty verdict, the jurors are discharged, and the jury trial proceedings are finished.

When a jury in a criminal trial is unable to agree on a unanimous verdict—or a majority in certain states—it returns with no decision. This is known as a **hung jury**. Following a hung jury, the judge will declare a *mistrial*, and the case will be tried again in front of a different jury if the prosecution decides to pursue the matter a second time. A judge can do little to reverse a hung jury, considering that "no decision" is just as legitimate a verdict as guilty or not guilty.

In some states, if there are only a few dissenters to the majority view, a judge can send the jury back to the jury room under a set of rules enunciated more than a century ago by the Supreme Court in *Allen v. United States* (1896).[31] The **Allen Charge**, as this instruction is called, asks the jurors in the minority to reconsider the majority opinion. Many jurisdictions do not allow *Allen* Charges on the ground that they improperly coerce jurors with the minority opinion to change their minds.[32]

APPEALS

Even if a defendant is found guilty, the trial process is not necessarily over. In our criminal justice system,

Verdict A formal decision made by the jury.

Hung Jury A jury whose members are so irreconcilably divided in their opinions that they cannot reach a verdict.

Allen Charge An instruction by a judge to a deadlocked jury that asks the jurors in the minority to reconsider the majority opinion.

CAREERPREP   JURY CONSULTANT

JOB DESCRIPTION:

- Pretrial: Research jurors' backgrounds, assist with juror selection, create favorable potential juror profiles, develop *voir dire* questions, and organize mock trials to aid trial attorneys.
- During trial: Carefully watch jurors' body language and behavior to determine if the client trial lawyer is communicating her or his arguments successfully, coach witnesses, and help trial lawyers develop strategies.

WHAT KIND OF TRAINING IS REQUIRED?

- Minimum of a bachelor's degree (although a master's degree or a Ph.D. is ideal) in sociology, political science, criminology, psychology, or behavioral science. Research and data analysis skills are also crucial for this profession.
- A strongly developed intuition. Jury consultants are not hired for their expertise in criminal law but for their insight into human behavior, decision making, and motivational patterns.

ANNUAL SALARY RANGE?

- $40,000–$100,000

For additional information, visit:
www.wisegeek.com/what-is-a-jury-consultant.htm.

Alina Solovyova-Vincent/iStockphoto

a person convicted of a crime has a right to appeal. An **appeal** is the process of seeking a higher court's review of a lower court's decision for the purpose of correcting or changing the lower court's judgment. A defendant who loses a case in a trial court cannot automatically appeal the conviction. The defendant normally must first be able to show that the trial court acted improperly on a question of law. Common reasons for appeals include the introduction of tainted evidence by the prosecution or faulty jury instructions delivered by the trial judge. In federal courts, about 19 percent of criminal convictions are appealed.[33]

Double Jeopardy

The appeals process is available only to the defense. If a jury finds the accused not guilty, the prosecution cannot appeal to have the decision reversed. To do so would infringe on the defendant's Fifth Amendment rights against multiple trials for the same offense. This guarantee against being tried a second time for the same crime is known as protection from **double jeopardy.**

The prohibition against double jeopardy means that once a criminal defendant is found not guilty of a particular crime, the government may not reindict the person and retry him or her for the same crime. The basic idea behind the double jeopardy clause, in the words of Supreme Court justice Hugo Black, is that the state should not be allowed to

> make repeated attempts to convict an individual for an alleged offense, thereby subjecting him to embarrassment, expense, and ordeal and compelling him to live in a continuing state of anxiety and insecurity, as well as enhancing the possibility that though innocent he may be found guilty.[34]

The bar against double jeopardy does not keep a victim from bringing a *civil* suit against the same person to recover damages. For example, in 2011, Charles Buck was acquitted of killing his wife, Leslie, who nine years earlier had been found dead at the bottom of the stairs of their home in Mystic, Connecticut, with unexplained head injuries. Although prosecutors could not prove Buck's guilt, a wrongful death lawsuit against him filed by Leslie's brother proceeded, unaffected. This was not considered double jeopardy because the wrongful death suit involved a civil claim, not a criminal one. Therefore, Buck was not being tried for the same *crime* more than once.

Note that a hung jury is *not* an acquittal for purposes of double jeopardy. So, if a jury is deadlocked, the government is free to seek a new trial. In another spousal murder case, from June 2010, a jury deliberated for thirty hours but could not decide whether Gary Widmer of Hamilton Township, Ohio, drowned his wife, Sarah, in their bathtub (see the photo on the facing page). Six months later, relying on a new "mystery witness" who heard Widmer admit to killing Sarah, prosecutors opted to try the defendant again for the same crime.

The Appeal Process

There are two basic reasons for the appeal process. The first is to correct an error made during the initial trial. The second is to review policy. Because of this second function, the appellate courts are an important part of the flexible nature of the criminal justice system. When existing law has ceased to be effective or no longer reflects the values of society, an appellate court can effectively change the law through its decisions and the precedents that it sets.[35] A classic example was the *Miranda v. Arizona* decision (see page 135), which, although it failed to change the fate of the defendant (he was found guilty on retrial), had a far-reaching impact on custodial interrogation of suspects.

It is also important to understand that once the appeal process begins, the defendant is no longer presumed innocent. The burden of proof has shifted, and the

Do you think that the government should be able to seek a new trial if a jury deadlocks in the previous one, as happened with Gary Widmer, shown here, who was convicted of murder in his second trial for the same crime? Why or why not? (AP Photo/The Cincinnati Enquirer, Cara Owsley)

defendant is obligated to prove that her or his conviction should be overturned. The method of filing an appeal differs slightly among the fifty states and the federal government, but the five basic steps are similar enough for summarization in **Figure 10.3** alongside. For the most part, defendants are not required to exercise their right to appeal. The one exception involves the death sentence. Given the seriousness of capital punishment, the defendant is required to appeal the case, regardless of his or her wishes. (CAREER TIP: Prosecutors can also choose to reopen a case if new evidence is discovered that casts doubt on the conviction. If you are interested in the use of DNA evidence to exonerate wrongly convicted people, you should consider seeking employment or volunteering with the *Innocence Project*. [Go to www.innocenceproject.org.])

HABEAS CORPUS

Even after the appeals process is exhausted, a convict might have access to one final procedure, known as *habeas corpus* (Latin for "you have the body"). *Habeas corpus* is a judicial order that commands a corrections official to bring a prisoner before a federal court so that the court can hear the convict's claim that he or she is being held illegally. A writ of *habeas corpus* differs from an appeal in that it can be filed only by someone who is imprisoned. In recent years, defense attorneys have made a number of successful *habeas corpus* claims stating that their death row clients have new DNA evidence proving their innocence.[36]

Habeas Corpus An order that requires correctional officials to bring an inmate before a court or a judge and explain why he or she is being held in prison.

Figure 10.3 The Steps of an Appeal

1. The defendant, or *appellant,* files a *notice of appeal*—a short written statement outlining the basis of the appeal.

2. The appellant transfers the trial court record to the appellate court. This record contains items such as evidence and a transcript of the testimony.

3. Both parties file *briefs*. A brief is a written document that presents the party's legal arguments.

4. Attorneys from both sides present *oral arguments* before the appellate court.

5. Having heard from both sides, the judges of the appellate court retire to deliberate the case and make their decision. As described in Chapter 8, this decision is revealed in a *written opinion*. Appellate courts generally do one of the following:

- *Uphold* the decision of the lower court;
- *Modify* the lower court decision by changing only a part of it;
- *Reverse* the decision of the lower court; or
- *Reverse and remand* the case, meaning that the matter is sent back to the lower court for further proceedings.

Brandon Laufenberg/iStockphoto.com

11 PUNISHMENT AND SENTENCING

Learning Outcomes

After studying this chapter, you will be able to . . .

LO 1 List and contrast the four basic philosophical reasons for sentencing criminals.

LO 2 Contrast indeterminate sentencing with determinate sentencing.

LO 3 List the six forms of punishment.

LO 4 Explain some of the reasons why sentencing reform has occurred.

LO 5 Identify the two stages that make up the bifurcated process of death penalty sentencing.

Bad Habits

The cases of John Patterson and Michael Albanesi were strikingly similar. In late 2008, the Pennsylvania Internet Crimes against Children Task Force raided Patterson's home in West Pittston, and the officers discovered nearly three hundred images of child pornography stored on various hard drives. A year later, the same task force raided Albanesi's home in Wyoming, Pennsylvania, located about three miles from Patterson's residence, and discovered computer hardware with about five hundred images of child pornography. Neither man had a criminal record. Both admitted to having a long history of downloading and trading sexually explicit images of children on the Internet.

When it came to sentencing, however, Patterson's and Albanesi's fates differed greatly. In November 2009, Patterson pleaded guilty to one count of receiving child pornography and is serving eleven years in prison. In April 2010, Albanesi pleaded guilty to 507 counts of child pornography possession, eleven counts of dissemination and one count of utilizing a computer to commit his crimes, and he was sentenced to twenty-three months behind bars.

Within the criminal justice system, opinions about the proper punishment for child pornography-related crimes vary just as widely as Patterson's and Albanesi's sentences do. A recent poll among federal judges showed that 70 percent believe the sentencing requirements for child pornography defendants are too harsh. Ingrid Cronin, a federal public defender, points out that these defendants often receive longer prison terms than those who are caught "actually having sex with a child." Luzerne County (Pennsylvania) detective Chaz Balogh counters that real children are harmed in the production of these images and rejects the argument that merely "curious" users of child porn should be treated with leniency. "Maybe they wouldn't be so curious if they knew they were going to do ten years [in prison]," Balogh insists.

(AP Photo/Eric Risberg)

U.S. Representative Debbie Wasserman, shown here, sponsored a bill that provides state and local law enforcement agencies $1 billion to help fight child pornography. What are the arguments in favor of treating child pornography as a serious crime deserving of harsh punishment? (Photo by Win McNamee/Getty Images)

NATIONAL CENTER FOR
MISSING & EXPLOITED
CHILDREN®

Retribution The philosophy that those who commit criminal acts should be punished based on the severity of the crime.

Just Deserts A sentencing philosophy based on the assertion that criminals deserve to be punished for breaking society's rules.

Why did John Patterson receive a dramatically stiffer punishment than Michael Albanesi for committing essentially the same crime? The main reason is that Patterson was prosecuted in federal court, while Albanesi was tried in Pennsylvania state court. Federal sentencing guidelines, which you will learn about later in the chapter, tend to be harsher than state requirements. In 2009, the average sentence in federal court for possessing or disseminating child pornography was seven years in prison. That same year, 47 percent of convicted child pornographers in Pennsylvania state court did not serve *any* time behind bars, having been sentenced to probation or house arrest instead.[1]

Is the federal approach better than Pennsylvania's approach when it comes to child pornography? A 2009 study, conducted at a North Carolina prison, reported that 85 percent of those convicted of possessing child pornography had also engaged in at least one "hands on" sexual offense against a minor.[2] This finding would suggest that the harsher federal approach is justified to deter potential abusers. However, in that same report the authors wrote, "We know less about online child pornographers than many other types of offenders," and they cautioned against a one-size-fits-all approach.[3] As you can see, punishment and sentencing present some of the most complex issues of the criminal justice system. One scholar has even asserted:

> There is no such thing as "accurate" sentencing; there are only sentences that are more or less just, more or less effective. Nothing in the recent or distant history of sentencing reform suggests that anything approaching perfection is attainable.[4]

In this chapter, we will discuss the various attempts to "perfect" the practice of sentencing over the past century and explore the consequences of these efforts for the American criminal justice system. Whereas previous chapters have concentrated on the prosecutor and defense attorney, this one will spotlight the judge and his or her role in making the sentencing decision. We will particularly focus on recent national and state efforts to limit judicial discretion in this area, a trend that has had the overall effect of producing harsher sentences for many offenders. Finally, we will examine the issues surrounding the death penalty, a controversial subject that forces us to confront the basic truth of sentencing: the way we punish criminals says a great deal about the kind of people we are.[5]

¿WHY DO WE PUNISH CRIMINALS?

Professor Herbert Packer has said that punishing criminals serves two ultimate purposes: the "deserved infliction of suffering on evil doers" and "the prevention of crime."[6] Even this straightforward assessment raises several questions. How does one determine the sort of punishment that is "deserved"? How can we be sure that certain penalties "prevent" crime?

Should criminals be punished solely for the good of society, or should their well-being also be taken into consideration? Sentencing laws indicate how any given group of people has answered these questions, but do not tell us why these questions were answered in that manner. To understand why, we must first consider the four basic philosophical reasons for sentencing—retribution, deterrence, incapacitation, and rehabilitation.

RETRIBUTION

The oldest and most common justification for punishing someone is that he or she "deserved it"—as the Old Testament states, "an eye for an eye and a tooth for a tooth." Under a system of justice that favors **retribution**, a wrongdoer who has freely chosen to violate society's rules must be punished for the offense. Retribution relies on the principle of **just deserts**, which holds that the severity of the punishment must be in proportion to the severity of the crime. Retributive justice is not the same as *revenge*. Whereas revenge implies that the wrongdoer is punished only with the aim of satisfying a victim or victims, retribution is more concerned with the needs of society as a whole.

CJ and Technology

THE DNA REVOLUTION, PART II

In Chapter 6, we saw how DNA fingerprinting has been a boon to law enforcement. As these techniques have become more effective, however, they have also brought the problem of wrongful convictions—which occur when an innocent person is found guilty—into the national spotlight. DNA exonerates (clears of blame) potential wrongdoers the same way it identifies them: by matching genetic material found at a crime scene to that of a suspect (or, conversely, by showing that the genetic material does not match the suspect's). For example, in 1980 Cornelius Dupree, Jr., was sentenced to seventy-five years in prison for the rape and robbery of a Dallas, Texas, woman. He subsequently spent three decades behind bars before being released in January 2011, when DNA tests proved his innocence. Dupree was the 265th person exonerated by DNA evidence in the United States.

THINKING ABOUT DNA AND WRONGFUL CONVICTIONS

How does the fact that some people who are convicted and punished by the courts are actually innocent influence your opinion of retribution as a justification for punishment?

Alex Williamson/Photodisc/Getty Images/iStockphoto.com

DETERRENCE

The concept of **deterrence** (as well as incapacitation and rehabilitation) takes the opposite approach: rather than seeking only to punish the wrongdoer, the goal of sentencing should be to prevent future crimes. By "setting an example," society is sending a message to potential criminals that certain actions will not be tolerated. Jeremy Bentham, a nineteenth-century British reformer who first expressed the principles of deterrence, felt that retribution was counterproductive because it does not serve the community. (See page 24 in Chapter 2 to review Bentham's utilitarian theories.) He believed that a person should be punished only when doing so is in society's best interests and that the severity of the punishment should be based on its deterrent value, not on the severity of the crime.[7]

Deterrence can take two forms: general and specific. The basic idea of **general deterrence** is that by punishing one person, others will be persuaded not to commit

a similar crime. **Specific deterrence** assumes that an individual, after being punished once for a certain act, will be less likely to repeat that act because she or he will not want to be punished again.[8] Both forms of deterrence have proved problematic in practice. General deterrence assumes that a person commits a crime only after a rational decision-making process, in which he or she deliberately weighs the benefits of the crime against the possible costs of the punishment. This is not necessarily the case, especially for young offenders, who tend to value the immediate rewards of crime over the possible future consequences. The argument for specific deterrence

> **Deterrence** The strategy of preventing crime through the threat of punishment.
>
> **General Deterrence** The theory that by punishing an individual, other individuals will be deterred from committing the same or similar offenses.
>
> **Specific Deterrence** The theory that an individual who has been punished once for criminal wrongdoing is less likely to commit further crimes, as he or she will not want to repeat the experience of punishment.

Incapacitation A strategy for preventing crime by detaining wrongdoers in prison.

Rehabilitation The philosophy that society is best served when wrongdoers are treated for the issues underlying their criminality.

INCAPACITATION

"Wicked people exist," said James Q. Wilson. "Nothing avails except to set them apart from innocent people."[9] Wilson's blunt statement summarizes the justification for **incapacitation** as a form of punishment. As a purely practical matter, incarcerating criminals guarantees that they will not be a danger to society, at least for the length of their prison terms. To a certain extent, the death penalty could be justified in terms of incapacitation, as it prevents the offender from committing any future crimes.

Several studies do support incapacitation's efficacy as a crime-fighting tool. Criminologist Isaac Ehrlich of the University of Buffalo estimated that a 1 percent increase in sentence length will produce a 1 percent decrease in the crime rate.[10] University of Chicago professor Steve Levitt has noticed a trend that further supports incapacitation. He found that violent crime rates rise in communities where inmate litigation over prison overcrowding has forced the early release of some inmates and a subsequent drop in the prison population.[11] More recently, Avinash Singh Bhati of the Urban Institute in Washington, D.C., found that higher is somewhat weakened by the fact that a relatively small number of habitual offenders are responsible for the majority of certain criminal acts.

> *"Men are not hanged for* **stealing** *horses, but that horses* **may not be stolen.** *"*
>
> —MARQUIS DE HALIFAX, *POLITICAL THOUGHTS AND REFLECTIONS* (1750)

levels of incarceration lead to fewer violent crimes but have little impact on property crime rates.[12]

REHABILITATION

For most of the past century, **rehabilitation** has been seen as the most "humane" goal of punishment. This line of thinking reflects the view that crime is a "social phenomenon" caused not by the inherent criminality of a person but by factors in that person's surroundings. By removing wrongdoers from their environment and intervening to change their values and personalities, the rehabilitative model suggests, criminals can be "treated" and possibly even "cured" of their tendencies toward crime. Although studies of the effectiveness of rehabilitation are too varied to be easily summarized, it does appear that in most instances, criminals who receive treatment are less likely to reoffend than those who do not.[13]

For the better part of the past three decades, the American criminal justice system has been characterized by a notable rejection of many of the precepts of rehabilitation in favor of retributive, deterrent, and incapacitating sentencing strategies that "get tough on crime." Recently, however, more jurisdictions are turning to rehabilitation as a cost-effective (and, possibly, crime-reducing) alternative to punishment, a topic that we will explore more fully in the next chapter. Furthermore, the American

In a Santa Ana, California, courtroom, Andrew Gallo reacts to his sentence of fifty-one years in prison for killing three people in a drunk driving automobile accident. How do theories of deterrence and incapacitation justify Gallo's severe punishment? (AP Photo/Mark Rightmire, Pool)

Jozsef Szasz-Fabian/iStockphoto.com

public may be more accepting of rehabilitative principles than many elected officials think. A survey by Zogby International, sponsored by the National Council on Crime and Delinquency, found that 87 percent of respondents favored rehabilitative services for nonviolent offenders, both before and after they leave prison.[14]

RESTORATIVE JUSTICE

It would be a mistake to view the four philosophies we have just discussed as being mutually exclusive. For the most part, a society's overall sentencing direction is influenced by all four theories, with political and social factors determining which one is predominant at any one time. Political and social factors can also support new approaches to punishment. The influence of victims, for example, has contributed to the small but growing *restorative justice* movement in this country.

Despite the emergence of victim impact statements, which we will discuss later in the chapter, victims have historically been restricted from participating in the punishment process. This policy has found support in the general assumption that victims are focused on vengeance rather than justice. According to criminologists Heather Strang of Australia's Center for Restorative Justice and Lawrence W. Sherman of the University of Pennsylvania, however, this is not always the case. After the initial shock of the crime has worn off, Strang and Sherman have found, victims are most interested in three things that have little to do with revenge: (1) an opportunity to participate in the process, (2) material reparations (compensation), and (3) an apology.[15]

Restorative justice strategies focus on these concerns by attempting to repair the damage that a crime does to the victim, the victim's family, and society as a whole. This outlook relies on the efforts of the offender to "undo" the harm caused by the criminal act

through an apology and **restitution**, or monetary compensation for losses suffered by the victim or victims. Theoretically, the community also participates in the process by providing treatment programs and financial support that allow both offender and victim to reestablish themselves as productive members of society.[16]

¿WHAT IS THE STRUCTURE OF SENTENCING?

Philosophy not only is integral to explaining *why* we punish criminals, but also influences *how* we do so. The history of criminal sentencing in the United

Restorative Justice An approach to punishment designed to repair the harm done to the victim and the community by the offender's criminal act.

Restitution Monetary compensation for damages done to the victim by the offender's criminal act.

CAREERPREP

MEDIATION SPECIALIST

JOB DESCRIPTION:

- Complement the standard adjudication of a crime by acting as a third party facilitator between the victim and the offender. Help resolve their conflicts through a face-to-face discussion of the criminal act.
- Encourage the increased presence of restorative justice in the criminal justice system.

WHAT KIND OF TRAINING IS REQUIRED?

- No formal licensing or certification process exists for mediators. Rather, training is available through independent mediation programs and mediation organizations. Some colleges and universities offer advanced degrees in conflict management and dispute resolution.
- Skills required include the ability to communicate, negotiate, solve problems, and analyze difficult situations. Successful mediators are also highly intuitive and able to meet clients' emotional needs during difficult times.

ANNUAL SALARY RANGE?

- $28,000–$102,200

For additional information, visit: www.voma.org.

Indeterminate Sentencing A period of incarceration that is determined by the judge, operating within a set of minimum and maximum sentences determined by the legislature.

Determinate Sentencing A period of incarceration that is fixed by a sentencing authority and cannot be reduced by judges or other corrections officials.

"Good Time" A reduction in time served by prisoners based on good behavior, conformity to rules, and other positive actions.

Truth-in-Sentencing Law A legislative attempt to ensure that convicts will serve approximately the terms to which they were initially sentenced.

States has been characterized by shifts in institutional power among the three branches of the government. When public opinion moves toward more severe strategies of retribution, deterrence, and incapacitation, *legislatures* have responded by asserting their power over determining sentencing guidelines. In contrast, periods of rehabilitative justice are marked by a transfer of this power to the *judicial* and *administrative* branches.

LEGISLATIVE SENTENCING AUTHORITY

Because legislatures are responsible for making laws, these bodies are also initially responsible for passing the criminal codes that determine the length of sentences.

Indeterminate Sentencing For a good part of the twentieth century, goals of rehabilitation dominated the criminal justice system, and legislatures were more likely to enact **indeterminate sentencing** policies. Penal codes with indeterminate sentences set a minimum and maximum amount of time that a person must spend in prison. For example, the indeterminate sentence for aggravated assault could be three to nine years, or six to twelve years, or twenty years to life. Within these parameters, a judge can prescribe a particular term, after which an administrative body known as the *parole board* decides at what point the offender is to be released. A prisoner is aware that he or she is eligible for *parole* as soon as the minimum time has been served and that good behavior can further shorten the sentence.

Determinate Sentencing Disillusionment with the ideals of rehabilitation has led to **determinate**

sentencing, or fixed sentencing. As the name implies, in determinate sentencing an offender serves exactly the amount of time to which she or he is sentenced (minus "good time," described below). For example, if the legislature deems that the punishment for a first-time armed robber is ten years, then the judge has no choice but to impose a sentence of ten years, and the criminal will serve ten years minus good time before being freed.

"Good Time" and Truth in Sentencing Often, the amount of time prescribed by a judge bears little relation to the amount of time the offender actually spends behind bars. In states with indeterminate sentencing, parole boards have broad powers to release prisoners once they have served the minimum portion of their sentence. Furthermore, all but four states offer prisoners the opportunity to reduce their sentences by doing "**good time**"—or behaving well—as assessed by prison administrators. (See **Figure 11.1** on the facing page for an idea of the effects of good-time regulations and other early-release programs on state prison sentences.)

Sentence-reduction programs promote discipline within a correctional institution and reduce overcrowding. Consequently, these programs are welcomed by many prison officials. The public, however, may react negatively to news that a violent criminal has served a shorter term than ordered by a judge and may pressure elected officials to "do something." In Illinois, for example, some inmates were serving less than half their sentences by receiving a one-day reduction in their term for each day of "good time." Under pressure from victims' groups, the state legislature passed a **truth-in-sentencing law** that requires murderers and others convicted of serious crimes to complete at least 85 percent of their sentences with no time off for good behavior.[17]

As their name suggests, the primary goal of these laws is to provide the public with more accurate information about the actual amount of time an offender will spend behind bars. They have also found support with those who believe that keeping offenders incapacitated for longer periods of time will reduce crime.[18] Today, forty states have instituted some form of truth-in-sentencing laws, though the future of such statutes is in doubt due to the pressure of overflowing prisons.

JUDICIAL SENTENCING AUTHORITY

Determinate sentencing is a direct encroachment on the long-recognized power of judges to make the final decision on sentencing. Historically, the judge bore most of the responsibility for choosing the proper sentence within the guidelines set by the legislature. In the twentieth century, this power was reinforced by the rehabilitative ethic. Each offender, it was believed, has a different set of problems and should therefore receive a sentence tailored to her or his particular circumstances. Legislators have generally accepted a judge as the most qualified person to choose the proper punishment.

Between 1880 and 1899, seven states passed indeterminate sentencing laws, and in the next dozen years, another twenty-one followed suit. By the 1960s, every state in the nation allowed its judges the freedom of operating under an indeterminate sentencing system.[19] In the 1970s, however, criticism of indeterminate sentencing began to grow. Marvin E. Frankel, a former federal district judge in New York, gained a great deal of attention when he described sentencing authority as "unchecked" and "terrifying and intolerable for a society that professes devotion to a rule of law."[20] As we shall see, the 1980s and 1990s saw numerous attempts on both the state and federal levels to limit this judicial discretion.

¿WHAT ROLE DO JUDGES PLAY IN SENTENCING?

During the pretrial procedures and the trial itself, the judge's role is somewhat passive and reactive. She or he is primarily a "procedural watchdog," ensuring that the rights of the defendant are not infringed on while the prosecutor and defense attorney dictate the course of action. At a traditional sentencing hearing, however, the judge is no longer an arbiter between the parties. She or he is now called on to exercise the ultimate authority of the state in determining the defendant's fate.

From the 1930s to the 1970s, when theories of rehabilitation held sway over the criminal justice system, indeterminate sentencing practices were guided by the theory

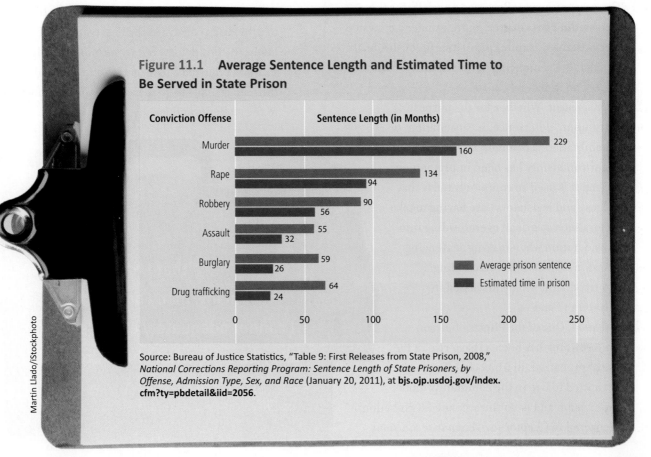

Figure 11.1 Average Sentence Length and Estimated Time to Be Served in State Prison

Conviction Offense — Sentence Length (in Months)

Conviction Offense	Average prison sentence	Estimated time in prison
Murder	229	160
Rape	134	94
Robbery	90	56
Assault	55	32
Burglary	59	26
Drug trafficking	64	24

Source: Bureau of Justice Statistics, "Table 9: First Releases from State Prison, 2008," *National Corrections Reporting Program: Sentence Length of State Prisoners, by Offense, Admission Type, Sex, and Race* (January 20, 2011), at **bjs.ojp.usdoj.gov/index.cfm?ty=pbdetail&iid=2056**.

Martin Llado/iStockphoto

of "individualized justice." Just as a physician gives specific treatment to individual patients depending on their particular health needs, the hypothesis goes, a judge needs to consider the specific circumstances of each individual offender in choosing the best form of punishment. Taking the analogy one step further, just as the diagnosis of a qualified physician should not be questioned, a qualified judge should have absolute discretion in making the sentencing decision. *Judicial discretion* rests on the assumption that a judge should be given ample leeway in determining punishments that fit both the crime and the criminal.[21] As we shall see later in the chapter, the growth of determinate sentencing has severely restricted judicial discretion in many jurisdictions.

FORMS OF PUNISHMENT

LO 3 Within whatever legislative restrictions apply, the sentencing judge has a number of options when it comes to choosing the proper form of punishment. These sentences, or *dispositions*, include:

1. *Capital punishment.* Reserved normally for those who commit first degree murder under aggravated circumstances, **capital punishment**, or the death penalty, is a sentencing option in thirty-four states and in federal courts.

2. *Imprisonment.* Whether for the purpose of retribution, deterrence, incapacitation, or rehabilitation, a common form of punishment in American history has been imprisonment. In fact, it is used so commonly today that judges—and legislators—are having to take factors such as prison overcrowding into consideration when making sentencing decisions. The issues surrounding imprisonment will be discussed in Chapters 13 and 14.

3. *Probation.* One of the effects of prison overcrowding has been a sharp rise in the use of probation, in which an offender is permitted to live in the community under supervision and is not incarcerated. (Probation is covered in Chapter 12.) *Alternative sanctions*

(also discussed in Chapter 12) combine probation with other dispositions such as electronic monitoring, house arrest, boot camps, and shock incarceration.

4. *Fines.* Fines can be levied by judges in addition to incarceration and probation or independently of other forms of punishment. When a fine is the only punishment, it usually reflects the judge's belief that the offender is not a threat to the community and does not need to be imprisoned or supervised. In some instances, mostly involving drug offenders, a judge can order the seizure of an offender's property, such as his or her home.

5. *Restitution and community service.* Whereas fines are payable to the government, restitution and community service are seen as reparations to the injured party or to the community. Restitution (see page 201) is a direct payment to the victim or victims of a crime. Community service consists of "good works"—such as cleaning up highway litter or tutoring disadvantaged youths—that benefit the entire community.

6. *Apologies.* As we saw earlier in this chapter, when the offender has committed a less serious crime, many judges are turning to restorative justice to provide a remedy. At the heart of restorative justice is the apology. So, for example, a judge in Texas required a teenager who had vandalized thirteen schools to go to each school and apologize to the students and faculty.

> "I am **painfully aware** that I have deeply hurt many, many people.... I cannot adequately express how sorry I am for what I have done."
>
> —BERNARD MADOFF, AFTER PLEADING GUILTY TO DEFRAUDING INVESTORS OUT OF AN ESTIMATED $65 BILLION (2009)

Mario Aguilar/iStockphoto.com

In some jurisdictions, judges have a great deal of discretionary power and can impose sentences that do not fall into any of these categories. This "creative sentencing," as it is sometimes called, has produced some interesting results. After being convicted of criminal damaging for throwing beer bottles at a car, Jason Householder and John Stockum were ordered by the judge to walk down Main Street in Coshocton, Ohio, in women's clothing (see the photo below).

A judge in Painesville, Ohio, ordered a man who had stolen from a Salvation Army kettle to spend twenty-four hours as a homeless person. In Harris County, Texas, a man who slapped his wife was sentenced to attend yoga classes. Although these types of punishments are often ridiculed, many judges see them as a viable alternative to incarceration for less dangerous offenders.

THE SENTENCING PROCESS

The decision of how to punish a wrongdoer is the end result of what Yale Law School professor Kate Stith and federal appeals court judge José A. Cabranes call the "sentencing ritual."[22] The two main participants in this ritual are the judge and the defendant, but prosecutors, defense attorneys, and probation officers also play a role in the proceedings. Individualized justice requires that the judge consider all the relevant circumstances in making sentencing decisions. Therefore, judicial discretion is often on par with *informed* discretion—without the aid of the other members of the courtroom work group, the judge would not have sufficient information to make the proper sentencing choice.

> **Presentence Investigative Report** An investigative report on an offender's background that assists a judge in determining the proper sentence.

The Presentence Investigative Report For judges operating under various states' indeterminate sentencing guidelines, information in the **presentence investigative report** is a valuable component of the sentencing ritual. Compiled by a probation officer, the report describes the crime in question, notes the suffering of any victims, and lists the defendant's prior offenses (as well as any alleged but uncharged criminal activity). The report also contains a range of personal data such as family background, work history, education, and community activities—information that is not admissible as evidence during trial. In putting together the presentence investigative report, the probation officer is supposed to gain a "feel" for the defendant and communicate these impressions to the judge.

Sentencing and the Jury Juries also play an important role in the sentencing process. As we will see later in the chapter, it is the jury, and not the judge, who decides whether a convict eligible for the death penalty will in fact be executed. Additionally, six states—Arkansas, Kentucky, Missouri, Oklahoma, Texas, and Virginia—allow juries, rather than judges, to make the sentencing decision even when the death penalty is not an option. In these states, the judge gives the jury instructions on the range of penalties available, and then the jury makes the final decision.[23] Juries have traditionally been assigned a relatively small

What reasons might a judge have for handing down a "creative" sentence such as the one given to Jason Householder, left, and John Stockum? (AP Photo/Dante Smith/ *Coshocton Tribune*)

role in felony sentencing, largely out of concern that jurors' lack of experience and legal expertise leaves them unprepared for the task. When sentencing by juries is allowed, the practice is popular with prosecutors because jurors are more likely than judges to give harsh sentences, particularly for drug crimes, sexual assault, and theft.[24]

FACTORS OF SENTENCING

The sentencing ritual strongly lends itself to the concept of individualized justice. With inputs—sometimes conflicting—from the prosecutor, attorney, and probation officer, the judge can be reasonably sure of getting the "full picture" of the crime and the criminal. In making the final decision, however, most judges consider two factors above all others: the seriousness of the crime and any *mitigating* or *aggravating circumstances*.

The Seriousness of the Crime As would be expected, the seriousness of the crime is the primary factor in a judge's sentencing decision. The more serious the crime, the harsher the punishment, for society demands no less. Each judge has his or her own methods of determining the seriousness of the offense. Many judges simply consider the "conviction offense." That is, they base their sentence on the crime for which the defendant was convicted.

Other judges—some mandated by statute—focus instead on the "**real offense**" in determining the punishment. The "real offense" is based on the actual behavior of the defendant, regardless of the official conviction. For example, through a plea bargain, a defendant may plead guilty to simple assault when in fact he hit his victim in the face with a baseball bat. A judge, after reading the presentence investigative report, could decide to sentence the defendant as if he had committed aggravated assault, which is the "real" offense. Although many prosecutors and defense attorneys are opposed to "real offense" procedures, which

can render a plea bargain meaningless, there is a growing belief in criminal justice circles that they bring a measure of fairness to the sentencing decision.[25]

Mitigating and Aggravating Circumstances
When deciding the severity of punishment, judges and juries are often required to evaluate the mitigating and aggravating circumstances surrounding the case. **Mitigating circumstances** are those circumstances, such as the fact that the defendant was coerced into committing the crime, that allow a lighter sentence to be handed down. In contrast, **aggravating circumstances**, such as a prior record, blatant disregard for the safety of others, or the use of a weapon, can lead a judge or jury to inflict a harsher penalty than might otherwise be warranted.

In 2006, for example, Zacarias Moussaoui pleaded guilty to taking part in the al Qaeda plot that led to the terrorist attacks of September 11, 2001. The defense asked the jury to consider twenty-four mitigating circumstances when deciding whether Moussaoui deserved the death penalty or life in prison. These included Moussaoui's hostile mother and physically abusive father, the racism that he had to face as an African in French society, and his limited knowledge of the September 11, 2001, attack plans. (CAREER TIP: One of the witnesses called to argue against the death penalty for Moussaoui was a *behavioral specialist,* or a health-care expert who focuses on diagnosing and reducing problem behavior.) For their part, the prosecutors offered

STUDY PREP

A neat study space is important. Staying tidy forces us to stay organized. When your desk is covered with piles of papers, notes, and textbooks, things are being lost even though you may not realize it. The only work items that should be on your desk are those that you are working with that day.

seven aggravating circumstances, including the great death and destruction caused by the terrorist attacks, Moussaoui's desire to harm Americans, and his lack of remorse for the victims. In choosing life imprisonment over the death penalty, the jury decided that the mitigating circumstances surrounding the defendant's crimes outweighed the aggravating circumstances.

¿WHAT ARE SOME PROBLEMS WITH SENTENCING?

For some, the natural differences in judicial philosophies, when combined with a lack of institutional control, raise important questions. Why should a bank robber in South Carolina and a bank robber in Michigan receive different sentences? Even federal indeterminate sentencing guidelines seem overly vague: a bank robber can receive a prison term from one day to twenty years, depending almost entirely on the judge.[26] Furthermore, if judges have freedom to use their discretion, do they not also have the freedom to misuse it?

A claim of improper judicial discretion is often the first reason given for two phenomena that plague the criminal justice system: *sentencing disparity* and *sentencing discrimination*. Although the two terms are often used interchangeably, they describe different statistical occurrences—the causes of which are open to debate.

 LO4

SENTENCING DISPARITY

Justice would seem to demand that those who commit similar crimes should receive similar punishments. **Sentencing disparity** occurs when this expectation is not met in one of three ways:

1 Criminals receive similar sentences for different crimes of unequal seriousness.

2 Criminals receive different sentences for similar crimes.

3 Mitigating or aggravating circumstances have a disproportionate effect on sentences. Prosecutors, for example, reward drug dealers who inform on their associates with lesser sentences. As a result, low-level drug sellers, who have no information to trade for reduced sentences, often spend more time in prison than their better-informed bosses.[27]

> **Sentencing Disparity** A situation in which those convicted of similar crimes do not receive similar sentences.
>
> **Sentencing Discrimination** A situation in which the length of a sentence appears to be influenced by the defendant's race or another factor not directly related to the crime he or she committed.

Most of the blame for sentencing disparities is placed at the feet of the judicial profession. Even with the restrictive presence of the sentencing reforms we will discuss shortly, judges have a great deal of influence over the sentencing decision, whether they are making that decision themselves or instructing the jury on how to do so. Like other members of the criminal justice system, judges have personal opinions, and their discretionary sentencing decisions reflect these opinions.

SENTENCING DISCRIMINATION

Sentencing discrimination occurs when disparities can be attributed to extralegal variables such as the defendant's gender, race, or economic standing.

Race and Sentencing At first glance, racial discrimination would seem to be rampant in sentencing practices. Research by Cassia Spohn of Arizona State University and David Holleran of the College of New Jersey suggests that minorities pay a "punishment penalty" when it comes to sentencing.[28] Spohn and Holleran found that in Chicago, convicted African Americans were 12.1 percent more likely to go to prison than convicted whites, and convicted Hispanics were 15.3 percent more likely. In Miami, Hispanics were 10.3 percent more likely to be imprisoned than either blacks or whites.[29] Nationwide, about 43 percent of all inmates in state and federal prisons are African American, even though that minority group makes up only about 13 percent of the country's population.[30]

Spohn and Holleran also found that the rate of imprisonment rose significantly for minorities who were young and unemployed. This led the researchers to

James V. Taylor was sentenced to fifteen years in a Missouri prison for possessing so little crack cocaine that the amount was unweighable. Do you think that individual states should follow the federal government's lead in addressing unequal punishments for crack and powder cocaine related crimes? Why or why not? (AP Photo/Jeff Roberson)

conclude that the disparities between races were not the result of "conscious" discrimination on the part of the sentencing judges. Rather, faced with limited time to make decisions and limited information about the offenders, the judges would resort to stereotypes, considering not just race, but age and unemployment as well.[31]

Crack Cocaine Sentencing Few sentencing policies have aroused as many charges of discrimination as those involving crack cocaine. Powder cocaine and crack, a crystallized form of the drug that is smoked rather than inhaled, are chemically identical. Under federal legislation passed in 1986, however, sentences for crimes involving crack are, in some instances, one hundred times more severe than for crimes involving powder cocaine.[32] The law was designed to combat the violence associated with the crack trade in American cities. Instead, say critics, it wound up harming those very areas, particularly African American communities. About 82 percent of federal crack defendants are African American.[33]

In November 2007, the U.S. Sentencing Commission voted to lessen the disparity between crack and powder cocaine sentences. The commission also decided that the changes would be retroactive, meaning that about 25,000 federal inmates were eligible for

sentence reductions. As of November 2010, federal judges had reduced the sentences of more than 16,000 of these inmates.[34] That same year, President Barack Obama signed the Fair Sentencing Act, which reduces the legal disparity between the two forms of cocaine to eighteen to one for federal sentencing purposes.[35] (CAREER TIP: A lobbying group called Crack the Disparity is dedicated to changing federal crack sentencing laws. A *lobbyist* is someone who, on behalf of a client, tries to influence the enactment of legislation and the decisions of government officials.)

Women and Sentencing Few would argue that race or ethnicity should be a factor in sentencing decisions—the system should be color-blind. Does the same principle apply to women? In other words, should the system be gender-blind as well—at least on a policy level? Congress answered that question in the Sentencing Reform Act of 1984, which emphasized the ideal of gender-neutral sentencing.[36]

In practice, however, this has not occurred. Women who are convicted of crimes are less likely to go to prison than men, and those who are incarcerated tend to serve shorter sentences. According to government data, the average sentence of a woman for a felony is fifteen months shorter than that of a man.[37]

In certain situations, however, a woman's gender can work against her. In 2010, Florida prosecutors asked that Emose Oceant receive eighteen years in prison after she was convicted of child abuse. Instead, circuit judge Margaret Steinbeck sentenced Oceant, who whipped her seven children with boards, belts, and wire hangers, to thirty years behind bars. According to Keith Crew, a professor of sociology and criminology at the University of Northern Iowa, defendants who are seen as bad mothers often "get the hammer" from judges and juries.[38]

¿HOW HAVE POLITICIANS TRIED TO "FIX" SENTENCING?

Judicial discretion, then, appears to be a double-edged sword. Although it allows judges to impose a wide variety of sentences to fit specific criminal situations, it appears to fail to rein in a judge's subjective biases, which can lead to disparity and perhaps discrimination.

Critics of judicial discretion believe that its costs (the lack of equality) outweigh its benefits (providing individualized justice). As Columbia law professor John C. Coffee noted:

> If we wish the sentencing judge to treat "like cases alike," a more inappropriate technique for the presentation could hardly be found than one that stresses a novelistic [storytelling] portrayal of each offender and thereby overloads the decisionmaker in a welter of detail.[39]

In other words, Coffee feels that judges are given too much information in the sentencing process, making it impossible for them to be consistent in their decisions. It follows that limiting judicial discretion would not only simplify the process but also lessen the opportunity for disparity or discrimination. Since the 1970s, this attitude has spread through state and federal legislatures, causing more extensive changes in sentencing procedures than in almost any other area of the American criminal justice system over that time period.

SENTENCING GUIDELINES

In an effort to eliminate the unfairness of disparity by removing judicial bias from the sentencing process, many states and the federal government have turned to **sentencing guidelines**, which require judges to dispense legislatively determined sentences based on factors such as the seriousness of the crime and the offender's prior record. In 1978, Minnesota became the first state to create a Sentencing Guidelines Commission with a mandate to construct and monitor the use of a determinate sentencing structure. The Minnesota Commission left no doubt as to the philosophical justification for the new sentencing statutes, stating unconditionally that retribution was its primary goal.[40]

Today, about twenty states employ some form of sentencing guidelines with similar goals. In general, these guidelines remove discretionary power from state judges by turning sentencing into a mathematical exercise. Members of the courtroom work group are guided by a *grid*, which helps them determine the proper sentence.

Federal Sentencing Guidelines In 1984, Congress passed the Sentencing Reform Act (SRA),[41] paving the way for federal sentencing guidelines that went into effect three years later. Similar in many respects to the state guidelines, the SRA also eliminated parole for federal prisoners and severely limited early release from prison due to good behavior.[42] The impact of the SRA and the state guidelines has been dramatic. Sentences have become harsher—by the middle of the first decade of the 2000s, the average federal prison sentence was fifty months, more than twice as long as in 1984.[43]

Furthermore, much of the discretion in sentencing has shifted from the judge to the prosecutor. Because the prosecutor chooses the criminal charge, she or he, in effect, can present the judge with the range of sentences. Defendants and their defense attorneys realize this and are more likely to agree to a plea bargain, which is, after all, a "deal" with the prosecutor.[44]

Judicial Departures Even in their haste to limit a judge's power, legislators realized that sentencing guidelines could not be expected to cover every possible criminal situation. Therefore, both state and federal sentencing guidelines allow an "escape hatch" of limited judicial discretion known as a **departure**. The SRA includes a proviso that a judge may "depart" from the presumptive sentencing range if a case involves circumstances that are not adequately covered in the

Sentencing Guidelines Legislatively determined guidelines that judges are required to follow.

Departure A stipulation that allows a judge to adjust his or her sentencing decision based on the special circumstances of a particular case.

Mandatory Sentencing Guidelines Statutorily determined punishments that must be applied to those who are convicted of specific crimes.

Habitual Offender Laws Statutes that require lengthy prison sentences for those who are convicted of multiple felonies.

guidelines. For example, in 2010, federal judge Jack Weinstein overturned a twenty-year child pornography sentence, ruling that "unless applied with care," the federal requirements "can lead to unreasonable sentences."[45] As we noted in the opening to this chapter, federal judges often react this way to child pornography punishments. Indeed, federal judges depart downward more often in child pornography cases—about 40 percent of the time—than in cases involving any other offense.[46]

MANDATORY SENTENCING GUIDELINES

In an attempt to close even the limited loophole of judicial discretion offered by departures, politicians (often urged on by their constituents) have passed sentencing laws even more contrary to the idea of individualized justice. These **mandatory** (minimum) **sentencing guidelines**

further limit a judge's power to deviate from determinate sentencing laws by setting firm standards for certain crimes. Forty-six states have mandatory sentencing laws for crimes such as selling illegal drugs, driving under the influence of alcohol, and committing any crime with a dangerous weapon. In Alabama, for example, any person caught selling illegal drugs must spend at least two years in prison, with five years added to the sentence if the sale takes place within three miles of a school or public housing project.[47] Similarly, Congress has set mandatory minimum sentences for more than one hundred crimes, mostly drug offenses. (See the feature *You Be the Judge—Minimum: Two Hundred Years* below to learn about the consequences of mandatory sentencing guidelines.)

Habitual Offender Laws Habitual offender laws are a form of mandatory sentencing that has become increasingly popular over the past decade. Also known as "three-strikes-and-you're-out" laws, these statutes require that any person convicted of a third felony must serve a lengthy prison sentence. The crime does not have to be of a violent or dangerous nature. Under Washington's habitual offender law, for example, a "persistent offender" is automatically sentenced to life

YOU BE THE JUDGE
Minimum: Two Hundred Years

THE FACTS An Arizona trial court found Morton guilty of twenty counts of sexual exploitation of a minor based on his possession of twenty pornographic images of children. Under the state's mandatory minimum sentencing laws, each count warrants a ten-year prison term, and the terms must be served consecutively. As a result, the trial judge had no choice but to sentence Morton to two hundred years in prison. Morton is appealing the sentence as unconstitutionally cruel and unusual punishment.

THE LAW The Eighth Amendment prohibition against cruel and unusual punishments guarantees individuals the right not to be subjected to excessive sanctions. That right flows from the basic precept of justice that punishment for crime should be proportional to the offense.

YOUR DECISION Morton's lawyers present evidence that in most other states, Morton would be allowed to serve his sentences concurrently and would spend no more than five years behind bars. Had Morton been prosecuted by federal prosecutors, they point out, federal sentencing guidelines would have mandated a five-year sentence. Prosecutors counter by saying, in effect, "the law is the law." If you were a judge hearing Morton's appeal of his sentence, how would you rule? Do you believe that this mandatory minimum sentence is "cruel and unusual" or that it reflects the will of Arizona residents and must be upheld?

[To see how the Arizona Supreme Court ruled in this case, go to Example 11.1 on page 350.]

even if the third felony offense happens to be "vehicular assault" (an automobile accident that causes injury), unarmed robbery, or attempted arson, among other lesser felonies.[48] Today, twenty-six states and the federal government employ "three-strikes" statutes, with varying degrees of severity.

"Three Strikes" in Court The United States Supreme Court paved the way for these three-strikes laws when it ruled in *Rummel v. Estelle* (1980)[49] that Texas's habitual offender statute did not constitute "cruel and unusual punishment" under the Eighth Amendment. Basically, the Court gave each state the freedom to legislate such laws in the manner that it deems proper. Twenty-three years later, in *Lockyer v. Andrade* (2003),[50] the Court upheld California's "three-strikes" law. The California statute allows prosecutors to seek penalties up to life imprisonment without parole on conviction of *any* third felony, including conviction for nonviolent crimes. Leandro Andrade (see the photo below) received fifty years in prison for stealing $153 worth of videotapes, his fourth felony conviction. A federal appeals court overturned the sentence, agreeing with Andrade's attorneys that it met the definition of cruel and unusual punishment.[51]

In a bitterly divided 5–4 decision, the Supreme Court reversed. Justice Sandra Day O'Connor, writing for the majority, stated that the sentence was not so "objectively" unreasonable that it violated the Constitution.[52] In his dissent, Justice David H. Souter countered that "[i]f Andrade's sentence is not grossly disproportionate, the principle has no meaning."[53] Basically, the justices who upheld the law said that if the California legislature—and by extension the California voters—felt that the law was reasonable, then the judicial branch was in no position to disagree.

Why did the United States Supreme Court uphold Leandro Andrade's sentence of fifty years in prison for stealing $153 worth of videotapes? (AP Photo/ California Dept. of Corrections/ Darren Hendley/iStockphoto. com)

> **Victim Impact Statement (VIS)** A statement to the sentencing body (judge, jury, or parole board) in which the victim is given the opportunity to describe how the crime has affected her or him.

VICTIM IMPACT EVIDENCE

The final piece of the sentencing puzzle involves victims and victims' families. Traditionally, crime victims were banished to the peripheries of the criminal justice system. This situation has changed dramatically with the emergence of the victims' rights movement over the past few decades. Victims are now given the opportunity to testify—in person or through written testimony—during sentencing hearings about the suffering they experienced as the result of the crime.

Every state and federal government has some form of victim impact legislation. In general, these laws allow a victim (or victims) to present a **victim impact statement (VIS)** that tells his or her side of the story to the sentencing body, be it a judge, jury, or parole board. In nonmurder cases, the victim can personally describe the physical, financial, and emotional impact of the crime.

When the charge is murder or manslaughter, relatives or friends can give personal details about the victim and describe the effects of her or his death. In the sentencing phase of the Zacarias Moussaoui trial, discussed earlier in this chapter, the prosecution called thirty-five witnesses to tell the jury how losing loved ones in the September 11 attacks had affected their lives. (As could have been expected, much of this testimony was heartbreaking, such as that of the Indian-born dentist whose sister hanged herself after her husband perished in one of the hijacked planes.) In almost all instances, the goal of the VIS is to increase the harshness of the sentence.

¿WHAT IS THE STATUS OF CAPITAL PUNISHMENT IN THE UNITED STATES?

"You do not know how hard it is to let a human being die," Abraham Lincoln (1809–1865) once said, "when you feel that a stroke of your pen will save him." Despite these misgivings, during his four years in office Lincoln approved the execution of 267 soldiers, including those who had slept at their posts.[54] Our sixteenth president's ambivalence toward capital punishment is reflected in America's continuing struggle to reconcile the penalty of death with the morals and values of society. Capital punishment has played a role in sentencing since the earliest days of the Republic and—having survived a brief period of abolition between 1972 and 1976—continues to enjoy public support.

Still, few topics in the criminal justice system inspire such heated debate. Death penalty opponents such as legal expert Stephen Bright wonder whether "there comes a time when a society gets beyond some of the more primitive forms of punishment."[55] They point out that two dozen countries have abolished the death penalty since 1985 and that the United States is the only Western democracy that continues the practice. Critics also claim that a process whose subjects are chosen by "luck and money and race" cannot serve the interests of justice.[56] Proponents believe that the death penalty serves as the ultimate deterrent for violent criminal behavior and that the criminals who are put to death are the "worst of the worst" and deserve their fate. (CAREER TIP: *Pollsters,* who conduct surveys of public opinion, have found that about 65 percent of Americans are in favor of the death penalty.)

Today, about 3,300 convicts are living on "death row" in American prisons, meaning they have been sentenced to death and are awaiting execution. In the 1940s, as many as two hundred people were put to death in the United States in one year. As **Figure 11.2** on the facing page shows, the most recent high-water mark was ninety-eight in 1999. Despite declines since then, states and the federal government are still executing convicts at a rate not seen in six decades. Consequently, the questions that surround the death penalty—Is it fair? Is it humane? Does it deter crime?—will continue to mobilize both its supporters and its detractors.

CAREERPREP

NATIONAL VICTIM ADVOCATE

JOB DESCRIPTION:

- Provide direct support, advocacy, and short-term crisis counseling to crime victims.
- Act as a liaison between victims or witnesses and district attorneys or law enforcement, and provide court support for victims.

WHAT KIND OF TRAINING IS REQUIRED?

- A bachelor's degree in criminal justice, social work/psychology, or a related field.
- A minimum of two years' experience in the criminal justice system, one year of which should have involved direct services with victims.

ANNUAL SALARY RANGE?

- $29,000–$44,000

For additional information, visit:
www.ncvc.org/ncvc/Main.aspx.

Aldo Murillo/iStockphoto.com

METHODS OF EXECUTION

In its early years, when the United States adopted the practice of capital punishment from England, it also adopted English methods, which included drawing and quartering and boiling the convict alive. In the nineteenth century, these techniques were deemed too barbaric and were replaced by hanging. Indeed, the history of capital punishment in America is marked by attempts to make the act more humane. The 1890s saw the introduction of electrocution as a less painful method of execution than hanging, and in 1890 in Auburn Prison, New York, William Kemmler became the first American to die in an electric chair.

The "chair" remained the primary form of execution until 1977, when Oklahoma became the first state to adopt lethal injection. Today, this method dominates executions in all thirty-four states that employ the death penalty. In the lethal injection process, the condemned convict is given a sedative, followed by a combination of deadly drugs administered intravenously. Seventeen states authorize at least two different methods of execution, meaning that electrocution (nine states), lethal gas (four states), hanging (three states), and the firing squad (three states) are still used on rare occasions.[57]

Regardless of the method, as **Figure 11.3** on the following page shows, a convict's likelihood of being executed is strongly influenced by geography. Six states (Alabama, Florida, Missouri, Oklahoma, Texas, and Virginia) account for more than two-thirds of all executions, while fifteen states and the District of Columbia do not provide for capital punishment within their borders. (CAREER TIP: Michael Graczyk, an Associated Press reporter, has witnessed more than three hundred executions in Texas. *Journalists* such as Graczyk present important information about the criminal justice system to the public.)

THE DEATH PENALTY AND THE SUPREME COURT

In 1890, William Kemmler challenged his sentence to die in New York's new electric chair (for murdering his mistress) on the grounds that electrocution infringed on his Eighth Amendment rights against cruel and unusual punishment.[58] Kemmler's challenge is historically significant in that it did not challenge the death penalty itself as being cruel and

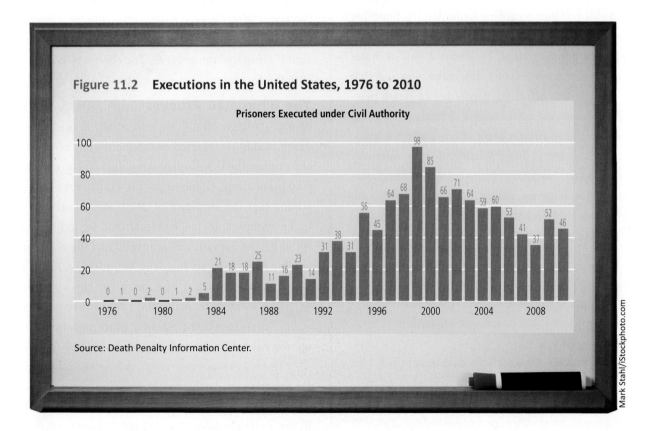

Figure 11.2   Executions in the United States, 1976 to 2010

Prisoners Executed under Civil Authority

Source: Death Penalty Information Center.

Mark Stahl/iStockphoto.com

unusual, but only the method by which it was carried out. Many constitutional scholars believe that the framers never questioned the necessity of capital punishment, as long as due process is followed in determining the guilt of the suspect.[59] Accordingly, the Supreme Court rejected Kemmler's challenge, stating:

> Punishments are cruel when they involve torture or a lingering death; but the punishment of death is not cruel, within the meaning of that word as used in the Constitution. It implies there something inhuman and barbarous, something more than the mere extinguishment of life.[60]

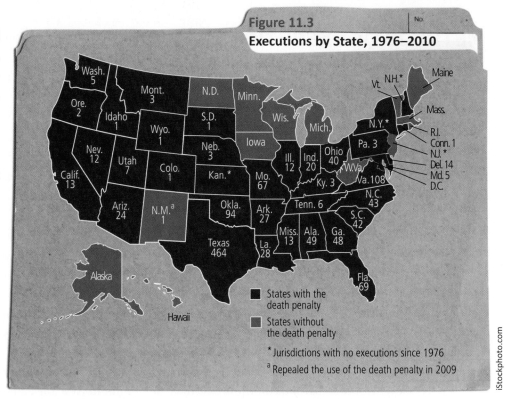

Figure 11.3

Executions by State, 1976–2010

Wash. 5
Ore. 2
Mont. 3
N.D.
Minn.
Vt.
N.H.*
Maine
Mass.
N.Y.*
R.I.
Conn. 1
N.J.*
Del. 14
Md. 5
D.C.
Idaho 1
Wyo. 1
S.D. 1
Wis.
Mich.
Pa. 3
Nev. 12
Utah 7
Colo. 1
Neb. 3
Iowa
Ill. 12
Ind. 20
Ohio 40
W.Va.
Calif. 13
Kan.*
Mo. 67
Ky. 3
Va. 108
Ariz. 24
N.M.a 1
Okla. 94
Ark. 27
Tenn. 6
N.C. 43
S.C. 42
Miss. 13
Ala. 49
Ga. 48
Texas 464
La. 28
Fla. 69
Alaska
Hawaii

■ States with the death penalty
■ States without the death penalty

* Jurisdictions with no executions since 1976
a Repealed the use of the death penalty in 2009

iStockphoto.com

Thus, the Court set a standard that it has followed to this day. No *method* of execution has ever been found to be unconstitutional by the Supreme Court.

Weems v. United States For nearly eight decades following its decision regarding Kemmler, the Supreme Court was silent on the question of whether capital punishment was constitutional. In *Weems v. United States* (1910),[61] however, the Court did make a ruling that would significantly affect the debate on the death penalty. The *Weems* case concerned a defendant who had been sentenced to fifteen years of hard labor, a heavy fine, and a number of other penalties for the relatively minor crime of falsifying official records. The Court overturned the sentence, ruling that the penalty was too harsh considering the nature of the offense. Ultimately, in the *Weems* decision, the Court set three important precedents concerning sentencing:

1. Cruel and unusual punishment is defined by the changing norms and standards of society and therefore is not based on historical interpretations.
2. Courts may decide whether a punishment is unnecessarily cruel with regard to physical pain.
3. Courts may decide whether a punishment is unnecessarily cruel with regard to psychological pain.[62]

REFORMING THE DEATH PENALTY

In the 1960s, the Supreme Court became increasingly concerned about what it saw as serious flaws in the way the states administered capital punishment. Finally, in 1967, the Court put a moratorium on executions until it could "clean up" the process. The chance to do so came with the *Furman v. Georgia* case, decided in 1972.[63]

The Bifurcated Process In its *Furman* decision, by a 5–4 margin, the Court essentially agreed that the death penalty, as carried out at the time, was so unfair as to violate the U.S. Constitution. Justice Potter Stewart was particularly eloquent in his concurring opinion, stating that the sentence of death was so arbitrary as to be comparable to "being struck by lightning."[64] Although the *Furman* ruling invalidated the death penalty for more than six hundred offenders on death row at the time, it also provided the states with a window to make the process less arbitrary, therefore bringing their death penalty statutes up to constitutional standards.

The result was a two-stage, or *bifurcated*, procedure for capital cases. In the first stage, a jury determines the guilt or innocence of the defendant for a crime that has, by state statute, been determined to be punishable by death. If the defendant is found guilty, the jury reconvenes in the second stage and considers all aggravating and mitigating factors (see page 206) to decide whether the death sentence is in fact warranted. Therefore, even if a jury were to find the defendant guilty of a crime that *may be* punishable by death, such as first degree murder, in the second stage it could decide that the circumstances surrounding the crime justified only a punishment of life in prison. In 2010, for example, a Bucks County (Pennsylvania) jury spared the life of Omar Sharif Cash, convicted of killing the fiancé of a woman he had kidnapped and raped. In deciding to be lenient, the jury appeared to accept the defense counsel's argument that, among other mitigating circumstances, Cash suffered from brain damage and had endured a stressful home life. Following the jury's decision, a judge sentenced Cash to two life terms plus 130 years behind bars, the maximum penalty for his crimes.

Court Approval The Supreme Court ruled in favor of the new bifurcated process in 1976, stating that the process removed the ability of a court to "wantonly and freakishly impose the death penalty."[65] On January 17, 1977, Gary Gilmore became the first American executed (by Utah) under the new laws, and today thirty-four

"Let's do it."

—CONVICTED MURDERER GARY GILMORE, SHORTLY BEFORE HIS EXECUTION BY A UTAH FIRING SQUAD (1977)

states and the federal government have capital punishment laws based on the bifurcated process. (Note that state governments are responsible for almost all executions in this country. The federal government has carried out only three death sentences since 1963.)

The Jury's Role The Supreme Court reaffirmed the important role of the jury in death penalties in *Ring v. Arizona* (2002).[66] The case involved Arizona's bifurcated process: after the jury determined a defendant's guilt or innocence, it would be dismissed, and the judge would decide whether execution was warranted. The Court found that this procedure violated the defendant's Sixth Amendment right to a jury trial, requiring that juries be involved in *both* stages of the bifurcated process. The decision invalidated death penalty laws in Arizona, Colorado, Idaho, Montana, and Nebraska, forcing legislatures in those states to hastily revamp their procedures.

Mitigating Circumstances Several mitigating circumstances will prevent a defendant found guilty of first degree murder from receiving the death penalty.

Insanity In 1986, the United States Supreme Court held that the Constitution prohibits the execution of a person who is insane. The Court failed to provide a test for insanity other than Justice Lewis F. Powell's statement that the Eighth Amendment "forbids the execution only of those who are unaware of the punishment they are about to suffer and why they are to suffer it."[67] Consequently, each state must come up with its own definition of insanity for death penalty purposes. A state may also force convicts on death row to take medication that will make them sane enough to be aware of the punishment they are about to suffer and why they are about to suffer it.[68]

Being Mentally Handicapped The Supreme Court's change of mind on the question of whether a mentally handicapped convict may be put to death underscores the continuing importance of the *Weems* test

TEST PREP

For multiple-choice questions, try to arrive at the answer in your head before looking at the possible answers. This may provide you with the correct choice. If not, eliminate obvious incorrect choices and watch for two similar answers. Usually, one of those is correct.

(see page 214). In 1989, the Court rejected the argument that execution of a mentally handicapped person was "cruel and unusual" under the Eighth Amendment.[69] At the time, only two states barred execution of mentally handicapped individuals. Thirteen years later, eighteen states had such laws, and the Court decided that this increased number reflected "changing norms and standards of society." In *Atkins v. Virginia* (2002),[70] the Court used the *Weems* test as the main rationale for barring the execution of mentally handicapped convicts.

The *Atkins* ruling, however, did not end the controversy in this area, as it allowed state courts to make their own determinations concerning which inmates qualified as "mentally impaired" for death penalty purposes. In December 2009, for example, Texas executed Bobby Wayne Woods even though some tests showed him to have an IQ below 70, the score accepted by many experts as the cutoff point for mental retardation. Although Woods's lawyers spent years challenging their client's fate, numerous appellate courts, including the Supreme Court, upheld the right of Texas to execute in this instance.[71]

Age Following the *Atkins* case, many observers, including four Supreme Court justices, hoped that the same reasoning would be applied to the question of whether convicts who committed the relevant crime when they were juveniles may be executed. These hopes were realized in 2005 when the Court issued its *Roper v. Simmons* decision, which effectively ended the execution of those who committed crimes as juveniles.[72] As in the *Atkins* case, the Court relied on the "evolving standards of decency" test, noting that a majority of the states, as well as every other civilized nation, prohibited the execution of offenders who committed their crimes before the age of eighteen.

The *Roper* ruling required that seventy-two convicted murderers in twelve states be resentenced and took the death penalty off the table for dozens of pending cases in which prosecutors were seeking capital punishment for juvenile criminal acts.

STILL CRUEL AND UNUSUAL?

As noted earlier, lethal injection is the dominant form of execution in this country. Most states employ the same three-drug process. First, the sedative sodium thiopen-

tal is administered to deaden pain. Then pancuronium bromide, a paralytic, immobilizes the prisoner. Finally, a dose of potassium chloride stops the heart. Members of the law enforcement and medical communities have long claimed that this procedure, if performed correctly, kills the individual quickly and painlessly. Many others, however, contend that the second drug—the paralytic—masks any outward signs of distress and thus keeps observers from knowing whether the inmate suffers extreme pain before death.[73] (CAREER TIP: A number of states require an *anesthesiologist* to mix the drugs used in the lethal injection process and oversee the execution. This can present a problem if these anesthetic specialists refuse to participate on moral grounds.)

In 2007, two convicted murderers in Kentucky asked the United States Supreme Court to invalidate the state's lethal injection procedure because of the possibility that it inflicted undetectable suffering. Nearly all of the scheduled executions in the United States were placed on hold while the Court deliberated this issue. In 2008, the Court ruled in *Baze v. Rees* that the mere possibility of pain "does not establish the sort of 'objectively intolerable risk of harm' that qualifies as cruel and unusual" punishment.[74] Within hours of the *Baze* decision, state governments began taking steps to resume their death penalty programs.[75] A year later, Ohio, reacting to concerns over the prevailing method, became the first state to use a new one-drug method—relying only on a large dose of sodium thiopental—to execute murderer Kenneth Biros.

The lethal injection apparatus outside the execution chambers at California's San Quentin Prison shows the three injection portals for the three different drugs used during execution. What are some of the drawbacks of this three-drug protocol?

(AP Photo/HO/California Dept. of Corrections)

USE THE TOOLS.

- Rip out the Review Cards in the back of your book to study.

Or Visit CourseMate for:

- Full, interactive eBook (search, highlight, take notes)
- Review Flashcards (Print or Online) to master key terms
- Test yourself with Auto-Graded Quizzes
- Bring concepts to life with Games, Videos, and Animations!

Go to CourseMate for **CJ** to begin using these tools.
Access at **www.cengagebrain.com**.

Complete the Speak Up
survey in CourseMate at
www.cengagebrain.com

f **Follow us at**
www.facebook.com/4ltrpress

©iStockphoto.com/A-Digit

12 PROBATION AND COMMUNITY CORRECTIONS

Learning Outcomes

After studying this chapter, you will be able to . . .

 LO1 Explain the justifications for community-based corrections programs.

 LO2 Describe the three general categories of conditions placed on a probationer.

 LO3 Explain the three stages of probation revocation.

 LO4 List the five sentencing options for a judge besides imprisonment and probation.

LO5 List the three levels of home monitoring.

Light Rap for Lil Wayne?

Usually, judges prefer that a defendant be in court during sentencing hearings. Lil Wayne, however, had a good excuse for his absence from the Yuma County (Arizona) Superior Court on June 30, 2010, when Judge Mark W. Reeves heard his case. The hip-hop artist, born Dwayne Carter, Jr., was incarcerated 2,600 miles to the east, already serving a yearlong sentence at the Rikers Island Prison Complex in New York City on a weapons violation. So, Lil Wayne was forced to watch via video monitor as Reeves decided his fate.

Lil Wayne's "appearance" in the Arizona court stemmed from an incident at a U.S. Border Patrol checkpoint near the Mexican border two and a half years earlier. Led onto the rapper's tour bus by drug-sniffing dogs, law enforcement agents found an ounce of cocaine, nearly four ounces of marijuana, forty-one grams of Ecstasy, and a .40-caliber handgun. Yuma County prosecutors charged Lil Wayne with felony possession of a narcotic drug for sale, possession of dangerous drugs, misconduct involving weapons, and possession of drug paraphernalia. If found guilty on all charges, Lil Wayne faced more than three years in a state prison.

Not wanting to risk a further stay behind bars, Lil Wayne negotiated a deal with Arizona authorities. He pleaded guilty to one count of possession of a dangerous drug in exchange for the dismissal of the other charges. As part of the plea bargain, Reeves sentenced Lil Wayne to three years' probation only, with the further conditions that he not consume any alcohol, take any illegal drugs, or consort with any individual involved in criminal activity during that time. Lil Wayne's probationary period started the instant he left Rikers Island on November 4, 2010, which didn't stop him from joining fellow rapper Drake onstage in Las Vegas two days later. "I'm fresh from vacation," he told the adoring crowd. "I swear to God ain't nothing, nothing, nothing like home."

How did the rapper Lil Wayne, shown here in a red baseball cap with his attorneys, avoid spending time behind bars in Arizona after committing several crimes in that state?

(AP Photo/Yuma Sun, Jared Dort)

Reintegration A goal of corrections that focuses on preparing the offender for a return to the community.

Lil Wayne's Arizona sentence sparked skepticism, particularly in light of his previous conviction in New York. Many felt he had been let off easy because of his fame and a high-priced defense attorney. In fact, Judge Reeves hardly broke new ground with Lil Wayne's sentence. Defendants found guilty of crimes far more serious than drug possession are routinely given *probation* in this country. A system that initially provided judges with the discretion to show leniency to first-time, minor offenders increasingly allows those who have committed serious crimes to serve their time in the community rather than prison or jail.

Just two months after Lil Wayne's release from Rikers Island, Illinois circuit court judge Daniel J. Rozak sentenced a sixty-nine-year-old man who had been found guilty of second degree murder to four years of probation. (The judge based the decision on the defendant's advanced age, his lack of a criminal record, and the fact that he had been provoked by the victim.)

Fifty-one percent of probationers have been convicted of a felony; about 800,000 have been found guilty of a violent crime such as assault or rape.[1] In total, about 4.2 million adults are under the supervision of state and federal probation organizations—a figure that has grown by approximately 1 million over the past decade.[2]

In this chapter, we will discuss the strengths and weaknesses of probation and other community or intermediate sanctions such as intensive probation, fines, boot camps, electronic monitoring, and home confinement. Given the scarcity of prison resources, decisions made today concerning these alternative punishments will affect the criminal justice system for decades to come.

¿WHY DO WE NEED COMMUNITY CORRECTIONS?

In the court of popular opinion, retribution and crime control take precedence over community-based correctional programs. America, says University of Minnesota law professor Michael Tonry, is preoccupied with the "absolute severity of punishment" and the "widespread view that only imprisonment counts."[3] Mandatory sentencing guidelines and "three-strikes" laws are theoretically the opposite of community-based corrections.[4] To a certain degree, correctional programs that are administered in the community are considered a less severe, and therefore less worthy, alternative to imprisonment.

REINTEGRATION

Supporters of probation and intermediate sanctions reject such views as not only shortsighted but also contradictory to the aims of the corrections system. A very small percentage of all convicted offenders have committed crimes that warrant capital punishment or life imprisonment. Most, at some point, will return to the community. Consequently, according to one group of experts, the task of the corrections system

> includes building or rebuilding solid ties between the offender and the community, integrating or reintegrating the offender into community life—restoring family ties, obtaining employment and an education, securing in the larger sense a place for the offender in the routine functioning of society.[5]

Considering that some studies have shown higher rearrest rates for offenders who are subjected to prison culture, a frequent justification of community-based corrections is that they help to reintegrate the offender into society.

Reintegration has a strong theoretical basis in rehabilitative theories of punishment. An offender is generally considered to be rehabilitated when he or she no longer represents a threat to other members of the community and therefore is believed to be fit to live in that community. In the context of this chapter and the two that follow, it will also be helpful to see reintegration as a process through which corrections officials such as probation and parole officers provide the offender with incentives to follow the rules of society. These incentives can be positive, such as enrolling the offender in a drug treatment program.

They can also be negative—in particular, the threat of return to prison or jail for failure to comply. In all instances, corrections system professionals must carefully balance the needs of the individual offender against the rights of law-abiding members of the community.

Diversion A strategy to divert those offenders who qualify away from prison and jail and toward community-based and intermediate sanctions.

In Dallas, street prostitutes such as the two shown here are often treated as crime victims and offered access to treatment and rehabilitation programs. How might society benefit if such offenders are kept out of jail or prison through diversion programs? (AP Photo/LM Otero, File)

DIVERSION

Another justification for community-based corrections, based on practical considerations, is **diversion**. As you are already aware, most criminal offenses fall into the category of "petty," and it is practically impossible, as well as unnecessary, to imprison every offender for every offense. Community-based corrections are an important means of diverting criminals to alternative modes of punishment so that scarce incarceration resources are consumed by only the most dangerous criminals. In his "strainer" analogy, corrections expert Paul H. Hahn likens this process to the workings of a kitchen strainer.

With each "shake" of the corrections "strainer," the less serious offenders are diverted from incarceration. At the end, only the most serious convicts remain to be sent to prison.[6] (CAREER TIP: In 2009, the state of Nevada passed a law allowing judges to sentence problem gamblers to treatment rather than prison. The new legislation has created a demand for *pathological gambling therapists,* who help problem gamblers overcome their addiction.)

The diversionary role of community-based punishments has become more pronounced as prisons and jails have filled up over the past three decades. In fact, probationers now account for nearly 60 percent of all adults in the American corrections systems (see **Figure 12.1** on the next page).

THE "LOW-COST ALTERNATIVE"

Not all of the recent expansion of community corrections can be attributed to acceptance of its theoretical underpinnings. Many politicians and criminal justice officials who do not look favorably on ideas such as reintegration and diversion have embraced programs to keep nonviolent offenders out of prison. The reason is simple: money. The cost of constructing and maintaining prisons and jails, as well as housing and caring for inmates, has placed a great deal of pressure on corrections budgets across the country. Indeed, to cut incarceration costs, states are taking such steps as installing windmills and solar panels to save energy and using medical schools to provide less costly health care to prisoners.[7]

Community corrections offer an enticing financial alternative to imprisonment. In the federal corrections system, for example, the annual cost of incarcerating an inmate is just over $25,800, compared with about $3,740 for a year of probation.[8] For states, the annual cost is $29,000 for a prison inmate versus $1,250 for a probationer.[9] Officials can also require criminals to pay the bill for their own supervision. In Loudoun County, Virginia, the $12 daily cost of wearing a transdermal alcohol ankle bracelet (see page 51) is covered by the offender.[10] Not surprisingly, many jurisdictions are adopting policies that favor moving offenders from their cells into the community. In Kansas, for example, corrections officials estimate that the state has saved $80 million in future prison construction costs with a program aimed at keeping probationers out of prison.[11]

¿HOW DOES PROBATION WORK?

As **Figure 12.1** below shows, **probation** is the most common form of punishment in the United States. Although it is administered differently in various jurisdictions, probation can be generally defined as

> the legal status of an offender who, after being convicted of a crime, has been directed by the sentencing court to remain

Figure 12.1 Probation in American Corrections

As you can see, the majority of convicts under the control of the American corrections system are on probation.

Prison 21%

Probation 58%

Jail 10%

Parole 11%

Source: Bureau of Justice Statistics, *Correctional Populations in the United States, 2009* (Washington, D.C.: U.S. Department of Justice, December 2010), Table 1, page 2.

C Squared Studios/Photodisc/ Getty Images

in the community under the supervision of a probation service for a designated period of time and subject to certain conditions imposed by the court or by law.[12]

(As you read this chapter, keep in mind the distinction between *probation* and *parole*. Although they sound similar and both involve community supervision of offenders, there are differences. Probation is a sentence handed down by a judge following conviction and usually does not include incarceration. Parole, explained in detail in Chapter 14, is a form of conditional release from prison.)

The theory behind probation is that certain offenders, having been found guilty of a crime, can be treated more economically and humanely by putting them under controls while still allowing them to live in the community. One of the advantages of probation has been that it provides for the rehabilitation of the offender while saving society the costs of incarceration. Despite probation's widespread use, certain participants in the criminal justice system question its ability to reach its rehabilitative goals. Critics point to the immense number of probationers and the fact that many of them are violent felons as evidence that the system is out of control. Supporters contend that nothing is wrong with probation in principle, but admit that its execution must be adjusted to meet the goals of modern corrections.[13]

SENTENCING CHOICES AND PROBATION

Probation is basically an arrangement between sentencing authorities and the offender. In traditional probation, the offender agrees to comply with certain terms for a specified amount of time in return for serving the sentence in the community. One of the primary benefits for the offender, besides not getting sent to a correctional facility, is that the length of the probationary period is usually considerably shorter than the length of a prison term (see **Figure 12.2** on the facing page).

The traditional form of probation is not the only arrangement that can be made. A judge can forgo probation altogether by handing down a **suspended sentence**. A suspended sentence places no conditions or supervision on the offender. He or she remains free for a certain length of time, but the judge keeps the option of revoking the suspended sentence and remanding (sending) the offender to prison or jail if circumstances call for such action.

Alternative Sentencing Arrangements

Judges can also combine probation with incarceration. Such sentencing arrangements include the following:

- *Split sentences.* In **split sentence probation**, also known as *shock probation*, the offender is sentenced to a specific amount of time in prison or jail, to be followed by a period of probation. According to the U.S. Department of Justice, about 10 percent of all probationers are also sentenced to some form of incarceration.[14]

- *Shock incarceration.* In this arrangement, an offender is sentenced to prison or jail with the understanding that after a period of time, she or he may petition the court to be released on probation. Shock incarceration is discussed more fully later in the chapter.

- *Intermittent incarceration.* With intermittent incarceration, the offender spends a certain amount of time each week, usually during the weekend, in a jail, workhouse, or other government institution.

Split Sentence Probation A sentence that consists of incarceration in a prison or jail, followed by a probationary period in the community.

Eligibility for Probation Not every offender is eligible for probation. In Bell County, Texas, for example, juries can recommend probation only for prison sentences of ten years or less. Generally, research has shown that offenders are most likely to be denied probation if they:

- Are convicted on multiple charges.
- Were on probation or parole at the time of the arrest.
- Have two or more prior convictions.
- Are addicted to narcotics.
- Seriously injured the victim of the crime.
- Used a weapon during the commission of the crime.[15]

Half of all probationers have been found guilty of a misdemeanor, and half have been found guilty of a felony.[16] As might be expected, the chances of a felon being sentenced to probation are highly dependent on the seriousness of the crime he or she has committed. Two out of every three felons on probation have been convicted of a property crime or a drug offense.[17]

CONDITIONS OF PROBATION

As we saw at the beginning of this chapter, a judge may decide to impose certain conditions as part of a probation sentence. In the case of Lil Wayne (see page 219), Judge Mark W. Reeves prohibited the rapper from consuming alcohol or associating with known criminals. These conditions represent a "contract" between the

Figure 12.2 Average Length of Sentence: Prison versus Probation

As you can see, the average probation sentence is much shorter than the average prison sentence for most crimes.

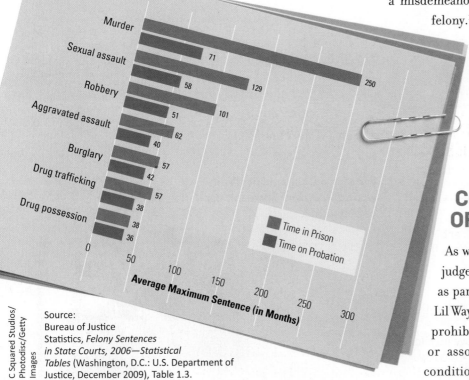

Source: Bureau of Justice Statistics, *Felony Sentences in State Courts, 2006—Statistical Tables* (Washington, D.C.: U.S. Department of Justice, December 2009), Table 1.3.

C Squared Studios/ Photodisc/Getty Images

judge and the offender, in which the latter agrees that if she or he does not follow certain rules, probation may be revoked. The probation officer usually recommends the conditions of probation, but judges also have the power to set any terms they believe to be necessary.

Principles of Probation This power is far-reaching, and a judge's personal philosophy is often reflected in the probation conditions that are set. In *In re Quirk* (1998),[18] for example, the Louisiana Supreme Court upheld the ability of a trial judge to impose church attendance as a condition of probation. Although judges have a great deal of discretion in setting the conditions of probation, they do operate under several guiding principles. First, the conditions must be related to the dual purposes of probation, which most federal and state courts define as (1) the rehabilitation of the probationer and (2) the protection of the community. Second, the conditions must not violate the U.S. Constituton. In other words, probationers are generally entitled to the same constitutional rights as other prisoners.[19]

Probationers do give up certain constitutional rights when they consent to the terms of probation. Most probationers, for example, agree to spot checks of their homes for contraband such as drugs or weapons, and they therefore have a diminished expectation of privacy. In *United States v. Knights* (2001),[20] the United States Supreme Court upheld the actions of deputy sheriffs in Napa County, California, who searched a probationer's home without a warrant or probable cause. The unanimous decision was based on the premise that because those on probation are more likely to commit crimes, law enforcement agents "may therefore justifiably focus on probationers in a way that [they do] not on the ordinary citizen."[21]

Types of Conditions Obviously, probationers who break the law are very likely to have their probation revoked. Other, less serious infractions may also result in revocation. The conditions placed on a probationer fall into three general categories:

- *Standard conditions*, which are imposed on all probationers. These include reporting regularly to the probation officer, notifying the agency of any change of address, not leaving the jurisdiction without permission, and remaining employed.
- *Punitive conditions*, which usually reflect the seriousness of the offense and are intended to increase the punishment of the offender. Such

CAREER**PREP**   PROBATION OFFICER

JOB DESCRIPTION:

- Work with offenders or clients who have been sentenced to probation and will not go to prison or jail for their offenses. In some departments, investigate offender backgrounds, write presentence reports, and recommend sentences.
- Includes extensive fieldwork to meet with and monitor offenders. May be required to carry a firearm or other weapon for protection.

WHAT KIND OF TRAINING IS REQUIRED?

- A bachelor's degree in criminal justice, social work, psychology, or a related field.
- Must be at least twenty-one years old, have no felony convictions, and have strong writing and interview skills. Experience in multicultural outreach is a plus.

ANNUAL SALARY RANGE?

- $31,500–$51,500

For additional information, visit:
www.careeroverview.com/probation-officer-careers.html.

Mark Evans/iStockphoto.com

LO2 conditions include fines, community service, restitution, drug testing, and home confinement (discussed later).

- *Treatment conditions,* which are imposed to reverse patterns of self-destructive behavior. Data show that more than 40 percent of probationers were required to undergo drug or alcohol treatment as part of their sentences, and an additional 18 percent were ordered to seek other kinds of treatment such as anger-control therapy.[22]

Some observers feel that judges have too much discretion in imposing overly restrictive conditions that no person, much less one who has exhibited antisocial tendencies, could meet. Citing prohibitions on drinking liquor, gambling, and associating with "undesirables," as well as requirements such as meeting early curfews, the late University of Delaware professor Carl B. Klockars claimed that if probation rules were taken seriously, "very few probationers would complete their terms without violation."[23]

As about six out of ten federal probationers do complete their terms successfully, Klockars's statement suggests that either probation officers are unable to determine that violations are taking place, or many of them are exercising a great deal of discretion in reporting minor probation violations. Perhaps the officers realize that punishing probationers for every single "slip-up" is unrealistic and would add to the already significant problem of jail and prison overcrowding.

THE SUPERVISORY ROLE OF THE PROBATION OFFICER

The probation officer has two basic roles. The first is investigative and consists of conducting the presentence investigation (PSI), which was discussed in Chapter 11. The second is supervisory and begins as soon as the offender has been sentenced to probation. (CAREER TIP: In smaller probation agencies, individual officers perform both tasks. In larger jurisdictions, the trend has been toward separating the responsibilities, with *pretrial services officers* handling the PSI and *line officers* concentrating on supervision.)

The Use of Authority

The ideal probation officer–offender relationship is based on trust. In reality, this trust does not often exist. Any incentive an offender might have to be completely truthful with a line officer is marred by one simple fact: self-reported wrongdoing can be used to revoke probation. Even probation officers whose primary mission is to rehabilitate are under institutional pressure to punish their clients for violating conditions of probation. One officer deals with this situation by telling his clients

> that I'm here to help them, to get them a job, and whatever else I can do. But I tell them too that I have a family to support and that if they get too far off track, I can't afford to put my job on the line for them. I'm going to have to violate them.[24]

In the absence of trust, most probation officers rely on their **authority** to guide an offender successfully through the sentence. An officer's authority, or ability to influence a person's actions without resorting to force, is based not only on her or his power to revoke probation, but also on her or his ability to impose a number of lesser sanctions. For example, if a probationer fails to attend a required alcohol treatment program, the officer can send him or her to a "lockup," or detention center, overnight. To be successful, a probation officer must establish this authority early in the relationship, as it is the primary tool in persuading the probationer to behave in a manner acceptable to the community.[25]

The Offender's Perspective The public perception of probationers is that they are lucky not to be in prison or jail and should be grateful for receiving a "second chance." Although they may not describe their situation in that way, many probationers are willing to comply with the terms of their sentences, if for no other reason than to avoid any further punishments. Such offenders can make a line officer's supervision duties relatively simple.

By the same token, as we discussed in Chapter 2, criminal behavior is often based on a lack of respect for authority. This attitude can be incompatible with the supervisory aspects of probation. The average probationer will have eighteen face-to-face meetings with her or his probation officer each year. Those under more

Authority The power designated to an agent of the law over a person who has broken the law.

restrictive probation conditions may see their supervising officers as many as eighty times a year.[26] Furthermore, to follow the conditions of probation, convicts may have to discontinue activities that they find enjoyable, such as going to a bar for a drink on Saturday night. Consequently, some probationers consider supervision as akin to babysitting and resist the strict controls placed on them by the government.

The Changing Environment of the Probation Officer The probation profession has seen considerable changes over the past three decades. As noted earlier, probation is being offered to more offenders with violent criminal histories than in the past. Inevitably, this has changed the job description of the probation officer, who must increasingly act as a law enforcement agent rather than concentrating on the rehabilitation of clients. Probation officers now conduct surveillance and search and seizure operations, administer drug tests, and accompany police officers on high-risk law enforcement assignments. Consequently, the work has become more dangerous. According to the National Institute of Corrections, more than half of the probation officers who directly supervise wrongdoers have been victims of a "hazardous incident" that endangered their safety.[27]

As a result, many probation officers are seeking permission to carry guns on the job.

Three probation officers take down a probation violator during a roundup in Tampa, Florida. Explain why probation officers' work is more dangerous today than it was several decades ago.

(AP Photo/Chris O'Meara)

Several years ago, for example, the Arizona Probation Officer Association convinced state authorities that probation officers should be able to wield firearms if they so desire. Making a similar argument, Los Angeles probation officer Janis Jones said, "We're not in the '70s anymore. We're not dealing with little dope dealers on the corner selling nickel bags of marijuana." Jones, whose unit collects about a dozen guns a week, added, "These guys are into hard-core, heavy firepower to protect their interests. You feel totally vulnerable [without a gun]."[28]

In the federal probation system, eighty-five of the ninety-four federal judicial districts permit their probation officers to carry firearms after receiving proper training, as do thirty-four states.

REVOCATION OF PROBATION

The probation period can end in one of two ways. Either the probationer successfully fulfills the conditions of the sentence, or the probationer misbehaves and probation is revoked, resulting in a prison or jail term. The decision of whether to revoke after a **technical violation**—such as failing to report a change of address or testing positive for drug use—is often a judgment call by the probation officer and therefore the focus of controversy.

"I try to get in the field two to three nights a week to see my offenders. It's really the only way to stop trouble before it happens. Otherwise, it's a free-for-all."

—KEVIN DUDLEY, SALT LAKE CITY PROBATION OFFICER

The Revocation Process As we have seen, probationers do not always enjoy the same protections under the U.S. Constitution as other members of society. The United States Supreme Court has not stripped these offenders of all rights, however. In *Mempa v. Rhay* (1967),[29] the Court ruled that probationers were entitled to an attorney during the **revocation process**. Then, in *Morrissey v. Brewer* (1972) and *Gagnon v. Scarpelli* (1973),[30] the Court established a three-stage procedure by which the "limited" due process rights of probationers must be protected in potential revocation situations:

- *Preliminary hearing.* In this appearance before a "disinterested person" (often a judge), the facts of the violation or arrest are presented, and it is determined whether probable cause for revoking probation exists. This hearing can be waived by the probationer.

- *Revocation hearing.* During this hearing, the probation agency presents evidence to support its claim of violation, and the probationer can attempt to prove this evidence false. The probationer has the right to know the charges being brought against him or her. Furthermore, probationers can testify on their own behalf and present witnesses in their favor, as well as confront and cross-examine adverse witnesses. A "neutral and detached" body must hear the evidence and rule in favor of the probation agency or the offender.

- *Revocation sentencing.* If the presiding body rules against the probationer, then the judge must decide whether to impose incarceration and if so, for what length of time. In a revocation hearing dealing with technical violations, the judge will often reimpose probation with stricter terms or intermediate sanctions.

In effect, this is a bare-bones approach to due process. Most of the rules of evidence that govern regular trials do not apply to revocation hearings. Probation officers are not, for example, required to read offenders their *Miranda* rights before questioning them about crimes they may have committed during probation. In *Minnesota v. Murphy* (1984),[31] the Supreme Court ruled that a meeting between probation officer and client does not equal custody, and therefore, the Fifth Amendment protection against self-incrimination does not apply, either.

DOES PROBATION WORK?

On June 2, 2010, apparently as part of a dispute over the sale of a used car, Frederick Hedgepeth fatally shot an elderly couple in Salisbury, North Carolina (see the photo on the following page). At the time of the murders, Hedgepeth was serving his second stint on probation for felony fraud. Indeed, probationers are responsible for a significant amount of crime. Each year, about 375,000 return to prison or jail, many because they have committed new crimes.[32] Such statistics raise a crucial question: Is probation worthwhile?

To measure the effectiveness of probation, one must first establish its purpose. Generally, the goal of probation is to protect public safety. Specifically, it is to prevent **recidivism**—the eventual rearrest of the probationer.[33] Given that most probationers are first-time, nonviolent offenders, the system is not designed to prevent outbursts of violence, such as the murders committed by Frederick Hedgepeth.

Revocation Process A three-stage procedure that offers limited due process protections to probationers facing revocation, including the opportunity to have the facts of the case heard by a judge and the right to testify on their own behalf.

Recidivism The commission of another crime after the offender has already been arrested and incarcerated for prior criminal activity.

STUDY PREP

Often, studying involves pure memorization. To help with this task, use flash (or note) cards. On one side of the card, write the question or term. On the other side, write the answer or definition. Then, use the cards to test yourself on the material.

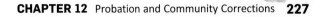

Caseload The number of individual probationers or parolees under the supervision of a probation or parole officer.

The Hybrid Approach A good deal of evidence suggests that probation is more effective than incarceration at preventing recidivism. A recent study of drug offenders in Kansas City, Missouri, for example, found that those who went to prison were 2.3 times more likely to be charged with a new offense than those on probation and 2.2 times more likely than the probationers to be sent back to a correctional facility.[34] Such findings are hardly surprising, though, because by definition, the criminal justice system considers probationers to be lower-risk offenders than prison inmates in the first place.

Do the benefits of our probation system outweigh the risks that probationers such as Frederick Hedgepeth, left, will commit violent crimes? Explain your answer. (Wayne Hinshaw)

Perhaps the better question is, Do certain types of probation work better than others? As far as preventing recidivism is concerned, the most effective probation strategy appears to be a mix of supervision (behavior monitoring) and treatment (behavior change). Researchers have labeled this a *hybrid approach* to probation, and numerous studies attest to the benefits of mixing "tough love" and treatment such as drug counseling and continuing education instead of focusing on one or the other.[35] Some experts even claim that supervision, by itself, has no effect on recidivism—a sobering conclusion, considering the resources dedicated to supervised probation.[36]

The Caseload Dilemma Even the most balanced, "firm but fair" approach to probation can be defeated by the problem of excessive *caseloads*.[37] A **caseload** is the number of clients a probation officer is responsible for at any one time. Although data vary from state to state, Professor Joan Petersilia of the University of California at Irvine estimates that on average, a probation officer in the United States has a caseload of 175 offenders.[38] Some cities report as many as 1,000 cases per officer.[39]

Heavy probation caseloads seem inevitable. Unlike a prison cell, a probation officer can always take "just one more" client. Furthermore, the ideal caseload size is very difficult to determine because different offenders require different levels of supervision. The consequences of disproportionate probation officer–probationer ratios are self-evident, however. When burdened with large caseloads, probation officers find it practically impossible to rigorously enforce the conditions imposed on their clients. Lack of surveillance leads to lack of control, which can undermine the very basis of a probationary system. Several years ago, for example, Dallas County (Texas) probation officers—struggling with high caseloads—lost track of more than 10,000 probationers, half of whom had committed felonies.[40]

¿WHAT ARE SOME TYPES OF INTERMEDIATE SANCTIONS?

Many observers feel that the most widely used sentencing options—imprisonment and probation—fail to reflect the immense diversity of crimes and criminals. **Intermediate sanctions** provide a number of additional sentencing options for those wrongdoers who require stricter supervision than that supplied by probation, but for whom imprisonment would be unduly harsh and counterproductive.[41] The intermediate sanctions discussed in this section are designed to match the specific punishment and treatment of an individual offender with a corrections program that reflects that offender's situation.

Dozens of different variations of intermediate sanctions are handed down each year. To cover the spectrum succinctly, two general categories of such sanctions will be discussed in this section: those administered primarily by the courts and those administered primarily by corrections departments, including day reporting centers, intensive supervision probation, shock incarceration, and home confinement. Remember that none of these sanctions is exclusive. The sanctions are often combined with imprisonment and probation, and with one another.

ishments are generally combined with incarceration or probation. For that reason, some critics feel the retributive or deterrent impact of such punishments is severely limited. Many European countries, in contrast, rely heavily on fines as the sole sanctions for a variety of crimes.

Forfeiture In 1970, Congress passed the Racketeer Influenced and Corrupt Organizations Act (RICO) in an attempt to prevent the use of legitimate business enterprises as shields for organized crime.[42] As amended, RICO and other statutes give judges the ability to implement forfeiture proceedings in certain criminal cases. **Forfeiture** is a process by which

> **Intermediate Sanctions** Sanctions that are more restrictive than probation and less restrictive than imprisonment.
>
> **Forfeiture** The process by which the government seizes private property attached to criminal activity.

JUDICIALLY ADMINISTERED INTERMEDIATE SANCTIONS

The lack of sentencing options is most frustrating for the person who, in the majority of cases, does the sentencing: the judge. Consequently, when judges are given the discretion to "color" a punishment with intermediate sanctions, they will often do so. In addition to imprisonment and probation, a

LO 4 judge has five sentencing options:

1. Fines.
2. Community service.
3. Restitution.
4. Forfeiture.
5. Pretrial diversion programs.

Fines, community service, and restitution were discussed in Chapter 11. In the context of intermediate sanctions, it is important to remember that these pun-

Why might corrections officials support the increased use of intermediate sanctions—such as the court-ordered community service performed by the two gang members in this photo—instead of probation or incarceration? (A. Ramey/PhotoEdit/Petoo/iStockphoto.com)

Pretrial Diversion Program An alternative to trial in which the offender agrees to participate in a specified counseling or treatment program in return for withdrawal of the charges.

Day Reporting Center (DRC) A community-based corrections center to which offenders report on a daily basis for purposes of treatment, education, and rehabilitation.

the government seizes property gained from or used in criminal activity. For example, if a person is convicted for smuggling cocaine into the United States from South America, a judge can order the seizure of not only the narcotics but also the speedboat the offender used to deliver the drugs to a pickup point off the coast of South Florida. In *Bennis v. Michigan* (1996),[43] the Supreme Court ruled that a person's home or car could be forfeited even though the owner was unaware that the property was connected to illegal activity.

Once property is forfeited, the government has several options. It can sell the property, with the proceeds going to the state and/or federal government law enforcement agencies involved in the seizure. Alternatively, the government agency can use the property directly in further crime-fighting efforts or award it to a third party, such as an informant. Forfeiture has proved highly profitable: federal law enforcement agencies impound over $2 billion worth of contraband and property from alleged criminals each year.[44] (CAREER TIP: Local and federal prosecutors often rely on *asset recovery professionals* to coordinate the collection, transportation, and storage of items that have been designated for forfeiture by the government.)

Pretrial Diversion Programs Not every criminal violation requires the courtroom process. Consequently, some judges have the discretion to order an offender into a **pretrial diversion program** during the preliminary hearing. (Prosecutors can also offer an offender the opportunity to join such a program in return for reducing or dropping the initial charges.) These programs represent an interruption of the criminal proceedings and are generally reserved for young or first-time offenders who have been arrested on charges of illegal drug use, child or spousal abuse, or sexual misconduct. Pretrial diversion programs usually include extensive counseling, often in a treatment center. If

the offender successfully follows the conditions of the program, the criminal charges are dropped.

Drug Courts With more than two thousand in operation, *drug courts* have become the fastest-growing form of pretrial diversion in the country. Although the specific procedures of drug courts vary widely from jurisdiction to jurisdiction, most follow a general pattern. Either after arrest or on conviction, the offender is given the option of entering a drug court program or continuing through the standard courtroom process. Those who choose the former come under the supervision of a judge who will oversee a mixture of treatment and sanctions designed to cure the offenders' addictions. When offenders successfully complete the program, the drug court rewards them by dropping all charges against them.

Drug courts operate on the assumption that when a criminal addict's drug use is reduced, his or her drug-fueled criminal activity will also decline. To test this assumption, researchers focused on the Multnomah County (Oregon) Drug Court, comparing postrelease behavior of participants and nonparticipants with similar backgrounds over a ten-year period. The recidivism rate of the participants was nearly 30 percent lower than that of their nonparticipating counterparts.[45] A larger study conducted by the National Institute of Justice produced almost identical results.[46]

DAY REPORTING CENTERS

First used in Great Britain, **day reporting centers (DRCs)** are mainly tools to reduce jail and prison overcrowding. Although the offenders are allowed to live in the community rather than jail or prison, they must spend all or part of each day at a reporting center. In general, being sentenced to a DRC is an extreme form of supervision. With offenders under a single roof, they are much more easily monitored and controlled.

DRCs are instruments of rehabilitation as well. They often feature treatment programs for drug and alcohol abusers and provide counseling for a number of psychological problems, such as depression and anger management problems. Many of those found guilty in the Roanoke (Virginia) Drug Court, for example, are ordered to participate in a year-long day reporting program. At the center, offenders meet with probation officers, submit to various forms of drug testing, and attend counseling and education programs, such as parenting and life-skills classes. After the year has passed, if the offender has completed the program to the satisfaction of the judge and has found employment, the charges will be dropped.[47]

INTENSIVE SUPERVISION PROBATION

Over the past several decades, a number of jurisdictions have turned to **intensive supervision probation (ISP)** to solve the problems associated with the burdensome caseloads we discussed earlier in the chapter. ISP offers a more restrictive alternative to regular probation, with higher levels of face-to-face contact between offenders and officers and frequent modes of control such as urine tests for drugs, or **urinalysis**. In New Jersey, for example, ISP officers have caseloads of only 20 offenders (compared with 115 for other probation officers in the state) and are provided with laptop computers to help them keep tabs on their charges.[48] Different jurisdictions have different methods of determining who is eligible for ISP, but a majority of states limit ISP to offenders who do not have prior probation violations.

The main goal of ISP is to provide prison-like control of offenders while keeping them out of prison. With this in mind, one researcher claims that ISP has had "uniformly dismal" results.[49] In an experiment that compared ISP-eligible probationers in traditional and ISP programs, Joan Petersilia and Susan Turner found that those in ISP programs were more likely to have a technical violation, equally likely to be rearrested and convicted, and more likely to return to prison or jail.[50] One theory is that ISP "causes" these high failure rates—more supervision increases the chances that an offender will be caught breaking conditions of probation. In those ISP programs that have produced low rates of recidivism, a mixture of manageable caseloads and offender access to treatment seems to make the difference.[51]

> **Intensive Supervision Probation (ISP)** A form of probation in which the offender is placed under stricter and more frequent surveillance and control than in conventional probation.
>
> **Urinalysis** The chemical analysis of urine to determine if the subject has been using prohibited substances such as illegal drugs.

CAREERPREP   SUBSTANCE ABUSE COUNSELOR

JOB DESCRIPTION:

- Assess the background and needs of patients suffering from substance abuse and addiction, and craft and execute a plan for recovery.
- Lead group and one-on-one counseling sessions geared toward providing the patient with a sense of accountability and a desire to change the direction of her or his life.

WHAT KIND OF TRAINING IS REQUIRED?

- A bachelor's degree from a counselor program, often found in the department of education or psychology in undergraduate institutions, as well as two years of counseling in a related field or equivalent life experience.
- For licensing and employment with a government agency, a master's degree in substance abuse counseling or rehabilitation counseling is often required.

ANNUAL SALARY RANGE?

- $40,000–$83,000

For additional information, visit: www.princetonreview.com/Careers.aspx?cid=172.

iStockphoto.com

SHOCK INCARCERATION

As the name suggests, **shock incarceration** is designed to "shock" criminals into compliance with the law. Following conviction, the offender is first sentenced to a prison or jail term. Then, usually within ninety days, he or she is released and resentenced to probation. The theory behind shock incarceration is that by getting a taste of the brutalities of the daily prison grind, the offender will be shocked into a crime-free existence.

Boot camp is a variation on traditional shock incarceration. Instead of spending the shock period of incarceration in prison or jail, offenders are sent to a boot camp. Modeled on military basic training, these camps are generally located within prisons and jails, though some can be found in the community. The programs emphasize strict discipline, manual labor, and physical training. They are designed to instill self-responsibility and self-respect in participants, thereby lessening the chances that they will return to a life of crime. More recently, boot camps have also emphasized rehabilitation, incorporating such components as drug and alcohol treatment programs, anger-management courses, and vocational training.[52]

The first boot camp opened in Georgia in 1983. At the peak of their popularity in the mid-1990s, about 120 local, state, and federal boot camps housed more than 7,000 inmates. Around that time, however, studies began to show that the camps were not meeting their goals of improving rearrest rates while reducing prison populations and corrections budgets.[53] By 2000, nearly one-third of the boot camps had closed, and in 2005 the Federal Bureau of Prisons discontinued its boot camp program. Because of their rehabilitative and disciplinarian features, boot camps remain popular in the juvenile corrections system, as we will see in Chapter 15. (CAREER TIP: Although boot camps have fallen out of public favor, wilderness therapy programs for teenagers with behavioral problems such as drug or alcohol abuse or antisocial tendencies have flourished. These programs rely on *field guides, outdoor instructors,* and *youth counselors* to succeed.)

HOME CONFINEMENT AND ELECTRONIC MONITORING

Various forms of **home confinement**—in which offenders serve their sentences not in a government institution but at home—have existed for centuries. It has often served, and continues to do so, as a method of political control, used by totalitarian regimes to isolate and silence dissidents. For purposes of general law enforcement, home confinement was impractical until relatively recently. After all, one could not expect offenders to keep their promises to stay at home, and the personnel costs of guarding them were prohibitive. In the 1980s, however, with the advent of **electronic monitoring**, or using technology to guard the prisoner, home confinement became more viable. Today, all fifty states and the federal government have home monitoring programs, with about 130,000 offenders participating at any one time.[54]

 LO 5 **The Levels of Home Monitoring and Their Benefits** Home monitoring has three general levels of restriction:

1. *Curfew,* which requires offenders to be in their homes at specific hours each day, usually at night.

Shock Incarceration A short period of incarceration that is designed to deter further criminal activity by "shocking" the offender with the hardships of imprisonment.

Home Confinement A community-based sanction in which offenders serve their terms of incarceration in their homes.

Electronic Monitoring A technique of probation supervision in which the offender's whereabouts are kept under surveillance by an electronic device.

2. *Home detention*, which requires that offenders remain home at all times, with exceptions being made for education, employment, counseling, or other specified activities such as the purchase of food or, in some instances, attendance at religious ceremonies.

3. *Home incarceration*, which requires the offender to remain home at all times, save for medical emergencies.

Under ideal circumstances, home confinement serves many of the goals of intermediate sanctions. It protects the community. It saves public funds and space in correctional facilities by keeping convicts out of institutional incarceration. It meets public expectations of punishment for criminals. Uniquely, home confinement also recognizes that convicts, despite their crimes, play important roles in the community, and allows them to continue in those roles. An offender, for example, may be given permission to leave confinement to care for elderly parents.

Home confinement is also lauded for giving sentencing officials the freedom to match the punishment with the needs of the offender. In Missouri, for instance, the conditions of detention for a musician required him to remain at home during the day, but allowed him to continue his career at night. In addition, he was obliged to make antidrug statements before each performance, to be verified by the manager at the club where he appeared.

Types of Electronic Monitoring

According to some reports, the inspiration for electronic monitoring was a *Spider-Man* comic book in which the hero was trailed by the use of an electronic device on his arm. In 1979, a New Mexico judge named Jack Love, having read the comic, convinced an executive at Honeywell, Inc., to begin developing similar technology to supervise convicts.[55]

Two major types of electronic monitoring have grown out of Love's initial concept. The first is a "programmed contact" arrangement, in which the offender is contacted periodically by telephone or beeper to verify his or her whereabouts. Verification is obtained via a computer that uses voice or visual identification techniques or by requiring the offender to enter a code in

How does an electronic monitoring device such as the one shown here meet many of the goals of intermediate sanctions? (AP Photo/CP/Tom Hanson)

an electronic box when called. The second type of electronic monitoring is a "continuously signaling" device, worn around the convict's wrist, ankle, or neck (see the photo above). A transmitter in the device sends out a continuous signal to a "receiver-dialer" device located in the offender's dwelling. If the receiver device does not detect a signal from the transmitter, it informs a central computer, and the police are notified.[56] (CAREER TIP: *Electronic monitoring technicians,* usually members of probation departments, are responsible for instructing offenders on the rules and regulations of the monitoring regime, installing the device, and notifying law enforcement when a breach has occurred.)

Technological Advances in Electronic Monitoring

As electronic monitoring technology has evolved, the ability of community corrections officials to target specific forms of risky behavior has greatly increased. A Michigan court, for example, has begun placing black boxes in the automobiles of repeat traffic law violators. Not only do these boxes record information about the offenders' driving habits for review by probation officers, but they also emit a loud beep when a car goes too fast or stops too quickly. As we saw in Chapter 3, another device—an ankle bracelet—is able to test a person's sweat for alcohol levels and transmit the results over the Internet.

CJ and Technology

GLOBAL POSITIONING SYSTEM (GPS)

San Bernardino County (California) probation officer Nathan Scarano had two reasons to believe that Christopher Henry was involved in a street gang fight earlier that night. First, Henry's face was bloodied. Second, the global positioning system (GPS) device strapped to Henry's ankle placed him at the scene. GPS technology is a form of tracking technology that relies on twenty-four military satellites orbiting thousands of miles above the earth. The satellites transmit signals to each other and to a receiver on the ground, allowing a monitoring station to determine the location of a receiving device to within a few feet. GPS provides a much more precise level of supervision than regular electronic monitoring. A probationer like Henry wears a transmitter, similar to a traditional electronic monitor, around his or her ankle or wrist. This transmitter communicates with a portable tracking device (PTD), a small box that uses the military satellites to determine the probationer's movements.

GPS technology can be used either "actively" to monitor constantly the subject's whereabouts, or "passively" to ensure that the offender remains within the confines of a limited area determined by a judge or probation officer. Inclusion and exclusion zones are also important to GPS supervision. Inclusion zones are areas such as a home or workplace, where the offender is expected to be at certain times. Exclusion zones are areas such as parks, playgrounds, and schools, where the offender is not permitted to go. GPS-linked computers can alert officials immediately when an exclusion zone has been breached and create a computerized record of the probationer's movements for review at a later time.

THINKING ABOUT GPS

How could GPS technology be used to ensure that a convicted sex offender complies with a judge's order to stay away from areas where large numbers of children are present?

AP Photo/Jeff T. Green/ iStockphoto.com

WIDENING THE NET

Widen the Net The criticism that intermediate sanctions designed to divert offenders from prison actually increase the number of citizens who are under the control of the corrections system.

Not surprisingly, most of the convicts chosen for intermediate sanctions are low-risk offenders. From the point of view of the corrections official doing the choosing, this makes sense. Such offenders are less likely to commit crimes and attract negative publicity. This selection strategy, however, appears to undermine one of the primary reasons intermediate sanctions exist: to reduce prison and jail popula-tions. If most of the offenders in intermediate sanctions programs would otherwise have received probation, then the effect on these populations is nullified. Indeed, studies have shown this to be the case.[57]

At the same time, such selection processes broaden the reach of the corrections system. In other words, they increase rather than decrease the amount of control the state exerts over the individual. Suppose a person is arrested for a misdemeanor such as shoplifting and, under normal circumstances, would receive probation. With access to intermediate sanctions, the judge may add a period of home confinement to the sentence. Critics contend that such practices **widen the net** of the corrections system by augmenting the number of citizens who are under the control and surveillance of the state and also *strengthen the net* by increasing the government's power to intervene in the lives of its citizens.[58] (See the feature *You Be the Judge—What's the Sentence?* below to make your own assessment as to how wide the net should be in a particular instance.)

¿WHAT IS ONE MAJOR CONCERN WITH COMMUNITY CORRECTIONS?

Despite their many benefits, including cost savings, treatment options, and the ability to divert hundreds of thousands of nonviolent wrongdoers from prisons and jails, community-based corrections programs suffer from a basic paradox: the more effectively offenders are controlled, the more likely they are to be caught violating the terms of their conditional release. As you may have noticed, the community supervision programs discussed in this chapter are evaluated according to rates of recidivism and revocation, with low levels of each reflecting a successful program. Increased control and surveillance, however, will necessarily raise the level of violations, thus increasing the probability that any single violation will be discovered. Therefore, as factors such as the number of conditions placed on probationers and the technological proficiency of electronic monitoring devices increase, so, too, will the number of offenders who fail to meet the conditions of their community-based punishment.

One observer calls this the "quicksand" effect of increased surveillance. Instead of helping offenders leave the corrections system, increased surveillance pulls them more deeply into it.[59] The quicksand effect can be quite strong, according to researchers Barbara Sims of Penn State University–Harrisburg and Mark Jones of East Carolina University. In a study of North Carolina corrections data, Sims and Jones found that 26 percent of the probationers whose probation terms were revoked had been guilty of violations such as failing a single drug test. The researchers believe this strategy is overly punitive—anybody who has tried to quit smoking is aware of the difficulties of breaking an addiction.[60]

YOU BE THE JUDGE
What's the Sentence?

Gina Sanders/Shutterstock

THE FACTS Marcus, a freshman at Florida College, wanted to join the Kappa Alpha Psi fraternity. Jason and four other fraternity brothers took twenty-seven pledges, including Marcus, to an abandoned warehouse for the initiation rites, in which the pledges were blindfolded, taunted, slapped, punched with boxing gloves, and paddled with wooden canes. The beatings left Marcus with a ruptured eardrum and a hematoma on his buttocks that required surgery. Although Marcus was a willing participant who could have left at any time, a Florida jury found Jason guilty of hazing that resulted in serious bodily injury.

THE LAW Under Florida law, hazing that results in serious bodily injury is a third degree felony. As such, it is punishable by penalties ranging from probation to five years in prison.

YOUR DECISION On the one hand, Jason's attorney has requested leniency, pointing out that his client has no previous record of wrongdoing and a fiancée who is four months pregnant. On the other hand, the Florida legislature passed the antihazing law after public outcry over a string of violent incidents on college campuses, including one that resulted in death. Given the range of punishment options you have learned about in the past two chapters, what is your sentence for Jason?

[To see how a Florida judge ruled in a case with similar facts, go to Example 12.1 on page 350.]

13 PRISONS AND JAILS

Learning Outcomes

After studying this chapter,
you will be able to . . .

LO 1 List the factors that have
caused the prison population
to grow dramatically in the
last several decades.

LO 2 List and briefly explain the
four types of prisons.

LO 3 Summarize the distinction
between jails and prisons,
and indicate the importance
of jails in the American correctional system.

LO 4 Explain how jails are
administered.

LO 5 Indicate some of the consequences of our high rates of
incarceration.

Incarceration Nation

How much does it cost to send someone to prison? As a rule, judges ignore such questions when it comes to making the sentencing decision. Missouri lawmakers, however, have decided that this rule was made to be broken. In August 2010, state corrections officials began providing judges with very specific information concerning the economics of sentencing. Missouri judges now know, for example, that a three-year prison sentence for someone convicted of endangering the welfare of a child would cost more than $37,000, compared with a $6,770 price tag if that same person was placed on probation. Similarly, the going rate for a five-year term in state prison for second degree robbery is $50,000, compared with $9,000 for intensive probation over that same time period.

The intent is clear: saddled with an ever-growing corrections budget, Missouri officials would rather that judges keep certain offenders out of expensive prison cells. Other states are taking comparable steps. California has recently extended the use of good-behavior credits to reduce the length of prison terms. Rhode Island has increased its commitment to rehabilitating offenders rather than incarcerating them. Michigan is closing five prisons. The consequences of these new policies, in the words of one corrections expert, "took us a little bit by surprise." In 2009, the number of inmates in state prisons nationwide declined for the first time since 1972.

To be sure, this decline was very small—less than 1 percent—and does little to threaten America's title as "the globe's leading incarcerator." The United States locks up six times as many of its citizens as Canada does, and seven times as many as most European democracies. Approximately 2.4 million Americans are in prison or jail. Still, the fact that so many state politicians are willing to seek bargains when it comes to corrections does represent a sea change in policy thinking. As one Missouri judge puts it, "We live in a what's-it-going-to-cost society now."

(David L Ryan/The Boston Globe via Getty Images)

What unusual step did Missouri lawmakers take to reduce the state's inmate population, which includes these four prisoners at the Western Missouri Correctional Center in Cameron? (Mike Ransdell/MCT/Landov)

Cost-cutting tactics aside, the American corrections system is a massive institution and will remain so for the foreseeable future.[1] Indeed, despite the decline in state prison populations noted above, the overall U.S. prison population continues to grow, thanks to more significant annual increases in the number of inmates in federal corrections facilities.[2] Throughout this textbook, we have discussed many of the social and political factors that help explain the prison population boom of the past forty years. In this chapter and the next, we turn our attention to the incarceration system itself. (CAREER TIP: Just as criminologists study crime, *penologists* study the corrections system, often with a focus on prison management and inmate rehabilitation.)

This chapter focuses on the organizational structures of prisons (which generally hold those who have committed serious felonies for long periods of time) and jails (which generally hold those who have committed less serious felonies and misdemeanors, and those awaiting trial, for short periods of time). Although the two terms are often used interchangeably, they refer to two very different institutions, each with its own responsibilities and its own set of seemingly unsolvable problems.

¿WHAT TRENDS ARE DRIVING THE AMERICAN PRISON POPULATION?

The number of Americans in prison or jail has more than tripled since 1985 (see **Figure 13.1** above). These numbers are not only dramatic, but also, say some

Figure 13.1 The Inmate Population of the United States

The total number of inmates in the United States has risen from 744,208 in 1985 to nearly 2.4 million in 2009.

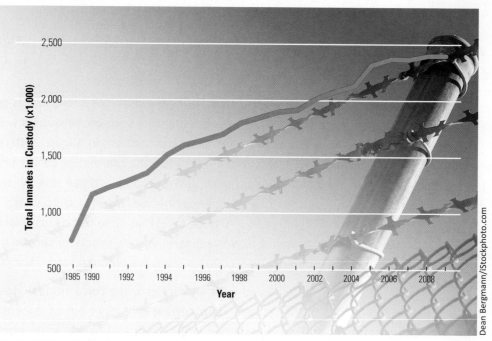

Source: U.S. Department of Justice.

observers, inexplicable, given the overall crime picture in the United States. According to the accepted theory, rising incarceration rates should come from a rise in crime. Yet, violent and property crime rates have been *declining* since the 1990s. "That's the puzzling piece" of the recent drop in state prison populations, says Marc Mauer of the Sentencing Project, a research group based in Washington, D.C. "Why did this take so long?"[3]

FACTORS IN PRISON POPULATION GROWTH

To a large degree, the dramatic growth of inmate populations is a consequence of the *penal harm movement*.[4] Characterized by "get tough" ideologies in sentencing and punishment, this movement has been particularly influential when it comes to the "war" on drugs. Indeed, much of the growth in the number of Americans behind bars can be attributed to the enhancement and stricter enforcement of the nation's drug laws. There are more people in prison and jail for drug offenses today than there were for *all* offenses in the early 1970s.[5] In 1980, about 19,000 drug offenders were incarcerated in state prisons, and 4,800 drug offenders were in federal prisons. Twenty-nine years later, state prisons contained about 264,000 inmates who had been arrested for drug offenses, and the number of drug offenders in federal prisons had risen to more than 95,200 (representing half of all inmates in federal facilities).[6]

Other reasons for the growth in incarcerated populations include the following:

- *Increased probability of incarceration.* Simply stated, the chance of someone who is arrested going to prison today is much greater than it was thirty years ago. Most of this growth took place in the 1980s, when the likelihood of incarceration in a state prison after arrest increased fivefold for drug offenses, threefold for weapons offenses, and twofold for crimes such as sexual assault, burglary, auto theft, and larceny.[7] For federal crimes, the proportion of convicted defendants being sent to prison rose from 54 percent in 1988 to 86 percent in 2009.[8]

- *Inmates serving more time for each crime.* After the Sentencing Reform Act of 1984, the length of time served by federal convicts for their crimes rose significantly. As noted in Chapter 11, in the fifteen years after the law went into effect, the average time served by inmates in federal prisons rose to fifty months—an increase of more than 50 percent.[9] For drug offenders, the average amount of time served in federal prison escalated from 39.3 months to 62.4 months, while the average

prison term for weapons offenses grew from 32.4 months to 64.5 months.[10] State sentencing reform statutes and "truth-in-sentencing" laws have had similar consequences. In the thirty-two states that require their inmates to serve at least 85 percent of their sentences, for example, violent offenders are expected to spend an average of fifteen months more in prison than violent offenders in states without such laws.[11]

- *Federal prison growth.* Thanks in part to federal sentencing policy, the federal prison system is now the largest in the country, with more than 208,000 inmates. In fact, since 1995 the federal prison population has more than doubled, whereas state prison populations have grown by "only" 37 percent.[12] Besides the increase in federal drug offenders already mentioned, this growth can be attributed to efforts by Presidents Bill Clinton and George W. Bush to federalize gun possession crimes: from 1995 to 2003, the number of inmates sent to federal prisons for weapons violations jumped by 120 percent.[13] Furthermore, between 1995 and 2009, immigration law offenders increased by more than 590 percent (3,612 to 21,395).[14] This trend has led to a surge in the number of Latino inmates in federal prison. In 2008, 40 percent of federal inmates were Latino, up from 24 percent sixteen years earlier.[15]

- *Rising incarceration rates of women.* In 1981, 14,000 women were prisoners in federal and state

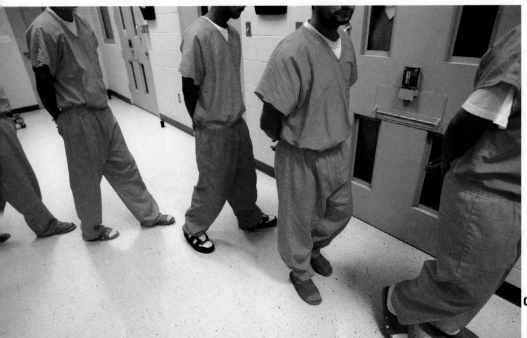

Several Latino inmates await health screening at the Val Verde Correctional Facility in Del Rio, Texas. What factor is most responsible for the surge in the number of Latinos incarcerated by the federal government? (Tom Pennington/MCT/Newscom)

Custodial Model A theory of prison organization that emphasizes security and discipline, and thus restricts the personal freedoms of inmates in the name of order.

Rehabilitation Model A theory of prison organization that emphasizes treatment and reform, with security concerns secondary to the well-being of the inmates.

Reintegration Model A theory of prison organization in which the correctional facility offers classes and programs designed to ease the inmate's reentry into society following her or his release from incarceration.

institutions. By 2009, the number had grown to about 113,500. Women still account for only 7 percent of all prisoners nationwide, but their rates of imprisonment are growing nearly twice as rapidly as those of men.[16]

DOWNSIZING AMERICA'S PRISONS

The escalation in the prisoner population has brought with it an increased demand for new prisons. In 1980, the Federal Bureau of Prisons had a budget of $330 million and operated forty-four prisons. Today, its budget exceeds $5 billion and there are 114 federal prisons. Over the past three decades, the number of state prisons has increased from fewer than 600 to more than 1,700.[17] Today, state governments spend more than $49 billion a year to operate their corrections systems, up from $12 billion in 1987. Nearly 90 percent of this spending goes to operating prisons, as opposed to probation, parole, or other community-based programs.[18] Consequently, states are increasingly focusing on reducing prison costs by revising mandatory-sentencing laws (see page 210), recalculating "good time" credits (see page 202), or in extreme cases, closing facilities down.

As we pointed out in the opening to this chapter, many states have taken extreme steps to cut prison costs. As another example, Illinois expects to reduce its corrections budget by $5 million annually by releasing low-level nonviolent offenders from prison to be monitored—either electronically or by parole officers—in the community. New York plans to save $250 million a year by repealing a series of harsh drug laws under which anyone convicted of selling two ounces or possessing four ounces of narcotics receives a prison term of fifteen years to life.[19] Arizona has even considered putting its entire prison system under private control.[20] (Prison privatization will be discussed later in the chapter.)

¿WHAT IS THE ROLE OF PRISONS IN SOCIETY?

The increase in prison populations also reflects the varied demands placed on penal institutions. As University of Connecticut sociologist Charles Logan once noted, Americans expect prisons to "correct the incorrigible, rehabilitate the wretched . . . restrain the dangerous, and punish the wicked."[21] Basically, prisons exist to make society a safer place. Whether this is to be achieved through retribution, deterrence, incapacitation, or rehabilitation—the four justifications of corrections introduced in Chapter 11—depends on the operating philosophy of the individual penal institution.

Three general models of prisons have emerged to describe the different schools of thought behind prison organization:

- The **custodial model** is based on the assumption that prisoners are incarcerated for reasons of incapacitation, deterrence, and retribution. All decisions within the prison—such as what form of recreation to provide the inmates—are made with an eye toward security and discipline, and the daily routine of the inmates is highly controlled. The custodial model has dominated the most restrictive prisons in the United States since the 1930s.

- The **rehabilitation model** stresses the ideals of individualized treatment that we discussed in Chapter 11. Security concerns are often secondary to the well-being of the individual inmate, and a number of treatment programs are offered to aid prisoners in changing their criminal and antisocial behavior. The rehabilitation model came into prominence during the 1950s and enjoyed widespread popularity until it began to lose general acceptance in the 1970s and 1980s.

- In the **reintegration model**, the correctional institution serves as a training ground for the inmate to prepare for existence in the community. Prisons that have adopted this model give the prisoners more responsibility during incarceration and offer halfway houses and work programs (both to be discussed in Chapter 14) to help them reintegrate into society. This model is becoming more influential as corrections officials react to problems such as prison overcrowding.[22]

Competing views of the prison's role in society are at odds with these three "ideal" perspectives. Professor Alfred Blumstein argues that prisons create new criminals, especially with regard to nonviolent drug offenders. Not only do these nonviolent felons become socialized to the criminal lifestyle while in prison, but the stigma of incarceration makes it more difficult for them to obtain employment on release. Their only means of subsistence "on the outside" is to apply the criminal methods they learned in prison.[23] A study by criminal justice professors Cassia Spohn of Arizona State University and David Holleran of the College of New Jersey found that convicted drug offenders who were sentenced to prison were 2.2 times more likely to be incarcerated for a new offense than those sentenced to probation.[24]

¿WHAT ARE THE DIFFERENT TYPES OF PRISONS?

Prison administrators have long been aware of the need to separate different kinds of offenders. In federal prisons, this led to a system with six levels based on the security needs of the inmates, from level 1 facilities with the lowest amount of security to level 6 with the harshest security measures. To simplify matters, most observers refer to correctional facilities as being one of three levels—minimum, medium, or maximum. A fourth level—the supermaximum-security prison, known as the "supermax"—is relatively rare and somewhat controversial due to its hyperharsh methods of punishing and controlling the most dangerous prisoners.

LO2

MAXIMUM-SECURITY PRISONS

Once wrongdoers enter a corrections facility, they are constantly graded on behavior. Those who serve "good time," as we have seen, are often rewarded with early release. Those who compile extensive misconduct records are usually housed, along with violent and repeat offenders, in **maximum-security prisons.** The names of these institutions—Folsom, San Quentin, Sing Sing, Attica—conjure up foreboding images of concrete and steel jungles, with good reason.

Maximum-security prisons are designed with full attention to security and surveillance. In these institutions, inmates' lives are programmed in a militaristic fashion to keep them from escaping or from harming each other or the prison staff. About a quarter of the prisons in the United States are classified as maximum security, and these institutions house about a third of the country's prisoners.

The Design Maximum-security prisons tend to be large—holding more than a thousand inmates—and they have similar features. The entire operation is usually surrounded by concrete walls that stand twenty to thirty feet high and have also been sunk deep into the ground to deter tunnel escapes. These facilities also feature fences reinforced with razor-ribbon barbed wire that can be electrically charged to supplement these barriers. The prison walls are studded with watchtowers, from which guards armed with shotguns and rifles survey the movement of

> **Maximum-Security Prison** A correctional institution designed and organized to control and discipline dangerous felons.

STUDYPREP

Mnemonic (*ne-MON-ik*) devices are tricks that increase our ability to memorize. One well-known mnemonic trick is "Every Good Boy Does Fine" to remember the sequence of musical notes E, G, B, D, F. The more fun you have coming up with mnemonics for yourself, the more useful they will be.

prisoners on the ground. The designs of these facilities, though similar, are not uniform. Although some correctional facilities still use the radial design first developed in the nineteenth century, several other designs have become prominent in more recently constructed institutions. For an overview of these designs, including the radial design, see **Figure 13.2** below.

Inmates live in cells, most of them with similar dimensions to those found in the I-Max maximum-security prison for women in Topeka, Kansas: eight feet by fourteen feet with cinder block walls.[25] The space contains bunks, a toilet, a sink, and possibly a cabinet or closet. Cells are located in rows of *cell blocks*, each of which forms its own security unit, set off by a series of gates and bars. A maximum-security institution is essentially a collection of numerous cell blocks, each constituting its own prison within a prison.

Inmates' lives are dominated by security measures. Whenever they move from one area of the prison to another, they do so in groups and under the watchful

Figure 13.2 Prison Designs

The Radial Design
The radial design has been utilized since the early nineteenth century. The wagon wheel form of the structure was created with the dual goals of separation and control.

The Courtyard Style
In the courtyard-style prison, a courtyard replaces the transportation function of the "pole" in the telephone-pole prison. The prison buildings form a square around the courtyard, and to get from one part of the facility to another, the inmates go across the courtyard.

The Telephone-Pole Design
The main feature of this design is a long central corridor that serves as a means for transporting inmates from one part of the facility to another. Branching off from this main corridor are the functional areas of the facility: housing, food services, workshops, a treatment programs room, and other services.

The Campus Style
Some of the newer minimum-security prisons have adopted the campus style, a style that had previously been used in correctional facilities for women and juveniles. Like a college campus, housing units are scattered among functional units such as the dining room, recreation area, and treatment centers.

Source: Adapted from Todd R. Clear, George F. Cole, and Michael D. Reisig, *American Corrections,* 9th ed. (Belmont, Calif.: Wadsworth Publishing Company, 2010), pages 267–268.

Courtesy of Leavenworth Area Development/Stefan Klein/iStockphoto.com

CJ and Technology

TRACKING INMATES

Technology has added significantly to the overall safety of maximum-security prisons. Walk-through metal detectors and X-ray body scanners, for example, can detect weapons or other contraband hidden on the body of an inmate. The most promising new technology in this field, however, relies on radio frequency identification (RFID). In the prison context, RFID works as a high-tech head count: inmates wear bracelets tagged with microchips, and correctional officers wear small RFID devices resembling pagers. Guided by a series of radio transmitters and receivers, the system is able to pinpoint the location of inmates and guards within twenty feet. Every two seconds, radio signals search out the location of each inmate and guard and relay this information to a central computer. On a grid of the prison, an inmate shows up as a yellow dot and a correctional officer as a blue dot. Many RFID systems also store all movements in a database for future reference. "[RFID] completely revolutionizes a prison because you know where everyone is—not approximately but exactly where they are," remarked an official at the National Institute of Justice.

THINKING ABOUT RFID TRACKING

Review the discussion of crime mapping and "hot spots" on page 109 in Chapter 6. Drawing on your knowledge of crime-mapping technology, discuss how RFID technology can reduce violence and other misconduct such as drug sales in prisons.

---

eyes of armed correctional guards. Television surveillance cameras may be used to monitor the prisoners' every move, even when sleeping, showering, or using the toilet. They are subject to frequent pat-downs or strip searches at the guards' discretion. Constant "head counts" ensure that every inmate is where he or she should be. Tower guards—many of whom have orders to shoot to kill in the case of a disturbance or escape attempt—constantly look down on the inmates as they move around outdoor areas of the facility.

Supermax Prisons About thirty states and the Federal Bureau of Prisons (BOP) operate **supermax** (short for supermaximum-security) **prisons**, which are supposedly reserved for the "worst of the worst" of America's corrections population. Most of the inmates in these facilities are deemed high risks to commit murder behind bars—about a quarter of the occupants of the BOP's U.S. Penitentiary Administrative Maximum (ADX) in Florence, Colorado, have killed other prisoners

or assaulted correctional officers elsewhere. In addition, many supermax inmates are either high-profile individuals who would be at constant risk of attack in a general prison population or convicted terrorists such as Zacarias Moussaoui (see page 206), Ted "the Unabomber" Kaczynski, and Terry Nichols, who was involved in the bombing of the federal building in Oklahoma City in 1995.

Supermax Prison A correctional facility reserved for those inmates who have extensive records of misconduct in maximum-security prisons.

A Controlled Environment The main purpose of a supermax prison is to control strictly the inmates' movement, thereby limiting (or eliminating) situations that could lead to breakdowns in discipline. The conditions at California's Security Housing Unit (SHU) at Pelican Bay State Prison are representative of most supermax institutions. Prisoners are confined to their one-person cells for twenty-two and a half hours each day under video camera surveillance; they receive meals through a slot in the door. The cells measure eight by ten feet and are windowless. No decorations of any kind are permitted on the walls.[26]

To a great extent, supermax prisons operate in a state of perpetual **lockdown,** in which all inmates are confined to their cells, and social activities such as meals, recreational sports, and treatment programs are nonexistent. For the ninety minutes of each day that SHU inmates are allowed out of their cells (compared with twelve to sixteen hours in regular maximum-security prisons), they may either shower or exercise in an enclosed, concrete "yard" covered by plastic mesh. Prisoners are strip-searched before and after leaving their cells and are placed in waist restraints and handcuffs on their way to and from the yard and showers.[27]

Supermax Syndrome Many prison officials support the proliferation of supermax prisons because they provide increased security for the most dangerous inmates. These proponents believe that the harsh reputation of the facilities will deter convicts from misbehaving for fear of transfer to a supermax. Nevertheless, the supermax has aroused a number of criticisms. Amnesty International and other human rights groups assert that the facilities violate standards for proper treatment of prisoners.

At Wisconsin's Supermax Correctional Facility, for example, the cells are illuminated twenty-four hours a day. Because they have no air-conditioning or windows, average temperatures in these cells during the summer top 100 degrees.[28] Furthermore, while studying prisoners at California's Pelican Bay facility, a Harvard University psychiatrist found that 80 percent suffered from what he called "SHU [security housing unit] syndrome," a condition brought on by long periods of isolation.[29] Further research on SHU syndrome shows that supermax inmates manifest a number of psychological problems, including massive anxiety, hallucinations, and acute confusion.[30]

MEDIUM- AND MINIMUM-SECURITY PRISONS

Medium-security prisons hold about 40 percent of the prison population and minimum-security prisons 20 percent. Inmates at **medium-security prisons** have for the most part committed less serious crimes than those housed in maximum-security prisons and are not considered high risks for escaping or causing harm. Consequently, medium-security institutions are not designed for control

Inside the Northern Correctional Institution, the supermax facility in Somers, Connecticut, a correctional officer, top left, enters a cell. In what ways does the supermax prison represent the ultimate controlled environment for its inmates?

(AP Photo/Steve Miller/Korhan Karacan/iStockphoto.com)

to the same extent as maximum-security prisons and have a more relaxed atmosphere. These facilities also offer more educational and treatment programs and allow for more contact between inmates. Medium-security prisons are rarely walled, relying instead on high fences. Prisoners have more freedom of movement within the structures, and the levels of surveillance are much lower. Living quarters are less restrictive as well—many of the newer medium-security prisons provide dormitory housing.

A **minimum-security prison** seems at first glance to be more like a college campus than an incarceration facility. Most of the inmates at these institutions are first-time offenders who are nonviolent and well behaved. A high percentage are white-collar criminals. Indeed, inmates are often transferred to minimum-security prisons as a reward for good behavior in other facilities. Therefore, security measures are lax compared with even medium-security prisons.

Unlike medium-security institutions, minimum-security prisons do not have armed guards. Prisoners are allowed amenities such as television sets and computers in their rooms, they enjoy freedom of movement, and they are allowed off prison grounds for educational or employment purposes to a much greater extent than those held in more restrictive facilities. (CAREER TIP: Many colleges now offer degrees in *recreation management*. Although geared toward corporate fitness/wellness programs, recreation management also has a place in the corrections system. For example, Danbury Women's Prison—where television personality Martha Stewart spent more than five months in the mid-2000s—has a track and a gymnasium that is used for Dancersize, Pilates, and yoga classes.)

Some critics have likened minimum-security prisons to "country clubs," but in the corrections system, everything is relative. A minimum-security prison may seem like a vacation spot when compared with the horrors of Sing Sing, but it still represents a restriction of personal freedom and separates the inmate from the outside world.

¿HOW ARE PRISONS MANAGED?

The security level of the institution generally determines the specific methods by which a prison is managed.

There are, however, general goals of prison administration, summarized by Charles Logan as follows:

> The mission of a prison is to keep prisoners—to keep them in, keep them safe, keep them in line, keep them healthy, and keep them busy—and to do it with fairness, without undue suffering and as efficiently as possible.[31]

Minimum-Security Prison A correctional institution designed to allow inmates, most of whom pose low security risks, a great deal of freedom of movement and contact with the outside world.

Considering the environment of a prison—an enclosed world inhabited by people who are generally violent and angry and would rather be anywhere else—Logan's mission statement may be highly idealistic. A prison staff must supervise the daily routines of hundreds or thousands of inmates, a duty that includes providing them with meals, education, vocational programs, and different forms of leisure. The smooth operation of this supervision is made more difficult—if not at times impossible—by budgetary restrictions, overcrowding, and continual inmate turnover.

FORMAL PRISON MANAGEMENT

In some respects, the management structure of a prison is similar to that of a police department, as discussed in Chapter 5. Both systems rely on a hierarchical (top-down) *chain of command* to increase personal responsibility. Both assign different employees to specific tasks, though prison managers have much more direct control over their subordinates than do police managers. The main difference is that police departments have a *continuity of purpose* that is sometimes lacking in prison organizations. All members of a police force, at least theoretically, are working to reduce crime and apprehend criminals.

In a prison, this continuity is less evident. An employee in the prison laundry service and one who works in the visiting center have little in common. In some cases, employees may even have cross-purposes: a prison guard may want to punish an inmate, while a counselor in the treatment center may want to rehabilitate her or him.

Consequently, a strong hierarchy is crucial for any prison management team that hopes to meet Charles

Warden The prison official who is ultimately responsible for the organization and performance of a correctional facility.

Logan's expectations. The **warden** (also known as a superintendent) is ultimately responsible for the operation of a prison. He or she oversees deputy wardens, who in turn manage the various organizational lines of the institution. The custodial employees, who deal directly with the inmates and make up more than half of a prison's staff, operate under a militaristic hierarchy, with a line of command passing from the deputy warden to the captain to the correctional officer. (CAREER TIP: With each inmate comes a significant amount of recorded information: criminal background, security designation, special needs, disciplinary restrictions, and the like. The *inmate records coordinator* is responsible for organizing this information and keeping it up to date.)

GOVERNING PRISONS

The implications of prison mismanagement can be severe. While studying a series of prison riots, sociologists Bert Useem and Peter Kimball found that breakdown in managerial control commonly preceded such acts of mass violence.[32] During the 1970s, for example, conditions at the State Penitentiary in New Mexico deteriorated significantly. Inmates were the targets of random and harsh treatment at the hands of the prison staff, while at the same time a reduction in structured activities left prison life "painfully boring."[33] The result, in 1980, was one of the more violent prison riots in this nation's history.

What sort of prison management is best suited to avoid such situations? Although there is no single "best" form of prison management, political scientist John DiIulio believes that in general, the sound governance of corrections facilities is a matter of order, amenities, and services:

- *Order* can be defined as the absence of misconduct such as murder, assault, and rape. Many observers, including DiIulio, believe that the state, having incarcerated a person, has a responsibility to protect that person from disorder in the correctional institution.

CAREERPREP

WARDEN

JOB DESCRIPTION:

- As chief managing officer of an adult correctional institution, the warden is responsible for the custody, feeding, clothing, housing, care, treatment, discipline, training, employment, rehabilitation, and well-being of inmates.
- The warden provides institutional staff with effective communications, training, and leadership.

WHAT KIND OF TRAINING IS REQUIRED?

- A bachelor's degree in criminal justice, social work, psychology, or a related field.
- One or more years of work experience in the management of a major division of a correctional institution.

ANNUAL SALARY RANGE?

- $42,000–$95,000 (depending on size of institution and geographic region)

For additional information, visit:
www.legal-criminal-justice-schools.com/
Criminal-Justice-Careers/prison-warden.html.

Jesse Karjalainen/iStockphoto.com

- *Amenities* are those comforts that make life "livable," such as clean living conditions, decent food, and entertainment. One theory of incarceration holds that inmates should not enjoy a quality of life comparable to life outside prison. Without the basic amenities, however, prison existence becomes unbearable, and inmates are more likely to lapse into disorder and violence.

- *Services* include programs designed to improve an inmate's prospects on release, such as vocational training, remedial education, and drug treatment. Again, many feel that a person convicted of a crime does not deserve to participate in these kinds of programs, but they have two clear benefits. First, they keep the inmate occupied and focused during her or his sentence. Second, they reduce the chances that the inmate will go back to a life of crime after she or he returns to the community.[34] (CAREER TIP: For spiritual guidance behind bars, inmates of all faiths turn to *prison chaplains,* who coordinate religious services in correctional facilities.)

According to DiIulio, in the absence of order, amenities, and services, inmates will come to see their imprisonment as not only unpleasant but also unfair, and they will become much more difficult to control.[35] Furthermore, weak governance encourages inmates to come up with their own methods of regulating their lives. As we shall see in the next chapter, the result is usually high levels of violence and the expansion of prison gangs and other unsanctioned forms of authority.

¿WHAT ARE PRIVATE PRISONS?

In addition to all the other pressures placed on wardens and other prison administrators, they must operate within a budget assigned to them by an overseeing governmental agency. Today, the great majority of all prisons are under the control of federal and state governments, but government-run prisons have not always been the rule. In the nineteenth century, some correctional facilities were not under the control of the state. In fact, the entire Texas prison system was privately operated from 1872 to the late 1880s. For most of the twentieth century, however, **private prisons,** or prisons run by private business firms to make a profit, could not be found in the United States.

That is certainly not the case today. With corrections exhibiting all appearances of, in the words of one observer, "a recession-proof industry," the American business community has eagerly entered the market. Fourteen private corrections firms operate more than two hundred facilities across the United States. The two largest corrections companies, Corrections Corporation of America (CCA) and the GEO Group, Inc., have contracted to supervise more than 100,000 inmates.

In 1997, the Federal Bureau of Prisons (BOP) awarded the first contract paying a private company to operate one of its prisons—the GEO Group received $88 million to run the Taft Correctional Institution in Taft, California. Today, the GEO Group operates nineteen federal corrections facilities. By 2009, private penal institutions housed more than 129,000 inmates, representing 8 percent of all prisoners in the state and federal corrections systems.[36]

WHY PRIVATIZE?

It would be a mistake to automatically assume that private prisons are less expensive to run than public ones. Nevertheless, the incentive to privatize is primarily financial.

Cost Efficiency In the 1980s and 1990s, a number of states and cities saved operating costs by transferring government-run services such as garbage collection and road maintenance to the private sector. Similarly, private prisons can often be run more cheaply and efficiently than public ones for the following reasons:

- *Labor costs.* The wages of public employees account for nearly two-thirds of a prison's operating expenses. Although private corrections firms pay base salaries comparable to those received by public prison employees, their nonunionized staffs receive lower levels of overtime pay,

Private Prison
A correctional facility operated by a private corporation instead of the government.

workers' compensation claims, sick leave, and health-care insurance.

- *Competitive bidding.* Because of the profit motive, private corrections firms have an incentive to buy goods and services at the lowest possible price.

- *Less red tape.* Private corrections firms are not part of the government bureaucracy and therefore do not have to contend with the massive amount of paperwork that can clog government organizations.[37]

In the middle of the first decade of the 2000s, the National Institute of Justice released the results of a five-year study comparing low-security public and private prisons in California. The government agency found that private facilities cost taxpayers between 6 and 10 percent less than public ones.[38] More recent research conducted at Vanderbilt University found that states saved about $15 million annually when they supplemented their corrections systems with privately managed institutions.[39]

Overcrowding and Outsourcing Private prisons are becoming increasingly attractive to state governments faced with the competing pressures of tight budgets and overcrowded corrections facilities. Lacking the funds to relieve overcrowding by building more prisons, state officials are turning to the private institutions for help. Often, the private prison is out of state, which leads to the "outsourcing" of inmates. Hawaii, for example, sends about one-third of its 6,000 inmates to private prisons in Arizona.[40] California, dealing with severe overcrowding and an annual corrections health-care budget of $1.5 billion, has increased the number of its inmates housed out of state to more than 15,000, placing them in private insti-

tutions in Arizona, Colorado, Michigan, Minnesota, Missouri, Montana, and Oklahoma.[41]

Quality of Service Executives at corrections firms claim that because their contracts can be canceled for poor performance, private prisons have a greater incentive to provide higher-quality service than their public counterparts. At least one study, conducted by Charles Logan, supports this contention. Logan found that according to statistical data and staff surveys, a private women's prison in New Mexico outperformed a state prison and a federal prison in a number of areas such as security, safety, living conditions, and management.[42]

THE ARGUMENT AGAINST PRIVATE PRISONS

Significantly, in Logan's study mentioned above, the inmates themselves gave the private prison lower scores than did the staff members. Opponents of private prisons worry that despite the assurances of corporate executives, private corrections companies will cut corners to save costs, denying inmates important security guarantees in the process.

Safety Concerns These criticisms find some support in the anecdotal evidence. On April 24, 2007, about five hundred inmates rioted at a medium-security facility operated by the GEO Group in New Castle, Indiana. The disturbance was started by newly transferred inmates from Arizona who were upset at the lack of rec-

Why would sending inmates to out-of-state private prisons be attractive to states such as California, whose Institution for Men in Chino is so overcrowded that, as this photo shows, inmates are forced to sleep in bunk beds in a gymnasium?

(Monica Almeida/*The New York Times*/Redux)

reation and other programs at their new "home." The Reeves County Detention Center in Pecos, Texas, also operated by the GEO Group, experienced two riots over a span of two months in late 2008 and early 2009.

Both disturbances were attributed to inmate discontent over medical services and food quality. Then, in the summer of 2010, Tracy Province, along with another inmate, escaped from the Management and Training Corporation's Arizona State Prison in Kingman using nothing more than a pair of contraband wire cutters. Province eventually made his way into New Mexico, where he allegedly murdered Linda and Gary Haas and stole their pickup truck before being apprehended by U.S. Marshals and local police in Meeteetse, Wyoming.

Apart from anecdotal evidence, various studies have also uncovered disturbing patterns of misbehavior at private prisons. For example, officials from the BOP discovered higher levels of serious inmate violence and drug abuse at California's Taft Correctional Institute, operated by the GEO Group, than at three similar government-run prisons.[43] In addition, research conducted by Curtis R. Blakely of the University of South Alabama and Vic W. Bumphus of the University of Tennessee at Chattanooga found that a prisoner in a private corrections facility was twice as likely to be assaulted by a fellow inmate as a prisoner in a public one.[44]

Financial Concerns Furthermore, some observers note, if a private corrections firm receives a fee from the state for each inmate housed in its facility, does that not give management an incentive to increase the amount of time each prisoner serves? Although government parole boards make the final decision on an inmate's release from private prisons, the company could manipulate misconduct and good behavior reports to maximize time served and, by extension, higher profits.[45]

Philosophical Concerns Other critics see private prisons as inherently unjust, even if they do save tax dollars or provide enhanced services. These observers believe that corrections is not simply another industry, like garbage collection or road maintenance, and that only the government has the authority to punish. In the words of John DiIulio:

It is precisely because corrections involves the deprivation of liberty, precisely because it involves the legally sanctioned exercise of coercion by some citizens over others, that it must remain wholly within public hands.[46]

Critics of private correctional facilities also believe that private prisons are constitutional contradictions, offering Article I of the U.S. Constitution as support. That passage states that "legislative powers herein granted shall be vested in a Congress of the United States." These powers include the authority to define penal codes and to determine the punishments that will be handed out for breaking federal law. Therefore, a strict interpretation of the Constitution appears to prohibit the passing of this authority from the federal government to a private company.[47]

THE FUTURE OF PRIVATIZATION IN THE CORRECTIONS INDUSTRY

The continued financial health of the "recession-proof" private prison industry seems assured by two factors. First, as we have noted, shrinking budgets have forced states to look for less costly alternatives to housing inmates in public prisons. Second, as the number of federal prisoners increases, the BOP has turned to private prisons to expand its capacity. Between 2000 and 2009, the number of federal inmates in private prisons effectively doubled, from about 15,500 to more than 34,000.[48] The current emphasis on imprisoning violators of immigration law seems likely to ensure

Jail A facility used to hold persons awaiting trial or those who have been found guilty of misdemeanors.

that this trend will continue. (CAREER TIP: Given the private prison industry's bright prospects, it is no surprise that Corrections Corporation of America is offering positions in all areas of corrections, including security, health care, and administration. For more information, go to the company's career Web page at *www.correctionscorp.com/careers/career-overview/training.*)

¿WHY ARE JAILS SO IMPORTANT?

Although prisons and prison issues dominate the public discourse on corrections, there is an argument to be made that jails are the dominant penal institutions in the United States. In general, a prison is a facility designed to house people convicted of felonies for lengthy periods of time, while a **jail** is authorized to hold pretrial detainees and offenders who have committed misdemeanors. On any given day, about 777,000 inmates are in jail in this country, and approximately 7 million Americans spend at least a day in jail each year. Furthermore, the jail population increased by 51 percent between 1995 and 2009.[49] Nevertheless, jail funding is often the lowest priority for the tight budgets of local governments, leading to severe overcrowding and other dismal conditions.

Many observers see this negligence as having far-reaching consequences for criminal justice. Jail is often the first contact that citizens have with the corrections system. It is at this point that treatment and counseling have the best chance to deter future criminal behavior.[50] By failing to take advantage of this opportunity, says Professor Franklin Zimring of the University of California at Berkeley School of Law, corrections officials have created a situation in which "today's jail folk are tomorrow's prisoners."[51]

THE FUNCTION OF JAILS

Until the eighteenth century, all penal institutions existed primarily to hold those charged with a crime until their trial. Although jails still serve this purpose,

they have evolved to play a number of different roles in the corrections system, including the following:

- Holding those convicted of misdemeanors.
- Receiving individuals pending arraignment and holding them while awaiting trial (if they cannot post bail), conviction, or sentencing.
- Temporarily detaining juveniles pending transfer to juvenile authorities.
- Holding the mentally ill pending transfer to health facilities.
- Detaining those who have violated conditions of probation or parole and those who have "jumped" bail.
- Housing inmates awaiting transfer to federal or state prisons.
- Operating community-based corrections programs such as home confinement and electronic monitoring.

Increasingly, jails are also called on to handle the overflow from saturated state and federal prisons. In Washington State, for example, corrections officials are forced to rent eight hundred jail cells a day to house convicts who have been sent back to prison for violating the terms of their parole.

According to sociologist John Irwin, the unofficial purpose of the jail is to manage society's "rabble," so called because

> [they] are not well integrated into conventional society, they are not members of conventional social organizations, they have few ties to conventional social networks, and they are carriers of unconventional values and beliefs.[52]

In Irwin's opinion, rabble who act violently are arrested and sent to prison. The jail is reserved for merely offensive rabble, whose primary threat to society lies in their failure to conform to its behavioral norms. Nearly seven out of ten jail inmates, for example, are dependent on or abuse alcohol or drugs.[53] This concept of rabble has been used by some critics of American corrections to explain the disproportionate number of poor and minority groups who may be found in the nation's jails at any time.

THE JAIL POPULATION

About 88 percent of jail inmates in the United States are male. As in other areas of corrections, however, women are becoming more numerous. Between 2000 and 2009, the adult female jail population increased by 32 percent, compared with a 22 percent increase for males.[54] Jails also follow the general corrections pattern in that, as mentioned, a disproportionate number of their inmates are members of minority groups. (For an overview of the characteristics of the jail population, see **Figure 13.3** below.)

Pretrial Detainees

A significant number—as many as a third, in some facilities—of those detained in jails technically are not prisoners. They are **pretrial detainees** who have been arrested by the police and, for a variety of reasons that we discussed in Chapter 9, are unable to post bail. Pretrial detainees, in many ways, are walking legal contradictions. According to the U.S. Constitution, they are innocent until proved guilty. At the same time, by being incarcerated while awaiting trial, they are denied a number of personal freedoms and are subjected to the poor conditions of many jails.

In *Bell v. Wolfish* (1979), the Supreme Court rejected the notion that this situation is inherently unfair by refusing to give pretrial detainees greater legal protections than sentenced jail inmates have.[55] In essence, the Court recognized that treating pretrial detainees differently from convicted jail inmates would place too much of a burden on corrections officials and was therefore impractical.[56]

Sentenced Jail Inmates

According to the U.S. Department of Justice, about 38 percent of those in jail have been convicted of their current charges.[57] In other words, they have been found guilty of a crime, usually a misdemeanor, and sentenced to time in jail. The typical jail term lasts between thirty and ninety days, and rarely does a prisoner spend more than one year in jail for any single crime. Often, a judge will credit the length of time the convict has spent in detention waiting for trial—known as **time served**—toward his or her sentence. This practice acknowledges two realities of jails:

1. Terms are generally too short to allow the prisoner to gain any benefit (that is, rehabilitation) from the jail's often limited or nonexistent treatment facilities. Therefore, the jail term can serve no other purpose than to punish the wrongdoer. (Judges who believe jail time can serve purposes of deterrence and incapacitation may not agree with this line of reasoning.)

> **Pretrial Detainee** An individual who spends the time prior to his or her trial incarcerated in jail.
>
> **Time Served** The period of time a person denied bail (or unable to pay it) has spent in jail prior to his or her trial.

Figure 13.3 The Characteristics of America's Jail Population

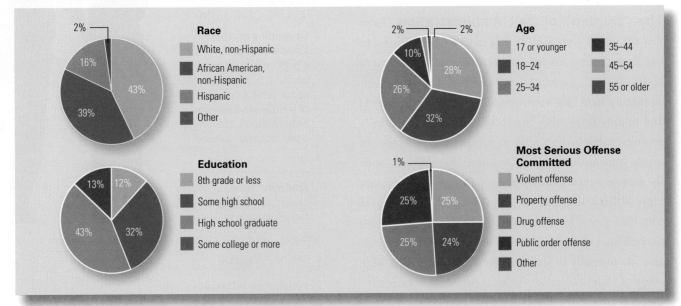

Sources: Bureau of Justice Statistics, *Profile of Jail Inmates, 2002* (Washington, D.C.: U.S. Department of Justice, July 2004), pages 1–4; and Bureau of Justice Statistics, *Jail Inmates at Midyear 2009—Statistical Tables* (Washington, D.C.: U.S. Department of Justice, June 2010), Table 6, page 9.

2. Jails are chronically overcrowded, and judges need to clear space for new offenders.

Other Jail Inmates Pretrial detainees and those convicted of misdemeanors make up the majority of the jail population. As mentioned earlier, jail inmates also include felons who are either waiting for transfer or have been assigned to jails because of prison overcrowding, probation and parole violators, the mentally ill, and juveniles. In addition, jails can hold those who require incarceration but do not "fit" anywhere else. A material witness or an attorney in a trial who refuses to follow the judge's instructions, for example, may be held in contempt of court and sent to jail.

JAIL ADMINISTRATION

LO 4 Of the nearly 3,370 jails in the United States, more than 2,700 are operated on a county level by an elected sheriff. Most of the remainder are under the control of municipalities, although six state governments (Alaska, Connecticut, Delaware, Hawaii, Rhode Island, and Vermont) manage jails. The capacity of jails varies widely. The Los Angeles County Men's Central Jail holds nearly 7,000 people, but jails that large are relatively rare. Almost two-thirds of all jails in this country house fewer than 50 inmates.[58]

The "Burden" of Jail Administration Given that the public's opinion of jails ranges from negative to indifferent, some sheriffs neglect their jail management duties. Instead, they focus on high-visibility issues such as putting more law enforcement officers on the streets and improving security in schools. In fact, a jail usually receives publicity only after an escape or an incident in which inmates are abused by jailers. Nonetheless, with their more complex and diverse populations, jails are often more difficult to manage than prisons. Jails hold people who have never been incarcerated before, people under the influence of drugs or alcohol at the time of their arrival, and the mentally ill. Jail inmates also engage in a wide range of violent behavior—from nonexistent to extreme—that only adds to the unpredictable atmosphere.[59]

Despite some sheriffs' general apathy toward jails, few would be willing to give up their management duties. As troublesome as they may be, jails can be useful in other ways. The sheriff appoints a jail administrator, or deputy sheriff, to oversee the day-to-day operations of the facility. The sheriff also has the power to hire other staff members, such as deputy jailers. The sheriff may award these jobs to people who helped her or him get elected, and in return, jail staffers can prove helpful to the sheriff in future elections. Furthermore, jails pay. In Kentucky, for example, jails receive $30.94 a day for every inmate transferred from the state's consistently overcrowded prison system.[60]

CAREER PREP

DEPUTY SHERIFF/JAIL DIVISION

JOB DESCRIPTION:

- Be responsible for supervising jail inmates by ensuring that order, discipline, safety, and security are maintained.

- Transport or escort inmates and defendants from jail to courtrooms, attorneys' offices, or medical facilities.

WHAT KIND OF TRAINING IS REQUIRED?

- Depending on the jurisdiction, possession of a high school diploma or bachelor's degree, as well as successful completion of written and physical examinations, training, and a probationary period.

- Some states require completion of a "jail academy" training course of up to sixteen weeks, including field training.

ANNUAL SALARY RANGE?   Kaupo Kikkas/iStockphoto.com

- $44,000–$55,000

For additional information, visit:
www.usdsa.org.

The Challenges of Overcrowding In many ways, the sheriff is placed in an untenable position when it comes to jail overcrowding. He or she has little control over the number of people who are sent to jail, a power that resides with prosecutors and judges. Nevertheless, the jail, regardless of its capacity, is expected to find space to hold all comers. A sheriff from Kane County, Utah, describes the situation:

> We have people who should get sixty or ninety days, and they just do a weekend and we kick them out. Unless we get a real habitual abuser, we have no choice but to set them free. Most of the time we're pretty sure they will be back in a couple of days with a new offense.[61]

Living Conditions Chronic overcrowding makes the jail experience a miserable one for most inmates. Cells intended to hold one or two people are packed with up to six. Often, inmates are forced to sleep in hallways. In such stressful situations, tempers flare, leading to violent, aggressive behavior. The close proximity and unsanitary living conditions also lead to numerous health problems. In the words of one observer, jail inmates

> share tight space day and night, struggle with human density never before experienced (unless earlier in jail), and

search hopelessly for even a moment of solitude. . . . [The congested conditions offer] inmates next to nothing except a stifling idleness that is almost sure to make them worse for the experience. If hard time in prison or jail is time without meaning, there might be no equal to long periods of time in the seriously overcrowded living areas of jails; for above all else (and clearly in comparison to time in prison), jail time is dead time.[62]

Such conditions also raise basic questions of justice: as we noted earlier, many of the inmates in jail have not yet been tried and must be presumed innocent.

A New Trend? Fortunately, at least for some jail managers, the situation seems to be improving. Between June 30, 2008, and June 30, 2009, the nation's jail inmate population declined for the first time since the early 1980s.[63] Spurred by the same factors that have led to a reduction in state prison inmates, as discussed earlier in this chapter, in 2009 U.S. jails averaged only 90 percent capacity, the lowest such rates in a decade.[64] Also, jails have continued to add new beds—more than 21,000 in 2008–2009—which helped relieve overcrowding, if not pressures on local and state budgets.[65]

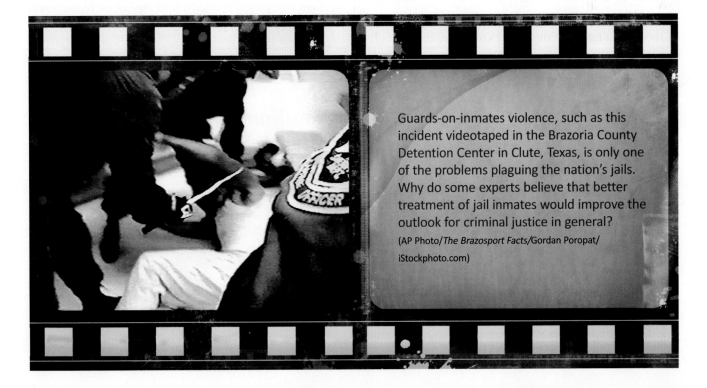

Guards-on-inmates violence, such as this incident videotaped in the Brazoria County Detention Center in Clute, Texas, is only one of the problems plaguing the nation's jails. Why do some experts believe that better treatment of jail inmates would improve the outlook for criminal justice in general?

(AP Photo/*The Brazosport Facts*/Gordan Poropat/iStockphoto.com)

¿WHAT ARE THE CONSEQUENCES OF OUR HIGH RATES OF INCARCERATION?

LO5 For many observers, especially those who support the crime control theory of criminal justice, America's high rate of incarceration has contributed significantly to the drop in the country's crime rates.[66] At the heart of this belief is the fact, which we discussed in Chapter 2, that most crimes are committed by a relatively small group of repeat offenders. Several studies have tried to corroborate this viewpoint, with varying results—estimates of the number of crimes committed each year by habitual offenders range from 3 to 187.[67] If one accepts the higher estimate, each year a repeat offender spends in prison prevents a significant number of criminal acts.

Criminologists, however, note the negative consequences of America's growing prison and jail population. For one, incarceration can have severe social consequences for communities and the families that make up those communities. About 1.7 million minor children—one in 43—have a parent in prison, putting them at greater risk of suffering financial hardship and reduced supervision and discipline.[68] As a result of the deterioration of the family structure, children of convicts are more likely to become involved in delinquent behavior.[69] Our high rates of incarceration also deny one of the basic rights of American democracy—the right to vote—to about 5.3 million Americans with criminal records.[70] (A number of states and the federal government *disenfranchise*, or take away the ability to vote, from those convicted of felonies. This has a disproportionate impact on minority groups, weakening their voice in the democratic debate).

Today, African American males are incarcerated at a rate more than six times higher than white males and almost three times higher than Latino males.[71] With more black men behind bars than enrolled in the nation's colleges and universities, Marc Mauer of the Sentencing Project believes that the "ripple effect on their communities and on the next generation of kids, growing up with their fathers in prison, will certainly be with us for at least a generation."[72]

Whether the American incarceration situation is "good" or "bad" depends to a large extent on one's personal philosophy. In the end, it is difficult to do a definitive cost-benefit analysis for each person incarcerated, weighing the benefits of preventing crimes that might (or might not) have been committed by an inmate against the costs to the convict's family and society. One thing that can be stated with some certainty is that even with the growing interest in diversion and rehabilitation described in the previous chapter, the American prison system will remain one of the largest in the world for the foreseeable future.

About 1.7 million minor children— one in 43—have a parent in prison.

What risks are children exposed to when separated from their incarcerated parents? (Suzanne DeChillo/*The New York Times*/Redux)

WHY CHOOSE?

Every 4LTR Press solution comes complete with a visually engaging textbook in addition to an interactive eBook. Go to CourseMate for **CJ** to begin using the eBook. Access at **www.cengagebrain.com**

14 BEHIND BARS: THE LIFE OF AN INMATE

Learning Outcomes

After studying this chapter, you will be able to . . .

LO1 Indicate some of the reasons for violent behavior in prisons.

LO2 List and briefly explain the six general job categories among correctional officers.

LO3 Contrast probation, parole, mandatory release, pardon, and furlough.

LO4 Describe typical conditions of parole.

LO5 Explain the goal of prisoner reentry programs.

Threepeat

On August 27, 2010, a riot involving about two hundred inmates broke out in the main exercise yard at California's Folsom State Prison. After first using gas grenades and then rubber bullets, correctional officers were forced to fire actual bullets into the mass of brawling convicts, sending five of them to the hospital. This disturbance should not have surprised anyone, as such outbreaks have become an annual occurrence at the Folsom prison. Nearly a year earlier, in October 2009, eight inmates were injured when a riot broke out in the facility's dining hall. A year before that, in September 2008, five inmates were treated for injuries following another disturbance in the exercise yard.

Today's penal institutions are often characterized by "grindingly dull routine interrupted by occasional flashes of violence and brutality." The situation is even worse in facilities such as Folsom that are plagued by overcrowding. The prison, built in 1880, houses more than 4,000 inmates even though it was designed for a capacity of 2,065. According to one Folsom inmate, more than anything else, the daily frustrations born of such congestion are to blame for the eruptions of disorder. "Imagine you have to wait in line to relieve yourself or take a shower," he says. "Then watching someone crowd his way in." A "no frills" movement in public policy and prison management has further succeeded in removing any comfort from inmates' lives. Many state prisons ban weight lifting, televisions, radios, adult magazines, and conjugal visits. All states and the federal government have limited smoking in their correctional facilities, and some institutions spend less than $2 a day per inmate on meals.

What are some of the reasons for eruptions of prison violence and brutality in correctional facilities such as California's Folsom State Prison, shown here in more peaceful times? (ZUMA Press/Newscom)

Total Institution An institution that provides all of the necessities for existence to those who live within its boundaries.

Argot A secret language used by inmates to make their speech difficult for outsiders to understand.

Figure 14.1 Prison Slang

Ace Another word for *dollar*.

Bang A fight to the death, or shoot to kill.

Base head A cocaine addict.

B.G. "Baby gangster," or someone who has never shot another person.

Booty bandit An incarcerated sexual predator who preys on weaker inmates, called "punks."

Bug A correctional staff member, such as a psychiatrist, who is deemed untrustworthy or unreliable.

Bumpin' titties Fighting.

Catch cold To get killed.

Chiva Heroin.

Dancing on the blacktop Getting stabbed.

Diddler A child molester or pedophile.

Green light A prison gang term for a contract killing.

Hacks Correctional officers.

Jug-up Mealtime.

Lugger An inmate who smuggles in and possesses illegal substances.

Punk An inmate subject to rape, usually more submissive than other inmates.

Ride with To perform favors, including sexual favors, for a convict in return for protection or prison-store goods.

Shank A knife.

Tits-up An inmate who has died.

Topped Committed suicide.

Korhan Karacan/iStockphoto.com

Source: **www.insideprison.com/glossary.asp**.

In "Folsom Prison Blues," country singer Johnny Cash tells the story of a murderer who laments, "I know I can't be free," as he hears the whistle of a train passing outside his cell window.[1] Most inmates, however, will at some point be free after release from incarceration. The Delancey Street Foundation, a self-supporting rehabilitation program headquartered about two hours south of Folsom State Prison in San Francisco, tries to help released prisoners adjust to their newfound freedom. It offers them a place to live, job training, and employment at one of the businesses owned by the group. Roderick Davis, who has worked at the Delancey Street Restaurant for ten years since his prison release, credits the foundation for accepting him despite "all the horrible and terrible things I've done in my life." He adds, "Nobody judged me because I did those things."[2]

In this chapter, we will look at the life of the imprisoned convict, starting with the realities of an existence behind bars and finishing with the challenges of living "on the outside." Along the way, we will discuss violence in prison, correctional officers, women's prisons, the mechanics of release, and several other issues that are at the forefront of the American corrections system today. To start, we must understand the forces that shape prison culture and how those forces affect the overall operation of the correctional facility.

¿HOW DO INMATES ADJUST TO LIFE IN PRISON?

Any institution, whether a school, a bank, or a police department, has an organizational culture—a set of values that help the people in the organization understand what actions are acceptable and what actions are unacceptable. According to a theory put forth by the influential sociologist Erving Goffman, prison cultures are unique because prisons are **total institutions** that encompass every aspect of an inmate's life. Unlike a student or a bank teller, a prisoner cannot leave the institution or have any meaningful interaction with outside communities. Others arrange every aspect of daily life, and all prisoners are required to follow this schedule in exactly the same manner.[3]

Inmates develop their own **argot**, or language (see **Figure 14.1** above). They create their own economy, which, in the absence of currency, is based on the barter of valued items such as food, contraband, and sexual favors. They establish methods of determining power, many of which, as we shall see, involve violence. Isolated and heavily regulated, prisoners create a social existence that is, out of both necessity and design, separate from the outside world.

WHO IS IN PRISON?

The culture of any prison is heavily influenced by its inmates, whose values, beliefs, and experiences will be reflected in the social order that exists behind bars. As we noted in the last chapter, the past three decades have seen incarceration rates of women and minority groups rise sharply. Furthermore, the arrest patterns of inmates have changed over that time period. A prisoner today is much more likely to have been incarcerated on a drug charge or immigration violation than was the case in the 1980s. Today's inmate is also more likely to behave violently behind bars—a situation that will be addressed shortly.

In recent years, the most significant demographic change in the prison population involves age. Although the majority of inmates are still under thirty-four years old, the number of state and federal prisoners over the age of forty has increased by about 170,000 in the last decade alone.[4] Several factors have contributed to this upsurge, including "get tough on crime" measures that impose mandatory sentences (discussed in Chapter 11), high rates of recidivism, higher levels of murder and sex crimes committed by older offenders, and the aging of the U.S. population as a whole.[5] (CAREER TIP: Given that older inmates experience more health problems than younger ones, prisons and jails are now housing more people with medical issues than in the past. As a result, *registered nurses* are in high demand in the corrections system.)

ADAPTING TO PRISON SOCIETY

On arriving at prison, each convict attends an orientation session and receives a "Resident's Handbook." The handbook provides information such as meal and official count times, disciplinary regulations, and visitation guidelines. The norms and values of the prison society, however, cannot be communicated by the staff or learned from a handbook. As first described by Donald Clemmer in his classic 1940 work, *The Prison Community*, the process of **prisonization**—or adaptation to the prison culture—advances as the inmate gradually understands what constitutes acceptable behavior in the institution. Generally, such norms and values are defined not by prison officials but by other inmates.[6]

In studying prisonization, criminologists have focused on two areas: how prisoners change their behavior to adapt to life behind bars, and how life behind bars has changed because of inmate behavior. Sociologist John Irwin has identified several patterns of inmate behavior, each one driven by the inmate's personality and values:

1. Professional criminals adapt to prison by "doing time." In other words, they follow the rules and generally do whatever is necessary to speed up their release and return to freedom.
2. Some convicts, mostly state-raised youths or those frequently incarcerated in juvenile detention centers, are more comfortable inside prison than outside. These inmates serve time by "jailing," or establishing themselves in the power structure of prison culture.
3. Other inmates take advantage of prison resources such as libraries or drug treatment programs by "gleaning," or working to improve themselves to prepare for a return to society.
4. Finally, "disorganized" criminals exist on the fringes of prison society. These inmates may have mental impairments or low levels of intelligence and find it impossible to adapt to prison culture on any level.[7]

The process of categorizing prisoners has a theoretical basis, but it serves a practical purpose as well, allowing administrators to reasonably predict how different inmates will act in certain situations. An inmate who

> **"One of the most amazing things about prisons is that they 'work' at all."**
>
> —DONALD RAY CRESSEY, AMERICAN PRISON EXPERT (1919–1987)

Prisonization
The socialization process through which a new inmate learns the accepted norms and values of the prison population.

Алексей Пинчук/IStockphoto.com

Deprivation Model
A theory that inmate aggression is the result of being deprived of freedom, consumer goods, sex, and other staples of life outside the institution.

is doing time generally does not present the same security risk as one who is jailing.

¿HOW VIOLENT ARE PRISONS?

Prisons and jails are dangerous places to live, as much of prison culture is predicated on violence. One observer calls the modern institution an "unstable and violent jungle."[8] Prison guards use the threat of violence (and, at times, its reality) to control the inmate population. Sometimes, the inmates strike back. Each year, federal correctional officers are subjected to approximately 80 assaults and 1,500 less serious attacks such as shoving and pushing.[9] Among the prisoners, violence is used to establish power and dominance.

On occasion, this violence leads to death. About fifty-five inmates in state prisons and twenty-five inmates in local jails are murdered by fellow inmates each year.[10] (Note, though, that this homicide rate is lower than the national average.) With nothing but time on their hands, prisoners have been known to fashion deadly weapons out of everyday items such as toothbrushes and mop handles.

VIOLENCE IN PRISON CULTURE

Until the 1970s, prison culture emphasized "noninterference" and did not support inmate-on-inmate violence. Prison "elders" would themselves punish any of their peers who showed a tendency toward assaulting fellow inmates. Today, in contrast, violence is used to establish the prisoner hierarchy by separating the powerful from the weak.

LO 1

Humboldt State University's Lee H. Bowker has identified several other reasons for violent behavior:

- It provides a deterrent against being victimized, as a reputation for violence may eliminate an inmate as a target of assault.
- It enhances self-image in an environment that does not respect other attributes, such as intelligence.
- In the case of rape, it gives sexual relief.
- It serves as a means of acquiring material goods through extortion or outright robbery.[11]

The **deprivation model** can be used to explain the high level of prison violence. According to this model, the stressful and oppressive conditions of prison life lead to aggressive behavior on the part of inmates. Prison researcher Stephen C. Light found that when conditions such as overcrowding worsen, inmate misconduct often increases.[12] In these circumstances, the violent behavior may not have any express purpose—it may just be a means of relieving tension.[13]

RIOTS

The deprivation model is helpful, though less convincing, in searching for the roots of collective violence. As far back as the 1930s, sociologist Frank Tannenbaum

A corrections official displays a set of homemade knives, also known as *shivs,* made by inmates at the Attica Correctional Facility in Attica, New York. What are some of the reasons that violence flourishes behind bars? (AP Photo/David Duprey/iStockphoto.com)

> ## "*I've seen seven* stabbings, *about six* bashings, *and three self-mutilations.* *Two* hangings, *one attempted hanging, any* *number of* overdoses. *And that's only me, in just* *seventy days.*"
>
> —ANONYMOUS JAIL INMATE

noted that harsh prison conditions can cause tension to build among inmates until it eventually explodes in the form of mass violence.[14] Living conditions among prisons are fairly constant, however, so how can the seemingly spontaneous outbreak of prison riots be explained?

Researchers have addressed these inconsistencies with the concept of **relative deprivation**, a theory that focuses on the gap between what is expected in a certain situation and what is achieved. Criminologist Peter C. Kratcoski has argued that because prisoners enjoy such meager privileges to begin with, any further deprivation can spark disorder.[15] A number of criminologists, including Bert Useem in his studies made in the wake of a major riot at the Penitentiary of New Mexico in 1980, have noted that collective violence occurs in response to heightened measures of security at corrections facilities.[16] Thus, the violence occurs in response to an additional reduction in freedom for inmates, who enjoy very little freedom to begin with.

Riots, which have been defined as situations in which a number of prisoners are beyond institutional control for a significant amount of time, are relatively rare. Because of their explosive nature and potential for high casualties, however, riots have a unique ability to focus public attention on prison conditions. The collective violence that took place in 1971 at the Attica Correctional Facility in upstate New York has been described as a turning point in the history of American corrections. The subject of intense media scrutiny, this riot alerted citizens to deteriorating living conditions in correctional facilities and spurred the prisoners' rights movement.[17]

> **Relative Deprivation** The theory that inmate aggression occurs when freedoms and services that the inmate has come to accept as normal are decreased or eliminated.

ISSUES OF RACE AND ETHNICITY

Race plays a major role in prison life, and prison violence is often an outlet for racial tension. Prison populations have changed over the past three decades, with African Americans and Hispanics becoming the majority in many penal institutions. Consequently, issues of race and ethnicity have become increasingly important to prison administrators and researchers.

Separate Worlds As early as the 1950s, researchers were noticing different group structures in inmate life. At that time, for example, prisoners at California's Soledad Prison informally segregated themselves according to geography as well as race: Tejanos (Mexicans raised in Texas), Chicanos, blacks from California, blacks from the South and Southwest, and the majority whites all formed separate social worlds.[18]

Leo Carroll, professor of sociology at the University of Rhode Island, has written extensively about how today's prisoners are divided into hostile groups, with race determining nearly every aspect of an inmate's life, including friends, job assignments, and cell location.[19] Carroll's research has also shown how minority groups in prison have seized on race to help form their prison identities.[20]

Prison Segregation Severe overcrowding has only worsened racial tensions in the American prison system. Several years ago, more than two thousand African American and Hispanic inmates at the Pitchless Detention Center in Castaic, California, battled each other for several hours, leaving one dead and fifty injured. Corrections officials responded by separating black and Hispanic inmates. Only a year earlier, the United States Supreme Court had struck down the California Department of Corrections' unwritten policy of **prison segregation**, under which prisoners were placed only with those of similar race or ethnicity for their first sixty days of incarceration. The Supreme Court held that such a practice was unconstitutional and might even contribute to race-based violence by reinforcing the idea that members of different racial groups pose a threat to one another.[21]

The Supreme Court, however, did, leave prison officials with an out. They can still segregate prisoners in an "emergency situation."[22] Most observers, including the local branch of the American Civil Liberties Union, agreed that the situation at the Pitchless Detention Center qualified as an emergency. Even so, segregation proved to be only a short-term remedy for the Los Angeles County jails. A week later, Hispanic inmates threw bunk beds and other items at their African American counterparts in a dayroom in the nearby Los Angeles Men's Central Jail, sparking a disturbance that resulted in the death of a black inmate. As one observer pointed out, racial segregation "will never solve the underlying problems in L.A. County's jails."[23]

PRISON GANGS AND SECURITY THREAT GROUPS (STGs)

In many instances, racial and ethnic identification is the primary focus of the **prison gang**—a clique of inmates who join together in an organizational structure. Gang affiliation is often the cause of inmate-on-inmate violence. Folsom State Prison, discussed in the opening of this chapter, is plagued by a variety of gangs such as the Mexican Mafia, comprised of U.S.-born inmates of Mexican descent, and their enemies, a spinoff organization called Nuestra Familia.

In part, the prison gang is a natural result of life in the modern prison. As one expert says of these gangs:

> Their members have done in prison what many people do elsewhere when they feel personally powerless, threatened, and vulnerable. They align themselves with others, organize to fight back, and enhance their own status and control through their connection to a more powerful group.[24]

In addition to their important role in the social structure of corrections facilities, prison gangs participate in a wide range of illegal economic activities within these institutions, including prostitution, drug selling, gambling, and loan sharking. A study released in 2011 by Alan J. Drury and Matt DeLisi of Iowa State University found that gang members were even more likely to be involved in prison misconduct than those offenders who had been convicted of murder.[25]

The Prevalence of Prison Gangs Recent research places the rate of gang membership at 11.7 percent in federal prisons, 13.4 percent in state prisons, and 15.6 percent in jails.[26] When the National Gang Crime Research Center surveyed prison administrators, however, almost 95 percent said that gang recruitment took place at their institutions, so the overall prevalence of gangs is probably much higher.[27] Los Angeles corrections officials believe that eight out of every ten inmates in their city jails are gang affiliated.

In many instances, prison gangs are extensions of street gangs. Indeed, investigators believe that leaders of the Mexican Mafia put out a contract for ("green lighted") the violence in the Los Angeles jails discussed earlier in retaliation for an attack that took place on the city streets. Although

A member of the Aryan Brotherhood in California's Calipatria State Prison. Why might an inmate join the Aryan Brotherhood or any other prison gang? (Mark Allen Johnson/ ZUMA Press)

the stereotypical gang is composed of African Americans or Hispanics, the majority of large prisons also have white, or "Aryan," gangs. One of the larger federal capital prosecutions in U.S. history, involving thirty-two counts of murder, focused on a major prison gang known as the Aryan Brotherhood (see the photo on the previous page).

Combating Prison Gangs In their efforts to combat the influence of prison gangs, over the past decade corrections officials have increasingly turned to the **security threat group (STG)** model. Generally speaking, an STG is an identifiable group of three or more individuals who pose a threat to the safety of other inmates or members of the corrections community.[28]

About two-thirds of all prisons have a correctional officer who acts as an STG coordinator.[29] This official is responsible for determining groups of individuals (not necessarily members of a prison gang) that qualify as STGs and taking appropriate measures. In many instances, these measures are punitive. Prison officials, for example, have reduced overall levels of violence significantly by putting gang members in solitary confinement, away from the general prison population. Treatment philosophies also have a place in these strategies. New York corrections administrators have increased group therapy and anger-management classes for STGs, a decision they credit for low murder rates (one a year) in their state prisons.[30]

¿ARE WOMEN'S PRISONS DIFFERENT?

When the first women's prison in the United States opened in 1839 on the grounds of New York's Sing Sing institution, the focus was on rehabilitation. Prisoners were groomed for a return to society with classes on reading, knitting, and sewing. Early women's reformatories had few locks or bars, and several contained nurseries for the inmates' young children. Today, the situation has changed dramatically. "Women's institutions are literally men's institutions, only we pull out the urinals," remarks Meda Chesney-Lind, a criminologist at the University of Hawaii.[31] Given the different circumstances surrounding male and female incarceration, this uniformity can have serious consequences for the women imprisoned in this country.

CHARACTERISTICS OF FEMALE INMATES

Male inmates outnumber female inmates by approximately thirteen to one, and there are only about 170 women's correctional facilities in the United States.[32] Consequently, most research concerning the American corrections system focuses on male inmates and men's prisons.

Enough data exist, however, to provide a useful portrait of women behind bars. Female inmates are typically low income and undereducated, and have a history of unemployment. Like male inmates, female prisoners are disproportionately African American, although the percentage of white female inmates has increased over the past two decades. Female offenders are much less likely than male offenders to have committed a violent offense. Particularly in federal prisons, most are incarcerated for a nonviolent drug or property crime (see **Figure 14.2** on the next page).

A History of Abuse The single factor that most distinguishes female prisoners from their male counterparts is a history of physical or sexual abuse. A self-reported study conducted by the federal government indicates that 55 percent of female jail inmates have been abused at some point in their lives, compared with only 13 percent of male jail inmates.[33] Fifty-seven percent of women in state prisons and 40 percent of women in federal prisons report some form of past abuse. Both these figures are significantly higher than those for male prisoners.[34] Health experts believe that these levels of abuse are related to the significant amount of drug and/or alcohol addiction that plagues the female prison population, as well as to the mental illness problems that such addictions can cause or worsen.[35]

Other Health Problems In fact, about 25 percent of women in state prisons have been diagnosed with serious mental disorders such as post–traumatic stress disorder (PTSD), depression, and substance abuse. PTSD, in particular, is found in women who have experienced sexual or physical abuse.[36] Furthermore, more women than men enter prisons and jails with health problems due to higher instances of poverty, inadequate health care, and substance abuse.[37]

Women prisoners are 50 percent more likely than men to be HIV positive and are at significantly greater risk for lung cancer. They also have high rates of breast and cervical cancer.[38] The health risks and medical needs are even higher for the 5 percent of the female prison population who enter the correctional facility while pregnant. One study estimates that 20 to 35 percent of women inmates visit the infirmary each day, compared with 7 to 10 percent of male inmates.[39]

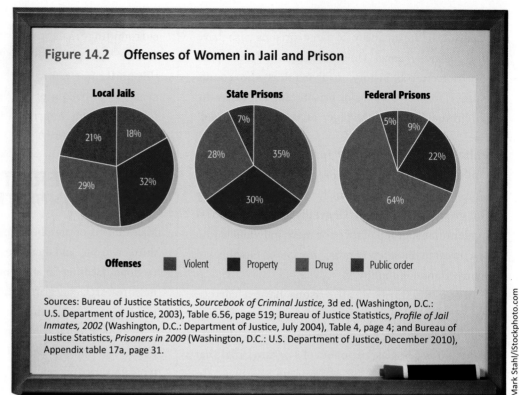

Figure 14.2   Offenses of Women in Jail and Prison

Sources: Bureau of Justice Statistics, *Sourcebook of Criminal Justice,* 3d ed. (Washington, D.C.: U.S. Department of Justice, 2003), Table 6.56, page 519; Bureau of Justice Statistics, *Profile of Jail Inmates, 2002* (Washington, D.C.: Department of Justice, July 2004), Table 4, page 4; and Bureau of Justice Statistics, *Prisoners in 2009* (Washington, D.C.: U.S. Department of Justice, December 2010), Appendix table 17a, page 31.

Mark Stahl/iStockphoto.com

THE MOTHERHOOD PROBLEM

Drug and alcohol use within a women's prison can be a function of the anger and depression many inmates experience due to being separated from their children. An estimated seven out of every ten female prisoners have at least one minor child, and many of these mothers face the potential termination of parental rights on release.[40] Given the scarcity of women's correctional facilities, inmates are often housed at great distances from their children. One study found that almost two-thirds of women in federal prison are more than five hundred miles from their homes.[41]

Further research indicates that an inmate who serves her sentence more than fifty miles from her residence is much less likely to receive phone calls or personal visits from family members. For most inmates and their families, the costs of staying in touch are too high.[42] This kind of separation can have serious consequences for the children of inmates. When a father goes to prison, his children are likely to live with their mother. When a mother is incarcerated, however, her children are likely to live with other relatives or, in about 11 percent of the cases, be sent to foster care.[43] Only six states—California, Indiana, Nebraska, New York, Ohio, and Washington—provide facilities where inmates and their infant children can live together, and even in these facilities nursery privileges usually end once the child is eighteen months old.

VIOLENCE IN WOMEN'S PRISONS

There are no federal maximum- or medium-security women's prisons. Any female inmate who requires a high level of security is housed in a special unit of a men's prison. This does not mean, of course, that women's prisons are free of violence. Compared with men's prisons, women's prisons have extremely low levels of race-based, gang-related physical aggression. Indeed, serious physical violence, particularly assaults involving weapons, is infrequent in women's correctional facili-

What are some factors that distinguish female inmates, such as those pictured here at a women's prison in Gatesville, Texas, from their male counterparts? (Andrew Lichtenstein/Corbis/Sygma)

ties.[44] This is not to say that female inmates are better behaved than male inmates. In many instances, officials at women's prisons report more "incidents," or petty offenses such as insubordination, verbal abuse of other inmates, and stealing, than their counterparts at male facilities.[45] The same is true of sexual misconduct.

Extensive research conducted by Nancy Wolff, a professor of urban studies at New Jersey's Rutgers University, and several colleagues indicates that the rate of inmate-on-inmate sexual victimization is four times higher for women than for men in prison. Most of the episodes, however, involve abusive sexual contacts such as unwanted touching rather than sexual assault or rape.[46]

¿HOW DO CORRECTIONAL OFFICERS MAINTAIN CONTROL?

Under model circumstances, the presence of correctional officers—the standard term used to describe prison guards—would moderate the levels of violence in American correctional institutions. To a large extent, this is indeed the case; without correctional officers, the prison would be a place of anarchy. But in the highly regulated, oppressive environment of the prison, correctional officers must use the threat of violence, if not actual violence, to instill discipline and keep order. Thus, the relationship between prison staff and inmates is marked by mutual distrust. Consider the two following statements, the first made by a correctional officer and the second by a prisoner:

> [My job is to] protect, feed, and try to educate scum who raped and brutalized women and children . . . who, if I turn my back, will go into their cell, wrap a blanket around their cellmate's legs, and threaten to beat or rape him if he doesn't give sex, carry contraband, or fork over radios, money, or other goods willingly. And they'll stick a shank in me tomorrow if they think they can get away with it.[47]

> The pigs in the state and federal prisons . . . treat me so violently, I cannot possibly imagine a time I could ever have anything but the deepest, aching, searing hatred for them. I can't begin to tell you what they do to me. If I were weaker by a hair, they would destroy me.[48]

It may be difficult for an outsider to understand the emotions that fuel such sentiments. French philosopher Michel Foucault points out that discipline, both in prison and in the general community, is a means of social organization as well as punishment.[49] Discipline is imposed when a person behaves in a manner that

STUDY PREP

Use colored pens to highlight key words and sentences in your reading. Doing so forces you to read actively and to make constant choices about what is important to study and retain. Don't go overboard, however. Read a section first without highlighting to get a sense of which parts are essential.

is contrary to the values of the dominant social group. Correctional officers and inmates have different concepts of the ideal structure of prison society, and as the two quotations just cited demonstrate, this conflict generates intense feelings of fear and hatred, which often lead to violence.

RANK AND DUTIES OF CORRECTIONAL OFFICERS

After local officials shut down the Montague County (Texas) Jail several years ago because it had become something of an "Animal House" behind bars, much of the blame fell on the custodial staff. Security at the facility had become lax, to put it mildly. With little interference, inmates were allowed to have sex with their girlfriends, bring in comfortable furniture from home, take drugs, and chat on cell phones. To avoid such problems, corrections facilities generally provide their employees with clearly delineated ranks and duties. The custodial staff at most prisons, for example, is organized according to four general ranks—captain, lieutenant, sergeant, and officer. In keeping with the militaristic model, captains are primarily administrators who deal directly with the warden on custodial issues. Lieutenants are the disciplinarians of the prison, responsible for policing and transporting the inmates. Sergeants oversee platoons of officers in specific parts of the prison, such as various cell blocks or work spaces.

LO 2 Lucien X. Lombardo, professor of sociology and criminal justice at Old Dominion University, has identified six general job categories among correctional officers:

1. *Block officers.* These employees supervise cell blocks containing as many as four hundred inmates, as well as the correctional officers on block guard duty. In general, the block officer is responsible for the well-being of the inmates. He or she makes sure the inmates do not harm themselves or other prisoners and also acts as something of a camp counselor, dispensing advice and seeing that inmates understand and follow the rules of the facility.

2. *Work detail supervisors.* In many penal institutions, the inmates work in the cafeteria, the prison store, the laundry, and other areas. Work detail supervisors oversee small groups of inmates as they perform their tasks.

3. *Industrial shop and school officers.* These officers perform maintenance and security functions in workshop and educational programs. Their primary responsibility is to make sure that inmates are on time for these programs and do not cause any disturbances during the sessions.

4. *Yard officers.* Officers who work the prison yard usually have the least seniority, befitting the assignment's reputation as dangerous and stressful. These officers must be constantly on alert for breaches in prison discipline or regulations in the relatively unstructured environment of the prison yard.

5. *Tower guards.* These officers spend their entire shifts, which usually last eight hours, in isolated, silent posts high above the grounds of the facility. Although their only means of communication are walkie-talkies or cellular devices, the safety benefits of the position can outweigh the loneliness that comes with the job.

6. *Administrative building positions.* Officers who hold these positions provide security at prison gates, oversee visitation procedures, act as liaisons for civilians, and handle administrative tasks such as processing the paperwork when an inmate is transferred from another institution.[50]

DISCIPLINE

As Erving Goffman noted in his essay on the "total institution," in the general society adults are rarely placed in a position where they are "punished" as a child would be.[51] Therefore, the strict disciplinary measures imposed on prisoners come as something of a shock and can provoke strong defensive reactions. Correctional officers who must deal with these responses often find that disciplining inmates is the most difficult and stressful aspect of their job.

Most correctional officers prefer to rely on the "you scratch my back and I'll scratch yours" model for controlling inmates. In other words, as long as the prisoner makes a reasonable effort to conform to institutional rules, the correctional officer will refrain from

CJ and Technology

CELL PHONES BEHIND BARS

Just because Justin Walker was incarcerated, he wasn't about to stop social networking. Walker, serving a thirty-year sentence at the Oklahoma State Penitentiary in Granite for killing a sheriff, took several photos of himself with a cell phone. One showed him licking a shank. Another featured him smoking a joint while holding a bag of marijuana and a bottle of liquor. Although controversy erupted in December 2010 after Walker managed to post these photos on Facebook, his technological misconduct was relatively benign. In other, more serious incidents, inmates have planned escapes, coordinated drug deals, organized prison riots, and even ordered murders, all via cell phone.

Of course, prison and jail inmates are not allowed to have cell phones. Still, California correctional officers confiscated nearly nine thousand of these devices from prisoners in 2010, and nearly every corrections facility in the country struggles to keep them out of the hands of their inmates. Attempts to combat the problem with cell phone–sniffing dogs and "managed access," which limits the transmission of calls from prison grounds, have been only marginally successful in solving the problem. "[Cell phones] are everywhere," complains Maryland prison administrator Carl Harmon.

THINKING ABOUT CELL PHONES BEHIND BARS

In recent years, more and more inmates are smuggling smartphones into prisons and jails, thus gaining access to the Internet. Why would one security expert say, "The smartphone is the most lethal weapon you can get inside a prison"?

---

taking disciplinary steps. Of course, the staff-inmate relationship is not always marked by cooperation, and correctional officers often find themselves in situations where they must use force.

Legitimate Security Interests Generally, courts have been unwilling to put too many restrictions on the use of force by correctional officers. Like police officers (see Chapter 5), correctional officers are given great leeway to use their experience to determine when force is warranted. In *Whitley v. Albers* (1986),[52] the Supreme Court held that the use of force by prison officials violates an inmate's Eighth Amendment protections only if the force amounts to "the unnecessary and wanton infliction of pain." Excessive force can be considered "necessary" if the *legitimate security interests* of the penal institution are at stake. Consequently,

an appeals court ruled that when officers at a Maryland prison formed an "extraction team" to remove the leader of a riot from his cell, beating him in the process, the use of force was justified given the situation.[53]

In general, courts have found that the **legitimate security interests** of a prison or jail justify the use of force when the correctional officer is:

1 Acting in self-defense.

2 Acting to defend the safety of a third person, such as a member of the prison staff or another inmate.

> **Legitimate Security Interests** A standard used by the U.S. Supreme Court to determine when correctional officers may use excessive force. Such conditions exist when, for example, a correctional officer is acting in self-defense or to prevent an escape.

Malicious and Sadistic Standard If a correctional officer's use of force is found to be "malicious and sadistic"—that is, mean-spirited or designed to cause pain for no acceptable reason—then that use of force may violate the prisoner's rights.

Parole The conditional release of an inmate before his or her sentence has expired.

3 Upholding the rules of the institution.

4 Preventing a crime such as assault, destruction of property, or theft.

5 Preventing an escape effort.[54]

In addition, most prisons and jails have written policies that spell out the situations in which their employees may use force against inmates. (CAREER TIP: Most high-security prisons also have *emergency response teams,* or ERTs, made up of specially trained correctional officers who respond to dangerous situations such as riots and other disruptive incidents.)

The "Malicious and Sadistic" Standard The judicial system has not, however, given correctional officers total freedom to apply force. In *Hudson v. McMillan* (1992), the Supreme Court ruled that minor injuries suffered by a convict at the hands of a correctional officer following an argument did violate the inmate's rights, because there was no security concern at the time of the incident.[55] In other words, the issue is not *how much* force was used, but whether the officer used the force as part of a good faith effort to restore discipline or acted maliciously and sadistically to cause harm.

This **malicious and sadistic standard** has been difficult for aggrieved prisoners to meet. In the ten years following the *Hudson* decision, only about 20 percent of excessive force lawsuits against correctional officials were successful.[56]

TEST PREP

When you finish a test early, your first instinct may be to hand it in and get out of the classroom as quickly as possible. It is *always* a good idea, however, to review your answers. You may find a mistake or an area where some extra writing will improve your grade.

¿WHEN AND HOW ARE INMATES RELEASED FROM PRISON?

LO3 At any given time, more than 800,000 Americans are living in the community on **parole**, the *conditional* release of a prisoner after a portion of his or her sentence has been served. Parole allows the corrections system to continue to supervise an offender who is no longer incarcerated. As long as parolees follow the conditions of their parole, they are allowed to finish their terms outside the prison. If parolees break the terms of their early release, however, they face the risk of being returned to a penal institution.

According to Todd Clear and George F. Cole, parole is based on three concepts:

1. *Grace.* The prisoner has no right to be given an early release, but the government has granted her or him that privilege.
2. *Contract of consent.* The government and the parolee enter into an arrangement whereby the latter agrees to abide by certain conditions in return for continued freedom.
3. *Custody.* Technically, though no longer incarcerated, the parolee is still the responsibility of the state. Parole is an extension of corrections. (Remember that an offender is sentenced to probation as an *alternative* to a prison or jail term, while parole is a form of *early release* for someone who has already spent time behind bars.)[57]

Because of good-time credits and parole, most prisoners do not serve their entire sentence in prison. In fact, the average felon serves only about half of the term handed down by the court.

TYPES OF PRISON RELEASE

Parole, a conditional release, is the most common form of prison release. About two-thirds of all inmates who leave incarceration do so under the supervision of a parole officer.[58] The remaining one-third are subject to various other release mechanisms. Prisoners receive an unconditional release when they have completed the terms of their sentence and no longer require incarceration or supervision. One form of unconditional release is **mandatory release** (also known as "maxing out"), which occurs when an inmate has served the maximum amount of time on the initial sentence, minus reductions for good-time credits.

Another, quite rare unconditional release is a **pardon**, a form of executive clemency (forgiveness). The president (on the federal level) and the governor (on the state level) can grant a pardon, or forgive a convict's criminal punishment. Most states have a board of pardons—affiliated with the *parole board* (discussed later)—which makes recommendations to the governor in cases in which it believes a pardon is warranted. Most pardons involve obvious miscarriages of justice, though sometimes a governor will pardon an individual to remove the stain of conviction from his or her criminal record.

Certain *temporary releases* also exist. Some inmates, who qualify by exhibiting good behavior and generally proving that they do not represent a risk to society, are allowed to leave the prison on **furlough** for a certain amount of time, usually between a day and a week. At times, a furlough is granted because of a family emergency, such as a funeral. Furloughs can be particularly helpful for an inmate who is nearing release and can use them to ease the readjustment period.

DISCRETIONARY RELEASE

As you may recall from Chapter 11, corrections systems are classified by sentencing procedure—indeterminate or determinate. Indeterminate sentencing occurs when the legislature sets a range of punishments for particular crimes, and the judge and the **parole board** exercise discretion in determining the actual length of the prison term. For that reason, states with indeterminate sentencing are said to have systems of **discretionary release**. Until the mid-1970s, all states and the federal government operated in this manner.

Eligibility for Parole Under indeterminate sentencing, parole is not a right but a privilege. This is a crucial point, as it establishes the terms of the

relationship between the inmate and the corrections authorities during the parole process. In *Greenholtz v. Inmates of the Nebraska Penal and Correctional Complex* (1979),[59] the Supreme Court ruled that inmates do not have a constitutionally protected right to expect parole, thereby giving states the freedom to set their own standards for determining parole eligibility.

In most states that have retained indeterminate sentencing, a prisoner is eligible to be considered for parole release after serving a legislatively determined percentage of the minimum sentence—usually one-half or two-thirds—less any good time or other credits.

Contrary to what is depicted in many films and television shows, a convict does not "apply" for parole. An inmate's case automatically comes up before the parole board a certain number of days—often ninety—before she or he is eligible for parole. The date of eligibility depends on statutory requirements, the terms of the sentence, and the behavior of the inmate in prison. The board has an eligibility report prepared, which provides information on the various factors that must be considered in making the decision. The board also reviews the case file to acquaint itself with the original crime and conducts an interview with the inmate. At some point before the eligibility date, the entire board, or a subcommittee of the board, votes on whether parole will be granted.

The Parole Board The cumulative efforts of the police, the courtroom work group, and corrections officials lead to a single question in most cases: When should an offender be released? This is a difficult question and is often left to the parole board to answer. When members of the parole board make what in retrospect was a mistake, they quickly draw the attention

Mandatory Release Release from prison that occurs when an offender has served the full length of his or her sentence, minus any adjustments for good time.

Pardon An act of executive clemency that overturns a conviction and erases mention of the crime from the person's criminal record.

Furlough Temporary release from a prison.

Parole Board A body of appointed civilians that decides whether a convict should be granted conditional release before the end of his or her sentence.

Discretionary Release The release of an inmate at the discretion of the parole board.

LO 4

of the media, the public, and the courts.

According to the American Correctional Association, the parole board has four basic roles:

1. To decide which offenders should be placed on parole.
2. To determine the conditions of parole and aid in the continuing supervision of the parolee.
3. To discharge the offender when the conditions of parole have been met.
4. If a violation occurs, to determine whether parole privileges should be revoked.[60]

Most parole boards are small, made up of five to seven members. In many jurisdictions, board members' terms are limited to between four and six years. The requirements for board members vary. Nearly half the states have no prerequisites, while others require a bachelor's degree or some expertise in the field of criminal justice.

Parole boards are either affiliated with government agencies or act as independent bodies. In the first instance, board members are usually members of the correctional staff appointed by the state department of corrections. In contrast, independent parole boards are made up of citizens from the community who have been chosen for the post by a government official, usually the governor. Because most states with independent boards have no specific criteria for the members, critics believe that these boards tend to be politicized by the appointment of members—who have limited knowledge of the criminal justice system—as a return for political favors.

The Parole Hearing In a system that uses discretionary parole, the actual release decision is made at a **parole grant hearing**. During this hearing, the entire board or a subcommittee reviews relevant information on the convict. Sometimes, but not always, the offender is interviewed. Because the board members have only limited knowledge of each offender, key players in the case are often notified in advance of the parole hearing and asked to provide comments and recommenda-

tions. These participants include the sentencing judge, the attorneys at the trial, the victims, and any law enforcement officers who may be involved. After these preparations, the typical parole hearing itself is very short—usually lasting just a few minutes. (CAREER TIP: Often, parole boards rely on *institutional parole assistants* to gather and summarize background information about inmates up for parole. These paraprofessionals also guide inmates through the parole hearing procedure.)

If parole is denied, the entire process is replayed at the next "action date," which depends on the nature of the offender's crimes and all relevant laws. This process can continue for long periods of time. On September 2, 2009, for example, Susan Atkins had her eighteenth parole hearing (see the photo below). In 1969, Atkins, a follower of Charles Manson, stabbed pregnant actress Sharon Tate sixteen times and wrote out the word "PIG"

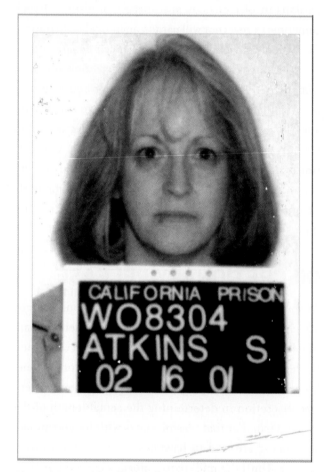

Given Susan Atkins's medical problems and her age, do you feel she should have been granted "compassionate parole" by the state of California? Or do you believe that some crimes are so horrific that the offender should never be given parole? (AP Photo/ California Department of Corrections and Rehabilitation)

on a door using Tate's blood. Forty years later, Atkins asked for "compassionate parole" from the California corrections system because she was dying of brain cancer. Atkins had been a model prisoner, and a psychiatric report stated that she would pose no immediate threat to the community if released. Nonetheless, Atkins's last parole attempt was unsuccessful, and on September 24, 2009, at age sixty-one, she died at the Central California Women's Facility. (Manson himself has been denied parole eleven times and has stated that he does not want to be released.) In some states, the parole board is required to give written reasons for denying parole, and some jurisdictions give the inmate, prosecution, or victims the option to appeal the board's decision.

Johnny plus alcohol plus women

equals trouble."

—EXCERPT FROM PAROLE REPORT ON JOHNNY ROBERT EGGERS, WHO WAS RELEASED ON PAROLE FIVE DIFFERENT TIMES BEFORE STABBING A YOUNG WOMAN TO DEATH

Parole Contract
An agreement between the state and the offender that establishes the conditions under which the latter will be granted parole.

Parole Revocation
The process of withdrawing parole and returning the parolee to prison.

PAROLE SUPERVISION

The term *parole* has two meanings. The first, as we have seen, refers to the establishment of a release date. The second relates to the continuing supervision of convicted felons after they have been released from prison.

Conditions of Parole Many of the procedures and issues of parole supervision are similar to those of probation supervision. Like probationers, when parolees are granted parole, they are placed under the supervision of correctional officers and must follow certain conditions. Some of these conditions are fairly uniform. All parolees, for example, must comply with the law, and they are generally responsible for reporting to their parole officer at certain intervals. The frequency of these visits, along with the other terms of parole, is spelled out in the **parole contract**, which sets out the agreement between the state and the paroled offender. Under the terms of the contract, the state agrees to release the inmate under certain conditions, and the future parolee agrees to follow these conditions.

Each jurisdiction has its own standard parole contract, although the parole board can add specific

provisions if it sees the need. Besides common restrictions, such as no illegal drug use, no association with known felons, and no change of address without notifying authorities, parolees have on occasion been ordered to lose weight and even to undergo chemical castration. Professional football player Michael Vick, who recently spent eighteen months in federal prison for running a pit bull fighting operation in Virginia, was prohibited from owning a dog as a condition of his early release.

Parole Officers The correctional agent assigned the responsibility of supervising parolees is the parole officer. In many respects, the parole officer's relationship with the parolee mirrors that of the probation officer and the probationer (see Chapter 12). In fact, many municipal and state departments of corrections combine the two posts to create probation/parole officers. Parole officers are required to enforce the conditions of parole and initiate revocation hearings when these conditions are not met. Furthermore, a parole officer is expected to help the parolee readjust to life outside the correctional institution by helping her or him find a place to live and a job, and seeing that she or he receives any treatment or rehabilitation that may be necessary.

Parole Revocation If convicts follow the conditions of their parole until the *maximum expiration date*, or the date on which their sentence ends, then they are discharged from supervision. A large number—about 38 percent—return to incarceration before their maximum expiration date, most because they were convicted of a new offense or had their parole revoked (see **Figure 14.3** on the following page). **Parole revocation** is similar in many aspects to probation revocation. If the parolee commits a new crime, then a return

Figure 14.3 Terminating Parole

As you can see, about half of all parolees successfully complete their terms of parole. The rest are either returned to incarceration or have their supervision terminated administratively for a variety of reasons, including disappearance, transfer to another jurisdiction, or death.

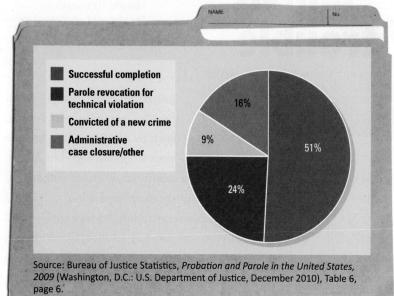

- ■ Successful completion
- ■ Parole revocation for technical violation
- ■ Convicted of a new crime
- ■ Administrative case closure/other

16%
9%
51%
24%

Source: Bureau of Justice Statistics, *Probation and Parole in the United States, 2009* (Washington, D.C.: U.S. Department of Justice, December 2010), Table 6, page 6.

iStockphoto.com

to prison is very likely. If, however, the individual breaks a condition of parole, known as a *technical violation*, the parole authorities have discretion as to whether revocation proceedings should be initiated. An example of a technical violation would be failure to report a change in address to parole authorities. As with probation revocation, many observers believe that parolees who commit technical violations should not be imprisoned, as they have not committed a crime.

¿WHAT HAPPENS TO EX-INMATES?

Even though Dominic Cinelli had a lengthy criminal history and was serving three consecutive life sentences for a series of armed robberies, the Massachusetts Parole Board decided that he deserved to be granted parole. Unfortunately, on December 26, 2010, just a year after his early release, Cinelli fatally shot Woburn police officer John Maguire during a failed attempt to rob a jewelry store. Ex-inmates such as Cinelli (who also died in the shootout) and the troubles they bring with them present a crucial challenge for the criminal justice system.

Prisoner Reentry A corrections strategy designed to prepare inmates for a successful return to the community.

Each year, more than 700,000 persons leave prison and return to the community. What steps can be taken to lessen the possibility that these ex-convicts will continue to harm society following their release? Efforts to answer that question have focused on programs that help inmates make the transition from prison to the "outside." In past years, these programs would have come under the general heading of "rehabilitation," but today corrections officials and criminologists refer to them as part of the strategy of **prisoner reentry.** The concept of reentry has many different meanings among corrections experts. For our purposes, keep in mind the words of Joan Petersilia of the University of California at Irvine, who defines *reentry* as encompassing "all activities and programming conducted to prepare ex-convicts to return safely to the community and to live as law abiding citizens."[61] In other words, whereas *rehab* is focused on the individual offender, *reentry* encompasses the released convict's relationship with society. (CAREER TIP: Organizations such as the Fortune Society, which operates out of New York City, provide aid for ex-inmates who may be struggling after release. These entities rely on *reentry counselors* to help ex-convicts deal with issues such as substance abuse, anger management, and joblessness.)

BARRIERS TO REENTRY

Perhaps the largest obstacle to successful prisoner reentry is the simple truth that life behind bars is very different from life on the outside. As one inmate explains, the "rules" of prison survival are hardly compatible with good citizenship:

> An unexpected smile could mean trouble. A man in uniform was not a friend. Being kind was a weakness. Viciousness and recklessness were to be respected and admired.[62]

The prison environment also insulates inmates. They are not required to make the day-to-day decisions that characterize a normal existence beyond prison bars. Depending on the length of incarceration, a released inmate must adjust to an array of economic, technological, and social changes that took place while she or he was behind bars. Common acts such as using an ATM or pumping gas may be completely alien to someone who has just completed a long prison term.

Life Challenges A number of other obstacles hamper reentry efforts. Housing can be difficult to secure, as many private property owners refuse to rent to someone with a criminal record, and federal and state laws restrict public housing options for ex-convicts. A criminal past also limits the ability to find employment, as does the lack of job skills of someone who has spent a significant portion of his or her life in prison.

Felix Mata, who works with ex-convicts in Baltimore, Maryland, estimates that the average male prisoner returning to that city has only $50 in his pocket; owes $8,000 in child support; and has no means of transportation, no place to live, and no ability to gain employment. At best, most ex-prisoners cannot expect to earn more than $10,000 annually the first few years after being released.[63] In addition, one study concluded that as many as one in five Americans leaving jail or prison is seriously mentally ill.[64]

Recidivism Rates It should come as no surprise that successful reentry is difficult to achieve for many offenders. Research conducted by the Bureau of Justice Statistics found that 67.5 percent of ex-prisoners are rearrested and 51.8 percent are returned to prison or jail within three years of their release dates.[65] These figures highlight the problem of recidivism among those released from incarceration.

POSITIVE REINFORCEMENT ON PAROLE

To help prepare prisoners for life on the outside, most American prisons and jails offer educational and counseling programs for inmates. For example, more than three-quarters of all prisons make available prerelease life skills classes, and many more provide counseling in areas such as drug and alcohol dependence, psychiatric health, and parenting and child rearing.[66]

(CAREER TIP: A typical life skills class includes topics such as finding and keeping a job, locating a residence, understanding family responsibilities, and budgeting. Most *prison teachers* are either corrections employees who have obtained the necessary certification or civilians with teaching credentials and previous career experience.) After release, however, former inmates often find it difficult to continue with educational programs and counseling as they struggle to readjust to life outside prison.

Corrections officials do have several options in helping certain parolees—usually low-risk offenders—find employment and a place to live during the supervision period. Nearly a third of correctional facilities offer **work release programs**, in which prisoners nearing the end of their sentences are given permission to work at paid employment in the community.[67] Inmates on work release must either return to the correctional facility in the evening or live in community residential facilities known as **halfway houses.**

These facilities, also available to other parolees and those who have finished their sentences, are often remodeled hotels or private homes. They provide a less institutionalized living environment than a prison or jail for a small number of offenders (usually between ten and twenty-five). Halfway houses can be tailored to the needs of the former inmate. Many communities, for example, offer substance-free transitional housing for those whose past criminal behavior was linked to drug or alcohol abuse.

THE SPECIAL CASE OF SEX OFFENDERS

Studies on the impact of reentry programs consistently show that they are beneficial, especially if they are initiated before the convicts leave incarceration.[68] Despite these data, one group of wrongdoers has consistently been denied access to the programs: sex offenders. The eventual return of these prisoners to society causes such high levels of community anxiety that the criminal justice system has not yet figured out

Work Release Program Temporary release of convicts from prison for purposes of employment.

Halfway House A community-based form of early release that places inmates in residential centers and allows them to reintegrate with society.

what to do with them. (A recent Gallup poll found that 66 percent of the respondents were "very concerned" about child molesters, compared with 52 percent who expressed such concern about violent crime and 36 percent about terrorism.[69])

Part of the problem is that efforts to reform sex offenders have produced inconsistent results. In one of the few long-term studies of the issue, researchers found that sex offenders who took part in therapy programs in California were actually more likely to reoffend than those who received no treatment whatsoever.[70] Thus, corrections officials are caught between public demands for protection from "these monsters" and the insistence of medical professionals that sex offenders represent a public health problem, albeit

> "*I don't care if we* **stomp on** *his civil liberties. Truly, I don't.*"
>
> —NEW JERSEY POLITICIAN MIKE HOWELL, REFERRING TO A LAW LIMITING WHERE SEX OFFENDERS ARE ALLOWED TO LIVE

one without any ready solution. Not surprisingly, strategies to control sex offenders on their release from prison have frustrated both the public and medical professionals.

Sex Offender Notification Laws In the summer of 1994, seven-year-old Megan Kanka of Hamilton Township, New Jersey, was raped and murdered by a twice-convicted pedophile (an adult sexually attracted to children) who had moved into her neighborhood after being released from prison on parole. The next year, in response to public outrage, the state passed a series of laws known collectively as the New Jersey Sexual Offender Registration Act, or "Megan's Law."[71] Today, all fifty states and the federal government have their own ver-

---

CAREERPREP HALFWAY HOUSE PROGRAM MANAGER

JOB DESCRIPTION:

- Coordinate recreational, educational, and vocational counseling, and other programs for residents. Also, maintain the security of the house and the residents.

- Serve as a mediator between the residents and the community and as an advocate for the halfway house with community groups.

WHAT KIND OF TRAINING IS REQUIRED?

- A bachelor's degree or master's degree in social work, career counseling, criminal justice, or psychology.

- Also helpful are internships, volunteer work with a halfway house, or community service work through an agency.

ANNUAL SALARY RANGE?

- $29,390–$45,550.

For additional information, visit:
www.michigan.gov/careers/
0,1607,7-170-46398-64300-,00.html.

Benjamin F. Fink, Jr./Brand X Pictures/Jupiterimages

sion of Megan's Law, or a **sex offender notification law**, which requires local law authorities to alert the public when a sex offender has been released into the community.

Active and Passive Notification No two sex offender notification laws have exactly the same provisions, but all are designed with the goal of allowing the public to learn the identities of convicted sex offenders living in their midst. In general, the laws demand that a paroled sex offender notify local law enforcement authorities on taking up residence in a state. In Georgia, for example, paroled sex offenders are required to present themselves to both the local sheriff and the superintendent of the public school district where they plan to live.[72] This registration process must be renewed every time the parolee changes address.

The authorities, in turn, notify the community of the sex offender's presence through the use of one of two models. Under the "active" model, the authorities directly notify the community or community representatives. This notification often takes the form of bulletins or posters, distributed and posted within a certain distance from the offender's home. In the "passive" model, information on sex offenders is made open and available for public scrutiny. All fifty states operate Web sites that provide citizens with data on registered sex offenders in their jurisdiction.

Conditions of Release Generally, sex offenders are supervised by parole officers and are subject to the same threat of revocation as other parolees. Paroled child molesters usually have the following conditions of release:

- Must have no contact with children under the age of sixteen.
- Must continue psychiatric treatment.
- Must receive permission from the parole officers to change residence.
- Must stay a certain distance from schools or parks where children are present.
- Cannot own toys that may be used to lure children.
- Cannot have a job or participate in any activity that involves children.

In addition, of course, they are required to register through the proper authorities. Today, more than 700,000 registered sex offenders live throughout the United States.

Jetseta Gage, shown here on a poster held by a protester in Des Moines, Iowa, was kidnapped, raped, and murdered by a convicted sex offender. How are notification laws designed to prevent these sorts of crimes? (AP Photo/Charlie Neibergall/Michael Krinke/iStockphoto.com)

15

THE JUVENILE JUSTICE SYSTEM

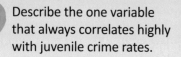

Forever Young

As a boy, Kenneth Young always admired local crack dealer Jacques Bethea, who would drive around their Tampa, Florida, neighborhood in a Buick Regal with gold rims. Still a boy, just fourteen years old, Young helped Bethea rob four hotels and an office building. His job was to grab the cash and disable the security cameras while Bethea held a gun to the night clerks' heads, shouting out orders. For his help, Bethea gave Young $50, a pair of Air Jordan sneakers, and a six-pack of Heineken beer. For committing armed robbery, Hillsborough County circuit judge J. Rogers Padgett gave Young four life terms in prison.

Although Young became something of a poster child for lawyers fighting Florida's harsh juvenile sentences, he spent a decade behind bars without hope of an early release. Then, hope arrived in the form of a decision by the United States Supreme Court. In May 2010, the Court ruled that judges could no longer sentence juveniles who commit crimes in which nobody is killed to life in prison without the possibility of parole. According to Justice Anthony Kennedy, who wrote the majority opinion, state officials must give these inmates "some meaningful opportunity to obtain release based on demonstrated maturity and rehabilitation."

"This is great for Kenneth Young," said his attorney, Paolo Annino, at the time of the Supreme Court's ruling. Indeed, Young had been a model prisoner, caring for elderly inmates and participating in educational classes. Judge Padgett admitted that his original sentence was overly harsh. Two of the victims in the robberies publicly supported him, including one woman who said that Young had kept Bethea from raping her. In December 2010, however, Florida governor Charlie Crist, taking advantage of a loophole in the Court's decision, refused to even consider early release for Young. Curtis Allen, who had prosecuted Young ten years earlier, agreed with Crist's hard stand. "I would tell anyone that I think Mr. Young is very, very dangerous," Allen said.

What are the arguments for and against giving juvenile offender Kenneth Young, shown here at the age of twenty-three, a chance at being released early from his life prison term on parole? (Cira Moro/ Laif/Redux)

The American juvenile justice system has been both hailed as one of the "greatest social inventions of modern times" and criticized for "failing to protect either the legal rights of the juvenile offenders or the public on whom they prey."[1] A difficult question—one that will be asked numerous times as defendants like Kenneth Young challenge their suddenly unconstitutional lifetime-without-parole prison sentences in court—lies at the heart of the juvenile justice debate: Should criminal acts by youths be given the same weight as those committed by adults or be seen as "mistakes" that can be "corrected" by the state?

For most of its 110-year history, the system was dominated by the latter philosophy. Only recently have opposing views summarized by the sound bite "old enough to do the crime, old enough to do the time" gained widespread acceptance—a change reflected in political trends. Since the 1980s, nearly every state has updated its laws to make it easier to try juveniles as adults. This shift has had a profound impact on a juvenile system that generally acts as a "compromise between rehabilitation and punishment, treatment and custody."[2]

In this chapter, we will discuss the successes and failures of this compromise and examine the aspects of the juvenile justice system that differentiate it from the criminal justice system. As you will see, observers on both sides of the rehabilitation versus punishment debate find many flaws with the present system. Some have even begun to call for its dismantling. Others blame social problems such as racism, poverty, and a culture dominated by images of violence for creating a system that no government agency or policy can effectively control.[3]

¿WHY DO WE HAVE A SEPARATE JUSTICE SYSTEM FOR JUVENILES?

In a recent poll, almost 60 percent of Americans indicated that they favored trying violent youths in adult criminal court instead of juvenile courts, which were perceived as too lenient.[4] To a certain degree, such opinions reflect a desire to return the focus of the American juvenile justice system toward punishment and incapacitation, as was the situation at the beginning of the 1800s. At that time, juvenile offenders were treated the same as adult offenders—they were judged by the same courts and sentenced to the same severe penalties. This situation changed throughout the nineteenth century, as urbanization and industrialization created an immigrant underclass that was, at least in the eyes of many reformers, predisposed to deviant activity. Certain members of the Progressive movement, known as the child savers, began to take steps to "save" children from these circumstances, introducing the idea of rehabilitating delinquents in the process.

THE CHILD-SAVING MOVEMENT

LO In general, the child savers favored the doctrine of *parens patriae*, which holds that the state has not only a right but also a duty to care for children who are neglected, delinquent, or in some other way disadvantaged. Juvenile offenders, the child savers believed, required treatment, not punishment, and they were horrified at the thought of placing children in prisons with hardened adult criminals. In 1967, then Supreme Court justice Abe Fortas said of the child savers:

> They believed that society's role was not to ascertain whether the child was "guilty" or "innocent," but "What is he, how

When our children make mistakes, are we going to lock them up and **throw away the key?**

—BRIAN GOWDY, DEFENSE ATTORNEY (2009)

Gabor Izso/iStockphoto.com

has he become what he is, and what had best be done in his interest and in the interest of the state to save him from a downward career." The child—essentially good, as they saw it—was made "to feel that he is the object of [the government's] care and solicitude," not that he was under arrest or on trial.[5]

Child-saving organizations convinced local legislatures to pass laws that allowed them to take control of children who exhibited criminal tendencies or had been neglected by their parents.

The efforts of the child savers culminated with the passage of the Illinois Juvenile Court Act in 1899. The Illinois legislature created the first court specifically for juveniles, guided by the principles of *parens patriae* and based on the concepts that children are not fully responsible for criminal conduct and are capable of being rehabilitated.[6]

The Illinois Juvenile Court and those in other states that followed in its path were (and, in many cases, remain) drastically different from adult courts:

- *No juries.* The matter was decided by judges who wore regular clothes instead of black robes and sat

The eight teenagers shown here, ranging in age from fourteen to eighteen, were charged in Polk County, Florida, with battery and kidnapping for beating a classmate so badly that she suffered a concussion. How might proponents of *parens patriae* suggest that authorities deal with these young offenders? (Photos Courtesy of Polk County Sheriff's Office/Blent Gültek/iStockphoto.com)

at a table with the other participants rather than behind a bench. Because the primary focus of the court was on the child and not the crime, the judge had wide discretion in disposing of each case.

- *Different terminology.* To reduce the stigma of criminal proceedings, "petitions" were issued instead of "warrants"; the children were not "defendants" but "respondents"; they were not "found guilty" but "adjudicated delinquent."
- *No adversarial relationship.* Instead of trying to determine guilt or innocence, the parties involved in the juvenile court worked together in the best interests of the child, with the emphasis on rehabilitation rather than punishment.
- *Confidentiality.* To avoid saddling the child with a criminal past, juvenile court hearings and records were kept sealed, and the proceedings were closed to the public.

By 1945, every state had a juvenile court system modeled after the first Illinois court. For the most part, these courts were able to operate without interference until the 1960s and the onset of the juvenile rights movement.

JUVENILE DELINQUENCY

After the first juvenile court was established in Illinois, the Chicago Bar Association described its purpose as, in part, to "exercise the same tender solicitude and care over its neglected wards that a wise and loving parent would exercise with reference to his [or her] own children under similar circumstances."[7] In other words, the state was given the responsibility of caring for those minors whose behavior seemed to show that they could not be controlled by their parents.

As a result, many **status offenders** found themselves in the early houses of refuge and continue to be placed in state-run facilities today. A status offense is an act that, if committed by a juvenile, is considered illegal and grounds for possible state custody. The same act, if committed by an adult, does not warrant law enforcement action. (See **Figure 15.1** below for a list of status offenses.) (CAREER TIP: Most states have attendance laws that require students to be in school during school hours. These states employ *truancy officers* to enforce such laws by working with parents and investigating suspicious patterns of absence.)

In contrast, **juvenile delinquency** refers to conduct that would also be criminal if committed by an adult. According to federal law and the laws of most states, a juvenile delinquent is someone who has not yet reached his or her eighteenth birthday, or the age of majority, at the time of the offense in question. In two states (New York and North Carolina), persons aged sixteen are considered adults, and ten other states

(Georgia, Illinois, Louisiana, Massachusetts, Michigan, Missouri, New Hampshire, South Carolina, Texas, and Wisconsin) confer adulthood on seventeen-year-olds.

Under certain circumstances, discussed later in this chapter, children below the age of majority can be treated as adults for the purposes of prosecution and trial. Remember that Kenneth Young was fourteen years old when he was tried and sentenced in adult court for his role in a series of robberies, described in the opening to this chapter.

CONSTITUTIONAL PROTECTIONS AND THE JUVENILE COURT

Although the ideal of the juvenile court seemed to offer the "best of both worlds" for juvenile offenders, in reality the lack of procedural protections led to many children arbitrarily being punished not only for crimes but for status offenses as well. Juvenile judges were treating all violators similarly, which led to many status offenders being incarcerated in the same institutions as violent delinquents. In response to a wave of lawsuits demanding due process rights for juveniles, the Supreme Court issued several rulings in the 1960s and 1970s that significantly changed the juvenile justice system.

Kent v. United States The first Supreme Court decision to extend due process rights to children in juvenile courts was *Kent v. United States* (1966).[8] The case concerned sixteen-year-old Morris Kent, who had been arrested for breaking into a woman's house, stealing her purse, and raping her. Because Kent was on juvenile probation, the state sought to transfer his trial for the crime to an adult court (a process to be discussed later in the chapter). Without giving any reasons for his decision, the juvenile judge consented to this judicial waiver, and Kent was sentenced in the adult court to a thirty- to ninety-year prison term.

The Court overturned the sentence, ruling that juveniles have a right to counsel and a hearing in any instance in which the juvenile judge is considering sending the case to an adult court. The Court stated that, in jurisdiction waiver cases, a child receives "the worst of both worlds,"

Figure 15.1 Status Offenses

1. Smoking cigarettes
2. Drinking alcohol
3. Being truant (skipping school)
4. Disobeying teachers
5. Running away from home
6. Violating curfew
7. Participating in sexual activity

THIS IS A DRUG FREE WEAPON FREE ALCOHOL FREE TOBACCO FREE SCHOOL ZONE

Stan Rohrer/iStockphoto.com/Cathleen Clapper/iStockphoto.com

getting neither the "protections accorded to adults" nor the "solicitous care and regenerative treatment" offered in the juvenile system.[9]

In re Gault The *Kent* decision provided the groundwork for the Supreme Court's *In re Gault* ruling one year later. Considered by many the single most important case concerning juvenile justice, *In re Gault* involved a fifteen-year-old boy who was arrested for allegedly making a lewd phone call while on probation.[10] In its decision, the Court held that juveniles are entitled to many of the same due process rights granted to adult offenders, including notice of charges, the right to counsel, the privilege against self-incrimination, and the right to confront and cross-examine witnesses.

Other Important Court Decisions Over the next ten years, the Supreme Court handed down three more important rulings on juvenile court procedure. *In re Winship* (1970)[11] required the government to prove "beyond a reasonable doubt" that a juvenile had committed an act of delinquency, raising the burden of proof from a "preponderance of the evidence."

In *Breed v. Jones* (1975),[12] the Court held that the Fifth Amendment's double jeopardy clause prevented a juvenile from being tried in an adult court for a crime that had already been adjudicated in juvenile court. In contrast, *McKeiver v. Pennsylvania* (1971)[13] represented the one instance in which the Court did not move the juvenile court further toward the adult model. It ruled that the Constitution did not give juveniles the right to a jury trial.

¿HOW IS DELINQUENCY DETERMINED?

In the eyes of many observers, the net effect of the Supreme Court decisions during the 1966–1975 period was to move juvenile justice away from the ideals of the child savers and toward a formalized system that is often indistinguishable from its adult counterpart. But, though the Court has recognized that minors possess certain constitutional rights, it has failed to indicate at what age these rights should be granted and at what age minors are to be held criminally responsible for delinquent actions. Consequently, the legal status of children in the United States varies depending on where they live, with each state making its own policy decisions on the crucial questions of age and competency.

THE AGE QUESTION

Several years ago, eleven-year-old Jordan Brown of New Galilee, Pennsylvania, shot his father's fiancée, Kenzie Houk, in the head with a shotgun while she slept, killing both Houk and her unborn child. Law enforcement officials believe that Brown was resentful of the impending birth of his half-brother, particularly because he was being asked to vacate his room for the infant. "He looked like a baby in an orange jumpsuit," the fifth-grader's father, Chris, said after the boy's first court appearance.[14]

As **Figure 15.2** on the next page shows, twenty-two states, including Pennsylvania, and the District of Columbia do not have age restrictions on prosecuting juveniles as adults. Thus, Pennsylvania officials had the option of charging Brown for murder as an adult, despite his tender years. On March 29, 2010, Judge Dominick Motto decided that, indeed, the boy could be tried as an adult for first degree murder, and the young defendant faced a possible life sentence (with a chance at parole) in adult prison. The judge based his

STUDY PREP

Take notes twice. First, take notes in class. Then, when you get back home, rewrite your notes. The rewrite will act as a study session by forcing you to think about the material. It will also, invariably, lead to questions that are crucial to the study process.

Competency The mental capacity of an individual to participate in legal proceedings, based on that person's ability to understand the nature of the those proceedings.

decision on the defendant's lack of remorse and the "execution-style" of the killing.[15]

Brown's attorneys had argued that their client would be better served by facing the charges in juvenile court, where he would receive treatment designed for younger offenders. For the most part, when juveniles who remain in juvenile court are found guilty, they receive "limited" sentences. Under these circumstances, they cannot remain incarcerated in juvenile detention centers past their eighteenth or twenty-first birthday. As the Brown case shows, when the underlying crime is a serious one such as rape or murder, judges and prosecutors are less likely to accept the juvenile justice option.

THE CULPABILITY QUESTION

Many researchers believe that by the age of fourteen, an adolescent has the same ability as an adult to make a *competent* decision.[16] Nevertheless, according to some observers, a juvenile's ability to theoretically understand the difference between "right" and "wrong" does not mean that she or he should be held to the same standards of **competency** as an adult.

Juvenile Behavior A study released in 2003 by the Research Network on Adolescent Development and Juvenile Justice found that 33 percent of juvenile defendants in criminal courts had the same low level of understanding of legal matters as mentally ill adults who had been found incompetent to stand trial.[17]

Legal psychologist Richard E. Redding believes that

> adolescents' lack of life experience may limit their real-world decision-making ability. Whether we call it wisdom, judgment, or common sense, adolescents may not have nearly enough.[18]

Figure 15.2   The Minimum Age at Which a Juvenile Can Be Tried as an Adult

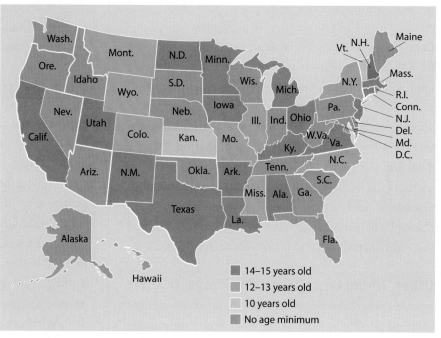

14–15 years old
12–13 years old
10 years old
No age minimum

Source: National Center for Juvenile Justice.

Juveniles are generally more impulsive, more likely to engage in risky behavior, and less likely to calculate the long-term consequences of any particular action. Furthermore, adolescents are far more likely to respond to peer pressure than are adults. The desire for acceptance and approval may drive them to commit crimes; juveniles are arrested as part of a group at much higher rates than adults.[19]

Diminished Guilt The "diminished culpability" of juveniles was one of the reasons given by the United States Supreme Court in its landmark decision in *Roper v. Simmons* (2005).[20] As we saw in Chapter 11, that case forbade the execution of offenders who were under the age of eighteen when they committed their crimes. In his majority opinion, Justice Anthony Kennedy wrote that because minors cannot fully comprehend the consequences of their actions, the two main justifications for the death penalty—retribution and deterrence—do not "work" with juvenile wrongdoers.[21]

Five years later, the Supreme Court applied the same reasoning in *Graham v. Florida* (2010).[22] The case involved two defendants who had committed violent crimes as juveniles: Joe Sullivan, who raped a woman when he was thirteen, and Terrance Graham, who committed armed burglary at sixteen. Both defendants claimed that their life-without-parole sentences violated the Eight Amendment's prohibition of "cruel and unusual punishment." By a close 5–4 vote, the Court agreed, holding that juveniles who commit crimes that do not involve murder may not be sentenced to life in prison without the possibility of parole (as we mentioned in the introduction to this chapter). In large part, the ruling was based on the assumption that most young offenders are not "lost causes" and should be given the chance to rehabilitate themselves and return to the community.[23]

¿WHAT HAPPENS AFTER A JUVENILE IS ARRESTED?

A young offender's first contact with the juvenile justice system usually comes through a police officer. Police arrest about 1.2 million youths under the age of eighteen each year. In most states, police officers must have probable cause to believe that the minor has committed an offense, just as they would if the suspect were an adult.

Police power with regard to juveniles is greater than with adults, however, because police can take youths into custody for status offenses, such as possession of alcohol or truancy. In these cases, the officer is acting *in loco parentis*, or in the place of the parent. The officer's role is not necessarily to punish the youths but to protect them from harmful behavior. With less serious offenses, the officer may simply issue a warning, but when a grave offense has occurred, the officer will formally arrest the offender and send him or her to juvenile court.

Law enforcement officers notify the juvenile court system that a particular young person requires its attention through a process known as a **referral**. Anyone with a valid reason, including parents, relatives, welfare agencies, and school officials, can refer a juvenile to the juvenile court. The vast majority of delinquency cases in juvenile courts, however, are referred by the police.[24] Once a youth has been referred, various decision makers are provided the opportunity to determine how the juvenile justice system will dispose of the case. The offender may be diverted to a social-services program

or detained in a juvenile lockup facility. In the most serious cases, the youth may even be transferred to adult court.

To ensure due process during pretrial procedures, offenders and their families may retain an attorney or have one appointed by the court. The four primary stages of this critical period—intake, diversion, waiver, and detention—are discussed below.

INTAKE

After an offender has **LO3** been referred, a complaint is filed with a special division of the juvenile court, and the **intake** process begins. During intake, an official of the juvenile court—usually a probation officer, but sometimes a judge—must decide, in effect, what to do with the offender. The intake officer has several options during intake:

1. Simply dismiss the case, releasing the offender without taking any further action.
2. Divert the offender to a social-services program, such as drug rehabilitation or anger management.
3. File a **petition** for a formal court hearing. The petition is the formal document outlining the charges against the juvenile.
4. Transfer the case to an adult court, where the offender will be tried as an adult.

With regard to status offenses, judges have sole discretion to decide whether to process the case or *divert* the youth to another juvenile service agency.

PRETRIAL DIVERSION

In a practical sense, the juvenile justice system started as a diversionary program with the goal of redirecting children from the punitive adult court to the more

---

In Loco Parentis
(Latin for "in place of the parents") In juvenile justice, the role of police officers who automatically assume parental status and take responsibility for the well-being of the juvenile offender.

Referral The notification process through which a law enforcement officer or other concerned citizen makes the juvenile court aware of a juvenile's unlawful or unruly conduct.

Intake The process during which an official of the court decides whether to file a petition, release the juvenile, or place the juvenile under some other form of supervision.

Petition The document alleging that a juvenile is a delinquent or a status offender and asking the juvenile court to hear the case.

rehabilitative juvenile court.[25] By the 1960s, many observers felt that juvenile courts had lost sight of this early mandate and were badly in need of reform. A particular concern was the growing number of status offenders who were being punished even though they had not committed a truly delinquent act. To provide an alternative for them, hundreds of diversion programs were put into effect. Today, diversion refers to the process of removing low-risk offenders from the formal juvenile justice system by placing them in community-based rehabilitation programs.

Diversion programs vary widely, but fall into three general categories:

1 *Probation.* In this program, the juvenile is returned to the community, but placed under the supervision of a juvenile probation officer. If the youth breaks the conditions of probation, he or she can be returned to the formal juvenile system. (CAREER TIP: As you will soon see, *juvenile probation officers* face different challenges from those who work with adults, primarily because juvenile officers become much more involved with their clients' often difficult home life.)

2 *Treatment and aid.* Many juveniles have behavioral or medical conditions that contribute to their delinquent behavior, and many diversion programs offer remedial education, drug and alcohol treatment, and other forms of counseling to help with these problems.

3 *Restitution.* In restitution programs, the offender "repays" her or his victim, either directly or, in the case of community service, symbolically.[26]

Proponents of diversion programs include many labeling theorists (see Chapter 2), who believe that contact with the formal juvenile justice system labels the youth a delinquent, which leads to further delinquent behavior.

TRANSFER TO ADULT COURT

One side effect of diversionary programs is that the youths who remain in the juvenile courts are more likely to be seen as "hardened" and less amenable to rehabilitation. This, in turn, increases the likelihood that the offender will be transferred to an adult court, a process in which the juvenile court waives jurisdiction over the youth. As the American juvenile justice system has shifted away from ideals of treatment and toward punishment, transfer to adult court has been one of the most popular means of "getting tough" on delinquents.

Methods of Transfer There are three types of transfer laws, and most states use more than one of

CAREERPREP

JUVENILE DETENTION OFFICER

JOB DESCRIPTION:

- Oversee the detention of juvenile offenders being held in temporary custody before the adjudicatory process begins. Observe the behavior of and, when necessary, counsel the juvenile offenders to ensure their safety during the detention period.

- Maintain personal relationships with the juvenile offenders so as to supervise their progress in educational, recreational, and therapeutic activities while housed at the detention center.

WHAT KIND OF TRAINING IS REQUIRED?

- A high school diploma plus at least three years of work experience involving children of school age (seven to seventeen years) or one year of college education for each year of experience lacking.

- Physical agility and strength, as well as a firm manner in dealing with juveniles who may present severe disciplinary problems.

ANNUAL SALARY RANGE?

- $29,000 to $62,000

For additional information, visit: www.npjs.org.

PhotoDisc

them, depending on the jurisdiction and the seriousness of the offense. Juveniles are most commonly transferred to adult courts through **judicial waiver,** in which the juvenile judge is given the power to determine whether a young offender's case will be transferred to adult court. As occurred with Jordan Brown (see page 281), the judge makes this decision based on the offender's age, the nature of the offense, and any criminal history. All but five states employ judicial waiver.

Twenty-nine states have taken the waiver responsibility out of judicial hands through **automatic transfer,** also known as *legislative waiver.* In these states, the legislatures have designated certain conditions—usually involving serious crimes such as murder and rape—under which a juvenile case is automatically "kicked up" to adult court. In Rhode Island, for example, a juvenile aged sixteen or older with two prior felony adjudications will automatically be transferred on being accused of a third felony.[27] Fourteen states also allow for **prosecutorial waiver,** in which prosecutors are allowed to choose whether to initiate proceedings in juvenile or criminal court when certain age and offense conditions are met.

Incidence of Transfer Each year, about seven thousand delinquency cases are waived to adult criminal court—less than 1 percent of all cases that reach

In 2009, Vernon Bartley, right, was convicted as an adult for raping and murdering his neighbor in Ewa Beach, Hawaii, when he was fifteen years old. What factors should be taken into consideration when deciding whether juveniles charged with violent crimes should be tried as adults?

(AP Photo/Richard Ambo, The Honolulu Advertiser)

juvenile court.[28] As we saw earlier in the chapter, those juveniles who commit the most violent of felonies are the most likely to be transferred. For example, when he was fifteen years old, Vernon Bartley raped and murdered a neighbor, Karen Ertell, who was scheduled to testify against him during a burglary trial in Ewa Beach, Hawaii.

Given the "gruesome, violent, detestable" nature of his crimes, there was little doubt that a judge would waive Bartley to adult court, where, in 2010, he was found guilty of second degree murder and sentenced to life in adult prison (see the photo below).

DETENTION

Once the decision has been made that the offender will face adjudication in a juvenile court, the intake official must decide what to do with him or her until the start of the trial. Generally, the juvenile is released into the custody of parents or a guardian—most jurisdictions favor this practice in lieu of setting money bail for youths. The intake officer may also place the offender in **detention,** or temporary custody in a secure facility, until the disposition process begins. Once a juvenile has been detained, most jurisdictions require that a **detention hearing** be held within twenty-four hours. During this hearing, the offender has several due process safeguards, including the right to counsel, the right against self-incrimination, and the right to cross-examine and confront witnesses.

In justifying its decision to detain, the court will usually address one of three issues:

1. Whether the child poses a danger to the community.

2. Whether the child will return for the adjudication process.

3. Whether detention will provide protection for the child.

The Supreme Court upheld the practice of preventive detention (see Chapter 9) for juveniles in *Schall v. Martin* (1984)[29] by ruling that youths can be detained if they are deemed a "risk" to the safety of the community or to their own welfare. Partly as a result, the number of detained juveniles increased by 48 percent between 1985 and 2007.[30]

¿HOW DOES A JUVENILE COURT OPERATE?

Over the past forty years, the one constant in the juvenile justice system has been change. Supreme Court rulings in the wake of *In re Gault* (1967) have increased the procedural formality and the overriding punitive philosophy of the juvenile court. Diversion policies have worked to remove many status offenders from the juvenile court's jurisdiction, and waiver policies ensure that the most violent juveniles are tried as adults. Some observers feel these adjustments have "criminalized" the juvenile court, effectively rendering it indistinguishable both theoretically and practically from adult courts.[31]

Along with a number of his colleagues, law professor Barry C. Feld thinks that the juvenile court has become obsolete and should be abolished. Feld believes the changes noted above have "transformed the juvenile court from its original model as a social-service agency into a deficient second-rate criminal court that provides young people with neither positive treatment nor criminal procedural justice."[32] Indeed, juvenile hearings do proceed along many of the same lines as the adult criminal court, with similar due process protections and rules of evidence (though minors do not enjoy the right to a jury trial). Nevertheless, juvenile justice proceedings may still be distinguished from the adult system of criminal justice, and these differences are evident in the adjudication and disposition of the juvenile trial.

ADJUDICATION

During the adjudication stage of the juvenile justice process, a hearing is held to determine the fate of the young offender. Most state juvenile codes dictate a specific set of procedures that must be followed during the **adjudicatory hearing**, with the goal of providing the respondent with "the essentials of due process and fair treatment."

Consequently, the respondent in an adjudicatory hearing has the right to notice of charges, counsel, confrontation and cross-examination, and the privilege against self-incrimination. Furthermore, "proof beyond a reasonable doubt" must be established to find the child delinquent. When the child admits guilt—that is, admits to the charges of the initial petition—the judge must ensure that the admission was voluntary.

At the close of the adjudicatory hearing, the judge is generally required to rule on the legal issues and evidence that have been presented. Based on this ruling, the judge determines whether the respondent is delinquent or in need of court supervision. Alternatively, the judge can dismiss the case based on a lack of evidence. It is important to remember that finding a child to be delinquent is *not* the same as convicting an adult of a crime. A delinquent does not face the same restrictions, such as those concerning the right to vote and to run for political office, as do adult convicts in some states (discussed in Chapter 13).

DISPOSITION

Once a juvenile has been adjudicated delinquent, the judge must decide what steps will be taken toward treatment and/or punishment. Most states provide for a *bifurcated* (two-part) *process* in which a separate **disposition hearing** follows the adjudicatory hearing. Depending on state law, the juvenile may be entitled to counsel at the disposition hearing.

Sentencing Juveniles In an adult trial, the sentencing phase is primarily concerned with the "needs" of the community to be protected from the convict. In contrast, a juvenile court judge uses the disposition hearing to determine a sentence that will serve the "needs" of the child. For assistance in this crucial process, the judge will order the probation department to gather information on the juvenile and present it in the form of a **predisposition report**. The report usually contains information concerning the respondent's family background, the facts surrounding the delinquent act, and interviews with social workers, teachers, and other important figures in the child's life.

Judicial Discretion In keeping with the rehabilitative tradition of the juvenile justice system, many judges have a great deal of discretion in choosing one of several disposition possibilities. A judge can tend toward leniency, delivering only a stern reprimand or warning before releasing the juvenile into the custody of parents or other legal guardians. Otherwise, the choice is among incarceration in a juvenile correctional facility, probation, or community treatment.

In most cases, seriousness of the offense is the primary factor used in determining whether to incarcerate a juvenile, though history of delinquency, family situation, and the offender's attitude are all relevant. (CAREER TIP: In many jurisdictions, the *juvenile court judge* is an elected position, meaning that, like their counterparts in the adult criminal justice system, these judges face the pressures of public opinion in dealing with juvenile offenders.)

¿HOW ARE JUVENILE OFFENDERS PUNISHED?

In general, juvenile corrections are based on the concept of **graduated sanctions**—that is, the severity of the punishment should fit the crime. Consequently, status and first-time offenders are diverted or placed on probation, repeat offenders find themselves in intensive community supervision or treatment programs, and serious and violent offenders are placed in correctional facilities.[33]

As society's expectations of the juvenile justice system have changed, so have the characteristics of its corrections programs. In some cities, for example, juvenile probation officers join police officers on the beat. Because the former are not bound by the same search and seizure restrictions as other law enforcement officials, this interdepartmental teamwork provides more opportunities to fight youth crime aggressively. Juvenile correctional facilities are also changing their operations to reflect public mandates that they both reform and punish. Also, note that at midyear 2009, 7,220 juveniles were in adult jails and another 2,778 were serving time in state prisons.[34]

Predisposition Report A report that provides the judge with relevant background material to aid in the disposition decision.

Graduated Sanctions The theory that a delinquent or status offender should receive a punishment that matches the severity of the wrongdoing.

JUVENILE PROBATION

The most common form of juvenile corrections is probation—33 percent of all delinquency cases disposed of by juvenile courts result in conditional diversion. The majority of all adjudicated delinquents will never receive a disposition more severe than being placed on probation.[35] These statistics reflect a general understanding among juvenile court judges and other officials that removing a child from her or his home should be considered primarily as a last resort.

TEST PREP

Be prepared. Make a list of everything you will need for an exam, such as a pen/pencil, watch, and calculator. Arrive at the exam early to avoid having to rush, which will only add to your stress. Good preparation helps you focus on the task at hand.

Residential Treatment Program A government-run facility for juveniles whose offenses are not deemed serious enough to warrant incarceration in a training school.

The organization of juvenile probation is very similar to adult probation (see Chapter 12), and juvenile probationers are increasingly subjected to electronic monitoring and other supervisory tactics. The main difference between the two programs lies in the attitude toward the offender. Adult probation officers have an overriding responsibility to protect the community from the probationer, while juvenile probation officers are expected to take the role of a mentor or a concerned relative in looking after the needs of the child.

CONFINING JUVENILES

About 92,000 American youths (up from 30,000 at the end of the 1970s) are incarcerated in public and private juvenile correctional facilities in the United States.[36] Most of these juveniles have committed crimes against people or property, but a significant number (about 15 percent) have been incarcerated for technical violations of their probation or parole agreements.[37] After deciding that a juvenile needs to be confined, the judge has two sentencing options: nonsecure juvenile institutions and secure juvenile institutions.

Nonsecure Confinement Some juvenile delinquents do not require high levels of control and can be placed in **residential treatment programs**. These programs, run by either probation departments or social-services departments, allow their subjects freedom of movement in the community. Generally, this freedom is predicated on the juveniles following certain rules, such as avoiding alcoholic beverages and returning to the facility for curfew. Residential treatment programs can be divided into four categories:

1. *Foster care programs*, in which the juveniles live with a couple who act as surrogate parents.
2. *Group homes*, which generally house between twelve and fifteen youths and provide treatment, counseling, and education services by a professional staff.
3. *Family group homes*, which combine aspects of foster care and group homes, meaning that a single family, rather than a group of professionals, looks after the needs of the young offenders.
4. *Rural programs*, which include wilderness camps, farms, and ranches where between thirty and fifty children are placed in an environment that provides recreational activities and treatment programs.[38]

This support class for fathers at the Hogan Street Regional Youth Center in St. Louis, Missouri, is one of many group-counseling classes offered at the juvenile facility. Why would the juvenile justice system emphasize rehabilitation for young offenders rather than adult-style punitive incarceration? (Dilip Vishwanat/*The New York Times*/Redux/MBPHOTO, INC./ iStockphoto.com)

Secure Confinement Secure facilities are comparable to the adult prisons and jails we discussed in Chapters 13 and 14. These institutions go by a confusing array of names depending on the state in which they are located, but the two best known are boot camps and training schools.

Boot Camps A **boot camp** is the juvenile variation of shock probation. As we noted in Chapter 12, boot camps are modeled after military training for new recruits. Boot camp programs are based on the theory that by giving wayward youths a taste of the hard life of military-like training for short periods of time, usually no longer than 180 days, they will be "shocked" out of a life of crime. New York's Camp Monterey Shock Incarceration Facility is typical of the boot camp experience. Inmates are grouped in platoons and live in dormitories. They spend eight hours a day training, drilling, and doing hard labor, and also participate in programs such as basic adult education and job skills training.[39]

Training Schools No juvenile correctional facility is called a "prison." This does not mean they lack a strong resemblance to prisons. The facilities that most closely mimic the atmosphere at an adult correctional facility are **training schools**, alternatively known as youth camps, youth development centers, industrial schools, and several other similar titles. Whatever the name, these institutions claim to differ from their adult countparts by offering a variety of programs to treat and rehabilitate the young offenders. In reality, training schools are plagued by many of the same problems as adult prisons and jails, including high levels of inmate-on-inmate violence, substance abuse, gang wars, and overcrowding.

Boot Camp A variation on traditional shock incarceration in which juveniles (and some adults) are sent to secure confinement facilities modeled on military basic training camps instead of prison or jail.

Training School A correctional institution for juveniles found to be delinquent or status offenders.

Aftercare The variety of therapeutic, educational, and counseling programs for juvenile delinquents (and some adults) after they have been released from a correctional facility.

Aftercare Juveniles leave correctional facilities through an early release program or because they have served the length of their sentences. Juvenile corrections officials recognize that many of these children, like adults, need assistance readjusting to the outside world. Consequently, released juveniles are often placed in **aftercare** programs.

Based on the same philosophy that drives the prisoner reentry movement (discussed in the last chapter), aftercare programs are designed to offer services for the juveniles, while at the same time supervising them to reduce the chances of recidivism. The ideal aftercare program includes community support groups, aid in finding and keeping employment, and continued monitoring to ensure that the juvenile is able to deal with the demands of freedom. (CAREER TIP: *Aftercare coordinators* help juvenile offenders during the critical transitional period immediately after discharge from a youth correctional facility, when old temptations, acquaintances, and stresses pose the greatest threat to rehabilitation.)

CAREERPREP

YOUTH WORKER

JOB DESCRIPTION:

- Provide safety, security, custodial care, discipline, and guidance for youths held in juvenile correctional facilities.

- Play a critical role in the rehabilitation of youthful offenders and, as a result, have a potentially great impact on their success during and after incarceration.

WHAT KIND OF TRAINING IS REQUIRED?

- A bachelor's degree in human services, behavioral science, or a related field.

- Professional and respectful communication skills and a commitment and dedication to the needs of adolescent offenders and their families.

ANNUAL SALARY RANGE?

- $33,000–$52,000

For additional information, visit: www.youthtoday.org.

Lisa F. Young/iStockphoto

¿HOW MUCH JUVENILE DELINQUENCY IS THERE IN THE UNITED STATES?

When asked, juveniles will admit to a wide range of illegal or dangerous behavior, including carrying weapons, getting involved in fights, driving after drinking alcohol, and stealing or deliberately damaging school property.[40] Have juvenile law enforcement efforts, juvenile courts, and juvenile corrections been effective in controlling and preventing this kind of misbehavior, as well as more serious acts?

To answer this question, many observers turn to the Federal Bureau of Investigation's Uniform Crime Report (UCR), initially covered in Chapter 3. Because the UCR breaks down arrest statistics by age of the arrestee, it has been considered the primary source of information on the presence of juveniles in America's justice system. This does not mean, however, that the UCR is completely reliable when it comes to measuring juvenile delinquency. The process measures only those juveniles who were caught and therefore does not accurately reflect all delinquent acts in any given year. Furthermore, it measures the number of arrests but not the number of arrestees, meaning that—due to repeat offenders—the number of juveniles actually in the system could be below the number of juvenile arrests.

DELINQUENCY BY THE NUMBERS

With these cautions in mind, UCR findings are quite clear as to the extent of the juvenile delinquency problem in the United States today. In 2009, juveniles accounted for 14 percent of the nation's total arrests.[41] According to the 2009 UCR, juveniles were responsible for

- ☑ 9 percent of all murder arrests;
- ☑ 12 percent of all aggravated assault arrests;
- ☑ 15 percent of all forcible rapes;
- ☑ 21 percent of all weapons arrests;
- ☑ 25 percent of all robbery arrests;
- ☑ 25 percent of all property crimes; and
- ☑ 10 percent of all drug offenses.

IS JUVENILE CRIME LEVELING OFF?

As **Figure 15.3** on the facing page shows, the juvenile violent crime rate has fluctuated dramatically over the past three decades, with highs in the mid-1990s and lows in the early years of this century. Today, the juvenile crime rate has leveled off, though in 2007 the juvenile property crime rate did rise for the first time in thirteen years, only to resume its downward trend a year later. In addition, juvenile arrest rates for some crimes—such as fraud, embezzlement, and driving under the influence—are still relatively high. The overall situation, however, is not nearly as bleak as it was fifteen years ago.[42]

Although the theory is not universally accepted, many observers see the rise and decline of juvenile arrests as mirroring the rise and decline of crack cocaine.[43] When inner-city youths took advantage of the economic opportunities offered by the crack trade in the 1980s, they found they needed to protect themselves against rival dealers. This led to the proliferation of firearms among juveniles, as well as the formation of violent youth gangs. As the crack epidemic has slowed in recent years, so have arrest and violent crime rates for juveniles.

Other theories have been put forth as well. Some observers point to the increase in police action against "quality-of-life" crimes such as loitering, which they believe stops juveniles before they have a chance to commit more serious crimes. Furthermore, many schools have adopted zero-tolerance policies that punish students harshly for bringing weapons or drugs onto school grounds. Alfred Blumstein, a criminologist at Carnegie Mellon University in Pittsburgh, thinks young Americans learned from the examples of their older acquaintances. "Kids saw what crack was doing to their siblings, friends, and parents and turned away from it," he says.[44]

SCHOOL VIOLENCE

One Wednesday afternoon in January 2011, seventeen-year-old Robert Butler, Jr., walked into an administrative office at Millard South High School in Omaha, Nebraska, and fatally shot assistant principal Vicki Kaspar. Butler, who had been suspended for misconduct earlier that day, also wounded principal Curtis Case before talking his own life. The incident was every teacher's (and student's and parent's) worst nightmare. Like other episodes of school violence, it received heavy media coverage, fanning fears that our schools are not safe.

In fact, school-age youths are about fifty times more likely to be murdered away from school than on a campus.[45] Furthermore, between 1995 and 2009, victimization rates of students for nonfatal crimes at school declined significantly, meaning that, in general, schools are safer today than they were in the recent past.[46] To a certain extent, these statistics mirror the downward trend of all criminal activity in the United States since the mid-1990s.

In addition, since the fatal shootings of fourteen students and a teacher at Columbine High School near Littleton, Colorado, in 1999, many schools have also improved security measures. From 1999 to 2007, the percentage of American schools using security cameras to monitor their campuses increased from 19 to 56 percent. Today, 90 percent of public schools control access to school buildings by locking or monitoring their doors.[47] Furthermore, in light of studies showing that bullying plays a significant role in school violence, forty-five states have passed legislation designed to curtail such behavior.[48]

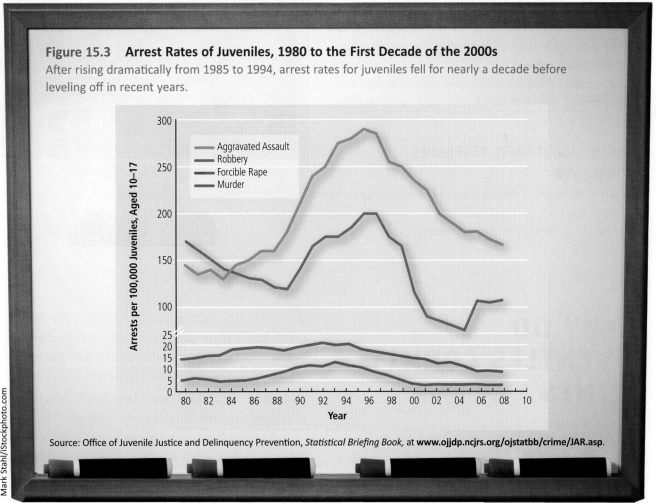

Figure 15.3 Arrest Rates of Juveniles, 1980 to the First Decade of the 2000s

After rising dramatically from 1985 to 1994, arrest rates for juveniles fell for nearly a decade before leveling off in recent years.

Source: Office of Juvenile Justice and Delinquency Prevention, *Statistical Briefing Book*, at www.ojjdp.ncjrs.org/ojstatbb/crime/JAR.asp.

CJ and Technology

THE RAPID RESPONDER

At 11:30 A.M., a sixteen-year-old student pulls out a 9-mm handgun during science class and shoots a hole in the wall. By 11:42 A.M., the entire school population of two thousand students has been evacuated, unharmed, and a SWAT team has the shooter surrounded. This incident, which took place at Lewis and Clark High School in Spokane, Washington, in the early 2000s, was an early example of the benefits of Rapid Responder technology. The password-protected software program—accessible either as a computer download or via the Internet—acts as an instant information clearinghouse during an emergency. It provides school officials and law enforcement officers with detailed floor plans, satellite and geospatial (GIS) imagery, photos of views from windows, student population figures, and even the locations of trees and bushes on school grounds. By the time the local SWAT team arrived at Lewis and Clark High School, for example, the team already knew the quickest route to Room 307, where the shooter had barricaded himself, and that this room was connected by an internal doorway to Room 305. (When the officers arrived, the shooter's first words were, "You got here too fast.") Furthermore, a Rapid Responder map of the school showed that the field where the evacuated students had gathered was in direct sight of Room 307's windows. These students were quickly moved.

Today, nearly three hundred school districts in the United States are using Rapid Responder software to protect their campuses.

THINKING ABOUT RAPID RESPONDER TECHNOLOGY

In what other emergency situations would this technology be helpful? Why do you think the U.S. Department of Homeland Security has certified Rapid Responder as "Qualified Anti-Terrorism Technology"?

¿WHY DO JUVENILES COMMIT CRIMES?

As we discussed in Chapter 2, an influential study conducted by Professor Marvin Wolfgang and several colleagues in the early 1970s introduced the "chronic 6 percent" to criminology. The researchers found that out of one hundred juvenile offenders, six will become "chronic" offenders, meaning that they are arrested five or more times before their eighteenth birthdays. Furthermore, Wolfgang and his colleagues determined that these chronic offenders are responsible for half of all crimes and two-thirds of all violent crimes within any given cohort (a group of persons who have similar characteristics).[49] Does this "6 percent rule" mean that no matter what steps society takes, six out of every hundred troubled juveniles are "bad seeds" and will act delinquently? Or does it point to a situation in which a small percentage of children may be more likely to commit crimes under certain circumstances?

Most criminologists favor the second interpretation. In this section, we will examine the four factors that have traditionally been used to explain juvenile criminal behavior and violent crime rates: age, substance abuse, family problems, and gangs. Keep in mind, however, that the factors influencing delinquency are not limited to these topics. Researchers are constantly interpreting and reinterpreting statistical evidence to provide fresh perspectives on this very important issue. A study released several years ago, for example, focused on low self-control as a predictor of juvenile violence. According to authors Matt DeLisi of Iowa State University and Michael G. Vaughn of the University of Pittsburgh, the inability of youths to avoid risky, impulsive decisions is a very strong predictor of delinquency and, indeed, of a long career in crime.[50]

THE AGE–CRIME RELATIONSHIP

Crime statistics are fairly conclusive on one point: the older a person is, the less likely he or she will exhibit criminal behavior. Self-reported studies confirm that most people are involved in some form of criminal behavior—however "harmless"—during their early years. In fact, Terrie Moffitt of the University of Wisconsin has said that "it is statistically aberrant to refrain from crime during adolescence."[51]

So, why do the vast majority of us not become chronic offenders? According to many criminologists, particularly Travis Hirschi and Michael Gottfredson, any group of at-risk persons—regardless of gender, race, intelligence, or class—will commit fewer crimes as they grow older.[52] This process is known as **aging out** (or, sometimes, *desistance*). Professor Sampson and his colleague John H. Laub believe that this phenomenon is explained by certain events, such as marriage, employment, and military service, which force delinquents to "grow up" and forgo criminal acts.[53]

SUBSTANCE ABUSE

As we have seen throughout this textbook, substance abuse plays a strong role in criminal behavior for adults. The same can certainly be said for juveniles. According

to the National Survey on Drug Use and Health (NSDUH), more than 11 million Americans between the ages of twelve and twenty consume alcohol on a regular basis, increasing the probability that they will become involved in violent behavior, delinquency, academic problems, and risky sexual behavior.[54] At the same time, 10 percent of those between the ages of twelve and seventeen admit using illegal drugs on a regular basis, a number that, as **Figure 15.4** below shows, rose in 2009 for the first time in several years. Almost 10 percent of all juvenile arrests involve a drug abuse violation.

Nearly all young offenders (94 percent) entering juvenile detention self-report drug use at some point in their lives, and 85 percent have used drugs in the previous six months.[55] According to the Arrestee Drug Abuse Monitoring Program, nearly 60 percent of male juvenile detainees and 46 percent of female juvenile detainees test positive for drug use at the time of their offense.[56]

CHILD ABUSE AND NEGLECT

Abuse by parents also plays a substantial role in juvenile delinquency. **Child abuse** can be broadly defined as the infliction of physical or emotional, or sexual damage

Aging Out A term used to explain the fact that criminal activity declines with age.

Child Abuse Mistreatment of children by causing physical, emotional, or sexual damage.

Figure 15.4 Drug Use among Juveniles

Among Americans aged twelve to seventeen, the percentage who admit to using illegal drugs in the past month dropped each year from 2002 until 2008 before rising in 2009.

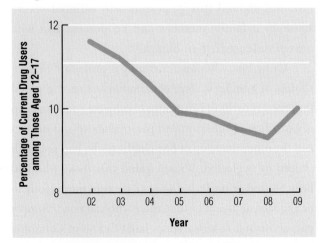

Source: National Survey on Drug Use and Health, 2003–2010

on a child, while **child neglect** refers to deprivations—of love, shelter, food, and proper care—children undergo by their parents. According to the National Survey of Children's Exposure to Violence, one in ten children in the United States suffers from mistreatment at the hands of a close family member.[57] (CAREER TIP: When the level of abuse and neglect becomes particularly severe, a court will decide that the parents cannot be trusted to look after the best interests of their child. When this occurs the court will assign a *guardian ad litem* to attend to the child's emotional and legal needs and monitor the family situation.)

Children in homes characterized by violence or neglect suffer from a variety of physical, emotional, and mental health problems at a much greater rate than their peers.[58] This, in turn, increases their chances of engaging in delinquent behavior. One survey of violent juveniles showed that 75 percent had suffered severe abuse by a family member and 80 percent had witnessed violence in their homes.[59]

Cathy Spatz Widom, currently a professor of psychology at John Jay College of Criminal Justice, compared the arrest records of two groups of subjects—one made up of 908 cases of substantiated parental abuse and neglect and the other made up of 667 children who had not been abused or neglected. Widom found that those who had been abused or neglected were 53 percent more likely to be arrested as juveniles than those who had not.[60] Simply put, according to researchers Janet Currie of Columbia University and Erdal Tekin of Georgia State University,

"**My homeboys became my family**—the older ones were father figures. Each time I shot someone, each time I put another gun on the set, each time I successfully recruited a combat soldier, I was congratulated by my older homeboys."

—SANYKA SHAKUR, FORMER GANG MEMBER

Duncan Walker/iStockphoto.com/Korhan Karacan/iStockphoto.com

"child maltreatment roughly doubles the probability that an individual engages in many types of crime."[61]

GANGS

When youths cannot find the stability and support they require in the family structure, they will often turn to their peers. This is just one explanation for why juveniles join **youth gangs**. Although jurisdictions may have varying definitions, for general purposes a youth gang is viewed as a group of three or more persons who (1) self-identify as an entity separate from the community by special clothing, vocabulary, hand signals, and names and (2) engage in criminal activity. Although the first gangs may have appeared in the 1780s, around the time of the American Revolution, there have been four periods of major gang activity in American history: the late 1800s, the 1920s, the 1960s, and the present.

According to an exhaustive survey of law enforcement agencies, there are probably around 20,000 gangs with approximately 1 million members in the United States.[62]

The Criminality of Gang Members To some degree, the violent and criminal behavior of youths in gangs has been exaggerated by information sources such as the media. In proportion to all gang activities, violence is a rare event; youth gang members spend most of their time "hanging out" and taking part in other normal adolescent behavior.[63] That having been said, gang members are responsible for a disproportionate amount of violent and nonviolent criminal acts by juveniles. Traditional gang activities such as using and trafficking in drugs, protecting their territory in turf battles, and graffiti/vandalism all contribute to high crime rates among members.

Gang Violence Nationwide, larger cities report the highest number of gang-related homicides.[64] Every year, more than half of the murders in Chicago and Los Angeles are attributed to gang violence. Statistics also show high levels of gang involvement in weapons trafficking, burglary, assault, and motor vehicle theft, while more than 50 percent of all youth gangs are believed to be involved in drug sales.[65] Furthermore, a study of criminal behavior among juveniles in Seattle found that gang members were considerably more likely to commit crimes than at-risk youths who shared many characteristics with gang members but were not affiliated with any gang. The gang members in Seattle were also much more likely to own firearms or to have friends who owned firearms.[66]

GUNS

It is hardly surprising that the gang members in Seattle were disproportionately involved with firearms. Studies have shown that youths who are members of gangs are three times as likely to own a handgun as those who are not.[67] Gang members are also much more inclined to believe that they need a gun for protection and to be involved in gun-related crimes.[68]

The harmful link between juveniles and guns is hardly limited to gang members, however. Indeed, one explanation for the increase in youth violence in the late 1980s and early 1990s points to the unprecedented access minors had to illegal weapons during that time. According to Carnegie Mellon's Alfred Blumstein:

> [Y]outh have always fought with each other. But when it's a battle with fists, the dynamics run much more slowly. With a gun, it evolves very rapidly, too fast for a third party to intervene. That also raises the stakes and encourages others to arm themselves, thereby triggering a preemptive strike: "I better get him before he gets me."[69]

In fact, the correlation between access to guns and juvenile homicide rates is striking. The juvenile arrest rate for weapons violations doubled between 1987 and 1993. By 1994, 82 percent of all homicides committed by juveniles involved a handgun. Then, as the homicide rate began to drop, so did the arrest rate for weapons offenses, and many experts believe that the downward trend in juvenile homicide arrests can be traced largely to a decline in firearm use.[70]

In what sort of criminal activity do youth gang members, such as this Crip from South Central Los Angeles, usually engage? (Ted Soqui/Corbis)

16 HOMELAND SECURITY

Learning Outcomes

After studying this chapter, you will be able to . . .

 LO 1 Identify three important trends in terrorism.

 LO 2 Explain why the Antiterrorism and Effective Death Penalty Act of 1996 (AEDPA) is an important legal tool against terrorists.

 LO 3 Describe the primary goals of an intelligence agency and indicate how it differs from an agency that focuses solely on law enforcement.

 LO 4 Explain how American law enforcement agencies have used preventive policing to combat terrorism.

 LO 5 Explain how the Patriot Act has made it easier for federal agents to conduct searches during terrorism investigations.

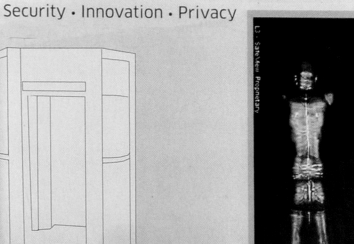

21st Century Technology
Security · Innovation · Privacy

Wrong Number

"Do you remember when 9/11 happened, when those people were jumping from the skyscrapers?" asked nineteen-year-old Mohamed Osman Mohamud. "I thought that was awesome." These are strong, even shocking, words, but Mohamud, a Somali American who had recently dropped out of Oregon State University at Corvallis, was willing to back them up. On July 30, 2010, Mohamud met for the first time with a person he knew only as "Abdulhadi" in nearby Portland to plan his own terrorist attack. When the two met again three weeks later, Mohaumud had chosen his target: the city's annual Christmas tree–lighting ceremony in Pioneer Square, held annually the day after Thanksgiving. "I want whoever is attending that event to leave . . . dead or injured," he said.

Abdulhadi, along with several associates, helped Mohamud work toward this goal. They provided him with nearly $3,000 to rent an apartment and purchase bomb components. They took him to a remote location near the Oregon coast for an operational dry run. Then, on November 26, Abdulhadi and Mohamud loaded a white van with six 55-gallon drums of explosives and diesel fuel, parked it near Pioneer Square, and retired to a safe distance. At 5:40 P.M., as thousands of people gathered in the downtown plaza to watch a tall Douglas fir tree laced with tiny Christmas lights, Mohamud took out his cell phone and dialed the number that he thought was going to detonate the huge bomb.

Nothing happened. As it turned out, Abdulhadi was a federal agent, and the bomb was a fake designed by Federal Bureau of Investigation (FBI) specialists. When Mohamud tried to dial a second time, he was arrested. Eventually, authorities charged him with attempted use of a weapon of mass destruction, which carries a maximum sentence of life in prison. Told of his exploits, friends were astounded that "Mo," a suburban teen who liked to play video games, was capable of such behavior. "When you think of someone doing what he did, you think of some crazy kind of guy," said one. "He wasn't like that. He was just like everybody else."

Zhang Jun/Xinhua/Landov

How did law enforcement agents prevent Mohamed Osman Mohamud from carrying out a terrorist attack during the annual Christmas tree–lighting ceremony in Portland, Oregon? (b37/ZUMA Press/Newscom)

Young Mohamed Osman Mohamud is only one in a series of recent American terrorists who seem "just like everybody else." In June 2009, Abdulhakim Muhammad, born Carl Bledsoe, opened fire on a military recruiting center in Little Rock, Arkansas, killing one soldier and wounding another. On November 5 of that year, Army major Nidal Malik Hasan fatally shot thirteen people during a surprise rampage at Fort Hood in Texas. In February 2011, Collen LaRose, a blonde Pennsylvanian woman who called herself "JihadJane," pleaded guilty to plotting the death of a Swedish cartoonist whose work had offended some Muslims.

These "homegrown" extremists present a grave new challenge for law enforcement. Because they have been raised in the United States, they know how to operate on American soil. Because they possess U.S. passports, they can move freely in and out of the country. Unless they draw attention to themselves by posting their views on the Internet—which is how the FBI was first alerted to Mohamud—they can go unseen until they take action. Consequently, the old terrorist profile has been "broken," according to Bruce Hoffman, a terrorism expert at Georgetown University in Washington, D.C.: "It's women as well as men, it's lifelong Muslims as well as converts, it's college students as well as jailbirds."[1]

Such unpredictability is one of the more striking, and unnerving, aspects of life in the United States, post–September 11. Terrorism and its uncertainties have been a constant theme throughout this textbook, and we have seen many instances in which law enforcement, the courts, and corrections have had to evolve to meet the challenge. In this chapter, we will focus solely on the criminal justice system's role in *homeland security*, defined by the federal government as

> a concerted national effort to prevent terrorist attacks within the United States, reduce America's vulnerability to terrorism, and minimize the damage and recover from attacks that do occur.[2]

We start with a continuation of our discussion of the phenomenon that has driven the homeland security movement in the United States since September 11, 2001—terrorism.

¿WHAT IS TERRORISM?

Relatively speaking, the term *terrorism* has had a short history. In the political context, its birth can be traced to the time during the French Revolution (1789–1799) when the French legislature ordered the public executions of nearly 18,000 "enemies" of the new government. As a result of this *régime de la terreur* (reign of terror), terrorism was initially associated with state-sponsored violence against the people. By the dawn of the twentieth century, this dynamic had shifted. Terrorists had evolved into **nonstate actors**, free of control by or allegiance to any nation, who used violence to further political goals such as the formation or destruction of a particular government.

Today, the dominant strain of terrorism mixes political goals with very strong religious affiliations. Modern terrorism is also characterized by extreme levels of violence. The January 24, 2011, suicide bombing at Russia's busiest airport in Moscow killed at least 35 people and injured 150 more. The three-day November 2008 raid on the financial district of Mumbai, India, left 173 dead and more than 300 wounded. And, of course, the September 11, 2001, attacks on New York and Washington, D.C., claimed nearly 3,000 lives. Indeed, the power of terrorism is a direct result of the fear caused by this violence—not only the fear that such atrocities will be repeated, but also that next time, they will be much worse.

DEFINING TERRORISM

Terrorism has always had a subjective quality, summed up by the useful cliché "one person's terrorist is another person's freedom fighter." Because it means different things to different people in different situations, politicians, academics, and legal experts alike have long struggled to determine which acts of violence qualify as terrorism and which do not. One observer has even compared these efforts to the legendary quest for the

Holy Grail, stating, "[P]eriodically, eager souls set out, full of purpose, energy and self-confidence, to succeed where so many others before have tried and failed."[3]

The FBI defines terrorism as

> the unlawful use of force or violence against persons or property to intimidate or coerce a government, the civilian population, or any segment thereof, in furtherance of political or social objectives.[4]

This definition is useful for our purposes because it is relatively straightforward and easy to understand. It is inadequate, however, in that it fails to capture the wide scope of international terrorism in the 2000s. Today, many observers are asking whether the state should consider terrorist violence merely "unlawful," as in the FBI definition, or an act of war. The answer is crucial in the homeland security context because, as we shall see later in the chapter, our rules for preventing crimes and fighting a war are markedly different.

Generally, wars are considered military actions undertaken by one state or nation against another. This would seem to remove terrorism from the realm of war, given that its participants are nonstate actors, as mentioned earlier. Professor David A. Westbrook of the University of New York at Buffalo points out, however, that the large scale and financial resources of some modern terrorist organizations makes them as powerful as many nations, if not more so. In addition, the high body counts associated with the worst terrorist acts seem better described in terms of war than of crime, which in most cases involves two people—the criminal and the victim.[5] Thus, as we see in **Figure 16.1** on the following page, perhaps the most satisfying, if not the most concise, definition of terrorism describes it as a "supercrime" that incorporates many of the characteristics of warfare.

> *Jihad* The struggle by a Muslim to reach a moral, spiritual, or political goal, interpreted by a small minority of Muslim religious leaders to require violence against non-Muslims.

THE CHANGING GLOBAL CONTEXT OF TERRORISM

On May 1, 2011, a team of U.S. Navy Seals killed Osama bin Laden in Abbottabad, Pakistan. For many Americans, the event marked a triumph in the struggle against international terrorism. Experts, however, noted that al Qaeda, the movement bin Laden had helped to start, already seemed to be moving on without him.

Osama bin Laden and al Qaeda Just as there has been some trouble coming up with a useful definition of terrorism, there has been a great deal of confusion concerning the terrorists themselves. To start with, the Arabic term *al Qaeda*, which can be roughly translated as "the base," has two meanings. One alludes to a diffuse, general anti-Western global social movement, while the other refers to a specific organization responsible for the September 11 attacks and numerous other terrorist activities over the past two decades.[6]

Osama bin Laden's al Qaeda organization grew out of a network of volunteers who migrated to Afghanistan in the 1980s to rid that country of its Communist occupiers. (Ironically, in light of later events, bin Laden and these volunteers received significant American financial aid.) For bin Laden, these efforts took the form of *jihad*, a controversial term that, once again, has been the subject of much confusion. *Jihad* does not, as many think, mean "holy war." Rather, it refers to three kinds of struggle, or exertion, required of the Muslim faithful: (1) the struggle against the evil in oneself, (2) the struggle against the evil outside of oneself, and (3) the struggle against nonbelievers.[7] Many Muslims

STUDY PREP

Notice that each major section heading in this textbook has been written in the form of a question. By turning headings or subheadings in *all* of your textbooks into questions—and then answering them—you will increase your understanding of the material.

Domestic Terrorism
Acts of terrorism that take place within the territorial jurisdiction of a country without direct foreign involvement.

believe that this struggle can be achieved without violence and denounce the form of *jihad* practiced by al Qaeda. Clearly, however, bin Laden and his followers rejected the notion that *jihad* can be accomplished through peaceable efforts.

Domestic Terrorism In the years following September 11, 2001, America's counterterrorism strategies proceeded under the assumption that there were two distinct strands of terrorism. First—and most dangerous—was international terrorism, represented by bin Laden and al Qaeda and possessing the resources to carry out massive, coordinated attacks. Second was **domestic terrorism**, which involves acts of terrorism that are carried out within one's own country, against one's own people, and with no direct foreign involvement.

Alienated and Online The long-accepted profile of the domestic terrorist in the United States is that of an alienated individual who becomes emboldened after meeting others who share his or her extreme views. Usually, such views focus on outrage at American military excursions against Muslims in Afghanistan and Iraq. These homegrown radicals often find support and encouragement on the Internet, which offers training manuals, audio and video propaganda, and communication with like-minded individuals through chat rooms.

Take, for example, Mohamed Osman Mohamud, whose attempt to bomb a Portland tree-lighting ceremony we discussed at the beginning of this chapter. Mohamud first caught the attention of federal law enforcement authorities when he began trading e-mails with a friend who had moved to Waziristan, an al Qaeda stronghold in northwestern Pakistan. He also wrote numerous articles for online extremist magazines, including one article entitled "Getting in Shape without

Figure 16.1   The "Supercrime" of Terrorism

To accommodate the idea of terrorism as a "supercrime," Professor George Fletcher of the Columbia University School of Law has devised eight variables that often—though not always—capture the essence of what we think about when we consider terrorism.

1. **The violence factor.** First and foremost, terrorism is an expression of violence.

2. **The intention.** Just as the goal of bank robbers is to get the cash, terrorists have an objective each time they act. In some instances, the very act of violence or destruction fulfills this intent.

3. **The victims.** Terrorist acts generally target civilians or "innocent" persons rather than military personnel.

4. **The wrongdoers.** Similarly, terrorists operate outside any military command structure.

5. **A "just cause."** Those who decide to use terror to further their aims believe that the ends justify the often-violent means.

6. **Organization.** Generally, terrorists act in concert with other like-minded individuals. The solo terrorist is only now becoming more common.

7. **Theater.** For a terrorist act to be truly effective, it must be dramatic. One expert has even said, "Terrorism is theater."

8. **The absence of guilt.** Terrorists are so certain of the righteousness of their cause that they act without feeling guilt or remorse.

New York City, September 2001

(Beth A. Keiser/AFP/Getty Images/ Korhan Karacan/iStockphoto.com)

Like a number of other terrorist suspects apprehended over the past few years, Faisal Shahzad, shown here on the Arabic-language television news channel Al Arabiya, is a U.S. citizen. What challenges does this trend pose for America's anti-terrorism efforts? (AP Photo/Al-Arabiya via AP Television Network)

Weights" that sought to help readers prepare "physically for *jihad*" using Pilates.[8]

Radical Planning As was the case with Mohamed Osman Mohamud, the process of self-radicalization can result in a plan to carry out a terrorist attack on U.S. soil. Given the lack of experience of the would-be domestic terrorists, when these plots do materialize, they are often haphazard and amateurish. On May 1, 2010, for example, Faisal Shahzad packed a Nissan Pathfinder with ten gallons of gasoline, sixty gallons of propane, 250 pounds of fertilizer, and hundreds of M-88 fireworks and parked the car in New York's Times Square.

Shahzad, a U.S. citizen born in Pakistan who lived in Bridgeport, Connecticut, lit a fuse connected to the fireworks and walked away, expecting the ensuing explosion to create a fireball of destruction. His plan failed, though, because he used the wrong type of fertilizer and the firecrackers weren't powerful enough to detonate the containers of propane and gasoline.[9] Instead, a street vendor noticed suspicious white smoke coming from the vehicle and alerted officials before the makeshift bomb could do any damage.

Evolving Threat Patterns After Faisal Shahzad was apprehended at New York's John F. Kennedy International Airport while trying to board a flight to the Middle East, he told interrogators that he had received five days of explosives training and $15,000 from the Pakistani Taliban, an extremist group operating out of Waziristan. (The Pakistani Taliban is not the same as the Taliban groups that the U.S. military is fighting in Afghanistan.) This confession was notable for two reasons: (1) it involved a terrorist organization other than al Qaeda operating in the United States, and (2) Shahzad's American citizenship and connections to a foreign enemy reflected a blurring of the lines between international and domestic terrorism.

The Diffusion of al Qaeda Because of successful U.S. military operations against al Qaeda bases and worldwide law enforcement efforts to cut off the organization's

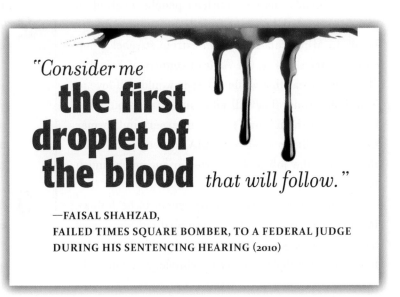

"Consider me **the first droplet of the blood** *that will follow."*

—FAISAL SHAHZAD, FAILED TIMES SQUARE BOMBER, TO A FEDERAL JUDGE DURING HIS SENTENCING HEARING (2010)

supply of funds, al Qaeda is no longer the powerful organization it was in the late 1990s and early 2000s. It now relies more on a loose organization of affiliates—"more of a McDonald's . . . than a General Motors," in the words of one expert.[10] Today, diffuse al Qaeda cells create their own strategies and pick their own targets. Even before Osama bin Laden's death, these groups tended to see him more as an inspirational figure than a hands-on leader.[11]

For example, an al Qaeda branch in the small, poor Middle Eastern country of Yemen has been particularly active on American soil. It was responsible for training Umar Farouk Abdulmutallab, a Nigerian who attempted to detonate a bomb hidden in his underwear on a Northwest flight as it landed in Detroit on December 25, 2009. Then, in October 2010, two packages containing bombs were shipped from Yemen to Jewish religious centers in Chicago. The packages were intercepted thanks to a tip from Saudi Arabian intelligence agents. Finally, the writings of al Qaeda associate Anwar al-Awlaki, a radical U.S.-born cleric hiding in Yemen, are known to have influenced Abdulmutallub, Army major Nidal Malik Hasan (who, as mentioned earlier, killed thirteen people at Fort Hood, Texas, in 2009), and the Oregon teenager Mohamed Osman Mohamud.[12]

The Internationalization of Domestic Terrorism

The newer version of al Qaeda, perhaps finding it difficult to execute large-scale operations such as the 9/11 attacks, has instead focused recently on smaller jobs involving American-born operatives. In August 2010, federal officials charged fourteen people involved in gathering potential recruits from immigrant neighborhoods in Minnesota to join an extremist rebel group with al Qaeda ties in the African country of Somalia. "It's pretty clear that while al Qaeda would still love to have home runs, they will take singles and doubles if they can get them," one terrorism expert and former Central Intelligence Agency (CIA) officer said. "And that makes the job of counterterrorism much, much harder."[13]

Other terrorist organizations seem to be following a similar strategy. After Faisal Shahzad, the Times Square suspect, was arrested, an Afghan Taliban leader bragged that with "all this new technology, it's not dif-

> ## "Terrorism cannot be 'defeated' because it is a tactic and not an enemy."
>
> —NORA BENSAHEL, POLITICAL SCIENTIST

ficult to recruit people in the West." He also claimed to have received hundreds of e-mails from potential homegrown American terrorists who "want to join us."[14]

Terrorism Trends for the Future Smaller operations involving American-born terrorists influenced by international sources are the result of several trends identified by homeland security expert Brian M. Jenkins. **LO** Notice how each of Jenkins's trends, which follow, deemphasize the importance of any single, dominant organization such as al Qaeda:

1 *Terrorists have developed more efficient methods of financing their operations* through avenues such as Internet fund-raising, drug trafficking, and money laundering schemes.

2 *Terrorists have developed more efficient organizations* based on the small-business model, in which individuals are responsible for different tasks including recruiting, planning, propaganda, and social services such as supporting the families of suicide bombers. These "employees" do not answer to a single leader but rather function as a network that is quick to adjust and difficult to infiltrate.

3 *Terrorists have exploited new communications technologies to mount global campaigns*, relying on the Internet for immediate, direct communication among operatives and as a crucial recruiting tool.[15]

As you may have noted, each of these trends favors the global terrorism movement. Indeed, Jenkins finds that today's *jihadists* are dangerous, resilient survivors who have achieved some strategic results and are determined to continue attacking their enemies. "Destroying their terrorist enterprise," he concludes, "will take years."[16]

THE TERRORIST THREAT

On September 18, 2001, just a week after the hijacked airplanes flew into the World Trade Centers and the Pentagon, a batch of envelopes containing several grams of anthrax powder were sent out to various media outlets from a post office in Trenton, New Jersey. Anthrax is a very dangerous infectious disease transmitted by bacteria so small that a thousand spores would not reach across the thin edge of a dime.[17] On October 5, Robert Stevens, a photo editor for the Florida-based newspaper *Sun*, died after inhaling some of the powder. Over the next few weeks, several more anthrax-filled envelopes infiltrated the U.S. Postal Service, including two mailed to U.S. senators, and twenty-one other people became infected. Four of them died.

This first-known deliberate use of bacteria to commit murder in the United States was almost completely unexpected. Only eighteen cases of inhaled anthrax spores were recorded in the entire twentieth century. Weapons experts knew that the bacteria could be disseminated from a germ-packed light bulb or a suitcase with holes punched in it, but nobody had considered the post office as an anthrax delivery service.[18] Thus, though the perpetrators and therefore their motives are still unknown, the incident was a very effective act of terrorism. Not only was it unpredictable and random, but it gave people a reason to fear a mainstay of their daily life—the mail.

The Weaponry of Terrorism While the images and memories of September 11, 2001, remain part of the national psyche, the anthrax mailings have largely been forgotten. For the most part, however, homeland security experts are more concerned about the dangers presented by minuscule bacteria than by the threat posed by two-hundred-ton airplanes. In 2007, Robert Mueller, the director of the FBI, said that "the biggest threat faced by the United States in the counterterrorism arena . . . is [a] WMD in the hands of terrorists."[19] **WMD** is the acronym for **weapons of mass destruction**, a term used to describe a wide variety of deadly instruments that represent significant security challenges for the United States and other targets of international terrorism. Anthrax is considered a WMD because a very small amount of it has the potential to cause a massive amount of destruction, killing and sickening thousands of people.

WMDs come in four categories: (1) *biological* weapons, (2) *chemical* weapons, (3) *nuclear* weapons, and (4) *radiological* weapons. **Biological weapons** are living organisms such as bacteria, viruses, and other microorganisms such as anthrax that cause disease and death. Because these weapons are "alive," they have unique capabilities to reproduce and spread undetected through large populations of humans, animals, and plants. In contrast, **chemical weapons** are manufactured for the purpose of causing harm or death. They can be inhaled or ingested, and they can seep into the body though the skin or eyes.

The "doomsday" terrorist attack scenario involves **nuclear weapons**. The destructive force of these bombs is caused by the massive release of heat and energy that accompanies their detonation. Only two such bombs have ever been used—by the U.S. military against the Japanese cities of Hiroshima and Nagasaki in August of 1945. About 70,000 people in Hiroshima and 40,000 people in Nagasaki were killed instantly. Adding to the devastating impact of these weapons is the **radiation** that is released following detonation. Radiological

Weapons of Mass Destruction (WMDs) A term that describes nuclear, radiological, chemical, or biological weapons that have the capacity to cause significant damage.

Biological Weapon Any living organism, such as a bacterium or virus, used to intentionally harm or kill adversaries in war or targets of terrorist attacks.

Chemical Weapon Any weapon that uses a manufactured chemical to harm or kill adversaries in war or targets of terrorist attacks.

Nuclear Weapon An explosive device that derives its massive destructive power from the release of nuclear energy.

Radiation Harmful energy that is transmitted outward from its source through rays, waves, or particles following the detonation of a nuclear device.

Antiterrorism and Effective Death Penalty Act of 1996 (AEDPA) Legislation giving law enforcement officers the power to arrest and prosecute any individual who provides "material support or resources" to a "foreign terrorist organization."

material destroys human cells, and exposure to high levels of radiation can lead to immediate death. Exposure to lower levels of radiation is also dangerous, greatly increasing the risk of long-term health problems such as cancer. (CAREER TIP: Homemade bombs, otherwise known as improvised explosive devices [IEDs], are also of great concern to homeland security officials. *Bomb appraisal officers* have the responsibility of responding to IED alarms, particularly in airports and other public transportation areas.)

The Incidence of WMDs For all the nightmarish possibilities, WMDs have been more a threat than a reality on American soil. Besides the anthrax mailings already discussed, only one instance of bioterrorism has occurred in the United States. In 1984, members of the Rajneesh cult spread salmonella bacteria through supermarkets and restaurants in The Dalles, Oregon, as part of an effort to influence local elections. About 750 residents fell ill, none fatally. Terrorist attacks using chemical agents have been rare throughout the world, and there have been no nuclear or radiological terrorism incidents.

There are a number of reasons why WMDs have been used only rarely. The biological agents most appropriate for terrorist attacks are short lived and easily destroyed, so there is no guarantee that they will be effective. The materials needed to carry out a chemical, nuclear, or radiological attack are heavily regulated by the world's governments, and their theft or purchase in significant amounts is likely to set off alarm bells. Furthermore, once a threat has been identified, governments respond by lessening the risks associated with that threat. Within two years of the anthrax scare, for example, U.S. post offices began installing alarm systems designed to detect the presence of anthrax spores in mail-handling facilities.[20] (CAREER TIP: U.S. Coast Guard *marine inspectors* have the authority to conduct inspections and board all vessels within U.S. waters to search for materials that may pose a threat to national security.)

¿HOW HAS THE U.S. GOVERNMENT RESPONDED TO TERRORISM?

On September 12, 2001, President George W. Bush made a public promise that the "United States of America will use all our resources to conquer this enemy."[21] About seven and a half years later, as Barack Obama assumed the presidency, he warned "those who seek to advance their aims by inducing terror and slaughtering innocents" that "[o]ur spirit is stronger and cannot be broken; you cannot outlast us, and we will defeat you."[22]

So far in this chapter we have concentrated on the nature of terrorism and the threat that it poses. Now we turn our attention to the "resources" that the United States has at its disposal to "defeat" this threat. Eventually, this discussion will lead us to an examination of the tactics used by law enforcement agents and other government actors to combat terrorism, along with the controversies that these tactics have sparked. We start, however, with an examination of the rules governing counterterrorism and the agencies and individuals that are bound by them.

THE ANTITERRORISM AND EFFECTIVE DEATH PENALTY ACT

LO2 Signed into law by President Bill Clinton on April 24, 1996, the Antiterrorism and Effective Death Penalty Act (AEDPA) was passed in response to the 1995 truck bombing of the Alfred P. Murrah Federal

Bart Everett/Shutterstock.com

Building in Oklahoma City, Oklahoma. The primary goal of the AEDPA is to hamstring terrorist organizations by cutting off their funding from outside sources. The law prohibits persons from "knowingly providing material support or resources" to any group that the United States has designated a "foreign terrorist organization," or FTO.[23] Each year, the U.S. secretary of state is required to provide Congress with a list of these FTOs, loosely defined to cover organizations that are (1) foreign, (2) engage in terrorist activity, and (3) threaten the security of U.S. citizens or the United States itself.[24] The latest edition of this list included forty-four such organizations, most of them based in the Middle East.[25]

"Material support" is defined very broadly in the legislation, covering funding, financial services, lodging, training, expert advice or assistance, communications equipment, transportation, and other physical assets.[26] The "knowingly" requirement applies to all material support except for direct monetary donations to FTOs—this act is a strict liability crime (see page 68). Consequently, even if a person is unaware that the recipient of charitable giving is involved in terrorist activity, he or she can be prosecuted under the AEDPA.[27]

THE PATRIOT ACT

The original AEDPA did not include the provision making a donation to an FTO a strict liability crime. This amendment was part of the far-reaching scope of the **Patriot Act**, signed into law by President George W. Bush on October 26, 2001, just six weeks after the September 11 terrorist attacks.[28]

"Leveling the Playing Field" As we have seen throughout this textbook, particularly in Chapters 7 and 10, the emphasis on the rights of the accused in the American criminal justice system often makes it difficult to arrest and convict suspected criminals. The Patriot Act resulted from a strong impulse to "level the playing field" when it comes to terrorists. The legislation makes it easier for law enforcement agents to collect information about those suspected of committing terrorist acts or having knowledge of terrorist activity and then detain them based on that information. It enhances the power of the federal gov-

ernment to keep non-citizens under suspicion of having terrorist sympathies from entering the United States, and, as we have seen, it targets the fund-raising of terrorist enterprises.

> **Patriot Act** Legislation passed in the wake of the September 11, 2001, terrorist attacks that greatly expanded the ability of government agents to monitor and apprehend suspected terrorists.

A massive piece of legislation, the Patriot Act is difficult to summarize. Selected aspects are listed here, however, to provide a general idea of the statute's goals, as well as its methods of achieving them:

- The act relaxes restrictions on information sharing between various U.S. law enforcement agencies and other governmental departments concerning suspected terrorists.
- It creates the crime of knowingly harboring a terrorist.
- It allows law enforcement agents greater freedom in seizing the e-mail records of suspected terrorists.
- It authorizes funds to triple the number of border patrol agents, customs inspectors, and immigration enforcement officers along the United States' northern border with Canada.
- It allows the federal government to detain non-U.S. citizens suspected of terrorist activity for up to seven days without informing them of the charges on which they are being held.
- It eliminates the statute of limitations (see page 181) for prosecution of the most serious terrorism-related crimes.[29]

Renewing the Patriot Act Partly because of the speed with which the Patriot Act was pieced together and approved, many lawmakers and their constituents were wary of its long-term impact on the civil rights of all Americans. Consequently, a "sunset provision" was added to the initial legislation, meaning that it would expire if not renewed by Congress at certain invervals. In 2011, President Barack Obama, despite having criticized the Patriot Act before taking office, signed a four-year extension of the legislation.[30] It seems that despite its perceived weaknesses, the Patriot Act has become an accepted part of America's antiterrorism arsenal.

THE DEPARTMENT OF HOMELAND SECURITY

While the Patriot Act transformed the legal landscape of America's counterterrorism efforts, the Homeland Security Act of 2002 had a similar effect on the inner workings of the U.S. government.[31] Prior to this legislation, disaster management at the federal level was primarily the responsibility of the Federal Emergency Management Agency (FEMA). The Patriot Act placed FEMA, as well as twenty-one other federal agencies, under the control of the Department of Homeland Security (DHS).

Descriptions of those agencies within the DHS that have traditionally been oriented toward law enforcement, such as U.S Customs and Border Protection (CBP) and U.S. Immigration and Customs Enforcement (ICE), can be found in Chapter 5, and we will not repeat that discussion here. A wide variety of other federal agencies, including the following, also answer directly to the secretary of homeland security, a post currently held by Janet Napolitano:

- The *Transportation Security Administration (TSA)* is responsible for the safe operation of our airline, rail, bus, and ferry services.
- *U.S. Citizenship and Immigration Services (USCIS)* handles the "paperwork" side of U.S. immigration law. The agency processes the more than 20 million applications made each year by individuals who want to visit the United States or reside or work in this country.
- *FEMA* retains its position as the lead federal agency in preparing for and responding to disasters such as hurricanes, floods, terrorist attacks, and *infrastructure* concerns. The term **infrastructure** refers to the facilities and systems that provide the daily necessities of modern life, such as electric power, food, water, transportation, and telecommunications.

Infrastructure The services and facilities that support the day-to-day needs of modern life, such as electricity, food, transportation, and water.

Some critics of the DHS argue that its immense bureaucratic structure has dulled the effectiveness of individual agencies, which must now go through a chain of command rather than relying on their own initiative. FEMA, in particular, was the target of a firestorm of criticism following its less-than-stellar response to Hurricane Katrina, which devastated the Gulf Coast of the United States in 2005. (CAREER TIP: When a natural disaster hits, FEMA responds by immediately sending *relief workers* into the area to provide the affected communities with emergency services.)

FEDERAL AGENCIES OUTSIDE THE DHS

The DHS does not directly control all federal efforts to combat terrorism. Since September 11, 2001, the FBI, a branch of the Department of Justice, has been the "lead federal agency" for all terrorism-related matters. Its Strategic Information Operations Center serves as an information clearinghouse for federal, state, and local law enforcement agents who want to share information on terrorism-related matters. Indeed, the agency now lists "protecting the United States from terrorist attack" as its highest organizational priority.[32]

The *intelligence* agencies of the U.S. government also play an important role in antiterrorism efforts. As opposed to a law enforcement agency, which works to solve crimes that have already occurred, an **intelligence agency** works to prevent crimes or other undesirable acts by gathering information, or intelligence, on potential wrongdoers and stopping the illegal conduct in the planning stage. Intelligence operations rely on the following strategies to collect information:

- *Electronic surveillance* of phone and e-mail communications, as well as advanced recording devices placed on satellites, aircraft, and land-based technology centers.
- *Human-source collection*, which refers to the recruitment of foreign agents and interviews with people who have particular knowledge about areas of interest.
- *Open-source collection*, or close attention to "open" data sources such as books, newspapers, radio and television transmissions, and Internet sites.
- *Intelligence sharing* with friendly foreign intelligence services.
- *Counterintelligence*, which involves placing undercover agents in a position to gain information from hostile foreign intelligence services.[33]

TEST PREP

Be sure to eat before taking a test. Having food in your stomach will give you the energy you need to concentrate. Don't go overboard, however. Too much food or heavy foods will make you sleepy during the exam.

In particular, two intelligence agencies are integral to American antiterrorism efforts. The first is the **Central Intelligence Agency (CIA)**, which is responsible for gathering and analyzing information on foreign governments, corporations, and individuals, and then passing that information on to the upper levels of our federal government.

> **Intelligence Agency** An agency that is primarily concerned with gathering information about potential criminal or terrorist events in order to prevent those acts from taking place.
>
> **Central Intelligence Agency (CIA)** The U.S. government agency that is responsible for collecting and coordinating foreign intelligence operations.
>
> **National Security Agency (NSA)** The intelligence agency that is responsible for protecting U.S. government communications and producing intelligence by monitoring foreign communications.

The second, the **National Security Agency (NSA)**, is also in the business of gathering and analyzing information, but it focuses primarily on communications. NSA agents eavesdrop on foreign conversations, whatever form they might take, while at the same time working to ensure that sensitive messages sent by the U.S. government are not subjected to similar scrutiny. (CAREER TIP: Both the CIA and the NSA need *Middle East specialists* to gather intelligence in countries such as Iraq and Iran and, more generally, to help government officials better understand the political and religious complexities of the region.)

¿HOW HAS AMERICAN LAW ENFORCEMENT RESPONDED TO TERRORISM?

Several years ago, the chair of an independent congressional panel investigating the September 11 attacks (the 9/11 Commission) said that the "most important failure" of the nation's leaders prior to the September 11 attacks was "one of imagination."[34] In other words, because our criminal justice and intelligence experts could not imagine such a scenario, they were powerless to prevent it.

Preventive Policing A law enforcement strategy that has proved popular against domestic terrorist suspects, in which police officers work to apprehend the suspects in the planning stages of a potential criminal act, rather than after the act has taken place.

Today, no such imagination is necessary. With memories of the falling towers and a smoldering Pentagon still potent, the U.S. homeland security apparatus has developed a wide variety of methods to protect America from terrorist activity. From 2008 to 2010, law enforcement and intelligence agencies foiled at least fifteen domestic terrorism plots,[35] and the likelihood of an American citizen dying at the hands of a terrorist is minuscule. Keeping in mind the ever-present possibility of a successful terrorism operation, in this section we will examine the various strategies that have been devised to detect American terrorist plots and prevent another attack.

PREVENTIVE POLICING

Twenty-year-old Mohamed Mahmood Alessa may not have been much of a criminal mastermind, but he was an expert braggart. "He's not better than me. I'll do twice what he did," Alessa, an American citizen of Palestinian descent, said of Major Nidal Hasan, who killed thirteen people at Fort Hood, Texas, in 2009.[36] "My soul cannot rest until I shed blood," Alessa boasted on another occasion. "I wanna, like, be the world's best known terrorist."[37] Unfortunately for Alessa, when he said these things he was talking to an undercover officer working for the New York Police Department. Consequently, in June 2010, Alessa and his friend Carlos Almonte were arrested as they tried to board a flight to Africa and were charged with conspiring to join the Somali terrorist group al-Shabaab.

Taking No Chances In Chapter 4, we saw that criminal law generally requires intent and action. That is, a person must have both intended to commit a crime and taken some steps toward doing so. In most cases, criminal law also requires that a harm has been done and that the criminal act caused the harm. According to federal officials, however, no evidence showed that either Mohamed Mahmood Alessa or Carlos Almonte had any successful contacts with established terrorist groups. The only weapons the two men possessed were folding knives, and they appeared to have spent most of their time lifting weights, playing violent video games, and watching *jihadist* videos on the Internet.

The case of Alessa and Almonte represents a growing trend in the criminal justice system brought about by the new challenges of fighting terrorism. The goal for many law enforcement agencies is no longer to solve crimes after they have occurred, but rather to prevent them from happening in the first place. Even though Alessa and Almonte did not pose any "known immediate threat to the public,"[38] federal authorities were not willing to take the risk that the actions of these men could eventually evolve into something dangerous to U.S. citizens at home or abroad. Although some observers claim that law enforcement officials are exaggerating the menace posed by many of these accused plotters, the government points to a record of successes to justify this new approach of **preventive policing**. (See **Figure 16.2** on the facing page.)

Informants and Entrapment To infiltrate homegrown terrorist cells, law enforcement relies heavily on intelligence provided by informants (first discussed in Chapter 6). Because these makeshift cells often need help to procure the weaponry necessary for their schemes, they are natural targets for well-placed informants and undercover agents (both discussed in Chapter 6). Hampered by their amateur approach to terrorist activities, these suspects also are natural targets for well-placed "insiders." According to the Center of Law and Security at New York University, 62 percent of the federal government's most significant terrorism prosecutions relied on evidence provided by informants.[39] As you may recall from the beginning of this chapter, FBI agents gave Mohamed Osman Mohamud funds to purchase explosive material and even provided him with a fake bomb in that young man's efforts to carry out an attack in Portland, Oregon.

These tactics have drawn criticism from some quarters. Following Mohamud's apprehension, for example, one commentator wrote an article entitled "The FBI Successfully Thwarts Its Own Terrorist Plot."[40] Stephen R. Sady, Mohamud's defense attorney, charged the FBI with "basically grooming" his client to commit a terrorist act.[41] As you learned in Chapter 4 (see page 76), entrapment is a possible defense for criminal behavior when a government agent plants the idea of committing a crime in a defendant who would not have considered it on his or her own. Although the entrapment defense has often been raised in terrorism cases involving informants or undercover agents, it has yet to succeed. In every instance, judges and juries have found that the defendant was predisposed to terrorist behavior without any help from the government.[42]

Accepting Change "Intelligence used to be a dirty word" for local police departments, according to David Carter, a professor of criminal justice at Michigan State University.[43] Today, however, hundreds of millions of dollars of support from the U.S. Department of Justice and the DHS have helped create more than one hundred nonfederal police intelligence units, with at least one in every state.[44] The New York Police Department, in a class by itself, has more than one thousand personnel assigned to homeland security and has stationed agents in six foreign countries. Thanks to the FBI's Joint Terrorism Task Forces and *fusion centers* that bring multiple agencies together in one location, state and local police departments also have more opportunities to share intelligence with their federal counterparts.

Figure 16.2 Preventive Policing: The Age of the Foiled Plot

Testifying before Congress in 2001, then attorney general John Ashcroft succinctly outlined the nation's new law enforcement strategy regarding domestic terrorists: "Prevent first, prosecute second." This blueprint has led to dozens of "quick strikes" against alleged terrorists, including the several examples listed here.

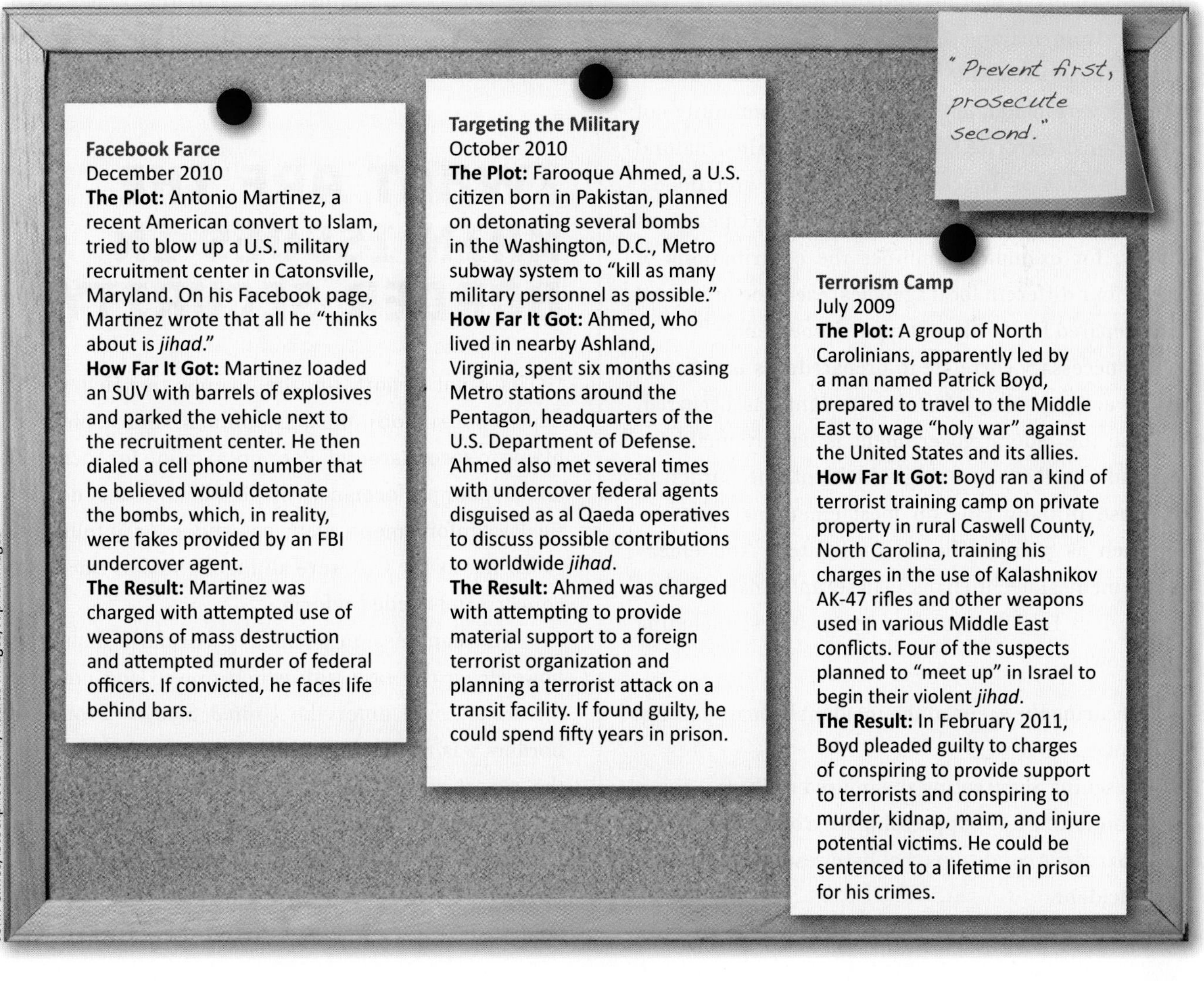

Facebook Farce
December 2010
The Plot: Antonio Martinez, a recent American convert to Islam, tried to blow up a U.S. military recruitment center in Catonsville, Maryland. On his Facebook page, Martinez wrote that all he "thinks about is *jihad*."
How Far It Got: Martinez loaded an SUV with barrels of explosives and parked the vehicle next to the recruitment center. He then dialed a cell phone number that he believed would detonate the bombs, which, in reality, were fakes provided by an FBI undercover agent.
The Result: Martinez was charged with attempted use of weapons of mass destruction and attempted murder of federal officers. If convicted, he faces life behind bars.

Targeting the Military
October 2010
The Plot: Farooque Ahmed, a U.S. citizen born in Pakistan, planned on detonating several bombs in the Washington, D.C., Metro subway system to "kill as many military personnel as possible."
How Far It Got: Ahmed, who lived in nearby Ashland, Virginia, spent six months casing Metro stations around the Pentagon, headquarters of the U.S. Department of Defense. Ahmed also met several times with undercover federal agents disguised as al Qaeda operatives to discuss possible contributions to worldwide *jihad*.
The Result: Ahmed was charged with attempting to provide material support to a foreign terrorist organization and planning a terrorist attack on a transit facility. If found guilty, he could spend fifty years in prison.

"Prevent first, prosecute second."

Terrorism Camp
July 2009
The Plot: A group of North Carolinians, apparently led by a man named Patrick Boyd, prepared to travel to the Middle East to wage "holy war" against the United States and its allies.
How Far It Got: Boyd ran a kind of terrorist training camp on private property in rural Caswell County, North Carolina, training his charges in the use of Kalashnikov AK-47 rifles and other weapons used in various Middle East conflicts. Four of the suspects planned to "meet up" in Israel to begin their violent *jihad*.
The Result: In February 2011, Boyd pleaded guilty to charges of conspiring to provide support to terrorists and conspiring to murder, kidnap, maim, and injure potential victims. He could be sentenced to a lifetime in prison for his crimes.

John Clines/iStockphoto.com/Radius Images/Jupiterimages

Members of a hazardous material team wear protective suits as they respond to an anthrax scare in Centennial, Colorado. Why are these emergency personnel called *first responders?* What role do first responders play in homeland security? (John Moore/Getty Images/iStockphoto.com)

EMERGENCY PREPAREDNESS AND RESPONSE

The White House defines **preparedness** as the "existence of plans, procedures, policies, training, and equipment necessary at the federal, state, and local level to maximize the ability to prevent, respond to, and recover from major events."[45] The term has come to describe a wide variety of actions taken at different governmental levels to protect a community not only against terrorist attacks but also against natural disasters such as hurricanes, tornadoes, and floods. The Oakland County (Michigan) Emergency Operations Center, for example, combines the contributions of thirty-four different local agencies, each one organized and prepared for a different type of emergency.

A necessary correlate to preparedness is *response*, or the actions taken after an incident has occurred. Because the federal government is usually unable to respond rapidly to any single incident, the burden of response initially falls on local emergency personnel such as police officers, firefighters, and emergency medical technicians. These aptly named **first responders** have several important duties, including the following:

- Securing the scene of the incident by maintaining order.
- Rescuing and treating any injured civilians.
- Containing and suppressing fires or other hazardous conditions that have resulted from the incident.
- Retrieving those who have been killed.[46]

First responders often show great bravery in carrying out their duties under extremely dangerous circumstances. On September 11, 2001, 343 firefighters and 75 police officers were killed in the line of duty.

¿WHAT ARE THE MAIN ISSUES IN BORDER SECURITY?

In its final report on the events that led up to September 11, 2001, the 9/11 Commission had plenty of blame to spread around. Poor preparation for a terrorist attack, poor performances by the FBI and other domestic law enforcement agencies, and poor intelligence gathering by the CIA were all highlighted as causes for concern and needed reform.

The commission seemed particularly disturbed, however, at the ease with which proved and potential terrorists could enter the United States. "Protecting borders was not a national security issue before 9/11," the report remarked, with more than a hint of disbelief.[47] The protection of our national borders has certainly become an issue since the commission published its report, though questions remain as to whether homeland security has significantly improved as a result.

REGULATED POINTS OF ENTRY

People and goods legally enter the United States through checkpoints at airports, seaports, and guarded land stations. At these regulated points of entry, government agents check documents such as passports and *visas* and inspect luggage and cargo to ensure compliance with immigration and trade laws. (A **visa** is a document issued by the U.S. State Department that indicates the conditions under which a holder can enter and travel within the United States.) The task is immense: close to 90 million foreign visitors arrive at America's more than one hundred international airports each year, with millions more passing through patrol stations along our borders with Mexico and Canada. (CAREER TIP: Millions of immigrants—both legal and illegal—rely on *immigration lawyers* to defend their rights and help them navigate the extremely complex world of immigration law.)

CAREERPREP

CUSTOMS AND BORDER PROTECTION AGENT

JOB DESCRIPTION:

- Ensure that laws are observed when goods and people enter the United States. Work at ports of entry and along the U.S. borders with Canada and Mexico to prevent smuggling and the entrance of illegal aliens.
- Conduct surveillance along the border using electronic sensors, infrared scopes, low-light television systems, and aircraft.

WHAT KIND OF TRAINING IS REQUIRED?

- Be fluent in Spanish or be able to learn the Spanish language.
- Pass a thorough background investigation, medical examination, fitness test, and drug test.

ANNUAL SALARY RANGE?

- $36,600–$46,500

For additional information, visit: www.cbp.gov.

(AP Photo/Roswell Daily Record, Andrew Poertner)

Increased Scrutiny

One of the hard lessons of the September 11 attacks was that regulation of points of entry does not ensure security. Every one of the nineteen hijackers involved in those attacks entered the United States legally—that is, with a valid visa. They were also able to easily board the airplanes that they used as flying bombs. Consequently, one of the hallmarks of homeland security has been increased scrutiny at points of entry—particularly airports. The DHS Transportation Security Administration (TSA) has overseen significant changes in the way airports screen passengers, luggage, and cargo. Border personnel, both at home and abroad, have been trained to look for "terrorist risk factors" for all foreigners entering the United States. The FBI's Terrorist Screening Center has also created a "No Fly" list of individuals who are deemed to pose a risk of terrorist activity and therefore are not allowed to board flights leaving or entering the United States.

Visa Official authorization allowing a person to travel to and within the issuing country.

Success and Failure Sometimes port-of-entry strategies succeed, and sometimes they fail. Two of the risk factors mentioned in the previous section are the purchase of a one-way plane ticket with cash and a failure to check any luggage for long flights. These behavior patterns may indicate that a traveler wishes to keep his or her identity hidden and that he or she may have no plans for a return flight. One troubling aspect of the "Christmas bomber" case that was discussed previously in this chapter is that Umar Abdulmutallab followed this pattern exactly and was still allowed to board Northwest Flight 253 in Amsterdam and fly to Detroit. At the same time, Faisal Shahzad, the attempted Times Square bomber, would have successfully fled the country had his name not been on the No Fly list, allowing federal agents to arrest him while his airplane destined for the Middle East was still at the gate in New York.[48]

The U.S. Border Patrol's unmanned aerial vehicle (UAV) uses thermal and night-vision equipment to detect illegal immigrants trying to sneak into the United States. Why is technology like the UAV so important to the Border Patrol's efforts? (AP Photo/John Miller)

UNREGULATED BORDER ENTRY

Every year about 300,000 non-U.S. citizens, unable to legally secure visas, enter the country *illegally* by crossing the large, unregulated stretches of our borders with Mexico and Canada. Securing these border areas has proved problematic, if not impossible, for the various homeland security agencies. As a result, the border areas provide a conduit for illegal drugs, firearms and other contraband, **illegal immigrants**, and, possibly, terrorists and WMDs to be smuggled into the country.

The main problem for the U.S. Border Patrol and local law enforcement agents in trying to stem this flow is logistics. The U.S.-Canadian border extends for 3,957 miles (not counting Alaska), and the border with Mexico stretches for 1,954 miles. Much of the borderland consists of uninhabited plains and woodland to the north and desert and scrubland to the south. To compensate, the homeland security presence on the Mexican border has never been greater. In September 2011, approximately 21,000 Border Patrol agents were monitoring the area, up from 9,000 in 2001.

Even with this small army of agents and physical barriers such as checkpoint stations, barbed-wire fences, and roadblocks in the most populous areas, effectively policing this

Illegal Immigrant A person who has entered the United States without passing through customs and immigration controls, and therefore has no legal right to be in the country.

immense expanse of land is nearly impossible. The crime surge on the border fueled by the drug war in Mexico, discussed earlier in this textbook, is putting further pressure on law enforcement and homeland security resources. An estimated 90 percent of the illegal drugs that enter the United States come from Mexico, and an estimated 90 percent of the weapons seized at crime scenes in Mexico come from the United States.[49] As of 2011, however, no high-level terrorist suspects are known to have taken an illegal land route into the United States.

¿HOW DO WE BALANCE HOMELAND SECURITY AND CIVIL LIBERTIES?

After Faisal Shahzad was arrested for attempting to detonate a bomb in New York's Times Square, he was interviewed by federal law enforcement agents without being read his *Miranda* rights. The officers were able to do so under an exception to the rules of interrogation, which we learned about in Chapter 7, that applies when public safety is believed to be at risk. After investigators determined there was no such threat, they did read Shahzad his rights to remain silent and then continued the interrogation.

Even this cautious approach angered many, including Republican senator John McCain of Arizona. "When we detain terrorism suspects, our top priority should be finding out what intelligence they have that could prevent future attacks and save American lives," he said. "Our priority should not be telling them they have a right to remain silent."[50]

The challenge of protecting personal freedoms in the era of homeland security requires difficult decisions. Magistrate Judge H. Kenneth Schroeder, Jr., who oversaw the trial of six young "wannabe" terrorists in Lackawanna, New York, several years ago, said he spent "some pretty restless, sleepless nights" trying to "balance the rights of the people of the community to be safe and the rights of the defendants."[51] As we have seen throughout this textbook, the need to balance the rights of society and the rights of the individual is a constant in the criminal justice system. As we will see in this section, nowhere is this challenge more fraught with difficulty than in the struggle against terrorism.

SEARCHES, SURVEILLANCE, AND SECURITY

The Fourth Amendment protects against unreasonable searches and seizures. According to the United States Supreme Court, the purpose of this amendment is to "prevent arbitrary and oppressive interference by enforcement officials with the privacy and personal security of individuals."[52] In practice, this has meant that a "neutral and detached" judge must, in most circumstances, decide whether a search or surveillance of a suspect's person or property is warranted. Law enforcement has often chafed against these restrictions, and this tension has only been exacerbated by the demands of counterterrorism search and surveillance strategies.

The Patriot Act and Searches

The case of Zacarias Moussaoui is "Exhibit A" for those who feel that the Fourth Amendment, as interpreted by the courts, is incompatible with homeland security. During the summer of 2001, FBI agents in Minnesota arrested Moussaoui for immigration violations and sought a warrant to search his apartment and laptop computer. Because their superiors felt the agents had not established Moussaoui's involvement in terrorist activities, they refused to ask a judge for the necessary search warrant until after the September 11 attacks. (For a review of these procedures, see pages 128–130.) According to a congressional report, the information on Moussaoui's computer would have helped provide a "veritable blueprint for 9/11."[53]

Addressing these concerns, several sections of the Patriot Act make it easier for law enforcement **LO5** agents to conduct searches. Previously, to search a suspect's apartment and examine the contents of his or her computer, they needed a court order based on probable cause that a crime had taken place or was about to take place. The Patriot Act amends the law to allow the FBI or other federal agencies to obtain warrants for

"terrorism" investigations, "chemical weapons" investigations, or "computer fraud and abuse" investigations as long as agents can prove that such actions have a "significant purpose."[54] In other words, no proof of criminal activity need be provided.

The Patriot Act and Surveillance Even before September 11, 2001, the Foreign Intelligence Surveillance Act of 1978 (FISA) had made it easier for intelligence agents to practice surveillance. Under FISA, the Foreign Intelligence Surveillance Court (FISC) would issue a warrant (technically known as a "special court order") without probable cause as long as the "primary purpose" of the surveillance was to investigate foreign espionage and not to engage in criminal law enforcement.[55]

Gene Chutka/iStockphoto.com

CAREERPREP

TRANSPORTATION SECURITY OFFICER

JOB DESCRIPTION:

- Protect the public by preventing any deadly or dangerous objects from being carried onto an aircraft, boat, train, or other public transit vehicle.

- Implement security-screening procedures of passengers, baggage, and cargo.

WHAT KIND OF TRAINING IS REQUIRED?

- Must be able to repeatedly lift and carry up to seventy pounds and maintain focus and awareness within a stressful work environment.

- Must meet job-related medical standards and pass a background investigation.

ANNUAL SALARY RANGE?

- $28,600–$67,000

For additional information, visit:
www.tsa.gov/join/index.shtm.

The Patriot Act gives federal agents even more leeway. It amends FISA to allow for searches and surveillance if a "significant purpose" of the investigation is intelligence gathering or any other type of antiterrorist activity.[56] The statute also provides federal agents with "roving surveillance authority," allowing them to continue monitoring a terrorist suspect on the strength of the original warrant even if the suspect moves to another jurisdiction.[57] Furthermore, the Patriot Act makes it much easier for law enforcement agents to avoid the notification requirements of search warrants, meaning that a person whose home has been the target of a search and whose voice mails or computer records have been seized may not be informed of these activities until weeks after they have taken place.[58]

Following a series of controversies concerning the ability of the NSA to monitor telephone and e-mail communications of terrorism suspects, several years ago Congress passed an amended version of FISA.[59] The new law allows the NSA to wiretap for seven days any person "reasonably believed" to be outside the United States, without a court order if necessary to protect national security. It also permits the wiretapping of Americans for seven days without a court order if the attorney general has probable cause to believe that the target is linked to terrorism.

Privacy versus Security

As far as many members of the general public are concerned, the most intrusive searches in the name of homeland security are taking place at airports. Complaints focus on body scanners, which enable screeners to see passengers' bodies underneath their clothing, and aggressive pat-downs, which include checking areas such as the groin and breasts for signs of explosives or weapons. The backlash against such techniques was neatly captured in a 2010 YouTube video of a traveler named John Tyner refusing a pat-down while telling TSA employees, "You touch my junk, and I'm going to have you arrested!"

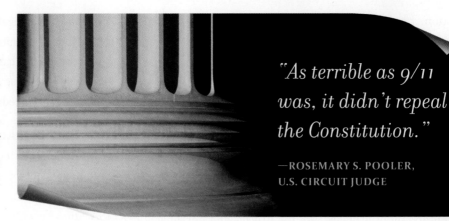

"As terrible as 9/11 was, it didn't repeal the Constitution."

—ROSEMARY S. POOLER, U.S. CIRCUIT JUDGE

Comstock Images/Jupiterimages

Necessary Intrusions

Despite the threat of airline passenger boycotts and lawsuits, federal officials insist that the security measures are necessary. "We know through intelligence that there are . . . terrorists who are trying to kill not only Americans but innocent people around the world," warns John Pistole, head of the TSA.[60] In particular, the measures are designed to detect an explosive powder called PETN, which was sewn into the underwear of Umar Abdulmutallab as he boarded Flight 253 for Detroit on December 25, 2009. PETN was also packed by al Qaeda operatives into computer printer cartridges and shipped to Chicago in October 2010. A white powder, PETN does not trigger metal detector alarms and is easily hidden, and only a small amount is needed to cause a serious explosion. With the body scanners and pat-down searches, security personnel hope to detect the devices needed to detonate PETN, which are more difficult to conceal.[61]

Terrorist Profiling

Criticizing the more invasive security measures at airports, Jason Chaffetz, a Republican congressman from Utah, said, "We don't need to look at naked eight-year-olds and grandmothers to secure airplanes."[62] Who do we "need to look at," then? Polls have found that a relatively high percentage of Americans favor using Muslim identity as a trigger for government surveillance and preflight boarding interrogations.[63] Indeed, when collecting domestic intelligence, FBI agents are permitted to use race or religion as a factor—though not the only factor—in choosing targets for security.[64]

These strategies raise concerns of racial and cultural profiling. In Chapter 7, you learned that because of the Fourth Amendment, law enforcement agents cannot

CJ and Technology

FUTURE ATTRIBUTE SCREEN TECHNOLOGY

In the aftermath of Umar Farouk Abdulmutallab's unsuccessful in-air bombing attempt over Detroit, security expert Philip Baum criticized America's general approach to screening airline passengers as "outdated" and insufficient to "respond to the threats of the 21st century." With funding from the Department of Homeland Security, one private company is doing its best to remedy the situation with a project called Future Attribute Screening Technology, or FAST. The goal of the technology is to track involuntary physiological reactions that characterize someone boarding an

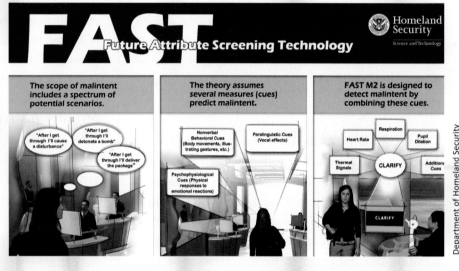

airplane with evil intent. As the subject answers a dozen questions, FAST employs several different sensors to search for "tip-offs" in the responses. An eye tracker notes gaze direction, blinks, and pupil dilation. A thermal camera measures the way heat changes on the face. Two separate devices track respiration and pulse rate. FAST can even detect fidgeting with a ground-level accessory normally used with the Nintendo Wii gaming system. Although it is unlikely that passengers will be subjected to FAST's methods anytime soon, the system's manufacturer does plan to start field testing the process by 2012.

THINKING ABOUT FUTURE ATTRIBUTE SCREEN TECHNOLOGY

What is your opinion of FAST as a viable new screening technology? What problems do you foresee with FAST, even if it works as advertised?

---

legitimately stop a suspect unless they have a reasonable suspicion of illegal behavior. Is a person's race or religion ever sufficient to create reasonable suspicion? The question has yet to be directly addressed by American courts in the context of homeland security. As the polls cited earlier show, however, because of the connection between Islamic extremists and international terrorism, the public does seem somewhat comfortable discriminating against Muslims based on their religious beliefs. For its part, the American Muslim community expects the federal government to protect its members against such attitudes. "We're not asking for special

treatment, just equal treatment," said Agha Saeed of the Council of American-Islamic Relations.[65]

DUE PROCESS AND INDEFINITE DETENTION

The Fifth Amendment provides that no *person* shall be deprived of life, liberty, or property without due process of law. (See pages 78–79 for a review of due process.) More than a century ago, the United States Supreme Court ruled that, because the amendment uses the word *person* and not *citizen*, due process protections extend

Military Tribunal
A court that is operated by the military rather than the criminal justice system and is presided over by military officers rather than judges. Often, the tribunals operate in secrecy and do not provide the suspect with the full range of constitutional protections.

to non-U.S. citizens under the jurisdiction of the U.S. government.[66]

Immediately after the September 11, 2001, attacks, however, the Office of the U.S. Attorney General set forth regulations that allowed homeland security officials to detain aliens of "special interest" without first charging them with any crime. The new rules also allowed for the indefinite detention of such non-U.S. citizens in the event of "emergency or other extraordinary circumstance."[67]

The GTMO Dilemma About eight hundred of these detainees were eventually transferred to a U.S. military detention center at the U.S. Naval Base in Guantánamo Bay, Cuba (GTMO), where, by 2011, about 170 remained (see the photo below). The detainees have been denied access to legal representation or contact with family members and subjected to harsh interrogation tactics such as waterboarding, sleep and food deprivation, physical stress positions, and isolation.[68] As a result of conditions at GTMO, the U.S. government has come under a great deal of international criticism, particularly from Arab and Muslim countries.

Meanwhile, members of the American legal community pointed out that those held at GTMO were being deprived of their liberty without being charged with a crime and without access to legal representation. Consequently, the administration of President

Barack Obama has stated, at various times, its preference that GTMO eventually be closed down.

Court Battles The primary challenge in closing GTMO is finding a way to disperse its remaining detainees without risking the safety of the American public. Many of the prisoners participated in significant terrorist incidents, including the September 11 attacks, and homeland security officials still believe they pose a threat. Furthermore, about one in seven of the detainees released from GTMO returned, or are suspected of having returned, to terrorist activity.[69] One former prisoner, Said Ali al-Shihri became the deputy leader of al Qaeda operations in Yemen.[70]

Military Justice For those who remain incarcerated at GTMO, the Obama administration would appear to have two options: provide them with a trial either in civilian criminal court or before a *military tribunal*. In a civilian court on U.S. soil, the detainees would enjoy all of the rights available to any criminal defendant, as described in Chapter 10.

By contrast, **military tribunals**, located at GTMO, offer a more limited set of protections. In these tribunals, the accused do not have the right to a trial by jury, as guaranteed by the Sixth Amendment. Instead, a panel of at least five military commissioners acts in the place of judge and jury and decides questions of both "fact

What have been some of the criticisms of the U.S. military detention center for terrorist suspects (such as these, in orange jumpsuits) at the U.S. Naval Base in Guantánamo Bay, Cuba? (Reuters NewMedia, Inc./ Corbis/iStockphoto.com)

Assistant U.S. Attorney Nicholas Lewin, foreground, gives his opening statement to the jury in the trial of Ahmed Khalfan Ghailani, left, in New York. Why did the verdict in this trial disappoint some observers?
(AP Photo/Elizabeth Williams)

and law." Only two-thirds of the panel members need to agree for a conviction, in contrast to the unanimous jury required by criminal trials. Furthermore, evidence that would be inadmissible in criminal court, such as some forms of hearsay testimony (see page 190), is allowed before these tribunals.[71]

Criticism of civilian criminal courts as too lenient for terrorist suspects increased following the 2010 trial of Ahmed Ghailani. A federal jury in New York acquitted Ghailani of all but 1 of more than 280 charges of conspiracy and murder related to his participation in the 1998 bombings of U.S. embassies in Kenya and Tanzania. During the trial, Judge Lewis A. Kaplan barred prosecutors from presenting certain strong evidence against Ghailani because it had been obtained via intense coercion by CIA agents. According to Republican senator Mitch McConnell of Kentucky, the Ghailani verdict "is all the proof we need that the administration's approach to prosecuting terrorists has been deeply misguided and indeed potentially harmful as a matter of national security" (see the courtroom sketch above).[72]

Political Pressure Ultimately, in early 2011, Judge Kaplan sentenced Ahmed Ghailani to life in prison for the one count of conspiracy to destroy govern-

ment property—the same sentence he would have received had he been found guilty on all the charges. Furthermore, as supporters of civilian trials point out, since September 11, 2001, civilian courts have resolved more than four hundred terrorism cases. In contrast, only five cases have been resolved by military tribunals, and two of those detainees were eventually set free.[73]

The Obama administration prefers trying GTMO detainees in civilian court. This preference, however, has been stymied by political realities. In 2010, the government was forced to abandon efforts to try self-described 9/11 mastermind Khalid Shaikh Mohammed and four other high-level terrorist suspects in a Manhattan federal court because of worries that the trial would place the citizens of New York in danger.[74] Fifteen months later, the federal government announced that Mohammed and his four alleged co-conspirators would appear before military tribunals after all. As of August 2011, no date had been set for these proceedings.[75] In addition, the Obama administration has identified at least forty GTMO detainees who will not be given any kind of trial because they are too dangerous to risk release.[76] Thus, despite any plans to the contrary, GTMO looks likely to remain open and operational for the foreseeable future.

17

CYBER CRIME AND THE FUTURE OF CRIMINAL JUSTICE

Learning Outcomes

After studying this chapter, you will be able to . . .

LO1 Distinguish cyber crime from "traditional" crime.

LO2 Explain the differences between cyberstalking and cyberbullying.

LO3 Describe the three following forms of malware: (a) botnets, (b) worms, and (c) viruses.

LO4 Explain how the Internet has contributed to the piracy of intellectual property.

LO5 Outline the three major reasons why the Internet is conducive to the dissemination of child pornography.

A Tragic End

Nobody involved could comment on the events that led to the death of eighteen-year-old Tyler Clementi, but a series of electronic messages tell the sad story well enough. On September 19, 2010, Dharun Ravi, Clementi's roommate at New Jersey's Rutgers University, tweeted that Clementi "asked for room until midnight. I went into Molly's room and turned on my webcam. I saw him making out with a dude. Yay." "Molly" was Molly Wei, another Rutgers student. Clementi quickly discovered that Ravi had set up a laptop video to spy on him, and he mused about how to respond. "Revenge never ends well for me, as much as I would have loved to pour pink paint all over [Ravi's] stuff," Clementi posted on a chat site. Later, Clementi found Ravi's laptop camera again aimed at his bed. Humiliated, he made one last posting on Facebook: "Jumping off the GW bridge sorry."

On September 22, Clementi did jump more than two hundred feet from the George Washington Bridge into the Hudson River, killing himself. Afterward, some observers called for officials to charge Ravi and Wei with a hate crime, which involves a criminal act committed specifically because of—in this case—the victim's sexual orientation. "Does anyone really think that this would have happened if [Clementi had been] with someone of the opposite sex?" asked Steven Goldstein of Garden State Equality, a gay rights organization. Others wanted the two charged with manslaughter, given that their callous actions led directly to Clementi's death. New Jersey law enforcement officials, however, could not determine that Ravi and Wei had intended to physically harm Clementi. Consequently, manslaughter was not an option. Instead, a grand jury indicted Ravi for fifteen lesser crimes, including invasion of privacy, and for acting with unlawful bias. In addition, Wei agreed to cooperate with prosecutors, who dropped all criminal charges against her. "Sometimes the laws don't always adequately address the situation," said Middlesex County prosecutor Bruce Kaplan.

Dharun Ravi, center right, is seen during his hearing in the webcam-spying case involving the suicide of Rutgers University student Tyler Clementi. (AP Photo/Julio Cortez)

David McGlynn/Getty Images

Computer Crime Any wrongful act that is directed against computers and computer parts or that involves wrongful use or abuse of computers or software.

Cyber Crime A crime that occurs online, in the virtual community of the Internet.

In the eyes of many, Dharun Ravi and Molly Wei shared the blame for causing Tyler Clementi's suicide with a third "player"—the Internet. According to the Associated Press, since 2003 at least twelve young people between the ages of eleven and eighteen, including Clementi, have killed themselves after have been teased, harassed, or intimidated via text message or online.[1] "Just as an assault rifle facilitates mass murder," wrote one commentator, "the Internet facilitates mass character assassination."[2] At the least, it seemed obvious that technology provided Ravi and Wei with both the means to secretly record Clementi's private behavior and the false sense of anonymity that allowed them to think they could get away with it.

In this final chapter of the textbook, we will examine the various types of crimes that take place in cyberspace and the efforts of law enforcement agencies to combat them. We will also look at private methods of fighting such crimes—just as technology provides opportunities for wrongdoers, it also provides individuals with the means to better protect themselves. Finally, we will explore the impact that the virtual explosion of technological advances has had on the criminal justice system and consider how these developments will affect the immediate future of law enforcement.

¿WHAT IS COMPUTER CRIME?

The U.S. Department of Justice broadly defines **computer crime** as "any violation of criminal law that involves a knowledge of computer technology for [its] perpetration, investigation, or prosecution."[3] More specifically, computer crimes can be divided into three categories, according to the computer's role in the particular criminal act:

1. The computer is the *object* of a crime, such as when the computer itself or its software is stolen.

2. The computer is the *subject* of a crime, just as a house is the subject of a burglary. This type of computer crime occurs, for example, when someone "breaks into" a computer to steal personal information such as a credit-card number.

3. The computer is the *instrument* of a crime, as when Dharun Ravi and Molly Wei used a computer to invade Tyler Clementi's privacy.[4]

A number of the white-collar crimes discussed in Chapter 1, such as fraud, embezzlement, and the theft of intellectual property, are now committed with the aid of computers and are thus considered computer crimes.

CYBER CRIME

In this chapter, we will be using a broader term, **cyber crime**, to describe any criminal activity occurring via a computer in the virtual community of the Internet. It is very difficult, if not impossible, to determine how much cyber crime actually takes place. Often, people never know that they have been the victims of this type of criminal activity. Furthermore, businesses sometimes fail to report such crimes for fear of losing customer confidence. Nonetheless, the Internet Crime Complaint Center (IC3), operated as a partnership between the Federal Bureau of Investigation (FBI) and the National White Collar Crime Center, receives more

"You know, you can do this just as easily online."

than 335,000 complaints annually.[5] Furthermore, the United States appears to have gained the unwanted distinction of being the world's leader in cyber crime: 19 percent of all global computer attacks originate in this country, and America is the target of nearly one-quarter of all illegal Internet activity.[6]

OPPORTUNITY AND ANONYMITY

Many experts believe that Internet-enabled crime is going to increase dramatically in the near future.[7] These predictions are based on several trends, in particular the growth in the number of potential victims of cyber crime. As the price of computer technology has dropped, its presence in daily life has surged. Nearly three-fourths of all American households now own a computer, and the proliferation of handheld Internet devices will only increase the amount of personal information stored online. Furthermore, nearly every business in today's economy relies on computers both to conduct its daily affairs and to gain easy access to consumers through *e-commerce* (buying and selling that take place in cyberspace).

In short, the Internet has become a place where large numbers of people interact socially and commercially. As in any such environment, crime has the opportunity to flourish. Until relatively recently, only individuals with a certain level of technological savvy were able to take advantage of this environment. Today,

however, even relative novices can carry out a variety of cyber crimes. The **anonymity** provided by the Internet also opens up a wealth of criminal possibilities, particularly for young people, who are on an equal footing with adults in cyberspace. Increased criminal activity on the Internet could have a number of serious consequences, including reduced confidence in online security, reduction in e-commerce, and, as we shall see later in the chapter, a marked increase in child pornography.

Anonymity The condition of not being recognized or having a traceable name or identity.

¿WHAT ARE THE MOST COMMON CYBER CRIMES AGAINST PERSONS AND PROPERTY?

LO 1 Most cyber crimes are not "new" crimes. Rather, they are existing crimes in which the Internet is the instrument of wrongdoing. In March 2010, for example, a religious fanatic named Norman Leboon made a YouTube video in which Leboon threatened to kill U.S congressman Eric Cantor, a Republican from Virginia, and Cantor's family. Federal authorities charged Leboon with communicating threats in interstate commerce, the same charge that would have been filed if Leboon had used a telephone or even the mail to make his menacing remarks. The challenge for law enforcement is to apply traditional laws, which were designed to protect persons from physical harm or to safeguard their physical property, to crimes committed in cyberspace. Here, we look at several types of activity that constitute "updated" crimes against persons and property—online consumer fraud, cyber theft, cyberstalking, and cyberbullying.

CYBER CONSUMER FRAUD

The expanding world of e-commerce has created many benefits for consumers. It has also led to some challenging problems, including fraud conducted via the

Internet. In general, fraud is any misrepresentation knowingly made with the intention of deceiving another and on which a reasonable person would and does rely to her or his detriment. **Cyber fraud**, then, is fraud committed over the Internet.

Scams that were once conducted solely by mail or phone can now be found online, and new technology has led to increasingly more creative ways to commit fraud. Several years ago, for example, online advertisements featuring adorable photos of "free" English bulldog puppies began appearing on the Internet. A number of respondents paid close to $1,000 in "shipping fees" (from West Africa), "customs costs," "health insurance," and other bogus charges before realizing that no puppy would be forthcoming.

As you can see in Figure 17.1 below, two widely reported forms of cyber crime are *online retail fraud* and *online auction fraud*. In the simplest form of online retail fraud, consumers order and pay for items that are never delivered. About a decade ago, for example, Virginian Jeremy Jaynes was grossing more than $75,000 per week selling nonexistent or worthless products such as "penny stock pickers" and Internet history erasers.

By the time he was arrested in 2003, he had amassed an estimated $24 million from various fraudulent schemes. Online auction fraud is also fairly simple in its basic form. A person puts up an item for auction, on either a legitimate or fake auction site, and then refuses to send the product after receiving payment. Or, as a variation, the wrongdoer may provide the purchaser with an item that is worth less than the one offered in the auction. (CAREER TIP: Online auc-

tion companies hire *Internet fraud investigators* to ensure the authenticity of their services. In some instances, investigators must travel to countries with a reputation for harboring cyber criminals, such as Romania, Russia, and Ukraine. "The fraudsters need to know we're coming after them," says the head of eBay's Trust and Safety Division.)

CYBER THEFT

In cyberspace, thieves are not subject to the physical limitations of the "real" world. A thief can steal data stored in a networked computer with network access from anywhere on the globe. Only the speed of the connection and the thief's computer equipment limit the quantity of data that can be stolen.

Identity Theft This freedom has led to a marked increase in **identity theft**, which occurs when the wrongdoer steals a form of identification—such as a name, date of birth, or Social Security number—and uses the information to access the victim's financial resources. This crime existed to a certain extent before widespread use of the Internet. Thieves would "steal" calling-card numbers by watching people using public telephones, or they would rifle through garbage to find bank account or credit-card numbers. The identity thief would then use the calling-card or credit-card number or withdraw funds from the victim's account until the theft was discovered.

The Internet has provided even easier access to personal data. Frequent Web surfers surrender a wealth of information about themselves without knowing it. Many Web sites use "cookies" to collect data on those who visit their sites. The data can include the areas of the site the user visits and the links the user clicks on.

Furthermore, Web browsers often store information such as the consumer's name and e-mail address. Finally,

Figure 17.1   Criminal Activities Online

In 2009, the Internet Crime Complaint Center (IC3) received about 335,000 complaints of online criminal behavior. As the graph shows, many of these complaints involved fraudulent behavior relating to e-commerce.

Other crimes 19%
Retail fraud 20%
Spam 4%
Computer damage 8%
Scams/confidence fraud 15%
Auction fraud 10%
Identity theft 14%
Credit/debit card fraud 10%

Source: National White Collar Crime Center and Federal Bureau of Investigation, *Internet Crime Report: 2009* (Washington, D.C.: Internet Crime Complaint Center, March 2010), Figure 5, page 6.

every time a purchase is made online, the item is linked to the purchaser's name, allowing Web retailers to amass a database of who is buying what.

As many consumers are discovering, any information that can be collected can be stolen. In 2010, about 8 million Americans reported being victims of identity fraud.[8]

Phishing A distinct form of identity theft known as **phishing** has added a different wrinkle to the practice. In a phishing attack, the perpetrators "fish" for financial data and passwords from consumers by posing as a legitimate business such as a bank or credit-card company. The "phisher" sends an e-mail asking the recipient to "update" or "confirm" vital information, often with the threat that an account or some other service will be discontinued if the information is not provided. Once the unsuspecting target enters the information, the phisher can use it to masquerade as the person or to drain his or her bank or credit account.

In 2010, dozens of companies, including Amazon.com, AT&T, and Zappos.com, were forced to warn consumers that recent e-mails they had supposedly sent out asking for personal and financial information were fraudulent. Government agencies can be misused as well. That same year, a bogus e-mail purporting to be from the Internal Revenue Service asked for Social Security and credit-card numbers to help clarify information contained in recent tax returns.

Phishing scams have also spread to other areas, such as text messaging and social-networking sites. Nearly 13 percent of all phishing, for example, takes place using Facebook alerts.[9] Although the true incidence of phishing is probably incalculable, one study estimates that about 3.6 million adults lose $3.2 billion to these tactics every year.[10]

> **Phishing** The sending of an unsolicited e-mail, falsely claiming to be from a legitimate organization, in an attempt to acquire sensitive information such as passwords or credit card details from the recipient.

CYBER AGGRESSION AND THE NEW MEDIA

Several years ago, Megan Meier of Dardenne Prairie, Missouri, killed herself after being taunted online by a neighbor's mother pretending to be a teenage boy. The suicide was a watershed moment in the way many people perceived the danger of the Internet. Even though the mother, Lori Drew, was eventually cleared of any wrongdoing, public outrage surrounding the case led nearly twenty states to pass new laws criminalizing aggressive behavior perpetrated through technology. For the most part, these laws focus on *cyberstalking* and *cyberbullying*, both of which are examples of common offline behavior that has been exacerbated by e-mail, social networking, instant and text messaging, and the generally far reach of the Internet.

Cyberstalking Several years ago, the U.S. Department of Justice released a landmark study that shed light on the high incidence of stalking in the United States. Defined as a "credible threat" that puts a person in reasonable

" *REPLY to My e-MAIL or YOU WiLL DiE.*"

—E-MAIL MESSAGE SENT BY A MALE UNIVERSITY OF SAN DIEGO UNDERGRADUATE TO A FEMALE CLASSMATE

Nina Malyna/iStockphoto.com

Cyberstalking The crime of stalking, committed in cyberspace through the use of e-mail or another form of electronic communication.

Cyberbullying Willful and repeated emotional harm inflicted through the use of electronic devices such as computers and cell phones.

fear for her or his safety or the safety of the person's immediate family, stalking, according to the study, affects approximately 3.4 million Americans each year.[11] About one in four of these victims experiences a form of **cyberstalking**, in which the perpetrator uses e-mail, text messaging, or some other form of electronic communication to carry out his or her harassment.[12]

The only limitations on a cyberstalker's methods are technological savvy and imagination. He or she may send threatening e-mail messages directly to the victim or menace the victim in a live chat room. Recently, social-networking sites such as Facebook have become particularly tempting for online stalkers. In 2010, for example, Travis Allen Davis of New Castle, Indiana, created a fake Facebook profile with the name of an ex-girlfriend. Using this falsified account, Davis, pretending to be the ex-girlfriend, contacted *another* of his ex-girlfriends and threatened to post images of the second girlfriend having sex with Davis online if she did not resume her relationship with him. Davis was charged with stalking, among other crimes. That same year, David Brandt of Colonie, New York, used Facebook to meet four underage girls and convince them to have sex with him. In 2011, Brandt pleaded guilty to four counts of statutory rape.

Cyberbullying In a recent poll conducted by Larry D. Rosen, a professor at California State University at Dominguez Hills, 83 percent of the parents surveyed said they were concerned about sexual predators on the Internet.[13] Although such fears are understandable, research suggests that the greatest threats to children and teenagers on the Internet are other children and teenagers, not adult pedophiles.[14] As one expert puts it, "Sure, there are crazy sexual predators out there. But the most common problem is kids being mean to each other."[15]

The legal term for "kids being mean to each other" is **cyberbullying**, which occurs when a person repeatedly uses computers, cell phones, or other electronic devices to inflict willful and repeated emotional harm. According to

the Cyberbullying Research Center, one in five American middle and high school students have either been the target of cyerbullying or have cyberbullied others.[16]

As we saw in our discussion of the subject that opened this chapter, it is difficult to determine when cyberbullying rises to the level of crime and, indeed, how to stop it. The forty-four state laws that specifically target this behavior have had little, if any, measurable impact. Many of these laws rely on school administrators to design antibullying measures, but most of the electronic communications that are involved originate outside school grounds and during the weekend, when students have the most free time.[17]

On January 14, 2010, Phoebe Prince hung herself following three months of harassment by classmates at South Hadley High School in South Hadley, Massachusetts, including Facebook postings calling her an "Irish bitch"[18] (see the photo below). Six different defendants were charged with crimes ranging from criminal harassment to stalking, but no charges

What punishment, if any, do you feel is appropriate for Ashley Longe, left, Flannery Mullins, center, Sharon C. Velazquez, right, and the other defendants who used the Internet to bully Phoebe Prince? (AP Photo/Michael S. Gordon, Pool, File)

specifically relating to cyberbullying were available to prosecutors.

¿WHAT ARE THE MOST COMMON CYBER CRIMES IN THE BUSINESS WORLD?

Just as cyberspace can be a dangerous place for consumers, it presents a number of hazards for businesses that wish to offer their services on the Internet. The same circumstances that enable companies to reach a wide number of consumers also leave them vulnerable to cyber crime.

CREDIT-CARD CRIME ON THE WEB

In the previous section, we mentioned credit-card theft in connection with identity theft. An important point to note, however, is that stolen credit cards are much more likely to hurt merchants than the consumer from whom the card or card number has been stolen. In most situations, the legitimate holders of credit cards are not held responsible for the costs of purchases made with a stolen number. That means the financial burden must be borne either by the merchant or by the credit-card company. Almost all of these companies require merchants to cover the costs—especially if the address to which the goods are sent does not match the billing address of the credit card.

Companies take further risks by storing their customers' credit-card numbers. In doing so, companies provide quicker service for the consumer, who can make a purchase by providing a code or clicking on a particular icon without entering the lengthy card number. These electronic warehouses, however, are quite tempting to cyber thieves. In January 2011, the Chinese version of eBay (taobao.com) began selling access codes to tens of thousands of iTunes accounts. The listings promised unlimited downloads for a twenty-four-hour period, with all the costs to be paid by unsuspecting account holders.[19]

HACKERS

The offenders who "broke into" iTunes' database to steal the account numbers were *hackers*. A **hacker** is someone who uses one computer to illegally access another. The danger posed by hackers has increased significantly because of **botnets,** or networks of computers that have been appropriated by hackers without the knowledge of their owners. A hacker will secretly install a program on thousands, if not millions, of personal computer "robots," or "bots," that allows him or her to forward transmissions to an even larger number of systems. The program attaches itself to the host computer when someone operating the computer opens a fraudulent e-mail. The Zeus Trojan, or Zbot, for example, uses a technique called *keystroke logging* to embed itself in a victim's computer and then record user names and passwords. Using this "banking Trojan," cyberthieves stole $4 million from American bank accounts in 2010.[20]

 LO3

Malware Programs that create botnets are one of the latest forms of *malware*, a term that refers to any program that is harmful to a computer or, by extension, a computer user. A **worm**, for example, is a software program that is capable of reproducing itself as it spreads from one computer to the next. A **virus**, another form of malware, is also able to reproduce itself, but it must be attached to an "infested" host file to travel from one computer network to another. Worms and viruses can be programmed to perform a number of functions, such as prompting host computers to continually crash and reboot, or otherwise infect the system.

On any given day in 2010, the Koobface worm infected 500,000 computers in the United States, spreading through social-networking outlets such as Facebook, MySpace, and Twitter.[21] The Koobface

Hacker A person who uses one computer to break into another.

Botnet A network of computers that have been appropriated without the knowledge of their owners and used to spread harmful programs via the Internet.

Worm A computer program that can automatically replicate itself over a network such as the Internet and interfere with the normal use of a computer.

Virus A self-replicating software program that attaches itself to a host file to move from one computer to the next.

worm allows its creators to steal usernames and passwords, along with any other personal or financial data entered in the affected computer.

The Scope of the Problem

Hackers who create worms and viruses are often romanticized as high-tech rebels. After Max R. Vision pleaded guilty in June 2009 to two counts of wire fraud for stealing 2 million credit-card numbers, his defense attorney called Vision a "hacker's hacker" who stole information "because he could."[22] In fact, these criminals cause considerable damage. Every day, as many as 60,000 malicious programs circulate on the Internet. David Jevans, chairman of the Anti-Phishing Working Group, estimates that American businesses lose up to $1 billion a year because of malware and other cyber crime.[23]

Furthermore, as technology advances, so do opportunities to hack into that technology. In Chapter 13, we discussed how radio frequency identification (RFID) chips might be used to track inmates. These chips are becoming commonplace on items such as passports and credit cards, allowing either government or business agencies quick and easy access to embedded information such as Social Security or bank account numbers. As it turns out, RFID chips are fairly easy to hack—by connecting an antenna to an RFID reader, available for less than $200, one can "skim" the data on RFID chips at a distance of twenty feet.[24]

THE SPREAD OF SPAM

Businesses and individuals alike are targets of **spam**, or unsolicited "junk e-mails" that flood virtual mailboxes with advertisements, solicitations, and other messages. Considered relatively harmless in the early days of the Internet, by 2010 nearly 300 billion spam messages were being sent each day, accounting for about 97 percent of all e-mails. Far from being harmless, the unwanted files can wreak havoc with computer systems. Bot networks, described earlier, are responsible for about 90 percent of spam e-mail.[25] To help this situation, in 2003 Congress passed the Controlling the

Assault of Non-Solicited Pornography and Marketing Act (CAN-SPAM), which requires all unsolicited e-mails to be labeled and to include opt-out provisions and the sender's physical address.[26] In December 2010, federal authorities in Wisconsin charged Oleg Y. Nikolaenko for violating CAN-SPAM. According to prosecutors, the twenty-three-year-old Russian used botnets to send out one of every three unwanted e-mails in the world. It seems that the prosecution and incarceration of spammers such as Nikolaenko have had some effect. According to Cisco Systems, an Internet security company, the amount of spam on the World Wide Web declined for the first time in 2010.[27]

A further explanation for this trend may be the increased use of mobile devices at the expense of personal computers, which are easier—so far—for cyber criminals to target.[28] (**CAREER TIP:** *Computer programmers* create antispam software to protect consumers and businesses from the negative effects of spam and other malware.)

PIRATING INTELLECTUAL PROPERTY ONLINE

Most people think of wealth in terms of houses, land, cars, stocks, and bonds. Wealth, however, also includes **intellectual property**, which consists of the products that result from intellectual, creative processes. The government provides various forms of protection for intellectual property, such as copyrights and patents. These protections ensure that a person who writes a book or a song or creates a software program is financially rewarded if that product is sold in the marketplace.

Intellectual property such as books, films, music, and software is vulnerable to piracy—the unauthorized copying and use of the property. In the past, copying intellectual products was time consuming, and the quality of the pirated copies was clearly inferior. In today's online world, however, things have changed. Simply clicking a mouse can now reproduce millions of unauthorized copies, and pirated duplicates of copyrighted works obtained via the Internet are often exactly the same as the original, or close to it.

The Business Software Alliance estimates that 43 percent of all business software is pirated, costing software makers more than $54 billion in 2009.[29] In the United States, digital pirates can be prosecuted under

Money Laundering The introduction of illegally gained funds into the legal financial system with the goal of covering up the funds' true origin.

the No Electronic Theft Act[30] and the Digital Millennium Copyright Act.[31] In 2005, the entertainment industry celebrated the United States Supreme Court's decision in *MGM Studios v. Grokster*.[32] The ruling provided film and music companies with the ability to file piracy lawsuits against Internet file-sharing Web sites that market software used primarily to illegally download intellectual property. In the near future, however, such "peer-to-peer" transmission may be the least of the entertainment industry's problems. With the advent of Internet TV and "cyberlocker" Web sites that store illegal content for computer viewing on demand, some industry insiders predict that these streaming pirate sites will surpass peer-to-peer use by 2013.[33]

ELECTRONIC BANKING AND ONLINE MONEY LAUNDERING

Few industries have benefited from the convenience of online operation more than the banking industry.

"The argument that I hear a lot, that 'music should be free,' must then mean that musicians should work for free. Nobody else works for free. Why should musicians?"

—DRUMMER LARS ULRICH OF THE ROCK GROUP METALLICA, TESTIFYING BEFORE CONGRESS ON THE ILLEGAL DOWNLOADING OF MUSIC

Cyberspace connections have allowed banks to transfer more funds in less time and to provide customers with more transfer and withdrawal options.

Cleaning Dirty Money With increased speed and efficiency, however, banks have lost a certain measure of control over the funds that pass through their computer systems. Bank officials have less information about where the funds are coming from or where they are headed. This blind spot has made online banking fertile ground for **money laundering**. Tax evaders, drug traffickers, and other criminals seek to "launder" their "dirty" money by moving it through as many bank accounts in as many countries as possible. In the past, uncovering money laundering was much easier for law enforcement agencies because large sums of cash had to be physically transported, often across international borders. Today, when transfers can be completed with the touch of a button, the criminals have the advantage.

U.S. law does require that banks "know their customers"—that is, a bank is required to know the source of a customer's funds.[34] The statute is clearly outdated, however, stemming from a time when bank officials enjoyed face-to-face relations with their clients. Banks can now use software filters to monitor the wire systems for suspicious transfers, but the filters are costly and may slow down legitimate transfers, thereby negating many of the benefits offered by cyber banking.

Cyber "Money Mules" When cyber criminals want to take their money-laundering operations one step further and avoid legitimate banks altogether, they can make use of cyber "money mules." These individuals are called mules because they do nothing more than "carry" stolen funds. For example, suppose that a hacker uses one of the methods described earlier in the chapter to steal $15,000 from several online bank accounts. He or she will quickly transfer the $15,000

CJ and Technology

SEXTING

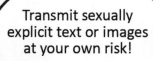

Transmit sexually explicit text or images at your own risk!

Until several years ago, *sexting* wasn't even a word. Now it's a crime, though the term isn't found in any criminal code. Generally defined as sending or receiving sexually explicit photos using a cell phone or computer, sexting is being prosecuted as a form of child pornography across the United States. In Iowa, eighteen-year-old Jorge Canal was convicted of distributing obscene materials to a minor after sending a picture of his genitals to a fourteen-year-old female friend. In New Jersey, a fourteen-year-old girl was arrested and charged with possession of child pornography after posting suggestive photos of herself on Myspace. Millions of teenagers run the risk of similar treatment under child pornography laws that ban the electronic transmission of sexually explicit images—a recent survey found that one in four has engaged in sexting. "Child pornography law was crafted to protect children from pedophiles," notes Amy Adler, a law professor at New York University. "But now what we have is the law applying to situations where the child him or herself is making the pornography."

THINKING ABOUT SEXTING

Florida lawmakers have proposed a bill that would treat sexting as a noncriminal offense, requiring only that the offender pay a small fine and perform community service. Do you agree that sexters should be treated leniently, or is sexting criminal behavior that should be punished accordingly? Explain your answer.

to a legitimate bank account owned by a mule, usually someone with no other connection to cyber crime who is paid a small percentage of the total amount as a fee. The mule then withdraws the stolen funds and sends them to a third party associated with the original hacker. In 2010, the FBI was working on 250 such money mule cases, involving hundreds of millions of dollars.[35]

¿HOW DOES THE INTERNET PROMOTE PORNOGRAPHY AND GAMBLING?

One of the greatest challenges cyberspace presents for law enforcement is how to enforce laws governing activities that are prohibited under certain circumstances but are not always illegal. Such laws generally reflect the will of the community, which recognizes behavior as acceptable under some circumstances and unacceptable under others. Thus, while it is legal in many areas to sell a pornographic video to a fifty-year-old, it is never legal to sell the same item to a fifteen-year-old. Similarly, placing a bet on a football game with a bookmaker in Las Vegas, Nevada, is legal, but doing the same thing with a bookmaker in Cleveland, Ohio, is not. Of course, in cyberspace it is often impossible to know whether the customer buying porn is aged fifty or fifteen, or if the person placing the bet is in Las Vegas or Cleveland.

ONLINE PORNOGRAPHY

The Internet has been a boon to the pornography industry. Twelve percent of all Web sites have pornographic content, and these sites generate $4.2 billion in revenue a year.[36] Although no general figures are available, the Internet has undoubtedly also been a boon to those who illegally produce and sell material depicting sexually

© Onur Döngel/iStockphoto.com

LO5 explicit conduct involving children, known as child pornography. As we have seen with other cyber crimes, the Internet is conducive to child pornography for a number of reasons:

- *Speed.* The Internet is the fastest means of sending visual material over long distances. Child pornographers can deliver their material faster and more securely online than through regular mail.

- *Security.* Any illegal material that is placed in the hands of a mail carrier is inherently in danger of being discovered. This risk is significantly reduced with e-mail. Furthermore, Internet sites that offer child pornography can protect their customers with passwords, which keep random Web surfers (or law enforcement agents) from stumbling on the sites of chat rooms.

- *Anonymity.* Obviously, anonymity is the most important protection offered by the Internet for sellers and buyers of child pornography, as it is for any person engaged in illegal behavior in cyberspace.[37]

Because of these three factors, courts and lawmakers have had a difficult time controlling the dissemination via the Internet of illegal sexual content that involves minors.

Even though it is technically illegal, more than 10 million Americans, including this one, regularly play online poker. What are the arguments for and against cracking down on gambling on the Internet?
(Rich Frishman/Getty Images/
Sports Illustrated/Bart Sadowski/
iStockphoto.com)

GAMBLING IN CYBERSPACE

Gambling Wagering on an event with an uncertain outcome by offering funds and/or material goods in the hope of winning additional funds and/or material goods.

In general, *gambling* is illegal. All states have statutes that regulate **gambling**—defined as any scheme that involves the distribution of property by chance among persons who have paid some amount for the opportunity to receive the property. In some states, certain forms of gambling, such as casino gambling or horse racing, are legal. Many states also have legalized state-operated lotteries, as well as lotteries, such as bingo, conducted for charitable purposes. A number of states also allow gambling on Native American reservations.

In the past, this mixed bag of gambling laws has presented a legal quandary: Can citizens in a state that does not allow gambling place bets to a Web site located in a state that does? After all, states have no constitutional authority over activities that take place in other states. Complicating the problem was the fact that many Internet gambling sites are located outside the United States, in countries where Internet gambling is legal, and no state government has authority over activities that take place in other countries. In 2006, Congress, concerned about money laundering stemming from online gambling, the problem of addiction, and underage gambling, passed legislation that greatly strengthened efforts to reduce online gaming. The Unlawful Internet Gambling Enforcement Act of 2006 cuts off the money flow to Internet gambling sites by barring the use of electronic payments, such as credit-card transactions, at those sites.[38]

¿WHAT ARE THE BEST STRATEGIES FOR FIGHTING CYBER CRIME?

Simply passing a law does not guarantee that the law will be effectively enforced. While the Unlawful Internet Gambling Enforcement Act may reduce visible Internet gambling, few believe that it will stop the practice altogether. "Prohibitions don't work," says Michael Bolcerek, president of the Poker Player's Alliance. "This [legislation] won't stop anything. It will just drive people underground."[39] In fact, despite the efforts of lawmakers and law enforcement, the United States represents the largest online betting market in the world, with some $6 billion illegally wagered each year.[40]

As we have already seen in this chapter, the Internet provides an ideal environment for the "underground" of society. With hundreds of millions of users reaching every corner of the globe, transferring unimaginable amounts of information almost instantaneously, the Internet has proved resistant to government regulation. In addition, although a number of countries have tried to "control" the Internet, the U.S. government has generally adopted a hands-off attitude to better promote the free flow of ideas and encourage the growth of electronic commerce. Thus, in this country cyberspace is, for the most part, unregulated, making efforts to fight cyber crime all the more difficult.

CAREERPREP — COMPUTER FORENSIC SPECIALIST

JOB DESCRIPTION:

- Investigate misbehavior on computer systems by collecting and analyzing computer-related evidence. Retrieve data that have been encrypted or electronically stored on a commercial or personal computer.
- Work for a law enforcement or homeland security agency to investigate crimes or terrorists' activities, or for a private company to protect commercial data and defend against worms, viruses, and other malware.

WHAT KIND OF TRAINING IS REQUIRED?

- An extensive knowledge of computers, computer programming, and data retrieval is essential. A number of colleges, universities, and online educational organizations offer computer forensic courses that provide the skills necessary for this career.
- A complete understanding of the rules of evidence in criminal courts and the ability to establish a proper chain of custody for all evidence retrieved from targeted computer databases.

ANNUAL SALARY RANGE?

- $50,000–$85,000

For additional information, visit: computer-forensics.sans.org.

ryasick/iStockphoto.com

ON THE CYBER BEAT: CHALLENGES FOR LAW ENFORCEMENT

In trying to describe the complexities of fighting cyber crime, Michael Vatis, former director of the FBI's National Infrastructure Protection Center, imagines a bank robbery during which the police arrive just as "the demand note and fingerprints are vanishing, the security camera is erasing its own images, and the image of the criminal is being erased from the mind of the teller."[41] The difficulty of gathering evidence is just one of the challenges that law enforcement officers face in dealing with cyber crime.

Cyber Forensics Police officers cannot put yellow tape around a computer screen or dust a Web site for fingerprints. The best, and often the only, way to fight computer crime is with technology that gives law enforcement agencies the ability to "track" hackers and other cyber criminals through the Internet. But, as Michael Vatis observed, these efforts are complicated by the fact that digital evidence can be altered or erased even as the cyber crime is being committed. In Chapter 6, we discussed *forensics*, or the application of science to find evidence of criminal activity. Within the past two decades, a branch of this science known as **cyber forensics** has evolved to gather evidence of cyber crimes.

The main goal of cyber forensics is to gather **digital evidence**, or information of value to a criminal investigation that is stored on, received by, or transmitted by an electronic device such as a computer.[42] Experts in cyber forensics often rely on software that retraces a suspect's digital movements. Such software works by creating a digital duplicate of the targeted hard drive, enabling cyber sleuths to break access codes, determine passwords, and search files.[43] "Short of taking your hard drive and having it run over by a Mack truck," says one expert, "you can't be sure that anything is truly deleted from your computer."[44]

Jurisdictional Challenges Regardless of what type of cyber crime is being investigated, law enforcement agencies are often frustrated by problems of jurisdiction (explained more fully in Chapter 8). Jurisdiction is primarily based on physical geography—each country, state, and nation has jurisdiction, or authority, over crimes that occur within its boundaries. The Internet, however, destroys these traditional notions because geographic boundaries simply do not exist in cyberspace.

Domestic Jurisdiction To see how jurisdictional challenges can affect law enforcement efforts, let's consider a hypothetical cyberstalking case. Phil, who lives in State A, has been sending e-mails containing graphic sexual threats to Stephanie, who lives in State B. Where has the crime taken place? Which police department has authority to arrest Phil, and which court system has authority to try him? To further complicate matters, what if State A has not yet added cyberstalking to its criminal code, while State B has? Does that mean that Phil has not committed a crime in his home state, but has committed one in Stephanie's?

Often, federal officials will answer this question by stating that Phil has committed a crime wherever they determine he has. The Sixth Amendment to the U.S. Constitution states that federal criminal cases should be tried in the district in which the offense was committed.[45] Because the Internet is "everywhere," the federal government has a great deal of leeway in choosing the venue in which an alleged cyber criminal will face trial. So, for example, British citizen David Carruthers, whose online gambling company operated out of Costa Rica, was charged for taking sports bets in St. Louis,

> **Cyber Forensics**
> The application of computer technology to finding and utilizing evidence of cyber crimes.
>
> **Digital Evidence**
> Information or data of value to a criminal investigation that is either stored or transmitted by electronic means.

TESTPREP

Identify the easiest questions on the exam and do them first. This will quickly get you in the proper thinking "mode" and enable you to tackle the more difficult questions with confidence.

Missouri, because an Internet user accessed his Web site from that area.

International Jurisdiction Issues of jurisdiction are even more pronounced when it comes to international cyber crime. Several years ago, U.S. officials charged Dimitry Ivanovich Golubov with a wide-ranging series of cyber crimes, including credit-card fraud. Police had recently arrested Golubov in his home country of Ukraine, and the U.S. government began the process of having him transported to the United States for trial. These efforts came to a halt when two high-ranking Ukrainian politicians inexplicably arranged for Golubov's release, an act over which the United States had no control because it lacks jurisdiction in Ukraine.

Federal law enforcement officials have worked to avoid such situations by building relationships with police in other countries. In 2010, for example, FBI agents, in cooperation with colleagues from Great Britain, the Netherlands, and Ukraine, infiltrated a ring of cyber money mules (discussed earlier in the chapter) who operated bank accounts in Estonia, Finland, Russia, Scotland, and the United States. Called Operation Trident Breach, these efforts recovered at least $14 million in stolen funds, mostly from small U.S. businesses.[46] Given the international scope of the Internet, such multinational cooperative investigations are likely to become the rule rather than the exception.

FEDERAL LAW ENFORCEMENT AND CYBER CRIME

Because of its freedom from jurisdictional restraints, the federal government has traditionally taken the lead in law enforcement efforts against cyber crime. This is not to say that little cyber crime prevention occurs on the local level. Most major metropolitan police departments have created special units to fight cyber crime. In general, however, only a handful of local police and sheriffs' departments have the resources to support a squad of cyber investigators.

The Federal Bureau of Investigation As the primary crime-fighting unit of the federal government, the FBI has taken the lead in law enforcement efforts against cyber crime. The FBI has the primary responsibility for enforcing all federal criminal statutes involving computer crimes. In 1998, the Bureau added a Cyber Division dedicated to investigating computer-based crimes. The Cyber Division and its administrators coordinate the FBI's efforts in cyberspace, specifically its investigations into computer crimes and intellectual property theft. The division also has jurisdiction over the Innocent Images National Initiative (IINI), the agency's online child-pornography subdivision.

In addition, the FBI has developed several Cyber Action Teams (CATs), which combine the skills of some twenty-five law enforcement agents, cyber forensics investigators, and computer programming experts.[47] Today, cyber crime is the FBI's third-highest priority (after counterterrorism and counterintelligence), and each of the Bureau's fifty-six field divisions has at least one agent who focuses solely on crimes com-

A special agent with U.S. Immigration and Customs Enforcement (ICE), stands in front of the agency's Cyber Crimes Center in Fairfax, Virginia. Why are federal agencies such as ICE generally better positioned to fight cyber crime than local law enforcement agencies? (Richard Clement/ Reuters/Landov)

mitted on the Internet. (**CAREER TIP:** One *FBI cyber agent* describes the "excitement" in his everyday work as "out-witting and out-thinking [those] who are committing crimes on the Internet." He continues: "They're anonymous online, so the chase is really on when you follow the trail of clues and evidence that ultimately reveals their identity and ties them to the crime.")

The United States Secret Service The Patriot Act greatly increased the Secret Service's role in fighting cyber crime. In the legal arena, the legislation gave the agency jurisdiction over some of the crimes that previously had been the sole responsibility of the FBI.[48] The Secret Service was authorized to develop a national network of electronic crime task forces based on the New York Electronic Crime Task Force, a collaboration among federal, state, and local law enforcement officers and a wide range of corporate sponsors.

PRIVATE EFFORTS TO COMBAT CYBER CRIME

In 2008, Congress passed the Identity Theft Enforcement and Restitution Act, giving federal authorities more power to prosecute those involved in identity theft, phishing, and spam.[49] Nevertheless, the government's ability to protect the integrity of all, or even most, computers and computer users is limited. Hence, the government must rely on the voluntary efforts of the private sector to secure both business and personal computer networks.

Online Security The fear of being hacked has spurred a billion-dollar industry that helps clients— either individuals or corporations—protect the integrity of their computer systems. Because every computer connected to the Internet is a potential security breach, cyber security companies help devise elaborate and ever-changing password systems to ensure that only authorized users can access data. These companies also install protective software and antivirus programs, which can limit outside access to a computer or a network. Such measures are credited with a positive development in one of the more troublesome arenas of cyber crime: according to one Internet security company, the

amount of identity theft in the United States fell 28 percent from 2010 to 2011.[50]

Encryption Perhaps the most successful way to protect computer information is to encrypt it. Through **encryption,** a message (plaintext) is transformed into something (ciphertext) that only the sender and receiver can understand. Unless a third party is able to break the code, the information will stay secure. Encryption is particularly useful in protecting the content of e-mails. The main drawback of this technology is the rate at which it becomes obsolete.

As a general rule, computing power doubles every eighteen months, which means that programs to break the "latest" encryption code are always imminent. Consequently, those who use encryption must ensure that they update their systems at the same rate as those who would abuse it. (**CAREER TIP:** Steganography is the science of secret codes. In the context of computers, it is a security tool that protects important digital information by "hiding" it in larger data files. *Steganographers,* therefore, are experts in the art of Internet confidentiality.)

> **Encryption** The process by which a message is transmitted into a form or code that the sender and receiver intend not to be understandable by third parties.

¿WHAT DOES THE FUTURE HOLD FOR CRIMINAL JUSTICE?

Deborah Norris, a resident of Indianapolis, Indiana, did not like the way her daughter Heather behaved around Joshua Bean, the teenager's boyfriend. "When he would call or text, she had to answer right away or there was trouble," Deborah said. "She became quiet and withdrawn around him, which wasn't like her."[51] After Heather turned twenty, she tried to end the relationship, even going as far as to seek court protection from Bean's attentions. The result: Bean stabbed Heather to death, dismembered her body, and discarded it in trash bags.

Earlier in this chapter, we discussed the prevalence of cyberbullying in the lives of young people. Unfortunately, such harassment sometimes goes beyond the relatively nonviolent forum of the Internet and cell phones. According to a recent survey, about 10 percent of adolescents report being hit or slapped by a romantic partner.[52] Victims of dating abuse are at risk of engaging in a host of self-destructive behaviors, including suicide attempts, binge drinking, and physical fights. Furthermore, they often do not know where to turn for help. "Few adolescents understand what a healthy relationship looks like," says Dr. Elizabeth Miller of the University of California at Davis.[53]

TRENDS FOR THE FUTURE

Throughout this textbook, you have learned about numerous innovations in law enforcement strategies and technology. Certainly, thanks to the Internet, the world of crime and crime control has changed dramatically from what it was even a decade ago. At its heart, however, the criminal justice equation remains a simple one: identify a threat to the community and take the necessary steps to protect the community from that threat. In the wake of Heather Norris's murder, Indianapolis officials started a program to train police officers in public schools to recognize the signs of dating abuse. Within the past few years, a number of states, including

New York, Rhode Island, and Texas, have passed legislation that brings dating abuse to the attention of educators, judges, and law enforcement officials.[54]

Thus, regardless of other changes, *crime fighting* remains the bedrock of criminal justice. Above all, criminal justice professionals are dedicated to reducing the opportunity for crime and apprehending those who have committed crimes. When experts consider the context in which crime fighting will take place over the next several decades, however, they generally point to the following trends:

- *Changing demographics.* By 2040, the proportion of males aged fifteen to twenty-nine—as we discussed in Chapters 3 and 15, the demographic group that commits the most crimes—will decline slightly. In contrast, the percentage of Americans over the age of thirty will increase, and the percentage of Americans over the age of sixty-five will increase dramatically.
- *Technological advances.* Many of the technologies we have discussed in this book, such as biometrics, DNA fingerprinting and analysis, electronic surveillance, and radio frequency identification, will continue to affect crime prevention and crime solving.

Police cadets draw practice weapons during a class at the Idaho Peace Officers Standards and Training Academy in Coeur d'Alene, Idaho. Despite an ever-changing environment, why do basic crime-fighting skills remain the bedrock of the American criminal justice system? (AP Photo/Jerome A. Pollos/ *Coeur d'Alene Press*/ iStockphoto.com)

- *Increasing diversity.* The growing number of foreign-born Americans will lead to even more diversity among criminal justice professionals and criminals, not to mention the general public. What will these immigrants expect of the U.S. criminal justice system? How will they regard the roles of criminal justice professionals such as police officers, judges, and defense attorneys?
- *Globalization of crime.* As we saw in Chapter 16, homeland security concerns have broken down many criminal justice borders. Given that international cooperation is a crucial component in antiterrorism efforts, the transfer of information and expertise between nations will undoubtedly become a hallmark of crime-fighting operations.[55]

YOUR FUTURE IN CRIMINAL JUSTICE

What role will you play in the future of criminal justice? As the CAREERpreps and Career Tips embedded in this textbook have shown, there are hundreds of choices for those interested in making criminal justice their career. Information on dozens of other criminal justice careers is available in the various supplements to this textbook, and, of course, the Internet can provide the answers to most other questions you might have.

In practical terms, the career prospects for those involved in the criminal justice system are excellent. In particular, the U.S. Department of Labor predicts double-digit growth in demand for law enforcement agents through at least 2016. The benefits of this field go beyond salary and job security, however. You will get the satisfaction of helping members of your community live safer lives. To be effective, the criminal justice system depends on well-trained and motivated individuals to serve the best interests of the American people. The authors of this textbook hope that this course has provided you with a strong sense of just how important this service can be. (CAREER TIP: For those of you who do choose to make criminal justice your life's work, you may also decide to help others do the same by becoming a *professor of criminal justice* at some point in your career.)

CAREERPREP — FORENSIC ANIMAL DOCTOR

JOB DESCRIPTION:
- Visit crime scenes and work closely with law enforcement to collect forensic evidence dealing with crimes against animals, such as cruelty or dog fighting.
- Protect evidence so that it is admissible in criminal court and testify in court on behalf of animal victims.

WHAT KIND OF TRAINING IS REQUIRED?
- A bachelor's degree in forensic science, plus training in crime scene investigation.
- A degree in veterinary medicine with a specialty in pathology, along with additional experience in animal cruelty investigation, animal handling, and/or disaster relief work.

ANNUAL SALARY RANGE?
- $50,000–$82,000

For additional information, visit:
www.aspca.org/fight-animal-cruelty.

Willie B. Thomas/iStockphoto.com

ONE APPROACH.
70 UNIQUE SOLUTIONS.

ENDNOTES

CHAPTER 1

1. "College Was on Alert for Giffords' Shooting Suspect," *Associated Press* (February 15, 2011).
2. Quoted in Eileen Sullivan, "Loners Like Tucson Gunman 'Fly Below the Radar,'" *Associated Press* (January 17, 2011).
3. Herman Bianchi, *Justice as Sanctuary: Toward a New System of Crime Control* (Bloomington: Indiana University Press, 1994), 72.
4. "Americans Split on Doctor-Assisted Suicide," *Associated Press* (May 29, 2007).
5. *2010 Report to the Nations: Occupational Fraud and Abuse* (Austin, TX: Association of Certified Fraud Examiners, 2012), 4.
6. President's Commission on Law Enforcement and Administration of Justice, *The Challenge of Crime in a Free Society* (Washington, D.C.: Government Printing Office, 1967), 7.
7. *Gonzales v. Oregon*, 546 U.S. 243 (2006). Many United States Supreme Court cases will be cited in this book, and it is important to understand these citations. *Gonzales v. Oregon* refers to the parties in the case that the Court is reviewing. "U.S." is the abbreviation for *United States Reports,* the official publication of the United States Supreme Court decisions, "546" refers to the volume of the *United States Reports* where the case appears, and "243" refers to the page number. The citation ends with the year the case was decided in parentheses. Most, though not all, Supreme Court case citations in this book will follow this formula.
8. President's Commission on Law Enforcement and Administration of Justice.
9. John Heinz and Peter Manikas, "Networks among Elites in a Local Criminal Justice System," *Law and Society Review* 26 (1992), 831–861.
10. James Q. Wilson, "What to Do about Crime: Blaming Crime on Root Causes," *Vital Speeches* (April 1, 1995), 373.
11. Herbert Packer, *The Limits of the Criminal Sanction* (Stanford, CA: Stanford University Press, 1968), 154–173.
12. *Ibid.*
13. Daniel Givelber, "Meaningless Acquittals, Meaningful Convictions: Do We Reliably Acquit the Innocent?" *Rutgers Law Review* 49 (Summer 1997), 1317.
14. William Yardley, "In Likely Obama Pick, Some Find Hope for Shift in Drug Policy," *New York Times* (February 16, 2009), A13.
15. Lawrence M. Friedman and Robert V. Percival, *The Roots of Justice* (Chapel Hill, NC: University of North Carolina Press, 1981).
16. Packer.
17. *Ibid.*
18. Givelber.
19. Guy-Uriel E. Charles, "Fourth Amendment Accommodations: (Un)-Compelling Public Needs, Balancing Acts, and the Fiction of Consent," *Michigan Journal of Race and Law* (Spring 1997), 461.
20. *Mapp v. Ohio*, 367 U.S. 643 (1961).
21. *Gideon v. Wainwright*, 372 U.S. 335 (1963); and *Miranda v. Arizona*, 384 U.S. 436 (1966).

CHAPTER 2

1. California Civil Code Sections 1746–1746.5 (2009).
2. Petition for Writ of Certiorari at 2, *Schwarzenegger v. Entertainment Merchants Association*, 130 S.Ct. 2398 (2009).
3. Dan Immergluck and Geoff Smith, "The Impact of Single-Family Mortgage Foreclosures on Neighborhood Crime," *Housing Studies* (November 2006), 851–866.
4. *Entertainment Software Association v. Blagojevich*, 404 F.Supp.2d 1078 (N.D. Ill. 2005).
5. James Q. Wilson and Richard J. Hernstein, *Crime and Human Nature: The Definitive Study of the Causes of Crime* (New York: Simon & Schuster, 1985), 515.
6. Jeremy Bentham, *An Introduction to the Principles of Morals and Legislation*, ed. W. Harrison (Oxford: Basil Blackwell, 1948).
7. Wilson and Hernstein, 44.
8. David C. Rowe, *Biology and Crime* (Los Angeles: Roxbury, 2002), 2.
9. Sarnoff A. Mednick and Karl O. Christiansen, eds., *Biosocial Bases in Criminal Behavior* (New York: Gardner Press, 1977).
10. David C. Rowe, "Genetic and Environmental Components of Antisocial Behavior: A Study of 265 Twin Pairs," *Criminology* 24 (1986), 513–532.
11. Raymond R. Crowe, "An Adoption Study of Antisocial Personality," *Archives of General Psychiatry* (1974), 785–791; Sarnoff A. Mednick, William F. Gabrielli, and Barry Hutchings, "Genetic Influences on Criminal Convictions: Evidence from an Adoption Cohort," *Science* (1994), 891–894; and Remi J. Cadoret, "Adoption Studies," *Alcohol Health & Research World* (Summer 1995), 195–201.
12. Gail S. Anderson, *Biological Influences on Criminal Behavior* (Boca Raton, FL: CRC Press, 2007), 105–118.
13. *Ibid.*, 118.
14. L. E. Kreuz and R. M. Rose, "Assessment of Aggressive Behavior and Plasma Testosterone in Young Criminal Population," *Psychosomatic Medicine* 34 (1972), 321–332.
15. H. Persky, K. Smith, and G. Basu, "Relation of Psychological Measures of Aggression and Hostility to Testosterone Production in Men," *Psychosomatic Medicine* 33 (1971), 265, 276.
16. Benjamin J. Sadock, Harold I. Kaplan, and Virginia A. Sadock, *Kaplan & Sadock's Synopsis of Psychiatry* (Philadelphia: Lippincott Williams & Wilkins, 2007), 865.
17. Robert J. Meadows and Julie Kuehnel, *Evil Minds: Understanding and Responding to Violent Predators* (Upper Saddle River, NJ: Pearson Prentice Hall, 2005), 156–157.
18. *Ibid.*, 157, 169.
19. Anderson, 210–216.
20. David G. Myers, *Psychology*, 7th ed. (New York: Worth Publishers, 2004), 576–577.
21. Philip Zimbardo, "Pathology of Imprisonment," *Society* (April 1972), 4–8.
22. David Canter and Laurence Alison, "The Social Psychology of Crime: Groups, Teams, and Networks," in *The Social Psychology of Crime: Groups, Teams, and Networks,* ed. David Canter and Laurence Alison (Hanover, NH: Dartmouth, 2000), 3–4.
23. Robert Park, Ernest Burgess, and Roderic McKenzie, *The City* (Chicago: University of Chicago Press, 1929).
24. Clifford R. Shaw, Henry D. McKay, and Leonard S. Cottrell, *Delinquency Areas* (Chicago: University of Chicago Press, 1929).
25. Clifford R. Shaw and Henry D. McKay, *Report on the Causes of Crime,* vol. 2: *Social Factors in Juvenile Delinquency* (Washington, D.C.: National Commission on Law Observance and Enforcement, 1931).
26. Elijah Anderson, *Code of the Street: Decency, Violence and the Moral Life of the Inner City* (New York: W. W. Norton, 2000), 35–65.
27. *Ibid.*, 180.
28. Karen F. Parker and Amy Reckdenwald, "Concentrated Disadvantage, Traditional Male Role Models and African-American Juvenile Violence," *Criminology* (August 2008), 711–735.
29. Emile Durkheim, *The Rules of Sociological Method,* trans. Sarah A. Solovay and John H. Mueller (New York: Free Press, 1964).
30. Robert K. Merton, *Social Theory and Social Structure* (New York: Free Press, 1957). See the chapter on "Social Structure and Anomie."
31. Philip G. Zimbardo, "The Human Choice: Individuation, Reason, and Order versus Deindividuation, Impulse, and Chaos," in *Nebraska Symposium on Motivation,* ed. William J. Arnold and David Levie (Lincoln, NE: University of Nebraska Press, 1969), 287–293.
32. Edwin H. Sutherland, *Criminology,* 4th ed. (Philadelphia: Lippincott, 1947).
33. Marcia Polansky, Augusta M. Villanueva, and Jeffrey Bonfield, "Responses to Violence Related Questionnaires by Delinquent, Truant, and State-Dependent Boys Receiving Treatment in an Extended Day Program," *Journal of Offender Rehabilitation* 47 (2008), 407, 415–416.
34. Prepared for Kevin Johnson, "For Many of USA's Inmates, Crime Runs in the Family," *USA Today* (January 29, 2008), 1A.
35. L. Rowell Huesmann, Jessica Moise-Titus, Cheryl-Lynn Podolski, and Leonard D. Eron, "Longitudinal Relations between Children's Exposure to TV Violence and Their Aggressive and Violent Behavior in Young Adulthood: 1977–1992," *Developmental Psychology* (March 2003), 201.

36. Telecommunications Act of 1996, 47 U.S.C. Section 303 (1999).

37. Travis Hirschi, *Causes of Delinquency* (Berkeley: University of California Press, 1969).

38. James Q. Wilson and George L. Kelling, "Broken Windows," *Atlantic Monthly* (March 1982), 29.

39. Quoted in Johnson.

40. Howard S. Becker, *Outsiders: Studies in the Sociology of Deviance* (New York: Free Press, 1963).

41. Lawrence L. Shornack, "Conflict Theory and the Family," *International Social Science Review* 62 (1987), 154–157.

42. Robert Meier, "The New Criminology: Continuity in Criminology Theory," *Journal of Criminal Law and Criminology* 67 (1977), 461–469.

43. Richard Quinney, *The Social Reality of Crime* (Boston: Little, Brown, 1970).

44. Carmen DeNavas-Walt, Bernadette D. Proctor, and Jessica C. Smith, *Income, Poverty, and Health Insurance Coverage in the United States: 2009* (Washington, D.C.: U.S. Census Bureau, September 2010), Table 1, page 5.

45. Nicole Hahn Rafter, *Partial Justice: Women, Prisons, and Social Control* (New Brunswick, NJ: Transaction Publishers, 1990).

46. Federal Bureau of Investigation, *Crime in the United States, 2009* (Washington D.C.: U.S. Department of Justice, 2010), at **www2.fbi.gov/ucr/cius2009/data/table_42.html.**

47. The Sentencing Project, at **www.sentencingproject.org/IssueAreaHome.aspx?IssueID=3.**

48. Bureau of Justice Statistics, *Bulletin: Prisoners in 2009* (Washington, D.C.: U.S. Department of Justice, December 2010), 9.

49. Becker.

50. Myers, 75–76.

51. Peter B. Kraska, "The Unmentionable Alternative: The Need for and Argument against the Decriminalization of Drug Laws," in *Drugs, Crime, and the Criminal Justice System,* ed. Ralph Weisheit (Cincinnati, OH: Anderson Publishing, 1990).

52. Bureau of Justice Statistics, *Substance Dependence, Abuse, and Treatment of Jail Inmates, 2002* (Washington, D.C.: U.S. Department of Justice, July 2005), 1.

53. *ADAM II: 2009 Annual Report* (Washington, D.C.: Office of National Drug Control Policy, June 2010), Figure 3.3, page 23.

54. Paul J. Goldstein, "The Drugs/Violence Nexus: A Tripartite Conceptual Framework," *Journal of Drug Issues* 15 (1985), 493–506.

55. James A. Inciardi, *The War on Drugs: Heroin, Cocaine, and Public Policy* (Palo Alto, CA: Mayfield, 1986), 148.

56. *Ibid.,* 106.

57. Quoted in Timothy Egan, "After Seven Deaths, Digging for an Explanation," *New York Times* (June 25, 2006), 12.

58. Marvin Wolfgang, Robert Figlio, and Thorsten Sellin, *Delinquency in a Birth Cohort* (Chicago: University of Chicago Press, 1972).

59. Lawrence W. Sherman, "Attacking Crime: Police and Crime Control," in *Modern Policing,* ed. Michael Tonry and Norval Morris (Chicago: University of Chicago Press, 1992), 159.

60. James Q. Wilson, "What to Do about Crime," *Commentary* (September 1994), 25–34.

61. Sarah J. Hart, "A New Way of Doing Business at the NIJ," *Law Enforcement News* (January 15/31, 2002), 9.

62. John H. Laub, "The Life Course of Criminology in the United States: The American Society of Criminology 2003 Presidential Address," *Criminology* (February 1, 2004), 1.

63. Benedict Carey, "Drug Rehabilitation or Revolving Door?" *New York Times* (December 23, 2008), D1.

64. Richard Rosenfeld, "Book Review: The Limits of Crime Control," *Journal of Criminal Law and Criminology* (Fall 2002).

CHAPTER 3

1. "Serial Murder" at **www.fbi.gov/stats-services/publications/serial-murder/serial-murder-1#two.**

2. Model Penal Code Section 1.04 (2).

3. *Federal Criminal Rules Handbook,* Section 2.1 (West 2008).

4. 625 Illinois Compiled Statutes Annotated Section 5/16-104 (West 2002).

5. Johannes Andenaes, "The Moral or Educative Influence of Criminal Law," *Journal of Social Issues* 27 (Spring 1971), 17, 26.

6. Federal Bureau of Investigation, *Uniform Crime Reporting Handbook* (Washington, D.C.: U.S. Department of Justice, 2004), 74.

7. Federal Bureau of Investigation, *Crime in the United States, 2009* (Washington, D.C.: U.S. Department of Justice, 2010), at **www2.fbi.gov/ucr/cius2009/about/index.html.**

8. *Ibid.*

9. *Ibid.,* at **www2.fbi.gov/ucr/cius2009/data/table_01.html.**

10. Jeffery Reiman, *The Rich Get Richer and the Poor Get Prison,* 4th ed. (Boston: Allyn & Bacon, 1995), 59–60.

11. *Crime in the United States, 2009,* at **www2.fbi.gov/ucr/cius2009/offenses/expanded_information/data/shrtable_10.html.**

12. *Ibid.,* at **www2.fbi.gov/ucr/cius2009/data/table_01.html.**

13. *Ibid.,* at **www2.fbi.gov/ucr/cius2009/data/table_29.html.**

14. Marcus Felson, *Crime in Everyday Life* (Thousand Oaks, CA: Pine Forge Press, 1994), 3.

15. Victor E. Kappeler, Mark Blumberg, and Gary W. Potter, *The Mythology of Crime and Criminal Justice,* 2d ed. (Prospect Heights, IL: Waveland Press, 1993), 31.

16. Franklin E. Zimring, *The Great American Crime Decline* (New York: Oxford University Press, 2007), 45–72.

17. David Garland, *The Culture of Control: Crime and Social Control in Contemporary Society* (Chicago: University of Chicago Press, 2001), 12–14.

18. James Q. Wilson, *Thinking about Crime* (New York: Basic Books, 1974), 12.

19. Howard N. Snyder and Melissa Sickmund, *Juvenile Offenders and Victims: A National Report* (Washington, D.C.: Office of Juvenile Justice and Delinquency Prevention, August 1995), 104–105.

20. Delbert S. Elliot and Scott Menard, "Delinquent Friends and Delinquent Behavior: Temporal Development Patterns," in Rolf Loeber and David P. Farrington, eds., *Delinquency and Crime: Current Theories* (Thousand Oaks, CA: Sage Publications, 1996), 47–66.

21. Bill McCarthy, "New Economics of Sociological Criminology," *Annual Review of Sociology* 28 (August 2002), 417, 426.

22. Zimring, 63.

23. Alfred Blumstein and Joel Wallman, eds., *The Crime Drop in America* (New York: Cambridge University Press, 2000), 39.

24. *Ibid.*

25. Northwest High Intensity Drug Trafficking Area Program, *Methamphetamine and Related Crime: The Impacts of Methamphetamine Abuse* (Washington, D.C.: Office of National Drug Control Policy, March 2006), 6, 10.

26. James Q. Wilson, "Concluding Essay in Crime," in James Q. Wilson and Joan Petersilia, eds., *Crime* (San Francisco: Institute for Contemporary Studies Press, 1995), 507.

27. John DiIulio, *How to Stop the Coming Crime Wave* (New York: Manhattan Institute, 1996), 4.

28. James A. Fox, *Trends in Juvenile Violence* (Boston: Northeastern University Press, 1996), 1.

29. Zimring, 6.

30. *Ibid.,* 197–198.

31. *Ibid.,* 82.

32. Quoted in Pete Yost, "Violent Crime Falls for Third Straight Year," *San Jose Mercury News* (September 15, 2010), 2B.

33. James A. Fox and Marc L. Swatt, *The Recent Surge in Homicides Involving Young Black Males and Guns: Time to Reinvest in Prevention and Crime Control* (December 2008), 2, at **www.jfox.neu.edu/Documents/Fox%20Swatt%20Homicide%20Report%20Dec%2029%202008.pdf.**

34. Quoted in Erik Eckholm, "Murders by Black Teenagers Rise This Decade, Bucking a Trend," *New York Times* (December 29, 2008), A12.

35. *Crime in the United States, 2009,* at **www2.fbi.gov/ucr/cius2009/data/table_43.html.**

36. *Targeting Blacks: Drug Law Enforcement and Race in the United States* (New York: Human Rights Watch, May 2008), 3.

37. Robert M. A. Johnson, "Racial Bias in the Criminal Justice System and Why We Should Care," *Criminal Justice* (Winter 2007), 1.

38. Robert J. Sampson, Jeffrey Morenoff, and Stephen W. Raudenbush, "Social Anatomy of Racial and Ethnic Disparities in Violence," *American Journal of Public Health* 95 (2005), 224–232.

39. Eric A. Stewart, Ronald L. Simons, and Rand D. Donger, "Assessing Neighborhood and Social Psychological Influence on Childhood Violence in an African American Sample," *Criminology* (November 2002), 801–829.

40. William A. Pridemore, "A Methodological Addition to the Cross-National Empirical Literature on Social Structure and Homicide: A First Test of the Poverty-Homicide Thesis," *Criminology* (February 2008), 133.

41. Caroline Wolf Harlow, *Education and Correctional Populations* (Washington, D.C.: Bureau of Justice Statistics, January 2003), 1.

42. Charles Tittle and Robert Meier, "Specifying the SES/Delinquency Relationship," *Criminology* 28 (1990), 270–301.

43. Mark Hugo Lopez and Michael T. Light, *A Rising Share: Hispanics and Federal Crime* (Washington, D.C.: Pew Hispanic Center, February 2009), i–iv.

44. Sampson, Morenoff, and Raudenbush, 231.

45. See **www.ojp.usdoj.gov/bjs/homicide/content/gender.htm.**

46. Bureau of Justice Statistics, *Jail Inmates at Midyear 2009—Statistical Tables* (Washington, D.C.: U.S. Department of Justice, June 2010), Table 6, page 9; Bureau of Justice Statistics, *Prison Inmates at Midyear 2009—Statistical Tables* (Washington, D.C.: U.S. Department of Justice, June 2010), Table 1, page 4; and *Crime in the United States, 2009*, at **www2.fbi.gov/ucr/cius2009/arrests/index.html.**

47. Bureau of Justice Statistics, *Prisoners in 2009* (Washington, D.C.: U.S. Department of Justice, December 2010), Table 1, page 2.

48. Jennifer Schwartz and Bryan D. Rookey, "The Narrowing Gender Gap in Arrests: Assessing Competing Explanations Using Self-Report, Traffic Fatality, and Official Data on Drunk Driving, 1980–2004," *Criminology* (August 2008), 637–638.

49. Quoted in Barry Yeoman, "Violent Tendencies: Crime by Women Has Skyrocketed in Recent Years," *Chicago Tribune* (March 15, 2000), 3.

50. *Crime in the United States, 2009*, at **www2.fbi.gov/ucr/cius2009/data/table_42.html.**

51. Schwarz and Rookey, 637–671.

52. Meda Chesney-Lind, "Patriarchy, Prisons, and Jails: A Critical Look at Trends in Women's Incarceration," *Prison Journal* (Spring/Summer 1991), 57.

CHAPTER 4

1. Quoted in DeeDee Correll, "Sweat Lodge Guru Is Held in 3 Deaths," *Los Angeles Times* (February 4, 2010), 1.

2. Arizona Revised Statutes, Section 31–1103(A)(1).

3. *Texas v. Johnson*, 491 U.S. 397 (1989).

4. "Ariz. Voters OK Medical-Marijuana Bill," *Boston Globe* (November 15, 2010), 2.

5. Clean Water Act Section 309.33 U.S.C.A. Section 1319 (1987).

6. Joel Feinberg, *The Moral Limits of the Criminal Law: Harm to Others* (New York: Oxford University Press, 1984), 221–232.

7. Flammable Fabrics Act, 15 U.S.C. Section 1196 (1994).

8. Henry M. Hart, Jr., "The Aims of the Criminal Law," *Law & Contemporary Problems* 23 (1958), 405–406.

9. John L. Diamond, "The Myth of Morality and Fault in Criminal Law Doctrine," *American Criminal Law Review* 34 (Fall 1996), 111.

10. Lawrence M. Friedman, *Crime and Punishment in American History* (New York: Basic Books, 1993), 34.

11. *Ibid.*, 10.

12. Thomas A. Mullen, "Rule without Reason: Requiring Independent Proof of the *Corpus Delicti* as a Condition of Admitting Extrajudicial Confession," *University of San Francisco Law Review* 27 (1993), 385.

13. *Hawkins v. State*, 219 Ind. 116, 129, 37 N.E.2d 79 (1941).

14. David C. Biggs, "'The Good Samaritan Is Packing': An Overview of the Broadened Duty to Aid Your Fellowman, with the Modern Desire to Possess Concealed Weapons," *University of Dayton Law Review* 22 (Winter 1997), 225.

15. Rhode Island General Laws Section 11-56-1 (1956); Vermont Statutes Annotated Title 12, Section 519 (2000); and Wisconsin Statutes Section 940.34 (West 2000).

16. Model Penal Code Section 2.02.

17. Texas Penal Code Section 46.13 (1995).

18. Model Penal Code Section 2.02(c).

19. Bryan A. Gardner, *Black's Law Dictionary*, 7th ed., (St. Paul, MN: West Publishing, Co., 1999), 1423.

20. *United States v. Dotterweich*, 320 U.S. 277 (1943).

21. New Jersey Statutes Annotated Section 2C:35-9 (West 2004).

22. *State v. Stiffler*, 763 P.2d 308, 311 (Idaho Ct. App. 1988).

23. *State v. Harrison*, 425 A.2d 111 (1979).

24. Richard G. Singer and John Q. LaFond, *Criminal Law: Examples and Explanations* (New York: Aspen Law & Business, 1997), 322.

25. *State v. Linscott*, 520 A.2d 1067 (1987).

26. Adam Liptak, "Serving Life for Providing Car to Killers," *New York Times* (December 4, 2007), A1.

27. *Morissette v. United States*, 342 U.S. 246, 251–252 (1952).

28. Federal Bank Robbery Act, 18 U.S.C.A. Section 2113.

29. New York Penal Law Sections 485.05–485.10 (2005).

30. *United States v. Jiminez Recio*, 537 U.S. 270 (2003).

31. Paul H. Robinson, *Criminal Law Defenses* (St. Paul, MN: West, 2008), Section 173, Ch. 5B1.

32. *M'Naghten's Case*, 10 Cl.&F. 200, Eng.Rep. 718 (1843). Note that the name is also spelled M'Naughten and McNaughten.

33. Model Penal Code Section 401 (1952).

34. Joshua Dressler, *Cases and Materials on Criminal Law*, 2d ed. (St. Paul, MN: West Group, 1999), 599.

35. Diane Jennings, "Killer's Case Fuels Debate on Texas' Insanity Defense Law," *Dallas Morning News* (April 11, 2009), A1.

36. Lawrence P. Tiffany and Mary Tiffany, "Nosologic Objections to the Criminal Defense of Pathological Intoxication: What Do the Doubters Doubt?" *International Journal of Law and Psychiatry* 13 (1990), 49.

37. Kenneth W. Simons, "Mistake and Impossibility, Law and Fact, and Culpability: A Speculative Essay," *Journal of Criminal Law and Criminology* 81 (1990), 447.

38. *United States v. Robinson*, 119 F.3d 1205 (5th Cir. 1997).

39. *Lambert v. California*, 335 U.S. 225 (1957).

40. Federal Bureau of Investigation, *Crime in the United States, 2009* (Washington, D.C.: U.S. Department of Justice, 2010), at **www2.fbi.gov/ucr/cius2009/offenses/expanded_information/data/shrtable_14.html**, and **www2.fbi.gov/ucr/cius2009/offenses/expanded_information/data/shrtable_15.html**.

41. Craig L. Carr, "Duress and Criminal Responsibility," *Law and Philosophy* 10 (1990), 161.

42. *United States v. May*, 727 F.2d 764 (1984).

43. *People v. Murillo*, 587 N.E.2d 1199, 1204 (Ill. Ct. App. 1992).

44. "Court Rejects 'Necessity' Defense in DUI Case," *Anchorage (Alaska) Daily News* (February 8, 2009), A10.

45. John Frank, "Hit-Run Driver Acquitted," *St. Petersburg (Fla.) Times* (February 4, 2009), 1B.

46. *People v. Petro*, 56 P.2d 984 (Cal. App. Ct. 1936); and *Regina v. Dudley and Stephens*, 14 Q.B.D. 173 (1884).

47. Fred Warren Bennett, "From *Sorrells* to *Jacobson*: Reflections on Six Decades of Entrapment Law and Related Defenses in Federal Court," *Wake Forest Law Review* 27 (1992), 829.

48. Henry J. Abraham, *Freedom and the Court: Civil Liberties in the United States*, 7th ed. (New York: Oxford University Press, 1998), 38–41.

49. *Skinner v. Switzer*, 131 S.Ct. 1289 (2011).

50. *Skinner v. Oklahoma*, 316 U.S. 535, 546–547 (1942).

CHAPTER 5

1. Egon Bittner, *The Functions of Police in a Modern Society*, Public Health Service Publication No. 2059 (Chevy Chase, MD: National Institute of Mental Health, 1970), 38–44.

2. Carl Klockars, "The Rhetoric of Community Policing," in *Community Policing: Rhetoric or Reality*, ed. Jack Greene and Stephen Mastrofski (New York: Praeger Publishers, 1991), 244.

3. Jack R. Greene and Carl B. Klockars, "What Do Police Do?" in *Thinking about Police*, 2d ed., ed. Carl B. Klockars and Stephen B. Mastrofski (New York: McGraw-Hill, 1991), 273–284.

4. John S. Dempsey and Linda S. Forst, *An Introduction to Policing*, 3d ed. (Belmont, CA: Thomson Wadsworth, 2005), 110.

5. Federal Bureau of Investigation, *Crime in the United States, 2009* (Washington, D.C.: U.S. Department of Justice, 2010), at **www2.fbi.gov/ucr/cius2009/data/table_29.html**.

6. Reprinted in *Police Chief* (January 1990), 18.

7. Eric J. Scott, *Calls for Service: Citizen Demand and Initial Police Response* (Washington, D.C.: U.S. Government Printing Office, 1981), 28–30.

8. Jerome H. Skolnick, "Police: The New Professionals," *New Society* (September 5, 1986), 9–11.

9. James Q. Wilson, "Looking for Crime's Smoking Gun," *Los Angeles Times* (January 8, 2009), 17.

10. Klockars, 250.

11. James Q. Wilson, *Varieties of Police Behavior: The Management of Law and Order in Eight Communities* (Cambridge, MA: Harvard University Press, 1968).

12. *Crime in the United States, 2009*, at **www2.fbi.gov/ucr/cius2009/data/table_74.html**.

13. *Ibid.*, at **www2.fbi.gov/ucr/cius2009/police/index.html**.

14. Bureau of Justice Statistics, *Local Police Departments, 2007* (Washington, D.C.: U.S. Department of Justice, December 2010), Table 3, page 9.

15. G. Robert Blakey, "Federal Criminal Law," *Hastings Law Journal* 46 (April 1995), 1175.

16. Vern L. Folley, *American Law Enforcement* (Boston: Allyn & Bacon, 1980), 228.

17. Bureau of Justice Statistics, *Sheriffs' Offices, 2003* (Washington, D.C.: U.S. Department of Justice, May 2006).

18. *Ibid.*, 15–18.

19. Bureau of Justice Statistics, *Sheriffs' Departments, 1997* (Washington, D.C.: U.S. Department of Justice, February 2000), 14.

20. Bureau of Justice Statistics, *Medical Examiners and Coroners' Offices, 2004* (Washington, D.C.: U.S. Department of Justice, June 2007), 1.

21. Robert Borkenstein, "Police: State Police," *Encyclopedia of Crime and Justice,* ed. Sanford H. Kadish (New York: Free Press, 1983), 1131.

22. Bureau of Justice Statistics, *Federal Law Enforcement Officers, 2004* (Washington, D.C.: U.S. Department of Justice, July 2006), 1.

23. Pub. L. No. 107-296, 116 Stat. 2135.

24. "Securing America's Borders: CBP Fiscal Year 2009 in Review Fact Sheet," at **www.cbp.gov/xp/cgov/newsroom/news_releases/archives/2009_news_releases/nov_09/11242009_5.xml**.

25. *U.S. Department of Homeland Security FY 2009 Annual Financial Report* (Washington, D.C.: U.S. Department of Homeland Security, 2010), 12.

26. Nick Miroff and William Booth, "Mexico's Marines Team with U.S. DEA," at **www.washingtonpost.com/wp-dyn/content/article/2010/12/03/AR2010120307106.html**.

27. *Private Security Services* (The Freedonia Group, November 2010), 15.

28. John B. Owens, "Westec Story: Gated Communities and the Fourth Amendment," *American Criminal Law Review* (Spring 1997), 1138.

29. California Penal Code Section 837 (West 1995).

30. Bruce L. Benson, "Guns, Crime, and Safety," *Journal of Law and Economics* (October 2001), 725.

31. "Private Protective Services: Armed Security Officer/Guard Requirements," at **state.tn.us/commerce/boards/pps/asgoReqs.shtml**.

32. Jeremy Bagott, "Security Standards Putting Public at Risk," *Chicago Tribune* (February 24, 2003), 15.

33. Mimi Hall, "Private Security Guards: Homeland Defense's Weak Link," *USA Today* (January 23, 2003), A1.

34. Brock N. Meeks, "Are 'Rent-a-Cops' Threatening Security?" *MSNBC Online* (March 9, 2005).

35. "Don Walker, CPP, Former President of ASIS International, Testifies before U.S. House of Representatives' Subcommittee on Crime, Terrorism and Homeland Security," *Business Wire* (March 31, 2004).

36. Pub. L. No. 108-458, Section 6402(d)(2) (2004).

37. David Bates, "New Law Allows Nationwide Checks by Security Firms," *Government Security News,* at **www.gsnmagazine.com/feb_05/security_checks.html**.

38. National Retail Federation, "Retail Fraud, Shoplifting Rates Decrease, According to National Retails Security Survey," at **www.nrf.com/modules,php?name=News&op=viewlive&sp_id=945**.

39. William C. Cunningham, John J. Strauchs, and Clifford W. Van Meter, *The Hallcrest Report II: Private Security Trends, 1970 to 2000* (Boston: Butterworth-Heinemann, 1990), 236.

40. Quoted in Dennis Wagner, "Private Security Guards Play Key Roles Post-9/11," *Arizona Republic* (January 22, 2006), A1.

41. A. J. Reiss, Jr., "Police Organization in the Twentieth Century," in *Modern Policing,* ed. Michael Tonry and Norval Morris (Chicago: University of Chicago Press, 1992), 51–98.

42. C. E. Pratt, "Police Discretion," *Law and Order* (March 1992), 99–100.

43. "More than a Hunch," *Law Enforcement News* (September 2004), 1.

44. Larry Copeland, "Chases by Police Yield High Fatalities," *USA Today* (April 23, 2010), 3A.

45. Bureau of Justice Statistics, *Local Police Departments, 2003* (Washington, D.C.: U.S. Department of Justice, May 2006), 24.

46. Jack Richter, "Number of Police Pursuits Drop Dramatically in Los Angeles," *Los Angeles Police Department Press Release* (August 20, 2003).

47. *County of Sacramento v. Lewis,* 523 U.S. 833 (1998).

48. *Scott v. Harris,* 550 U.S. 372 (2007).

CHAPTER 6

1. Quoted in Kim Murphy, "Shooting by Police Stirs Anger in Seattle," *Los Angeles Times* (September 17, 2010), A10.

2. *Ibid.*

3. Quoted in Gordon Witkin, "When the Bad Guys Are Cops," *U.S. News and World Report* (September 11, 1995), 22.

4. James H. Chenoweth, "Situational Tests: A New Attempt at Assessing Police Candidates," *Journal of Criminal Law, Criminology and Police Science* 52 (1961), 232.

5. Bureau of Justice Statistics, *Local Police Departments, 2007* (Washington, D.C.: U.S. Department of Justice, December 2010), 11.

6. *Ibid.,* Table 5, page 11.

7. D. P. Hinkle, "College Degree: An Impractical Prerequisite for Police Work," *Law and Order* (July 1991), 105.

8. *Local Police Departments, 2007,* Table 6, page 11.

9. Bureau of Justice Statistics, *State and Local Law Enforcement Training Academies, 2006* (Washington, D.C.: U.S. Department of Justice), 7.

10. Henry M. Wrobleski and Karen M. Hess, *Introduction to Law Enforcement and Criminal Justice,* 7th ed. (Belmont, CA: Wadsworth/Thomson Learning, 2003), 119.

11. Connie Fletcher, "What Cops Know," *On Patrol* (Summer 1996), 44–45.

12. David H. Bayley, *Police for the Future* (New York: Oxford University Press, 1994), 20.

13. Samuel Walker, *The Police in America: An Introduction,* 2d ed. (New York: McGraw-Hill, 1992), 103.

14. Eric J. Scott, *Calls for Service: Citizens Demand an Initial Police Response* (Washington, D.C.: National Institute of Justice, 1981), 28–30.

15. William G. Gay, Theodore H. Schell, and Stephen Schack, *Routine Patrol: Improving Patrol Productivity,* vol. 1 (Washington, D.C.: National Institute of Justice, 1977), 3–6.

16. Gary W. Cordner, "The Police on Patrol," in *Police and Policing: Contemporary Issues,* ed. Dennis Jay Kenney (New York: Praeger Publishers, 1989), 60–71.

17. Anthony V. Bouza, *The Police Mystique: An Insider's Look at Cops, Crime, and the Criminal Justice System* (New York: Plenum Press, 1990), 27.

18. Peter W. Greenwood and Joan Petersilia, *The Criminal Investigation Process: Summary and Policy Implications* (Santa Monica, CA: RAND Corporation, 1975).

19. Fletcher, 46.

20. Federal Bureau of Investigation, *Crime in the United States, 2009* (Washington, D.C.: U.S. Department of Justice, 2010), at **www2.fbi.gov/ucr/cius2009/data/table_25.html**.

21. Karen Hawkins, "More Are Getting Away with Murder," *Associated Press* (December 8, 2008).

22. Quoted in *ibid.*

23. James M. Cronin, Gerard R. Murphy, Lisa L. Spahr, Jessica I. Toliver, and Richard E. Weger, *Promoting Effective Homicide Investigations* (Washington, D.C.: Police Executive Research Forum, August 2007), 102–103.

24. Timothy G. Keel, "Homicide Investigations: Identifying Best Practices," *FBI Law Enforcement Bulletin* (February 2008), 5.

25. Ronald F. Becker, *Criminal Investigations,* 2d ed. (Sudbury, MA: Jones & Bartlett, 2004), 7.

26. Simon A. Cole, "More Than Zero: Accounting for Error in Latent Fingerprinting Identification," *Journal of Criminal Law and Criminology* (Spring 2005), 985–1078.

27. Quoted in "New DNA Database Helps Crack 1979 N.Y. Murder Case," *Miami Herald* (March 14, 2000), 18A.

28. Judith E. Lewter, "The Use of Forensic DNA in Criminal Cases in Kentucky as Compared with Other Selected States," *Kentucky Law Journal* (1997–1998), 223.

29. "CODIS—NDIS Statistics," at **www2.fbi.gov/hq/lab/codis/clickmap.htm**.

30. Hawkins.

31. Wrobleski and Hess, 173.

32. *Local Police Departments, 2007,* Table 6, page 12.

33. Lawrence W. Sherman, "Policing for Crime Prevention," in *Contemporary Policing: Controversies, Challenges, and Solutions,* ed. Quint C. Thurman and Jihong Zhao (Los Angeles: Roxbury Publishing Co., 2004), 62.

34. David Weisburd and Cynthia Lum, "The Diffusion of Computerized Crime Mapping in Policing: Linking Research and Practice," *Police Practice and Research* 6 (2005), 419–434.

35. Quoted in "New Model Police," *Economist* (June 9, 2007), 29.

36. Sherman, 63–66.

37. *Ibid.,* 65.

38. Steven Deitz, "Evaluating Community Policing: Quality Police Service and Fear of Crime," *Policing: An International Journal of Police Strategies and Management* 20 (1997), 83–100.

39. Herman Goldstein, "Improving Policing: A Problem-Oriented Approach," *Crime and Delinquency* 25 (1979), 236–258.

40. Bureau of Justice Assistance, *Problem-Oriented Drug Enforcement: A Community-Based Approach for Effective Policing* (Washington, D.C.: Office of Justice Programs, 1993), 5.

41. Quoted in Associated Press. "Philadelphia Cadets Get Straight Talk about Job," June 29, 2009.

42. *Ibid.*

43. Harry J. Mullins, "Myth, Tradition, and Ritual," *Law and Order* (September 1995), 197.

44. William Westly, *Violence and the Police: A Sociological Study of Law, Custom, and Morality* (Cambridge, MA: MIT Press, 1970).

45. Bureau of Labor Statistics, "Selected Occupations with High Fatality Rates, 2007," at **www.bls.gov/iif/oshwc/cfoi/cfch0006.pdf**.

46. "The Officer Down Memorial Page, Inc.," at **www.odmp.org/year.php?year=2010**.

47. Rebecca Kanable, "Going Home at Night," *Law Enforcement Technology* (January 2009), 23.

48. Federal Bureau of Investigation, *Law Enforcement Officers Killed and Assaulted, 2009*, at **www2.fbi.gov/ucr/killed/2009/data/table_64. html**.

49. Geoffrey P. Alpert, Robert C. Dunham, and Meghan S. Stroshine, *Policing: Continuity and Change* (Long Gove, IL: Waveland Press, 2006), 170.

50. University of Buffalo, "Impact of Stress on Police Officers' Physical and Mental Health," *Science Daily*, March 12, 2010, at **www.sciencedaily.com/ releases/2008/09/080926105029.htm**.

51. Bureau of Justice Statistics, *Contacts between Police and the Public, 2005* (Washington, D.C.: U.S. Department of Justice, April 2007), 1.

52. Bureau of Justice Statistics, *Arrest-Related Deaths in the United States, 2003–2005* (Washington, D.C.: U.S. Department of Justice, October 2007), 1.

53. H. Range Hutson, Deirdre Anglin, Phillip Rice, Demetrious N. Kyriacou, Michael Guirguis, and Jared Strote, "Excessive Use of Force by Police: A Survey of Academic Emergency Physicians," *Emergency Medicine Journal* (January 2009), 20–22.

54. Independent Commission on the Los Angeles Police Department, *Report of the Independent Commission on the Los Angeles Police Department* (1991), ix.

55. Joel Garner, John Buchanan, Tom Schade, and John Hepburn, *Research in Brief: Understanding the Use of Force by and against the Police* (Washington, D.C.: Office of Justice Programs, November 1996), 5.

56. *Ibid.*, 1.

57. 471 U.S. 1 (1985).

58. 471 U.S. 1, 11 (1985).

59. 490 U.S. 386 (1989).

60. *Brosseau v. Haugen*, 543 U.S. 194 (2004).

61. Joycelyn M. Pollock and Ronald F. Becker, "Ethics Training Using Officers' Dilemmas," *FBI Law Enforcement Bulletin* (November 1996), 20–28.

62. *Ibid.*

63. Linda S. Miller and Karen M. Hess, *Police in the Community: Strategies for the 21st Century*, 2d ed. (Belmont, CA: Wadsworth Publishing, 1998), 81.

CHAPTER 7

1. *Illinois v. Rodriguez*, 497 U.S. 177 (1990).

2. *Brigham City v. Stuart*, 547 U.S. 398, 403 (2006).

3. *Michigan v. Fisher*, 130 S.Ct. 546 (2009).

4. *Thompson v. Louisiana*, 469 U.S. 17 (1984).

5. *Michigan v. Summers*, 452 U.S. 692, (1981).

6. *Brinegar v. United States*, 338 U.S. 160 (1949).

7. Rolando V. del Carmen, *Criminal Procedure for Law Enforcement Personnel* (Monterey, CA: Brooks/Cole Publishing Co., 1987), 63–64.

8. *Maryland v. Pringle*, 540 U.S. 366 (2003).

9. 500 U.S. 44 (1991).

10. *United States v. Leon*, 468 U.S. 897 (1984).

11. Arizona Revised Statutes Sections 11-1051(B), 13-1509, 13-2929(C).

12. Quoted in Arian Campo-Flores, "Will Arizona's New Immigration Law Lead to Racial Profiling?" *Newsweek* (April 27, 2010), at **www.news-week.com/2010/04/26/will-arizona-s-new-immigration-law-lead-to-racial-profiling.html**.

13. Karen M. Hess and Henry M. Wrobleski, *Police Operation: Theory and Practice* (St. Paul, MN: West Publishing Co., 1997), 122.

14. 392 U.S. 1 (1968).

15. *Ibid.*, 20.

16. *Ibid.*, 21.

17. See *United States v. Cortez*, 449 U.S. 411 (1981); and *United States v. Sokolow*, 490 U.S. 1 (1989).

18. *United States v. Arvizu*, 534 U.S. 266 (2002).

19. *Ibid.*, 270.

20. *United States v. Place*, 462 U.S. 696 (1983).

21. *Hibel v. Sixth Judicial District Court*, 542 U.S. 177 (2004).

22. *Ibid.*, 182.

23. *Minnesota v. Dickerson*, 508 U.S. 366 (1993).

24. *Arizona v. Johnson*, 555 U.S. ___ (2009).

25. Rolando V. del Carmen and Jeffrey T. Walker, *Briefs of Leading Cases in Law Enforcement*, 2d ed. (Cincinnati, OH: Anderson, 1995), 38–40.

26. *Florida v. Royer*, 460 U.S. 491 (1983).

27. See also *United States v. Mendenhall*, 446 U.S. 544 (1980).

28. del Carmen, 97–98.

29. 514 U.S. 927 (1995).

30. Linda J. Collier and Deborah D. Rosenbloom, *American Jurisprudence*, 2d ed. (Rochester, NY: Lawyers Cooperative Publishing, 1995), 122.

31. 547 U.S. 586 (2006).

32. *United States v. Banks*, 540 U.S. 31, 41 (2003).

33. *Hudson v. Michigan*, 547 U.S. 586, 593 (2006).

34. Tom Van Dorn, "Violation of Knock-and-Announce Rule Does Not Require Suppression of All Evidence Found in Search," *Police Chief* (October 2006), 10.

35. Wayne R. LeFave and Jerold H. Israel, *Criminal Procedure* (St. Paul, MN: West Publishing Co., 1985), 141–144.

36. David Orlin, Jacob Thiessen, Kelli C. McTaggart, Lisa Toporek, and James Pearl, "Warrantless Searches and Seizures," in "Twenty-sixth Annual Review of Criminal Procedure," *Georgetown Law Journal* 85 (April 1997), 847.

37. *Atwater v. City of Lago Vista*, 532 U.S. 318, 346–347 (2001).

38. *California v. Greenwood*, 486 U.S. 35 (1988).

39. *Ibid.*

40. 389 U.S. 347 (1967).

41. *Ibid.*, 361.

42. 486 U.S. 35 (1988).

43. *Ibid.*

44. *Illinois v. Caballes*, 543 U.S. 405 (2005).

45. *Coolidge v. New Hampshire*, 403 U.S. 443, 467 (1971).

46. del Carmen, 158.

47. *Katz v. United States*, 389 U.S. 347, 357 (1967).

48. *Brigham City v. Stuart*, 547 U.S. 398 (2006).

49. 414 U.S. 234–235 (1973).

50. 395 U.S. 752 (1969).

51. *Ibid.*, 763.

52. Carl A. Benoit, "Questioning 'Authority': Fourth Amendment Consent Searches," *FBI Law Enforcement Bulletin* (July 2008), 24.

53. *Bumper v. North Carolina*, 391 U.S. 543 (1968).

54. *State v. Stone*, 362 N.C. 50, 653 S.E.2d 414 (2007).

55. 267 U.S. 132 (1925).

56. *United States v. Ross*, 456 U.S. 798, 804–809 (1982); and *Chambers v. Maroney*, 399 U.S. 42, 44, 52 (1970).

57. 453 U.S. 454 (1981).

58. *Arizona v. Gant*, 556 U.S. ___ (2009).

59. Quoted in Adam Liptak, "Justices Significantly Cut Back Officers' Searches of Cars of People They Arrest," *New York Times* (April 22, 2009), A12.

60. Dale Anderson and Dave Cole, "Search and Seizure after *Arizona v. Gant*," *Arizona Attorney* (October 2009), 15.

61. 517 U.S. 806 (1996).

62. 519 U.S. 408 (1997).

63. 403 U.S. 443 (1971).

64. 388 U.S. 42 (1967).

65. 18 U.S.C. Sections 2510(7), 2518(1)(a), 2516 (1994).

66. *Lee v. United States*, 343 U.S. 747 (1952).

67. Christopher K. Murphy, "Electronic Surveillance," in "Twenty-Sixth Annual Review of Criminal Procedure," *Georgetown Law Journal* (April 1997), 920.

68. *United States v. Nguyen*, 46 F.3d 781, 783 (8th Cir. 1995).

69. "Someone's Watching You," *The Week* (September 28, 2007), 13.

70. Sharon B. Franklin, "Watching the Watchers: Establishing Limits on Public Video Surveillance," *Champion* (April 2008), 40.

71. *People v. Clark*, 350 N.W. 2d 754, 758 (Mich. App. 1984).

72. *Brown v. Mississippi*, 297 U.S. 278 (1936).

73. *Miranda v. Arizona*, 384 U.S. 436 (1966).

74. H. Richard Uviller, *Tempered Zeal* (Chicago: Contemporary Books, 1988), 188–198.

75. *Orozco v. Texas*, 394 U.S. 324 (1969); *Oregon v. Mathiason*, 429 U.S. 492 (1977); and *California v. Beheler*, 463 U.S. 1121 (1983).

76. *Orozco*, at 325.

77. *Pennsylvania v. Muniz*, 496 U.S. 582 (1990).

78. del Carmen, 267–268.

79. *Moran v. Burbine*, 475 U.S. 412 (1986).

80. *Michigan v. Mosley*, 423 U.S. 96 (1975).

81. *Fare v. Michael C.*, 442 U.S. 707, 723–724 (1979).

82. 512 U.S. 452 (1994).

83. 560 U.S. ___ (2010).

CHAPTER 8

1. Andrea Vogt, "The Debate Continues over Knox's Guilt," *Seattle Post-Intelligencer* (December 15, 2009), at **www.seattlepi.com/local/413244_knox15.html**.

2. Quoted in Alessandro Rizzo, "Amanda Knox Makes Emotional Address in Appeal," *Seattle Times* (December 12, 2010), B10.

3. Roscoe Pound, "The Administration of Justice in American Cities," *Harvard Law Review* 12 (1912).

4. Russell Wheeler and Howard Whitcomb, *Judicial Administration: Text and Readings* (Englewood Cliffs, NJ: Prentice Hall, 1977), 3.

5. Herbert Packer, *The Limits of the Criminal Sanction* (Stanford, CA: Stanford University Press, 1968), 154–173.

6. Herbert Packer, "The Courts, the Police and the Rest of Us," *Criminal Law, Criminology & Political Science* 57 (1966), 238–239.

7. Larry J. Siegel, *Criminology: Instructor's Manual*, 6th ed. (Belmont, CA: West/Wadsworth Publishing Co., 1998), 440.

8. Gerald F. Velman, "Federal Sentencing Guidelines: A Cure Worse Than the Disease," *American Criminal Law Review* 29 (Spring 1992), 904.

9. Stephanie Martz, "Verbatim," *Champion* (July 2006), 42.

10. 21 U.S.C. Section 801 (2006).

11. Wayne R. LaFave, "Section 4.6. Multiple Jurisdiction and Multiple Prosecution," *Substantive Criminal Law*, 2d ed. (C.J.S. Criminal Section 254), 2007.

12. William Wan, "Snipers to Be Tried in Maryland," *Baltimore Sun* (May 11, 2005), 1A.

13. David W. Neubauer, *America's Courts and the Criminal Justice System*, 5th ed. (Belmont, CA: Wadsworth Publishing Co., 1996), 41.

14. 372 U.S. 335 (1963).

15. 384 U.S. 436 (1966).

16. 408 U.S. 238 (1972).

17. 428 U.S. 153 (1976).

18. 18 U.S.C. Section 48 (1999).

19. *United States v. Stevens*, 559 U.S. ___ (2010).

20. 130 S.Ct. 1213 (2010).

21. *Singleton v. Commissioner of Internal Revenue*, 439 U.S. 940 (1978).

22. Barry R. Schaller, *A Vision of American Law: Judging Law, Literature, and the Stories We Tell* (Westport, CT: Praeger, 1997).

23. Harlington Wood, Jr., "Judiciary Reform: Recent Improvements in Federal Judicial Administration," *American University Law Review* 44 (June 1995), 1557.

24. Pub. L. No. 76-299, 53 Stat. 1223, codified as amended at 28 U.S.C. Sections 601–610 (1988 & Supp. V 1993).

25. James E. Lozier, "The Missouri Plan a.k.a. Merit Selection Is the Best Solution for Selecting Michigan's Judges," *Michigan Bar Journal* 75 (September 1996), 918.

26. William Ballenger, "In Judicial Wilderness, Even Brickley's Not Safe," *Michigan Politics* 28 (1996), 1–3.

27. Roy B. Fleming, Peter F. Nardulli, and James Eisenstein, *The Craft of Justice: Politics and Work in Criminal Court Communities* (Philadelphia: University of Pennsylvania Press, 1992).

28. Neubauer.

29. Alissa P. Worden, "The Judge's Role in Plea Bargaining: An Analysis of Judges' Agreement with Prosecutors' Sentencing Recommendations," *Justice Quarterly* 10 (1995), 257–278.

30. Kimberly Jade Norwood, "Shopping for Venue: The Need for More Limits," *University of Miami Law Review* 50 (1996), 295–298.

CHAPTER 9

1. Quoted in Linda Deutsch, "Michael Jackson Doctor To Stand Trial for Involuntary Manslaughter," *Pittsburgh Post-Gazette* (January 12, 2011), C4.

2. Daniel B. Wood, "Michael Jackson Trial: Did Conrad Murray Act as a Doctor or an Enabler?" *Christian Science Monitor* (January 12, 2011), at **www.csmonitor.com/USA/Justice/2011/0112/Michael-Jackson-trial-Did-Conrad-Murray-act-as-a-doctor-or-an-enabler**.

3. Bennett L. Gershman, "Abuse of Power in the Prosecutor's Office," in *Criminal Justice 92/93*, ed. John J. Sullivan and Joseph L. Victor (Guilford, CT: The Dushkin Publishing Group, 1991), 117–123.

4. 295 U.S. 78 (1935).

5. Celesta Albonetti, "Prosecutorial Discretion: The Effects of Uncertainty," *Law and Society Review* 21 (1987), 291–313.

6. *Gideon v. Wainwright*, 372 U.S. 335 (1963); *Massiah v. United States*, 377 U.S. 201 (1964); *United States v. Wade*, 388 U.S. 218 (1967); *Argersinger v. Hamlin*, 407 U.S. 25 (1972); and *Brewer v. Williams*, 430 U.S. 387 (1977).

7. Larry Siegel, *Criminology*, 6th ed. (Belmont, CA: West/Wadsworth Publishing Co., 1998), 487–488.

8. Center for Professional Responsibility, *Model Rules of Professional Conduct* (Washington, D.C.: American Bar Association, 2003), Rules 1.6 and 3.1.

9. *United States v. Wade*, 388 U.S. 218, 256–258 (1967).

10. 372 U.S. 335 (1963).

11. 387 U.S. 1 (1967).

12. 407 U.S. 25 (1972).

13. Peter A. Joy and Kevin C. McMunigal, "Client Autonomy and Choice of Counsel," *Criminal Justice* (Fall 2006), 57.

14. *United States v. Gonzalez-Lopez*, 548 U.S. 140 (2006).

15. *Wheat v. United States*, 486 U.S. 153, 159 (1988).

16. Bureau of Justice Statistics, *Defense Counsel in Criminal Cases* (Washington, D.C.: U.S. Department of Justice, 2000), 3.

17. Catherine Bean, "Indigent Defense: Separate and Unequal," *Champion* (May 2004), 54.

18. 466 U.S. 668 (1984).

19. Adam Liptak, "Despite Flawed Defense, a Death Sentence Stands," *New York Times* (November 2, 2006), A17.

20. *Model Rules of Professional Conduct*, Rule 1.2(c)–(d).

21. Randolph Braccialarghe, "Why Were Perry Mason's Clients Always Innocent?" *Valparaiso University Law Review* (Fall 2004), 65.

22. John Kaplan, "Defending Guilty People," *University of Bridgeport Law Review* (1986), 223.

23. 491 U.S. 554 (1989).

24. Johannes F. Nijboer, "The American Adversary System in Criminal Cases: Between Ideology and Reality," *Cardozo Journal of International and Comparative Law* 5 (Spring 1997), 79.

25. Gordon Van Kessel, "Adversary Excesses in the American Criminal Trial," *Notre Dame Law Review* 67 (1992), 403.

26. James Eisenstein and Herbert Jacob, *Felony Justice* (Boston: Little, Brown, 1977), 24.

27. Jerome Skolnick, "Social Control in the Adversary System," *Journal of Conflict Resolution* 11 (1967), 52–70.

28. Abraham S. Blumberg, "The Practice of Law as Confidence Game: Organizational Cooption of a Profession," *Law and Society Review* 4 (June 1967), 115–139.

29. Malcolm Feeley, "The Adversary System," in *Encyclopedia of the American Judicial System*, ed. Robert J. Janosik (New York: Scribners, 1987), 753.

30. Blumberg, 115.

31. *Riverside County, California v. McLaughlin*, 500 U.S. 44 (1991).

32. Bureau of Justice Statistics, *Pretrial Release of Felony Defendants in State Courts* (Washington, D.C.: U.S. Department of Justice, November 2007), 2.

33. Illinois Annotated Statutes Chapter 725, Paragraph 5/110-5.

34. David W. Neubauer, *America's Courts and the Criminal Justice System*, 5th ed. (Belmont, CA: Wadsworth Publishing Co., 1996), 179–181.

35. Roy Flemming, C. Kohfeld, and Thomas Uhlman, "The Limits of Bail Reform: A Quasi Experimental Analysis," *Law and Society Review* 14 (1980), 947–976.

36. Los Angeles County Superior Court, *Felony Bail Schedule 2011*, at **www.lasuperiorcourt.org/bail/pdf/felony.pdf**.

37. Wayne H. Thomas, Jr., *Bail Reform in America* (Berkeley, CA: University of California Press, 1976), 4.

38. 18 U.S.C. Sections 3141–3150 (Supp. III 1985).

39. 481 U.S. 739 (1987).

40. Bureau of Justice Statistics, *Felony Defendants in Large Urban Counties, 2004* (Washington, D.C.: U.S. Department of Justice, April 2008), Appendix table F.

41. *Gerstein v. Pugh*, 420 U.S. 103 (1975).

42. Andrew D. Leipold, "Why Grand Juries Do Not (and Cannot) Protect the Accused," *Cornell Law Review* 80 (January 1995), 260.

43. Sam Skolnick, "Grand Juries: Power Shift?" *The Legal Times* (April 12, 1999), 1.

44. New York Court of Appeals Judge Sol Wachtler, quoted in David Margolik, "Law Professor to Administer Courts in State," *New York Times* (February 1, 1985), B2.

45. Ryan Blitstein, "Online Crooks Often Escape Prosecution," *San Jose Mercury News* (November 18, 2007), 1A.

46. Henry K. Lee, "D.A. Cuts Efforts on Lesser Crimes," *San Francisco Chronicle* (April 22, 2009), B1.

47. Milton Hirsh and David Oscar Markus, "Fourth Amendment Forum," *Champion* (December 2002), 42.

48. Barbara Boland, Paul Mahanna, and Ronald Scones, *The Prosecution of Felony Arrests, 1988* (Washington, D.C.: Bureau of Justice Statistics, 1992).

49. Richard Felson and Paul-Philippe Pare, *The Reporting of Domestic Violence and Sexual Assault by Nonstrangers to the Police* (Washington, D.C.: U.S. Department of Justice, March 2005), 6.

50. Tom Lininger, "Evidentiary Issues in Federal Prosecutions of Violence against Women," *Indiana Law Review* 36 (2003), 709.

51. 18 U.S.C. Section 3553(e) (2006).

52. Code of Alabama Section 26-15-3.2 (Act 2006-204, Section 2).

53. Quoted in Adam Nossiter, "In Alabama, Crackdown on Pregnant Drug Users," *New York Times* (March 15, 2008), A10.

54. 404 U.S. 257 (1971).

55. Fred C. Zacharias, "Justice in Plea Bargaining," *William and Mary Law Review* 39 (March 1998), 1121.

56. Bureau of Justice Statistics, *Felony Sentences in State Courts, 2006—Statistical Tables* (Washington, D.C.: U.S. Department of Justice, December 2009). 1.

57. Albert W. Alschuler, "The Prosecutor's Role in Plea Bargaining," *University of Chicago Law Review* 36 (1968), 52.

58. Milton Heumann, *Plea Bargaining: The Experiences of Prosecutors, Judges, and Defense Attorneys* (Chicago: University of Chicago Press, 1978), 58.

59. Albert W. Alschuler, "The Defense Attorney's Role in Plea Bargaining," *Yale Law Journal* 84 (1975), 1200.

60. Stephen J. Schulhofer, "Plea Bargaining as Disaster," *Yale Law Journal* 101 (1992), 1987.

CHAPTER 10

1. Quoted in Keith L. Alexander and Henri E. Cauvin, "Ingmar Guandique Convicted of First-Degree Murder of Former Intern Chandra Levy," *Washington Post* (November 23, 2010), at **www.washingtonpost.com/wp-dyn/content/article/2010/11/22/AR2010112203633.html**.

2. Ben Conery, "Prosecution, Defense Agree: Levy's Murder Probe Botched," *Washington Times* (October 26, 2010), A1.

3. Jerome Frank, *Courts on Trial: Myth and Reality in American Justice* (New York: Atheneum, 1969), 14–33.

4. 407 U.S. 514 (1972).

5. 725 Illinois Compiled Statutes Section 5/103-5 (1992).

6. 18 U.S.C. Section 3161.

7. 391 U.S. 145 (1968).

8. *Blanton v. Las Vegas*, 489 U.S. 538 (1989).

9. 332 U.S. 46 (1947).

10. Barton L. Ingraham, "The Right of Silence, the Presumption of Innocence, the Burden of Proof, and a Modest Proposal," *Journal of Criminal Law and Criminology* 85 (1994), 559–595.

11. 397 U.S. 358 (1970).

12. Quoted in Curt Anderson, "Padilla Trial Trouble," (March 29, 2007), at **www.nysun.com/article/51492?page_no=2**.

13. *Lockhart v. McCree*, 476 U.S. 162 (1986).

14. *Witherspoon v. Illinois*, 391 U.S. 510 (1968).

15. 380 U.S. 224 (1965).

16. 476 U.S. 79 (1986).

17. 499 U.S. 400 (1991).

18. 502 U.S. 1056 (1992).

19. *Snyder v. Louisiana*, 552 U.S. 472 (2008).

20. 511 U.S. 127 (1994).

21. Harry Kalven and Hans Zeisel, *The American Jury* (Boston: Little, Brown, 1966), 163–167.

22. Douglas D. Koski, "Testing the Story Model of Juror Decision Making," *Sex Offender Law* (June/July 2003), 53–58.

23. Nancy Pennington and Reid Hastie, "The Story Model for Juror Decision Making," in *Inside the Juror: The Psychology of Juror Decision Making* (Cambridge, MA: Harvard University Press, 1983), 192, 194–195.

24. Quoted in Katie Zezima, "Judge Will Allow Jurors to See Video of 8-Year-Old Being Killed by Uzi at Gun Show," *New York Times* (December 8, 2010), A15.

25. Thomas J. Reed, "Trial by Propensity: Admission of Other Criminal Acts Evidenced in Federal Criminal Trials," *University of Cincinnati Law Review* 50 (1981), 713.

26. *Ibid.*

27. Charles McCormick, *Handbook on Evidence* (St. Paul, MN: West Publishing Co., 1987), Chapter 1.

28. Douglas D. Koski, "Alcohol and Rape Study," *Criminal Law Bulletin* 38 (2002), 21–159.

29. Roger LeRoy Miller and Mary S. Urisko, *West's Paralegal Today*, 3d ed. (St. Paul, MN: West Publishing Co., 2003), 443.

30. *People v. Haran*, 109 P.3d 616 (Colo. 2005).

31. 164 U.S. 492 (1896).

32. *United States v. Fioravanti*, 412 F.2d 407 (3d Cir. 1969).

33. Bureau of Justice Statistics, *Federal Justice Statistics, 2005* (Washington, D.C.: U.S. Department of Justice, September 2008), 5–6.

34. *Green v. United States*, 355 U.S. 184 (1957).

35. David W. Neubauer, *America's Courts and the Criminal Justice System*, 5th ed. (Belmont, CA: Wadsworth Publishing Co. 1996), 254.

36. William J. Morgan, Jr., "Justice in Foresight: Past Problems with Eyewitness Identification and Exoneration by DNA Technology," *Southern Regional Black Law Students Association Law Journal* (Spring 2009), 87.

CHAPTER 11

1. Terrie Morgan-Beseeker, "Feds, Pa. Differ on Kid Porn," *The Times-Leader (Wilkes-Barre, PA)* (January 16, 2011), at **www.timesleader.com/news/Feds_Pa_differ_on_kid_porn_01-16-2011.html**.

2. Michael L. Bourke and Andres E. Hernandez, "The 'Butner Study' Redux: A Report on the Incidence of Hands-on Child Victimization by Child Pornography Offenders," *Journal of Family Violence* (2009), 183–191.

3. *Ibid.* 188.

4. David Yellen, "Just Deserts and Lenient Prosecutors: The Flawed Case for Real Offense Sentencing," *Northwestern University Law Review* 91 (Summer 1997), 1434.

5. Brian Forst, "Prosecution and Sentencing," in *Crime*, ed. James Q. Wilson and Joan Petersilia (San Francisco: ICS Press, 1995), 386.

6. Herbert L. Packer, "Justification for Criminal Punishment," in *The Limits of Criminal Sanction* (Palo Alto, CA: Stanford University Press, 1968), 36–37.

7. Jeremy Bentham, *An Introduction to the Principles of Morals and Legislation* 1789 (New York: Hafner Publishing Corp., 1961).

8. Forst, 376.

9. James Q. Wilson, *Thinking about Crime* (New York: Basic Books, 1975), 235.

10. Isaac Ehrlich, "Participation in Illegitimate Activities: A Theoretical and Empirical Investigation," *Journal of Political Economy* 81 (May/June 1973), 521–564.

11. Steve Levitt, "The Effect of Prison Population Size on Crime Rates," *Quarterly Journal of Economics* 111 (May 1996), 319.

12. Avinash Singh Bhati, *An Information Theoretic Method for Estimating the Number of Crimes Averted by Incapacitation* (Washington, D.C.: Urban Institute, July 2007), 18–33.

13. Robert J. Meadows and Julie Kuehnel, *Evil Minds: Understanding and Responding to Violent Predators* (Upper Saddle River, NJ: Pearson Prentice Hall, 2005), 256–258.

14. Barry Krisberg and Susan Marchionna, *Attitudes of U.S. Voters toward Prisoner Rehabilitation and Reentry Policies* (Oakland, CA: National Council on Crime and Delinquency, April 2006), 1.

15. Heather Strang and Lawrence W. Sherman, "Repairing the Harm: Victims and Restorative Justice," *Utah Law Review* (2003), 15, 18, 20–25.

16. Todd R. Clear, George F. Cole, and Michael D. Reisig, *American Corrections*, 7th ed. (Belmont, CA: Thomson Wadsworth, 2006), 68–69.

17. Gregory W. O'Reilly, "Truth-in-Sentencing: Illinois Adds Yet Another Layer of 'Reform' to Its Complicated Code of Corrections," *Loyola University of Chicago Law Journal* (Summer 1996), 986, 999–1000.

18. Marc Mauer, "The Truth about Truth-in-Sentencing," *Corrections Today* (February 1, 1996), 1–8.

19. Marvin Zalman, "The Rise and Fall of the Indeterminate Sentence," *Wayne Law Review* 24 (1977), 45, 52.

20. Marvin E. Frankel, *Criminal Sentences: Law without Order* (New York: Hill & Wang, 1972), 5.

21. Paul W. Keve, *Crime Control and Justice in America: Searching for Facts and Answers* (Chicago: American Library Association, 1995), 77.

22. Kate Stith and José A. Cabranes, "Judging under the Federal Sentencing Guidelines," *Northwestern University Law Review* 91 (Summer 1997), 1247.

23. Nancy J. King and Rosevelt L. Noble, "Felony Jury Sentencing in Practice: A Three-State Study," *Vanderbilt Law Review* (2004), 1986.

24. Jena Iontcheva, "Jury Sentencing as Democratic Practice," *Virginia Law Review* (April 2003), 325.

25. Julie R. O'Sullivan, "In Defense of the U.S. Sentencing Guidelines Modified Real-Offense System," *Northwestern University Law Review* 91 (1997), 1342.

26. 18 U.S.C. Section 2113(a) (1994).

27. Bob Barr and Eric Sterling, "The War on Drugs: Fighting Crime or Wasting Time?" *American Criminal Law Review* (Fall 2001), 1545.

28. Cassia Spohn and David Holleran, "The Imprisonment Penalty Paid by Young, Unemployed Black and Hispanic Male Offenders," *Criminology* 35 (2000), 281.

29. *Ibid.*

30. Bureau of Justice Statistics, *Prison Inmates at Midyear 2008—Statistical Tables* (Washington, D.C.: U.S. Department of Justice, April 2009), Table 16, page 17.

31. Spohn and Holleran.

32. Anti-Drug Abuse Act of 1986, Pub. L. No. 99-570, 100 Stat. 3207 (1986).

33. Solomon Moore, "Justice Department Seeks Equity in Sentences for Cocaine," *New York Times* (April 30, 2009), A17.

34. *U.S. Sentencing Commission Preliminary Crack Cocaine Retroactivity Data Report* (Washington, D.C.: U.S. Sentencing Commission, November 2010), Table 1.

35. Public Law No., 111-220, Section 2, 124 Statute 2372.

36. 28 U.S.C. Section 991 (1994).

37. Bureau of Justice Statistics, *State Court Sentencing of Convicted Felons, 2006—Statistical Tables* (Washington, D.C.: U.S. Department of Justice, December 2009), Table 3.5.

38. Quoted in Kareem Fahim and Karen Zraik, "Seeing Failure of Mother as Factor in Sentencing," *New York Times* (November 17, 2008), A24.

39. John C. Coffee, "Repressed Issues of Sentencing," *Georgetown Law Journal* 66 (1978), 987.

40. J. S. Bainbridge, Jr., "The Return of Retribution," *ABA Journal* (May 1985), 63.

41. Pub. L. No. 98-473, 98 Stat. 1987, codified as amended at 18 U.S.C. Sections 3551-3742 and 28 U.S.C. Sections 991-998 (1988).

42. Julia L. Black, "The Constitutionality of Federal Sentences Imposed under the Sentencing Reform Act of 1984 after *Mistretta v. United States*," *Iowa Law Review* 75 (March 1990), 767.

43. *Fifteen Years of Guidelines Sentencing: An Assessment of How Well the Federal Criminal Justice System Is Achieving the Goals of Sentencing Reform* (Washington, D.C.: U.S. Sentencing Commission, November 2004), 46.

44. Clear, Cole, and Reisig, 86.

45. Quoted in A. G. Sulzberger, "Defiant Judge Takes on Child Pornography Laws," *New York Times* (May 22, 2010), A1.

46. Tim McGlone, "Leniency Often Granted in Child Porn Cases." *The Virginian-Pilot (Norfolk, VA)* (January 16, 2011) at **hamptonroads.com/2011/01/leniency-often-grated-porn-cases**.

47. Alabama Code 1975 Section 20-2-79.

48. Washington Revised Code Annotated Section 9.94A.030.

49. 445 U.S. 263 (1980).

50. 538 U.S. 63 (2003).

51. *Lockyer v. Andrade*, 270 F.3d 743 (9th Cir. 2001).

52. *Ibid.*, 83.

53. *Lockyer v. Andrade*, 538 U.S. 63, 76 (2003).

54. Walter Berns, "Abraham Lincoln (Book Review)," *Commentary* (January 1, 1996), 70.

55. Comments made at the Georgetown Law Center, "The Modern View of Capital Punishment," *American Criminal Law Review* 34 (Summer 1997), 1353.

56. David Bruck, quoted in Bill Rankin, "Fairness of the Death Penalty Is Still on Trial," *Atlanta Constitution-Journal* (July 29, 1997), A13.

57. Bureau of Justice Statistics, *Capital Punishment, 2005* (Washington, D.C.: U.S. Department of Justice, December 2006), 4.

58. Larry C. Berkson, *The Concept of Cruel and Unusual Punishment* (Lexington, MA: Lexington Books, 1975), 43.

59. John P. Cunningham, "Death in the Federal Courts: Expectations and Realities of the Federal Death Penalty Act of 1994," *University of Richmond Law Review* 32 (May 1998), 939.

60. *In re Kemmler*, 136 U.S. 447 (1890).

61. 217 U.S. 349 (1910).

62. Pamela S. Nagy, "Hang by the Neck until Dead: The Resurgence of Cruel and Unusual Punishment in the 1990s," *Pacific Law Journal* 26 (October 1994), 85.

63. 408 U.S. 238 (1972).

64. 408 U.S. 309 (1972) (Stewart, concurring).

65. 428 U.S. 153 (1976).

66. 536 U.S. 584 (2002).

67. *Ford v. Wainwright*, 477 U.S. 399, 422 (1986).

68. Vidisha Barua, "'Synthetic Sanity': A Way Around the Eighth Amendment?" *Criminal Law Bulletin* (July/August 2008), 561-572.

69. *Penry v. Lynaugh*, 492 U.S. 302 (1989).

70. 536 U.S. 304 (2002).

71. James C. McKinley, "Killer with Low I.Q. Is Executed in Texas," *New York Times* (December 5, 2009). A19.

72. 543 U.S. 551 (2005).

73. *Baze v. Rees*, 217 S.W.3d 207 (Ky. 2006).

74. 553 U.S. 35 (2008).

75. Adam Liptak, "Moratorium May Be Over, but Hardly the Challenges," *New York Times* (April 17, 2008), A18.

CHAPTER 12

1. Bureau of Justice Statistics, *Probation and Parole in the United States, 2009* (Washington, D.C.: U.S. Department of Justice, December 2010), Appendix table 6, page 26.

2. *Ibid.*, Appendix table 2, page 23.

3. Michael Tonry, *Sentencing Matters* (New York: Oxford Press, 1996), 28.

4. Todd Clear and Anthony Braga, "Community Corrections," in *Crime*, ed. James Q. Wilson and Joan Petersilia (San Francisco: ICS Press, 1995), 444.

5. Corrections Task Force of the President's Commission on Law Enforcement and Administration of Justice (1967).

6. Paul H. Hahn, *Emerging Criminal Justice: Three Pillars for a Proactive Justice System* (Thousand Oaks, CA: Sage Publications, 1998), 106-108.

7. "Cutting Costs: How States Are Addressing Corrections Budget Shortfalls," *Corrections Directions* (December 2009), 2.

8. U.S. Courts, "Costs of Imprisonment Far Exceed Supervision Costs," at **www.uscourts.gov/newsroom/2009/costsofimprisonment.cfm**.

9. *One in 31: The Long Reach of American Corrections* (Washington, D.C.: The Pew Center on the States, March 2009), 12.

10. Frederick Kunkle and Derek Kravitz, "Sweat Becomes Offenders' New Snitch," *Washington Post* (September 25, 2009), A1.

11. Kevin Johnson, "To Save Money on Prisons, States Take a Softer Stance," *USA Today* (March 18, 2009), 2A.

12. Paul W. Keve, *Crime Control and Justice in America* (Chicago: American Library Association, 1995), 183.

13. Andrew R. Klein, *Alternative Sentencing, Intermediate Sanctions and Probation*, 2d ed. (Cincinnati: Anderson Publishing Co., 1997), 72.

14. *Probation and Parole in the United States, 2009*, Appendix table 3, page 24.

15. Joan Petersilia and Susan Turner, *Prison versus Probation in California: Implications for Crime and Offender Recidivism* (Santa Monica, CA: Rand Corporation, 1986).

16. *Probation and Parole in the United States, 2009*, Appendix table 5, page 24.

17. Bureau of Justice Statistics, *State Court Sentencing of Convicted Felons, 2002* (Washington, D.C.: U.S. Department of Justice, May 2005), Table 3.6.

18. 705 So.2d 172 (La. 1997).

19. Neil P. Cohen and James J. Gobert, *The Law of Probation and Parole* (Colorado Springs, CO: Shepard's/McGraw-Hill, 1983), Section 5.01, 183-184; Section 5.03, 191-192.

20. 534 U.S. 112 (2001).

21. *Ibid.*, 113.

22. Bureau of Justice Statistics, *Substance Abuse and Treatment for Adults on Probation, 1995* (Washington, D.C.: U.S. Department of Justice, March 1998), 11.

23. Carl B. Klockars, Jr., "A Theory of Probation Supervision," *Journal of Criminal Law, Criminology, and Police Science* 63 (1972), 550-557.

24. *Ibid.*, 551.

25. Hahn, 116-118.

26. Camille Graham Camp and George M. Camp, *The Corrections Yearbook: 1999* (Middletown, CT: Criminal Justice Institute, 1999).

27. National Institute of Corrections, *New Approaches to Staff Safety* (Washington, D.C.: U.S. Department of Justice, March 2003), 16.

28. Nicholas Riccardi, "Probation Dept. Divided over Rule Prohibiting Guns," *Los Angeles Times* (January 2, 1999), B1.

29. 389 U.S. 128 (1967).

30. *Morrissey v. Brewer*, 408 U.S. 471 (1972); and *Gagnon v. Scarpelli*, 411 U.S. 778 (1973).

31. 465 U.S. 420 (1984).

32. *Probation and Parole in the United States, 2009*, Table 2, page 3.

33. Jennifer L. Skeem and Sarah Manchak, "Back to the Future: From Klockars' Model of Effective Supervision to Evidence-Based Practice in Probation," *Journal of Offender Rehabilitation* 47 (2008), 231.

34. Cassie Spohn and David Holleran, "The Effect of Imprisonment on Recidivism Rates of Felony Offenders: A Focus on Drug Offenders," *Criminology* (May 1, 2002), 329-357.

35. Skeem and Manchak, 226-229.

36. James Bonta, Tanya Rugge, Terri-Lynne Scott, Guy Bourgon, and Annie K. Yessine, "Exploring the Black Box of Community Supervision," *Journal of Offender Rehabilitation* 47 (2008), 248-270.

37. Samuel Walker, "Too Many Sticks, Not Enough Carrots: Limits and New Opportunities in American Crime Policy," *University of Saint Thomas Law Journal* (Spring 2006), 430.

38. Joan Petersilia, "Community Corrections," in *Crime: Public Policies for Crime Control*, ed. James Q. Wilson and Joan Petersilia (Oakland, CA: ICS Press, 2002), 483-508.

39. Greg Berman, "Redefining Criminal Courts: Problem Solving and the Meaning of Justice," *American Criminal Law Review* (Summer 2004), 1313.

40. Brooks Egerton, "Losing Track of Crooks," *Dallas Morning News* (August 7, 2005), 1A.

41. Norval Morris and Michael Tonry, *Between Prison and Probation: Intermediate Punishments in a Rational Sentencing System* (Oxford, UK: Oxford University Press, 1990).

42. 18 U.S.C. Sections 1961-1968.

43. 516 U.S. 442 (1996).

44. U.S. Marshals Service, "Fact Sheets: Asset Forfeiture Program," at **www.justice.gov/marshals/duties/factsheets/afd-1209.html**.

45. Michael W. Finigan, Shannon M. Carey, and Anton Cox, *The Impact of a Mature Drug Court over Ten Years of Operation: Recidivism and Costs* (Portland, OR: NPC Research, April 2007), II.

46. John Roman, Wendy Townsend, and Avinash Singh Bhati, *Recidivism Rates for Drug Court Graduates: Nationally Based Estimates, Final Report* (Washington, D.C.: Urban Institute and Caliber Associates, July 2003), 27–42.

47. Model State Drug Court Legislation Committee, *Model State Drug Court Legislation: Model Drug Offender Accountability and Treatment Act* (Alexandria, VA: National Drug Court Institute, May 2004), 42.

48. Kate Coscarelli, "A Model Program for Model Prisoners," *Star-Ledger* (February 24, 2004), 25.

49. William Burrell, "Caseload Standards for Probation and Parole" (Lexington, KY: American Probation and Parole Association, September 2006), 4, at **www.appa-net.org/ccheadlines/docs/Caseload_Standards_PP_0906.pdf**.

50. Joan Petersilia and Susan Turner, "Intensive Probation and Parole," *Crime and Justice* 17 (1993), 281–335.

51. Skeem and Manchak, 235–236.

52. Dale Parent, *Correctional Boot Camps: Lessons from a Decade of Research* (Washington, D.C.: U.S. Department of Justice, June 2003), 6.

53. *Ibid.*, 8, 11–12.

54. Robert S. Gable, "Left to Their Own Devices: Should Manufacturers of Offender Monitoring Be Liable for Design Defect?" *University of Illinois Journal of Law, Technology, and Policy* (Fall 2009), 334.

55. Josh Kurtz, "New Growth in a Captive Market," *New York Times* (December 31, 1989), 12.

56. Edna Erez, Peter R. Ibarra, and Norman A. Lurie, "Electronic Monitoring of Domestic Violence Cases—A Study of Two Bilateral Programs," *Federal Probation* (June 2004), 15–20.

57. Michael Tonry and Mary Lynch, "Intermediate Sanctions," in *Crime and Justice*, vol. 20, ed. Michael Tonry (Chicago: University of Chicago Press, 1996), 99.

58. Dennis Palumbo, Mary Clifford, and Zoann K. Snyder-Joy, "From Net Widening to Intermediate Sanctions: The Transformation of Alternatives to Incarceration from Benevolence to Malevolence," in *Smart Sentencing: The Emergence of Intermediate Sanctions*, ed. James M. Byrne, Arthur Lurigio, and Joan Petersilia (Newbury Park, CA: Sage, 1992), 231.

59. Keve, 207.

60. Barbara Sims and Mark Jones, "Predicting Success or Failure on Probation: Factors Associated with Felony Probation Outcomes," *Crime and Delinquency* (July 1997), 314–327.

CHAPTER 13

1. Bureau of Justice Statistics, *Prisoners in 2009* (Washington, D.C.: U.S. Department of Justice, December 2010), 1.

2. Bureau of Justice Statistics, *Correctional Populations in the United States, 2009* (Washington, D.C.: U.S. Department of Justice, December 2010), Table 1, page 2.

3. Quoted in John Schwarz, "Report Finds States Holding Fewer Prisoners," *New York Times* (March 17, 2010), A15.

4. Cheryl L. Jonson, Francis T. Cullen, and Edward J. Latessa, "Cracks in the Penal Harm Movement: Evidence from the Field," *Criminology & Public Policy* (August 2008), 423.

5. Steven D. Levitt, "Understanding Why Crime Fell in the 1990s: Four Factors that Explain the Decline and Six that Do Not," *Journal of Economic Perspectives* (Winter 2004), 177.

6. *Prisoners in 2009*, Appendix table 16a, page 29; and Appendix table 18, page 33.

7. Allen J. Beck, "Growth, Change, and Stability in the U.S. Prison Population, 1980–1995," *Corrections Management Quarterly* (Spring 1997), 9–10.

8. Bureau of Justice Statistics, "Sentences Imposed in Cases Terminated in U.S. District Courts," *Sourcebook of Criminal Justice Statistics Online*, Table 5.25, at **www.albany.edu/sourcebook/pdf/t5252009.pdf**.

9. *Fifteen Years of Guidelines Sentencing: An Assessment of How Well the Federal Criminal Justice System Is Achieving the Goals of Sentencing Reform* (Washington, D.C.: U.S. Sentencing Commission, November 2004), 46.

10. Bureau of Justice Statistics, *Federal Criminal Case Processing, 2002* (Washington, D.C.: U.S. Department of Justice, January 2005), 1.

11. Bureau of Justice Statistics, *Prison and Jail Inmates, 1995* (Washington, D.C.: U.S. Department of Justice, August 1996), 1; and *Prisoners in 2009*, Table 1, page 2.

12. *Prisoners in 2009*, 1.

13. Bureau of Justice Statistics, *Prisoners in 2005* (Washington, D.C.: U.S. Department of Justice, November 2006), Table 14, page 10.

14. *Prisoners in 2009*, Appendix table 18, page 33.

15. Mark Hugo Lopez and Michael T. Light, *A Rising Share: Hispanics and Federal Crimes* (Washington, D.C.: Pew Hispanic Center, February 18, 2009), i.

16. *Prisoners in 2009*, Appendix table 5, page 20; and Appendix table 7, page 22.

17. Bureau of Justice Statistics, *Census of State and Federal Correctional Facilities, 2005* (Washington, D.C.: U.S. Department of Justice, October 2008), Appendix table 1, page 9.

18. *One in 100: Behind Bars in America 2008* (Washington, D.C.: The Pew Center on the States, February 2008), 11.

19. Deborah Hastings, "States Pull Back after Decades of Get-Tough Laws," *Associated Press* (April 4, 2009).

20. Monica Davey, "Touching Off Debate, Missouri Tells Judges Cost of Sentences," *New York Times* (September 19, 2010), 1.

21. Charles H. Logan, *Criminal Justice Performance Measures in Prisons* (Washington, D.C.: U.S. Department of Justice, 1993), 5.

22. Todd R. Clear and George F. Cole, *American Corrections*, 4th ed. (Belmont, CA: Wadsworth Publishing Co., 1997), 245–246.

23. Alfred Blumstein, "Prisons," in *Crime*, ed. James Q. Wilson and Joan Petersilia (San Francisco: ICS Press, 1995), 392.

24. Cassia Spohn and David Holleran, "The Effect of Imprisonment on Recidivism Rates of Felony Offenders: A Focus on Drug Offenders," *Criminology* (May 1, 2002), 329–357.

25. Tony Izzo, "I-Max Awaits Green," *Kansas City Star* (May 26, 1996), A1.

26. Charles A. Pettigrew, "Technology and the Eighth Amendment: The Problem of Supermax Prisons," *North Carolina Journal of Law and Technology* (Fall 2002), 195.

27. "Facts about Pelican Bay's SHU," *California Prisoner* (December 1991).

28. *Jones-El et al. v. Berge and Lichter*, 164 F.Supp.2d 1096 (2001).

29. Robert Perkinson, "Shackled Justice: Florence Federal Penitentiary and the New Politics of Punishment," *Social Justice* (Fall 1994), 117–123.

30. Terry Kuppers, *Prison Madness: The Mental Health Crisis behind Bars and What We Must Do about It* (San Francisco: Jossey-Bass, 1999), 56–64.

31. Charles H. Logan, "Well Kept: Comparing Quality of Confinement in a Public and Private Prison," *Journal of Criminal Law and Criminology* 83 (1992), 580.

32. Bert Useem and Peter Kimball, *Stages of Siege: U.S. Prison Riots, 1971–1986* (New York: Oxford University Press, 1989).

33. Bert Useem, "Disorganization and the New Mexico Prison Riot of 1980," *American Sociology Review* 50 (1985), 685.

34. John J. DiIulio, *Governing Prisons* (New York: Free Press, 1987), 12.

35. *Ibid.*

36. *Prisoners in 2009*, Appendix table 19, page 33.

37. "A Tale of Two Systems: Cost, Quality, and Accountability in Private Prisons," *Harvard Law Review* (May 2002), 1872.

38. Douglas C. McDonald and Kenneth Carlson, *Contracting for Imprisonment in the Federal Prison System: Cost and Performance of the Privately Operated Taft Correctional Institution* (Cambridge, MA: Abt Associates, Inc., October 2005), vii.

39. Vanderbilt University Law School, "New Study Shows Benefits of Having Privately and Publicly Managed Prisons in the Same State" (November 25, 2008), at **law.vanderbilt.edu/article-search/article-detail/index.aspx?nid=213**.

40. Nelson Daranciang, "Isle Inmates Brought Home," *Honolulu Star-Advertiser* (January 28, 2011), A3.

41. John Tunison, "Baldwin Prisoners Will Be Classified Medium Security," *Grand Rapids (Michigan) Press* (December 11, 2010), A4.

42. Logan, "Well Kept," 577.

43. Harley G. Lappin et al., *Evaluation of the Taft Demonstration Project: Performance of a Private-Sector Prison and the BOP* (Washington, D.C.: Federal Bureau of Prisons, 2005), 57–59.

44. Curtis R. Blakely and Vic W. Bumphus, "Private and Public Sector Prisons," *Federal Probation* (June 2004), 27.

45. Richard L. Lippke, "Thinking about Private Prisons," *Criminal Justice Ethics* (Winter/Spring 1997), 32.

46. John J. DiIulio, "Prisons, Profits, and the Public Good: The Privatization of Corrections," in *Criminal Justice Center Bulletin* (Huntsville, TX: Sam Houston State University, 1986).

47. Ira P. Robbins, "Privatization of Prisons, Privatization of Corrections: Defining the Issues," *Vanderbilt Law Review* 40 (1987), 823.

48. *Prisoners in 2009*, Appendix table 19, page 33.

49. Bureau of Justice Statistics, *Jail Inmates at Midyear 2009—Statistical Tables* (Washington, D.C.: U.S. Department of Justice, June 2010), 1.

50. Arthur Wallenstein, "Jail Crowding: Bringing the Issue to the Corrections Center Stage," *Corrections Today* (December 1996), 76–81.

51. Quoted in Fox Butterfied, "Defying Gravity: Inmate Population Climbs," *New York Times* (January 19, 1998), A10.

52. John Irwin, *The Jail: Managing the Underclass in American Society* (Berkeley, CA: University of California Press, 1985), 2.

53. Bureau of Justice Statistics, *Substance Dependence, Abuse, and Treatment of Jail Inmates, 2002* (Washington, D.C.: U.S. Department of Justice, July 2005), 1.

54. *Jail Inmates at Midyear 2009—Statistical Tables*, Table 6, page 9.

55. 441 U.S. 520 (1979).

56. *Ibid.*, 546.

57. *Jail Inmates at Midyear 2009—Statistical Tables*, Table 7, page 10.

58. Bureau of Justice Statistics, *Bulletin* (Washington, D.C.: U.S. Department of Justice, May 2004), 10.

59. Philip L. Reichel, *Corrections: Philosophies, Practices, and Procedures*, 2d ed. (Boston: Allyn & Bacon, 2001), 283.

60. John Cheves, "Cramming in the Inmates," *Lexington Herald-Leader* (January 13, 2008), A1.

61. Quoted in Greg Burton, "Jail Builders Race to Keep Up with Demand," *Salt Lake City Tribune* (May 8, 1998), N31.

62. Robert G. Lawson, "Turning Jails into Prisons—Collateral Damage from Kentucky's 'War on Crime,'" *Kentucky Law Journal* (2006–2007), 1.

63. *Jail Inmates at Midyear 2009—Statistical Tables*, 2.

64. *Ibid.*, Table 2, page 5.

65. *Ibid.*, Table 5, page 8.

66. Dan Seligman, "Lock 'Em Up," *Forbes* (May 23, 2005), 216–217.

67. Franklin E. Zimring and Gordon Hawkins, *Incapacitation: Penal Confinement and the Restraint of Crime* (New York: Oxford University Press, 1995), 38, 40, 145.

68. Sarah Schirmer, Ashley Nellis, and Marc Mauer, *Incarcerated Parents and Their Children* (Washington, D.C.: The Sentencing Project, February 2009), 2.

69. Todd R. Clear and Dina R. Rose, "A Thug in Jail Can't Shoot Your Sister: The Unintended Consequences of Incarceration," paper presented to the American Sociological Association (August 18, 1996).

70. The Sentencing Project, "Felony Disenfranchisement," at **www.sentencingproject.org/IssueAreaHome.aspx?IssueID=4**.

71. *Prisoners in 2009*, 9.

72. Quoted in Fox Butterfield, "Study Finds 2.6% Increase in U.S. Prison Population," *New York Times* (July 28, 2003), A8.

CHAPTER 14

1. Johnny Cash, "Folsom Prison Blues," (Sun Records, 1955).

2. Roderick Davis, "The Road from Prison to Rehabilitation," *New York Times* (January 21, 2011), at **www.nytimes.com/interactive/2011/01/22/opinion/20110122_Fixes_Delancey.html?emc=etal**.

3. Erving Goffman, "On the Characteristics of Total Institutions," in *Asylums: Essays on the Social Situation of Mental Patients and Other Inmates* (New York: Doubleday, 1961), 6.

4. Bureau of Justice Statistics, *Prisoners in 2000* (Washington, D.C.: U.S. Department of Justice, August 2001), Table 14, page 10; and Bureau of Justice Statistics, *Prisoners in 2009* (Washington, D.C.: U.S. Department of Justice, December 2010), Appendix table 13, page 27.

5. Robert Aday, *Aging Prisoners: Crisis in American Corrections* (Westport, CT: Praeger, 2003), 1–5.

6. Donald Clemmer, *The Prison Community* (Boston: Christopher, 1940).

7. John Irwin, *Prisons in Turmoil* (Boston: Little, Brown, 1980), 67.

8. Robert Johnson, *Hard Time: Understanding and Reforming the Prison*, 2d ed. (Belmont, CA: Wadsworth, 1996), 133.

9. Federal Bureau of Prisons report, cited in Kevin Johnson, "Report Points to Prison Security Failures," *USA Today* (June 8, 2009), 3A

10. "Table 1. Number of State Prisoner Deaths, by Cause of Death, 2001–2007," at **http://bjs.ojp.usdoj.gov/content/derp/tables/dcst07spt1.pdf**; and Bureau of Justice Statistics, *Mortality in Local Jails, 2001–2007* (Washington, D.C.: U.S. Deparment of Justice, July 2010), Appendix Table 2, page 16.

11. Lee H. Bowker, *Prison Victimization* (New York: Elsevier, 1981), 31–33.

12. Stephen C. Light, "The Severity of Assaults on Prison Officers: A Contextual Analysis," *Social Science Quarterly* 71 (1990), 267–284.

13. Lee H. Bowker, "An Essay on Prison Violence," in *Prison Violence in America*, ed. Michael Braswell, Steven Dillingham, and Reid Montgomery, Jr. (Cincinnati, OH: Anderson Publishing Co., 1985), 7–18.

14. Frank Tannenbaum, *Crime and Community* (Boston: Ginn & Co., 1938).

15. Randy Martin and Sherwood Zimmerman, "A Typology of the Causes of Prison Riots and an Analytical Extension to the 1986 Virginia Riot," *Justice Quarterly* 7 (1990), 711–737.

16. Useem, 677–688.

17. Stuart B. Klein, "Prisoners' Rights to Physical and Mental Health Care: A Modern Expansion of the Eighth Amendment's Cruel and Unusual Punishment Clause," *Fordham University Law Journal* 7 (1978), 1.

18. Irwin, 47.

19. Leo Carroll, "Race, Ethnicity, and the Social Order of the Prison," in *The Pains of Imprisonment*, ed. R. Johnson and H. Toch (Beverly Hills, CA: Sage, 1982).

20. Leo Carroll, *Hacks, Blacks, and Cons: Race Relations in a Maximum-Security Prison* (Lexington, MA: Lexington Books, 1988), 78.

21. *Johnson v. California*, 543 U.S. 499 (2005).

22. *Ibid.*, 508.

23. Jody Kent, "Race Walls Won't End Jail Riots," *Los Angeles Times* (February 12, 2006), M3.

24. Craig Haney, "Psychology and the Limits of Prison Pain," *Psychology, Public Policy, and Law* (December 1977), 499.

25. Alan Jr. Drury and Matt DeLisi, "Gangkill: An Exploratory Empirical Assessment of Gang Membership. Homicide Offending, and Prison Misconduct," *Crime & Delinquency* (January 2011), 130–146.

26. *A Study of Gangs and Security Threat Groups in America's Adult Prisons and Jails* (Indianapolis: National Major Gang Task Force, 2002).

27. George W. Knox, "The Problem of Gangs and Security Threat Groups (STGs) in American Prisons Today: Recent Research Findings from the 2004 Prison Gang Survey," at **www.ngcrc.com/corr2006.html**.

28. David M. Allender and Frank Marcell, "Career Criminals, Security Threat Groups, and Prison Gangs: An Interrelated Threat," *FBI Law Enforcement Bulletin* (June 2003), 8.

29. Knox.

30. Alan Gomez, "States Make Prisons Far Less Deadly," *USA Today* (August 22, 2008), 3A.

31. Quoted in Alexandra Marks, "Martha Checks in Today," *Seattle Times* (October 8, 2004), A8.

32. Robert Kravitz, "Women in Prisons" (April 5, 2010), at **www.corrections.com/articles/23873-women-in-prisons**.

33. Bureau of Justice Statistics, *Profile of Jail Inmates, 2002* (Washington, D.C.: U.S. Department of Justice, July 2004), 10.

34. Bureau of Justice Statistics, *Prior Abuse Reported by Inmates and Probationers* (Washington, D.C.: U.S. Department of Justice, April 1999), 2.

35. *Caught in the Net: The Impact of Drug Policies on Women and Families* (Washington, D.C.: American Civil Liberties Union, 2004), 18–19.

36. Allen J. Beck and Laura M. Maruschak, *Mental Health Treatment in State Prisons, 2000* (Washington, D.C.: U.S. Department of Justice, July 2001), 1.

37. Barbara Bloom, Barbara Owen, and Stephanie Covington, *Gender Responsive Strategies: Research, Practice, and Guiding Principles for Women Offenders* (Washington, D.C.: National Institute of Corrections, 2003), 6.

38. *Ibid.*, 7.

39. *Ibid.*, 6.

40. Sarah Schirmer, Ashley Nellis, and Marc Mauer, *Incarcerated Parents and Their Children: Trends 1991–2007* (Washington, D.C.: The Sentencing Project, February 2009), 2.

41. Kelly Bedard and Eric Helland, "Location of Women's Prisons and the Deterrent Effect of 'Harder' Time," *International Review of Law and Economics* (June 2004), 152.

42. *Ibid.*

43. Schirmer, Nellis, and Mauer, 5.

44. Barbara Owen *et al.*, *Gendered Violence and Safety: A Contextual Approach to Improving Security in Women's Facilities*, December 2008, 12–14.

45. Mary Bosworth, "Creating the Responsible Prisoner: Federal Admission and Orientation Packs," *Punishment and Society* 9 (2007), 67–85.

46. Nancy Wolff, Cynthia Blitz, Jing Shi, Jane Siegel, and Ronet Bachman, "Physical Violence inside Prisons: Rates of Victimization," *Criminal Justice and Behavior* 34 (2007), 588–604.

47. Quoted in John J. DiIulio, Jr., *No Escape: The Future of American Corrections* (New York: Basic Books, 1991), 268.

48. Jack Henry Abbott, *In the Belly of the Beast* (New York: Vintage Books, 1991), 54.

49. Michel Foucault, *Discipline and Punish: The Birth of the Prison* (New York: Pantheon Books, 1977), 128.

50. Lucien X. Lombardo, *Guards Imprisoned: Correctional Officers at Work* (Cincinnati, OH: Anderson Publishing Co., 1989), 51–71.

51. Goffman, 7.

52. 475 U.S. 312 (1986).

53. *Stanley v. Hejirika*, 134 F.3d 629 (4th Cir. 1998).

54. Christopher R. Smith, *Law and Contemporary Corrections* (Belmont, CA: Wadsworth, 1999), Chapter 6.

55. 503 U.S. 1 (1992).

56. Darrell L. Ross, "Assessing *Hudson v. McMillan* Ten Years Later," *Criminal Law Bulletin* (September/October 2004), 508.

57. Todd R. Clear and George F. Cole, *American Corrections*, 4th ed. (Belmont, CA: Wadsworth, 1997), 416.

58. Bureau of Justice Statistics, *Probation and Parole in the United States, 2005* (Washington, D.C.: U.S. Department of Justice, November 2006), 8.

59. 442 U.S. 1 (1979).

60. William Parker, *Parole: Origins, Development, Current Practices, and Statutes* (College Park, MD: American Correctional Association, 1972), 26.

61. Joan Petersilia, *When Prisoners Come Home: Parole and Prisoner Reentry* (New York: Oxford University Press, 2003), 39.

62. Victor Hassine, *Life without Parole: Living in Prison Today*, ed. Thomas J. Bernard and Richard McCleary (Los Angeles: Roxbury Publishing Co., 1996), 12.

63. John H. Tyler and Jeffrey R. King, "Prison-based Education and Reentry into the Mainstream Labor Market," in *Barriers to Reentry? The Labor Market for Released Prisoners in Post-Industrial America*, ed. Shawn D. Bushway, Michael A. Stoll, and David F. Weiman (New York: Russell Sage Foundation, 2007), 237.

64. *Ill Equipped: U.S. Prisons and Offenders with Mental Illness* (New York: Human Rights Watch, 2003).

65. Bureau of Justice Statistics, *Recidivism of Prisoners Released in 1994* (Washington, D.C.: U.S. Department of Justice, June 2002), 1.

66. *Census of State and Federal Correctional Facilities, 2005*, 6.

67. *Ibid.*, Table 6, page 5.

68. Joan Petersilia, "What Works in Prisoner Reentry," *Federal Probation* (September 2004), 4.

69. "The Greatest Fear," *The Economist* (August 26, 2006), 25.

70. Janice Marques, Mark Wiederanders, David Day, Craig Nelson, and Alice Ommeren, "Effects of a Relapse Prevention Program on Sexual Recidivism: Final Results from California's Sex Offender Treatment and Evaluation Project (SOTEP)," *Sexual Abuse: A Journal of Research and Treatment* (January 2005), 79–107.

71. New Jersey Revised Statute Section 2C:7-8(c) (1995).

72. Georgia Code Annotated Section 42-9-44.1(b)(1).

CHAPTER 15

1. Peter W. Greenwood, "Juvenile Crime and Juvenile Justice," in *Crime*, ed. James Q. Wilson and Joan Petersilia (San Francisco: ICS Press, 1995), 91.

2. Jennifer M. O'Connor and Lucinda K. Treat, "Getting Smart about Getting Tough: Juvenile Justice and the Possibility of Progressive Reform," *American Criminal Law Review* 33 (Summer 1996), 1299.

3. Eric K. Klein, "Dennis the Menace or Billy the Kid: An Analysis of the Role of Transfer to Criminal Court in Juvenile Justice," *American Criminal Law Review* 35 (Winter 1998), 371.

4. "Attitudes toward the Treatment of Juveniles Who Commit Violent Crimes," *Sourcebook of Criminal Justice Statistics 2003*, Table 2.48, at **www.albany.edu/sourcebook/pdf/t248.pdf**.

5. *In re Gault*, 387 U.S. 1, at 15 (1967).

6. Samuel Davis, *The Rights of Juveniles: The Juvenile Justice System*, 2d ed. (New York: C. Boardman Co., 1995), Section 1.2.

7. Quoted in Anthony Platt, *The Child Savers* (Chicago: University of Chicago Press, 1969), 119.

8. 383 U.S. 541 (1966).

9. *Ibid.*, 556.

10. 387 U.S. 1 (1967).

11. 397 U.S. 358 (1970).

12. 421 U.S. 519 (1975).

13. 403 U.S. 528 (1971).

14. Quoted in Sadie Gurman, "Hearing to Focus on Boy's Rehab Possibilities," *Pittsburgh Post-Gazette* (March 12, 2010), B1.

15. Sadie Gurman, "Boy Faces Murder Trial as Adult," *Pittsburgh Post-Gazette* (March 30, 2010), A1.

16. Gary B. Melton, "Toward 'Personhood' for Adolescents: Autonomy and Privacy as Values in Public Policy," *American Psychology* 38 (1983), 99–100.

17. Research Network on Adolescent Development and Juvenile Justice, *Youth on Trial: A Developmental Perspective on Juvenile Justice* (Chicago: John D. & Catherine T. MacArthur Foundation, 2003), 1.

18. Richard E. Redding, "Juveniles Transferred to Criminal Court: Legal Reform Proposals Based on Social Science Research," *Utah Law Review* (1997), 709.

19. Howard N. Snyder and Melissa Sickmund, *Juvenile Offenders and Victims: 2006 National Report* (Washington, D.C.: National Center for Juvenile Justice, March 2006), 47.

20. 543 U.S. 551 (2005).

21. *Ibid.*, 567.

22. 560 U.S. ___ (2010).

23. *Ibid.*

24. Charles Puzzanchera, Benjamin Adams, and Melissa Sickmund, *Juvenile Court Statistics 2006–2007* (Washington, D.C.: National Center for Juvenile Justice, March 2010), 31.

25. Frederick Ward, Jr., "Prevention and Diversion in the United States," in *The Changing Faces of Juvenile Justice*, ed. V. Lorne Stewart (New York: New York University Press, 1978), 43.

26. S'Lee Arthur Hinshaw II, "Juvenile Diversion: An Alternative to Juvenile Court," *Journal of Dispute Resolution* (1993), 305.

27. Rhode Island General Laws Section 14-1-7.1 (1994 and Supp. 1996).

28. Puzzanchera, Adams, and Sickmund, 40.

29. 467 U.S. 253 (1984).

30. Puzzanchera, Adams, and Sickmund, 32.

31. Barry C. Feld, "Criminalizing the American Juvenile Court," *Crime and Justice* 17 (1993), 227–254.

32. Barry C. Feld, "Abolish the Juvenile Court," *Journal of Criminal Law and Criminology* 88 (Fall 1997), 68.

33. Eric R. Lotke, "Youth Homicide: Keeping Perspective on How Many Children Kill," *Valparaiso University Law Review* 31 (Spring 1997), 395.

34. Bureau of Justice Statistics, *Jail Inmates at Midyear 2009—Statistical Tables* (Washington, D.C.: U.S. Department of Justice, June 2010), Table 6, page 9; and Bureau of Justice Statistics, *Prison Inmates at Midyear 2009—Statistical Tables* (Washington, D.C.: U.S. Department of Justice, June 2010), 2.

35. Sarah Livsey, "Juvenile Delinquency Probation Caseload, 2005," *OJJDP Fact Sheet* (Washington, D.C.: Office of Juvenile Justice and Delinquency Prevention, June 2009), 1.

36. Office of Juvenile Justice and Delinquency Prevention, *Juvenile Residential Facility Census 2006: Selected Findings* (Washington, D.C.: U.S. Department of Justice, December 2009), 2.

37. Snyder and Sickmund, 98.

38. Melissa Sickmund and Howard N. Snyder, *Juvenile Offenders and Victims: 1999 National Report* (Washington, D.C.: Office of Juvenile Justice and Delinquency Prevention, 1999), 182.

39. Dean John Champion, *The Juvenile Justice System: Delinquency, Processing, and the Law*, 5th ed. (Upper Saddle River, NJ: Pearson Prentice Hall, 2007), 581–582.

40. *Surveillance Summaries: Youth Risk Behavior Surveillance—United States, 2001* (Washington, D.C.: Centers for Disease Control and Prevention, June 28, 2002).

41. Federal Bureau of Investigation, *Crime in the United States, 2009* (Washington, D.C.: U.S. Department of Justice, 2010), at **www2.fbi.gov/ucr/cius2009/data/table_39.html**.

42. Office of Juvenile Justice and Delinquency Prevention, *Juvenile Arrests 2008* (Washington, D.C.: U.S. Department of Justice, December 2009).

43. Alfred Blumstein, "Youth Violence, Guns, and Illicit Drug Markets," *NIJ Research Journal* (Washington, D.C.: National Institute of Justice, 1995).

44. Quoted in Frank Greve, "Teens Not in As Much Trouble," *Arizona Daily-Star* (March 12, 2006), A7.

45. National Center for Education Statistics and Bureau of Justice Statistics, *Indicators of School Crime and Safety: 2010* (Washington, D.C.: U.S. Department of Justice, November 2010), 6.

46. *Ibid.*, 10–15.

47. *Ibid.*, Figure 20.2, page 78.

48. "Bully Police USA," at **bullypolice.org**.

49. Marvin E. Wolfgang, *From Boy to Man, from Delinquency to Crime* (Chicago: University of Chicago Press, 1987).

50. Matt DeLisi and Michael G. Vaughn, "The Gottfredson–Hirschi Critiques Revisited," *International Journal of Offender Therapy and Comparative Criminology* 52 (October 2008), 520–537.

51. Quoted in John H. Laub and Robert J. Sampson, "Understanding Desistance from Crime," in *Crime and Justice: A Review of Research* (Chicago: University of Chicago Press, 2001), 6.

52. Travis Hirschi and Michael Gottfredson, "Age and the Explanation of Crime," *American Journal of Sociology* 89 (1982), 552–584.

53. Robert J. Sampson and John H. Laub, "A Life-Course View on the Development of Crime," *Annals of the American Academy of Political and Social Science* (November 2005), 12.

54. "State Estimates of Underage Alcohol and Self-Purchase of Alcohol," *The NSDUH Report* (Rockville, MD: Office of Applied Studies, Substance Abuse and Mental Health Services Administration, April 1, 2010), 1.

55. Gary McClelland, Linda Teplin, and Karen Abram, "Detection and Prevalence of Substance Abuse among Juvenile Detainees," *Juvenile Justice*

Bulletin (Washington, D.C.: Office of Juvenile Justice and Delinquency Prevention, June 2004), 10.

56. Arrestee Drug Abuse Monitoring Program, *Preliminary Data on Drug Use and Related Matters among Adult Arrestees and Juvenile Detainees* (Washington, D.C.: National Institute of Justice, 2003).

57. David Finckhor *et al.*, *Children's Exposure to Violence: A Comprehensive National Survey* (Washington, D.C.: Office of Juvenile Justice and Delinquency Prevention, October 2009), 1.

58. Kimberly A. Tyler and Katherine A. Johnson, "A Longitudinal Study of the Effects of Early Abuse on Later Victimization among High-Risk Adolescents," *Violence and Victims* (June 2006), 287–291.

59. Grover Trask, "Defusing the Teenage Time Bombs," *Prosecutor* (March/April 1997), 29.

60. Cathy Spatz Widom, *The Cycle of Violence* (Washington, D.C.: National Institute of Justice, October 1992).

61. Janet Currie and Erdal Tekin, *Does Child Abuse Cause Crime?* (Atlanta: Andrew Young School of Policy Studies, April 2006), 27–28.

62. *National Gang Threat Assessment 2009* (Washington, D.C.: National Gang Intelligence Center, January 2009).

63. Sara R. Battin, Karl G. Hill, Robert D. Abbott, Richard F. Catalano, and J. David Hawkins, "The Contribution of Gang Membership to Delinquency beyond Delinquent Friends," *Criminology* 36 (1998), 93–115.

64. "Measuring the Extent of Gang Problems," *National Youth Gang Survey Analysis* at **www.nationalgangcenter.gov/Survey-Analysis/Measuring-the-Extent-of-Gang-Problem**.

65. *National Gang Threat Assessment 2009*, 8–9.

66. Karl G. Hill, Christina Lui, and J. David Hawkins, *Early Precursors of Gang Membership: A Study of Seattle Youth* (Washington, D.C.: Office of Juvenile Justice and Delinquency Prevention, December 2001).

67. Joseph F. Sheley and James D. Wright, *In the Line of Fire: Youth, Guns, and Violence in Urban America* (Hawthorne, NY: Aldine De Gruyter, 1995), 100.

68. Beth Bjerregaard and Alan J. Lizotte, "Gun Ownership and Gang Membership," *Journal of Criminal Law and Criminology* 86 (1995), 49.

69. Quoted in Gracie Bond Staples, "Guns in School," *Fort Worth Star-Telegram* (June 3, 1998), 1.

70. Office of Juvenile Justice and Delinquency Prevention, *1999 National Report Series: Juvenile Justice Bulletin—Kids and Guns* (Washington, D.C.: U.S. Department of Justice, March 2000), 4.

CHAPTER 16

1. Quoted in Richard A. Serrano, "'JihadJane' Indictment Unsealed," *Los Angeles Times* (March 10, 2010), 1.

2. *National Strategy for Homeland Security* (Washington, D.C.: Office of Homeland Security, 2002), 2.

3. Geoffrey Levitt, "Is 'Terrorism' Worth Defining?" *Ohio Northern University Law Review* 13 (1986), 97.

4. "Domestic Terrorism Program," at **baltimore.fbi.gov/domter.htm**.

5. David A. Westbrook, "Bin Laden's War," *Buffalo Law Review* (December 2006), 981–1012.

6. Marc Sageman, "Understanding Al-Qaida Networks," in *The McGraw-Hill Homeland Security Handbook*, ed. David G. Kamien (New York: McGraw-Hill, 2006), 53–54.

7. Ahmed S. Hashim, "Al-Qaida: Origins, Goals, and Grand Strategy," in *The McGraw-Hill Homeland Security Handbook*, ed. David G. Kamien (New York: McGraw-Hill, 2006), 24.

8. Bob Drogin and April Choi, "Oregon Man, 19, Is Held in Plan to Bomb Tree-Lighting," *Los Angeles Times* (November 29, 2010), A24.

9. Evan Thomas and Mark Hosenball, "53 Hours in the Life of a Near Disaster," *Newsweek* (May 17, 2010), 27.

10. Quoted in Josh Meyer, "Small Groups Seen as Biggest Threat in U.S.," *Los Angeles Times* (August 16, 2007), 1.

11. Even F. Kohlman, "'Homegrown' Terrorists: Theory and Cases in the War on Terror's Newest Front," *Annals of American Academy of Political and Social Science* (July 2008), 95–99.

12. Robert F. Worth, "Yemen: U.S.-Born Cleric Is Sentenced," *New York Times* (January 19, 2011), A7.

13. Quoted in Lolita C. Baldor, "Success of Lone Gunmen May Shift al-Qaida Strategy," *Associated Press* (March 11, 2010).

14. Quoted in Thomas and Hosenball, 29.

15. Brian Michael Jenkins, "The New Age of Terrorism," in *The McGraw-Hill Homeland Security Handbook*, ed. David G. Kamien (New York: McGraw-Hill, 2006), 117–129.

16. *Ibid.*, 128.

17. Leonard A. Cole, "WMD and Lessons from the Anthrax Attacks," in *The McGraw-Hill Homeland Security Handbook*, ed. David G. Kamien (New York: McGraw-Hill, 2006), 167.

18. *Ibid.*, 168.

19. Quoted in David Cook, "Robert Mueller," *Christian Science Monitor* (May 10, 2007), 25.

20. Cole, 169.

21. Quoted in Jim Lobe, "Nation Girds for War with Unidentified Enemy" (September 12, 2001), at **ipsnews.net/news.asp?idnews=34634**.

22. "Transcript: President Obama's Inaugural Address," *New York Times* (January 21, 2009), P2.

23. 18 U.S.C. Section 2339B(a)(1) (1996).

24. 8 U.S.C. Section 1182(a)(3)(B) (Supp. I 2001); and 8 U.S.C. Section 1189(a)(1)(C) (Supp I 2001).

25. U.S. Department of State, "Country Reports on Terrorism," at **www.state.gov/s/ct/rls/crt/2009/140900.htm**.

26. 18 U.S.C. Section 2339A(b) (Supp I 2001).

27. 8 U.S.C. Section 1182(a)(3)(B)(iv)(VI) (Supp. I 2001), amended by the Patriot Act of 2001, Pub. L. No. 107-56, Section 411(a), 115 Stat. 272.

28. Uniting and Strengthening America by Providing Appropriate Tools Required to Intercept and Obstruct Terrorism Act of 2001, Pub. L. No. 107-56, 115 Stat. 272 (2001).

29. Jane A. Bullock *et al.*, *Introduction to Homeland Security*, 2d ed. (Burlington, MA: Butterworth-Heinemann, 2006), 41–42.

30. "House Endorses Patriot Act," *Chicago Tribune* (February 15, 2011), 13.

31. Pub. L. No. 107-296, 116 Stat. 2135.

32. Federal Bureau of Investigation, "Facts and Figures: FBI Priorities," at **www.fbi.gov/priorities/priorities.htm**.

33. Bullock *et al.*, 198.

34. National Commission on Terrorist Attacks upon the United States, *The 9/11 Commission Report: Executive Summary* (Washington, D.C.: National Commission on Terrorist Attacks upon the United States, 2004), 9.

35. Bob Drogin and April Choi, "Defense Takes Aim at FBI," *Los Angeles Times* (November 30, 2010), A24.

36. Quoted in Bruce Shipkowski and Matt Apuzzo, "N.J. Man Held at JFK: I'll Outdo Fort Hood Killer," *Associated Press* (June 7, 2010).

37. *Ibid.*

38. Press Release, "Two New Jersey Men Arrested and Charged with Conspiring to Kill Persons Outside the United States," *United States Attorney, District of New Jersey*, at **www.state.nj.us/njhomelandsecurity/press-room/press-releases/2010/06-06-10-alessa-mohamed-and-almont-carlos-arrest-complaint-pr.pdf**.

39. The Center on Law and Security, *Terrorist Trial Report Card: September 11, 2009–September 11, 2009* (New York: New York University School of Law, January 2010), 42–44.

40. Glenn Greenwalk, "The FBI Successfully Thwarts Its Own Terrorist Plot," *Salon.com* (November 28, 2010), at **www.salon.com/news/opinion/glenn_greenwald/2010/11/28/fbi**.

41. Quoted in Drogin and Choi, A10.

42. Eric Schmitt and Charlie Savage, "In U.S. Sting Operations, Questions of Entrapment," *New York Times* (November 30, 2010), A22.

43. "Spies among Us," *U.S. News & World Report* (May 8, 2006), 43.

44. *Ibid.*, 41–43.

45. "Homeland Security Presidential Directive/HSPD-8," at **www.fas.org/irp/offdocs/nspd/hspd-8.html**.

46. Bullock *et al.*, 315.

47. National Commission on Terrorist Attacks upon the United States, 14.

48. Thomas and Hosenball, 30.

49. Ginger Thompson, "U.S. Taking Steps to Control Violence on the Mexican Border," *New York Times* (March 25, 2009), A10.

50. Quoted in Peter Baker, "A Renewed Debate over Suspect Rights," *New York Times* (May 5, 2010), A25.

51. Quoted in Susan Sachs, "Murky Lives, Fateful Trip in Buffalo Terrorism Case," *New York Times* (September 20, 2002), A1.

52. *INS v. Delgado*, 466 U.S. 215 (1983).

53. Quoted in Philip Shenon, "Senate Report on Pre-9/11 Failure Tells of Bungling at FBI," *New York Times* (August 28, 2002), A14.

54. Pub. L. No. 107-56, Section 201-2-2, 115 Stat. 272, 278 (2001).

55. 50 U.S.C. Section 1803 (2000).

56. Patriot Act, Section 203(d)(1), 115 Stat. 272, 280 (2001).

57. Patriot Act, Section 206, amending Section 105(c)(2)(B) of the Foreign Intelligence Surveillance Act.

58. Patriot Act, Section 213.

59. FISA Amendments Act of 2008, Pub. L. No. 110-261, 122 Stat. 2436 (2008).

60. Quoted in Jim Puzzanghera, "TSA Won't Back Off on Pat-Downs," *Los Angeles Times* (November 22, 2010), A8.

61. Brian Bennett, "Pat-Downs Aimed at Finding Explosive," *Los Angeles Times* (November 24, 2010), A1.

62. Quoted in David G. Savage, "Scanners Pit Privacy against Security," *Los Angeles Times* (January 13, 2010), 11.

63. "Anti-Muslim Sentiments Fairly Commonplace," *The Gallup Poll* (August 10, 2006), at **www.gallup.com/poll/24073/antimuslim-sentiments-fairly-commonplace.aspx**.

64. Charlie Savage, "Wider Authority for FBI Agents Stirs Concerns," *New York Times* (October 29, 2009), A1.

65. Quoted in Samantha Henry, "Some Muslims Rethink Close Ties to Law Enforcement," *Associated Press* (May 4, 2009).

66. *Wong Wing v. United States*, 163 U.S. 228 (1896).

67. 66 *Federal Register* 48334 (September 20, 2001).

68. Michael Greenberger, "You Ain't Seen Nothin' Yet: The Inevitable Post-*Hamdan* Conflict between the Supreme Court and the Political Branches," *Maryland Law Review* 66 (2007), 805, 807.

69. "One in 7 Who Leave Guantanamo Involved in Terrorism," *Reuters* (May 26, 2009).

70. Brian Bennett, "Former Detainees Now Plot in Yemen," *Los Angeles Times* (November 2, 2010), A1.

71. Military Commission Act of 2009, Public Law No. 111-84, Sections 1801-1807, 123 Stat. 2190 (2009).

72. Quoted in Richard A. Serrano and David G. Savage, "Obama to Stay Course on Terrorism Trials," *Los Angeles Times* (November 19, 2010), A9.

73. Carol J. Williams, "The Guantanamo Puzzle," *Los Angeles Times* (November 3, 2010), A9.

74. Al Baker, "In New York, Relief and Disappointments as 9/11 Trial is Headed Elsewhere," *New York Times* (January 31, 2010), 19.

75. Kevin Johnson, "Pollitical Sparring Snarls Terror Suspects Trials," *USA Today* (December 10, 2010), 5A.

76. *Ibid.*

CHAPTER 17

1. "Suicide Highlights Torment of the Internet," *Kansas City Star* (October 1, 2010), A1.

2. Sally Kalson, "Bad Intentions: The Rutgers Suicide Shows the Ugly Side of 'Sharing,'" *Pittsburgh Post-Gazette* (October 10, 2010), B3.

3. National Institute of Justice, *Computer Crime: Criminal Justice Resource Manual* (Washington, D.C.: U.S. Department of Justice, 1989), 2.

4. *Ibid.*

5. Internet Crime Complaint Center, "IC3 2009 Annual Report on Internet Crime Released," at **www.ic3.gov/media/2010/100312.aspx**.

6. *Symantec Global Internet Security Threat Report: Trends for 2009* (Mountain View, CA: Symantec Corporatiion, April 2010), 16.

7. Charlotte Decker, "Cyber Crime 2.0: An Argument to Update the United States Criminal Code to Reflect the Changing Nature of Cyber Crime," *Southern California Law Review* (July 2008), 959–1016.

8. *2011 Identity Fraud Survey Report* (Pleasanton, CA: Javelin Strategy and Research, 2011), 1.

9. Benny Evangelista and Alejandro Martinez-Cabrera, "Big Jump in Number of People on Twitter," *San Francisco Chronicle* (September 4, 2010), D2.

10. "Gartner Survey Shows Phishing Attacks Escalated in 2007; More than $3 Billion Lost to These Attacks" (December 17, 2007), at **www.gartner.com/it/page.jsp?id=565125**.

11. Bureau of Justice Statistics, *Stalking Victimization in the United States* (Washington, D.C.: U.S. Department of Justice, 2009), 1.

12. *Ibid.*

13. Melissa Healy, "Greatest Internet Threat to Teens May Be Teens Themselves," *Los Angeles Times* (January 26, 2009), 1.

14. Internet Safety Technical Task Force, *Enhancing Child Safety & Online Technologies* (Cambridge, MA: The Berkman Center for Internet & Society, December 31, 2008).

15. Quoted in Healy.

16. Sameer Hinduja and Justin W. Patchin, *Cyberbullying: Indentifications, Prevention, and Response* (**www.cyberbullying.us**: Cyberbullying Research Center, 2010), 1.

17. Jan Hoffman, "Online Bullies Pull Schools into the Fray," *New York Times* (June 28, 2010), A1.

18. Jessica Bennett, "From Lockers-to-Lockup," *Newsweek* (October 11, 2010), 39.

19. BBC Mobile, "Thousands of Stolen iTunes Accounts for Sale in China," (January 6, 2011), at **www.bbc.co.uk/news/technology-12127603**.

20. Geraldine Baum and Stuart Pfeifer, "Dozens Charged in Bank Thefts," *Los Angeles Times* (October 1, 2010), B1.

21. Byron Acohido, "An Invitation to Crime," *USA Today* (March 2010), 1A.

22. Quoted in Jason Cato, "'Hacker's Hacker' from San Francisco Pleads Guilty in $86 Million Fraud," *Pittsburgh Tribune-Review* (June 30, 2009), B1.

23. Quoted in Kelly Jackson Higgins, "U.S. Business Could Lose Up to $1 Billion in Online Banking Fraud This Year," *Tech Center: SMB Security* (September 1, 2010), at **www.darkreading.com/smb-security/167901073/security/attacks-breaches/227200174/index.html**.

24. Todd Lewan, "Chips in Official IDs Raise Privacy Fears," *Associated Press* (July 11, 2009).

25. *Symantec Global Internet Security Threat Report*, 16.

26. 15 U.S.C. Sections 7701–7713 (2003).

27. *Cisco 2010 Annual Security Report* (San Jose, CA: Cisco Systems, Inc., 2010).

28. *Ibid.*, 30.

29. *Seventh Annual BSA and IDC Global Software Piracy Study* (Washington, D.C.: Business Software Alliance, May 2010), 2.

30. 17 U.S.C. Section 23199(c) (1998).

31. 17 U.S.C. Sections 2301 et seq. (1998).

32. 545 U.S. 913 (2005).

33. Dawn C. Chmielewski, "A New Wave of Piracy Feared," *Los Angeles Times* (September 21, 2010), B3.

34. Bank Secrecy Act of 1970, 31 U.S.C. Sections 1051–1709 (2000).

35. Siobhan Gorman, "FBI Targets Cyber 'Mules,'" *Wall Street Journal* (May 11, 2010), at **online.wsj.com/article/SB10001424052748703565804575238531980928488.html**.

36. "The Internet Porn 'Epidemic': By the Numbers," *The WEEK* (June 17, 2010), at **theweek.com/article/index/204156/the-internet-porn-epidemic-by-the-numbers**.

37. William R. Graham, Jr., "Uncovering and Eliminating Child Pornography Rings on the Internet," *Law Review of Michigan State University Detroit College of Law* (Summer 2000), 466.

38. 31 U.S.C. Sections 5361 et seq. (2006).

39. Quoted in Michael McCarthy, "Feds Go after Offshore Online Betting Industry," *USA Today* (July 19, 2006), 6C.

40. Steve Chapman, "More Freedom Is a Sound Bet," *Chicago Tribune* (August 1, 2010), 21.

41. Quoted in Richard Rapaport, "Cyberwars: The Feds Strike Back," *Forbes* (August 23, 1999), 126.

42. National Institute of Justice, "What Is Digital Evidence?" in *Electronic Crime Scene Investigation: A Guide for First Responders*, 2d ed. (Washington, D.C.: U.S. Department of Justice, April 2008), ix.

43. Matthew Boyle, "The Latest Hit: CSI in Your Hard Drive," *Fortune* (November 14, 2005), 39.

44. Quoted in "Cybersleuths Find Growing Role in Fighting Crime," *HPC Wire*, at **www.hpcwire.com/hpc-bin/artread.pl?direction=Current&articlenumber=19864**.

45. Laurie P. Cohen, "Internet's Ubiquity Multiplies Venues to Try Web Crimes," *Wall Street Journal* (February 12, 2007), B1.

46. Alicia A. Caldwell and Pete Yost, "Cyberthieves Still Rely on Human Foot Soldiers," *Associated Press* (November 22, 2010).

47. Federal Bureau of Investigation, "Cyber Investigations," at **www.fbi.gov/cyberinvest/cyberhome.htm**.

48. Heather Jacobson and Rebecca Green, "Computer Crimes," *American Criminal Law Review* (Spring 2002), 283.

49. Pub. L. No. 326-110, 122 Stat. 3561.

50. Javelin Strategy and Research, "Identity Fraud Fell 28 Percent in 2010 According to New Javelin Strategy & Research Report" (February 8, 2011), at **www.javelinstrategy.com/news/1170/92/Identity-Fraud-Fell-28-Percent-in-2010-According-to-New-Javelin-Strategy-Research-Report/d,pressRoomDetail**.

51. Quoted in Elizabeth Olson, "Killings Prompt Effort to Spot and Reduce Abuse of Teenagers in Dating," *New York Times* (January 4, 2009), 16.

52. Danice K. Eaton, Kristen S. Davis, Lisa Barrios, Nancy D. Brenner, and Rita K. Noonan, "Associations of Dating Violence Victimization with Lifetime Participation, Co-Occurrence, and Early Initiation of Risk Behaviors among U.S. High School Students," *Journal of Interpersonal Violence* 22 (2007), 586–602.

53. Quoted in Olson, 12.

54. *Ibid.*

55. Nancy M. Ritter, "Preparing for the Future: Criminal Justice in 2040," *National Institute of Justice Journal*, No. 225 (2006), 8–11.

2.1 The judge required Philip to redo his rehabilitation, a twelve-step Sexaholics Anonymous program. Unfettered by his tumor, Philip kept his hands to himself and successfully completed the requirement. Eventually, he returned home to his family. Interestingly, about one year later the headaches returned and Philip resumed collecting child pornography. A brain scan showed that the tumor had begun to reform. As before, doctors removed the tumor, and the deviant behavior ceased. Source: Jeffrey M. Burns and Russell H. Swerdlow, "Right Orbifrontal Tumor with Pedophilia Symptom and Constructional Apraxia Sign," *Archives of Neurology* (March 2003), 437.

5.1 The United States Supreme Court ruled that individuals do not have a right to protection by law enforcement agencies and, therefore, Jessica could not sue the Castle Rock Police Department. In his majority opinion, Justice Antonin Scalia said that, while the restraining order did seem to mandate an arrest in these circumstances, "a well-established tradition of police discretion has long coexisted with apparently mandatory arrest statutes." Source: *Town of Castle Rock v. Gonzales,* 545 U.S. 748 (2005). The full text of this case can be found online at **supreme.justia.com/us/545/04-278/case.html**.

7.1 The United States Supreme Court ruled that the evidence was valid and could be presented against Harold. If the police officers had known, or should have known, that the third floor contained two apartments before they entered Harold's residence, then they would have been required to search only Larry's lodging. But, the Court said, "honest mistakes" by police officers do not equal an "unreasonable

search" under the Fourth Amendment. Source: *Maryland v. Garrison,* 480 U.S. 79 (1987). The full text of this case can be found online at **supreme.justia.com/us/480/79/case.html**.

11.1 The Arizona Supreme Court ruled that the sentence was "not so grossly disproportionate as to constitute cruel and unusual punishment," and upheld Morton's 200-year prison term. While admitting that the sentence might be unusual, the court felt that it was in keeping with the Arizona state legislature's goal of eradicating child pornography. Morton filed a petition for a writ of *certiorari* with the United States Supreme Court, but the Court declined to hear the case. The decision shows how reluctant judges are to strike down sentences as excessive. Source: For the full text of the Arizona Supreme Court's decision, go to **www.azcourts.gov/Portals/23/pdf2006/CR050101PR.pdf**.

12.1 The trial judge sentenced Jason and another fraternity brother who participated in the hazing to two years in prison, followed by three years on probation. The judge also ordered Jason to attend an antihazing class and refrain from communicating with any "Greek" (fraternity) organization while on probation. The judge said that she had considered limiting the sentence to one year, but added a second year to make sure that the punishment was seen as a deterrent. "I want to save the victims who will quietly go along because they want to belong," she said. "I want schools to be furious and mad and upset [and] come down hard on hazing." She added that she wanted other students to say, "Those guys, they got two years, Oh my God." Source: "Two Sentenced in FAMU Hazing" at **www.pks.org/pdf/updates/FAMUHazingturnstoJail.pdf**.

INDEX

CRIMINAL JUSTICE THEORIES

THEORY	SUMMARY	NOTED THEORISTS	RELATED THEORIES	CRIME PREVENTION STRATEGY
Choice Theories	A school of criminology that holds that wrongdoers act as if they weigh the possible benefits of criminal or delinquent activity against the expected costs of being apprehended.	Cesare Beccaria (1738–1794) Jeremy Bentham (1748–1832)	**Classical Criminology**—Individuals have free will to engage in criminal behavior. **Rational Choice Theory**—Individuals are rational, and engage in a decision making process prior to offending.	The punishment must outweigh the benefits of committing the crime. In addition, punishments must be swift and certain.
Trait Theories	A school of the social sciences that sees criminal and delinquent behavior as the result of biological and psychological forces.	Cesare Lombroso "Father of Criminology" (1835–1909)	Modern **biological theories** focus on the links between physiological elements such as genetics, hormones, and neurophysiology to explain offending. Modern **psychological theories** focus on the psychoanalysis, social psychology, and mental illness to explain criminal offending.	Offenders should be diagnosed and treated for the underlying causes of their behavior rather than punished.
Sociological Theories	A school of criminology that suggests that criminal behavior is the result of social and physical environmental factors. Established by a group of scholars who were collectively known as the "Chicago School."	Ernest Burgess (1886–1966) Robert Ezra Park (1864–1944)	**Social Disorganization Theory**—Deviant behavior is more likely in communities where social institutions fail to exert control over the population. (Shaw and McKay) **Strain Theory**—Crime is the result of frustration felt by individuals who cannot reach their financial and personal goals through legitimate means. (Durkheim and Merton) **Culture Deviance Theory**—Members of certain subcultures reject the values of the dominant culture through deviant behavior patterns. (Miller)	To address and prevent crime, the government should focus on building strong neighborhood environments by decreasing unemployment, reducing poverty, and improving educational facilities for low-income Americans.
Social Process Theories	Crime is not something that one is "born to do." Rather, crime is the result of the social conditions in which a person finds himself or herself.	Edwin Sutherland (1883–950) Travis Hirschi (1935–present)	**Learning Theory**—Delinquents and criminals must be taught both the practical and emotional skills necessary to participate in illegal activity. (Sutherland) **Control Theory**—All individuals have the potential for criminal behavior, but are restrained by the damage that such actions would do to their relationships with family friends, and members of the community. (Hirschi) **Labeling Theory**—Society creates crime and criminals by labeling certain behavior and certain people as deviant. (Becker)	To address and prevent crime, the criminal justice system should focus on encouraging positive social controls, such as mentoring programs and community groups, and prevent the labeling of criminal offenders
Social Conflict Theories	This movement views criminal behavior as the result of class conflict. Through criminal laws, the dominant members of society control minority members, using institutions such as the police, courts, and prisons as tools of oppression.	Richard Quinney (1934–present)	Supporters of this theory align themselves with **Marxist, radical, conflict, and feminist** schools of criminology.	In order to prevent and address criminal behavior, the criminal justice system should strive to ensure there is no disparity between the powerful and powerless members of society, particularly in the forms of poverty, racism, and sexism.

STEPS OF THE CRIMINAL JUSTICE SYSTEM

Step 1:
Entry into the System

Reported and Observed Crime

tifsonburg/iStockphoto

Investigation

POLICE LINE DO NOT CROSS POLICE LINE DO

tifsonburg/iStockphoto

Unsolved or Not Arrested

Arrest

arfo/iStockphoto

Released without Prosecution

Charges Filed

Step 2: Prosecution and Pretrial Services

Initial Court Appearance

PierreDesrosiers/iStockphoto

Released without Prosecution

Charges Dropped or Dismissed

- Admitted Guilt
- Penalty Assigned
- Diversion Program Ordered

AllinasSS/iStockphoto

Preliminary Hearing

Bail or Detention Hearing

Misdemeanors

Charges Dropped or Dismissed

Felonies

Grand Jury

dcdebs/iStockphoto

Refusal to Indict

Unsuccessful Diversion

Information

Carol Oostman/iStockphoto

Step 3: Adjudication

Arraignment

Charges Dismissed or Reduced

Guilty Plea

Trial

ftwitty/iStockphoto

Acquitted

Convicted

Step 4:
Sentencing and Sanctions

Appeal

Sentencing

Felonies

Intermediate Sanctions

vm/iStockphoto

Misdemeanors

Sentencing

Step 5: Corrections

Probation

Revocation

Out of System

Prison

leeznow/iStockphoto

Revocation

Parole

Out of System

- *Habeas Corpus*
- Pardon and Clemency
- Capital Punishment

Probation

Revocation

Out of System

Jail

wsmahar/iStockphoto

Out of System

STEPS OF THE CRIMINAL JUSTICE SYSTEM

Step 1: Entry into the System

● Once a law enforcement agency has established that a crime has been committed, a suspect must be identified and apprehended for the case to proceed through the system.

● Sometimes a suspect is apprehended at the scene of the crime; at other times, however, identification of a suspect requires an extensive investigation.

● Often, no one is identified or apprehended. In some instances, a suspect is arrested, and later the police determine that no crime was committed and the suspect is released.

Step 2: Prosecution and Pretrial Services

● After an arrest, law enforcement agencies present information about the case and about the accused to the prosecutor, who will decide if formal charges will be filed with the court.

● A suspect charged with a crime must be taken before a judge without unnecessary delay.

● At the initial appearance, the judge informs the accused of the charges and decides whether there is probable cause to detain the accused person.

● If the offense is not serious, the determination of guilt and an assessment of a penalty may also occur at this stage.

● Often, the defense counsel is assigned at the initial appearance. All suspects charged with serious crimes have a right to be represented by an attorney. If the suspect cannot afford a defense attorney, the court will provide one for him or her at the public's expense.

● A pretrial release decision may also be made at the initial appearance. The court may decide that the suspect poses a threat to society and place him or her in jail until the trial.

● The court may decide to release the suspect with the understanding that he or she will return for the trial, or release the suspect on bail (meaning he or she must provide the court with monetary payment [bail], which will be returned when the suspect appears for the trial).

● In many jurisdictions, the initial appearance may be followed by a preliminary hearing. The main function of this hearing is to discover if there is probable cause to believe that the accused committed a known crime within the jurisdiction of the court. If the judge does find probable cause or the accused waives his or her right to the preliminary hearing, the case may be sent to a grand jury.

● A grand jury hears evidence against the accused presented by the prosecutor and decides if there is sufficient evidence to cause the accused to be brought to trial. If the grand jury finds sufficient evidence, it submits to the court an indictment, a written statement of the essential facts of the offense charged against the accused.

● Misdemeanor cases and some felony cases proceed by the issuance of an information, a formal, written accusation submitted to the court by a prosecutor.

● In some jurisdictions, defendants—often those without prior criminal records—may be eligible for diversion programs. In these programs, the suspect does not go to trial and instead must complete a rehabilitation program, such as drug treatment. If he or she is successful, the charges may be dropped, and his or her criminal record may remain clear.

Step 3: Adjudication

● Once an indictment or information has been filed with the trial court, the accused is scheduled for an arraignment.

● At the arraignment, the accused is informed of the charges, advised of his or her rights, and asked to enter a plea to the charges.

● Sometimes a plea of guilty is the result of negotiations between the prosecutor and the defendant. If the defendant pleads guilty and this plea is accepted by the judge, no trial is held and the defendant is sentenced.

● If the accused pleads not guilty, a date is set for the trial. A person accused of a serious crime is guaranteed a trial by jury.

● During the trial, the prosecution and defense present evidence and the judge decides issues of law. The jury then decides whether the defendant will be acquitted (found not guilty) or convicted (found guilty of the initial charges or of other offenses).

● If the defendant is found guilty, he or she may request that the trial be reviewed by a higher court to assure that the rules of trial procedure were followed.

Step 4: Sentencing and Sanctions

● After a conviction, a sentence is imposed. In most cases, the judge decides the sentence, though sometimes the jury makes this decision.

● Some of the sentencing choices available to judges and juries include: the death penalty, incarceration in prison or jail, probation (allowing the convicted person to remain in the community as long as he or she follows certain rules), and fines. In many jurisdictions, persons convicted of certain types of offenses must serve a prison term.

Step 5: Corrections

● Offenders sentenced to incarceration usually serve time in a local jail or a prison. Offenders sentenced to less than one year usually go to jail, while those sentenced to more than one year go to prison.

● A prisoner may become eligible for parole after serving part of his or her sentence. Parole is the release of a prisoner before the full sentence has been served. If released under parole, the convict will be supervised in the community for the balance of his or her sentence.

SELECTED CRIMINAL JUSTICE CAREERS

POSITION	PRIMARY RESPONSIBILITIES	REQUIREMENTS	FOR MORE INFORMATION
F.B.I. Special Agent	Activities include investigating organized and white-collar crime, public corruption, civil rights violations, bank robberies, air piracy, terrorism, and other federal statutes violations.	U.S. citizenship; four-year degree from a U.S. accredited college or university; 23 years of age, but not older than 36; ability to relocate; excellent vision, health; valid driver's license.	www.fbi.gov
Federal Police	Enforce federal laws through patrol, apprehension of criminals, and investigation of crimes. Respond to incidents and emergencies and assist state and local police as needed.	U.S. citizenship; a bachelor's degree or experience in law enforcement; pass background screening and physical exam; valid driver's license.	www.usajobs.opm.gov
United States Marshal	Enforce all federal laws that aren't covered by other federal agencies, administer federal court proceedings, and apprehend fugitives.	U.S. citizenship; bachelor's degree or three years' work experience or a combination of the two; age 21–37; excellent health and physical fitness.	www.usdoj.gov/marshals/careers/career.html
County Sheriff	Responsibilities vary account to size of the county. In addition to law enforcement, sheriff's departments typically perform court-related functions, such as providing courtroom security.	U.S. citizenship; high school diploma or equivalent; age 21–37; good physical condition (meet vision, hearing standards and height/weight ratio); valid driver's license.	www.sheriffs.org
Municipal Police	Uphold laws, promote public safety, provide services, maintain order. Typical duties include evidence gathering when responding to incidents, reporting suspicious activities, communicating with community to promote safety, apprehending suspects.	High school diploma; police academy is typically three to seven months; most departments require continuing education.	www.officer.com
Private Investigator	Generally employed by private and public organizations to protect their businesses and employees.	Education and licensing varies by state. Minimum: high school diploma; some jobs require college degree. Screening can include background checks, fingerprinting, apptitude test.	www.bls.gov/oco/ocos157.htm
Judge	Apply the law through hearings and trials, ensuring that they are conducted in fairness to all parties, issuing sentences and penalties to guilty parties. Judges hear the facts and evidence of a case from prosecution and defense counsels to decided whether a trial is necessary.	Bachelor's degree Juris Doctorate degree Pass the state bar exam Practicing attorney experience	www.fjc.gov www.judges.org
Attorney	Attorneys practice in criminal law as prosecutors or defense counsel. Activities include researching and examining evidence and facts of each case and interpreting the law based on the purposes of the laws and prior judicial decisions.	Bachelor's degree Juris Doctorate degree Pass the state bar exam	www.americanbar.org/aba.htm
Paralegal	Research laws and prior cases, investigate facts and evidence, write legal documents and briefs, coordinate communications, keep records of all documents.	Varies among law firms and employers. Generally a college degree or paralegal certification is required.	www.nala.org
Correctional Officer	Monitor prisoners, enforce rules, maintain order, inspect correctional facilities and prisoners for illegal substances and weapons.	U.S. citizenship; high school diploma or equivalent; 18 years of age. Federal Bureau of Prisons requires one of the following: bachelor's degree, three years' work experience or a combination of college courses and work experience.	www.corrections.com
Probation Officer	Counseling and rehabilitating criminal offenders without the use of incarceration. Probation officers also assist in sentencing by preparing presentence reports. Monitor and keep records of the offender's behavior for the courts.	U.S. citizenship; bachelor's degree and/or experience in probation or intermediate corrections; pass drug, medical, and psychological screening tests; valid driver's license.	www.appa-net.org
Parole Officer	Responsible for legal custody of offenders following release from incarceration and ensuring adherence to conditions of parole.	Bachelor's degree or work experience in parole or probation; written and oral exams typically required.	www.appa-net.org

CRIMINAL JUSTICE TIMELINE

	Supreme Court Criminal Justice Decisions	Legal Events
1900s	1903 Lottery ticket ban upheld	
1910s	1914 *Weeks v. U.S.:* Exclusionary rule adopted for federal courts 1919 *Schenck v. U.S.:* Socialist found guilty of obstructing war effort	1914 Harrison Narcotics Act passed 1919 Prohibition begins
1920s	1923 *Frye v. U.S.:* Scientific evidence admissible if it has gained general acceptance 1927 *Tumey v. Ohio:* Paying a judge only if defendant is found guilty is unconstitutional 1928 *Olmstead v. U.S.:* Wiretaps legal if no trespass	1921 William Taft becomes Chief Justice 1925 Federal Probation Act
1930s	1932 *Powell v. Alabama:* Limited right to counsel in capital cases established 1939 *U.S. v. Miller:* Right to bear arms limited to militia	1930 Charles Evans Hughes becomes Chief Justice 1931 National Commission on Law Observance and Enforcement—Wickersham Commission 1933 Prohibition ends 1935 199 executions in U.S.; highest rate in 20th century 1937 FDR's court packing plan defeated 1939 Administrative Office of U.S. Courts created
1940s		1941 Harlan Stone becomes Chief Justice 1946 Fred Vinson becomes Chief Justice
1950s	1956 *Griffin v. Illinois:* Indigents entitled to court appointed attorney for first appeal	1953 Earl Warren becomes Chief Justice
1960s	1961 *Mapp v. Ohio:* Exclusionary rule required in state courts 1963 *Fay v. Noia:* Right to *habeas corpus* expanded *Brady v. Maryland:* Prosecutors must turn over evidence favorable to defense *Gideon v. Wainwright:* Indigents have right to counsel 1966 *Sheppard v. Maxwell:* Conviction reversed based on prejudicial pretrial publicity *Miranda v. Arizona:* Suspects must be advised of rights before interrogation 1967 *In Re Gault:* Requires counsel for juveniles	1966 Bail Reform Act favors pretrial release 1967 President's Commission on Law Enforcement and Administration of Justice 1969 Warren Burger becomes Chief Justice
1970s	1972 *Furman v. Georgia:* Declares state death penalty laws unconstitutional *Barker v. Wingo:* Adopts flexible approach to speedy trial 1975 *Gerstein v. Pugh:* Arrestee entitled to a prompt hearing 1976 *Gregg v. Georgia:* Upholds death penalty *North v. Russell:* Non-lawyer judges are upheld 1979 *Burch v. Louisiana:* Six member juries must be unanimous	1970 Organized Crime Control Act 1971 Prison riot in Attica, New York 1972 Break-in at Watergate 1973 National Advisory Commission on Criminal Justice Standards and Goals 1973 Nixon declares war on drugs 1977 Determinate sentencing enacted in 4 states
1980s	1986 *Baston v. Kentucky:* Jurors cannot be excluded because of race 1987 *U.S. v. Salerno:* Preventive detention upheld 1989 *Mistretta v. U.S.:* U.S. sentencing guidelines upheld	1982 Victim and Witness Protection Act 1984 Bail Reform Act: judge may consider if defendant is a danger to the community 1985 DNA first used in criminal case 1986 William Rehnquist becomes Chief Justice 1987 U.S. Sentencing Guidelines begin
1990s	1991 *Payne v. Tennessee:* Victim impact statements admissible during sentencing *Burns v. Reed:* Prosecutors have qualified immunity in civil lawsuits *Chisom v. Roemer:* Voting Rights Act applies to elected judges 1995 *U.S. v. Lopez:* Federal law barring guns in school unconstitutional	1993 Three-strikes laws gain currency 1994 New Jersey passes Megan's Law 1995 U.S. prison population tops one million 1996 Antiterrorism and Effective Death Penalty Act limits habeas petitions in federal court
2000s	2004 *Hamdi v. Rumsfeld:* U.S. citizens seized overseas during antiterror military operations must be given access to U.S. courts 2005 *Roper v. Simmons:* Capital punishment for crimes committed when the offender was under eighteen years of age is unconstitutional 2008 *Baze v. Rees:* The lethal injection cocktail used by states to execute inmates does not violate the Eighth Amendment's prohibition of cruel and unusual punishment	2002 The Patriot Act enacted into law; Department of Homeland Security established 2005 John Roberts, Jr., becomes Chief Justice 2006 Louisiana becomes the fifteenth state to pass a "stand your ground" law allowing greater use of deadly force in self-defense 2010 The United States prison and jail population levels off at approximately 2.3 million

CRIMINAL JUSTICE TIMELINE CONTINUED

		Famous Trials			Leading Crimes
1900s			1901		President McKinley assassinated by anarchist
			1908		Butch Cassidy and the Sundance Kid killed in Bolivia
1910s			1915		Anti-Semitic lynching of Leo Frank in Atlanta
			1919		Black Sox scandal in baseball
1920s	1921	Sacco and Vanzetti sentenced to death for murder	1921		Charles Ponzi sentenced to prison for pyramid scheme
	1925	Scopes "Monkey Trial"	1924		Leopold and Loeb plead guilty to thrill murder
	1927	Teapot Dome trials become symbol of government corruption	1929		St. Valentine's Day massacre, ordered by Al Capone in Chicago
1930s	1931	Chicago mobster Al Capone found guilty of income tax evasion	1934		Bonnie and Clyde killed
	1935	Bruno Hauptman convicted of kidnapping Charles Lindbergh's young son			"Baby Face" Nelson and "Pretty Boy" Floyd killed
	1939	Crime boss "Lucky" Luciano found guilty of compulsory prostitution			
1940s	1941	Murder, Inc. trials	1945		Bank robber Willie Sutton escapes from prison
	1948	Caryl Chessman sentenced to death for kidnapping and robbery	1947		Hollywood hopeful Black Dahlia's mutilated body found
	1949	Alger Hiss found guilty of perjury in the onset of the Cold War			
1950s	1951	Julius and Ethel Rosenberg sentenced to death for espionage	1950		Brinks armored car robbery in Boston
	1954	Dr. Samuel Sheppard convicted of murder	1957		George Metesky confesses to a string of New York City bombings
	1958	Daughter of movie actress Lana Turner found not guilty of killing mom's hoodlum lover	1959		Murder of Kansas farm couple becomes basis of *In Cold Blood*
1960s	1964	Teamster President Jimmy Hoffa found guilty	1962		French Connection drug bust
	1966	Dr. Sam Sheppard acquitted in second trial	1963		President Kennedy assassinated
	1968	Black Panther Huey Newton found guilty of voluntary manslaughter	1964		Boston Strangler arrested
			1966		Richard Speck kills eight Chicago nurses
	1969	Chicago 7 found guilty of incitement to riot and conspiracy	1968		Martin Luther King, Jr. and Robert Kennedy assassinated
			1969		Manson family commits Helter Skelter murders
1970s	1971	Lt. William Calley found guilty of murder in My Lai massacre	1971		Skyjacker D.B. Cooper disappears
	1976	Heiress Patty Hearst found guilty of bank robbery	1974		Heiress Patty Hearst kidnapped by terrorists
	1977	Maryland governor Marvin Mandel found guilty of mail fraud	1975		Jimmy Hoffa disappears
			1977		Serial murderer Son of Sam arrested in New York
			1978		Jonestown massacre
1980s	1980	John Wayne Gacy convicted of killing 33 boys	1980		Headmistress Jean Harris kills Scarsdale Diet Doctor
	1982	Automaker John DeLorean acquitted of cocaine trafficking	1981		President Ronald Reagan survives assassination attempt by John Hinckley
	1984	Mayflower Madam pleads guilty to misdemeanor of promoting prostitution	1984		21 killed at San Diego McDonalds
	1987	Subway vigilante Bernhard Goetz acquitted of attempted murder	1987		Savings and loan mogul Charles Keating accused of millions in fraud
	1989	Televangelist Jim Baker found guilty of fraud	1989		Junk bond king Michael Milken pays $600 million fine
1990s	1993	L.A. police officers found guilty in federal court of civil rights violations against Rodney King	1992		Boxer Mike Tyson charged with rape
	1995	OJ Simpson found not guilty of murdering his ex-wife Nicole and her friend, Ronald Goldman	1994		Fire in Waco kills Branch Davidians
			1995		Oklahoma City bombing
	1996	During second trial, Menendez brothers found guilty of killing wealthy parents	1997		Nanny in Boston charged with child murder
	1997	Timothy McVeigh sentenced to death for Oklahoma City bombing			
2000s	2000	NYPD officers acquitted for killing Amadou Diallo	2001		Terrorists strike targets in New York City and the Washington, D.C.-area
	2003	Washington state's Gary Ridgway sentenced as worst serial killer in U.S. history	2007		Student Cho Seung Hui murders five faculty members and twenty-seven students on the campus of Virginia Tech in Blacksburg, Virginia
	2006	Zacarias Moussaoui convicted for conspiring to kill U.S. citizens as part of the September 11, 2001, terrorist attacks			
	2011	Casey Anthony found not guilty of first degree murder in the death of her two-year-old daughter, Caylee, by a Florida jury	2009		Bernard Madoff pleads guilty to running a $65 billion Ponzi scheme
			2011		Jared Loughner kills six and injures thirteen during a shooting spree in Tucson, Arizona

Key Terms

assault A threat or an attempt to do violence to another person that causes that person to fear immediate physical harm. 7

battery The act of physically contacting another person with the intent to do harm, even if the resulting injury is minor. 7

burglary The act of breaking into or entering a structure (such as a home office) without permission for the purpose of committed a crime. 8

civil rights The personal rights and protections guaranteed by the Constitution, particularly the Bill of Rights. 17

conflict model A criminal justice model in which the content of criminal law is determined by the groups that hold economic, political, and social power in a community. 5

consensus model A criminal justice model in which the majority of citizens in a society share the same values and beliefs. 5

crime An act that violates criminal law and is punishable by criminal sanctions. 4

crime control model A criminal justice model that places primary emphasis on the right of society to be protected from crime and violent criminals. 17

criminal justice system The interlocking network of law enforcement agencies, courts, and corrections institutions designed to enforce criminal laws. 9

deviance Behavior that is considered to go against the norms established by society. 6

discretion The ability of individuals in the criminal justice system to make operational decisions based on personal judgment instead of formal rules. 14

due process model A criminal justice model that places primacy on the right of the individual to be protected from the power of government. 17

federalism A form of government in which a written constitution provides for a division of powers between a central government and several regional governments. 10

homeland security A concerted national effort to prevent terrorist attacks within the United States and reduce the country's vulnerability to terrorism. 19

justice The quality of fairness that must exist in the processes designed to determine whether citizens are guilty of criminal wrongdoing. 10

larceny The act of taking property from another person without the use of force with the intent of keeping that property. 8

morals Principles of right and wrong behavior, as practiced by individuals or by society. 5

ARCHIE CARPENTER/UPI /Landov

Chapter Summary
& Learning Outcomes

 LO 1 **Define crime and identify the different types of crime.** A crime is an act that violates criminal law and is punishable by criminal sanctions. Types of crime include (a) violent crime; (b) property crime; (c) public order crime; (d) white-collar crime; (e) organized crime; and (f) high-tech crime.

 LO 2 **Outline the three levels of law enforcement.** (a) Local and county law enforcement; (b) state law enforcement; and (c) federal law enforcement.

LO 3 **List the essential elements of the corrections system.** (a) Probation; (b) incarceration; and (c) community-based corrections.

 LO 4 **Explain the difference between the formal and informal criminal justice processes.** The formal criminal justice process involves the somewhat mechanical steps that are designed to guide criminal defendants from arrest to possible punishment. For every step in the formal process, though, someone has discretion, and such discretion leads to an informal process.

 LO 5 **Contrast the crime control and due process models.** The *criminal control model* places primary emphasis on the right of society to be protected from crime, while the *due process model* shifts the emphasis to protecting individual citizens from the power of government. (See next page for more detail.)

Figure 1.2 Discretion in the Criminal Justice System

Criminal justice officials must make decisions every day concerning their duties. The officials listed below, whether they operate on a local, state, or federal level, rely heavily on discretion when meeting the following responsibilities.

Police
- ✓ Enforce laws
- ✓ Investigate specific crimes
- ✓ Search people or buildings
- ✓ Arrest or detain people

Judges
- ✓ Set conditions for pretrial release
- ✓ Accept pleas
- ✓ Dismiss charges
- ✓ Impose sentences

Prosecutors
- ✓ File charges against suspects brought to them by the police
- ✓ Drop cases
- ✓ Reduce charges

Correctional Officials
- ✓ Assign convicts to prison or jail
- ✓ Punish prisoners who misbehave
- ✓ Reward prisoners who behave well

There are even MORE study aids for Chapter 1 at
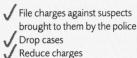

murder The unlawful killing of one human being by another. 7

organized crime Illegal acts carried out by illegal organizations engaged in the market for illegal goods or services. 9

public order crime Behavior that has been labeled criminal because it is contrary to shared social values, customs, and norms. 8

robbery The act of taking property from another person through force, threat of force, or intimidation. 7

sexual assault Forced or coerced sexual intercourse (or other sexual act). 7

system A set of interacting parts that, when functioning properly, achieve a desired result. 14

terrorism The use or threat of violence to achieve political objectives. 19

"wedding cake" model A many-layered model that explains how different cases receive different treatment in the criminal justice system. 15

white-collar crime Nonviolent crimes committed by business entities or individuals to gain a personal or business advantage. 8

STUDYPREP

Read textbook chapters actively! Underline the most important topics. Put a check mark next to material that you do not understand. After you have completed the entire chapter, take a break. Then, work on better comprehension of the check-marked material.

To help you refresh your understanding of each major chapter section, **go online to access the relevant Self-Assessment quiz.** You'll know right away whether you need to go back and read that section again to cement your understanding of major concepts!

Mastering Concepts | Crime Control vs. Due Process

CRIME CONTROL MODEL

Goals of the Criminal Justice System:
- Deter crime.
- Protect the public from crime.
- Incapacitate criminals.
- Provide quick and efficient justice.

Goals Can Best Be Met by:
- Promoting discretion and limiting bureaucratic red tape in criminal justice institutions.
- Making it easier for police to arrest criminals.
- Reducing legal restrictions on proving guilt in a criminal trial.

Favored Policies:
- Hire more police.
- Build more jails and prisons.
- Institute harsher penalties (including increased use of the death penalty) and longer sentences.

View of Criminality:
- Wrongdoers are responsible for their own actions.
- Wrongdoers have violated the social contract and can therefore be deprived of many of the rights afforded to law-abiding citizens.

DUE PROCESS MODEL

Goals of the Criminal Justice System:
- Protect the individual against the immense power of the state.
- Rehabilitate those convicted of crimes.

Goals Can Best Be Met by:
- Limiting state power by ensuring the constitutional rights of the accused.
- Providing even guilty offenders with full protection of the law and allowing those offenders to go free if due process procedures are not followed.
- Ensuring that all accused criminals receive the same treatment from the law, regardless of class, race, gender, or sexual orientation.
- Protecting the civil rights of prisoners.

Favored Policies:
- Open the criminal justice process to public scrutiny.
- Abolish the death penalty.
- Limit police powers to arbitrarily search, interrogate, and seize criminal suspects.
- Limit discretion and formalize criminal justice procedures so that all suspects and convicted offenders receive the same treatment.
- Increase funding for rehabilitation and education programs in jails and prisons.

View of Criminality:
- Criminal behavior can be attributed to social and biological factors.
- Criminals can be rehabilitated and returned to the community after incarceration.

Sample Self-Assessment

To protect against a too—powerful central government, the framers of the U.S. Constitution relied on the principle of _____ to balance power between the national government and the states. Consequently, the United States has a _____ court system—one at the federal level and one at the _____ level. At every level, the criminal justice system relies on the _____ of its employees to keep it from being bogged down by formal rules. Some critics think that this freedom to make decisions leads to the _____ model of court proceedings, in which only the "top" layer of criminal court cases meets ideal standards.

Key Terms

anomie A condition in which the individual suffers from the breakdown or absences of social norms. 32

biology The science of living organisms, including their structure, function, growth, and origin. 26

cause The relationship in which a change in one measurement or behavior creates a recognizable change in another measurement or behavior. 23

choice theory A school of criminology that holds that wrongdoers act as if they weigh the possible benefits of criminal or delinquent activity against the expected costs of being apprehended. 24

chronic offender A delinquent or criminal who commits multiple offenses. 39

classical criminology A school of criminology based on the belief that individuals have free will to engage in any behavior, including criminal behavior. 24

control theory A series of theories that assume that all individuals have the potential for criminal behavior but are restrained by the damage that such actions would do to their relationships with family, friends, and members of the community. 34

correlation The relationship between two measurements or behaviors that tend to move in the same direction. 22

criminal model of addiction An approach to drug abuse that treats illegal drug use as a criminal act. 38

criminologist A specialist in the field of crime and the causes of criminal behavior. 22

criminology The scientific study of crime and the causes of criminal behavior. 22

cultural deviance theory A theory based on the assumption that members of certain subcultures reject the values of the dominant culture through deviant behavior patterns. 32

drug Any substance that modifies biological, psychological, or social behavior; in particular, any illegal substance with those properties. 36

drug abuse The use of drugs that results is physical or psychological problems for the user or third parties. 37

genetics The study of how certain traits or qualities are transmitted from parents to their offspring. 26

hormone A chemical substance that controls certain cellular and bodily functions such as growth and reproduction. 27

hypothesis A possible explanation for an observed occurrence that can be tested by further investigation. 23

labeling theory The hypothesis that society creates crime and criminals by labeling certain behavior and certain people as deviant. 34

learning theory The hypothesis that delinquents and criminals must be taught both the practical and emotional skills necessary to participate in illegal activity. 32

Ronaldo Schemidt/AFP/Getty Images

Chapter Summary & Learning Outcomes

 Discuss the difference between a hypothesis and a theory in the context of criminology. A hypothesis is a proposition that can be tested by researchers to determine if it is valid. If enough authorities find a hypothesis to be valid, it will become a theory. Theories are explanations for criminal behavior based on observation, experimentation, and reasoning.

LO 2 Contrast positivism with classical criminology. According to positivism, criminal behavior is determined by biological, psychological, and social forces beyond the control of the individuals. Classical criminology argues that criminal behavior is a personal choice made by an offender exercising free will.

LO 3 List and briefly explain the three branches of social process theory. (a) Learning theory suggests that offenders are taught to behave criminally; (b) control theory assumes that all people have the potential to behave criminally, but most are restrained by their relationships; and (c) labeling theory claims that society creates criminals by labeling certain people as deviant.

 Contrast the medical model of addiction with the criminal model of addiction. The medical model views addiction as a mental or physical illness, while the criminal model of addiction views illegal drug use as a criminal act.

LO 5 Explain the theory of the chronic offender and its importance for the criminal justice system. The theory of the chronic offender explains that a small number of offenders are responsible for the majority of crime. By devising strategies that target chronic offenders, crime can be drastically reduced.

STUDYPREP

As a rule, do school work as soon as possible when you get home after class. The longer you wait, the more likely you will be distracted by television, video games, phone calls from friends, or social networking.

There are even MORE study aids for Chapter 2 at
www.cengagebrain.com

medical model of addiction An approach to drug addiction that treats drug abuse as a mental or physical illness. 38

neurotransmitter A chemical that transmits nerve impulses between nerve cells and from nerve cells to the brain. 28

positivism A school of the social sciences that sees criminal and delinquent behavior as the result of biological, psychological, and social forces. Because wrongdoers are driven to deviance by external factors, they should not be punished but treated to lessen the influence of those factors. 25

psychoactive drug A chemical that affects the brain, causing changes in emotions, perceptions, and behavior. 36

psychoanalytic theory Sigmund Freud's theory that attributes our thoughts and actions to unconscious motives. 29

psychology The scientific study of mental processes and behaviors. 26

social conflict theories A school of criminology that views criminal behavior as the result of class conflict. 34

social disorganization theory The theory that deviant behavior is more likely in communities where social institutions fail to exert control over the population. 30

social process theories A school of criminology that considers criminal behavior to be the predictable result of a person's interaction with his or her environment. 32

social psychology A branch of psychology that studies how people's thoughts and behaviors are influenced by the presence of others. 29

social reality of crime The theory that criminal laws are designed by those in power to help them keep power at the expense of those who do not have power. 35

strain theory The assumption that crime is the result of frustration felt by individuals who cannot reach their financial and personal goals through legitimate means. 31

subculture A group exhibiting certain values and behavior patterns that distinguish it from the dominant culture. 32

testosterone The hormone primarily responsible for the production of sperm and the development of male secondary sex characteristics. 27

theory An explanation of a happening or circumstance that is based on observation, experimentation, and reasoning. 23

utilitarianism An approach to ethical reasoning in which the "correct" decision is the one that results in the greatest amount of good for the greatest number of people affected by the decision. 24

Mastering Concepts | Theories of Crime

CHOICE THEORIES Crime is the result of rational choices made by those who decide to engage in criminal activity for the rewards it offers. The rewards may be financial, or they may be psychological—criminals enjoy the "rush" that comes with committing a crime. According to choice theorists, the proper response to crime is harsh penalties, which force potential criminals to weigh the benefits of wrongdoing against the costs of punishment if they are apprehended.

BIOLOGICAL AND PSYCHOLOGICAL TRAIT THEORIES Criminal behavior is explained by biological and psychological attributes of the individual. Those who support biological theories of crime believe that the secret to crime is locked in the human body: in genes, brain disorders, reaction to improper diet or allergies, and the like. Psychological theories attempt to explain crime based on the study of personality and intelligence and the development of a person's behavioral patterns during infancy.

SOCIOLOGICAL THEORIES Crime is not something a person is "born to do." Instead, it is the result of the social conditions under which a person finds himself or herself. Those who are socially disadvantaged—because of poverty or other factors such as racial discrimination—are more likely to commit crimes because other avenues to "success" have been closed off. High-crime areas will develop their own cultures that are in constant conflict with the dominant culture and create a cycle of crime that claims the youths who grow up in the area and go on to be career criminals.

SOCIAL PROCESS THEORIES The major influence on any individual is not society in general but the interactions that dominate everyday life. Therefore, individuals are drawn to crime not by general factors such as "society" or "community" but by family, friends, and peer groups. Crime is "learned behavior"; the "teacher" is usually a family member or friend. Everybody has the potential to become a criminal. Those who form positive social relationships instead of destructive ones have a better chance of avoiding criminal activity. Furthermore, if a person is labeled "delinquent" or "criminal" by the authority figures or organizations in his or her life, there is a greater chance he or she will create a personality and actions to fit that label.

SOCIAL CONFLICT THEORIES Criminal laws are a form of social control. Through these laws, the dominant members of society control the minority members, using institutions such as the police, courts, and prisons as tools of oppression. Crime is caused by the conflict between the "haves" and "have-nots" of society. The poor commit crimes because of the anger and frustration they feel at being denied the benefits of society.

Sample Self-Assessment

Researchers who study the causes of crime are called _____. These researchers test hypotheses, or educated guesses, using the _____ method. If a hypothesis proves valid, it can be used to support a _____, or explanation based on observation and reasoning, that explains a possible cause of crime.

To help you refresh your understanding of each major chapter section, **go online to access the relevant Self-Assessment quiz.** You'll know right away whether you need to go back and read that section again to cement your understanding of major concepts!

Key Terms

beyond a reasonable doubt The degree of proof required to find the defendant in a criminal trial guilty of committing the crime. 43

civil law The branch of law dealing with the definition and enforcement of all private and public rights, as opposed to criminal matters. 42

crack cocaine A highly addictive form of cocaine, crystallized into "rock" and smoked rather than snorted. 52

dark figure of crime A term used to describe the actual amount of crime that takes place. The "figure" is "dark," or impossible to detect, because a great number of crimes are never reported to the police. 49

defendant In a civil court, the person or institution against whom an action is brought. In a criminal court, the person or entity who has been formally accused of violating a criminal law. 42

felony A serious crime, punishable by imprisonment by a year or longer or, on rare occasions, death. 44

infraction In most jurisdictions, a noncriminal offense for which the penalty is a fine rather than incarceration. 45

involuntary manslaughter A negligent homicide in which the offender had no intent to kill his or her victim. 45

liability In a civil court, legal responsibility for one's own or another's actions. 43

mala in se A descriptive term for acts that are inherently wrong, regardless of whether they are prohibited by law. 46

mala prohibita A descriptive term for acts that are made illegal by criminal statute and are not necessarily wrong in and of themselves. 46

malice aforethought A depraved state of mind in which the offender's behavior shows a lack of concern for the well-being of his or her victims. 44

methamphetamine (meth) A synthetic stimulant that creates a strong feeling of euphoria in the user and is highly addictive. 53

misdemeanor A criminal offense that is not a felony; usually punishable by a fine and/or a jail term of less than one year. 45

Part I offenses Crimes reported annually by the FBI in its Uniform Crime Report. 47

Part II offenses All crimes recorded by the FBI that do not fall in the category of Part I offenses. 48

plaintiff The person or institution that initiates a lawsuit in civil court proceedings by filing a complaint. 42

preponderance of the evidence The degree of proof required to decide in favor of one side or the other in a civil case. In general, this requirement is met when a plaintiff proves that a fact is more likely than not true. 43

Chapter Summary & Learning Outcomes

LO 1 **Discuss the primary goals of civil law and criminal law, and explain how those goals are realized.** The criminal justice system is concerned with protecting society from harm by preventing and prosecuting crimes, which are considered harms directed toward society. Civil law is concerned with disputes between private individuals and between entities.

LO 2 **Explain the differences between crimes *mala in se* and *mala prohibita*.** Crimes that are *mala in se* are considered inherently wrong, regardless of whether they are prohibited by law. Crimes which are *mala prohibita* are illegal, but are not necessarily wrong in and of themselves.

LO 3 **Identify the publication in which the Federal Bureau of Investigation (FBI) reports crime data and list the three ways in which the data are reported.** The FBI publishes the Uniform Crime Report (UCR) annually. The UCR includes three measurements — (a) the number of persons arrested; (b) the number of crimes reported; and (c) the number of police officers.

LO 4 **Distinguish between the National Crime Victimization Survey (NCVS) and self-reported surveys.** The National Crime Victimization Survey (NCVS) is a method of gathering crime data from victims. Self-reported surveys involve asking offenders to detail their own criminal behavior.

LO 5 **Identify the three factors most often used by criminologists to explain increases and declines in the nation's crime rate.** (a) Imprisonment; (b) youth populations; and (c) the economy.

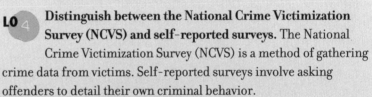

STUDY PREP

Ask questions! When you come across an issue or idea while studying that you don't fully understand, make an appointment with your professor to discuss it. Or, e-mail your question to him or her. Friends and family can also be important sources of information.

AP Photo/Joseph Kaczmarek

There are even MORE study aids for Chapter 3 at
www.cengagebrain.com

self-reported survey A method of gathering crime data that relies on participants to reveal and detail their own criminal or delinquent behavior. 49

Uniform Crime Report (UCR) An annual report compiled by the FBI to give an indication of criminal activity in the United States. 47

victim survey A method of gathering crime data that directly surveys participants to determine their experiences as victims of crime. 49

voluntary manslaughter A homicide in which the intent to kill was present in the mind of the offender, but malice was lacking. 45

Sample Self-Assessment

To produce its annual _____, the FBI relies on the cooperation of law enforcement agencies across the nation. The FBI often presents its findings to the public in terms of a crime _____, or the frequency with which offenses occur for every 100,000 inhabitants of the United States. Although _____ offenses are more likely to be covered by the media, _____ offenses are much more commonplace in the American crime landscape.

To help you refresh your understanding of each major chapter section, **go online to access the relevant Self-Assessment quiz.** You'll know right away whether you need to go back and read that section again to cement your understanding of major concepts!

Figure 3.1 Civil Law versus Criminal Law

Area of Concern	CIVIL LAW Rights and duties between individuals	CRIMINAL LAW Offenses against society as a whole
Wrongful act	Harm to a person or business entity	Violation of a statute that prohibits some type of activity
Party who brings suit	Person who suffered harm (plaintiff)	The state (prosecutor)
Party who responds	Person who supposedly caused harm (defendant)	Person who allegedly committed a crime (defendant)
Standard of proof	Preponderance of the evidence	Beyond a reasonable doubt
Remedy	Damages to compensate for the harm	Punishment (fine or incarceration)

Figure 3.2   Part I Offenses

Every month, local law enforcement agencies voluntarily provide information on serious offenses in their jurisdiction to the FBI. These serious offenses, known as Part I offenses, are defined here.

Criminal homicide.
  a. **Murder and nonnegligent manslaughter:** The willful (nonnegligent) killing of one human being by another.
  b. **Manslaughter by negligence:** The killing of another person through gross negligence.

Forcible rape. The carnal knowledge of a female forcibly and against her will. Included are rapes by force and attempted rapes or assaults as part of a rape.

Robbery. The taking or attempting to take anything of value from the care, custody, or control of a person or persons by force or threat of force or violence and/or by putting the victim in fear.

Aggravated assault. An unlawful attack by one person on another for the purpose of inflicting severe, or aggravated, bodily injury.

Burglary—breaking or entering. The unlawful entry of a structure to commit a felony or a theft. Attempted forcible entry is included.

Larceny/theft (except motor vehicle theft). The unlawful taking, carrying, leading, or riding away of property from the possession of another.

Motor vehicle theft. The theft or attempted theft of a motor vehicle.

Arson. Any willful or malicious burning or attempt to burn, with or without intent to defraud, a dwelling house, public building, motor vehicle or aircraft, personal property of another, and the like.

Source: Federal Bureau of Investigation, *Crime in the United States, 2009* (Washington, D.C.: U.S. Department of Justice, 2010), at www2.fbi.gov/ucr/cius2009/about/offense_definitions.html.

Key Terms

act of omission The act of neglecting or forgetting to do something that is required by law. 65

actus reus (pronounced *ak*-tus *ray*-us). A guilty (prohibited) act. 64

attempt The act of taking substantial steps toward committing a crime while having the ability and the intent to commit the crime, even if the crime never takes place. 66

attendant circumstances The facts surrounding a criminal event. 69

ballot initiative A procedure in which the citizens of a state, if they collect enough signatures, can force a public vote on a proposed change to state law. 61

Bill of Rights The first ten amendments to the U.S. Constitution. 77

case law The rules of law announced in court decisions. 62

constitutional law Law based on the U.S. Constitution and the constitutions of various states. 60

corpus delicti The body of circumstances that must exist for a criminal act to have occurred. 64

domestic violence The act of willful neglect or physical violence that occurs within a familial or other intimate relationship. 67

due process clause The provisions of the Fifth and Fourteenth Amendments to the Constitution that guarantee that no person shall be deprived of life, liberty, or property without due process of law. 78

duress Unlawful pressure brought to bear on a person, causing the person to perform an act that he or she would not otherwise perform. 74

duty to retreat The requirement that a person claiming self-defense prove that she or he first took reasonable steps to avoid the conflict that resulted in the use of deadly force. 75

entrapment A defense in which the defendant claims that he or she was induced by a public official —usually an undercover agent or police officer—to commit a crime that he or she would otherwise not have committed. 76

ex post facto **law** Latin for "after the fact," it refers to a law making a certain act illegal after that act was committed. That is, when the act took place, it was still legal. 77

felony-murder An unlawful homicide that occurs during the attempted commission of a felony. 69

hate crime law A statute that provides for greater sanctions against those who commit crimes motivated by bias against an individual or a group based on race, ethnicity, gender, sexual orientation, disability, or age. 70

inchoate offense Conduct deemed criminal without actual harm being done, provided that the harm that would have occurred is one the law tries to prevent. 70

Chapter Summary
& Learning Outcomes

 List the four written sources of American criminal law. (a) The U.S. Constitution and the constitutions of the various states; (b) statutes passed by congress and the state legislatures; (c) regulations created by regulatory agencies; and (d) case law (court decisions).

 Explain the two basic functions of criminal law. The primary legal function of the law is to maintain social order by protecting citizens from criminal harm. The social function of the law serves to reflect the norms and values of society.

 List and briefly define the most important excuse defenses for crimes. (a) **Infancy** excuses young wrongdoers of criminal behavior; (b) **insanity** asserts a lack of criminal responsibility for those whose mental state is such that they cannot comprehend the nature of their acts; (c) **intoxication** is a defense in which the defendant claims that intoxicants rendered him or her unable to form intent; and (d) **mistake** asserts that the defendant lacked the knowledge necessary to form criminal intent.

 Describe the four most important justification criminal defenses. (a) **Duress** exists when the defendant is induced to act by wrongful threat; (b) **self-defense** is the legally justified use of force to protect oneself from injury; (c) **necessity** involves circumstances that require the defendant to commit the crime; and (d) **entrapment** occurs when the defendant is induced by a public official to commit an act that he or she would not normally have committed.

 Distinguish between substantive and procedural criminal law. Substantive criminal law defines the rights and duties of individuals with respect to one another. Procedural criminal law defines the manner in which the rights and duties of individuals may be enforced.

REUTERS/Jessica Rinaldi

There are even MORE study aids for Chapter 4 at
www.cengagebrain.com

infancy A condition that, under early American law, excused young wrongdoers of criminal behavior because presumably they could not understand the consequences of their actions. 71

insanity A defense for criminal liability that asserts a lack of criminal responsibility. 71

intoxication A defense for criminal liability in which the defendant claims that the taking of intoxicants rendered him or her unable to form the requisite intent to commit the criminal act. 73

irresistible-impulse test A test for the insanity defense under which a defendant who knew his or her action was wrong must establish that he or she was unable to resist the urge to commit the crime. 72

mens rea (pronounced *mehns ray*-uh). Mental state, or intent. 66

M'Naghten Rule A common law test of criminal responsibility that relies on the defendant's inability to distinguish between right and wrong. 72

necessity A defense against criminal liability in which the defendant asserts that circumstances required her or him to commit an illegal act. 75

negligence A failure to exercise the standard of care that a reasonable person would exercise in similar circumstances. 66

precedent A court decision that is used as a guideline for deciding a subsequent case with similar facts. 62

procedural criminal law Rules that define the manner in which the rights and duties of individuals may be enforced. 76

procedural due process A provision in the Constitution that states that the law must be carried out in a fair and orderly manner. 79

recklessness The state of being aware that a risk does or will exist and nevertheless acting in a way that consciously disregards this risk. 67

self-defense The legally recognized privilege to protect one's self or property from injury by another. 75

statutory law The body of law enacted by legislative bodies. 61

statutory rape A strict liability crime in which an adult engages in a sexual act with a minor. 68

strict liability crimes Certain crimes, such as traffic violations, in which the defendant is guilty regardless of her or his state of mind at the time of the act. 68

substantive criminal law Law that defines the rights and duties of individuals with respect to one another. 76

substantive due process The constitutional requirement that laws used in accusing and convicting persons of crime must be fair. 79

substantial-capacity test (ALI/MPC Test) A test that states that a person is not responsible for criminal behavior if he or she had no awareness of wrongdoing or was unable to control his or her actions. 72

Mastering Concepts — The Elements of a Crime

Carl Robert Winchell walked into the SunTrust Bank in Volusia County, Florida, and placed a bag containing a box on a counter. Announcing that the box held a bomb, he demanded to be given an unspecified amount of cash. After being provided with several thousand dollars in cash, Winchell fled, leaving the box behind. A Volusia County Sheriff's Office bomb squad subsequently determined that the box did not in fact contain any explosive device. Winchell was eventually arrested and charged with robbery.

Winchell's actions were criminal because they satisfy the three elements of a crime:

1. ***ACTUS REUS*** The physical act of a crime took place. In this case, Winchell committed bank robbery.

2. ***MENS REA*** The offender must intentionally, knowingly, or willingly commit the criminal act. In this case, Winchell obviously planned to rob the SunTrust Bank using the false threat of a bomb.

3. **A CONCURRENCE of *actus reus* and *mens rea*** The criminal act must be the result of the offender's intention to commit that particular criminal act. In this case, the robbery was the direct result of Winchell's intent to take property using the threat of the fake bomb. If, in addition, a bank customer had died of a heart attack during the robbery attempt, in most jurisdictions Winchell could not have been charged with first degree murder because he did not intend to harm anyone.

Note that the fact that there was no bomb in the box has no direct bearing on the three elements of the crime. It could, however, lead to Winchell receiving a lighter punishment than if he had used a real bomb.

Sample Self-Assessment

The _____ function of the law is to protect citizens from _____ harm by assuring their physical safety. The _____ function of the law is to teach citizens proper behavior and express public _____ by codifying the norms and values of the community.

To help you refresh your understanding of each major chapter section, **go online to access the relevant Self-Assessment quiz.** You'll know right away whether you need to go back and read that section again to cement your understanding of major concepts!

STUDYPREP

Many students are tempted to take class notes on a laptop computer. This is a bad idea for two reasons. First, it is hard to copy diagrams or take other "artistic" notes on a computer. Second, it is easy to get distracted by checking e-mail or surfing the Web.

Key Terms

Bureau of Alcohol, Tobacco, Firearms, and Explosives (ATF) A federal law enforcement agency primarily concerned with criminal activity involving firearms and explosives, the illegal trafficking of alcohol and tobacco products, and acts of arson. 92

coroner The medical examiner of a county, usually elected by a popular vote. 86

Drug Enforcement Administration (DEA) The federal agency responsible for enforcing the nation's laws and regulations regarding narcotics and other controlled substances. 91

Federal Bureau of Investigation (FBI) The branch of the Department of Justice responsible for investigating violations of federal law. 91

mandatory arrest policy Departmental order that requires a police officer to detain a person for committing a certain type of crime as long as probable cause exists that he or she committed the crime. 96

private security The practice of private corporations or individuals offering services traditionally performed by police officers. 93

sheriff The primary law enforcement officer in a county, usually elected to the post by popular vote. 85

U.S. Border Patrol The mobile law enforcement branch of U.S. Customs and Border Protection, responsible for protecting this country's borders with Mexico and Canada. 89

U.S. Customs and Border Protection (CBP) The federal agency responsible for protecting U.S. borders and facilitating legal trade and travel across those borders. 89

U.S. Immigration and Customs Enforcement (ICE) The federal agency that enforces the nation's immigration and customs laws. 89

U.S. Secret Service A federal law enforcement organization with the primary responsibility of protecting the president, the president's family, the vice president, and other important political figures. 90

There are even MORE study aids for
Chapter 5 at
www.cengagebrain.com

Chapter Summary
& Learning Outcomes

List the four basic responsibilities of the police. (a) To enforce laws; (b) to provide services; (c) to prevent crime; and (d) to preserve the peace.

List five main types of law enforcement agencies. (a) Local police departments; (b) sheriff's departments; (c) special police agencies, limited to policing parks, schools, airports, and other areas; (d) state police departments; and (e) federal law enforcement agencies.

LO3 Indicate some of the most important law enforcement agencies under the control of the Department of Homeland Security. (a) U.S. Customs and Border Protection; (b) U.S. Immigration and Customs Enforcement; and (c) U.S. Secret Service.

Analyze the importance of private security today. Even with increasing numbers of local, state, and federal law enforcement officers, the police do not have the ability to prevent every crime. As a result, private security services are used to prevent criminal offending.

LO5 Indicate why patrol officers are allowed discretionary powers. The Supreme Court asserts that patrol officers are in a unique position to be allowed discretionary powers because they (a) are trustworthy and honest; (b) have experience and training that gives them the ability to determine potential threats to society; (c) are extremely knowledgeable in human and criminal behavior; and (d) must have the ability to protect themselves from personal, physical harm encountered on the job.

Stan Rohrer/iStockphoto.com

John Moore/Getty Images

STUDYPREP

We study best when we are free from distractions such as the Internet, cell phones, and our friends. That's why your school library is often the best place to work. Set aside several hours a week of "library time" to study in peace and quiet. Remember to turn off your cell phone and other Web devices.

Sample Self-Assessment

Private security is designed to _____ crimes rather than solve them. The majority of states require _____ hours of training and _____ background checks before a person can become a security guard. This perceived lack of standards in the industry is changing, however, as private security companies are responsible for protecting many of the country's likely _____ targets.

To help you refresh your understanding of each major chapter section, **go online to access the relevant Self-Assessment quiz.** You'll know right away whether you need to go back and read that section again to cement your understanding of major concepts!

Figure 5.1 Full-Time Police Personnel, by Size of Population Served

66191
14%

95,053
21%

51,973
11%

161,168
35%

88,763
19%

Population Served

■ 1,000,000 or more

□ 500,000 to 999,999

■ 100,000 to 499,999

□ 10,000 to 99,999

■ 9,999 or below

Source: Bureau of Justice Statistics, *Local Police Departments, 2007* (Washington, D.C.: U.S. Department of Justice, December 2010, Table 3, page 9).

Naomi Bassitt/iStockphoto

Stan Rohrer/iStockphoto.com

Key Terms

authority The legal power of law enforcement officers to enforce rules and give orders when circumstances require. 114

ballistics The study of firearms, including the firing of the weapon and the flight of the bullet. 107

blue curtain A metaphorical term used to refer to the value placed on secrecy and the general mistrust of the outside world shared by many police officers. 113

broken windows theory Wilson and Kelling's theory that law enforcement should crack down on quality-of-life crimes to reduce overall crime. 111

clearance rate A comparison of the number of crimes cleared by arrest and prosecution with the number of crimes reported during any given time period. 105

cold case A criminal investigation that has not been solved after a certain amount of time. 106

cold hit The establishment of a connection between a suspect and a crime in the absence of an ongoing criminal investigation. 108

community policing A police philosophy that emphasizes community support for and cooperation with the police in preventing crime. 111

confidential informant (CI) A human source for police who provides information concerning illegal activity in which he or she is involved. 105

crime mapping Technology that allows crime analysts to identify trends and patterns of criminal behavior within a given area. 109

deadly force Force applied by a police officer that is likely or intended to cause serious injury or death. 114

detective The primary police investigator of crimes. 104

directed patrol A patrol strategy that is designed to focus on a specific type of criminal activity at a specific time. 109

DNA fingerprinting The identification of a person based on a sample of her or his DNA, the genetic material found in the cells of all living organisms. 107

duty The moral sense of a police officer that she or he should apply authority in a certain manner. 117

ethics The rules or standards of behavior governing a profession; aimed at ensuring the fairness and rightness of actions. 116

field training The segment of a police recruit's training in which he or she is removed from the classroom and placed on the beat, under the supervision of a senior officer. 102

forensics The application of science to establish facts and evidence during the investigation of crimes. 106

CHALLENGES TO EFFECTIVE POLICING

Chapter Summary & Learning Outcomes

 Identify the differences between the police academy and field training as learning tools for recruits. The police academy is a controlled, militarized environment, run by the state or a police agency, that provides recruits instruction in the essentials of police work. Field training takes place outside the confines of the police academy. The recruit is paired with an experienced officer known as a field training officer, or FTO.

 List the three primary purposes of police patrol. (a) The deterrence of crime by maintaining a visible police presence; (b) the maintenance of public order and a sense of security in the community; and (c) the twenty-four-hour provision of services that are not crime related.

 Describe how forensic experts use DNA fingerprinting to solve crimes. DNA fingerprinting is useful because no two people, except for identical twins, have the same genetic code. Therefore, a DNA sample from the suspect can be compared to DNA taken from the scene of a crime to conclusively determine a match.

 Determine when police officers are justified in using deadly force. As a result of the Supreme Court's ruling in *Tennessee v. Garner* (1985), police officers may use deadly force if they have probable cause to believe that the fleeing suspect poses a threat of serious injury or death to the officers or others.

 Explain what an ethical dilemma is and name four categories of ethical dilemmas typically facing a police officer. An ethical dilemma is a situation in which the officer (a) does not know the right course of action; (b) has difficulty doing the right thing; and (c) finds the wrong choice very tempting. Four categories of ethical dilemmas involve (a) discretion; (b) duty; (c) honesty; and (d) loyalty.

STUDYPREP

Reward yourself for studying! From time to time, allow yourself a short break for surfing the Internet, going for a jog, taking a nap, or doing something else that you enjoy. These interludes will refresh your mind and enable you to study longer and more efficiently.

There are even MORE study aids for Chapter 6 at
www.cengagebrain.com

The Star-Ledger / Sarah Rice / The Image Works

general patrol A patrol strategy that relies on police officers monitoring a certain area with the goal of detecting crimes in progress or preventing crime due to their presence; also known as random or preventive patrol. 109

hot spot A concentrated area of high criminal activity that draws a directed police response. 109

incident-driven policing A reactive approach to policing that emphasizes a speedy response to calls for service. 109

nondeadly force Force applied by a police officer that does not pose the threat of serious bodily harm or death. 114

police corruption The abuse of authority by a law enforcement officer for personal gain. 116

police subculture The values and perceptions that are shared by law enforcement agents. 112

proactive arrest An arrest that occurs because of concerted efforts by law enforcement agencies to respond to a particular type of criminal or criminal behavior. 110

probationary period A period of time at the beginning of a police officer's career during which he or she may be fired without cause. 101

problem-oriented policing A policing philosophy that requires police to identify potential criminal activity and develop strategies to prevent or respond to that activity. 111

reactive arrest An arrest that comes about as part of the ordinary routine of police patrol and responses to calls for service. 110

reasonable force The degree of force that is appropriate to protect the police officer or other citizens and is not excessive. 114

recruitment The process by which law enforcement agencies develop a pool of qualified applicants from which to select new members. 100

socialization The process through which a police officer is taught the values and expected behavior of the police subculture. 112

sworn officer A law enforcement agent who has been authorized to make arrests and use force, including deadly force, against civilians. 102

trace evidence Evidence such as a fingerprint, blood, or hair found in small amounts at the crime scene. 106

Spectral-Design, 2009. Used under license from Shutterstock.com

The San Diego Police Department's Use-of-Force Matrix

The San Diego Police Department has a mission to "train its officers in the use of the safest, most humane restraint procedures and force options currently known." As part of this mission, the department provides its officers with this use-of-force matrix, which details the appropriate response to various forms of suspect behavior.

RUNG 5

Suspect's Behavior: **Life Threatening**

Officer's Response: Firearms and hard impact with weapons.

RUNG 4

Suspect's Behavior: **Assaultive**

Officer's Response: Hard impact with weapons such as nightsticks and flashlights and personal body weapons such as head, hands, elbows, knees, and feet.

RUNG 3

Suspect's Behavior: **Active Resistance**

Officer's Response: Tasers, neck restraints, takedown techniques, chemical agents such as pepper spray, and K-9.

RUNG 2

Suspect's Behavior: **Passive Resistance**

Officer's Response: Light pushes or jabs with impact weapons such as nightsticks and flashlights, control holds with or without light-impact weapons, and body strength.

RUNG 1

Suspect's Behavior: **Compliant**

Officer's Response: Touch and verbal control such as orders, explanations, and requests.

Sample Self-Assessment

Given the authority they command, police officers are held to high standards of _____ behavior by society. A police officer is often guided by his or her sense of _____, which obliges him or her to act in a certain manner depending on the circumstances. Feelings of _____ for a partner who is acting improperly can keep a police officer from reporting the partner's behavior to a superior.

To help you refresh your understanding of each major chapter section, **go online to access the relevant Self-Assessment quiz.** You'll know right away whether you need to go back and read that section again to cement your understanding of major concepts!

Key Terms

affidavit A written statement of facts, confirmed by the oath or affirmation of the party making it. 129

arrest warrant A written order commanding that the person named on the warrant be arrested by the police. 126

coercion The use of physical force or mental intimidation to compel a person to do something—such as confess to a committing a crime—against her or his will. 135

consent search A police search that is made after the subject of the search has agreed to the action. 131

custodial interrogation The questioning of a suspect after that person has been taken into custody. 136

custody The forceful detention of a person, or the perception that a person is not free to leave the immediate vicinity. 136

electronic surveillance The use of electronic equipment to record or observe conduct that is meant to be private. 133

exclusionary rule A rule under which any evidence that is obtained in violation of the accused's rights will not be admissible in criminal court. 122

exigent circumstances Situations that require extralegal or exceptional actions by the police. 126

frisk A pat-down or minimal search by police to discover weapons. 125

fruit of the poisoned tree Evidence that is acquired through the use of illegally obtained evidence and is therefore inadmissible in court. 122

interrogation The direct questioning of a suspect to gather evidence of criminal activity and to try to gain a confession. 135

***Miranda* rights** The constitutional rights of accused persons taken into custody by law enforcement officials. 135

***Miranda* waiver** A decision by a suspect to voluntarily give up his or her right to remain silent, with the understanding that his or her answers may be used as evidence in criminal court. 137

plain view doctrine The legal principle that objects in plain view of a law enforcement agent who has the right to be in a position to have that view may be seized without a warrant. 133

probable cause Reasonable grounds to believe the existence of facts warranting certain actions, such as the search or arrest of a person. 120

racial profiling The practice of targeting people for police action based solely on their race, ethnicity, or national origin. 123

reasonable In the context of criminal law, an action by a law enforcement agent that is appropriate under the circumstances. 120

CHAPTER REVIEW

POLICE AND THE CONSTITUTION:
THE RULES OF LAW ENFORCEMENT

7

Chapter Summary
& Learning Outcomes

LO 1 **Outline the four major sources that may provide probable cause.** The Supreme Court has ruled that any arrest or seizure is unreasonable unless it is supported by probable cause. Police officers may use personal observation, information, evidence, and association as sources of probable cause.

LO 2 **Distinguish between a stop and a frisk, and indicate the importance of the case *Terry v. Ohio*.** A police officer can stop, or briefly detain, a person for questioning when reasonable suspicion exists. During a stop an officer can frisk, or pat down, that person as a protective measure. The precedent for stop and frisks supported by reasonable suspicion was established by the Supreme Court in *Terry v. Ohio* (1968).

LO 3 **List the four elements that must be present for an arrest to take place.** (a) The intent to arrest; (b) the authority to arrest; (c) seizure or detention; and (d) the understanding of the person that he or she has been arrested.

LO 4 **Explain when searches can be made without a warrant.** An officer can conduct a search without a warrant (a) in an emergency; (b) incidental to arrest; (c) with voluntary consent; (d) when searching automobiles; (e) when the items are in plain view; and (f) when consent is provided to use electronic surveillance.

LO 5 **Indicate situations in which a *Miranda* warning is unnecessary.** (a) When the questions are testimonial in nature; (b) when the police have not focused on a suspect; (c) when the statements are volunteered by the suspect; (d) when the suspect has made a private statement to a third party; (e) during a stop and frisk; and (f) during a traffic stop.

STUDYPREP

When you are given a writing assignment, make sure you allow yourself enough time to revise and polish your final draft. Good writing takes time—you may need to revise a paper several times before you are satisfied with its quality.

There are even MORE study aids for Chapter 7 at
www.cengagebrain.com

search The process by which police examine a person or property to find evidence that will be used to prove guilt in a criminal trial. 128

searches incidental to an arrest Searches for weapons and evidence of persons who have just been arrested. 130

search warrant A written order commanding that criminal investigators search a specific person, place, or property to obtain evidence. 128

searches and seizures The legal term that generally refers to the searching for and the confiscating (taking) of evidence by law enforcement agents. 120

seizure The forcible taking of a person or property in response to a violation of the law. 129

stop A brief detention of a person by law enforcement agents for questioning. 124

warrantless arrest An arrest made without first seeking a warrant for the action. 127

Sample Self-Assessment

A police officer can make a _____ , which is not the same as an arrest, if she or he has a _____ suspicion that a criminal act is taking place or is about to take place. Then, the officer has the ability to _____ the suspect for weapons as a protective measure.

To help you refresh your understanding of each major chapter section, **go online to access the relevant Self-Assessment quiz.** You'll know right away whether you need to go back and read that section again to cement your understanding of major concepts!

The Differences between a Stop and an Arrest

Both stops and arrests are considered seizures because both police actions involve the restriction of an individual's freedom to "walk away." Both must be justified by a showing of reasonableness as well. You should be aware, however, of the differences between a stop and an arrest.

During a stop, police can interrogate the person and make a limited search of his or her outer clothing. If anything occurs during the stop, such as the discovery of an illegal weapon, then officers may arrest the person. If an arrest is made, the suspect is now in police custody and is protected by the U.S. Constitution in a number of ways.

	Stop	Arrest
Justification	Reasonable suspicion only	Probable cause
Warrant	None	Required in some, but not all, situations
Intent of Officer	To investigate suspicious activity	To make a formal charge against the suspect
Search	May frisk or "pat down" for weapons	May conduct a full search for weapons or evidence
Scope of Search	Outer clothing only	Area within the suspect's immediate control or "reach"

PhotoDisc

Jan Tyler/iStockphoto.com

Key Terms

appellate court A court that reviews decisions made by lower courts, such as trial courts; also known as *courts of appeals*. 145

bailiff of the court A law enforcement officer from the local sheriff's department who maintains courtroom order and oversees the activities of the jurors. 155

clerk of the court A court employee whose main duties include maintaining court records, coordinating jury selection, and managing case flow. 155

concurrent jurisdiction The situation that occurs when two or more courts have the authority to preside over the same criminal case. 143

concurring opinion A separate opinion prepared by a judge who supports the decision of the majority. 151

court reporter Also known as a stenographer. A court employee who provides a word-for-word written record of all court proceedings. 155

courtroom work group The social organization consisting of the judge, prosecutor, defense attorney, and other court workers. 154

dissenting opinion A separate opinion in which a judge disagrees with the conclusion reached by the majority of the court. 151

docket The list of cases entered on a court's calendar and thus scheduled to be heard by the court. 152

dual court system The separate but interrelated court system of the United States, made up of the courts on the national level and the courts on the state level. 145

extradition The process by which one jurisdiction surrenders a person accused or convicted of violating another jurisdiction's crime law to the second jurisdiction. 143

judicial review The power of a court to review the actions of the executive and legislative branches. 149

jurisdiction The authority of a court to hear and decide cases within an area of law or a geographic territory. 142

Missouri plan A method of selecting judges that combines appointment and election. 153

nonpartisan election An election in which candidates are presented on the ballot without any party affiliation. 153

opinion A statement made by a judge expressing the reasons for the court's decision in a case. 145

oral arguments The verbal arguments presented in person by attorneys to an appellate court. 151

partisan election An election in which candidates are affiliated with and receive support from political parties. 153

rule of four A rule of the United States Supreme Court that the Court will not issue a writ of *certiorari* unless at least four justices approve of the decision to hear the case. 150

specialty court A lower court that has jurisdiction over one specific area of criminal activity, such as illegal drugs or domestic violence. 146

Chapter Summary & Learning Outcomes

LO 1 **Define and contrast the four functions of the courts.** The primary concern of the due process function of the courts is to protect the rights of individuals against the power of the state. The crime control function of the courts is to punish criminal offenders for their wrongdoings. The rehabilitation function of the courts is to treat offenders in order to prevent further crimes, and the bureaucratic function of the courts is concerned with dealing with cases with speed and efficiency.

LO 2 **Define *jurisdiction* and contrast geographic and subject-matter jurisdiction.** Jurisdiction is the authority of the court to hear and decide cases. Geographic jurisdiction provides that a court can exercise its authority over residents of a certain area. Subject-matter jurisdiction defines the types of cases that a particular court may hear.

LO 3 **Explain the difference between trial and appellate courts.** Trial courts, or courts of original jurisdiction, are the courts in which criminal trials take place and guilt or innocence is determined. Appellate courts are courts of review. Cases can be brought before the appellate court to determine whether or not the trial court erred in reaching its decision.

LO 4 **Explain briefly how a case is brought to the U.S. Supreme Court.** A party petitions the court for a writ of *certiorari*, with which the Supreme Court orders a lower court to send it the record of a case for review. The court will not issue a writ unless at least four justices approve of it.

LO 5 **List and describe the members of the courtroom work group.** The courtroom work group includes (a) the judge; (b) the prosecutor; (c) defense counsel; (d) the bailiff of the court, who is responsible for maintaining order and security in the courtroom; (d) the clerk of the court, who manages the paperwork of the court; and (e) the court reporter, who records every word that is said during the course of the trial.

(AP Photo/Michael P. King, Pool)

There are even MORE study aids for Chapter 8 at
www.cengagebrain.com

STUDY PREP

You can outline as you read, after you've finished a reading assignment, or when you reread each section within a chapter before going on to the next section. The act of physically writing an outline for a chapter improves most students' ability to retain the material.

Mastering Concepts   Typical State Court System

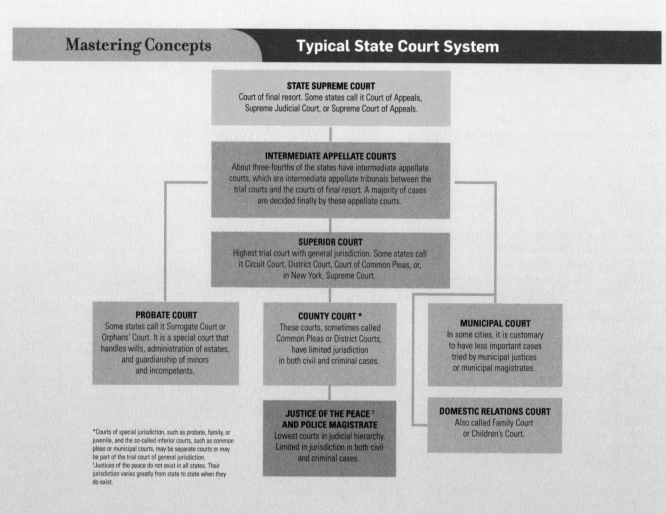

STATE SUPREME COURT
Court of final resort. Some states call it Court of Appeals, Supreme Judicial Court, or Supreme Court of Appeals.

INTERMEDIATE APPELLATE COURTS
About three-fourths of the states have intermediate appellate courts, which are intermediate appellate tribunals between the trial courts and the courts of final resort. A majority of cases are decided finally by these appellate courts.

SUPERIOR COURT
Highest trial court with general jurisdiction. Some states call it Circuit Court, District Court, Court of Common Pleas, or, in New York, Supreme Court.

PROBATE COURT
Some states call it Surrogate Court or Orphans' Court. It is a special court that handles wills, administration of estates, and guardianship of minors and incompetents.

COUNTY COURT *
These courts, sometimes called Common Pleas or District Courts, have limited jurisdiction in both civil and criminal cases.

MUNICIPAL COURT
In some cities, it is customary to have less important cases tried by municipal justices or municipal magistrates.

**JUSTICE OF THE PEACE †
AND POLICE MAGISTRATE**
Lowest courts in judicial hierarchy. Limited in jurisdiction in both civil and criminal cases.

DOMESTIC RELATIONS COURT
Also called Family Court or Children's Court.

*Courts of special jurisdiction, such as probate, family, or juvenile, and the so-called inferior courts, such as common pleas or municipal courts, may be separate courts or may be part of the trial court of general jurisdiction.
† Justices of the peace do not exist in all states. Their jurisdiction varies greatly from state to state when they do exist.

To help you refresh your understanding of each major chapter section, **go online to access the relevant Self-Assessment quiz.** You'll know right away whether you need to go back and read that section again to cement your understanding of major concepts!

Sample Self-Assessment

The _____ function of American courts is to protect _____ from the unfair advantages that the government enjoys during legal proceedings. In contrast, the _____ function of the courts emphasizes punishment—criminals must suffer for the harm they do to _____. A third view of the court system focuses on the need to _____ a criminal, in much the same way as a doctor would treat a patient.

Key Terms

adversary system A legal system in which the prosecution and defense are opponents, or adversaries, and present their cases in the light most favorable to themselves. The court arrives at a just solution based on the evidence presented by the contestants and determines who wins and who loses. 165

arraignment A court proceeding in which the suspect is formally charged with the criminal offense stated in the indictment or information. 174

attorney-client privilege A rule of evidence requiring that communications between a client and his or her attorney be kept confidential, unless the client consents to disclosure. 164

attorney general The chief law officer of a state. Also, the chief law officer of the nation. 161

bail The amount or conditions set by the court to ensure that an individual accused of a crime will appear for further criminal proceedings. 167

bail bond agent A business person who agrees, for a fee, to pay the bail amount if the accused fails to appear in court as ordered. 169

case attrition The process by which prosecutors effect an overall reduction in the number of persons prosecuted. 172

defense attorney The lawyer representing the defendant. 162

discovery Formal investigation prior to trial. 171

The *Gideon* protection The rule, established in the 1963 Supreme Court case *Gideon v. Wainwright*, that the government must provide a public defender for those defendants too poor to hire one for themselves. 163

grand jury The group of citizens called to decide whether probable cause exists. 171

indictment A written accusation that probable cause exists to believe that a named person has committed a crime. 171

information The formal charge against the accused issued by the prosecutor after a preliminary hearing has found probable cause. 171

initial appearance An accused's first appearance before a judge or magistrate following arrest. 166

nolle prosequi (nol-e pro-sekwi) A Latin term describing the prosecutor's decision not to prosecute a defendant based on his or her determination that a conviction is either unlikely or undesirable. 172

nolo contendere Latin for "I will not contest it." A criminal defendant's plea, in which he or she chooses not to challenge, or contest, the charges brought by the government. 174

plea bargaining The process by which the accused and the prosecutor work out a mutually satisfactory conclusion to the case, subject to court approval. 174

Chapter Summary & Learning Outcomes

LO 1 **List the different names given to public prosecutors and indicate the general powers they have.** The prosecutor in federal criminal cases is called a U.S. attorney. In state and local courts, the prosecutor is referred to as a prosecuting attorney, state prosecutor, district attorney, county attorney, or city attorney. Prosecutors have the power to charge offenders with criminal violations and prosecute them in a court of law.

LO 2 **Delineate the responsibilities of defense attorneys.** The defense attorney is responsible for representing the defendant at each stage of the custodial process, beginning with arrest, and at each stage of the criminal court process, including the appeals process.

LO 3 **List the three basic features of an adversary system of justice.** (a) A neutral decision maker, either a judge or a jury; (b) the presentation of evidence from both parties; and (c) a highly structured set of procedures that must be followed in the presentation of evidence.

LO 4 **Explain how a prosecutor screens potential cases.** The screening process varies from one jurisdiction to the next, but most prosecutors evaluate several factors when screening potential cases. These factors include whether there is sufficient evidence for conviction, whether the case is a priority for the prosecutor, and whether the victim and witnesses are cooperative and reliable.

LO 5 **List and briefly explain the different forms of plea bargaining agreements.** (a) In charge bargaining the defendant pleads guilty in exchange for a reduction of the charges; (b) in sentence bargaining the defendant pleads guilty for a reduction in the sentence; and (c) in count bargaining the defendant pleads guilty for a reduction in the counts against him or her.

STUDYPREP

To make an effective outline, you have to be selective. Outlines that contain all the information in the text are not very useful. Your objectives in outlining are, first, to identify the main concepts and, then, to add the details that support those main concepts.

There are even MORE study aids for Chapter 9 at
www.cengagebrain.com

Joe Burbank/MCT /Landov

preliminary hearing An initial hearing in which a judge decides if there is probable cause to believe that the defendant committed the crime with which he or she is charged. 170

preventive detention The retention of an accused person in custody due to fears that he or she will commit a crime if released before trial. 170

property bond The defendant gains pretrial release with property valued at double the bail amount that the defendant provides to the court as assurance that he or she will return for trial. 169

public defender A court-appointed attorney who is paid by the state to represent defendants who are unable to hire private counsel. 162

public prosecutor A lawyer who initiates and conducts cases in the government's name and on behalf of the people. 160

release on recognizance (ROR) A judge's order that releases an accused from jail with an understanding that he or she will return for further proceedings of his or her own will. 168

uncooperative victim A crime victim who decides, for reasons of his or her own, not to provide information concerning the alleged crime to police or prosecutors, therefore making it difficult or impossible to pursue a conviction. 173

Sample Self-Assessment

If a case is to proceed to trial, the prosecutor must establish _____ that the defendant committed the crime in question. One way of doing this involves a _____ hearing, in which a judge or magistrate rules whether the prosecutor has met this burden. In the other method, the decision rests with a group of citizens called a _____ who will hand down an _____ if they believe the evidence is sufficient to support the charges.

To help you refresh your understanding of each major chapter section, **go online to access the relevant Self-Assessment quiz.** You'll know right away whether you need to go back and read that section again to cement your understanding of major concepts!

Mastering Concepts   **The Criminal Justice Funnel**

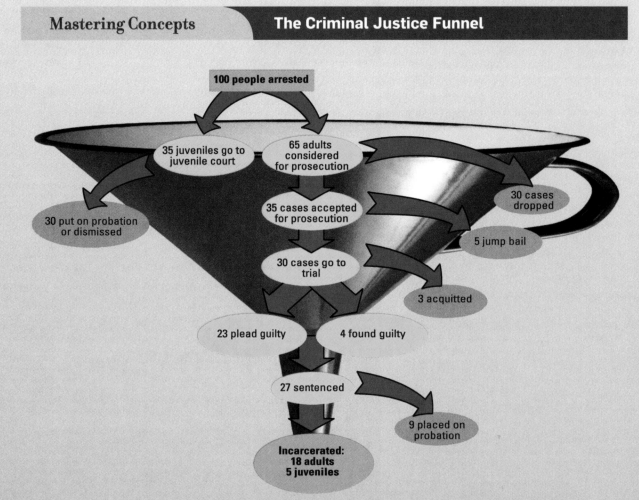

Source: Adapted from Todd R. Clear, George F. Cole, and Michael D. Reisig, *American Corrections,* 9th ed. (Belmont, Calif.: Wadsworth, 2011), 134.

Key Terms

acquittal A declaration following a trial that the individual accused of the crime is innocent. 182

Allen **charge** An instruction by a judge to a dead-locked jury that asks the jurors in the minority to reconsider the majority opinion. 193

appeal The process of seeking a higher court's review of a lower court's decision for the purpose of correcting or changing the lower court's judgment or decision. 194

bench trial A trial conducted without a jury, in which a judge makes the determination of the defendant's guilt or innocence. 182

challenge for cause A *voir dire* challenge in which an attorney states the reason why a prospective juror should not be included on the jury. 184

charge The judge's instructions to the jury following the attorney's closing arguments. 192

circumstantial evidence Indirect evidence that is offered to establish, by inference, the likelihood of a fact that is in question. 188

closing arguments An argument made by each side's attorney after the cases for the plaintiff and defendant have been presented. 192

confrontation clause The part of the Sixth Amendment that guarantees all defendants the right to confront witnesses against them during the criminal trial. 190

cross-examination The questioning of an opposing witness during trial. 190

direct evidence Evidence that establishes the existence of a fact that is in question without relying on inference. 188

direct examination The examination of a witness by the attorney who calls the witness to the stand to testify. 189

double jeopardy To be tried twice for the same criminal offense. 194

evidence Anything that is used to prove the existence or nonexistence of a fact. 187

expert witness A witness with professional training or substantial experience qualifying him or her to testify on a certain subject. 187

habeas corpus An order that requires correctional officials to bring an inmate before a court or a judge and explain why he or she is being held in prison. 195

hearsay An oral or written statement made by an out-of-court speaker that is later offered in court by a witness (not the speaker) concerning a matter before the court. 190

hung jury A jury whose members are so irreconcilably divided in their opinions that they cannot reach a verdict. 193

immunity A special status, granted by the prosecutor, protecting a witness from being prosecuted for any acts about which the witness testifies in criminal court. 182

(AP Photo/Knoxville News Sentinel, J. Miles Car)

Chapter Summary
& Learning Outcomes

LO 1 **Identify the basic protections enjoyed by criminal defendants in the United States.** In all criminal prosecutions, the Sixth Amendment provides the accused with (a) the right to a speedy and public trial; (b) an impartial jury of the state where the crime was committed; (c) to be informed of the nature of the accusation; (d) to be confronted with the witnesses against him or her; (e) to obtain witnesses in his or her favor; and (f) to have the assistance of counsel for his or her defense.

LO 2 **Explain what "taking the Fifth" really means.** "Taking the fifth" means that the defendant has the right to exercise his or her Fifth Amendment right not to testify at a trial if to do so would implicate him or her in the crime.

LO 3 **Contrast challenges for cause and peremptory challenges during *voir dire*.** If a defense attorney or prosecutor concludes that a prospective juror is unfit to serve, the attorney may exercise a challenge for cause, stating sound, legally identifiable reasons why that juror should not serve. A peremptory challenge allows a defense attorney or prosecutor to exclude a juror from serving without a reason or cause.

LO 4 **List the standard steps in a criminal jury trial.** (a) Opening statements; (b) the prosecution's case; (c) the defendant's case; (d) rebuttal and surrebuttal; (e) closing arguments; (f) jury deliberation; and (g) the verdict.

LO 5 **List the five basic steps of an appeal.** (a) The defendant files notice of appeal; (b) the trial court record is transferred to the appellate court; (c) both parties file briefs; (d) attorneys from both sides present oral arguments; and (e) the judges of the appellate court deliberate and make their decision.

There are even MORE study aids for Chapter 10 at
www.cengagebrain.com

jury trial A trial before a judge and a jury. 182

lay witness A witness who can truthfully and accurately testify on a fact in question without having specialized training or knowledge. 187

master jury list The list of citizens in a court's district from which the jury is selected. 184

opening statement An attorney's statement to the jury at the beginning of the trial. 186

peremptory challenge A *voir dire* challenge to exclude potential jurors from serving on the jury without any supporting reason or cause. 185

real evidence Evidence that is brought into court and seen by the jury. 187

rebuttal Evidence given to counteract or disprove evidence presented by the opposing party. 192

redirect examination The questioning of a witness following cross-examination, designed to reestablish the credibility of the witness in the minds of the jurors. 190

relevant evidence Evidence tending to make a fact in question more or less probable than it would be without the evidence. 188

sequestration A judge's decision during a high-profile case to isolate the jury following the attorney's closing arguments. 192

statute of limitations A law limiting the amount of time prosecutors have to bring criminal charges against the suspect after the crime has occurred. 181

testimony Verbal evidence given by witnesses under oath. 187

venire The group of citizens from which the jury is selected. 184

verdict A formal decision made by the jury. 193

voir dire The process that allows trial attorneys to determine the qualifications and suitability of prospective jurors. 184

Mastering Concepts The Steps of an Appeal

1. The defendant, or *appellant*, files a *notice of appeal*—a short written statement outlining the basis of the appeal.

2. The appellant transfers the trial court record to the appellate court. This record contains items such as evidence and a transcript of the testimony.

3. Both parties file *briefs*. A brief is a written document that presents the party's legal arguments.

4. Attorneys from both sides present *oral arguments* before the appellate court.

5. Having heard from both sides, the judges of the appellate court retire to deliberate the case and make their decsion. As described in Chapter 8, this decision is revealed in a *written opinion*. Appellate courts generally do one of the following:

   • *Uphold* the decision of the lower court;

   • *Modify* the lower court decision by changing only a part of it;

   • *Reverse* the decision of the lower court; or

   • *Reverse and remand* the case, meaning that the matter is sent back to the lower court for further proceedings.

STUDY PREP

An outline should consist of several levels written in a standard format. The most important concepts are assigned Roman numerals; second most important, the capital letters; the third most important, numbers; and the fourth most important, lowercase letters.

TEST PREP

Some professors make old exams available, either by posting them online or putting them on file in the library. Old tests can help you by providing an idea of the kinds of questions the professor likes to ask. You can also use them to take practice exams.

Sample Self-Assessment

The defendant in any felony case is entitled to a trial by _____. If the defendant waives this right, a _____ trial takes place, in which the _____ decides questions of law and fact. Another benefit for the defendant is the privilege against _____, which gives her or him the right to "take the Fifth." Perhaps the most important protection for the defendant, however, is the presumption in criminal law that she or he is _____ until proved _____. Thus, the burden is on the _____ to prove the defendant's culpability beyond a _____.

To help you refresh your understanding of each major chapter section, **go online to access the relevant Self-Assessment quiz.** You'll know right away whether you need to go back and read that section again to cement your understanding of major concepts!

Key Terms

aggravating circumstances Any circumstances accompanying the commission of a crime that may justify a harsher sentence. 206

capital punishment Another term for the death penalty. Crimes that are punishable by the death penalty are known as *capital* crimes or *capital* offenses. 204

departure A stipulation that allows a judge to adjust his or her sentencing decision based on the special circumstances of a particular case. 209

determinate sentencing A period of incarceration that is fixed by a sentencing authority and cannot be reduced by judges or other correctional officials. 202

deterrence The strategy of preventing crime through the threat of punishment. 199

general deterrence The theory that by punishing an individual, other individuals will be deterred from committing the same or similar offense. 199

"good time" A reduction in time served by prisoners based on good behavior, conformity to rules, and other positive actions. 202

habitual offender laws Statutes that require lengthy prison sentences for those who are convicted of multiple felonies. 210

incapacitation A strategy for preventing crime by detaining wrongdoers in prison. 200

indeterminate sentencing A period of incarceration that is determined by the judge, operating within a set of minimum and maximum sentences determined by the legislature. 202

just deserts A sentencing philosophy based on the assertion that criminals deserve to be punished for breaking society's rules. 198

mandatory sentencing guidelines Statutorily determined punishments that must be applied to those who are convicted of specific crimes. 210

mitigating circumstances Any circumstances accompanying the commission of a crime that may justify a lighter sentence. 206

presentence investigative report An investigative report on an offender's background that assists a judge in determining the proper sentence. 205

"real offense" The actual offense committed, as opposed to the charge levied by the prosecutor as the result of a plea bargain. 206

rehabilitation The philosophy that society is best served when wrongdoers are treated for the issues underlying their criminality. 200

restitution Monetary compensation for damages done to the victim by the offender's criminal act. 201

restorative justice An approach to punishment designed to repair the harm done to the victim and the community by the offender's criminal act. 201

Chapter Summary & Learning Outcomes

 LO 1 **List and contrast the four basic philosophical reasons for sentencing criminals.** (a) Retribution, the oldest justification for punishment, is the philosophy that those who commit crimes should be punished based on the severity of that crime; (b) deterrence is the strategy of preventing crime through the threat of punishment; (c) incapacitation is a strategy of preventing crime through detaining offenders; and (d) rehabilitation is the philosophy that offenders should be treated for the underlying causes of their criminality.

LO 2 **Contrast indeterminate sentencing with determinate sentencing.** Indeterminate sentencing is a period of incarceration that is determined by a judge, operating within a set of minimum and maximum terms determined by the legislature. Determinate sentencing is a fixed period of incarceration determined by the sentencing authority.

 LO 3 **List the six forms of punishment.** (a) Capital punishment; (b) imprisonment; (c) probation; (d) fines; (e) restitution and community service; and (f) apologies.

LO 4 **Explain some of the reasons why sentencing reform has occurred.** Sentencing reform often involves concerns that judicial discretion has been used improperly, resulting in sentencing disparity and sentencing discrimination.

 LO 5 **Identify the two stages that make up the bifurcated process of death penalty sentencing.** In the first stage of death penalty sentencing, a jury must determine the guilt or innocence of the defendant. In the second stage, the jury must determine if the death sentence is appropriate for the convicted offender.

(AP Photo/Eric Risberg)

There are even MORE study aids for Chapter 11 at
www.cengagebrain.com

retribution The philosophy that those who commit criminal acts should be punished based on the severity of the crime. 198

sentencing discrimination A situation in which the length of a sentence appears to be influenced by the defendant's race or another factor not directly related to the crime he or she committed. 207

sentencing disparity A situation in which those convicted of similar crimes do not receive similar sentences. 207

sentencing guidelines Legislatively determined guidelines that judges are required to follow. 209

specific deterrence The theory that an individual who has been punished once for criminal wrong-doing is less likely to commit further crime, as he or she will not want to repeat the experience of punishment. 199

truth-in-sentencing law A legislative attempt to ensure that convicts will serve approximately the term to which they were initially sentenced. 202

victim impact statement (VIS) A statement to the sentencing body (judge, jury, or parole board) in which the victim is given the opportunity to describe how the crime has affected her or him. 211

STUDY PREP

A neat study space is important. Staying tidy forces us to stay organized. When your desk is covered with piles of papers, notes, and text-books, things are being lost even though you may not realize it. The only work items that should be on your desk are those that you are working with that day.

TEST PREP

For multiple-choice questions, try to arrive at the answer in your head before looking at the possible answers. This may provide you with the correct choice. if not, eliminate obvious incorrect choices and watch for two similar answers. Usually, one of those is correct.

Mastering Concepts · **The Bifurcated Death Penalty Process**

Stage 1 — The Criminal Trial Phase

If found NOT guilty or guilty of a lesser offense: No Death Penalty

If found guilty of a capital crime: Move to Stage 2

Stage 2 — Sentencing Hearing Phase

Jury decides: Do the circumstances surrounding the crime justify the death penalty?

If no: Life in prison with or without parole

If yes: Execution

Sample Self-Assessment

Sentencing _____ occurs when similar crimes are punished with dissimilar sentences, while sentencing _____ is the result of judicial consideration of extralegal variables such as the defendant's race or gender.

To help you refresh your understanding of each major chapter section, **go online to access the relevant Self-Assessment quiz.** You'll know right away whether you need to go back and read that section again to cement your understanding of major concepts!

Chapter Summary & Learning Outcomes

LO 1 **Explain the justifications for community-based corrections programs.** Community-based corrections is often justified because it assists offenders in reintegration. A second justification for community-based corrections is that it diverts offenders from incarceration. A final justification is that it is a low-cost alternative to incarceration in prison or jail.

LO 2 **Describe the three general categories of conditions placed on a probationer.** (a) Standard conditions are imposed on all probationers; (b) punitive conditions reflect the seriousness of the offense and are intended to increased the punishment of the offender; and (c) treatment conditions are imposed to reverse patterns of self-destructive behavior.

LO 3 **Explain the three stages of probation revocation.** (a) During the preliminary hearing it is determined whether probable cause for revoking probation exists; (b) the purpose of the revocation hearing is to ascertain whether the probationer is guilty of the violations; and (c) if a probationer has in fact committed a violation, the judge will decide upon the sanction at the revocation sentencing.

LO 4 **List the five sentencing options for a judge besides imprisonment and probation.** (a) Fines, (b) community service, (c) restitution, (d) forfeiture, and (e) pretrial diversion programs.

LO 5 **List the three levels of home monitoring.** (a) Curfew, (b) home detention, and (c) home incarceration.

Key Terms

authority The power designated to an agent of the law over a person who has broken the law. 225

caseload The number of individual probationers or parolees under the supervision of a probation or parole officer. 228

day reporting center (DRC) A community-based corrections center to which offenders must report on a daily basis for purposes of treatment, education, and rehabilitation. 230

diversion A strategy to divert those offenders who qualify away from prison and jail and toward community-based and intermediate sanctions. 221

electronic monitoring A technique of probation supervision in which the offender's whereabouts are kept under surveillance by an electronic device. 232

forfeiture The process by which the government seizes private property attached to criminal activity. 229

home confinement A community-based sanction in which offenders serve their terms of incarceration in their homes. 232

intensive supervision probation (ISP) A form of probation in which the offender is placed under stricter and more frequent surveillance and control than in conventional probation. 231

intermediate sanctions Sanctions that are more restrictive than probation and less restrictive than imprisonment. 229

pretrial diversion program An alternative to trial in which the offender agrees to participate in a specified counseling or treatment program in return for withdrawal of the charges. 230

probation A criminal sanction in which a convict is allowed to remain in the community rather than be imprisoned as long as she or he follows certain conditions set by the court. 222

recidivism The commission of another crime after the offender has already been arrested and incarcerated for prior criminal activity. 227

reintegration A goal of corrections that focuses on preparing the offender for a return to the community. 220

There are even MORE study aids for Chapter 12 at www.cengagebrain.com

© BC/Retna Ltd./Corbis

Stan Rohrer/iStockphoto.com

revocation process A three-stage procedure that offers limited due process protections to probationers facing revocation, including the opportunity to have the facts of a case heard by a judge and the right to testify on their own behalf. 227

shock incarceration A short period of incarceration that is designed to deter further criminal activity by "shocking" the offender with the hardships of imprisonment. 232

split sentence probation A sentence that consists of incarceration in a prison or a jail, followed by a probationary period in the community. 223

suspended sentence A judicially imposed condition in which an offender is sentenced after being convicted of a crime, but is not required to begin serving the sentence immediately. 222

technical violation An action taken by a probationer that, although not criminal, breaks the terms of probation as designated by the court. 226

urinalysis The chemical analysis of urine to determine if the subject has been using prohibited substances such as illegal drugs. 231

widen the net The criticism that intermediate sanctions designed to divert offenders from prison actually increase the number of citizens who are under the control of the corrections systems. 234

STUDY PREP

Often, studying involves pure memorization. To help with this task, use flash (or note) cards. On one side of the card, write the question or term. On the other side, write the answer or definition. Then, use the cards to test yourself on the material.

TEST PREP

With essay questions, look for key words such as *compare*, *contrast*, and *explain*. These will guide your answer. If you have time, make a quick outline. Most important, as you write, get to the point without wasting your (or your professor's) time with statements such as "There are many possible reasons for . . . ."

Sample Self-Assessment

The three basic justifications for community corrections are: (1) _____, which focuses on building or rebuilding the offender's ties with the community; (2) _____, a strategy that attempts to allocate scarce jail and prison space to only the most dangerous criminals; and (3) _____ considerations, as community corrections are generally _____ expensive than incarceration.

To help you refresh your understanding of each major chapter section, **go online to access the relevant Self-Assessment quiz.** You'll know right away whether you need to go back and read that section again to cement your understanding of major concepts!

Figure 12.1 Probation in American Corrections
As you can see, the majority of convicts under the control of the American corrections system are on probation.

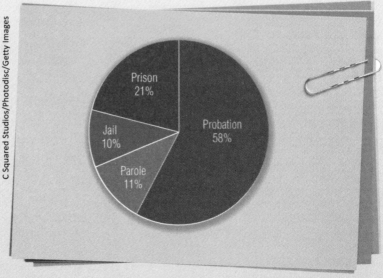

C Squared Studios/Photodisc/Getty Images

- Prison 21%
- Jail 10%
- Parole 11%
- Probation 58%

Source: Bureau of Justice Statistics, *Correctional Populations in the United States, 2009* (Washington, D.C.: U.S. Department of Justice, December 2010), Table 1, page 2.

Key Terms

custodial model A theory of prison organization that emphasizes security and discipline, and thus restricts the personal freedoms of inmates in the name of order. 240

jail A facility used to hold persons awaiting trial or those who have been found guilty of misdemeanors. 250

lockdown A disciplinary action taken by prison officials in which all inmates are ordered to their quarters and nonessential prison activities are suspended. 244

maximum-security prison A correctional institution designed and organized to control and discipline dangerous felons. 241

medium-security prison A correctional institution that houses less dangerous inmates. 244

minimum-security prison A correctional institution designed to allow inmates, most of whom pose low security risks, a great deal of freedom of movement and contact with the outside world. 245

pretrial detainee An individual who spends the time prior to his or her trial incarcerated in jail. 251

private prison A correctional facility operated by a private corporation instead of the government. 247

rehabilitation model A theory of prison organization that emphasizes treatment and reform, with security concerns secondary to the well-being of the inmates. 240

reintegration model A theory of prison organization in which the correctional facility offers classes and programs designed to ease the inmate's reentry into society following her or his release from incarceration. 240

supermax prison A correctional facility reserved for those who have extensive records of misconduct in maximum-security prisons. 243

time served The period of time a person denied bail (or unable to pay it) has spent in jail prior to his or her trial. 251

warden The prison official who is ultimately responsible for the organization and performance of a correctional facility. 246

Chapter Summary & Learning Outcomes

 List the factors that have caused the prison population to grow dramatically in the last several decades.
(a) The penal harm movement, characterized by "get-tough" ideologies; (b) the increased probability of incarceration; (c) inmates are serving more time for each crime; and (d) federal prison growth.

 List and briefly explain the four types of prisons.
(a) Maximum-security prisons are designed to control dangerous felons; (b) supermax prisons are reserved for inmates with extensive records of misconduct in maximum-security facilities; (c) medium-security prisons house less dangerous inmates; and (d) minimum-security prisons hold inmates who pose low security risks and are often preparing for a return to the community.

 Summarize the distinction between jails and prisons, and indicate the importance of jails in the American correctional system. Prisons are designed to hold those who have been convicted of felonies, while jails are authorized to hold pretrial detainees and those convicted of misdemeanors. While jails are chronically underfunded, they serve as the first contact that citizens have with the corrections system and are arguably the dominant penal institutions in the United States.

 Explain how jails are administered. The majority of jails are operated on a county level by an elected sheriff. Most of the remainder are under the control of municipalities, and six state governments manage jails.

LO5 **Indicate some of the consequences of our high rates of incarceration.** One positive consequence of high rates of incarceration is a corresponding decline in criminal offending. On the other hand, high incarceration rates also have severe social consequences for communities and families, including the deterioration of the family structure, the increased risk of delinquency among the children of the incarcerated, and the disenfranchisement of offenders.

There are even MORE study aids for Chapter 13 at
www.cengagebrain.com

David L. Ryan/The Boston Globe via Getty Images

Figure 13.3 The Characteristics of America's Jail Population

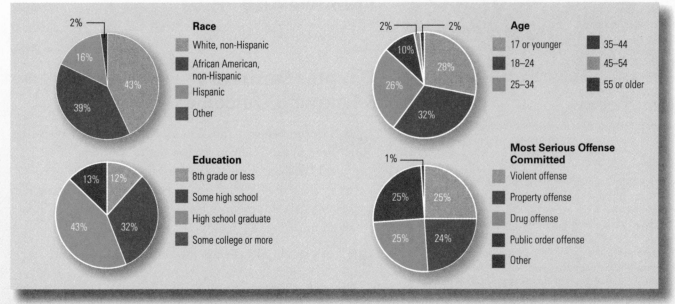

Sources: Bureau of Justice Statistics, *Profile of Jail Inmates, 2002* (Washington, D.C.: U.S. Department of Justice, July 2004), pages 1–4; and Bureau of Justice Statistics, *Jail Inmates at Midyear 2009—Statistical Tables* (Washington, D.C.: U.S. Department of Justice, June 2010), Table 6, page 9.

STUDYPREP

Mnemonic (ne-MON-ik) devices are tricks that increase our ability to memorize. One well-known mnemonic trick is "Every Good Boy Does Fine" to remember the sequence of musical notes E, G, B, D, F. The more fun you have coming up with mnemonics for yourself, the more useful they will be.

TESTPREP

Cramming just before the exam is a dangerous proposition. Cramming tires the brain unnecessarily and adds to stress, which can severely hamper your testing performance. If you've studied wisely, have confidence that the information will be available to you when you need it.

Sample Self-Assessment

Of all the factors in the growth of the prison population in the last several decades, stricter enforcement of the nation's _____ laws has had the greatest impact. Other factors contributing to this growth include (1) increased probability of _____, (2) increased _____ of time served in prison, (3) the growth of the _____ prison system, and (4) rising incarceration rates of _____.

To help you refresh your understanding of each major chapter section, **go online to access the relevant Self-Assessment quiz.** You'll know right away whether you need to go back and read that section again to cement your understanding of major concepts!

Key Terms

argot A secret language used by inmates to make their speech difficult for outsiders to understand. 258

deprivation model A theory that inmate aggression is the result of being deprived of freedom, consumer goods, sex, and other staples of life outside the institution. 260

discretionary release The release of an inmate at the discretion of the parole board. 269

furlough Temporary release from a prison. 269

halfway house A community-based form of early release that places inmates in residential centers and allows them to reintegrate with society. 273

legitimate security interests A standard used by the U.S. Supreme Court to determine when correctional officers may use excessive force. Such conditions exist when, for example, a correctional officer is acting in self-defense or to prevent an escape. 267

malicious and sadistic standard If a correctional officer's use of force is found to be "malicious and sadistic"—that is, mean-spirited or designed to cause pain for no acceptable reason—then that use of force may violate the prisoner's rights. 268

mandatory release Release from prison that occurs when an offender has served the full length of his or her sentence, minus any adjustments for good time. 269

pardon An act of executive clemency that overturns a conviction and erases mention of the crime from the person's criminal record. 269

parole The conditional release of an inmate before her or his sentence has expired. 268

parole board A body of appointed civilians that decides whether a convict should be granted conditional release before the end of her or his sentence. 269

parole contract An agreement between the state and the offender that establishes the conditions under which the latter will be granted parole. 271

parole grant hearing A hearing in which the parole board determines whether to grant parole. 270

parole revocation The process of withdrawing parole and returning the parolee to prison. 271

prison gang A group of inmates who band together within the corrections system to engage in social and criminal activities. 262

prison segregation The practice of separating inmates based on a certain characteristic, such as age, gender, type of crime committed, or race. 262

prisoner reentry A corrections strategy designed to prepare inmates for a successful return to the community. 272

Chapter Summary
& Learning Outcomes

LO 1 **Indicate some of the reasons for violent behavior in prisons.** (a) Violence is used to establish the prisoner hierarchy by separating the powerful from the weak; (b) it provides a deterrent against being victimized; (c) in enhances self-image; (d) in the case of rape, it gives sexual relief; and (e) it serves as a means of acquiring material goods.

LO 2 **List and briefly explain the six general job categories among correctional officers.** (a) Block officers supervise cell blocks; (b) work detail supervisors oversee small groups of inmates as they perform their tasks; (c) industrial shop and school officers perform maintenance and security functions in workshop and educational programs; (d) yard officers supervise the yard; (e) tower guards work in the towers overlooking the grounds; and (f) administrative building positions involve handling administrative tasks for the facility.

LO 3 **Contrast probation, parole, mandatory release, pardon, and furlough.** (a) Probation is conditional release into the community in place of incarceration; (b) parole is conditional release into the community after a period of incarceration; (c) mandatory release occurs when an inmate has served the maximum amount of time on the initial sentence and is unconditionally released; (d) pardon is a form of unconditional release as the result of executive clemency; and (e) a furlough is a temporary release from prison.

LO 4 **Describe typical conditions of parole.** Most parole conditions are uniform and involve requiring the parolee to comply with the law, report to his or her parole officer at regular intervals, abstain from drug use, and abide by any additional conditions set forth in the parole contract.

LO 5 **Explain the goal of prisoner reentry programs.** The goal of prisoner reentry programs is to prepare inmates for their eventual release back into the community.

Hal Yeager/Birmingham News/Landov

There are even MORE study aids for Chapter 14 at
www.cengagebrain.com

prisonization The socialization process through which a new inmate learns the accepted norms and values of the prison population. 259

relative deprivation The theory that inmate aggression occurs when freedoms and services that the inmate has come to accept as normal are decreased or eliminated. 261

security threat group (STG) A group of three or more inmates who engage in activity that poses a threat to the safety of other inmates or the prison staff. 263

sex offender notification law Legislation that requires law enforcement authorities to notify people when convicted sex offenders are released into their community. 275

total institution An institution that provides all of the necessities for existence to those who live within its boundaries. 258

work release program Temporary release of convicts from prison for purposes of employment. 273

Sample Self-Assessment

The majority of female inmates are members of _____ groups who have been arrested for nonviolent _____ or property crimes. On admission to a correctional facility, women report much higher levels of physical and sexual _____ than their male counterparts, and female inmates often suffer from depression because they are separated from their _____.

To help you refresh your understanding of each major chapter section, **go online to access the relevant Self-Assessment quiz.** You'll know right away whether you need to go back and read that section again to cement your understanding of major concepts!

Mastering Concepts	**Probation vs. Parole**	
	Probation and parole have many aspects in common. In fact, probation and parole are so similar that many jurisdictions combine them into a single agency. There are, however, some important distinctions between the two systems, as noted below. Because of these differences, many observers believe that probation and parole should not be combined in the same agency. Limited financial resources, however, will ensure that many jurisdictions will continue the practice.	
	PROBATION	**PAROLE**
Basic Definition	**An alternative to imprisonment** in which a person who has been convicted of a crime is allowed to serve his or her sentence in the community subject to certain conditions and supervision by a probation officer.	**An early release** from a correctional facility as determined by an administrative body (the parole board), in which the convicted offender is given the chance to spend the remainder of his or her sentence under supervision in the community.
Timing	The offender is sentenced to a probationary term in place of a prison or jail term. If the offender breaks the conditions of probation, he or she is sent to prison or jail. Therefore, probation occurs *before imprisonment.*	Parole is a form of early release. Therefore, parole occurs *after* an offender has spent time behind bars.
Authority	Probation falls under the domain of **the judiciary.** In other words, judges make the decision whether to send a convicted offender to prison or jail or to give her or him a sentence of probation. If a person violates the terms of probation, a judge ultimately decides whether she or he should be sent to a correctional facility as punishment.	Parole falls under the domain of an administrative body (often appointed by an executive such as a state governor) known as **the parole board.** The parole board determines whether the prisoner is qualified for early release, and under which conditions he or she will be allowed to remain in the community. When a parolee violates the conditions of parole, the parole board must decide whether to send him or her back to prison.
Characteristics of Offenders	As a number of studies have shown, probationers are normally less involved in the criminal lifestyle. Most of them are first-time offenders who have committed nonviolent crimes.	Many parolees have spent months or even years in prison and, besides abiding by conditions of parole, must make the difficult transition to "life on the outside."

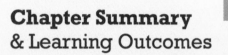
THE JUVENILE JUSTICE SYSTEM

Chapter Summary & Learning Outcomes

 Describe the child-saving movement and its relationship to the doctrine of *parens patriae*. Members of the progressive movement, known as child savers, took steps to save children from poverty and deviance during the nineteenth century. Child savers favored the doctrine of *parens patriae*, which holds that the state has the right and the duty to care for children who are delinquent, neglected, or in some way disadvantaged.

 List the four major differences between juvenile courts and adult courts. (a) No juries, (b) different terminology, (c) no adversarial relationship, and (d) confidentiality.

LO 3 **Describe the four primary stages of the pretrial juvenile justice procedure.** The first stage of the process in intake, during which an official of the juvenile court determines whether to petition the court for a formal hearing. During pretrial diversion, low-risk offenders are removed from the formal juvenile justice system and placed in community-based rehabilitation programs. Some juveniles, through a variety of methods, will be transferred to adult court for criminal proceedings. Once it has been determined that the youth will go to juvenile court, a detention hearing is held to decide whether the youth will remain in custody prior to the hearing.

LO 4 **Explain the distinction between an adjudicatory hearing and a disposition hearing.** During adjudication the court determines the culpability of the youth by assessing the evidence provided in support of and disputing the petition. Once a juvenile has been adjudicated delinquent, a disposition hearing is held to determine the appropriate treatment and/or punishment.

 Describe the one variable that always correlates highly with juvenile crime rates. Age is the variable that correlates most strongly with juvenile crime rates. The older a person is, the less likely he or she will exhibit criminal behavior.

Key Terms

adjudicatory hearing The process through which a juvenile court determines whether there is sufficient evidence to support the initial petition. 286

aftercare The variety of therapeutic, educational, and counseling programs for juvenile delinquents (and some adults) after they have been released from a correctional facility. 289

aging out A term used to explain the fact that criminal activity declines with age. 293

automatic transfer The process by which a juvenile is transferred to adult court as a matter of state law. 285

boot camp A variation on traditional shock incarceration in which juveniles (and some adults) are sent to secure confinement facilities modeled on military basic training camps instead of prison or jail. 289

child abuse Mistreatment of children causing physical, emotional, or sexual damage. 293

child neglect A form of child abuse in which the child is denied certain necessities such as shelter, food, care, and love. 294

competency The mental capacity of an individual to participate in legal proceedings, based on that person's ability to understand the nature of those proceedings. 282

detention The temporary custody of a juvenile in a secure facility. 285

detention hearing A hearing to determine whether a juvenile should be detained while waiting for the adjudicatory process to begin. 285

disposition hearing A hearing in which the juvenile court judge or officer decides the appropriate punishment for a youth found to be delinquent or a status offender. 286

graduated sanctions The theory that a delinquent or status offender should receive a punishment that matches the severity of the wrongdoing. 287

in loco parentis (Latin for "in place of the parents") In juvenile justice, the role of police officers who automatically assume parental status and take responsibility for the well-being of the juvenile offender. 283

intake The process during which an official of the court decides whether to file a petition, release the juvenile, or place the juvenile under some other form of supervision. 283

judicial waiver The process in which the juvenile court judge decides that the alleged offender should be transferred to adult court. 285

juvenile delinquency Behavior that is illegal under federal or state law that has been committed by a person who is under an age limit specified by statute. 280

parens patriae A doctrine that holds that the state has a responsibility to look after the well-being of children. 278

petition The document alleging that a juvenile is a delinquent or status offender and asking the juvenile court to hear the case. 283

predisposition report A report that provides the judge with relevant background material to aid in the disposition sanction. 287

prosecutorial waiver A process in which the prosecutor decides whether a juvenile offender's case will be heard in juvenile or adult court. 285

referral The notification process through which a law enforcement officer or other concerned citizen makes the juvenile court aware of a juvenile's unlawful or unruly conduct. 283

residential treatment program A government-run facility for juveniles whose offenses are not deemed serious enough to warrant incarceration in a training school. 288

status offender A juvenile who has been found to have engaged in behavior deemed unacceptable for those under a certain statutorily determined age. 280

training school A correctional institution for juveniles found to be delinquent or status offenders. 289

youth gang A self-formed group of youths who participate in illegal activities. 294

Sample Self-Assessment

The most common form of juvenile corrections is _____. If the judge decides that the juvenile needs more stringent supervision, he or she can sentence the offender to a _____ facility such as a residential treatment program. If the juvenile's offense has been particularly serious, she or he will most likely be sent to a secure confinement facility such as a _____ camp or a _____ school.

To help you refresh your understanding of each major chapter section, **go online to access the relevant Self-Assessment quiz.** You'll know right away whether you need to go back and read that section again to cement your understanding of major concepts!

STUDYPREP

Take notes twice. First, take notes in class. Then, when you get back home, rewrite your notes. The rewrite will act as a study session by forcing you to think about the material. It will also, invariably, lead to questions that are crucial to the study process.

Mastering Concepts

Juvenile vs. Criminal Justice Systems

SIMILARITIES

- The right to receive the *Miranda* warnings.
- Procedural protections when making an admission of guilt.
- Prosecutors and defense attorneys play equally important roles.
- The right to be represented by counsel at the crucial stages of the trial process.
- Access to plea bargains.
- The right to a hearing and an appeal.
- The standard of guilt is proof beyond a reasonable doubt.
- Offenders can be placed on probation by the judge.
- Offenders can be held before adjudication if the judge believes them to be a threat to the community.
- Following trial, offenders can be sentenced to community supervision.

DIFFERENCES

	Juvenile System	Adult System
Purpose	Rehabilitation of the offender.	Punishment.
Arrest	Juveniles can be arrested for acts (status offenses) that are not criminal for adults.	Adults can be arrested only for acts made illegal by the relevant criminal code.
Wrongdoing	Considered a "delinquent act."	A crime.
Proceedings	Informal; closed to public.	Formal and regimented; open to public.
Information	Courts may NOT release information to the press.	Courts MUST release information to the press.
Parents	Play significant role.	Play no role.
Release	Into parent/guardian custody.	May post bail when appropriate.
Jury trial	In most, but not all, states, juveniles do NOT have this right.	All adults have this right.
Searches	Juveniles can be searched in school without probable cause.	No adult can be searched without probable cause.
Records	Juvenile's record is sealed at age of majority.	Adult's criminal record is permanent.
Sentencing	Juveniles are placed in separate facilities from adults.	Adults are placed in county jails or state prisons.
Death penalty	No death penalty.	Death penalty for certain serious crimes under certain circumstances.

Key Terms

Antiterrorism and Effective Death Penalty Act of 1996 (AEDPA) Legislation giving law enforcement officers the power to arrest and prosecute any individual who provides "material support or resources" to a "foreign terrorist organization." 304

biological weapon Any living organism, such as a bacterium or virus, used to intentionally harm or kill adversaries in war or targets of terrorist attacks. 303

Central Intelligence Agency (CIA) The U.S. government agency that is responsible for protecting U.S. government communications and producing intelligence by monitoring foreign communications. 307

chemical weapon Any weapon that uses a manufactured chemical to harm or kill adversaries in war or targets of terrorist attacks. 303

domestic terrorism Acts of terrorism that take place within the territorial jurisdiction of a country without direct foreign involvement. 300

first responder An individual who is responsible for the protection and preservation of life and property immediately following a disaster. 310

illegal immigrant A person who has entered the United States without passing through customs and immigration controls, and therefore has no legal right to be in the country. 312

infrastructure The services and facilities that support the day-to-day needs of modern life, such as electricity, food, transportation, and water. 306

intelligence agency An agency that is primarily concerned with gathering information about potential criminal or terrorist events in order to prevent those acts from taking place. 307

jihad The struggles by a Muslim to reach a moral, spiritual, or political goal, interpreted by a small minority of Muslim religious leaders to require violence against non-Muslims. 299

military tribunal A court that is operated by the military rather than the criminal justice system and is presided over by military officers rather than judges. Often, the tribunals operate in secrecy and do not provide the suspect with the full range of constitutional protections. 316

National Security Agency (NSA) The intelligence agency that is responsible for protecting U.S. government communications and producing intelligence by monitoring foreign communications. 307

nonstate actor An entity that plays a role in international affairs but does not represent any established state or nation. 298

nuclear weapon An explosive device that derives its power from the release of nuclear energy. 303

Patriot Act Legislation passed in the wake of September 11, 2001, terrorist attacks that greatly expanded the ability of government agents to monitor and apprehend suspected terrorists. 305

Chapter Summary
& Learning Outcomes

 Identify three important trends in terrorism. (a) Terrorists have developed more efficient methods of financing their operations; (b) terrorists have developed more efficient organizations; and (c) terrorists have exploited new communications technologies to mount global campaigns.

 Explain why the Antiterrorism and Effective Death Penalty Act of 1996 (AEDPA) is an important legal tool against terrorists. The AEDPA is an important tool against terrorists because it makes providing financial or material support to terrorist organizations a federal offense.

 Describe the primary goals of an intelligence agency and indicate how it differs from an agency that focuses solely on law enforcement. The goal of intelligence agencies is to gather information about potential criminal or terrorist events in order to prevent them. Intelligence agencies differ from law enforcement agencies because they focus on preventing criminal events rather than responding to them after they have already occurred, as law enforcement does.

 Explain how American law enforcement agencies have used preventive policing to combat terrorism. Preventive policing is a strategy in which law enforcement officers apprehend suspects in the planning stages of terrorist attacks, rather than after the terrorist attacks have occurred.

Explain how the Patriot Act has made it easier for federal agents to conduct searches during terrorism investigations. The Patriot Act amends the law to allow the FBI and other federal agencies to obtain warrants for terrorism investigations as long as agents can prove that such actions have a "significant purpose."

preparedness An umbrella term for the actions taken by governments to prepare for large-scale catastrophic events such as terrorist attacks. 310

preventive policing A law enforcement strategy that has proved popular against domestic terrorist suspects, in which police officers work to apprehend the suspects in the planning stages of a potential criminal act, rather than after the act has taken place. 308

radiation Harmful energy that is transmitted outward from its source through rays, waves, or particles following the detonation of a nuclear device. 303

visa Official authorization allowing a person to travel to and within the issuing country. 311

weapons of mass destruction (WMDs) A term that describes nuclear, radiological, chemical, or biological weapons that have the capacity to cause significant damage. 303

Sample Self-Assessment

Since September 11, 2001, law enforcement agencies have been taking steps to _____ terrorist-related wrongdoing before it gets beyond the planning stage. In doing so, the FBI and other agencies have relied heavily on the use of _____, who infiltrate groups of would-be terrorists to gather_____ on their activities.

To help you refresh your understanding of each major chapter section, **go online to access the relevant Self-Assessment quiz.** You'll know right away whether you need to go back and read that section again to cement your understanding of major concepts!

TEST PREP

Be sure to eat before taking a test. Having food in your stomach will give you the energy you need to concentrate. Don't go overboard, however. Too much food or heavy foods will make you sleepy during the exam.

Mastering Concepts — The Bill of Rights in the Age of Terrorism

	PROVISION	CONSTITUTIONAL BURDEN	THE BALANCING ACT
First Amendment	The government shall not prohibit "the free exercise" of religion or abridge the "freedom of speech."	If a person—for religious reasons or otherwise—voices her or his support of terrorism, the government cannot punish that speech unless it causes "imminent lawless action and is likely to incite or produce such action."	Terrorists rely on propaganda to spread their message, particularly via the Internet. Terrorist incitement rarely leads to an "imminent" terrorist undertaking. Rather, it plants the idea in the mind of a potential terrorist, who may take years to act. Also, it is impossible to know whether the incitement is likely to "produce such action" until grave harm has already been done.
Fourth Amendment	Individuals have the right to be "secure in their persons" against "unreasonable searches and seizures."	Government agents must obtain a search warrant before any search or seizure. To obtain the warrant, the agent must provide a judge with probable cause that a criminal act has been or is being committed.	Search warrants require specificity—of the premises to be searched, the illegal activities taking place, and the items to be seized. Terrorism investigators often need to move against suspects long before any specific proof of criminal activity exists.
Fifth Amendment	No one can be deprived of life, liberty, or property without due process of law.	The government cannot indefinitely detain a suspect without informing that suspect of the charges against her or him and providing the suspect with the chance to defend herself or himself against those charges.	Terrorists are ideological fighters who, if released for any reason, pose a danger to U.S. troops abroad and civilians at home. Therefore, their indefinite detention is justified, at least until the end of the present conflict.
	No person can be required to incriminate himself or herself.	Any information that is gained from a suspect as a result of improper coercion cannot be used to help convict that suspect of wrongdoing.	Military and intelligence agents are often required to "coerce" crucial information from terrorism suspects to prevent future terrorist activity.
Sixth Amendment	An accused person is guaranteed a speedy and public trial before an impartial jury.	The government must provide the suspect with an open trial in a reasonable amount of time before a jury of her or his peers.	Open trials and rules of evidence make it very difficult to protect "classified information" critical to counterterrorism intelligence operations. Furthermore, an accused terrorist might escape conviction on a "technicality" if tried in a civilian criminal court.

Key Terms

anonymity The condition of not being recognized or having a traceable name or identity. 321

botnet A network of computers that have been appropriated without the knowledge of their owners and used to spread harmful programs via the Internet. 325

computer crime Any wrongful act that is directed against computers and computer parts or that involves wrongful use or abuse of computers or software. 320

cyber crime A crime that occurs online, in the virtual community of the Internet. 320

cyber forensics The application of computer technology to finding and utilizing evidence of cyber crimes. 331

cyber fraud Any misrepresentation knowingly made over the Internet with the intention of deceiving another and on which a reasonable person would and does rely to his or her detriment. 322

cyberbullying Willful and repeated emotional harm inflicted through the use of electronic devices such as computers and cell phones. 324

cyberstalking The crime of stalking, committed in cyberspace through the use of e-mail or another form of electronic communication. 324

digital evidence Information or data of value to a criminal investigation that is either stored or transmitted by electronic means. 331

encryption The process by which a message is transmitted into a form or code that the sender and receiver intend not to be understandable by third parties. 333

gambling Wagering on an event with an uncertain outcome by offering funds and/or material goods in the hope of winning additional funds and/or material goods. 329

hacker A person who uses one computer to break into another. 325

identity theft The theft of personal information, such as a person's name, driver's license number, or Social Security number. 322

intellectual property Property resulting from intellectual, creative processes. 326

money laundering The introduction of illegally gained funds into the legal financial system with the goal of covering up the funds' true origin. 327

phishing The sending of an unsolicited e-mail, falsely claiming to be from a legitimate organization, in an attempt to acquire sensitive information such as passwords or credit card details from the recipient. 323

spam Bulk e-mails, particularly of commercial advertising, sent in large quantities without the consent of the recipient. 326

Chapter Summary & Learning Outcomes

 Distinguish cyber crime from "traditional" crime. Cyber crimes are generally existing crimes that have been committed using the Internet. Law enforcement officers must apply traditional laws to events taking place in cyberspace.

 Explain the differences between cyberstalking and cyberbullying. Cyberstallking is the crime of stalking committed through the use of e-mail or another form of electronic communication. Cyberbullying, while similar, involves the willful and repeated infliction of emotional harm.

 Describe the three following forms of malware: (a) botnets, (b) worms, and (c) viruses. (a) A botnet is a network of computers that have been appropriated by the offender and are being used to spread harmful programs via the Internet; (b) a worm is a computer program that can automatically replicate itself over the Internet and interfere with the normal use of a computer; and (c) a virus is a self-replicating software program that attaches itself to a host file and moves from one computer to the next.

 Explain how the Internet has contributed to the piracy of intellectual property. Intellectual property consists of the products of intellectual, creative processes. Intellectual property such as books, films, music, and software is vulnerable to piracy because traditionally, copying these items was time consuming and difficult. It is both quick and easy to generate high-quality unauthorized copies of intellectual materials over the Internet.

LO5 Outline the three major reasons why the Internet is conducive to the dissemination of child pornography. The Internet is conducive to the dissemination of child pornography because (a) it is the fastest way of sending visual material over long distances, (b) it offers a measure of security for those who post and retrieve materials, and (c) it provides anonymity for those engaged in the illegal behavior.

There are even MORE study aids for Chapter 17 at
www.cengagebrain.com

virus A self-replicating software program that attaches itself to a host file to move from one computer to the next. 325

worm A computer program that can automatically replicate itself over a network such as the Internet and interfere with normal use of a computer. 325

Sample Self-Assessment

The practice of cyber _____ is greatly aided by software that allows investigators to retrace a suspect's online activities. In general, however, law enforcement on the Internet is complicated by the lack of geographic boundaries in cyberspace, which leads to problems of _____. Private parties can help protect sensitive information on their computers by installing _____ software, which renders digital text unreadable without the proper code.

To help you refresh your understanding of each major chapter section, **go online to access the relevant Self-Assessment quiz.** You'll know right away whether you need to go back and read that section again to cement your understanding of major concepts!

STUDY PREP

When one of the tasks is studying, multitasking is generally a bad idea. You may think you can study and surf the Internet at the same time, but your ability to retain course information will almost certainly suffer. Give yourself Facebook breaks from schoolwork, but avoid combining the two.

TEST PREP

Identify the easiest questions on the exam and do them first. This will quickly get you in the proper thinking "mode" and enable you to tackle the more difficult questions with confidence.

Federal Laws and Computer Crime

18 U.S.C. Section 1030—
It is a crime to do any of the following to and/or by means of a computer used by a financial institution, used by the federal government, or used in interstate or foreign commerce or communication:

1. gain unauthorized entry into a government computer and thereby discover information which is intended to remain confidential, information which the perpetrator either unlawfully discloses to someone not authorized to receive it or retains in violation of the law;

2. gain unauthorized entry to a computer and thereby gain access to information to which the perpetrator is not entitled to have access;

3. gain unauthorized access to a computer and thereby further the perpetration of a fraud;

4. cause damage to a computer as the result either of gaining unauthorized access to it or of inserting a program, code, or information into the computer;

5. transmit, in interstate or foreign commerce, a threat to cause damage to a computer in order to extort money or property from a person or other legal entity;

6. traffic, with intent to defraud, in passwords which either permit unauthorized access to a government computer or affect interstate or foreign commerce; or

7. transmit in interstate or foreign commerce any threat to cause damage to a protected computer with intent to extort something of value.

18 U.S.C. Section 1462—
It is a crime to use a computer to import obscene material into the United States.

18 U.S.C. Section 1463—
It is a crime to transport obscene material in interstate or foreign commerce.

18 U.S.C. Section 2251—
It is a crime to employ a minor or induce a minor to participate in making a visual depiction of a sexually explicit act if the depiction was created using materials that had been transported (including the transportation by computer) in interstate or foreign commerce.

18 U.S.C. Section 2252—
It is a crime to transport child pornography in interstate or foreign commerce.

18 U.S.C. Section 1028—
It is a crime to produce, transfer, or possess a device, including a computer, that is intended to be used to falsify identification documents.

Many traditional crimes encompass the use of a computer as well; for example, threatening the president's life or infringing a copyright.

Sources: Susan W. Brenner, "State Cybercrime Legislation in the United States of America: A Survey," *Richmond Journal of Law and Technology* 7 (Winter 2001), 1–5; Heather Jacobson and Rebecca Green, "Computer Crimes," *American Criminal Law Review* (Spring 2002), 280–284; and Computer Fraud and Abuse Act, 18 U.S.C. Section 1030.